THE RELIGIOUS HISTORY OF
THE ROMAN EMPIRE

The series provides students and scholars with a representative selection of the best and most influential articles on a particular author, work, or subject. No single school or style of approach is privileged: the aim is to offer a broad overview of scholarship, to cover a wide variety of topics, and to illustrate a diversity of critical methods. The collections are particularly valuable for their inclusion of many important essays which are normally difficult to obtain and for the first-ever translations of some of the pieces. Many articles are thoroughly revised and updated by their authors or are provided with addenda taking account of recent work. Each volume includes an authoritative and wide-ranging introduction by the editor surveying the scholarly tradition and considering alternative approaches. This pulls the individual articles together, setting all the pieces included in their historical and cultural contexts and exploring significant connections between them from the perspective of contemporary scholarship. All foreign languages (including Greek and Latin) are translated to make the texts easily accessible to those without detailed linguistic knowledge.

D1563629

OXFORD READINGS IN CLASSICAL STUDIES

Aeschylus
Edited by Michael Lloyd

Ovid
Edited by Peter E. Knox

The Attic Orators
Edited by Edwin Carawan

Lucretius
Edited by Monica R. Gale

Catullus
Edited by Julia Haig Gaisser

Seneca
Edited by John G. Fitch

Vergil's *Eclogues*
Edited by Katharina Volk

Vergil's *Georgics*
Edited by Katharina Volk

Homer's *Odyssey*
Edited by Lillian E. Doherty

Livy
Edited by Jane D. Chaplin and Christina S. Kraus

Persius and Juvenal
Edited by Maria Plaza

Horace: *Odes* and *Epodes*
Edited by Michèle Lowrie

Horace: *Satires* and *Epistles*
Edited by Kirk Freudenburg

Thucydides
Edited by Jeffrey S. Rusten

Lucan
Edited by Charles Tesoriero, with Frances Muecke and Tamara Neal

Xenophon
Edited by Vivienne J. Gray

All available in paperback

The Religious History of the Roman Empire

Pagans, Jews, and Christians

Edited by

J. A. NORTH AND S. R. F. PRICE

OXFORD
UNIVERSITY PRESS

OXFORD
UNIVERSITY PRESS

Great Clarendon Street, Oxford OX2 6DP

Oxford University Press is a department of the University of Oxford.
It furthers the University's objective of excellence in research, scholarship,
and education by publishing worldwide in

Oxford New York

Auckland Cape Town Dar es Salaam Hong Kong Karachi
Kuala Lumpur Madrid Melbourne Mexico City Nairobi
New Delhi Shanghai Taipei Toronto

With offices in

Argentina Austria Brazil Chile Czech Republic France Greece
Guatemala Hungary Italy Japan Poland Portugal Singapore
South Korea Switzerland Thailand Turkey Ukraine Vietnam

Oxford is a registered trade mark of Oxford University Press
in the UK and in certain other countries

Published in the United States
by Oxford University Press Inc., New York

British Library Cataloguing in Publication Data
Data available

Library of Congress Cataloging in Publication Data
Data available

Typeset by SPI Publisher Services, Pondicherry, India
Printed in Great Britain
on acid-free paper by
MPG Books Group, Bodmin and King's Lynn

ISBN 978–0–19–956734–8 (Hbk.)
978–0–19–956735–5 (Pbk.)

1 3 5 7 9 10 8 6 4 2

Acknowledgements

We would like to record how much we have enjoyed thinking together about the contours of this field, and about how best to bring to a wider readership the current debates. We would also like to thank the numerous friends and colleagues whom we have consulted, and who generously gave us their thoughts and suggestions for possible contributions.

Contents

I: CHANGES IN RELIGIOUS LIFE:
ROMAN AND CIVIC CULTS

II: ELECTIVE CULTS

III: CO–EXISTENCE OF RELIGIONS,
OLD AND NEW

IV: LATE ANTIQUITY

Contents   ix

List of Abbreviations

AE	*L'année épigraphique*
ANRW	W. Haase and H. Temporini (eds.), *Aufstieg und Niedergang der römischen Welt*. Berlin: De Gruyter, 1972–
ARG	*Archiv für Religionsgeschichte*
BCH	*Bulletin de correspondance hellénique*
BMCRE	H. Mattingly et al., *Coins of the Roman Empire in the British Museum*, 2nd edn. London: British Museum Publications, 1976–
Bull. Ép.	J. and L. Robert et al., 'Bulletin épigraphique', annually in *Revue des études grecques*
CIDelphes	F. Lefèvre (ed.), *Corpus des inscriptions de Delphes iv. Documents amphictioniques*. Athens: École française d'Athènes, 2002
CIL	*Corpus inscriptionum latinarum*
CIS	*Corpus inscriptionum semiticarum*
Coll.	*Collatio legum Mosaicarum et Romanarum* (in S. Riccobono et al. (eds.), *Fontes iuris Romani anteiustiniani*, 2nd edn. Florence, 1940–3, ii. 543–89)
CRAI	*Comptes rendus de l'Académie des inscriptions et belles-lettres*
EA	*Epigraphica Anatolica*
ÉPRO	*Études préliminaires aux religions orientales dans l'Empire romain*
HTR	*Harvard Theological Review*
IKosS	M. Segre, *Iscrizioni di Cos*. Rome: 'L'Erma' di Bretschneider, 1993
IDélos	*Inscriptions de Délos*
IDidyma	A. Rehm, *Didyma. ii. Die Inschriften*. Berlin: Gebr. Mann, 1958
IG	*Inscriptiones graecae*
IGBulg	G. Mihailov (ed.), *Inscriptiones graecae in Bulgaria repertae*, 2nd edn., 5 vols. Seredica: Academia Litterarum Bulgarica, 1970–

IGLS	*Inscriptions grecques et latines de la Syrie*
IGR	R. Cagnat (ed.), *Inscriptiones graecae ad res Romanas pertinentes*, 3 vols. Paris: Leroux, 1906–27 (repr. Chicago: Ares, 1975)
IGVR	L. Moretti, *Inscriptiones graecae urbis Romae*, 4 vols. Rome: Istituto italiano per la storia antica, 1968–90
IK	*Inschriften griechischer Städte aus Kleinasien.* Bonn: Habelt, 1972–
ILS	H. Dessau (ed.), *Inscriptiones latinae selectae*, 3 vols in 5. Berlin: Weidmann, 1892–1916
IPergamon	C. Habicht, *Die Inschriften von Pergamum 3: Die Inschriften des Asklepieions*, Altertümer von Pergamum 8. Berlin: De Gruyter, 1969
JRA	*Journal of Roman Archaeology*
JRS	*Journal of Roman Studies*
LIMC	*Lexicon iconographicum mythologiae classicae.* Zurich and Munich: Artemis Verlag, 1981–99
MAMA	*Monumenta Asiae Minoris antiqua*
OGIS	W. Dittenberger (ed.), *Orientis Graecae inscriptiones selectae*, 2 vols. Leipzig: Hirzel, 1903–5
RE	A. F. von Pauly, G. Wissowa, W. Kroll, and K. Witte (eds.), *Real-Encyclopädie der classischen Altertumswissenschaft.* Stuttgart and Munich: J. B. Metzler and Alfred Druckenmuller, 1894–
RGRW	Religions in the Graeco–Roman World
RIC	*The Roman Imperial Coinage.* London: Spink, 1923–
SB	*Sammelbuch griechischer Urkunden aus Ägypten*
SEG	*Supplementum epigraphicum Graecum*
SIG	W. Dittenberger, *Sylloge inscriptionum Graecarum*, 3rd edn. Leipzig: Hirzel, 1915–24
TAM	*Tituli Asiae Minoris*
ZPE	*Zeitschrift für Papyrologie und Epigraphik*

List of Illustrations

List of Contributors

NICOLE BELAYCHE is Directeur d'Études at l'École Pratique des Hautes Études (Sciences religieuses), Paris, with a chair in 'Religions de Rome et du monde romain'. Emphasizing epigraphy as crucial evidence for Graeco–Roman religious lives, she is interested both in the representation of the plurality of the divine (she heads a European research group 'FIGVRA', 2008–11) and in the relationships between religious milieux (polytheistic and monotheistic) and their interactions in the Eastern Roman Empire. Her works include: *Iudaea-Palaestina: Pagan Cults in Roman Palestine* (2001); *Les communautés 'religieuses' dans le monde gréco-romain* (2003, co-edited with S. C. Mimouni); *Nommer les dieux: Théonymes, épithètes, épiclèses dans l'Antiquité* (2005, co-edited with P. Brulé and others); *Entre lignes de partage et territoires de passage: Les identités religieuses dans les mondes grec et romain* (2009, co-edited with S. C. Mimouni); *L'oiseau et le poisson: Cohabitations religieuses dans les mondes grec et romain* (2010, co-edited with J.-D. Dubois).

ANDREAS BENDLIN teaches Classics at the University of Toronto. His current main research interest is in the field of ancient religion, and his publications focus on religion in Republican Rome and on the religious pluralism of the Roman Empire.

PETER BROWN is the Philip and Beulah Rollins Professor of History at Princeton University and Director of the Program in Hellenic Studies there. His central intellectual interests throughout his career have been with the world of late antiquity, its transition to the early medieval world, and the rise and development of Christianity. His books from *Augustine of Hippo* (1967) to *Poverty and Leadership in the Later Roman Empire* (2002) have had a world-wide influence on the subject, recognized by many honours and awards.

AVERIL CAMERON has been Warden of Keble College, Oxford, since 1994, a post from which she retired in 2010. Previously she taught late antique and Byzantine history at King's College London. Her Sather lectures, published as *Christianity and the Rhetoric of Empire* (1991) argued for the importance of Christian rhetoric for the Christianization of the Roman Empire, and she has since published with Stuart G. Hall a translation and commentary of Eusebius's *Life of Constantine* (1999).

MARTIN GOODMAN is Professor of Jewish Studies at the University of Oxford. He is a Fellow of Wolfson College and a Fellow of the Oxford Centre for Hebrew and Jewish Studies. He works particularly on Jewish history in the Roman period and has written *Apologetics in the Roman Empire: Pagans, Jews and Christians* (1991), co-edited with Mark Edwards and Simon Price, *Mission and Conversion* (1994), *The Roman World, 44 BC–AD 180* (1997), *Judaism in the Roman World: Collected Essays* (2007) as well as *Rome and Jerusalem: The Clash of Ancient Civilizations* (2007).

RICHARD GORDON taught Ancient History, Literature, and 'Civilization' (what would now be called Cultural History) in the School of European Studies at the University of East Anglia, Norwich from 1970–1988, and is now Honorary Professor of the Religions of Antiquity at the University of Erfurt in Germany. His main interest is in the imbrication of social and political structures with religious belief and practices. Apart from the cult of Mithras (e.g. *Image and Value in the Graeco–Roman World* (1996)) and other so-called 'oriental cults', he has worked extensively on Graeco–Roman magic (most recently, *Magical Practice in the Latin West* (2010), edited with F. Marco Simón) and is now working in a project at Erfurt on religion and individualization in the Roman Empire.

PHILIP A. HARLAND teaches ancient history and religious studies at York University, Toronto. His research focuses primarily on the comparative study of associations in the cities of the Roman Empire, including Judaean and early Christian groups. His recent works include *Associations, Synagogues, and Congregations* (2003) and *Dynamics of Identity in the World of the Early Christians* (2009). He is also editor of a volume on *Travel and Religion in Antiquity* (2010).

JUDITH LIEU is the Lady Margaret's Professor of Divinity at the University of Cambridge (since 2007), having previously taught at King's College London and Macquarie University, Sydney. Within the New Testament her primary focus has been the Johannine literature, as in a recent commentary *I, II, and III John* (2008). She is also interested in the emergence of Christianity in the second century in the context of Judaism and the Graeco–Roman world, and particularly in the construction of a distinctive identity in relation to the Jews and through the concept of heresy, as seen in

Image and Reality: The Jews in the World of the Christians in the Second Century (1996), *Neither Jew nor Greek? Constructing Early Christianity* (2002), and *Christian Identity in the Jewish and Graeco–Roman World* (2004).

JOHN NORTH taught ancient history at University College London from 1963 to 2003, and is now Emeritus Professor of History. His primary interest has been the religious history of Rome in the Republican period, and in the changing character of religious life in the Roman Empire down to the fourth century AD, as expressed in *Religions of Rome* (1998), written with Mary Beard and Simon Price, and in *The Jews among Pagans and Christians in the Roman Empire* (1992), co-edited with Judith Lieu and Tessa Rajak.

SIMON PRICE taught ancient history at the University of Oxford from 1981 to 2008, and is now an Emeritus Fellow of Lady Margaret Hall. He is especially interested in the variety of and relationships between religious traditions in the Roman Empire, as seen in *Religions of Rome* (1998), written with John North and Mary Beard, and also in *Religions of the Ancient Greeks* (1999), and *Apologetics in the Roman Empire: Pagans, Jews and Christians* (1999), co-edited with Mark Edwards and Martin Goodman.

J. B. RIVES is Kenan Eminent Professor of Classics at the University of North Carolina at Chapel Hill, where he moved in 2006 after teaching at Columbia University and at York University in Toronto. His interests focus on religion in the Roman imperial period, particularly the relationship of religion to social and political authority and the nature of religious change. His books include *Religion and Authority in Roman Carthage* (1995) and *Religion in the Roman Empire* (2007).

JÖRG RÜPKE teaches history of religion at The University of Erfurt (since 1999) and is now Fellow of its Max Weber Centre. His particular interest is in the history of Roman religion. His publications include *Religion of the Romans* (2007), *A Companion to Roman Religion* (2007), and *Fasti sacerdotum* (2008), a prosopography of priests at Rome down to the fifth century AD.

JOHN SCHEID has been Professor at the Collège de France since 2001, having previously been Directeur d'études in Roman Religions at the École Pratique des Hautes Études. His early work focused on the history, archaeology, and inscribed records of the Arval Brothers in Rome. He has directed excavations in Rome (la Magliana) and in Tunisia (Jebel Oust) and published on many aspects of Roman religion, especially their rituals—most recently *Quand faire c'est croire: Les rites sacrificiels des Romains* (2005).

GIULIA SFAMENI GASPARRO teaches History of Religions at Messina University. Her research work concerns the religions of the ancient world and late antiquity, most recently: *Problemi di religione ellenistica: Dèi, dèmoni, uomini: tra antiche e nuove identità* (2009). She has concentrated on mystery cults, as in *Soteriology and Mystic Aspects in the Cult of Cybele and Attis* (1985); on hermetism, magic, and prophecy, as in *Oracoli, Profeti, Sibille. Rivelazione e salvezza nel mondo antico* (2002); and—in the context of Early Christianity—on Encratites, Gnostics, and Manichaeans.

GUY G. STROUMSA is Professor of the Study of the Abrahamic Religions and Fellow of Lady Margaret Hall, University of Oxford, and Martin Buber Professor of Comparative Religion, Emeritus, at the Hebrew University of Jerusalem. His recent publications include: *The End of Sacrifice: Religious Transformations of Late Antiquity* (2009) and *A New Science: The Discovery of Religion in the Age of Reason* (2010).

WILLIAM VAN ANDRINGA is Professor of Ancient History at The University of Lille 3 (France). He is especially interested in the evolution of provincial religions in the western part of the Roman Empire. Works of his in this field include: *La Religion en Gaule romaine: piété et politique (Ier-IIIe siècle après J.-C.)* (2002), the editing of *Archéologie des sanctuaires en Gaule romaine* (2000) and of *Sacrifices, marché de la viande et pratiques alimentaires dans les cités du monde romain* (2007), and also of *Archéologie du sacrifice animal en Gaule romaine* (2008), co-edited with Sébastien Lepetz. Another major interest of his is religions in Roman Pompeii, as seen in *Quotidien des dieux et des hommes: La vie religieuse dans les cités du Vésuve à l'époque romaine* (2009) and in his recent excavations at the necropolis of Porta Nocera (conducted with Sébastien Lepetz) and in the sanctuary of Fortuna Augusta.

Introduction

John North and Simon Price

In recent years there have been dramatic changes in the thinking and research of those who work on the religious history of the Roman Empire. The purpose of this collection of papers is to illustrate the work of some of the scholars who have influenced the arguments and to indicate some of the key moments in these debates, which have caused the reconsideration of many of the elements of ancient religious life, whether we should classify them as pagan, Jewish, Christian, or some combination of the three.

Traditionally, these three areas of religious history have been the concern of groups of scholars working in different disciplines: the history of the pagan religions has mostly been written by scholars of the classical world; the history of Christianity mostly by those working in Faculties of Christian Theology; the history of Judaism by those with a commitment to Jewish Studies. Naturally enough the result of the separation has been a tendency to assume that the religions themselves all developed separately, though occasionally coming into contact or conflict; and that change took place mostly within the separate communities, not as a result of interaction between them. It is one of the chief objectives of this collection to illustrate how much can be achieved, and has recently been achieved, by breaking down these inter-disciplinary boundaries and conceiving of the process of religious change as resulting from the interaction of the various communities and also of the many people in the Roman Empire who moved between the different religious options, or stayed away from all of them.

Each of the disciplines has up to a point provided an effective way of studying a religious tradition during the period when pagans and Jews lived mostly separate lives and Christianity did not yet exist; but from the second century BC onwards there was considerable movement of population within and into the Mediterranean area, so that the cities of the Roman Empire came to contain communities speaking different languages and inheriting different traditions, including religious ones. There came to be communities of Jews, Egyptians, and Syrians in the cities of the West; and Roman citizens of Italian origin settled over the whole Empire including areas of the East. 'Roman' soldiers too, who might be of any ethnic origin, moved around the whole Empire with their units. The result was on occasion open conflict between groups of different origin, as for instance in Alexandria, where Greek, Jewish, and Egyptian communities lived side-by-side in uneasy co-existence with occasional outbreaks of violence. For most of the time, however, in most cities the various groups lived together, sharing the same community spaces. In this context, conversion to Christianity or other groups emerged as a possibility, if at first an extremely unusual and uncertain one, but in the course of the first three centuries AD all the inhabitants of the Empire must have come to have awareness of religious traditions other than their own and of individuals who moved between religious communities. We think it extremely important to emphasize the point that studying any one of these traditions in isolation from the others will always result in a warped and partial view of their histories.

In making our selection we had a series of issues in mind, where ideas have been changing most strikingly in recent years:

(a) the pagan religious tradition in the centuries after Augustus, once thought to have been in terminal decline, is now seen as showing surprisingly persistent vigour and even creativity, both in the Greek-speaking and the Latin-speaking areas of the Empire;

(b) in relation to the evolution of pagan religion in areas of the Empire outside Italy, the degree of Roman influence, the strength of local traditions, and the emergence of mixed forms have all been radically re-assessed;

(c) various types of elective cult have been much debated, both those within the pagan tradition, such as Mithraism or the mystery-cults, and those from outside that tradition, such as Christianity, Manichaeism, and the various groups formed within Judaism, of which Christianity was to be the most long-lived;

(d) questions about the nature of Christianity in the first three centuries AD, have increasingly led to the conviction that there was no single dominant tradition, that many different forms of Christianity co-existed, before it evolved the structure and doctrines characteristic of later centuries;

(e) it has been increasingly recognized that the awareness of pagan practices as constituting a single 'religion', eventually to be called pagan-ism, emerged slowly, and mostly even then in the writings of Christians not of pagans, as a result of the competition between the different religious communities.

None of these themes is completely new in the last ten or twenty years: contemporary work is always building on the achievements of the nineteenth and twentieth centuries, even where new work or new evidence has led to radical revision of earlier conclusions. All the themes are, however, touched on somewhere in the selection we have made, some of them from more than one point of view. Taking all these developments together, it is not too much to say that there has been a revolution in our way of thinking about the subject and that the pieces collected here will give the reader an opportunity to grasp the current situation of debate, which has reached a position where the basic significance of 'religion', both as word and as phenomenon, must be put into question. Had the people of the Roman Empire, whether pagan, Jewish, Christian, Manichaean, or devotees of many other religious convictions, developed a shared conception of their various different 'religions' as co-existing and competing? Or did they think of their own tradition as the only religion, from which the others were mere aberrations? Or did they have no conception of a religion in the modern sense and think about their lives and their gods in quite different terms? It seems clear enough that the co-existence of radically different groups and ideas in contact with one another had produced new ideas and new vocabulary as well as new practices, but the implications of the new situation are still being actively explored from many points of view.

In making our selection, we have aimed primarily at recent work that we regard as leading the development of the subject, as well as building on the work of earlier decades. The great majority of the pieces we are recommending were first published within the last fifteen years. We are acutely aware that we were making our selection from a very rich range of possibilities and much excellent work has had to be excluded to keep within the space allowed by the series. We have sought out work that has appeared in the form either of articles or of lectures, rather than as chapters in monographs, on the grounds that readers will find such pieces, designed to be free-standing expositions of a subject, a more accessible introduction to each author's work. On the religious history of the Roman Empire, work of the highest quality has been appearing in many different European languages. We have therefore included seven pieces that have appeared previously only in French, German, or Italian. The authors concerned will mostly be familiar to those who work on Classical history and pagan religions, perhaps, less familiar to those whose interest is especially in the rise of Christianity or in the history of Judaism.

We have divided the selection under four headings, all four of them relating to the central theme of the nature of religious change in the Roman Empire, in the centuries after the establishment of the imperial monarchy in the late first century BC:

1. *Changes in Religious Life* (covers the character and development of pagan religious life both in Rome and in the Empire);

2. *Elective Cults* (covers the part played by cults of various kinds which, unlike the traditional civic cults, were based on groups of peoples who had made a deliberate choice to practise a particular form of religion);

3. *Co-existence of Religions, Old and New* (covers the evolution within the Empire of religious movements of a radically new type, particularly Judaism and Christianity, and the relationship between these and the older forms of religious life);

4. *Late Antiquity* (covers the nature of the transformation of religious life in the period from the late third century AD onwards, in which old and new religions still co-exist, but in which Christianity becomes progressively more established).

The papers have not been re-written for this re-publication. In some cases authors have chosen to update by adding a brief 'Afterword', or by supplementing their bibliography with recent publications. Some authors have adjusted details in their text and where the original was not in English, there has inevitably been more adjustment in rethinking the text into a different language. In all cases, our intention has been to keep the arguments as near as practicable to the form in which they were first published. We have, however, been very concerned to make the papers accessible to the widest possible readership: all Greek and Latin is translated or glossed; references are in a form that can be interpreted without technical knowledge; the titles of ancient works are in English wherever there are available translations—we have as far as possible used the titles from the Loeb Classical Library. We have had it in mind throughout that both the selection of work to be included and the style of presentation should be designed to cater for those taking courses, whether in History, Religious Studies, Classics, or any other related discipline. It is our hope that students in all these areas and at various stages of higher education should find this a valuable introduction to the study of developments in ancient religious history. They are, after all, developments that have had profound effects on the whole religious experience of later generations in many parts of the world.

I

Changes in Religious Life

Roman and Civic Cults

1

Roman Religion and the Religion of Empire

Some Reflections on Method

Jörg Rüpke

The main focus of the following reflections will be on the conceptualization of the 'religion of the Roman Empire'.[1] This should in turn
provide a new perspective on two other territorial concepts, namely
'provincial religion' and 'local religion'. My aim here is not to present
a comprehensive *history* of this concept, since the materials available
are inadequate for such a reconstruction. One can however point up
certain prejudices and methodological dead-ends, as well as highlight
some potentially fruitful new approaches, which I will use to suggest
a few perspectives for further research on the subject.

When we speak about ancient religion, we tend typically to place
Greek and Roman religion in parallel (or in contrast, in the case of a
comparative study). 'Greek religion'—and nowadays this is a commonplace—includes more than just the religion of Athens. It is a
system of religious cults that includes a great number of locally

[1] This paper was delivered at the inaugural conference that prepared the 'Priority
programme 1080' of the German Science Foundation 'Römische Reichsreligion und
Provinzialreligion: Globalisierungs- und Regionalisierungsprozesse in der antiken
Religionsgeschichte', initiated by Hubert Cancik and co-ordinated by myself. The
conference at Bad Homburg, housed and financed by the Werner-Reimers-Stiftung,
attempted to formulate and test a number of analytical terms and lines of inquiry.
The proceedings were published in Cancik and Rüpke 1997. I am grateful to Richard
Gordon for a critical re-reading and have taken advantage of the opportunity to
remove some mistakes.

variable elements. Already in his day, Otto Gruppe planned to write a history of Greek religion based on the tribal structure of Greece (an idea obviously influenced by Karl Otfried Müller's mythological studies); a book like Fritz Graf's on the cults of Northern Ionia is certainly an integral part of the study of Greek religion (Graf 1985). Greek religion is the religion of a certain cultural area held together by shared political structures and literary communication. But the arrival of the Hellenistic period complicates matters. Religions developed in the Hellenistic kingdoms which were obviously not identical with the cults of Greek citizens in Alexandria, for example—perhaps indeed had nothing in common with them. Nevertheless, the concept 'Hellenistic religion' does seem to be a kind of meta-system capable of encompassing and influencing this great diversity of cults (Martin 1987). Glen Bowersock has traced the influence of this form of Hellenism up to Islamic times (1990).

Roman religion, on the other hand, is essentially or even exclusively the religion of a single city, the religion of Rome itself. Of course, Rome was not any old city, but the central city of Latium whose language was to become dominant in Italy, and the administrative language and the lingua franca of the western and—up to a point—also of the eastern Mediterranean empire. If we focus on the imperial phase, the *imperium Romanum* was the outcome of an uneven process of political and military expansion that gave rise to a number of very different administrative structures. For the moment, I just need to say that this expansion led to the integration of the large and ancient cultural area of the Mediterranean and its adjacent regions into a political system with Rome as its centre, a system that lasted until the beginning of the fourth century AD.

The basic question for someone concerned with the history of religion must be whether there were any cultural and especially religious institutions that can be understood as parallel to the political construct *imperium Romanum*, and which could by that token be called 'religion of Empire'? The second obvious question would concern the role of the centre and its religion for such a religion of Empire—or would it be more justifiable here too to say that the common denominator was *Hellenism*? Right at the start, however, we can state that, say, 'The North African Cults of Roman Religion' would be a very odd title for a book. A term such as *Romanism*, denoting the historical effects of the encounter with Roman religion, could only be applied, if at all, to Latin Christianity—and the centre of that was the *city* of Rome.

THE 'RELIGION OF EMPIRE' IN THE LITERATURE OF THE NINETEENTH AND TWENTIETH CENTURIES

Johann Adam Hartung (1802–67)

I begin with Hartung's very important work on Roman religion, published in 1836. He emphasized the parallel development of social and religious relations, because 'all corporations were based on the religious community' (Hartung 1836: i. 229). He also (1836: i. 230) observed this political aspect of religion at higher levels of social organization: 'every political conjunction that took place with other states or nations always included the establishment of a religious community or was even caused by it'. The example given by Hartung is the phenomenon of synoecism. For the establishment of the empire, however, such processes were irrelevant. Hartung can show that:

They [the Romans] were interested in extending the dominance of the Roman name and the Roman gods as far as possible without forcing the conquered nations to worship them. [...] In exchange every religion could be freely practised not only in the empire, but also in Rome itself and the conquered nations were allowed to keep their gods in the same way as they were allowed to keep their institutions and constitutions, as long as they did not impede Roman dominance. All foreign religions were categorized as *sacra privata, gentilitia* and *municipalia* (private, gentilician, municipal rituals), which affected the state religion to such a low degree that it even cared for their continuation and unaltered practice (Hartung 1836: i. 231).

Hartung has here evidently misunderstood a passage of Festus,[2] derived from Verrius Flaccus, who was in fact referring to the support

---

[2] Festus p.146.9–12 L.: *Municipalia sacra vocantur, quae ab initio habuerunt ante civitatem Romanam acceptam; quae observare eos voluerunt pontifices, et eo more facere, quo adsuessent antiquitus* (Municipalia is the word for cults which the communities had from the beginning, before acquiring Roman citizenship, and which the *pontifices* wanted them to maintain and perform as they had of old).

of the *pontifices* for the continuation of traditional cults in those *municipia* of Italy that had been granted Roman citizenship. At least the term *municipalia sacra*, which is evidently complementary to *sacra publica*, shows that even in Republican times there had been some reflection about the religious duties of Roman citizens not only with regard to familial and individual obligations (*sacra gentilicia*, *sacra privata*), but also to local, non-Roman obligations. As to how far these obligations were to extend beyond the *municipalia sacra*, neither Festus nor Hartung provides any answer. Whenever he mentions the 'state religion' thereafter, Hartung (1836: i. 237) is really referring to the religion of the city of Rome, which disintegrated when the city itself fell. Even the extension of Roman citizenship to the whole of the Empire did not change the local restriction of Roman religion: it only allowed complete freedom of religion (Hartung 1836: i. 271).

I want to offer two specific reasons for Hartung's position on the subject. They are both connected to the character of the Empire as a political structure consisting of many nations and to the historically-charged concept of 'nation'. My two keywords are 'diffusion' and 'state'. Hartung explicitly argued that processes of diffusion and reception are of no importance for the creation of a supranational religion: 'The only means by which customs and religions could be passed on was by inheritance, because all nations tried to protect themselves against the adoption of foreign customs as though they were an infectious disease' (Hartung 1836: i. 238). The genealogy itself has to be reconstructed by analysing language: this is Hartung's main paradigm, in favour of which he resolutely rejects mythological research (1836: i. 238f.). This also explains his choice of synoecism as an example for the creation of political communities: in a genealogical model, this phenomenon would correspond to marriage. By comparison, all 'proliferation by means of physical contact or intellectual communication' is unintentional and uncontrolled (1836: i. 238). So what we have to expect is that the religion of the city of Rome and the religions of the Empire existed side by side without interfering with each other.

Adopting the language of Romantic nationalism, one might say that religion is not the only direct form of expression available to the *Volksgeist* (the national spirit), since the state itself is also a manifestation of it. According to Hegel, a nation's constitution, its religion, and its art form a coherent whole that transforms the *Geist* (spirit), which is concretely represented by the state, into an 'individual totality': (Hegel 1837/1928: xi. 79) 'The state is the divine will, in the sense that it is mind present on earth, unfolding itself to be the actual shape and organization of a world' (Hegel 1820/2001: § 270).[3] Religion, which 'contains absolute truth', (Hegel 1837/1928: xi. 79) is oriented toward the state, because it is the historical form of the divine idea; religion reflects the Absolute that is granted physical form by the state, and makes it apprehensible. In this respect, religion—or at least the 'veritable kind' of religion—has a political function, because it acknowledges and confirms the state.[4]

It would be interesting to investigate the consequences of this concept of the national state in relation to supranational political structures. However the concept of *Reich* (empire) does not seem to have been widely used in this context in nineteenth-century philosophy of the state. Even in Hegel's work, only a footnote in the *Philosophie der Geschichte* (Philosophy of History) takes the Roman Empire seriously as a political structure: it is precisely by being constructed on a supranational level that this state was capable of turning the multiplicity of individuals bound up in their national ethical traditions into subjects. In so doing it created the right of personality.[5] With regard to religion, this involved agglutination: the Roman state made every attempt to 'assemble all gods and spirits in the pantheon of world domination in order to transform them into an abstract and shared entity' (Hegel 1837/1928: xi. 361f.). Here 'world domination' is the higher level to be attained, whereas the national state aims at a supranational, but nevertheless diverse, political structure.

[3] The quotations that follow are also taken from this section.
[4] Hegel himself also considers other possible developments: 'Religion is the relationship to the Absolute in the form of emotion, of imagination, and of belief. Inside its all-containing core, everything is coincidental or even evanescent.' As a consequence, a fanatical religion can certainly assume an adversarial attitude towards the state, because it no longer accepts the binding character of the state's laws as far as the direct access to the absolute and the resulting alignment are concerned. But in such a case, the religion is no longer of a 'veritable kind', because the criteria that would lead to this valuation are no longer fulfilled.
[5] Hegel 1837/1928: 11.361f. In Hegel's theory, a 'person' is a subject aware of its subjectivity, a unit of freedom aware of its sheer independence.

Theodor Mommsen (1817–1903)

By the end of the nineteenth century, views concerning the religion of Empire had hardly changed, in spite of the intense interest that the Roman Empire and the complex history of its religion had attracted. A reference to Theodor Mommsen will illustrate this. Although the concept of the religion of Empire is not to be found in his *Römisches Staatsrecht* (1871–75[1]; 1887–88[3]) it does occur in his *Strafrecht* (1899). On the basis of the *crimen laesae Romanae religionis*—an expression found in Tertullian,[6] but which can hardly be considered a technical term of Roman sacral law—he postulates a 'religion of Empire' that extended beyond the geographical bounds of Rome. However, in his opinion, this was by no means a new phenomenon, but rather a wider version of the 'official religion' of Rome. That is, Mommsen understood the religious *crimen* as a *crimen laesae maiestatis populi Romani*, 'which viewed offences against the *dii populi Romani* to be insults to the ruling nation' (Mommsen 1907: 395; cf. Mommsen 1899: 567f.).

This passage of Mommsen's work implies a dual model of nationality, according to which the old nationalities were overlaid by an imperial Roman nationality, which was in turn defined by the dominance of the city of Rome:

As the gods of the Roman nation as such were also gods of the Roman Empire and thus had to be granted a position equal or superior to the native gods of any subjected community [in order to express the community's acceptance of its subjection], the transformation of the Roman national religion into an 'imperial religion' does not seem to have been met with general resistance (1899: 571).

The redundancy of this argument reveals that Mommsen remained on the level of terminological definition, trying to cope with a new

---

[6] *Omnis ista confessio illorum, qua se deos negant esse quaque non alium deum respondent praeter unum cui nos mancipamur satis idonea est ad depellendum crimen laesae maxime Romanae religionis.* (That total admission of theirs—by which they deny that the gods exist and by which they concede that there is no god other than the one to whom we are bound—is perfectly sufficient to refute the charge of causing special harm to the religion of Rome.) Tertullian, *Apology* 24. 1: cf. *Against the nations* 1. 17; *ad Scapulam* 2.

phenomenon by means of old concepts, and without a closer analysis of its actual content. Mommsen neither tells us what functions this 'imperial religion' was supposed to fulfil on the local level, nor what happened to Roman religion after its transformation. Within the limits of Mommsen's system, his 'religion of the Roman Empire' might just be able to function as the consistent legal basis for the persecution of Christians in the Empire, the lack of which scholars have always pointed out. However, it is obvious that his attempt to create a more general concept is heavily influenced by the massive shift in the understanding of the *imperium Romanum* brought about by use of the term *Reich*, Empire. As a *Reich*—and in this context one must take into account the contemporary history of this concept in connection with the unification of Germany—the Empire is immediately assumed to have had a dense political and administrative structure, similar to a modern state. By analogy, the function of a 'religion of Empire' must be primarily political. This narrowing of the concept has had unfortunate consequences for subsequent work in this area, especially in Germany.

Georg Wissowa (1859–1931)

The obscurities we encountered in Mommsen's work are no longer present in the work of his pupil, Georg Wissowa. His standard work, *Religion und Kultus der Römer* (1912), is strongly influenced by the spirit of Mommsen's legal approach to Roman religion, and he explicitly claims that this is consistent with the Roman view of the matter: 'The crucial point is whether a scholar who attempts to investigate a single aspect of a people, its laws, its language, or its art can manage to understand this aspect with a clear and well founded notion of the character and mindset of these people, and to use the resulting insights to further refine this understanding of them.' (Wissowa 1912: viii, Preface to the 2nd edition.)

Wissowa (1912: 79) saw the consequences of the Empire for Roman religion in terms of the contrast between self and other. The rise of the imperial cult is naturally of the utmost importance in this context, as it transformed the Roman 'state religion' into a 'court religion'. But there were other processes which still have to be taken into consideration.

The alienation of the Roman gods from their traditional role was increased even more by the proliferation of their cult throughout the whole Roman Empire, which caused them to assimilate the gods of the barbarians and to conceal the worship of foreign deities in the provinces beneath their own names. The government of the Empire definitely allowed the inhabitants of the provinces to maintain their native beliefs and only interfered if these violated the general laws of the Empire; [at this point, Wissowa does not refer to Tertullian, but to human sacrifices by the Druids and in Africa] but Roman officials and soldiers carried the cult of the gods of the Roman state to every part of the Empire and thus stimulated a process of convergence and adjustment between them and native religious beliefs (Wissowa 1912, 85).

Wissowa saw Roman citizens as the primary agents of *interpretatio Romana*, and later elaborated on this idea in a long article (Wissowa 1919).[7] *Interpretatio Romana* is primarily evidence for a certain Roman mindset that understood gods as 'functionaries with specific responsibilities and competences' and all too often asserted identifications on the basis of arbitrary individual characteristics. In his earlier book, however, he stressed the reciprocal effects, the 'genuine exchange', that thereby came about (1912: 86). However, these processes are dependent on regional factors and may take a variety of different forms. Wissowa therefore concludes by saying:

There was no 'religion of Empire', but rather a transparent film of Roman names that covered an inexhaustible diversity of religious beliefs, only loosely connected to the whole by the worship of Jupiter Optimus Maximus and the imperial cult in all its variety and nuance. The actual religion of the state always remained tied to the area around the city of Rome and could never develop into a religion for the empire as a whole (1912: 87).

The only exception that Wissowa acknowledges, a little further on, is the worship of the sun-god, which was promoted by the emperors in the third century to such an extent that he 'really became a "god of

---

[7] Wissowa's interest in this topic is also evident from the dissertation of his pupil Franz Richter 1906.

the Empire" in its last centuries' (1912: 90).[8] In this context, it is the connection with the state's religious structures, the 'state cult', that is important for Wissowa's understanding of the religion of Empire. This is not true of the oriental religions: they strove for exclusive dominance at the expense of the other religions:

all worked toward the total destruction of the [. . .] Roman state religion from within [. . .] and after the completion of this task would have fought one another to become the religion of Empire, a world religion, if a still mightier opponent had not appeared in the form of Christianity and forced all others to withdraw (1912: 95).

In sum, then, Wissowa virtually fused the concept 'religion of Empire' with that of 'state religion', thus explicitly emphasizing its political aspect. This narrow focus on religion does not admit a functional analysis of the matter: he takes into account neither the expectations such a religious system had to fulfil, nor the political consequences of its absence. He did not believe in a religion of Empire either in the sense of Mommsen's sacral law, or in the form of the worship of Roman gods by administrative and military personnel. The only thing left is a process without a proper name, i.e. the highly variable religious encounters between the religious praxis of the city of Rome and the provincial cults, invoked as *interpretatio Romana*, which, according to Wissowa, certainly influenced 'Roman religion' but is nowhere analysed in detail. Note that he speaks of provincial and not national worship in this context. The imperial cult and worship of Jupiter are seen as integrating factors, yet their role remains conceptually undefined, though they definitely did not constitute a religion of Empire. At any rate, Wissowa is completely vague about the level at which they worked: was it political; was it religious? He also failed to examine the consequences of the existence of universal (i.e. 'oriental') cults and religions, and their dynamic relation to the other relevant institutions.

Wissowa evidently thought that the main reason for this thwarted development was the fact that the identity of the Roman gods was constructed historically and topographically: they were bound to

---

[8] Wissowa here refers to Usener 1905: 'Aurelian . . . ensur[ed] the position of *Sol* as the highest god of court and Empire.'

Rome both by locative rules—*intra* or *extra pomerium*—and by temporal ones—by the calendar, which marked the foundation dates of temples. And because the gods were only to a very limited degree personified, they could not develop a trans-local identity.[9]

Other positions

From the point of view of the history of the church, the problem looks quite different. In the context of the confrontation between Christianity and the 'state', the latter, in its religious aspect, appears as a relatively homogeneous entity in opposition to the churches, which were progressively (but not exclusively) modelling themselves on the self-same political structures and becoming more centralized (Markschies 1997). The far-reaching religious decisions taken during the reign of Constantine were interpreted in political terms. The matter has seldom been as well phrased as it was by Ernst Troeltsch, who spoke of 'the creation of a religion of Empire (*Reichsreligion*) to keep the Empire together'.[10] Troeltsch simply presupposed the functional necessity of a 'religious basis for the creation of the Empire', concretely identified with the imperial cult. If we disregard the explicit reflection on the Empire as a political entity—which in turn has implications for a 'catholic church of the Empire'—then the basic assumptions correspond to the concepts of 'state religion' and 'state cult', identified with the imperial cult. It is obvious that the latter was eminently political, but its direct sacralization of a particular state-form to some extent discredited the concept of a 'state religion' as far as Christians were concerned.[11] Troeltsch thus hastens

---

[9] This becomes evident from the book on Roman religion by Wissowa's pupil Aust (1899): 'The cordial acceptance of the foreign gods in Rome was not mirrored by the provincial inhabitants: Roman politics had conquered the world, but the Roman gods remained at home; we only encounter the national cult in places where Roman citizens lived. And how could a religion that failed to appeal to the people in its own native country suddenly be expected to attract the masses in a foreign environment!' (Aust 1899: 33).

[10] Troeltsch 1925: 89 (emphasis in the original). The phrasing and especially the italicization show that Troeltsch intended to establish a new concept.

[11] Cf. Harnack 1924: 306: '...the battle against the *deification of humans*...the culmination of which was the radical rejection of the imperial cult, also resulted in

to depreciate Christianity's newly-acquired function, predicated upon its Empire-wide expansion, and hails the reduction of emphasis on the emperor's divine status as an advance.[12] The internal consequences he presents in terms of the 'church of the Empire' (*Reichskirche*) or the 'Catholic church of the Empire' (*Reichskatholische Kirche*). This analytical restriction of the problem of the religion of Empire, which represents Christianity positively as in effect a political religion, really only fits the theories of a very few individuals, in particular the 'theology of Empire' of Eusebius of Caesarea, the 'bishop of Empire' (Cancik 1985).

As a contribution to the formation of a viable historical concept, theological terminology is only of limited use. It can reflect various aspects of a religion co-extensive with the Empire, such as the preconditions required for successful expansion (e.g. the Empire as a political unit; Christianity's own 'syncretism')[13] and its consequences for the internal structure of the church (according to Troeltsch, this already began in the period of the 'Early-Catholic church'), as well as its use of the state's structures and political functions. However, the concentration on early henotheist forms of what was to become

determined protest against the *blending of religion and patriotism*, which refers to the state cult that included the veneration of the state itself, or rather its representation in the form of the emperor. A central intention and success of Christian religion was to draw a sharp line between the worship of god and the veneration of the state and its leaders. '*Christianity uprooted political religion.*'

[12] See the previous note. On the Christian attitude towards the divinization of the emperor, see Schumacher 1995.

[13] This plays an important part in historical theology, for example in the work of Leo the Great (although he heavily concentrates on the role of Rome itself): *Ut autem inenarrabilis gratiae per totum mundum diffunderetur effectus, Romanum regnum divina providentia praeparavit; cuius ad eos limites incrementa perducta sunt, quibus cunctarum undique gentium vicina et contigua esset universitas. Dispositio namque divinitus operi maxime congruebat, ut multa regna confoederarentur imperio, ut cito pervios haberet populos praedicatio generalis, quos unius teneret regimen civitatis.* (In order that the accomplishment of grace beyond description should be disseminated throughout the whole world, divine providence arranged rule by the Romans, whose expansion attained such boundaries that the society of all the peoples from every land should be neighbouring and adjacent. For this arrangement was providentially the best adapted to the purpose that many kingdoms should be joined together in the empire, that the universal proclamation should speedily reach accessible peoples, subject to the rule of a single state.) (Leo, *Sermons* 82 [80]; Migne, *Patrologia Latina* 54. 423). On the subject of syncretism, see Harnack 1924.

Christian monotheism,[14] the alleged isolation of Christianity as well as the construction of a homogeneous ecclesiastical subject (if we disregard heretical splinter-groups) mean that Troeltsch's concept can only be transposed to a limited degree.

While the discussion about the link between monotheism and political empire continued,[15] the concept 'religion of Empire' only played a minor role among scholars dealing with the history of religion. In his *History of Greek Religion*—interestingly enough, the second volume is the sole handbook concerned with the history of the religion of the *Roman* Empire—Martin Nilsson pointed out the politically-integrative effect of ruler-cults in the Hellenistic kingdoms, as well as the imperial cult. But Nilsson only uses the term 'imperial cult' in his interpretation of a letter by Antiochus III from the year 194/3 bc, which provides evidence for an empire-wide organization of high-priests, ἀρχιερεῖς, of the cult (1961: 168f.).[16] In Roman times he saw no evidence for an empire-wide cult or religion of Empire until Aurelian's cult of Sol Invictus, at a period when there was anyway a strong drift towards monotheism.[17]

Nilsson's view (1961: 573) that this 'religion of Empire was an artificial political construct and not an organic popular development' makes clear that his concept cannot be understood in terms of the traditional concept in nineteenth-century Germany. It thus 're-mained more of an official state religion than a popular religion' (Nilsson 1961: 708). It is no longer assumed that political function and popular emotional attachment must go together; they are now two completely separate aspects of religion, which do not usually coincide in the case of the Roman Empire. Many scholars believe this to be true, especially in the case of the imperial cult.[18] In the late

[14] Cf. Schneider 1954: 1.4: civic gods turn into gods of the Empire and the world: the ever expanding homogeneous areas form the external side of the monotheistic movement. On local vs. supra-regional identity, see Markschies 1997.

[15] E.g. Peterson 1935; Momigliano 1986; on 'political religion', see Faber 1997.

[16] *OGIS* no. 224 = Welles 1934: no. 36. Two other letters from the king on the same topic are known: Robert 1949 and 1967.

[17] Nilsson 1961: 573. Latte agrees with this position, when he says that the late third century emperors had defined imperial religion as certain cults that were standardized throughout the whole Empire (1967: 364f.). Together with Aurelian's sun-cult, the 'reform of the imperial cult was intended to maintain the unity of the Empire.'

[18] Dessau (1924: 356) contradicts this, viewing the imperial cult as the solution to a crisis: 'the people had to be enthused. There was a lack of lofty aims . . .'.

seventies, Duncan Fishwick (1978: 1253) could still write: 'Emperor worship must be considered not really worship at all but homage', 'a purely mechanical exercise'—administrative practice, not religion.

Two implicit assumptions collide here. On the one hand, religion is supposed to be able to legitimate the political order, precisely because it can draw upon the non-political. On the other, within the gamut of the religious spectrum as a whole, the imperial cult seems to be so dedicated to legitimating the political that it is no longer 'religious' but purely 'political'. As a consequence, it can no longer fulfil its intended function. For that very reason, many recent publications have attempted to establish that it was the widespread acceptance of the imperial cult that enabled it to perform such a political function.[19] Concentrating on the imperial cult when investigating the religion of Empire is problematic, however, since such a procedure simply continues to highlight the political aspect of such a religion.

The concept of a religion of Empire is problematical for another reason too. Asking questions about the functions of religion in specific local contexts has led to wondering about the status of the higher entity, namely the Empire itself. Could there have been a religion of Empire if no organized 'Empire' in fact existed? If there was only an arbitrary agglomeration of territorial units, with an administration cobbled together according to the circumstances, needs and possibilities of the moment? What if it was only in the third and fourth centuries that the goal of a well-organized political 'Empire' was even approximately achieved?[20] By concentrating on the political function of religion, we would be returning to the deliberate silence of the nineteenth century, with the difference that a politico-philosophical problem has now become a historical one, and the entities we are talking about are no longer defined 'nationally' but 'locally'. In view of the complexity of the problems involved

---

[19]   See esp. Price 1984, emphasizing the local functions of the Roman imperial cult in Asia Minor. See also the essays in Small 1996, notably the contribution by Hänlein-Schäfer (1996) on the integration of the imperial cult into the domestic cult.

[20]   Rives 1995 not only disputes the existence but also the very possibility of a religion of Empire in his study of Carthage. He uses the term 'official religion' that 'narrowly defines religious identity and controls it by means of the central authority' (at p. 310).

in establishing the nature of the *imperium Romanum*, the historian of religion should not simply wait for the political historians to make their minds up, but help solve the problem by rethinking the religious angle.

PROBLEMATIZATION: RELIGION AS COMMUNICATION

In this situation, we cannot simply continue with any ready-made concept of the religion of Empire: there is no *communis opinio* whose contours I might be able to define more precisely. I will therefore try to develop a few of my own ideas, not drawing directly on the earlier discussion that I have summarized, but attempting to systematize and enrich it—on a very abstract level—with a model of my own. The results will require the creation of new terms and concepts.

My starting point is the following question: where are we to look for the religion of Empire? My answer begins with the idea of religious action. I understand religious action—even cult—as communicative action, as symbolic communication. This communication can be described in the following categories:

- Who is communicating with whom? Who are the participants?
- What are they communicating about? What are the contents of the communication?
- How is this communication conducted? What media are involved?

If we look beyond the mere act of communication, we might also ask:

- Who organizes and controls the communication?
- Why does the communication take place? What is its purpose?

Participants

The first question can be answered clearly: in the case of ancient religion, religion is a local, even private, action. The participants, male or female, communicate with each other; through texts, clothing, and choreography, religious roles strengthen or modify social roles. The local aspect is also dominant in the case of the imperial cult and the cult of the Capitoline triad (Mitchell 1993: 1. 102–17, esp. 113–17), but is also a feature of ritual action in more strongly centralized religions like Judaism and Christianity.[21] A ritual act can be perpetuated by means of an inscription and thereby overcome the temporal limitations of the actual performance. Spatial limitations can be overcome by reporting specific ritual actions, but this is only possible in a few special cases, e.g. exceptional oaths for the emperor or the daily reports of the performance of regular cult-acts in military units.[22] Only in these cases are local rituals conceptualized as translocal communication.

The exclusively local reach of ritual communication can of course be compromised by the presence of foreign guests in the θεωρία, the festive legation. However, senior Roman administrators evidently did not usually perform such duties, so this level can offer no answers in the search for regular symbolic communication on the level of the Empire. Rituals related to the emperor's *adventus* (arrival) were also exceptional. Personal representation is the inverse: representatives of various cities in a region perform a cult together at a central location. Historically, a grid of regional networks seems to have developed during the imperial period, of which we have only fragmentary evidence. We do not know whether such networks were territorially extensive or whether they were limited to the individual provinces. Nor do we know whether they were co-ordinated at some higher level (though this is likely). Such regional structures were almost certainly not identical everywhere.[23] The major characteristic of this form of cult was not supra-regional uniformity but competition between individual cities in a given regional category, i.e. local pride and local engagement.[24] The obvious conclusion must be that the

---

[21] Cf. Mellor 1992. Green 1992 has demonstrated the local character of religion in a diachronic perspective by using the example of Harran (Carrhae) in Syria.

[22] See for example Fink 1971: nos. 49; 50; 52 frg.b (taking *excubatio ad signa* as part of the symbolic system 'religion').

[23] This is the starting point of Marquardt 1888, with large amounts of useful material.

[24] For cities' efforts to obtain the title of *neokoros*, see Friesen 1993; Collas-Heddeland 1995; the importance of local prestige as a motivating factor is also demonstrated

primary political functions of local—i.e. practically all—rituals were tied to the local context. Such a point of view hardly leaves room for a religion of Empire. If it did exist, it had local character.

But such a model of communication must not lead us to a dead end. The generally small scale of pre-modern societies did condition the character of larger units, but did not as a rule prevent the creation of larger territorial structures. It is very important here to take account of the frequency of short-term and long-term movement. Besides the 'classical' long-distance merchants, we also have to consider military personnel as functional elites in military and administrative positions, economic migrants and itinerant professionals, such as artist-craftsmen and orators, as well as tourists. Precisely because they could not rely on well-developed supra-regional communicative networks, we need to ask how quickly these groups were able to participate in local religious communication. Were there forms of religious communication in the Empire that were similar or even identical to each other? The answer to this question depends on the content and media of religious discourse, to which I now turn.

Content

Whenever we speak of symbolic communication, we imply that the contents of this communication are expressed in communicative media. This is especially true in view of the type of source-materials at our disposal, i.e. mostly votive inscriptions that concentrate on the divine addressees and the donors. I want nevertheless to try to keep content and medium analytically separate. The occasion for the performance of the ritual or consecration may be entirely private, or local or supra-regional considerations might play a part. An example of the latter is provided by the dedications to Victoriae in Africa (Smadja 1986). It is not surprising to find much evidence for worship of a goddess of victory near the borders of the Empire and at strategically-important locations; but dedications to Victoria

by the example of Hispellum in the time of Constantine (Bowersock 1983: 177 = 1994: 333, on *ILS* no. 705).

Parthica or Armeniaca in the same area indicate that the donors saw their own situation in the context of the Empire as a whole (Smajda 1986: 509; 514).

A comparable awareness of a link between local action and the Empire as a whole, represented by the emperor, is suggested by the stereotyped dedications *pro salute imperatoris*, which can be combined with a great variety of addressees and concerns. This 'content' can be found throughout the Roman Empire, and can thus be considered as religion of Empire in a double sense.

Dates and festivals that were celebrated all over the Empire, above all those of the *domus Augusta* (Augustan house), also offered identical content. These are especially important in the military calendar, as we can see from the *feriale Duranum* (Fink 1971: 422–9 no.117, *c.* AD 223–7). But in the civil sphere too, as we can see from the Flavian municipal laws, such days are defined as days on which no court business can be done *propter venerationem domus Augustae*.[25] They are also very important as occasions for local public and private rituals (Herz 1975). In a world with a multitude of local calendars, the value of shared and correctly correlated festival dates is not to be underestimated, since they could confirm long-standing personal temporal grids and likewise affirm the supra-local importance of this aspect of religious communication.

Identical content does not necessarily have to be presented in identical form. This is clear from Tertullian's discussion about Christian prayer for the *imperator* (not for the *imperium*).[26] This prayer to God allows the Christian to maintain his (precarious) identity as *civis Romanus* and goes some way to accommodate the efforts from the Severan period to create a (civil-)religious basis for the Empire.[27] But

---

[25] '...because of the acts of veneration towards the Augustan house.' *Lex Flavia municipalis* <c.LXXXXII> = *Lex Irnitana.* X B 29, 44f., 49 (González 1986: 180); see Rüpke 1995: 540–46.

[26] For the emperor, not for the Empire: see 1 Timothy 2. 2; Tertullian, *Apology* 30. 1: *Nos enim pro salute imperatorum Deum invocamus aeternum, Deum verum...* (For we, in the interest of our emperors' safety, invoke the eternal God, the true God...).

[27] See Kehrer 1997: 25–33. In this context I should also refer to the religious aspect of Caracalla's extension of citizen status in the *constitutio Antoniniana* (*P. Giess.* 40 = Riccobono 1941: 445–9, no. 88). [cf. now Beard, North and Price 1998: i. 241]

such a prayer does not extend the religious communication beyond the confines of Christianity.

Media

I would define the 'media' of symbolic communication primarily as rituals, but also sacral architecture and the documentation of religious acts by means of inscriptions. In order to be able to establish whether or not there was a religious *koine*, allowing even outsiders to identify and practise local religion, it is important to analyse the extent to which certain forms managed to establish themselves. The role of such a *koine* in creating a specific identity could be read in terms of a contrast with the surrounding barbarian areas, insofar as such a contrast was perceptible. However, I doubt whether we can identify, for example in the extension of animal sacrifice, a religious content on this level which was valid throughout the whole Empire. Nevertheless, it is important to determine the extension of such media and their emblematic significance, meaning how in their specific local context they refer to the central system of values (Shils 1975: 3–13). The issue of a religious *koine* is absolutely central, above all for the definition of local and regional (provincial) religious systems, including their local particularities. The practice of making vows, including the requirement that they be documented by means of an inscription, the organization of cults as mysteries, the spread of specific patterns of priestly organization, the triumph of astrology, the definition of magical practice, and the exclusion of maleficent forms—all these combine supra-regional patterns with regional variation.[28]

In my opinion, we should include the gods addressed in the rituals (and the votive inscriptions) in the category 'media'. The very fact that they determine the specific religious action turns it into a medium of real symbolic communication. These gods are

[28] H. G. Kippenberg (1997: 157–9) has noted the differences between the western and eastern (or Roman and Greek) Empires regarding the acceptance of secret cults; on votive religion, see van Straten 1981; on magic, Graf 1996; in general, Rüpke 2009a.

also, in a polytheistic context, part of the local pantheon. Yet this pantheon is only up to a point defined by the temples and religious facilities on the ground; the individual's freedom to address gods not (yet) present in the area was, or might be, virtually unlimited.[29] Despite the great importance of traditional pre-Roman local deities, especially for those outside the local elites, we must not overlook the fact that the media of symbolic communication were often gods with Roman or even, in the west, Greek names.[30] The agents of this *interpretatio Romana* were thus not only Roman citizens but also natives who were not comfortable using indigenous names, at least in written and politically significant contexts[31]—though one can usually make out a local god behind the name taken from the central culture. In the name of realism we can of course play down the importance of these names, but a nominalist position is still tenable: new gods, marked as such by their names, are being introduced into local contexts. The fact that these names are to be found throughout the Empire, however, does not necessarily indicate the existence of Empire-wide cults. Such names were usually more or less learned constructions based on (older) texts and not on directly-communicated ritual tradition.[32] We can observe a high degree of formal stability, especially in the case of mystery cults, which were typically highly organized. This allowed them to become standing options in local cult-structures, and suggests long-term membership[33] as well as the possibility of migrants renewing their membership of the cult at their new location.

[29] For Rives 1995 this lack of control was a central reason for the failure of the civic model in the cities of the Empire. But because his model is the official religion of Republican Rome, he assumes a close monitoring of the pantheon which can never have existed in fact.

[30] Février 1976: 310 offers Pluto at Carthage as an example.

[31] See the observations by Derks 1992 on the differences in the treatment of local female gods and male gods being connected to *civitates* and *pagi* in Germania Inferior.

[32] See Scheid 1995: 106–09 on the deities of the temple area of the Altbachtal at Trier.

[33] On the problems of the concept of membership in relation to 'mystery-religions', see Burkert 1987: 21f.; 33ff., who links the mysteries closely to 'votive religion'.

Controlling communication

At this point we should also address the meta-question of how this communication was controlled and organized. The first point to make is that Roman religious policy was usually concerned with Rome alone, regardless of whether it was a matter of the location of temples or the eviction of undesirable religious groups. Such issues, e.g. the extension of the *pontifices'* authority over the recognition of prodigies (MacBain 1982 [now challenged by Rosenberger 2005: 87]) into Italy, or the dedication of votives outside Rome which had been made inside it (Tacitus, *Annals* 3. 71. 1f. (*aedes Fortunae Equestris* in Antium, AD 22)), were mostly motivated by immediate political circumstances, and were thus one-off decisions rather than a systematic enforcement of a fixed sacral law. The rather lax treatment of sacral *ius soli* points in the same direction, meaning the classification of property in the provinces used for religious purposes as *pro sacro* even though it was not consecrated *ex auctoritate populi Romani* (Gaius, *Institutes* 2. 7). Local temples were almost never built on initiative from higher levels. On the other hand, the requests for approval prior to the erection of large cult-complexes or festival games connected with the imperial cult show that approval from the centre was indeed sought, and that the centre considered granting it as a form of control over the symbolic inventory (Rüpke 1996). Once again, despite its polymorphism, we find the imperial cult to be a privileged site of supra-regional communication.

Supra-regional control was not however limited to the senate or the emperor and his cult. Synods or *concilia* might also exert 'media control' in other religions, and bring together Egyptian priests or Christian bishops; the intermediaries between Jewish communities and the patriarch were called ἀπόστολοι (Krauss 1905). Such structures might be congruent with the Empire, or with its administrative sub-units, but they might also extend beyond them. Even if they lack direct functional links to the political structure of the Empire, such connections are interesting for what they suggest about the development of regional and supra-regional systems, at any rate in so far as their centres coincided with the political centre, or the number of centres within a given area increased. After all, the Isiac, Jewish, and

Christian communities of Rome acquired disproportionate weight within their several organizations even though the historical and ideological centres of these cults were elsewhere.[34] In such cases, we can say that the political functions of the religion of Empire were being fulfilled quite unintentionally.

Function

This leads us on to the second meta-question, concerning conscious intentions and actual functions. The issue is whether a religion of Empire needed to have a positive relationship to the *imperium*, whether it had to reinforce the political system. If one works from local 'state religion' to religion of Empire, a connection of this kind can be taken for granted, but not if one starts from 'local religion', i.e. the totality of all local religious practices. After all, one cult that spread everywhere, namely Christianity, was certainly at odds with the Empire.

CONCEPTUAL PERSPECTIVES

What are the implications of this model for the selection of an appropriate set of terms for investigating the extent to which the religion of Rome, and other centres, was present on the periphery of the Roman Empire (and conversely, the extent to which the periphery was present in the centre) and for writing a history of religion in the Empire that acknowledges the influence of such regionally differentiated perceptions? Our starting point was the concept of the religion of Empire. The concept itself is heuristically important, because it addresses the religious aspect of the formation of the Roman Empire. The attempt to see it in terms of a supra-regional correlate of the 'state religion' of the city of Rome (the 'civic model') has not proved very satisfactory, since such an account can really only

---

[34] See Markschies 1997 on the development of regional religious structures in contrast to Roman political geography.

be applied to integrative features of institutions controlled from the centre (above all the army and certain parts of the administration), which largely prescribed both the participants and the contents of such communication. A functional approach, however, might produce significant insights into the process of the formation of the Empire, into the conceptualization of territorial domination and its practical implementation. At any rate, religion does not necessarily have to play second fiddle to political developments, but might itself be an area for experiment and a medium for the creation of new structures.

The analysis of local situations has shown that the concept of a religion of Empire is problematical in that context. Here I would like to argue in favour of Gladigow's purely territorial, inclusive concept of 'regional religion', i.e. 'urban religion', meaning religion of the city and not 'state religion'. Such a concept of the local history of religion does not exclude inner differences, even serious ones, but allows us to study all the cults/religions in a given area together and in relation to the local community. This does not imply that the local society must be seen as an absolute value: the role of supra-local but non-divine reference-points in local religion and in different social groups remains an important empirical question.

By concentrating solely on the religious aspect of the Empire and the history of local religion, however, we neglect essential parts of the picture. The religion of Empire in this sense and regional religion are not binary concepts. If we limited ourselves to these two themes, we would neglect the spread of religions diffused from the centre and from elsewhere, processes that differed markedly from region to region; likewise the shared features in the regional reception of central influence. This is where Wissowa's call (1912: 87) for a *Geographia sacra imperii Romani* (sacred geography of the Roman Empire) comes in, which he saw as a prerequisite for a history of the religion of the Empire. The fact that the media employed, although they are at least to some extent identical, differ in their range means that such a project involves investigating the periodization, the functions and the limits of a Mediterranean–European 'religious *koine*', whose centre was surely not exclusively at Rome.

A further aspect of the research-project is the definition of the units to be examined. If we are to form meaningful categories on the basis of the various local enquiries, we would need to establish common features in the reactions to and modifications of the processes of diffusion from the various centres. I would therefore propose using, at least provisionally, the concept of 'provincial religion'. This is not intended to substitute the framework of Roman administrative structures for research into the formation of cultural areas, as is the case with the 'archaeology of the Roman provinces', even though provinces (but also κοινά, provincial assemblies, whose territorial extent could be different) might occasionally be units in the required sense, i.e. centres of specific cults. On the contrary, the term is intended to link a geographical, regional perspective with a supra-regional system of reference, namely the Roman Empire. If we define the field in territorial terms, we can investigate not only status-specific religious systems, such as the religion of the army and cult acts by Roman officials, but also the expansion of single elements, as well as entire organizations, of external cults and regionally unrestricted religions, as well as locally-defined religious systems. The issues of what 'Roman religion' and its territorial limits are will then have to be the subject of a new debate.

AFTERWORD

The term 'religion of Empire' has proved heuristically fruitful throughout the research programme of the same name. It turned out, however, that the functional analysis suggested at the end of my contribution produced only very limited results. Intentional relationship with the centre on a religious level was restricted to very few phenomena, among which emperor worship was dominant. Yet even the cult of the emperors was not organized on a geographical scale or at a speed which would suggest that it was intended to serve as a 'religion of Empire', even if in fact it may actually have fulfilled that function. Positively, two developments stand out. First, we can register a plurifocal diffusion of religious symbols, practices, and standards, the development of a 'global' communication about religion, and hence the development of a religious *koiné*, a kind of institutional isomorphism. This development modified religion both in the centre as well as on the periphery, and caused archaisms as well as regional developments of new 'provincial religions'. Second, within the vast expanse of, and the intensive exchange within, the Roman Empire, the notion and shape of 'religion' itself changed. Religion grew in importance, defining ethics and behaviour, forming social bonds, and legitimizing power on a new scale. For both aspects many of the reflections reproduced above proved helpful. Terminologically, however, the notion of 'religion of empire' as a comparative category had to be stripped of some of its functional implications and has to be replaced by the historical notion of a new understanding and type of religion shaped in, and by the Roman Empire (see Rüpke 2007; 2009a and b).

BIBLIOGRAPHY

Aust, E. (1899). *Die Religion der Römer*. Darstellungen aus dem Gebiete der nichtchristlichen Religionsgeschichte 13. Münster: Aschendorff.

Beard, M., North, J., and Price, S. (1998). *Religions of Rome*, 2 vols. Cambridge: Cambridge University Press.

Bowersock, G. W. (1982). 'The Imperial Cult: Perceptions and Persistence', in B. F. Mayer and E. P. Sanders (eds.), *Jewish and Christian Self-Definition*. London: SCM Press, iii. 171–82 (text), 238–41 (notes), reprinted in his *Studies on the Eastern Roman Empire: Social, Economic and Administrative History, Religion, Historiography*. Bibliotheca Eruditorum 9. Goldbach: Keip (1994), 327–42.

——(1990). *Hellenism in Late Antiquity*. Cambridge: Cambridge University Press.

Burkert, W. (1987). *Ancient Mystery Cults*. Cambridge MA and London: Harvard University Press.

Cancik, H. (1985). 'Augustin als constantinischer Theologe', in Jacob Taubes (ed.), *Der Fürst dieser Welt: Carl Schmitt und die Folgen* (2nd edn.). Paderborn: Schöningh, 136–52. (First edn. 1983).

——and J. Rüpke (eds.) (1997). *Römische Reichsreligion und Provinzialreligion*. Tübingen: Mohr Siebeck.

Collas-Heddeland, E. (1995). 'Le culte impérial dans la compétition des titres sous le haut-empire: Une lettre d'Antonin aux Éphésiens', *Revue des études grecques*, 108: 410–429.

Derks, T. (1992). 'La perception du panthéon romain par une élite indigéne: Le cas des inscriptions votives de la Germanie inférieure', *Mélanges d'archéologie et d'histoire de l'École française de Rome, Antiquité*, 104: 7–23.

Dessau, H. (1924). *Geschichte der römischen Kaiserzeit* (2 vols.). Berlin: Weidmann.

Faber, R. (ed.) (1997). *Politische Religion—religiöse Politik*. Würzburg: Königshausen & Neumann.

Février, P.-A. (1976). 'Religion et domination dans l'Afrique romaine', *Dialogues d'histoire ancienne*, 2: 305–36.

Fink, R. O. (1971). *Roman Military Records on Papyrus*. Philological Monographs of the American Philological Association 26. Cleveland: Case Western Reserve Press for the American Philological Association, Philadelphia.

Fishwick, D. (1978). 'The Development of Provincial Ruler Worship in the Western Roman Empire', *ANRW*, 2. 16. 2: 1201–53.

Friesen, S. J. (1993). *Twice Neokoros: Ephesus, Asia and the Cult of the Flavian Imperial Family*. Religions in the Graeco–Roman World 116. Leiden: Brill.

Gladigow, B. (1979). 'Der Sinn der Götter: Zum kognitiven Potential der persönlichen Gottesvorstellung', in P. Eicher (ed.), *Gottesvorstellung und Gesellschaftsentwicklung*. Forum Religionswissenschaft 1. Munich: Kösel, 41–62.

——(1983). 'Strukturprobleme polytheistischer Religionen', *Saeculum*, 34: 292–304.

González, J. (1986). 'The Lex Irnitana: A New Copy of the Flavian Municipal Law', *JRS*, 76: 147–243.

Gordon, R. (1990). 'Religion in the Roman Empire: The Civic Compromise and its Limits', in M. Beard and J. North (eds.), *Pagan Priests: Religion and Power in the Ancient World*. London: Duckworth, 235–55.

Graf, F. (1985). *Nordionische Kulte: Religionsgeschichte und epigraphische Untersuchungen zu den Kulten von Chios, Erythrai, Klazomenai und Phokaia*. Bibliotheca Helvetica Romana 21. Rome: Istituto Svizzero di Roma.

——(1996). *Gottesnähe und Schadenzauber: Die Magie in der griechisch-römischen Antike*. Munich: Beck.

Green, T. M. (1992). *The City of the Moon God: Religious Traditions of Harran*. Religions in the Graeco–Roman World 114. Leiden: Brill.

Hänlein-Schäfer, H. (1996). 'Die Ikonographie des Genius Augusti im Kompital- und Hauskult der früheren Kaiserzeit', in Small 1996: 73–98.

Harnack, A. von. (1924). *Die Mission und Ausbreitung des Christentums in den ersten drei Jahrhunderten*. 4th improved and extended edn. Leipzig: Hinrich.

Hartung, J. A. (1836). *Die Religion der Römer: Nach den Quellen dargestellt* (2 vols.). Erlangen: J. Palm and E. Enhe.

——(1820/2001). *Grundlinien der Philosophie des Rechts*, in K. Grotsch (ed.), *Gesammelte Werke* 14.1. Hamburg: Meiner. [Eng. trans. by H. B. Nisbet, as *Elements of the Philosophy of Right*. Cambridge: Cambridge University Press (2001).]

Hegel, G. F. W. (1837/1928). *Vorlesungen über die Philosophie der Geschichte*, in H. Glockner (ed.), *Sämtliche Werke* xi. Stuttgart: Frommanns Verlag. [First edn. 1837; Eng. trans. by J. Sibree, as *Lectures on the Philosophy of History*. London: Clowes and Sons (1857).]

Herz, P. (1975). *Untersuchungen zum Festkalender der römischen Kaiserzeit nach datierten Weih- und Ehreninschriften* (2 vols.). Diss. Mainz.

Kehrer, G. (1997). 'Civil religion und Reichsreligion', in Cancik and Rüpke 1997: 25–33.

Kippenberg, H. G. (1997). 'Why Rituals could be Illegal', in P. Schäfer and H. G. Kippenberg (eds.), *Envisioning Magic: A Princeton Seminar & Symposium*. Studies in the History of Religions 75. Leiden; New York: Brill, 137–63.

Krauss, S. (1905). 'Die jüdischen Apostel', *Jewish Quarterly Review*, 17: 370–83.

Latte, K. (1960). *Römische Religionsgeschichte*. Handbuch der Altertumswissenschaft 5,4. Munich: Beck. [reprinted 1967]

MacBain, B. (1982). *Prodigy and Expiation: A Study in Religion and Politics in Republican Rome*. Collection Latomus 177. Brussels: Latomus.

Markschies, C. (1997). 'Stadt und Land. Beobachtungen zu Ausbreitung und Inkulturation des Chistentums in Palästina', in Cancik and Rüpke 1997: 265–98.

Marquardt, J. (1888). 'De provinciarum Romanarum conciliis et sacerdotibus', *Ephemeris epigraphica*, 1: 200–14.

Martin, L. H. (1987). *Hellenistic Religions: An Introduction*. New York: Oxford University Press.

Mellor, R. (1992). 'The Local Character of Roman Imperial Religion', *Athenaeum*, 80: 385–400.

Mitchell, S. (1993). *Anatolia: Land, Men, and Gods in Asia Minor* 1: *The Celts and the Impact of Roman Rule. 2: The Rise of the Church*. Oxford: Clarendon Press.

Momigliano, A. D. (1986). 'The Disadvantages of Monotheism for a Universal State', *Classical Philology*, 81: 285–97, reprinted in his *On Pagans, Jews and Christians*. Middletown, Connecticut: Wesleyan University Press (1987), 142–58.

——(1899). *Römisches Strafrecht*. Systematisches Handbuch der deutschen Rechtswissenschaft 1,4. Leipzig: Duncker & Humblot.

Mommsen, T. (1907). 'Der Religionsfrevel nach römischem Recht', in his *Gesammelte Schriften 3: Juristische Schriften*. Berlin: Weidmann, 389–422. Repr. from *Historische Zeitschrift*, 64 (1890), 389–429.

Nilsson, M. P. (1961). *Geschichte der griechischen Religion 2: Die hellenistische und römische Zeit* (2nd edn.). Handbuch der Altertumswissenschaft 5, 2, 2. Munich: Beck.

Peterson, E. (1935). *Der Monotheismus als politisches Problem: Ein Beitrag zur Geschichte der politischen Theologie im Imperium romanum.* Leipzig: Hegner (repr. Gütersloh: Gütersloher Verlagshaus Mohn, 1978).

Price, S. R. F. (1984). *Rituals and Power: The Roman Imperial Cult in Asia Minor.* Cambridge: Cambridge University Press.

Riccobono, S. (1941). *Fontes Iuris Romani Antejustiniani I (Leges).* (2nd edn.) Florence: Barbèra.

Richter, F. (1906). *De deorum barbarorum interpretatione Romana quaestiones selectae.* [Diss. Halle.] Halle: Kaemmerer.

Rives, J. B. (1995). *Religion and Authority in Roman Carthage from Augustus to Constantine.* Oxford: Clarendon Press.

Robert, L. (1949). 'Inscriptions Séleucides de Phrygie et d'Iran', *Hellenica*, vii: 5–29.

——(1967). 'Encore une inscription grecque de l'Iran', *CRAI*, Année 1967, 281–96, repr. in his *Opera Minora Selecta* v. Amsterdam: Hakkert (1989), 469–84.

Rosenberger, V. (2005). 'Divination, römische: C. Prodigien', in *Thesaurus cultus et rituum antiquorum 3.* Los Angeles: Getty, 85–8.

Rüpke, J. (1995). *Kalender und Öffentlichkeit: Die Geschichte der Repräsentation und religiösen Qualifikation von Zeit in Rom.* Religionsgeschichtliche Versuche und Vorarbeiten 40. Berlin: de Gruyter.

——(1996). 'Charismatics or Professionals? Analyzing Religious Specialists', *Numen*, 43: 241–62.

——(2007). 'Roman Religion—Religions of Rome', in J. Rüpke (ed.), *A Companion to Roman Religion.* Oxford: Blackwell, 1–9.

——(2009a). 'Religiöser Pluralismus und das römische Reich', in H. Cancik and J. Rüpke (eds.), *Die Religion des Imperium Romanum: Koine und Konfrontationen.* Tübingen: Mohr Siebeck, 331–54.

——(2009b). 'Wie verändert ein Reich Religion—und wie die Religion ein Reich? Bilanz und Perspektiven der Frage nach der "Reichsreligion"', in ibid. 5–18.

Scheid J. (1995). 'Der Tempelbezirk im Altbachtal zu Trier: Ein "Nationalheiligtum"?', in J. Metzler et al. (eds.), *Integration in the Early Roman West: The Role of Culture and Ideology.* Dossiers d'Archéologie du Musée National d'Histoire et d'Art 4. Luxembourg, 101–10; in French as 'Les temples de l'Altbachtal à Trèves: un "sanctuaire national"?', *Cahiers du Centre Glotz*, 6 (1995), 227–43.

Schneider, C. (1954). *Geistesgeschichte des antiken Christentums* (2 vols.). Munich: Beck.

Schuhmacher, L. (1995). 'Zur "Apotheose" des Herrschers in der Spätantike', *Atti dell'Accademia Romanistica Costantiniana: X Convegno Internazionale*. Perugia: Edizioni Scientifiche Italiane, 105–25.

Shils, E. (1975). 'Center and Periphery', in idem. *Center and Periphery: Essays in Macrosociology. Selected Papers of Edward Shils* 2. Chicago: University of Chicago Press, 3–16.

Smadja, E. (1986). 'La Victoire et la religion impériale dans les cités d'Afrique du nord sous l'Empire romain', in P. Lévêque and M.-M. Mactoux (pref.), *Les grandes figures religieuses: Fonctionnement pratique et symbolique dans l'antiquité*. Centre de recherches d'histoire ancienne 68 = Annales Littéraires de l'Université de Besançon 329 (Lire les polythéismes 1). Paris: Les Belles Lettres, 503–19.

Small, A. (ed.) (1996). *Subject and Ruler: The Cult of the Ruling Power in Classical Antiquity*. JRA, Suppl. 17. Ann Arbor, MI: Journal of Roman Archaeology.

Troeltsch, E. (1925). *Gesammelte Schriften* 4. Tübingen: Mohr.

Usener, H. (1905). 'Sol Invictus'. *Rheinisches Museum*, 60 (1905), 465–91 = *Das Weihnachtsfest*. Bonn: Cohen (1908), 348–78.

Van Straten, F. T. (1981). 'Gifts for the Gods', in H. S. Versnel (ed.), *Faith, Hope and Worship*. Leiden: Brill, 65–151.

Welles, C. B. (1934). *Royal Correspondence in the Hellenistic Period: A Study in Greek Epigraphy*. New Haven, CT: Yale University Press.

Wissowa, G. (1912). *Religion und Kultus der Römer* (2nd edn.). Handbuch der Altertumswissenschaft 5,4. Munich: Beck.

——(1919). '*Interpretatio Romana*: Römische Götter im Barbarenlande', *ARW*, 19 [1916/19]: 1–49.

2

The Roman Imperial Cult and the Question of Power

Richard Gordon

The historian is ever on the look-out for telling contexts.[1] But how to judge, in the market-place of interesting contexts, between competing wares?[2] Nowhere is this puzzle more pressing than in relation to religion, whether in ancient history[3] or in a modern, but remote, society. A brief illustration will serve. It was recently reported that Shibani Mullik, a 27-year-old Hindu woman, had sacrificed with a knife her two children, a seven-year-old girl and a five-year-old boy, to the goddess Kālī in a temple in the city of Tārās in northern Bangladesh (*Süd-deutsche Zeitung* 22. 11. 2000 (dpa report)). When arrested and charged with murder, she claimed to have had a dream in which the goddess demanded the deaths of the children.

Confronted with this report, we might judge simply that Mullik was mad. That would certainly be a plausible account if someone were to do such a thing in our society; and it would certainly help us

---

[1] A version of this paper was delivered to the 'C' Caucus Ancient History seminar, Cambridge, 'The Religions of Rome', organized by C. Kelly and W. Horbury, in November 2000. It was originally written, at short notice, as a contribution to a Festschrift for John Onians, of the School of Fine Arts and Music at the University of East Anglia, Norwich, now renamed the School of World Art and Music. His *Art and Thought in the Hellenistic World* (London 1979) remains as fresh as it then seemed.

[2] Jordanova 2000: 59–90; Potter 1963 remains worth reading.

[3] Note Hopkins 1999, confessedly an 'experiment', which seeks to highlight the difficulty of writing the religious history of the Roman Empire. Judgements on his success differ widely.

maintain commitment to a favoured story, mother-love. But such an account would also have costs attached, for it would be to ignore completely her own reported rationale. If we choose to use this as a clue, one possible context for her act would be the associations of the goddess Kālī. Kālī (Sanskr. 'the Black') is one manifestation of Umā/Devī, the female counterpart of Śiva, who represents in some of her avatars the great mother, the benevolent goddess, refuge from sorrows, the protectress. But Devī was created by the gods as a destroyer to defeat Mahiṣa, the leader of the demonic powers, and is represented in this role as the divinities Pārvatī and Durgā. In the *Devi-Mahatmya*, Kālī emerges from Durgā's forehead,[4] bedecked with severed heads and arms, blood dripping from her mouth. In art, she is represented as a black-skinned woman with four (or more) arms; her face and breasts are smeared with blood; her ear-rings are the corpses of children and she wears a necklace of skulls. Kālī represents the belief that birth and death, *genesis* and *apogenesis*, horror and joy are all part of the same universal process: in Tantric exegesis, her left arms signify her destructive aspect, her right arms the creative and beneficent.[5] Devout worship of her brings protection and prosperity; but the price is the acceptance of death—blood sacrifice is regularly offered to her.[6] All of this suggests a plausible set of themes for Mullik's act, if not a direct motive.

At the same time, a Classicist will not be able to ignore the possible analogy between Mullik and Medea. At least in Euripides' version, Medea's motive in murdering her children was to take revenge on her husband Jason, who had decided to abandon her to marry more advantageously. How better could she pay him back than by cutting off his house? Might the deaths of Mullik's children have less to do with Kālī—even granted that she dreamed of her—than with family

---

[4] In other accounts, Kālī emerges from the forehead of Caṇḍī (Sanskrit. 'the horrible').

[5] The protective, beneficent side of Kālī was first stressed by the poet Rama Prasada Sen (1718–75), and is the aspect now predominant in Bengal and in the Hinduisms represented in the West.

[6] On Kālī, see Kinsley 1992; 2000. There can be little doubt that in the past human sacrifice was offered to the goddess, and her worship may still be felt to demand ritual suicide: Gonda 1963: 209–11. Among Kālī's mythical followers are the Dākīnī, demonic attendants who eat human flesh.

politics? What was Mullik's relation to her husband? Was she the victim of pressure from her parents-in-law over her dowry? And what of the status of Hindus in Bangladesh, where they form only 12% of the population? Kālī is especially worshipped among the Hindus of Bengal, including Bangladesh. Might the children's deaths have been a means of calling attention to the plight of a religious minority in an increasingly Islamicized host culture? Might the Hindu temple where Mullik killed her children be a site claimed by Muslims as holy, just as in the north Indian city of Ayodhya a mosque was destroyed in 1992 by a Hindu mob claiming that it had been built on the site of an older Hindu temple?

It might at first sight be supposed that these possible contexts are an invitation to a post-modernist shrug of the shoulders, implying the impossibility of doing more than linking events to a range of 'discourses'. There could be many interpretations, all correct, depending merely on point of view. Among many literary critics, and some art historians, certainly, that would now be taken for granted. But I think it preferable to understand them as invitations to research, both of a proximate (what about Mullik's husband?; where is the temple?) and of a more general kind (the cult of Kālī in Bangladesh). In the course of such work, the anthropologist—or, *mutatis mutandis*, the historian—would seek to assemble a hierarchy (or perhaps simply a series) of interpretative contexts, which bear in different ways upon the event in question, leaving the reader to judge whether, and in what sense, there is a privileged level of discourse. Indeed, the deployment, the rhetorical ordering, of invocable contexts is one main measure of the investigator's skill; and many historical disputes concern precisely the choice between possible contexts, and their arrangement in an imaginary hierarchy. The inevitability of disputes does not mean that some contexts are not more illuminating than others.

Such a view implies that explanation need not be central to the historian's agenda (Jordanova 2000: 107–10). At the same time, there is a justified feeling that historians need to pay more attention to the concepts they invoke, from periodization to moral categories. The point here is not to encourage a neurotic self-consciousness, but to maintain as freshly as possible a sense both of the otherness of the past and of the delicacy of the historian's negotiation between two worlds.

My topic is one which begins in the Hellenistic world, with Alexander and the successor kings of his far-flung empire.[7] I want to re-open the question, which of late has become rather muffled, of the sense in which ruler cult, and in particular the cult of the Roman emperors, contributed to the maintenance of political power; and how we may envisage the part that images played in that process. Why did Roman emperors consider the multiplication of their likeness and that of members of their house, not merely in Rome and Italy, but throughout the provinces, by official fiat and by private initiative, and in many modes, so important?[8] Is it possible to move away from conceiving the surviving imperial images, which I take loosely as manifestations of the imperial cult, as illustrations, as contributions to a notional catalogue, which is still how we mostly encounter them, towards thinking of them as elements in a discourse of power?

The tradition of German art history, to which we owe the great bulk of work on such images, has tended towards the formalistic.[9] This approach certainly has its justification, given our ignorance of the archaeological context in which most such images were found, and the sheer difficulty of assembling corpora of imperial images.[10] Contextualism of a kind has however long been familiar in the field, and there have been many attempts to associate particular monuments with specific historical events (Torelli 1982; cf. Torelli 1977; 1998). This approach has been brilliantly extended into Augustan politico-cultural history by Paul Zanker,[11] and we may note individual attempts to contextualize imperial images by means of their dedicatory inscriptions (Fejfer 1988; Hahn 1994) and in terms of gender considerations.[12] But none of this work by classical

---

[7] On Hellenistic ruler-cult, Habicht 1970; Fishwick 1987–92: i.2. 6–45. On images, Smith 1988.

[8] The documentary evidence for the roles of imperial images is well discussed by Pekáry 1985.

[9] e.g. Niemayer 1968; Eck et al. 1986; Schindler 1986; and the incomplete series *Das römische Herrscherbild*. Berlin: Mann (1940–).

[10] Note the comments of Gazda and Haeckl 1993: 300f.; Rose 1996.

[11] Zanker 1987/1988; see also Vierneisel and Zanker 1979; Haussmann 1981; Hofter 1988; Rose 1997.

[12] Bartman 1999. It is, however, extremely doubtful whether Livia, as Bartman claims, can be supposed to have had a hand in the creation of her official portraiture; cf. Walker 2000.

archaeologists and art-historians has addressed the issue of power very directly.

Recently however, in a magisterial book, Marianne Bergmann has argued that the divine imagery employed in the context of imperial iconography constitutes a claim to special status negotiated between emperor and audience (Bergmann 1998; cf. Smith 2000). Divine attributes are marks of honour, expressing a partial overlap between emperor and divinity, an overlap created by the acceptance of an analogy between the emperor's virtues and the blessings emanating from the other world.[13] Good emperors are good in the same way that the gods are good. The symbols of divinity are specific to a particular discourse: for an emperor actually to appear in public dressed like a god would be absurd or blasphemous. But as the Principate progressed, say under Commodus (AD 180–96), and even more strikingly in the (now much-debated) third-century crisis (AD 236–70), the fit between image and real consent became increasingly tenuous, and the now-stereotyped symbols dwindle into references to claims once made, references to a consensus now impossible. On this account, the primary context for the imperial cult would be that of the imperial virtues, not merely the abstractions denoting 'euergetic' qualities such as *liberalitas* (liberality), *iustitia* (justice), *clementia* (clemency), but also 'salvific' ones such as *pietas* (piety), *moderatio* (moderation), *providentia* (providence) or *virtus* (courage), and the desirable states or utopias such as *Victoria* (victory), *felicitas* (good fortune), or *renovatio* (renewal), all so familiar from the official coinage and Pliny the Younger's *Panegyric* in honour of Trajan (AD 100) (Beaujeu 1955; Fears 1981). The implication is that the imperial cult is best understood as a bid for legitimacy through the medium of values widely shared both by the élites and by the urban population of the Empire.[14] Its keynote text is Plutarch's observation, 'Rulers serve god for the care and preservation of men in order that, of the excellent gifts which god bestows on mankind, they may distribute some and safeguard others' (Plutarch, *ad Principem ineruditum* 3, 780d).

---

[13] A key text is Philo, *Embassy to Gaius* 98: 'Yet these accessories (lit. "phylacteries") and ornaments are placed on images and statues (of the emperor) to signify the blessings which those who are so honoured bestow upon the mass of humankind.'

[14] Legitimacy is also the key for Turcan 1978: 1002.

The main advantage of this view is its concreteness. It views the imperial cult in transactional terms, and grounds it firmly in the context of the actors' horizons of expectation. As such it responds to the now-dominant view, first articulated by Simon Price in 1984, which looks at the imperial cult as a form of negotiation (Price 1984). 'Emperor worship was not a political subterfuge, designed to elicit the loyalty of untutored provincials, but was one of the ways in which Romans themselves and provincials alongside them defined their own relationship with a new political phenomenon, an emperor whose powers and charisma were so transcendent that he appeared to them as both man and god' (Mitchell 1993: 103). In this perspective, the emperor is located between two worlds, the ordinary human world and the world of the gods, and can be represented in a variety of stations on this continuum, in such a way as to make him a key mediator of transactions between Here and There. This Geertzian view was a reaction to the then general accounts of the imperial cult, either as an instrument of *Staatsräson*, an imposition from the centre, or, seen from below, as an idiosyncratic variety of political flattery. Price's perspective enabled him to view the masses of epigraphic evidence for the introduction and maintenance of the cult in different cities, which had hitherto been considered as mere administrative detail, as the very process of negotiation with the superordinate power. As one review had it, 'Nourries des faits et de détails signifiants, [ses analyses] nous font vivre le quotidien et le concret de ce culte, comme aucun livre n'y était encore parvenu'.[15]

The continuing persuasiveness of the transactional view has recently been confirmed by Manfred Clauss, whose *Kaiser und Gott* (1999) extends to the western Empire the insights which Price offered for Asia Minor. His slogan is, 'Antike Religion ist Handlung nicht Haltung' (p. 23).[16] To say 'Augustus is a god' is not an ontological statement in the philosophical sense, but a pragmatic statement recording the fact that Augustus received cult: 'eine Gottheit ist, wer

---

[15] Gros 1986: 'Nourished by facts and by significant details, [his analyses] make us live the everyday reality of the cult, in a way that had not been achieved by any other book'; Fishwick (1986) spoke of a 'tour de force in historical analysis'.

[16] 'Ancient religion is action not just an attitude of mind.'

einen Kult erhält'.[17] Clauss' interest is not so much in the details of the institution of emperor-worship. For him what count are anecdotes, stories of the emperors' extraordinary powers, the 'exaggerations' and 'rhetoric' of the poets, especially of the silver age, the stereotyped formulae of the inscriptions, the dust and fluff that hang round in the corners of the great hall of evidence, and which betray most tellingly characteristic modes of popular thinking that challenge modern good sense and right-thinking. He sees this right-thinking as anchored in the *doxa* that God is fundamentally other than man: too many scholars still fail to appreciate the centrality of the notion of 'deus praesens', the living god, in the imperial cult. Belief in the emperor's divinity was made possible by the sheer unclarity in antiquity of the distinction between man and divinity. 'Die Trennlinie zwischen Gottheit und Mensch [war] unscharf', the dividing-line between god and man [was] blurred (Clauss 1999: 30).

These transactional views are all modern variations upon Otto Weinreich's fundamental insight that the emperor's status was inherently ambiguous, and that he can be represented as the meeting-point between two worlds.[18] Wealth, status, and power are met with awe, respect—and cult. So far as it goes, this representation is irreproachable. But, as Peter Herz has pointed out, the institution of the imperial cult is too complex to be hung on a single theoretical peg (Herz 1988). Once one begins to examine the very considerable bulk of documentary, epigraphic, architectural, numismatic, and sculptural evidence in detail, there appears not one phenomenon but many.[19] Herz distinguishes between: the dedication by communities, groups, and individuals of sacral buildings and other sacral objects (e.g. altars) to the ruler and his family; the regional and local development of cult organization complete with priesthoods, sacrifices, public feasts, and festivals; the re-presentation of the emperor's features and actions in an iconographic language taken from the

---

[17] 'Anyone to whom worship is offered is a god.'

[18] Weinreich 1926; cf. Nock's observation, 'Powerful as the gods, sprung from them, he is the effective present power... this aspect of the ruler is central in homage paid to him in his life' (1928: 37).

[19] Bickerman 1973: 9f. In the discussion after his paper (26ff.), Bickerman was taken by den Boer, and others, to be implying that the notion of the 'imperial cult' is a modern invention.

religious sphere; the assimilation of the emperor to divinity; the dedication of votives to the emperor, the use of the emperor's statue as an index of political and religious loyalty.

One legitimate way of responding to this fact is to call for ever-more detailed examination of specific problems, provinces, and documents.[20] In the long run, close examination will undoubtedly throw up new general views. But we should also consider the issues at a more general level, and reflect upon issues which the transactional account obscures or neglects. One question it obscures is precisely the issue of the relation between power and the imperial cult: what kind of benefit did the ruling power get out of all this? How are we to envisage the paraphernalia of senatorial and council decrees, voting and erection of statues, the creation of priesthoods, the institution of festivals, processions and sacrifices, the dedication of votives, epigraphic formulae, and all the rest, contributing to the creation, maintenance, or aggrandizement of power? One preliminary answer might be to say that effort correlates with seriousness, and the product of effort is consent, which is more than the half of power. It might be then that all the imperial cult did was to achieve the precondition for power, consent, and not power itself. If we are to go further, we need to consider the issue of power more closely. Working with different notions of power, we can suggest different ways of conceptualizing the links between power and imperial cult. I propose in what follows to confine myself to two possibilities, the naturalization through religion of the social and political order; and the notion of power as essentially fictional, a matter of the possible options for future action that lie open to the individual.

*

There is a perfectly respectable view, shared for example by the authors of the article 'Macht' in the *Historisches Wörterbuch der Philosophie*, that all uses of the notion 'power' are metaphors of the key, fundamental concept, which is political power (Kobusch and Oeing-Hanhoff 1980; cf. also Gehlen 1961; Gibson 1971; Groetschy 1981). The classic version of this view is Weber's, according to which power is to be understood as a specific opportunity, when an actor is

---

[20] The need for still more detailed studies is a theme in Fishwick 1987–92; Friesen 1993; and Lietz 1998.

in a position to impose his or her 'will' or 'interests' on the interests and will of another, when this other might wish to prefer his own will, and the situation is therefore potentially one of conflict. The stress here is upon decisions and negotiations. The stark version of this view has since the 1960s generally been superseded by what can loosely be termed a systemic view, associated with Talcott Parsons, which takes account also of the general conditions within which decisions may be taken in a given society, in its major and subordinate structures (Parsons 1963). On this view, power is not merely a matter of the ability of the political system to decide upon the allocation of scarce goods and resources in the face of varying claims and desires, but also of the system's own drive towards ensuring its continuity and ability to function and develop *quâ* system. On this view, the imperial cult would belong less within the context of the unmediated application of power, that is of conflicts over allocation, than within that of the system's ability to maintain itself. In practice, the two aspects are not always easy to distinguish. The issue of consecration produced numerous conflicts, especially in the second and third centuries, precisely over 'allocation'—conflicts over which members of the imperial household were to receive divine honours: there were disputes between emperors, the imperial *consilium*, and the Senate over Trajan's homonymous father, for example; over L. Aelius Caesar, the adopted son of Hadrian; over Iulia Maesa, grandmother of Elagabalus and Severus Alexander, who was consecrated in 223 or 224, damned in 235, but restored sometime before May/June 238; to say nothing of Traianus Decius, who was consecrated in early June 251 but damned before 15 July. But the theoretical distinction is clear enough.

If we adopt some such view as this (granted of course that plenty has been said about power since Parsons), we might situate the imperial cult as a specific instance of the ability of religious institutions and discourse to naturalize the existing socio-economic order. Religion reinforces the divisions of the social and political order by tacitly proposing and imposing a scheme of perception in terms of which the distribution of power and social advantage is as it must and can only be.[21] The Princeps and his family do not represent the

---

[21] Cf. the account of Bell 1992: 169–223, developing the position argued in the 1970s by Bourdieu.

apex of a social hierarchy, but a mid-point in a vaster hierarchy of being without a meaningful beginning as it has no thinkable end. The socio–political order is not so much legitimated directly, as fitted into a wider order of things in such a way that it cannot readily be detached from that wider order and represented in and for itself. The contribution of the imperial cult, as a specialized sub-set of the religious system as a whole, is thus not so much legitimation of political power as its obfuscation, its re-description as an aspect not of politics but of the order of things. As Pierre Bourdieu observes, 'Les topologies cosmologiques sont toujours des topologies politiques naturalisées' (Bourdieu 1971).[22] At the same time, the imperial cult offered plenty of scope within the context of that process of naturalization for the furtherance of group interests.

In this connection, much of the most interesting material comes from Asia Minor. The keynote here was certainly given by Octavian in 29 BC when he permitted the inhabitants of Asia and Bithynia to set up sanctuaries of the goddess Roma and the deified Julius Caesar where the resident Roman citizens could worship, and at the same time allowed the Greek inhabitants to set up shrines for himself at the provincial 'capitals' Pergamum and Nicomedia (Cassius Dio 51. 20. 5–7). The second crucial move was evidently his decision to assume an impersonal name, Augustus, in Greek *Sebastos*, in 27 BC, which, connoting as it did solemnity, dignity, reverence, and numinosity, became part of the official titulature of all Roman emperors (Kienast 1999: 245f.). The institution of provincial cults of the new emperor rapidly gave rise also to city cults: 56 cities in the empire are known to have had cults of Augustus, at least 50 of which date to his life-time (Hänlein-Schäfer 1985). The driving force behind these foundations was mainly of two kinds. Many, especially in the Greek-speaking half of the Empire, were instituted by resident Roman citizens, who thereby expressed their role as mediators between the centre, at Rome, and the Greek-speaking provincials among whom they lived: in worshipping the emperor in, say, Ephesus or Ancyra, they presented themselves as a privileged subordinate power deriving its authority from the far-off centre. They also, of course, entered into a

---

[22] 'Cosmological topologies are always political ones naturalized.'

process of negotiation with that centre, expecting to gain privilege and notice by gestures which to a human being would have amounted to shameless self-abasement; but to a god, were nothing out of the ordinary.

Initially, then, the cult of the emperor masked from the worshippers themselves their own loss of political freedom and enabled them to negotiate a new relation to the centre. But once routinized, the cult conferred upon individual rulers a kind of temporary immortality until the point of eventual consecration, the official transition to the status of 'god in heaven' (*divus*). An official announcement of the accession of Hadrian in AD 117, probably issued by the governor of Egypt, reads: 'Be it known to you that for the salvation of the whole race of mankind the imperial rule has been taken over from the god his father by Imperator Caesar Traianus Hadrianus Optimus Augustus Germanicus Dacicus Parthicus. Therefore we shall pray to all the gods that his continuance may be preserved to us for ever and shall wear garlands for ten days.' (*Oxyrhynchus Papyri* 55. 3781, dated 11 May 117)

The other main group of initiators were members of local élites, and especially former kings and tribal leaders, or their descendants, who found in the establishment of the cult of the emperor, both provincial and municipal, a means of giving political edge to their roles as benefactors of their communities or, as the case may be, their former subjects. Assumption of the provincial priesthood of the emperor involved often enormous expense, not merely for the immediate costs of sacrificial animals and processions, but for the extended celebrations that accompanied the imperial festivals. There is a fascinating inscription from Ancyra, which lists the early priests of the deified Augustus and the goddess Roma in Galatia for the years between AD 19/20 and *c*.36/7 (*OGIS* 533 = Ehrenburg and Jones 1976, #109, cf. Mitchell 1993, 107–13). The earliest name that can be read, probably Castor the son of King Brigatus, who may have been the king of Amaseia until his kingdom was annexed in 3/2 BC, is recorded as giving a public banquet, olive oil for a month, a gladiatorial show with 30 pairs of gladiators, bull hunts and other hunts of wild animals; in AD 22/23 the fourth priest, Pylaemenes, son of the last tetrarch of Galatia, King Amyntas, who had been murdered in 26 or 25 BC, was even more generous, as befitted his enormous personal properties: he gave 2 public banquets, 2 gladiatorial shows, competitions for athletes, chariots and horse races; a bull fight; a wild animal hunt; olive oil. But he also made permanent gifts of land: the site where the temple of Augustus, the *Sebasteion*, stood, where the horse-races were held, and the site for the public market held in connection with the festival, the *panegyris*.

In displaying such generosity, the most eminent members of local élite groups represented here and now one aspect of the emperor, his beneficent care for the peoples of the empire, his *cura, sollicitudo, providentia*,[23] and could impersonate through the imperial priesthood the emperor himself. By so doing they symbolically justified the massive inequalities of wealth, privilege, and power which the empire maintained. Inequality seemed to be the pre-condition for access to the pleasures of the festival, the free wine and food, the spectacles that turned the spectators into judges of life and death (Schmitt Pantel 1992: 359–420; Kyle 1998). Moreover, in the non-urbanized provinces of the empire, the buildings of the imperial cult, such as the grand temple-complex at Antioch in Pisidia, which was visible for miles from the west, or the temple of Claudius at Colchester in Britain, were often the very first intimations of Roman civic magnificence, of the idea of the civilizing city, to arrive in these provinces.[24] They emblematized the sheer givenness of the Principate as an institution, suggesting that it was of a kind with the permanence of the gods, and with the permanence of human tendance of the divine.

The death of the emperor, the transition from one sort of godhead to another, may enable us to make a final observation about the naturalization of imperial power. Augustus' wife, Livia, made a present of 1 million sesterces—the wealth qualification of a senator—to a man of praetorian rank, Numerius Atticus, who took an oath that he had seen the dead emperor ascending to heaven just as Romulus, the founder of Rome, had appeared after his death to Julius Proculus (Cassius Dio 56. 46. 2, cf. Suetonius, *Augustus* 100. 4; cf. Price 1987). The historian Herodian describes how at least by

---

[23] Care, solicitude, foresight: on these imperial virtues, cf. Béranger 1953: 186–217; Martin 1982.

[24] Mitchell 1993: 103–7; Drury 1984; Fishwick, 'Templum divo Claudio constitutum', in Fishwick 1987–92: i.2. 195–218.

the late second century AD an eagle was released from the top of an
emperor's multi-storeyed funeral-pyre as the flames consumed the
body below: 'the bird is supposed by the Romans to bear the emperor's
soul from earth to heaven'.[25] So many pious fictions, so much more
or less acknowledged pretence. But hardly anyone, outside the ranks of
the philosophers, and one or two historians such as Hieronymus of
Cardia, and often enough not even they, cared about the truth. There
were few Plutarchs who cared to write: 'Have not many kings been told
they were Apollo just because they could hum a tune, or Dionysus
because they got drunk, or Heracles because they had distinguished
themselves in battle, and, in their delight, been led into utter disgrace
by flattery?' (Plutarch, *de adulatore et amico* 12, 56f.; cf. Taeger 1935).
For this was the point at which the senate, speaking for the empire as a
whole, was empowered to decide whether the deceased was worthy of
becoming a *divus*, that is, a true inhabitant of heaven, a full divinity
within the succession going back to Julius Caesar.[26] The senate's right
to choose, to deify or to damn, served to underpin the moral authority
of the imperial system as a whole. The pious spectacle enacted that
moral legitimacy before the eyes of the empire's inhabitants just as it
confirmed that true emperors truly were not of this world.[27]

At the level of public rhetoric, political power and religion were
so closely interwoven that they could not and cannot meaningfully
be separated. The decree of the senate in the celebrated case of
the treason of the consular Cn. Calpurnius Piso, delivered on 10
December AD 20, opens with the words:

The Senate and the Roman people above all else thank the immortal gods for
not allowing the present peaceable condition of the state, which could not be
wished to be better and which we are able to enjoy through the *beneficium* of

---

[25] Herodian 4. 2. 11. A similar account by Cassius Dio of the consecration of
Pertinax in June or July 193 AD: 74. 4. 2–5. 5: 'Then at last the consuls applied fire to
the structure, and thereupon an eagle flew up out of it'; cf. Clauss 1999: 360–8.

[26] For a convenient list of the 72 emperors and their relatives who are known to
have been created *divi* up to and including Theodosius (but excluding Antinoüs), see
Clauss 1999: 533–5.

[27] At one of the high points of the 'third-century crisis' Traianus Decius (AD
249–51) issued a coin-series showing the hallowed sequence of eleven 'real' *divi*—
including Commodus but not Pertinax—stretching back to Augustus: Mattingly
1949.

the emperor, to be destroyed by the impious conspiracy of Cn. Piso the elder; and second, they thank the emperor Ti. Caesar Augustus....

(*AE* 1996: no. 885 = *CIL* ii². 5, no. 900, ll.12–15 (El Tajar, Cordoba))

The existence of the emperor makes political and social life possible. Nearly three hundred years later, the emperor Maximinus claimed in his rescript of AD 312 encouraging persecution of the Christians: 'Who is so obtuse as not to see that the benevolent concern of the gods is responsible for the fertility of the earth, for keeping the peace and defeating unrighteous enemies, for curbing storms at sea, tempests and earthquakes, which have occurred only when the Christians with their ignorant and futile beliefs have come to afflict almost the entire world with their shameful practices?'.[28] At any rate from the emperors' point of view, the safety of the Roman Empire was a matter of constant and unremitting concern to the Other World. If to the people emperors looked very much like gods, to the emperors the gods looked very much like themselves—part of the order of things.

*

What of the role of images, however, about which I have as yet said nothing? Some of the themes I have mentioned can certainly be illustrated. Several consecration issues (Fig. 2.1) depict the elaborate four-storey cremation-tower. The bier bearing the wax effigy of the corpse, which the new emperor (if the dead were his predecessor) kissed in farewell, is depicted on the second tier. The top tier is surmounted by an imperial quadriga—evidently a real one: the short-lived Emperor Pertinax, for example, took his favourite chariot to heaven with him. We must of course imagine the rest—all the magistrates of the state in full gear, the entire senatorial and equestrian orders, the imperial family on its tribunal, the consuls setting fire to the tower, the scent of burning wood, offerings and spices, the intricate exhibition marching of the massed infantry and cavalry, the eagle rising heavenward bearing the new god. And the theme of the emperors' self-identification with the cares of the gods is neatly

---

[28] Eusebius, *History of the Church* 9. 7. 8, cf. Mitchell 1988: 120; Mitchell 1993, ii. 64f.; 101, fig. 22.

Fig. 2.1. Consecration *aureus* for Antoninus Pius, depicting (reverse) the four-storey cremation-tower, decorated with garlands and statues: on top, chariot, on second tier, a door (AD 161). Legend: *Consecratio*.

suggested by the type (Fig. 2.2) issued on a considerable scale in commemoration of the recovery in 19 BC by negotiation (*signis receptis*) of the legionary standards lost by the triumvir M. Licinius Crassus at Carrhae. Augustus planned, but never executed, a temple on the Capitol to house the standards, which eventually found a permanent home in the temple of Mars Ultor, the Avenger, dedicated in the Forum in 2 BC.[29] On the coin, we find Mars hurrying along to Rome with the standards, looking back as though to say 'farewell' to Parthia, a divine top-speed parcel-service. The image expresses: the divine favour that enabled Augustus to make good the Parthian

---

[29] Rich 1999. Augustus had probably vowed that the standards would be dedicated to Mars Ultor before their recovery. I think Zanker's view (Zanker 1987: 186) that the image depicts an archaizing statue of Mars in the Capitoline temple, implausible. Rich (1999) has in my view rightly argued that, despite Cassius Dio 54. 8. 3, the senatorial decree for a Capitoline temple remained a dead-letter.

Fig. 2.2. Reverse of denarius, 17 BC, depicting the god Mars carrying the legionary standards lost to the Parthians at Carrhae in 53 BC and recovered by Augustus' diplomacy in 19 BC. Legend: *signis receptis* 'standards recovered'.

insult to Roman arms, his restoration of the *pax deorum* destroyed by the civil wars,[30] the recovery of Roman military power, the consolidation of the army, but more than any of these, the congruence between the care exercised by the gods and by the emperor.

Illustration however is not quite enough. If we are to make fuller use of ancient images related to the imperial cult, we need to appeal to a different notion of power from that of Parsons and Bourdieu. We may perhaps appeal here to some suggestions offered by Kurt Röttgers in the light of Kant's reflections, in the aftermath of the great Lisbon earthquake of 1755, on the problem of what it means to ascribe power to Nature (Röttgers 1990: 488–537). Röttgers suggests that there can

[30] Cf. the excellent study by Jal 1963: 360–488.

be a non-metaphoric notion of power which is not centred upon the political, citing Thomas Reid, Adam Smith's successor (1764) in the chair of moral philosophy at Glasgow and founder of the Scottish school of moral philosophy: 'Power is not an object of any of our external senses, nor even an object of consciousness... Indeed every operation of the mind is the exertion of some power of the mind; but we are conscious of the operation only, the power lies behind the scene' (Reid 1788. On Reid, see Haakonssen 1990; Holcomb 1995). There can be a transcendental conception of power. On this account, power is a non-normative, relative notion, essentially identical to the notion of possibility. In social processes, the primary function of power is to ensure the continuity of action. It is the creation and maintenance of options. Options are representations or images of possible forms of action, so that the content of power is basically fictional. Power prefers the invocation of the possibility of action, images of action, to action itself. From this perspective, power is best defined as the asymmetrical distribution of possibilities or options among potential actors. The person who has most conception of the opportunities available for action is most truly powerful. The most important aspect of acquiring possibilities of action is disposing of ideas about conceiving possibilities of action.[31] To increase one's power is to increase one's power over possibilities of action, i.e. to acquire power over power. In that sense the drive for power can indeed never be satisfied, for it is constantly found wanting by the thought of new options, new possibilities.

If we apply this conception to the case of the imperial cult, we might look at the surviving iconographic (and indeed epigraphic) evidence not so much as illustrations of a process of naturalization, as themselves assertions of, or claims to, the inexpressible variety of the emperor's choices of action, a variety which constantly nudges against that traditionally ascribed to the gods. Whatever the actual restrictions of emperors' existences, their political choices, and administrative responsibilities,[32] the imagery deployed for them,

---

[31] 'Das Verfügenkönnen über die Vorstellungen über das Verfügenkönnen zukunftiger Handlungen ist bereits der wahrscheinlich wichtigste Teil des Verfügenkönnens über zukünftige Handlungen' (p. 494).
[32] Best described by Millar 1977.

and in particular the imagery of the imperial cult, suggests a limitless freedom of action, and in that sense unlimited power, a power that could be unfettered precisely because it existed only in and through the images.

I will limit myself here to a few suggestive images, deliberately ignoring considerations of time, space, and development. We may start with the well-known bust of Caracalla (AD 211–17) in the Berlin Antikensammlung (Fig. 2.3). Traditionally, imperial portraiture had distinguished between the emperor's different roles. This one suggests a desire to transcend such limitations. Who is Caracalla? The image, which draws on the iconography of the victorious athlete but also of the military commander (the sword belt, the military cloak), suggests first that the emperor can somehow simultaneously occupy both roles, that he can at the same time be active in the gymnasium while he is commanding his troops. But the image also suggests an unbridled physical energy, as though the real Caracalla wished somehow to burst out of the confining marble. The features of the face, the brow drawn down towards the nose, and the jutting chin, convey a sense of remorseless, unbroken concentration and determination. More than any other single feature, the vigorously unruly curling of the hair (present for the first time in imperial portraits) suggests unlimited possibility: some curls are tightly coiled and convey potential but suppressed action; others are already dancing upwards into space (Fittschen and Zanker 1985: 106 no. 1; Kunze et al. 1992: 213–15 no. 104). It may be true that 'l'état est le contraire de l'histoire' (Serres 1980: 33),[33] but this image conveys the sense that an emperor is capable even of mediating the opposition between *stasis* and movement.

One of the central themes of traditional discourse about the gods is their ubiquity. The multiplicity of imperial images enabled emperors in a sense to emulate the gods' ability to defy the limits of space and time. The living god could be 'present' in each of his temples, all over the empire, but also in public spaces, fora, cycles, odea, amphitheatres, and in rooms in private houses. Not merely that, he could be present in different scales, in different fractions or segments,

[33] '... Being is the opposite of History.'

Fig. 2.3. Marble bust of Caracalla, 58 cm high, AD 212–17, allegedly from Rome.

each alluding to the real person but at the same time suggesting a transcendence of human limitation. A small bronze bust of Augustus, with the features of Octavian, now in the Louvre, may have stood in a Gallic temple (Fig. 2.4). It is dedicated to him as a god by a certain Atespatus, a non-citizen Gaul whose name has nevertheless been Latinized.[34] One of a pair with Livia, it employs the skills of naturalism to convey a sense of disembodied presence, principally conveyed

[34] This point has been much disputed, cf. Fishwick 1987–92: ii.1. 544f.; Clauss 1999: 31–3.

Fig. 2.4. Bronze bust of Augustus, one of a pair with Livia, from Neuilly-le-Réal, now in the Louvre. The inscription reads: *Caesari Augusto Atespatus Crixi fil. v(otum) s(olvit) l(ibens) m(erito)*, the normal formula for a votive (*CIL* XIII 1366).

by the exaggeratedly large inlaid irides and pupils, and by the tension set up between direction of gaze and that of the suggested torso. Moreover, it has rightly been observed that one of the values of the miniature in the Hellenistic period was the paradox implied in the suggestion that something very small could embody all the strength of something huge (Onians 1979: 126). The miniature introduces a domestic scale, which it simultaneously subverts by calling attention to its referent through naturalist virtuosity. But scale is of course entirely relative. The colossal statue of Augustus, which was visible through the pierced exedra in the theatre at Emerita in Lusitania (Fig. 2.5), as in numerous other known theatres, nevertheless seems dwarfed by its surroundings.[35] In such theatres, the emperor is a kind of spectator, but a spectator not only of the play—he also spectates the spectators in the *cavea*, thus turning them into subjects of his imagined gaze. Elsewhere, again, colossal scale can be de-emphasized, as in the case of the seated togate statue (Fig. 2.6), probably of Hadrian (AD 117–38), found in the 'Byzantine esplanade' near the Crusader fort in Caesarea Maritima in northern Israel. It may have served as the cult statue in his temple, or have been set up in the council-building. In this case, the nature of the stone (porphyry) and the seated pose serve to reduce the true scale, simultaneously suggesting super-human magnificence and normal humanity. It is thus not merely the ubiquity of the emperor that was emphasized by the

Fig. 2.5. The *scaenae frons* of the theatre at Mérida, Spain, with the colossal statue of Augustus in the centre.

---

[35] Similar statues are known from the theatres at Orange, Arles, Lepcis Magna, and Bulla Regia; perhaps also at Tarraco, Vienne, Vaison-les-Romains, Cherchel, and elsewhere: Fishwick 1987–92: ii.1. 522f.

Fig. 2.6. Porphyry statue of a seated emperor, probably Hadrian, from Caesarea Maritima (2.45 m high).

imperial cult, but also, once again, his ceaseless capacity to mediate between oppositions, to be as it were at least two things at once. It is the plurality of the emperor's options for acting that are stressed—his manifold *Handlungsmöglichkeiten*. A quite different kind of option is suggested by an over-lifesized cuirassed statue from the theatre at Cherchel (Shirshāll) in Algeria, probably set up in honour of Caius Caesar, Augustus' ill-fated adoptive heir (Fig. 2.7). As usual in Augustan imperial iconography, the cuirass is elaborately decorated with symbolic figures. The human figure 'carries' divine figures, thus

Fig. 2.7. Marble torso of a cuirassed statue, probably of Caius Caesar, who died in AD 4 (2.28 m high).

setting it apart from mortals unequal to such burdens. That suggests
one relation to divinity. Among the figures depicted is Caius himself,
at centre-right, heroically draped to resemble the image of the divi-
nized Julius Caesar, solemnly offering a statue of Victoria, Victory,
over the navel of the 'real' Caius, to an armed Venus, ancestor of the
Iulii, who is depicted on the same scale, though slightly smaller, as
befits a woman.[36] Caius is on the same footing as the inhabitants of
heaven. But above them is represented the bust of Mars *velatus*
(veiled), suggesting the supremacy of the divine-imperial mission of
universal victory and conquest.[37] Here Caius not only 'bears' the gods
on his cuirass, he is descended from one and so equal to her (Venus),
he is master of another (the statue of Victoria), but subordinate to—
or beneath the protection of—yet another, Mars Ultor. Of course in
one sense this can be read as 'symbolism', as a series of claims. What
interests me in the present connection is the suggestion of the options
that Caius, as a member of the Julian house, can exercise simultaneously in relation to the divine world.

The emperor may have been a god, but he was also the key
mediator between his empire and the Other World. This role is
repeatedly depicted in imperial art (Scott Ryberg 1955), for example
in the panel from his arch showing Marcus Aurelius, *capite velato*,
with his head covered, taking the incense from the *acerra*, incense
box, as he prepares to sacrifice in front of the temple of Capitoline
Jupiter (Fig. 2.8). The emperor's key role in the state is connoted by
his position between a *flamen*, presumably of Jupiter (to his right),
and the bearded *Genius Senatus* to his left (Scott Ryberg 1955: 157f.;
Turcan 1988: ii. 32 no. 69). Even though they may denote an actual
ritual, in this case, say, his *decennalia* celebration in AD 171, such
images also connote the emperor's role as exemplary sacrificant,
which models the sacrificial acts of all magistrates, officials, military
commanders, central and local, and even of every *paterfamilias*. The
imperial images summarize, subsume, these thousands of daily

[36] Caius Caesar (COS. AD 1) was sent with *imperium proconsulare* to the East in AD
2 to settle the political situation in Armenia. On 9 Sept. AD 3 he was wounded
at Atagira and died at Limyra in Caria on 21 Feb. the following year.
[37] See the fine account by Zanker 1987: 223. The statue may have been erected by
King Juba of Mauretania.

Fig. 2.8. Relief plaque of M. Aurelius sacrificing, probably from his triumphal arch on the Capitol. Palazzo dei Conservatori, 3.14 x 2.10 m.

sacrifices. But the claims made for the emperor's sacrificial role, in maintaining the *pax deorum* and so the welfare and physical well-being of the entire population of the empire, are better expressed on the reverse of a Trajanic *as* from Caesarea Maritima (Fig. 2.9), showing the emperor, *capite velato*, in an abbreviated sacrificial gesture, dropping grains of incense on a portable altar. In his left hand he holds the cornucopia, the symbol of domestic peace and agricultural fecundity. The image conveys the claimed real consequences, in daily life all over the empire, of the totality of ritual acts that maintain the *pax deorum*, the return for the deaths of all the victims, the gods' respect for Roman piety. And an essential aspect of that piety is sacrifice on behalf of, for, and even to, the succession of the *divi*, and the living emperor.

Fig. 2.9. Reverse of *as* of Trajan, AD 115–17, mint of Caesarea: Trajan sacrificing, holding the cornucopia.

The notion of totality is also suggestive for the issue of 'transcendental' power. On his succession in AD 79, Titus issued a number of coins (Fig. 2.10) showing his father Vespasian passing a globe to Titus, who already stands beside the rudder of state. The legend, *providentia august(a)*, suggests Vespasian's foresight in naming Titus his successor already in 69 (Clauss 1999: 109f.). The globe is a condensed symbol, connoting rule over the empire, of course, which the Romans liked to think as extending over the entire world (Vogt 1960: 151–71; Nicolet 1988); but it also connotes the permanence of the imperial system, denoted by the phrase *aeternitas Augusti*, of the universe, and the weight of ages (Schneider 1997). The scale of this responsibility is overwhelming. But the emperors are a match for the task: for they are vast enough to pass the world from hand to hand as though it were indeed a ball. Moreover, insofar as the globe denotes power, power is represented as a quantum, as a concrete totality, reified as a sphere, almost as a possession. This

Fig. 2.10. Reverse of *sestertius* of Titus (AD 80–1), showing Vespasian (l.) giving his son the world-globe. Legend: *Provident(ia) august(a)/ S.C.*

power cannot leak away, is dependent neither upon negotiation nor political calculation, fears not the mood of the military nor the assassin's dagger. 'The ideal social process of succession outflanks mere time' (Bloch 1987).

Re-thinking power may also involve a deliberate subversion of the usual rules for reading Roman iconographic language, a decision to read them for what they might tell us about 'transcendence', about power as option, possibility, the mediation of oppositions, being in more than one place at once. If there is anything at all in this effort at re-thinking, others will be able to turn it to their own ends. Duncan Fishwick ends one of his excellent essays on the imperial cult with the observation: 'Generalizations are always risky and a piecemeal analysis clearly provides the soundest approach.'[38] Details of course naturally delight the scholarly mind, but without contexts they remain mere details. Transactionalism will not remain the last word. The questions return. What ends are served by the imagery of the imperial cult? How are we to think of power?

AFTERWORD (2009)

Work on the numerous facets of the imperial cult continues unabated. The proceedings of two conferences give a good idea of the spread of recent interests: Cancik (ed.) 2003 and Navarro Caballero (ed.) 2003. Gradel (2002) has competently applied Simon Price's approach to Italy. On municipal imperial cycles and the Augustales in the peninsula: Wohlmayr 2004. Augustus himself is the focus of Rehak 2006 [2007]. 'Mentality': Herz 2007. Imperial funerary monuments: Davies (2004). Useful monographs on aspects of provincial cults: Witulski (2007) on Asia Minor; Hardin (2008) on the *Epistle to the Galatians*; (I pass over several other discussions of the relation of Christianity to the imperial cult, and of the background to *Revelations*); Lozano 2002 on Athens. The crisis of legitimation: Kolb 2001.

---

[38] Fishwick, 'The Augustales and the Imperial cult', in Fishwick 1987–92: ii.1. 607–16 at 616.

BIBLIOGRAPHY

Bartman, E. (1999). *Portraits of Livia. Imaging the Imperial Woman in Augustan Rome*. Cambridge: Cambridge University Press.

Beaujeu, J. (1955). *La religion romaine à l'apogée de l'Empire*, 1: *la politique religieuse des Antonins (96–192)*. Paris: Les Belles Lettres.

Bell, C. (1992). *Ritual Theory, Ritual Practice*. New York and Oxford: Oxford University Press.

Béranger, J. (1953). *Recherches sur l'aspect idéologique du Principat*, Schweizerische Beiträge zur Altertumswissenschaft 6. Basel: Reinhardt.

Bergmann, M. (1998). *Die Strahlen der Herrscher. Theomorphes Herrscherbild und politische Symbolik im Hellenismus und der römischen Kaiserzeit*. Mainz: von Zabern.

Bickerman, E. J. (1973). 'Consecratio', in W. den Boer (ed.), *Le culte des souverains dans l'Empire romain*, Entretiens Fondation Hardt 19. Vandoeuvres: Fondation Hardt, 179–206.

Bourdieu, P. (1971). 'Genèse et structure du champ religieux', *Revue française de sociologie*, 12: 295–334.

Bloch, M. (1987). 'The Ritual of the Royal Bath in Madagascar: The Dissolution of Death, Birth, and Fertility into Authority', in D. Cannadine and S. Price (eds.), *Rituals of Royalty*. Cambridge: Cambridge University Press, 271–97, repr. in his *Ritual, History and Power: Selected Papers in Anthropology*. London: Athlone Press (1989), 187–211.

Cancik, H. (ed.) (2003). *Die Praxis der Herrscherverehrung in Rom und seinen Provinzen*. Tübingen: Mohr Siebeck.

Clauss, M. (1999). *Kaiser und Gott. Herrscherkult im römischen Reich*. Stuttgart and Leipzig: Teubner.

Davies, P. J. E. (2000). *Death and the Emperor: Roman Funerary Monuments from Augustus to Marcus Aurelius*. Cambridge: Cambridge University Press.

Drury, P. (1984). 'The Temple of Claudius at Colchester Reconsidered', *Britannia*, 15: 7–50.

Eck, W., Fittschen K., and Naumann F. (1986). *Kaisersaal. Porträts aus den Kapitolinischen Museen in Rom*. Rome: de Luca.

Ehrenberg, V. and Jones, A. H. M. (eds.) (1976). *Documents Illustrating the Reigns of Augustus and Tiberius*, 2nd edn. Oxford: Clarendon Press.

Fears, J. R. (1981). 'The Cult of Virtues and Roman Imperial Ideology', *ANRW* 2. 17. 2: 827–948.

Fejfer, J. (1988). 'Official Portraits of Julia Domna', in N. Boncasa and G. Rizza (eds.), *Ritratto ufficiale e ritratto privato: Atti del II conferenza intern. sul ritratto romano, Roma sett. 1984*. Rome: Consiglio nazionale delle ricerche, 288–304.

Fishwick, D. (1986). *Phoenix*, 40: 225–30 (Review of Price 1984).

——(1987–92). *The Imperial Cult in the Latin West*, EPRO 108. Leiden: Brill.

Fittschen K. and Zanker, P. (1985). *Katalog der römischen Porträts in den Capitolinischen Museen*, Mainz: von Zabern.

Friesen, S. J. (1993). *Twice Neokoros: Ephesus, Asia and the Cult of the Flavian Imperial Family*, RGRW 116. Leiden: Brill.

Gazda E. K. and Haeckl, A. E. (1993). 'Roman Portraiture: Reflections on the Question of Context', *JRA*, 6: 289–302.

Gehlen, A. (1961). *s.v.* 'Macht', in *Handbuch der Sozialwissenschaften*, 7: 77–81.

Gibson, Q. (1971). *s.v.* 'Power', in *Philosophy of the Social Sciences*, 1: 101–12.

Gonda, J. (1963). *Die Religionen Indiens*, 2: *Der jüngere Hinduismus*. Stuttgart: Kohlhammer.

Gradel, I. (2002). *Emperor Worship and Roman Religion*. Oxford: Oxford University Press.

Groetschy, J. (1981). 'Les théories du pouvoir', *Sociologie du Travail*, 23: 447–67.

Gros, P. (1986). *Revue des Études Latines*, 64: 321–3 (review of Price 1984).

Haakonssen, K. (1990). *Introduction* to T. Reid, *Practical Ethics*. Princeton: Princeton University Press.

Habicht, C. (1970). *Gottmenschentum und griechische Städte*, 2nd edn. Munich: Beck.

Hahn, U. (1994). *Die Frauen des römischen Kaiserhauses und ihre Ehrungen im griechischen Osten anhand epigraphischer und numismatischer Zeugnisse von Livia bis Sabina*. Saarbrücken: Sahrbrucker Druckerei und Verlag.

Hänlein-Schäfer, H. (1985). *Veneratio Augusti: eine Studie zu den Tempeln des ersten römischen Kaisers*, Archaeologica 39. Rome: Bretschneider.

Hardin, J. K. (2008). *Galatians and the Imperial Cult: A Critical Analysis of the First-Century Social Context of Paul's Letter*. Tübingen: Mohr Siebeck.

Haussmann, U. (1981). 'Zur Typologie und Ideologie des Augustusporträts', *ANRW*, 2. 12. 2: 513–98.

Herz, P. (1988). 'Der römische Kaiser und der Kaiserkult: Gott oder primus inter pares?', in D. Zeller (ed.), *Menschwerdung Gottes—Vergöttlichung von Menschen*, Novum testamentum et orbis Antiquus 7. Fribourg, Suisse: Universitätsverlag—Göttingen: Vanderhoeck and Ruprecht, 115–40.

——(2007). 'Emperors Caring for the Empire and their Successors', in J. Rüpke (ed.), *A Companion to Roman Religion*. Malden, MA, and Oxford: Blackwell, 304–16.

Hofter, M. (1988). 'Porträt', in *Kaiser Augustus und die verlorene Republik*. Mainz: von Zabern, 291–343.

Holcomb, K. (1995). 'T. Reid in the Glasgow Literary Society', in A. Hook and R. B. Sher (eds.), *The Glasgow Enlightenment*. East Linton, Scotland: Tuckwell Press, 95–110.

Hopkins, K. (1999). *A World Full of Gods: Pagans, Jews and Christians in the Roman Empire*. London: Weidenfeld and Nicolson.

Jal, P. (1963). *La Guerre civile à Rome: étude littéraire et morale*. Paris: Presses universitaires de France.

Jordanova, L. (2000). *History in Practice*. London: Arnold.

Kienast, D. (1999). *Augustus. Prinzeps und Monarch*, 3rd edn. Darmstadt: Wissenschafliche Buchgesellschaft.

Kinsley, D. R. (1992). *Hindu Goddesses: Visions of the Divine Feminine in Hindu Religious Tradition*. Berkeley: University of California Press.

——(2000). *The Sword and the Flute: Kali and Krishna: Dark Visions of the Terrible and Sublime in Hindu Mythology*. Berkeley: University of California Press.

Kobusch T. and Oeing-Hanhoff, L. (1980). *s.v.* 'Macht', in *Historisches Wörterbuch der Philosophie*. Basel and Stuttgart: Schwabe, vol. 5. cols. 585–8.

Kolb, F. (2001). *Herrscherideologie in der Spätantike*. Berlin: Akademie Verlag.

Kyle, D. G. (1998). *Spectacles of Death in Ancient Rome*. London and New York: Routledge.

Kunze, M., Giuliani, L., et al. (1992). *Die Antikensammlung im Pergamonmuseum und in Charlottenburg*. Staatliche Museen zu Berlin. Mainz: von Zabern.

Lietz, U.-M. (1998). *Kult und Kaiser. Studien zur Kaiserkult und Kaiserverehrung in den germanischen Provinzen und in Gallia Belgica zur römischen Kaiserzeit*, Acta Instituti Romani Finlandiae 20. Rome: Institutum Romanum Finlandiae.

Lozano, F. (2002). *La religión del poder: el culto imperial en Atenas en época de Augusto y los emperadores Julio-Claudios*, British Archaeological Reports, international series 1087. Oxford: Archaeopress.

Martin, J.-P. (1982). *Providentia deorum: aspects religieux du pouvoir romain*, Collection de l'école française de Rome 61. Rome: École française de Rome.

Mattingly, H. (1949). 'The Coins of the *"Divi"* issued by Trajan Decius', *Numismatic Chronicle*, 9: 75–82.

Millar, F. G. B. (1977). *The Emperor in the Roman World (31 BC–AD 337)*. London: Duckworth.

Mitchell, S. (1988). 'Maximinus and the Christians in AD 312: A New Latin Inscription', *JRS*, 78: 105–24.

——(1993). *Anatolia: Land, Men and Gods in Asia Minor*. Oxford: Clarendon Press.

Navarro Caballero, M. (ed.) (2003). *La transmission de l'idéologie impériale dans l'Occident romain*. Bastia; Pessac; Ausonius; Paris: Comité des Travaux Historiques et Scientifiques.

Nicolet, C. (1988). *L'inventaire du monde: géographie et politique aux origines de l'Empire romain*. Paris: Fayard., Eng. trans. *Space, Geography and Politics in the Early Roman Empire*. Ann Arbor: University of Michigan Press (1990).

Niemayer, H. G. (1968). *Studien zur statuarischen Darstellung der römischen Kaiser*. Berlin: Gebr. Mann.

Nock A. D. (1928). 'Notes on Ruler-Cult, I–IV', *Journal of Hellenic Studies*, 48: 21–43, reprinted in Z. Stewart (ed.), *Essays on Religion and the Ancient World*. Oxford: Oxford University Press (1972), ii. 135–58.

Onians, J. B. (1979). *Art and Thought in the Hellenistic Age*. London: Thames and Hudson.

Parsons, T. (1963). 'On the Concept of Power', *Proceedings of the American Philosophical Society*, 107: 232–62, reprinted in his *Sociological Theory and Modern Society*. New York and London: Collier-Macmillan. (1967), 297–354.

Pekáry, T. (1985). *Das römische Kaiserbildnis in Staat, Kult und Gesellschaft*, Das römische Herrscherbild 3. 5. Berlin: Mann Verlag.

Potter, D. M. (1963). 'Explicit Data and Implicit Assumptions in Historical Study', in L. Gottschalk (ed.), *Generalization in the Writing of History*. Chicago: University of Chicago Press, 178–94.

Price, S. R. F. (1984). *Rituals and Power: The Roman Imperial Cult in Asia Minor*. Cambridge: Cambridge University Press.

——(1987). 'From Noble Funerals to Divine Cult: The Consecration of Roman Emperors', in D. Cannadine and S. R. F. Price (eds.), *Rituals of Royalty: Power and Ceremonial in Traditional Societies*. Cambridge: Cambridge University Press, 56–105.

Rehak, P. (2006 [2007]). *Imperium and Cosmos: Augustus and the Northern Campus Martius*. Madison, Wi.: University of Wisconsin Press.

Reid, T. (1788). *Essays on the Active Powers of Man*. Edinburgh: John Bell. London: J. & J. Robinson; reprinted 1977, New York and London: Garland Publishing.

Rich, J. W. (1999). 'Augustus's Parthian Honours, the Temple of Mars Ultor and the Arch in the Forum Romanum', *Papers of the British School at Rome*, 53: 71–128.

Rose, C. B. (1996). 'The Portraits of Agrippina the Elder', *JRA*, 9: 353–4.

——(1997). *Dynastic Commemoration and Imperial Portraiture in the Julio–Claudian Period*. Cambridge: Cambridge University Press.

Röttgers, K. (1990). *Spuren der Macht: Begriffsgeschichte und Systematik*. Freiburg and Munich: Karl Alber.

Schindler, W. (1986). *Römische Kaiser: Herrscherbild und Imperium*. Vienna: Bohlau.

Schmitt Pantel, P. (1992). *La cité au banquet: histoire des repas publics dans les cités grecques romain*, Collection de l'école française de Rome 157. Rome: École française de Rome.

Schneider, R. M. (1997). 'Rome aeterna—aurea Roma. Der Himmelsglobus als Zeitzeichen und Machtsymbol', in J. Assmann and E. W. B. Hess-Lüttich (eds.), *Kult, Kalender und Geschichte. Semiotisierung von Zeit als kulturelle Konstruktion*. Tübingen: Narr (special issue of *Kodikas/Code: Ars Semeiotica* 20. 1–2), 103–33.

Scott Ryberg, I. (1955). *Rites of the State Religion in Roman Art*, Memoirs of the American Academy in Rome 22. Rome: American Academy in Rome.

Serres, M. (1980). *Le parasite*. Paris: Grasset.

Smith, R. R. R. (1988). *Hellenistic Royal Portraits*. Oxford: Oxford University Press.

——(2000). 'Nero and the Sun-God: Divine Accessories and Political Symbols in Roman Imperial Images', *JRA*, 13: 532–42.

Taeger, F. (1935). 'Zum Kampf gegen den antiken Herrscherkult', *Archiv für Religionswissenschaft*, 32: 282–92.

Torelli, M. (1977). *Il rango, il rito e l'immagine: alle origine della rappresentazione storica romana*. Milan: Electa.

——(1982). *Typology and Structure of Roman Historical Reliefs*. Ann Arbor: University of Michigan Press.

——(1998) *Tota Italia: Essays in the Cultural Formation of Roman Italy*. Oxford: Clarendon Press.

Turcan, R. (1978). 'Le culte impérial au IIIe siècle', in *ANRW*, 2. 16. 2: 996–1084.

——(1988). *Religion romaine*, Iconography of Religions 17. 1. Leiden: Brill.

Vierneisel, K. and Zanker, P. (eds.) (1979). *Die Bildnisse des Augustus. Herrscherbild und Politik im kaiserlichen Rom*. Munich: Glyptothek Munich.

Vogt, J. (1960). 'Orbis Romanus', in his *Orbis: Ausgewählte Schriften zur Geschichte des Altertums*. Freiburg: Herder, 152–72.

Walker, S. (2000). 'The Imperial Image of Livia', *JRA*, 13: 529–31.

Weinreich, O. (1926). 'Antikes Gottmenschentum', *Neue Jahrbücher für Wissenschaft und Jugendbildung*, 6: 633–51.

Witulski, T. (2007). *Kaiserkult in Kleinasien: die Entwicklung der kultisch-religiösen Kaiserverehrung in der römischen Provinz Asia von Augustus bis Antoninus Pius.* Göttingen: Vanderhoeck & Ruprecht.

Wohlmayr, W. (2004). *Kaisersaal.* Vienna: Phoibos.

Zanker, P. (1987). *Augustus und die Macht der Bilder.* Munich: Beck. English trans. (1988). *The Power of Images in the Age of Augustus.* Ann Arbor: University of Michigan Press.

3

Magic in Roman Law
The Reconstruction of a Crime[1]

J. B. Rives

As Book Four of *The Aeneid* draws to its climax, Dido begins to make plans for her self-immolation and enlists her sister's help with the preparations. In order to hide from Anna the true significance of her requests, she explains that she has found a way either to get Aeneas back or to loosen the hold of love: a priestess (*sacerdos*) of the Massylii can by means of chants (*carmina*) free her mind from cares. But before giving Anna her instructions, Dido makes a short but emotional apology: 'Dear sister, I call the gods to witness, and you and your sweet life, that unwillingly do I resort to magical arts' (*Aeneid* 4. 492–3). An innocent reader might wonder why she feels the need to apologize in this way. The ancient commentator Servius, writing probably in the early fifth century CE, provides a plausible answer: 'because, although the Romans adopted many rites (*sacra*), they always condemned those of magic (*semper magica damnarunt*); for that reason she excuses herself' (Servius on *Aeneid* 4. 493). Since

[1] Earlier versions of this paper were presented at Columbia University, Loyola University in Chicago, the University of Manchester, McMaster University, the University of Pennsylvania, Yale University, and York University in Toronto. I am indebted to the audiences on all those occasions for their probing questions and helpful comments. I also owe thanks to Timothy Barnes for advice on the *The Opinions of Paulus* (*Pauli Sententiae*); to Michael Peachin for his comments on the penultimate draft; to Robert Phillips for his valuable feedback and suggestions on many occasions; and to Kathleen McCarthy and the two anonymous referees for *Classical Antiquity* for their thoughtful and helpful criticism.

Servius was writing as an ancient *grammaticus*, concerned above all
with the linguistic exposition of his text for young students, it is not
surprising that his comment is somewhat lacking in nuance. It is not,
however, inapposite: if we understand that both the author and his
readers condemned magical rites, a character who was meant to appear
sympathetic would naturally express shame at recourse to them.

Nor did Servius' observation lack historical basis. By using the
verb *damnare*, with its strong legal connotations, Servius almost
certainly meant to suggest that *sacra magica* were not merely
improper but actually illegal. At the time that he was writing, this
was indeed the case.[2] Moreover, Servius had good reason to believe
that it had in fact 'always' been the case, for he knew of a law from the
Twelve Tables, the ancient compilation of Roman laws written some
eight and a half centuries before, that concerned a specific magical
rite. Commenting on the second half of Vergil's eighth *Eclogue*, a
poem in which a young girl attempts by ritual means to bring her
lover back from town, he elucidates her claim that certain herbs,
herbae, and potent substances, *venena*, can be used to transfer crops
from one field to another (*Eclogue* 8. 99) by remarking that 'this came
about by means of certain magical arts; hence in the Twelve Tables
there is the clause "nor entice the crop of others"'.[3] It was therefore
with some justification that he could assert that the Romans had
'always' condemned magical rites.

Although most scholars since Servius would agree with his assessment that magic was always illegal in the Roman world, there have
been relatively few detailed discussions of the extent to which and,
more importantly, the senses in which this was true. Until the latter
part of the twentieth century, most classical scholars interested in the
legal status of magic tended to accept 'magic' as an unproblematic,
objective category that required little examination or definition. Many
seem to have operated with an implicit version of the triangulated
definition expressed most succinctly by Frazer, who characterized

---

[2] See especially *The Opinions of Paulus* 5. 23. 17–18, discussed below, and *Codex
Theodosianus* 9. 16. 3–7 (translated in Beard, North, and Price 1998: ii. 263).
[3] Since Augustine made the same connection between this passage of the *Eclogues*
and the Twelve Tables (*City of God* 8. 19), it may have been a piece of stock knowledge
in the repertoire of a *grammaticus*. For a discussion of this law, see Rives 2002: 273–9.

magic by contrasting it with religion and science.[4] The lack of any need to worry over what was magic and what was not greatly simplified the task of these scholars, since they could proceed merely by collecting references to the legal status of anything that was 'obviously' magic. This approach, which I will refer to as the 'realist' school, resulted in some studies that still provide the most comprehensive collections of material.[5] Yet they are generally quite weak in analysis, because the failure to consider the nature of magic tended to obviate the need for careful interpretation. It was not necessary to consider the specific issues at stake in any given case, since the fact that it concerned 'magic' was considered explanation enough. Hence these older studies often leave an aftertaste of tautology: 'these various magical practices were illegal, and they were illegal because they were cases of magic'.

Over the last twenty-five years or so, however, the revival of scholarly interest in ancient magic has led to a sea change in methodology. The category 'magic' has become a highly charged one, and even scholars disinclined to engage with theoretical issues now feel compelled to address questions about its meaning and applicability.[6] A dominant approach in current scholarship, although by no means the only one, is to treat 'magic' as an evaluative term used to mark off activities or beliefs that the speaker regards with disapproval. Moreover, the cultural sphere to which this evaluative term referred is generally, although not universally, understood to be what we would call religion, i.e., interactions with the divine. In short, there exists today a widespread tendency to regard 'magic' simply as a label that people gave to religious practices they considered immoral,

---

[4] For Frazer 1922: 56–60, magic, like science, assumes 'the order and uniformity of nature', so that the same causes always produce the same effects; the difference is that magic postulates causal connections where none in fact exist, so that magic is 'the bastard sister of science'. Religion, in contrast to both, assumes that the world is governed by conscious and personal powers, whose favour people must win by propitiation or conciliation; hence where the magician attempts to manipulate and control, the worshipper humbly supplicates.

[5] In particular, Pharr 1932 and Massonneau 1934: 136–241; Mommsen 1899: 639–43 remains valuable for its sensitivity to the evidence.

[6] For example, Dickie (2001: 18) asserts that 'my own reaction on coming across yet another attempt at defining the notion of magic is dismay combined with a sense of foreboding'; nevertheless he spends two chapters discussing the emergence of a concept of magic in the Greek and the Roman worlds.

fraudulent, or otherwise unacceptable.[7] This is what I will call the 'nominalist' approach.

For the purposes of analysing the legal situation, the nominalist approach constitutes a tremendous advance over the realist approach, in that it calls explicit attention to an underlying issue rather than simply relying on the term 'magic' as a self-evident explanatory term. Yet it is not without limitations of its own: if realist assumptions obviated the need for analysis, nominalist assumptions tend to restrict analysis to one set of issues. Indeed, if we pursue the nominalist insight to its logical conclusion, we should dispense with 'magic' altogether, and focus instead on issues of religious deviance.[8] The problem with this, I would argue, is that the issues behind the criminalization of certain activities shifted over time, as those activities came to be perceived in new ways. In an earlier paper I examined the laws in the Twelve Tables that dealt with 'wicked chants', *mala carmina*, and with the enchantment of crops (i.e., the law cited by Servius in the passage quoted above). I argued that the notion of 'magic' hinders rather than aids our efforts to understand these laws in their original historical context, although I also pointed out that Servius and other later Roman writers understood them precisely as laws against magic. I thus concluded that these laws both did and did not constitute laws against magic, insofar as they criminalized certain actions that were later reconceptualized as instances of magic (Rives 2002). It is this sort of reconceptualization, the possibility that the same set of actions might be treated as crimes over a long period but for reasons that gradually shifted, that the nominalist focus on religious deviance renders very difficult to analyse.

It thus seems important to retain 'magic' as a heuristic category if we wish to achieve a broader and richer analysis of Roman legal developments. This does not mean that we should return to the old

---

[7] For important expositions of this approach, see M. Smith 1978: 68–93; Phillips 1986: 2711–32, 1991, and 1994; cf. J. Z. Smith 1975: 22–5; Gager 1992: 24–5; Beard, North, and Price 1998: i. 154–6; Janowitz 2001: 9–26; Dickie 2001: 20–2, 39–40, and 461; it is anticipated by Nock 1933: 169–75 (= 1972: 313–18). For a critique, see Versnel 1991 and J. Z. Smith 1995: 16–20; for general reflections, see Remus 1999.

[8] As argued most cogently by Phillips: 'instead of looking for legal repression of ancient magic, we could more accurately—and hence more profitably—look for legal repression of unsanctioned religious activity' (1991: 269).

realist approach, but rather that we should extend the nominalist approach in order to take into account issues other than religious deviance; 'magic', it seems to me, provides the most convenient overarching category to encompass these various issues. It will be useful at this point to invoke the distinction between emic and etic levels of analysis, that is, between 'magic' as a Roman conceptual category and 'magic' as a modern heuristic category.[9] If we hope to understand the issues at stake in the criminalization of any particular action, we must do our best to reconstruct emic categories. It is for this reason that in my earlier article I resisted describing the laws of the Twelve Tables as laws against magic, since that term does not seem to correspond to any contemporary conceptual category and consequently implies issues and concerns that have little relevance to archaic Rome. As several scholars have argued, however, a conceptual category of magic, what Richard Gordon has called a 'strong view' of magic, did eventually develop in the Roman world, probably some-time during the first centuries BCE and CE.[10] This development in turn had an impact on Roman law, so that at some point people became liable to general charges of engaging in the magical arts, *artes magicae*; as I shall argue below, in this sort of charge issues of religious deviance could indeed play a central part. If we restrict ourselves to an emic level of analysis, therefore, if we are talking only about what Romans themselves described as the *artes magicae*, then the nominalist approach is an effective one.

Yet to restrict ourselves to an emic level of analysis is to make it virtually impossible to trace lines of continuity between shifting emic categories. Roman authorities criminalized the enchantment of crops long before a strong view of magic gained currency in the Roman world and for reasons that apparently had nothing to do with religious deviance, yet later Romans like Servius could associate that law with the later legal treatment of magicians, *magi*, and evil-doers, *malefici*. From Servius' perspective the archaic law on the

---

[9] For a brief and convenient discussion of these terms, see Harris 1979: 32–41; on their role in the study of ancient magic, see Versnel 1991.

[10] Gordon 1999: 164–5, 207, and 229–31; see also Garosi 1976: 33–73; Beard, North, and Price 1998: i. 154–6; Dickie 2001: 124–41.

enchantment of crops had 'always' been about magic, even though from our own perspective we can see how the underlying issues shifted as emic categories changed. But we can see these changes only because our perspective is precisely not that of contemporary actors, because we employ an overarching etic category that can encompass the shifting emic categories. For better or worse, 'magic' is the most suitable and convenient label for that category. It is useful not only because it is familiar and commonly accepted, but also because it is such a fluid term, able to function as an inclusive but not rigid rubric for a shifting cluster of concerns.[11] Thus the adoption of 'magic' as an explicitly etic, heuristic category allows us to analyse much more effectively the sorts of reconceptualization that I have traced in connection with the Twelve Tables.

In this paper I examine another more complex case of continuity and change in the Roman legal treatment of magic, the development of the *Lex Cornelia de sicariis et veneficiis*, 'the Cornelian law concerning assassins and poisoners'. Since it is not possible in a single paper to scrutinize all the pertinent material, I have chosen to focus on three key 'moments': the original *Lex Cornelia*, insofar as we can reconstruct it; the legal context of the *Apology* of Apuleius; and the situation represented by a passage from *The Opinions of Paulus*. I will argue that the concern of the original *Lex Cornelia* was with harmful and uncanny actions, and that this broadened out over time into a wider concern with religious deviance, even though the latter never entirely displaced the former. My purpose is two-fold. On the one hand, I hope my analysis will serve as a specific exploration of the general methodological issues that I have outlined above. On the other hand, I hope to demonstrate that these issues are not merely abstract, but significantly affect our understanding of historical developments in the Roman world. I thus conclude by discussing some

---

[11] In other words, the term 'magic' is well suited to a polythetic definition, in which the category is defined not by the invariable presence of a single feature or group of features, but instead by the variable presence of one or more features from a general pool; see Versnel 1991: 185–7, who stresses the advantages of such a definition for the study of magic in the ancient world. For a convenient overview of polythetic classification in the biological and social sciences, see Needham 1975; for an influential application to the study of ancient religion, see J. Z. Smith 1980.

of the connections between these changes in the Roman legal treatment of magic and other large-scale developments within the Roman world.

THE *LEX CORNELIA DE SICARIIS ET VENEFICIIS*

The original *Lex Cornelia de sicariis et veneficiis* was one of the laws passed in 81 BCE under L. Cornelius Sulla, by which he reorganized and augmented the system of standing courts that had been developing since the middle of the second century BCE (e.g. Brunt 1988: 216–22). None of these laws is extant in its original form, and we depend for our knowledge of them on later references and quotations. This evidence indicates that the original *Lex Cornelia de sicariis et veneficiis* had at least six sections, and provides a good idea of the contents of three. The first section (dealing with *sicarii*) concerned those 'armed with a weapon for the purpose of killing a person or perpetrating a theft' as well as those who killed someone or arranged for someone to be killed; its purview was restricted to cases in Rome itself or within one mile. The fifth section, (dealing with *venefici*), the one that most concerns us here, dealt with a person 'who for the purpose of killing a person' prepared, sold, bought, possessed, or administered a dangerous drug (*venenum malum*). The sixth section concerned people who caused someone to be wrongfully condemned on a capital charge. There is no evidence regarding the contents of sections two through four, although it is very likely that one of them concerned cases like those in section one that took place more than a mile outside Rome.[12]

At least for those sections whose contents are known, it is clear that this law was not a new creation of Sulla, but instead a reworking of pre-existing laws; Sulla's contribution may have been simply to combine previously separate laws.[13] What were the common elements in these

---

[12] I follow the reconstruction of Ferrary 1996 and his more detailed discussion in Ferrary 1991; for the title *de veneficiis*, instead of *de veneficis*, see Cloud 1968: 140–1.

[13] There was a specific court, the *quaestio inter sicarios*, already in 142 BCE (Cicero, *de Finibus* 2. 54), and section six of the Sullan law incorporated a law of C. Gracchus 'that no one should be convicted unjustly in trial' (Cicero, *For Cluentius* 151). An inscription (*ILS* 45 = *Inscriptiones Italiae* xiii. 3. 70b) records that C. Claudius

laws that caused him to group them together? The most obvious
connection is the idea of murder: the first section was clearly directed
against violent forms of murder, and the sixth against the manipula-
tion of the courts to condemn an innocent person on a capital charge.
Yet there may have been further considerations. We should note that
the clause concerning *sicarii* dealt not only with actual killing but also
with the possession of arms 'for the purpose of killing a person or
committing theft'; a person who in a fit of rage bludgeoned someone
to death would presumably not be tried as a *sicarius*. The term *sicarius*
implied planning and concealment, and so meant something more like
'assassin' than simply 'murderer'.[14] We can thus see a more precise
connection between these two laws: not murder in general, but wrongful death brought about through stealth and malice aforethought.

It is easy to see why Sulla also included the law against *veneficium*
in this grouping. *Veneficium* was in general the use of *venena*, substances that had the power to affect something else. The law on
veneficium, however, did not concern all types of *venena*, but only
those that were dangerous, *venena mala*.[15] Secondly, it did not
concern even all *venena mala*, but only those possessed 'for the
purpose of killing a person'.[16] In these respects, *veneficium*, as defined
by the *Lex Cornelia*, was something very close to the modern idea of

Pulcher was *iudex quaestionis veneficiis* probably in 98 BCE, and Cicero (*de Inventione*
2. 58) implies the existence of such a court *c.*84 BCE; see further Brunt 1988: 220–1.
We know from Livy that earlier *quaestiones*, presumably ad hoc, were established to
deal with cases of *veneficium* in 331 BCE (8. 18), 184 BCE (39. 38. 3; 41. 5); 180 BCE (40.
37. 4; 43. 2–3); 179 BCE (40. 44. 6); and 152 BCE (Livy, *Periochae* 48; cf. Valerius
Maximus 6. 3. 8); note also Polybius (6. 13. 4), who says that cases of poisoning and
murder come under the jurisdiction of the senate.

[14] This clause is attested by Ulpian (*Coll.* 1. 3. 1) and Marcian (*Digest* 48. 8. 1. pr.);
cf. Cicero, *For Rabirius, Charged with Treason* 19; *For Milo* 11; *Paradoxes of the Stoics*
31. Cloud 1969 interprets *sicarius* as 'gangster'.

[15] Cf. Gaius in *Digest* 50. 16. 236. pr.: 'Whoever says *venenum* ought to add
whether bad or good; for *medicamenta* are also *venena*, since under that word is
contained everything that, when administered to something, changes the nature of
that to which it was administered'; see also Marcian in *Digest* 48. 8. 3. 2; Servius on
Georgics 1. 129, and on *Aeneid* 11. 458.

[16] Marcian (in *Digest* 48. 8. 3. 2): 'only this [kind of *venenum*] is specified in the
law, that which is possessed for the purpose of killing a person'; cf. *Digest* 48. 8. 1. 1
and 3. pr. 1; *The Opinions of Paulus* 5. 23. 1; Cicero, *For Caelius* 51.

poisoning.[17] If anything, then, the clause concerning *veneficium* implied even more strongly than the other two the notion of wrongful death brought about through stealth. The limited physiological and pharmacological knowledge of the day meant that the presence of *venena* was difficult to detect and their effectiveness even more difficult to explain; consequently, their use was in many cases simply inferred from the effects. In such circumstances it was relatively easy to suspect *veneficium*, and allegations of *veneficium* were liable to follow on any death regarded as unusual or suspicious. Moreover, the difficulty in assigning responsibility meant that these allegations often allowed free rein to suspicions of conspiracy and the venting of personal hostilities. Consequently, charges of *veneficium* tended both to feed on and to reinforce fears about the hidden enemy, the seemingly innocuous who wielded deadly power.[18]

Was the law on *veneficium* a law against magic? Yes and no. A number of scholars have stressed the ambiguity of the word *venenum*, which they rightly point out can be translated as either 'poison' or 'magic potion', and have accordingly argued that the *Lex Cornelia* embraced both magic and poisoning.[19] This distinction, however, depends on the conceptual categories of modern western science rather than on those of contemporary Romans. When we distinguish 'poison' from 'magic potion', we mean in general that the effects of the former can be explained and to some extent predicted within a scientific understanding of nature, while the effects of the latter

---

[17] This is apparent in the only trials in the republican period known to have taken place under the Sullan law, those connected with A. Cluentius Habitus: Cicero, *For Cluentius* esp. 55; 147–8. We may also note that both Cicero and the author of the *Rhetorica ad Herennium*, when using the terms *venenum, veneficium,* or *veneficus/a* in a legal context, always do so in reference to substances intended to cause death, i.e., poisons: *Rhetorica ad Herennium* 2. 8 and 44; 3. 33; 4. 23; Cicero, *de Inventione* 2. 58; *For Roscius of Ameria* 90; *For Cluentius* 1–2 and 166; *On the Orator* 2. 105.

[18] Women were especially associated with *veneficium*; for the most spectacular example, see Livy's account of the matronly poisoners of 331 BCE (8. 18).

[19] e. g., Pharr 1932: 272–4; M. Smith 1978: 75; Beard, North, and Price 1998: i. 233; Ogden 1999: 83; Dickie 2001: 15; it is misleading to infer the scope of the original *Lex Cornelia* from much later texts, such as *The Opinions of Paulus* (as Castello 1990: 673) or the *Institutes of Justinian* (as Hunink 1997: i. 13). *Pace* Phillips 1991: 264, Kippenberg 1997: 148, and Graf 1997: 46–7, it is unlikely that the original *Lex Cornelia*, by specifying *venena*, also covered maleficent rituals, although as I argue below they were eventually assimilated.

cannot: hence poisons are natural and magical potions are supernatural. The Romans, however, would not have made the same distinction. They may well have regarded the operation of *venena* as occult and uncanny, in the literal sense of 'concealed' and 'unknown', insofar as they could not observe or explain how certain substances produced certain effects. In our own culture, we tend to equate the occult and uncanny with the supernatural: something is uncanny only if it has no obvious explanation within the scientific framework of 'nature', and so is necessarily 'supernatural' as well. In the Roman world, by contrast, it would have been perfectly possible for people to regard something as occult or uncanny and yet not supernatural.[20] Within this conceptual framework, the word *venenum*, far from being ambiguous, denoted a consistent and fairly simple concept, namely, any natural substance that had an occult or uncanny power to affect something else. On an emic level, therefore, i.e., in Roman terms, it would be better to describe the law on *veneficium* as dealing not with both magic and poisoning, but rather with wrongful death effected through occult and uncanny means.

On an etic level, however, we might reasonably regard it as a law concerning magic, provided that by 'magic' we do not mean religious deviance. As I suggested above, it was the occult and uncanny aspect that endowed the concept of *veneficium* with its distinctive social implications, since any unexpected death could be attributed to the malice of some unknown agent who had used *venena* to bring it about. This pattern of attributing misfortune to the occult powers of a malicious agent is something that occurs cross-culturally: E. E. Evans-Pritchard's study of the Azande and Clyde Kluckhohn's study of the Navaho provide classic anthropological analyses (Evans-Pritchard 1937: 63–106; Kluckhohn 1944/1967; cf. Graf 1997: 47). Most scholars tend to describe this combination of occult powers and malicious intent as 'witchcraft' or 'sorcery' or 'black magic'. It is easy enough to understand the *Lex Cornelia* as a law dealing with 'magic' in this sense of the word. Moreover, it is useful

---

[20] For example, Cicero, *On Divination* 1. 13 and 16. See especially Phillips 1991: 263–4 and 267–8 on the lack of a generally accepted theory of naturalistic causation in the Roman world.

for analysis, since it allows us to label the common element that bound together the original law with its later extensions.

For it is important to keep in mind that Roman law was not a static system. Statutes were subject to a process of ongoing alteration and expansion in which three different activities could play a part: the application of the law in actual trials, the passage of new laws that modified earlier statutes, and the work of jurists in interpreting and codifying earlier laws. As a result, the scope of the original *Lex Cornelia* was gradually extended. On the one hand, there were tendencies to apply it to malicious actions effected by occult means other than *venena*. For example, a senatorial decree of unknown date, but probably prior to the mid-second century CE, decreed that anyone responsible for 'wicked sacrifices', *mala sacrificia*, should be condemned and punished under the *Lex Cornelia*.[21] The text as we have it does not specify the nature of these *mala sacrificia*, but comparison with other evidence suggests that they were primarily cursing rituals, *devotiones*.[22] Certainly Tacitus, in reporting some of the political trials in the reigns of Tiberius and Claudius, suggests that *devotiones* were easily assimilated to *venena* (e.g., *Annals* 4. 52. 1, 12. 65. 1), and Quintilian similarly implies that in his day it was an open question whether 'the chants of *magi*', *carmina magorum*, might be considered a type of *veneficium* (*Institutes* 7. 3. 7). On the other hand, the *Lex Cornelia* was also gradually extended to malicious actions other than murder. Quintilian suggests that there were debates whether love potions could be regarded as *venena* under

[21] Modestinus (*Digest* 48. 8. 13): 'In accordance with a senatorial decree, whoever conducts or organizes *mala sacrificia* is ordered to be condemned to the punishment of that law.' Modestinus' *floruit* in the second quarter of the third century CE provides a *terminus ante quem* for the senatorial decree, and the fact that jurists were much more likely to refer to the initial motions of emperors than to the subsequent senatorial decrees for laws passed after the reign of Hadrian (Talbert 1984: 438–50) suggests an earlier date.

[22] Cf. *The Opinions of Paulus* 5. 23. 15, quoted in section three below. Attempts to bring the use of *devotiones* under the law against *veneficium* may go back to the reign of Tiberius, if Tacitus is correct in saying that Germanicus' friends accused Piso of killing him by means of *devotiones et venenum* (*Annals* 3. 13. 2; cf. 2. 79. 1 and Pliny, *Natural History* 11. 187; see further Eck et al. 1996: 154–5); by the start of the third century CE, Tertullian can regard it as obvious that *homicidium* can be accomplished equally by sword, *venenum*, or magical binding spells (*de Spectaculis* 2).

Magic in Roman Law

the *Lex Cornelia*, and other evidence suggests that *venena* meant to cause madness might also come under this law. Although at least some jurists continued to insist on its limitation to *venena* that cause death, there was clearly a tendency to apply it to other types as well.[23] In both respects, then, the purview of the *Lex Cornelia* was gradually extended.

At the same time as the scope of the *Lex Cornelia* was being extended to include actions other than those defined in the original law, some Romans were also starting to change the way that they thought about them, by associating them with a range of other practices and ideas in a new conceptual category. Evidence for this change lies in lexical developments: alongside *veneficium* and its cognates, two new word groups appeared, those of *magus* and *maleficium*. *Magus* was a loan word from Persian by way of Greek, and originally denoted a Persian wise man or religious specialist. In our extant sources it does not appear in Latin before the 50s BCE; the first authors who use it do so in its original sense, as do prose writers down to the late first century CE.[24] Vergil is the earliest extant author to use the adjective *magicus*, and he does so in reference to what we would call magical rites; the word is thereafter very common in poetry with this meaning.[25] *Maleficium* was a native Latin term, originally with the generic meaning of 'wicked deed, crime'. By the

---

[23] Love potions: Quintilian, *Institutes* 7. 3. 10; 7. 3. 30; 7. 8. 2; 8. 5. 31; Pseudo-Quintilian, *Declamationes Minores* 385; *Declamationes Maiores* 14 (a 'hate potion'); Julius Victor, *Ars Rhetorica* 3. 3; Marcian (*Digest* 48. 8. 3. 2) notes that the term *venenum* can apply to a love potion, *amatorium*, but then says expressly that the *Lex Cornelia* applies only to *venena* intended to cause death; see further Gordon 1999: 256–8. Madness: Quintilian, *Institutes* 9. 2. 105; cf. Philo, *On Specific Laws* 3. 98–9; Numantina, accused in 24 CE of driving her husband mad 'by means of *carmina* and *veneficia*' (Tacitus, *Annals* 4. 22. 3), may have been tried under the *Lex Cornelia* (Dickie 2001: 146–7).
[24] Earliest examples: Cicero, *On Laws* 2. 26; *On the Nature of the Gods* 1. 43; *On Divination* 1. 46 and 90–1; *Tusculan Disputations* 1. 108; *de Finibus* 5. 87; Catullus 90. 1 and 3; Nigidius Figulus fgt. 67 (Swoboda 1889). Later examples in prose: Vitruvius 8. pr. 1; Valerius Maximus 8. 7. ext. 2, 1. 6. ext. 1b; Velleius Paterculus 2. 24. 31; Curtius 3. 3. 10; 5. 1. 22; Seneca, *Letters* 58. 31; *Dialogues* 5. 16. 3; the elder Pliny is the first prose author to use the term *magus* in a looser sense, e.g., *Natural History* 16. 249; 22. 20; 24. 156 and 160–7. See in general Nock 1933; Graf 1997: 20–61; Bremmer 1999: 1–9; Gordon 1999: 163–5.
[25] Vergil, *Eclogue* 8. 66; *Aeneid* 4. 493; Tibullus 1. 2. 41–63; 1. 5. 11–12; Propertius 1. 1. 19–24; 2. 28. 35–6; 4. 1. 103–6; Ovid, *Amores* 1. 8. 5-6 (*magus*); *The Art of Love* 2.

time of Apuleius, however, it and its cognates had apparently become closely identified with *magus* and its cognates, and by the fourth century CE had even started to displace them.[26] Although it is fairly easy to trace these semantic developments, it is more difficult to chart the conceptual shift that presumably lay behind them. Many scholars would agree, however, that an idea of 'magic' was fairly well established in Roman culture by the time of the elder Pliny, who gives a rambling and somewhat chaotic account of the magical art, *magica ars*.[27] The importance of these developments for us lies in the fact that the concept of magic provided a new umbrella category under which the various actions now associated with the *Lex Cornelia* could be classed. We can see its effects in the trial of Apuleius.

THE *APOLOGY* OF APULEIUS

Our information about the trial of Apuleius comes entirely from his *Apology*, which represents the speech that he delivered in his own defence before the proconsul of Africa around 158/9 CE.[28] Briefly, the

99–106, etc.; *magicus* does not appear in prose before the elder Pliny (*Natural History* 8. 106; 11. 203, etc.).

[26] Despite some hints in earlier writers (Festus. 414. 23–27 L; Tacitus, *Annals* 2. 69. 3), Apuleius is the first in whom this usage is clearly discernible: see *Golden Ass* 3. 16; 6. 16; 9. 29; 9. 31, and note especially the phrase *magica maleficia* that he commonly uses in the *Apology* (1. 5; 9. 2; 42. 2; 61. 2 and 69. 4; cf. 51. 10 and 96. 2). It may have begun as a popular usage, as later writers suggest (Lactantius, *Divine Institutes* 2. 16. 4; Constantius in *Codex Theodosianus* 9. 16. 4 and 6; Augustine, *City of God* 10. 9), but eventually assumed virtually 'official' status: see further below, n. 57.

[27] See above, n. 10. Gordon (1999: 260–1) likewise insists on the legal implications of these conceptual shifts, although his analysis differs somewhat from my own. For Pliny see *Natural History* 30. 1–15; partly translated in Beard, North, and Price 1998: ii. 263–4.

[28] The trial is dated by the proconsulship of Claudius Maximus, on which see Thomasson 1996: 62–3, nos. 76–7. I cite the text by the numbering of Paul Vallette's Budé edition (1924); Hunink (1997) and Harrison (2000: 39–88) provide valuable recent guides. Although there have been varying opinions about its historical value, with some scholars regarding it essentially as a literary exercise (e.g. Gaide 1993) I follow the majority opinion in seeing it as a version of the actual courtroom speech, probably with some revision for publication; Hunink (1997: i. 25–7) conveniently summarizes the debate, although I cannot agree with his conclusion that by approaching the text as 'a literary work of art' one 'rises above the level of historical, biographical, and legal records'.

background is as follows. Apuleius, a stranger to Oea, the modern Tripoli, had married a wealthy widow named Aemilia Pudentilla. She had two sons from her first marriage: Sicinius Pontianus, a friend of Apuleius' from Athens who at first encouraged the union, and Sicinius Pudens, who reached adulthood not long before the trial. Some connections of the family, however, strongly disapproved of the marriage: Sicinius Aemilianus, the brother of Pudentilla's first husband, and Herennius Rufinus, Pontianus' father-in-law. They spread the story that Apuleius was a *magus* and had used love charms to win Pudentilla, who they alleged had previously vowed never to remarry. They even managed for a while to turn Pontianus against his friend, although the two were reconciled shortly before Pontianus' unexpected death. This they also attributed to Apuleius, and even taxed him with it in the course of another legal case conducted before the governor of Africa, Claudius Maximus. At this point Apuleius challenged Aemilianus to bring a formal charge against him, which he did.

It is the nature of this charge that concerns us here. Unfortunately, to determine it is no simple matter, since our only evidence is Apuleius' speech itself. The scholarly consensus has been that Apuleius was tried under the *Lex Cornelia de sicariis et veneficiis*.[29] Although this may be true, it does not really help to illuminate the underlying issues at stake. As I noted above, the *Lex Cornelia* was no longer restricted to cases of *veneficium* as defined in the original law, that is, wrongful death effected through uncanny and occult means. So far as we can determine, Aemilianus' indictment reflected this development. It is clear that the issue of wrongful death was only peripheral to the case. Since Aemilianus had dropped the murder of Pontianus, the only remaining point relevant to such a charge was Apuleius' alleged attempt to buy a *lepus marinus*, a type of poisonous mollusc (Pliny, *Natural History* 9. 155 and 32. 8–9). More importantly, Apuleius several times implicitly denies that he was accused of

---

[29] Massonneau 1934: 168 and 190; Graf 1997: 66; Hunink 1997: i. 13 (with further references); Beard, North, and Price 1998: i. 235; Gordon 1999: 263; Dickie 2001: 147. This view, however, downplays both the loose structure of criminal trials, especially in the provinces, and the judges' often haphazard knowledge of law: see Peachin 1996: 7–9 and 25–53.

veneficium. For example, he argues that even if fish were used in magic, the mere purchasing of fish would not make someone a *magus* (*Apology* 30–2); similarly, 'if I had bought hellebore or hemlock or poppy-juice … who would endure it with equanimity, if on these grounds you were to indict me for poisoning (*veneficium*), because a man can be killed by them?'[30] But if wrongful death was not the issue, in what sense was the charge brought under the *Lex Cornelia*?

At the very end of the speech, Apuleius quotes from the actual indictment that Sicinius Aemilianus brought against him: 'This is the man, my lord Maximus, whom I have decided to indict before you … for numerous wicked deeds (*maleficia*), openly committed.'[31] Thanks to Apuleius' rebuttal, we know what Aemilianus cited as specific instances of *maleficia*: Apuleius had sought to purchase certain kinds of fish, presumably for use as *venena*; he had used chants to send a slave boy into a trance; he kept a secret object wrapped up among the household gods of Pontianus; he had performed a nocturnal sacrifice; he had commissioned the carving of a ghoulish wooden statuette to which he paid cult; and last but not least, he had used *carmina et venena* (*Apology* 69. 4) to seduce Pudentilla. Some of these activities clearly came under the *Lex Cornelia*, especially with its extended purview: the nocturnal sacrifice recalls the senatorial decree on *mala sacrificia*, and the secret object and ghoulish statuette may also have been meant to suggest *devotiones*. Whether or not the use of love potions came under the *Lex Cornelia* was, as we have seen, a matter of debate, but Aemilianus could well have hoped that in this case the debate would be settled in his favour. Although the alleged enchantment of the slave boy seems rather remote from the concerns of the *Lex Cornelia*, we have little idea what the prosecution made of it: Apuleius focuses on the issue of

[30] *Apology* 32. 8; cf. 41. 6: 'Indeed, I am glad that my opponents are unaware that I have also read Theophrastus' *On Animals that Bite and Sting* and Nicander's *Antidotes for Poisonous Bites*; otherwise they would be indicting me for poisoning (*veneficium*) as well'; see also *Apology* 26. 8–9, where he contrasts people who accuse *magi* with those who accuse *sicarii, venenarii*, or thieves.

[31] *Apology* 102. 9–103. 1; I owe thanks to an anonymous referee for calling my attention to the importance of this passage. See also *Apology* 90. 1 and especially 28. 4, where Apuleius suggests that he would even concede being a *magus* so long as it was understood that he had not been involved in any *maleficium*.

divination, but Aemilianus may have intended it as an example of harmful *carmina*. In general, however, the concern with harmful actions that informed the original *Lex Cornelia* seems fairly attenuated here; after all, the only people said to have been affected were Pudentilla and the slave boy. The focus seems thus to have been not so much on the harm caused by these actions as on the actions themselves. As I shall argue below, this shift in focus is significant.

Apuleius himself, although he also employs the term *maleficium*, insists that the charge was in essence one of *magia* or being a *magus*, two phrases that he uses interchangeably. He does this from the very start of his speech. Only a few days before the trial, he claims, Aemilianus' advocates 'began to accuse me of magical misdeeds (*magica maleficia*) and even of the murder of my stepson Pontianus' (*Apology* 1. 5). But when Apuleius challenged him to bring a formal charge, he changed his tune: he conveniently forgot about the murder of his nephew and instead 'based his indictment solely on the slanderous charge of magic (*calumnia magiae*), which brings disgrace more readily than conviction' (2. 2). This is how Apuleius presents the charge throughout the speech. For example, after he has dealt in the first part of the speech with general attacks on his character, he introduces its main section by saying 'I come now...to the actual charge of magic (*ad ipsum crimen magiae*)' (25. 5); indeed, all the allegations that Aemilianus has made are aimed at one idea, 'that I am a *magus*' (25. 8). Therefore, his primary task in the main section will be to demonstrate that 'their evidence has nothing at all to do with magic' (*Apology* 28. 4; cf. 29. 1, 47. 1, 66. 3, 67. 1, 79. 2, and 83. 5). According to Apuleius himself, then, the charge against which he was defending himself was that he was a *magus* or practiced *magia*.

This representation of the charge was well suited to the rhetorical strategy around which Apuleius shaped his defence. According to ancient rhetorical handbooks, speakers for the defence had three basic choices: they could deny the actions in question, they could dispute their characterization as crimes, or they could plead extenuating circumstances (e.g., *Rhetorica ad Herennium* 1. 18–25). Apuleius certainly avails himself of the first option, especially but not exclusively in connection with the charges concerning Pudentilla. But for his overall strategy he relied on the second option. Instead of denying the points alleged against him, he simply provided an alternative explanation of them: they were the actions, not of a *magus*, but of a philosopher, and it was only his accuser's ignorance that led him to think otherwise.[32] Apuleius proclaims this strategy in his address to the governor at the very start of his speech: 'I congratulate myself, by God, that with you as judge I have the opportunity and occasion to exonerate philosophy among the ignorant and to clear my own name' (*Apology* 1. 3). In the course of the speech, he reinterprets virtually every allegation brought by Aemilianus. He claims that his interest in fish is not that of a *magus* seeking out *venena*, but that of a philosopher exploring the mysteries of nature, as Aristotle and Theophrastus had done before him (36–8). Similarly, the slave boy whom he allegedly entranced is in fact an epileptic who happened to have a seizure; Apuleius treats his audience to a long philosophical discussion of this condition (49–51). The secret object that he kept wrapped up among the household gods of Pontianus was the token of an initiation into a mystery cult: his zeal for truth and piety towards the gods have led him to undergo countless such initiations (53–6). And the skeletal figure that he had carved is in reality an image of Mercury to whom he piously makes offerings on holidays (61–5).

Apuleius thus makes the case hinge on the distinction between a philosopher and a *magus*. As this very strategy shows, the distinction was by no means cut and dried: one person's philosopher might be another's *magus*.[33] The key issue therefore became one of perceived deviance. A wide range of acts that from one point of view might mark the actor as a *magus* could from another point of view appear

---

[32] *Apology* 28. 2: 'And none of those charges, whether true or false, will I deny, but will confess them just as if they were facts, so that this whole crowd . . . may clearly understand that not only can no true objections be brought against philosophers, but not even false ones be devised'; see the useful discussions of Graf 1997: 69–88; Bradley 1997: 212–19; Harrison 2000: 45–7.

[33] Philostratus' defense of Apollonius of Tyana provides a useful parallel: without denying any of the feats attributed to Apollonius, Philostratus, like Apuleius, argues that he should not be regarded as a *magus* but as a philosopher (*Life of Apollonius* 1. 2). Again, Philostratus can provide no clear-cut criteria for distinguishing the philosopher from the *magus*; the best he can do is to insist that Apollonius performed his feats of prognostication by means of wisdom rather than magical art. See the stimulating discussion of Francis 1995: 108–29.

entirely innocuous.[34] The matter was thus essentially one of accepted
norms and their limits: someone whose behaviour was judged to lie
beyond the accepted limits could by that very fact be regarded as a
magus. It became the task of the judge to decide whether Apuleius'
activities were acceptable, and thus those of a philosopher, or were
instead deviant, and thus those of a *magus*. Furthermore, although
Apuleius treats philosophy as the non-deviant term against which the
deviant term magic is defined, a modern observer might classify
much of what he discusses as religion: the secret object hidden
among the household gods, the performance of a nocturnal sacrifice,
the allegedly demonic object of cult, perhaps even the enchantment
of a boy, all relate in some way to interactions with the divine. We
should also note what Apuleius presents as the popular definition of
a *magus*: one 'who by an exchange of speech with the immortal gods
exerts power in any matter he chooses through some amazing force
of chants' (*Apology* 26. 6). On this definition it is his distinctive
ability to communicate with the gods that gives the *magus* his
unusual powers. But that Apuleius, in discussing all this, should
have used the language of philosophy rather than that of religion is
not surprising: in neither Latin nor Greek did there exist a word
entirely equivalent to the modern term 'religion'.[35] In short, we may
reasonably regard religious deviance, as we would describe it, as one
of the key issues in the trial of Apuleius.

Whether or not the introduction of this issue was due solely to
Apuleius' choice of rhetorical strategy is a more difficult question to
answer, since his version of the case is the only one to which we have
direct access. Two observations, however, suggest that it was not.
First, the issue of philosophy versus magic was probably not entirely
of Apuleius' making. His public persona as a philosopher must
already have been well established, and his opponents had apparently
made explicit attempts to undermine it in their prosecution; in other
words, they understood that proving their charge of *maleficia*

---

[34] A point Apuleius makes much of: note especially *Apology* 54. 6–7.

[35] See M. Smith 1956: 79 (= 1996. i. 113). Note also the Greek and Roman
tendency to identify as philosophers the religious specialists of other cultures, such
as Egyptian priests, Persian *magi*, Indian Brahmans, and Celtic Druids: see, e.g., Dio
Chrysostom 49. 7–8; Numenius Fgt.1a (des Places 1973); Clement of Alexandria,
Stromateis 1. 15; Diogenes Laertius 1. 1–11.

depended to some extent on denying Apuleius' claims to be a philosopher.[36] Second, there is the issue that I sketched above, that Aemilianus' charge of *maleficia* seems to assume something more than actual or even potential harm to specific individuals. The allegations were undoubtedly meant to give the impression that Apuleius could indeed harm someone, if he chose, and had already harmed Pudentilla (although in her case the harm was presumably to her pocketbook and reputation rather than her body). Nevertheless, it is difficult to avoid the sense that the charge of *maleficia* also involved the assumption that these actions were simply wrong in and of themselves; as I noted in the previous section, the term *maleficium* was in this very period acquiring the specific connotations of 'magic' that came to dominate in late antiquity. In short, it seems that Apuleius' characterization of the charge as one of *magia*, with all the implications of deviance that it involved, may not have significantly misrepresented Aemilianus' intentions.

But although we can deduce a great deal about Apuleius' thinking and make some reasonable guesses about Aemilianus', we know virtually nothing about that of Claudius Maximus, the representative of Roman authority and law. It is impossible to say whether his decision to accept Aemilianus' indictment was motivated solely by a concern for the sorts of harmful actions that traditionally came under the *Lex Cornelia*, or by a more general concern with *magia* and issues of deviance, or by some of both. We do not even know what verdict he reached, although the probability is strong that he decided to acquit Apuleius.[37] If so, we might reasonably suppose that Apuleius' rhetorical strategy paid off. Certainly he had assessed the situation shrewdly: it is likely that Maximus was himself a philosopher, and Apuleius may therefore have counted on his sympathy for a

[36] e. g., *Apology* 4. 1: 'So you heard a little earlier the following statement made at the beginning of the indictment: "We accuse before you a philosopher who is handsome and most eloquent"—for shame!—"in Greek as well as Latin"'; cf. 13. 5: 'Pudens almost split his sides shouting, "A philosopher has a mirror, a philosopher owns a mirror!"'.

[37] This is suggested not only by the very survival of his defence speech, but also by the fact that a few years later he was alive and well in Carthage, and indeed a local celebrity: he delivered speeches before Severianus, governor in 162/3 CE (*Florida* 9. 39), and Scipio Orfitus, governor in 163/4 CE (*Florida* 17. 1 and 21).

man of similar culture, with a cosmopolitan background and connections to the highest society, assailed by locals whom he could
depict as vicious and ignorant bumpkins.[38] What we do know,
however, is that Apuleius' decision to highlight the definitional
issue of philosophy versus magic meant that Maximus was in effect
required to make a decision about a general charge of magic, regardless of whether or not this was his initial concern.

Although the trial of Apuleius is the only trial of this kind for
which we have any substantial evidence, it is unlikely to have been the
only one that took place. I would suggest that we may regard it as
representative of a gradual shift in the interpretation of the *Lex
Cornelia*, away from an exclusive focus on harmful actions accomplished through occult and uncanny means, towards a more general
concern with issues of religious deviance. The lexical shift, from
veneficus and *veneficium* to *magus* and *maleficium*, is clear enough,
and the evidence also strongly suggests an associated shift in the
conceptualization of the legal issues involved. As more and more
actions involving *venena* and *mala sacrificia* and the like were
brought into association with the *Lex Cornelia*, and as a 'strong
view' of magic that encompassed all these things became more and
more widely spread in society, the *Lex Cornelia* came to serve as a
precedent for what was in effect a general charge of being a *magus* or
practicing *magia*, a charge in which issues of religious deviance
tended to play an important part.[39] Once this became established in
practice, it was only a matter of time before the charge of magic *tout*

---

[38]　The proconsul's identity with the Stoic Claudius Maximus who taught Marcus
Aurelius (*Historia Augusta, Life of Marcus Aurelius* 3. 2; Marcus Aurelius, *Meditations*
1. 15. 1 and 1. 17. 4) seems to be widely accepted: e.g., Champlin 1980: 32–3; Birley
1987: 96–7; and Bradley 1997: 216.

[39]　In my general views about the emergence of an actionable charge of magic in
Roman law I follow the observation of Mommsen (1899: 639–40) that the term
magus 'appeared from the Trajanic period as a delictual category for the wicked
magician'. For his Trajanic date, Mommsen cites Tacitus (*Annals* 2. 27. 3 and 32. 3; 6.
29. 3–4; 12. 22. 1 and 59. 11; 16. 30. 2 and 31. 1); I would argue that in all these cases
the word has particular reference to divination, so that the trial of Apuleius is the
earliest evidence for the usage that Mommsen had in mind, and that even in this case
it is not certain that actual charge brought by Aemilianus was one of being a *magus*.
For other accounts of the development of the *Lex Cornelia* with respect to magic, see
MacMullen 1966: 124–5; Gordon 1999: 255–60; Dickie 2001: 145–8.

court, with its implications of religious deviance, entered into the formal discourse of Roman law. As I argue in the next section, it is this stage of development that is discernible in *The Opinions of Paulus*.

THE OPINIONS OF PAULUS

The first significant appearance of the term *magus* and its cognates in an extant legal text is a passage from a work entitled *The Opinions of Paulus* (*Pauli Sententiae*), one of the most frequently cited texts pertaining to the Roman legal treatment of magic.[40] The Paulus of the title is Julius Paulus, one of the great jurists of the early third century CE whose work summed up the legal developments of the classical period and became canonical in the post-classical period. The popularity of this passage is due to a number of perceived advantages: it provides the text of an actual law rather than an account of a trial; it is guaranteed by the authority of a famous jurist; it is a complete text and not a reconstruction from later citations and allusions. Unfortunately, almost all these advantages are illusory. First, as the work of a jurist, it was not in fact an actual law, in the same way that the *Lex Cornelia de sicariis et veneficiis* was a law; I shall deal with this issue at greater length below. Second, virtually all legal historians now agree that it is not the work of Paulus himself, but an epitome compiled at the end of the third century CE; it is not even possible to know what sort of documents lay behind it.[41] Lastly, the passage is probably not even complete, since what is normally cited as *The Opinions of Paulus* is in fact a reconstruction compiled by Paul

[40] The very first appearance is in a passage of Ulpian (*Digest* 10. 2. 4) that equates magical books, *libri magici*, with *mala medicamenta* and *venena*.

[41] This has been overlooked by a number of scholars who discuss the Roman law on magic, e.g., MacMullen 1966: 125; Garosi: 1976: 80; Francis 1995: 91; Graf 1997: 55; and Ogden 1999: 83; although Kippenberg 1997: 148–50 describes the text as a later compilation, he nevertheless consistently cites it as Paulus' own opinions. Pharr 1932: 288–9 and Massonneau 1934: 192 also attribute the text to Paulus, but were simply following the scholarship of their day.

Krüger in 1878 from a number of late antique sources.[42] Yet despite all these considerable problems, this text nevertheless provides extremely valuable evidence for the further development of the *Lex Cornelia*.

It is best to begin with the passage itself. Because a sense of its context is necessary for an understanding of its significance, I will quote from the relevant section at some length.[43]

The Opinions of Paulus 5. 23: On the *Lex Cornelia de sicariis et veneficiis.*

14. Those who give abortifacients or love potions (*abortionis aut amatorium poculum*), even if they do not act with malicious intent (*dolo*), nevertheless, because it sets a bad example (*mali exempli res est*): persons of low status (*humiliores*) are relegated to the mines, persons of high status (*honestiores*) to an island, with partial forfeiture of their property; but if as a result a woman or a man has died, they suffer the supreme punishment. 15. Those who perform, or arrange for the performance of, impious or nocturnal rites (*sacra impia nocturnave*), in order to enchant (*obcantarent*), transfix (*defigerent*), or bind (*obligarent*) someone, shall either be crucified or thrown to the beasts. 16. Those who sacrifice a man or obtain omens from his blood (*hominem immolaverint exve eius sanguine litaverint*), or pollute a shrine or a temple, shall be thrown to the beasts or, if persons of high status, be punished capitally. 17. It is agreed that those guilty of the magic art (*magicae artis conscios*) be inflicted with the supreme punishment, i.e., be thrown to the beasts or crucified. Actual magicians (*magi*), however, shall be burned alive. 18. No one is permitted to have in their possession books of the magic art (*libri artis magicae*); anyone in whose possession they are found shall have their property confiscated and the books publicly burnt, and they themselves shall be deported to an island; persons of low status shall be punished capitally. Not only is the profession of this art but also the

---

[42] The fullest extant version of the text is an epitome made for the *Lex Romana Visigothorum* in 506 CE; other compilations such as the *Digest* quote individual sentences: Levy 1943: 17; Liebs 1993: 28–9; Robinson 1997: 63–4. Krüger's edition (Krüger et al. 1878–1927, vol. ii) is essentially followed by other standard editions, e.g., Riccobono et al. 1940–3. Liebs 1993: 121–210 offers an alternative reconstruction.

[43] It is worth noting that sentences 15–19 are preserved only in the *Lex Romana Visigothorum* (sentence 14 is also found as *Digest* 48. 19. 38. 5); apparently none of the other compilers who drew on this text were interested in the material on magic. On the legal differentiation of *humiliores* and *honestiores*, see Garnsey 1970 and cf. below, p. 96.

knowledge (*scientia*) prohibited.[44] 19. If a person has died from a medicine (*medicamen*) given for human health or recovery, the one who gave it, if a person of high status, is relegated to an island; a person of low status, however, is punished capitally.

The great interest of this text is immediately apparent. But to understand its exact significance, we must consider more generally what it is that Roman jurists did. In the imperial period, the main sources of law were senatorial decrees, which steadily declined in importance, and imperial pronouncements or 'constitutions'; as I discussed earlier, such decrees could extend the purview of previous laws as well as define entirely new areas. But these decrees were almost entirely ad hoc, concerned with specific problems arising out of specific circumstances. They were not, with very few exceptions, concerned with defining or redefining the general scope of a law or elaborating its underlying legal principle. Nor were they automatically incorporated into some comprehensive code, since no such code existed: it was only in the 290s CE that lawyers, apparently at imperial instigation, produced the first authoritative collections of imperial constitutions, the *Codex Gregorianus* and the *Codex Hermogenianus*.[45]

These two deficiencies were in part made good by the jurists. In their expository works they would cite a range of material concerning a particular issue and discuss the general legal principles involved. With few exceptions, these works are now represented only as excerpts in later compilations, such as the *Digest* of Justinian; nevertheless, enough survives to indicate their original nature. As a relevant example we may consider the exposition of the *Lex Cornelia de sicariis et veneficiis* in the elementary textbook, the *Institutiones*, of

---

[44] This sentence was rejected as an interpolation by Krüger, on the assumption that Paulus was the author. If we accept that the author was a later compiler, I see no objections to its authenticity. It bears some resemblance to Ulpian's discussion of astrology, in which he asks whether the *scientia* or the 'exercise and profession', *exercitio et professio*, is punishable (*Coll.* 15. 2. 2); similarly, *The Opinions of Paulus* itself notes à propos of astrologers that it is better to stay away not only from divination, but also from 'the science itself and the books that deal with it' (*The Opinions of Paulus* 5. 21. 4).

[45] On the sources of law in the imperial period, see Peachin 1996: 14–25; on the Diocletianic codes, Corcoran 1996: 25–42.

the early third century CE jurist Marcian (*Digest* 48. 8. 1). Marcian
apparently begins by quoting the chief provisions of the original law.
He then proceeds to cite a rescript of Hadrian that those who
committed murder without intending to kill could be acquitted,
while those who wounded a person they had intended to kill should
be found guilty of murder. At this point he pauses to consider the
various implications of this ruling, before going on to cite two
further rescripts, another of Hadrian and one of Antoninus Pius.
What Marcian in effect does here is to gather later laws that modified
or supplemented the original *Lex Cornelia* and to discuss some of the
associated principles and problems. Such works as these did not
themselves constitute law, although the senatorial decrees and imperial constitutions that they cited did. Yet because they provided the
only coherent and systematic treatments of the law, they were by far
the most convenient sources of information. Moreover, the knowledge and expertise of the jurists meant that their opinions were
highly influential and in some cases even authoritative.[46]

Now *The Opinions of Paulus* is also the work of a jurist, but of a
rather peculiar type. It covers more or less the entire scope of Roman
law, civil as well as criminal. In overall organization it follows the
pattern established by the first comprehensive treatments of Roman
law, the *Digests* of Salvius Julianus and Juventius Celsus written
under Hadrian. It thus treats civil law first, following the order of
the praetorian edict and organizing the material under rubrics that
define the general topic, e.g., 'On Wills' (*The Opinions of Paulus* 3. 4).
There then follows a section, dealing mostly with criminal law, in
which the rubrics usually refer to specific laws of republican and early
imperial date. Hence the chapter of *The Opinions of Paulus* with
which we are concerned comes under the rubric of the *Lex Cornelia
de sicariis et veneficiis*. Yet we notice immediately that the treatment
of this topic in *The Opinions of Paulus* is, despite certain broad
parallels, strikingly different from that of Marcian in his textbook.
Both begin with citations from the original law, and follow with

---

[46] The responses of jurists to particular inquiries by officials could have the force
of law, provided that the jurists were unanimous in their opinion (Gaius, *Institutes* 1.
7; cf. Papinian in *Digest* 1. 1. 7. pr.), but the opinions they expressed in their literary
works had only the authority of their learning; see in general Kunkel 1973: 105–24.

supplementary material. But whereas Marcian cites specific rescripts by the name of the emperor and pauses to ponder various issues, *The Opinions of Paulus* proceeds with a set of cut and dried rules that baldly list specific crimes and assign specific punishments. This abrupt and summary treatment is what allows for a comprehensive treatment of Roman law in only five books, as opposed, for example, to the ninety of Julianus' *Digest.*

It is this abbreviated and simplistic style, so different from the usual method of Paulus as seen in the remains of his work, that initially raises suspicion of authorship. More detailed examination has served to demonstrate that the text is not in fact a genuine work of Paulus at all, but rather a compilation dating to *c.*300 CE.[47] The first advocates of this view believed that the compiler took his material from authentic works of Paulus, and this continues to be the general consensus (e.g. Robinson 1997: 63; note, however, Kunkel 1973: 149). More recently, however, Detlef Liebs has argued that the compiler instead drew on works by a number of classical jurists, as well as the *Codex Gregorianus* and *Codex Hermogenianus*.[48] The compiler more or less extensively altered his material by greatly simplifying it, sometimes to the point of unintelligibility, and by combining under the same rubric material from different sources.[49] That he has done this in the passage under consideration is likely enough.[50]

---

[47] Levy 1930 and 1943: 18–20; Barnes 1981: 289, n.73 notes that the fragment of the full text discovered in the mid-twentieth century is dated on palaeographical grounds to *c.*300 CE, and so was presumably written shortly after the composition of the text itself (personal communication). Liebs 1993: 29–43 gives detailed arguments for a date around 300 CE, although his attempt to locate the author in Africa should be treated with caution.

[48] Liebs 1993: 29–31 and 43–93. Liebs identifies a maximum of forty-seven passages that may derive from Ulpian or pseudo-Ulpian, fourteen from Paulus, thirteen from the *Codex Gregorianus*, seven from Marcian, six from Papinian, four from Modestinus, and three from the *Codex Hermogenianus*. As Barnes has pointed out to me (personal communication), our very fragmentary knowledge of legal literature makes many of these identifications uncertain, although the general hypothesis that the compiler drew on a variety of sources is no doubt correct.

[49] For example, Liebs argues that the rubric on buying and selling (*The Opinions of Paulus* 2. 17) contains material from Ulpian's commentary on the praetor's edict, the *Responsa* of Papinian and Paulus, and the *Codex Gregorianus* (Liebs 1993: 46, 54–5, 60, and 82–3).

[50] *The Opinions of Paulus* 5. 23. 12 perhaps derives from Paulus (cf. *Digest* 9. 2. 31 and *Digest* 48. 8. 7), although Liebs (1993: 53) points out that since Paulus himself

It would be quite interesting to know the sources from which the compiler derived the prescriptions on magic, and how he changed them. Unfortunately, there is little to go on. The general severity of the punishments probably reflects the situation after the Severan period, but whether the compiler added these or found them in his sources we cannot say.[51] The only sentence that we can plausibly link to a specific source is that dealing with *sacra impia nocturnave* (*The Opinions of Paulus* 5. 23. 15), which may ultimately depend on the senatorial decree on *mala sacrificia* discussed above in section two. The former is much more specific in describing the purpose of the rites in question as well as in prescribing punishments, but since we do not have the senatorial decree in its full original form, we cannot determine how much the compiler may have changed it.[52] Regarding the most interesting of these prescriptions, those that deal generally with the *magicae artes* and *magici libri* (*The Opinions of Paulus* 5. 23. 17–18), we can only speculate.

One possibility is that the two sentences in question derive from decrees of Diocletian, since in certain respects they are reminiscent of known Diocletianic measures. First, the lack of a distinction between *humiliores* and *honestiores* in sentence 17 may reflect the developments of the Tetrarchic period, when people of high status began to lose their exemption from harsher penalties.[53] Second, its distinction between *magi* and *conscii magicae artis*, presumably those in some

---

cites Q. Mucius Scaevola another source is also possible. *The Opinions of Paulus* 5. 23. 13 almost certainly derives from Marcian (*Digest* 48. 8. 3. 4–5; cf. *The Opinions of Paulus* 5. 23. 13); see also n. 52 below.

[51] Garnsey 1970: 109–11; MacMullen 1986: 209–10. See especially Marcian in *Digest* 48. 8. 3. 5: 'The penalty under the *Lex Cornelia de sicariis et veneficis* is deportation to an island and forfeiture of all property. But today capital punishment is normal, except for those of a status too high to be subject to the penalty of the law: persons of low status are normally crucified or thrown to the beasts, while their superiors are deported to an island.'

[52] Liebs (1997: 146–7) proposes that sentences 14 and 19 depend on a senatorial decree mentioned by Marcian (*Digest* 48. 8. 3. 2: 'But as the result of a senatorial decree it is ordered that a woman be relegated who, not indeed maliciously but unadvisedly, has administered a drug for fertility, which caused the death of the woman who took it'). But although similar legal principles are invoked, the differences are so great as to make a direct connection implausible.

[53] Liebs 1993: 35; so for example Diocletian's rescript on the Manichees (*Coll.* 15. 3. 7) distinguishes *honestiores* but condemns them to the mines nonetheless.

way involved with magic without being real *magi*, recalls the distinction made by Diocletian in his rescript on the Manichees between the leaders of the movement and their followers: like *magi*, the leaders are to be burnt alive, while their followers suffer capital punishment and confiscation of property (*Coll.* 15. 3. 6). Lastly, the phrase *ars magica* recalls *ars mathematica*, which Diocletian condemned in a private rescript of 294 CE (*Codex Justinianus* 9. 18. 2), although it also has a long pedigree in Latin literature (e.g. Vergil, *Aeneid* 4. 493; Ovid, *Metamorphoses* 7. 195; Manilius 5. 34–5; Curtius 7. 4. 8). The rule in sentence 18 that *libri magici* be publicly burnt likewise recalls several measures of Diocletian: his rescript on the Manichees directed that their leaders be burnt 'together with their abominable writings' (*Coll.* 15. 3. 6), his first edict against the Christians ordered that their 'writings be destroyed by fire' (Eusebius, *History of the Church* 8. 2. 4; cf. *Martyrs of Palestine* praef. 1), and he allegedly ordered that books of alchemy in Egypt be collected and burnt.[54] We should note, however, that book burning was not novel to Diocletian.[55] None of these parallels is in any way decisive, however, and the traces of Diocletianic sources in *The Opinions of Paulus* are otherwise slight.[56]

It seems more likely that the compiler instead derived these two rules from an earlier juristic discussion of magic. As we saw in the example from Marcian, it was not uncommon for jurists to cite various specific precedents and then draw from them more general conclusions. For the sake of comparison, we may consider Ulpian's discussion of astrologers and prophets in his handbook for proconsuls (*Coll.* 15. 2. 1–6). Ulpian begins by saying that there is a long-standing prohibition of 'the clever trickery and obstinate conviction of astrologers', and cites as evidence a senatorial decree from the reign of Tiberius that ordered their punishment. He then discusses the

---

[54] John of Antioch, in Müller 1885: iv. 601–2, fgt. 165, reproduced in the *Suda* (Adler 1928–38: ii. 104 = Letter D, entry 1156; text and translation are available at http://www.stoa.org).

[55] For example, Augustus collected and burned all books of prophecy in Greek and Latin except those considered genuine Sibylline oracles (Suetonius, *Augustus* 31. 1), and Septimius Severus removed from the sanctuaries in Egypt all books containing secret lore (Dio Cassius 75. 13. 2); see further Speyer 1981.

[56] Liebs (1993: 80–9) identifies only five sentences that may derive from constitutions of Diocletian, and in no case is the connection entirely secure.

question whether it is only the practice of astrology that is punishable or also the mere knowledge of it, and explains that different sorts of inquiries merit different types of penalties. He next considers the issue of prophets who disturb the peace, citing specific rulings of Antoninus Pius and Marcus Aurelius. Ulpian concludes that 'men of this sort, who under the pretext of divine admonition issue proclamations or boasts or knowingly devise fabrications, ought not to escape punishment'. It is easy enough to read *The Opinions of Paulus* 5. 23. 14–18 as a summary of this sort of discussion, in which the compiler has omitted references, smoothed out complexities, and transformed the concluding observations of the jurist into cut and dried prescriptions.

Although this seems to me a more plausible origin of these sentences than a derivation from decrees of Diocletian, it is no less hypothetical. In either case, however, they demonstrate that by 300 CE the terminology of *magus* and its derivatives had in one way or another entered into the formal language of Roman law. As I discussed above, the trial of Apuleius shows no more than that a Roman governor accepted a case in which the general issue of *magia* came to play a central role. *The Opinions of Paulus*, in contrast, indicates that this charge had become more formally established, through either imperial decree or juristic discussion or both. And since Constantine was to recognize *The Opinions of Paulus* itself as authoritative (*Codex Theodosianus* 1. 4. 2), its own prescriptions soon acquired the force of law.

The extremely concise form of these prescriptions and the lack of any discussion means that we cannot be sure of the issues that underlay them or of the emic categories involved. But general considerations make it likely that they involved a concern with religious deviance as well as with malicious and uncanny actions. In favour of the latter is the organization of these prescriptions under the rubric of the *Lex Cornelia*. Although there were historical reasons for this placement, as I have suggested, the fact that the compiler chose to retain it suggests that he regarded the sentences concerning *magi* and the *artes magicae* as specific examples of the general issue with which the *Lex Cornelia* was concerned. Moreover, some of the prescriptions that precede the general rules on magic clearly address the sorts of uncanny and malicious actions that had long been associated with the *Lex Cornelia*: the use of *venena* to cause abortions and create desire (*The Opinions of Paulus* 5. 23. 14), and the use of impious rites to bind someone (5. 23. 15). On the other hand, the ruling about human sacrifice and the pollution of temples (5. 23. 16) suggests a concern with religious deviance. More importantly, the general prescriptions on magic (5. 23. 17–18) do nothing to define a *magus* or the *ars magica*, but merely indicate how an official should handle them once they have been identified. The identification itself was presumably the responsibility of the individual official, who would thus have been faced with the same problem as Claudius Maximus. If so, the issue of religious deviance must again have played at least a part. In both respects, this passage of *The Opinions of Paulus* reveals a later stage in the same development whose beginnings can be seen in Apuleius' *Apology*, when charges of *maleficia* under the *Lex Cornelia* were leading to the more general charge of magic and its associated issues of religious deviance.

SOME IMPLICATIONS

The trajectory that I have charted in this paper could be extended further. Starting in the reign of Diocletian, for example, jurists seem to have reclassified laws on magic, removing them from the rubric of the *Lex Cornelia* and assigning them to a new rubric covering other unacceptable religious activities, including eventually divination; this new classification suggests that the connotations of religious deviance had perhaps finally come to overshadow the original concern with harmful occult actions.[57] But I hope that what I have already

---

[57] A rubric 'concerning evil-doers and Manichees', *de maleficis et Manichaeis*, is attested for the *Codex Gregorianus* of *c*.292 CE (*Coll*. 15. 3), and the Theodosian Code has a rubric 'concerning evil-doers and astrologers and the others like them', *de maleficis et mathematicis et ceteris similibus* (9. 16); the latter seems to collapse the rubric from the *Codex Gregorianus* with an earlier rubric 'concerning astrologers and soothsayers', *de mathematicis et vaticinatoribus* attested for Ulpian (*Coll*. 15. 2) and in *The Opinions of Paulus* (5. 21). We should note the presence in these rubrics of the term *maleficus* rather than *magus*, which suggests that the notion of harm was still significant; note too Constantine's distinction between those who use the *artes magicae* to attack someone's health or chastity and those who employ medical or weather charms (*Codex Theodosianus* 9. 16. 3).

presented is enough to illustrate the methodological issues that I discussed at the start. The use of 'magic' as an explicitly etic, heuristic category allows us to bring together evidence from different periods and contexts, and thereby to trace a significant shift in emic conceptual categories and in lexical usage. The Roman law on magic that was grounded in the *Lex Cornelia de sicariis et veneficiis* moves from a classification of harmful and uncanny actions denoted primarily by the word *veneficium* to a classification in which the notion of religious deviance played an equally if not more important role, a classification denoted chiefly by the word-groups *magus* and *maleficium*. The advantage of 'magic' as a heuristic device lies in the fact that it can encompass both 'harmful and uncanny actions' and 'religious deviance', and other concerns as well.[58]

These methodological considerations are not important merely in the abstract. They are important because they allow for a more precise analysis of the Roman legal treatment of magic. As a result, we can see not only that the conceptualization of magic in legal thinking shifted over time, but also that this shift corresponds to significant large-scale developments in the Roman world. I will here mention only two. The first is the emergence of religion as an increasingly autonomous discourse within Graeco–Roman culture (Beard, North, and Price 1998: i. 149–56). With the development of a 'strong view' of magic, certain acts that were already punishable because they were uncanny and malicious, such as *veneficium*, began to be viewed as acts of religious deviance as well; in other words, they were brought into an association with religion that evidently did not exist before. I would suggest that this new association is a byproduct of the emerging discourse of religion, which necessarily involved a discussion of what did or did not fall within

---

[58] That these concerns eventually included divination seems clear: see the preceding note. Yet the tendency of some modern scholars to assume that this association held good in all periods, as do Castello 1990 and Fögen 1993, is quite mistaken; Liebs (1997) is right to distinguish cases of *Schadenzauberei*, harmful magic, from those of *Wahrsagerei*, divination. This is not to say that there was no overlap: for example, men called *magi* could act as experts in divination (see above, n. 39). The conceptual relationship between 'magic' and divination in the Graeco–Roman world needs further analysis; Graf 1999 provides a good start.

its parameters.[59] *Veneficium* and the like were gradually brought within, although neither completely nor unambiguously.

The second development is the transformation of the Roman world from an empire ruled by Rome to an empire of Romans. Although Roman authorities had long made at least periodic attempts to police the limits of acceptable religious behaviour, such attempts were restricted in the republican period to the city of Rome or at most the Italian peninsula. Behind most of them we can discern an underlying concern to maintain the boundary between Roman and non-Roman. For example, the worship of Isis might be ejected from within the *pomerium*, the sacred boundary of the city of Rome, but it was not forbidden in other cities, much less in Egypt. Similarly, Roman authorities might expel Jews from Rome while at the same time recognizing their legitimacy elsewhere. In contrast, once it became standard practice for Roman officials to countenance a charge of being a *magus*, that charge was valid wherever they exercised authority. In this way, the new law on magic, as we see it in the trial of Apuleius, extended official concern with religious propriety to the entire empire. It is perhaps not a coincidence that it developed at much the same time as another empire-wide religious concern, that with Christians: in both cases Roman officials worked to establish empire-wide limits of acceptable religious behaviour.[60]

But the legal handling of magic provided in some respects a more supple and useful instrument than did the persecution of Christians. As we saw in the case of Apuleius, a trial on a charge of magic was to some extent a two-way process: a local inhabitant would bring the charge on the basis of what he considered unacceptable behaviour, and the presiding Roman official would evaluate his arguments according to general precedents as well as his own standards. A trial of this sort accordingly provided a context in which Roman

---

[59] See Woolf 2000: 617–21, who sketches an approach to the religious history of the Roman empire that interprets it in terms of 'competing ideas of what a religion is'.

[60] See Gordon 1999: 166: 'we find during the Principate an inclination to deploy magic... as part of a wider, hesitant, attempt to give substance to the imagined community of the Roman empire... through its negative inversions, atheists on the one hand (that is, Christians and Epicureans), and practitioners of illicit religion, magicians and private diviners, on the other'; on the 'boundaries of Roman religion'; see further Beard, North, and Price 1998: i. 211–44.

authorities and the inhabitants of the provinces could to some extent
work together in defining and policing the boundaries of the acceptable, even though the officials acted as final arbiters. It therefore
helped to create a consensus about acceptable and unacceptable
religious behaviour that could in theory apply to the entire empire.[61]

This analysis of the development of the *Lex Cornelia* is not
intended to be a comprehensive interpretation of the Roman legal
treatment of magic, nor is my identification of a shift in legal focus
from harmful and uncanny actions to religious deviance meant to be
a comprehensive account of the issues that could arise. Indeed, it is
easy enough to think of other significant factors: political concerns,
cultural identity, distinctions of status and gender. But an analysis of
these issues, I would argue, requires a nuanced awareness of the
complex methodological problems involved. I hope that this paper
will help further that awareness, as well as provide an account of one
significant historical development.

AFTERWORD (2009)

When I wrote this paper, I was still inclined to accept received opinion
on two crucial points, although with some qualifications. Further
reflection has led me to reject it altogether. The first point is the
assumption that the passage from *The Opinions of Paulus* quoted
above proves that the *Lex Cornelia* was the basis for the Roman
criminalization of magic throughout the imperial period. A more
detailed examination of the available evidence, however, revealed that
The Opinions of Paulus is in fact the only clear-cut evidence for this; all
the other evidence, at least through the Severan period, tends to suggest
that the *Lex Cornelia* remained limited to cases involving wrongful
death. I am thus now inclined to believe that the author of *The
Opinions of Paulus*, in including magic in general under the rubric of
the *Lex Cornelia*, was either following a late and an otherwise unattested line of legal thought or simply advancing an idiosyncratic

---

[61] On the importance of consensus in the Roman empire, see Ando 2000.

interpretation of his own (Rives 2006); even in late antiquity the majority tendency was to classify magic not under the *Lex Cornelia* but under the new rubric *de maleficis et mathematicis* (see above, n. 57).

The second point, closely related to the first, is the assumption that Apuleius was charged under the *Lex Cornelia*. Although this remains the *communis opinio* (e.g., Puccini-Delbey 2004: 28; Collins 2008: 152), I have become convinced that it is wrong. If the *Lex Cornelia* remained limited to cases involving wrongful death, then it was effectively irrelevant to Apuleius' case. Two other scholars have recently adopted a similar position, although they develop it to very different ends: Lamberti (2002) to postulate an unattested law that specifically criminalized magic, Riemer (2006) to support her case against the historicity of Apuleius' speech (see also Gaide 2005: 103–4). Both arguments assume that without a specific law on magic there could have been no legal case against Apuleius at all. But this seems to me a faulty assumption. The trial was clearly a *cognitio extra ordinem,* and as such all the prosecution had to do was to argue that Apuleius had engaged in socially disruptive behavior and that the governor should accordingly take action against him; I have elsewhere (Rives 2008) discussed in more detail how this understanding of the legal context affects our assessment of Apuleius' strategy in his defence speech.

I would thus modify the sketch of the legal developments that I outlined here. I remain convinced that changing social concerns gradually resulted in the criminalization of 'magic' as a form of religious deviance, and that this process involved the reclassification of certain practices previously criminalized on other grounds within the new category of magic. But I would now identify as the chief arena for this legal development not so much the ongoing interpretation of the *Lex Cornelia*, although that certainly played a role, as the kind of ad hoc *cognitiones extra ordinem* represented for us by the trial of Apuleius. It was in trials like these, in which the culpability of the accused depended almost entirely on what the presiding official regarded as acceptable or unacceptable behaviour, that the idea of *magia* as a type of legally actionable religious deviance was actually worked out.

On the emergence of a concept of magic in the Roman world (see above, n. 10), see also Marco Simón 2001; on the meaning of *magus* and related terms in classical Latin (nn. 24–5), see my more detailed analysis (Rives 2010).

BIBLIOGRAPHY

Adler, A. (1928–38). *Suidae Lexicon*. Stuttgart: Teubner, reprinted 1967–71.

Ando, C. (2000). *Imperial Ideology and Provincial Loyalty in the Roman Empire*. Berkeley and London: University of California Press.

Ankarloo, B. and Clark, S. (eds.) (1999). *Witchcraft and Magic in Europe: Ancient Greece and Rome*. London: Athlone Press.

Barnes, T. D. (1981). *Constantine and Eusebius*. Cambridge, Mass: Harvard University Press.

Beard, M., North, J., and Price, S. (1998). *Religions of Rome*, 2 vols. Cambridge: Cambridge University Press.

Birley, A. R. (1987). *Marcus Aurelius: A Biography*. Rev. edn. London: Batsford.

Bradley, K. R. (1997). 'Law, Magic, and Culture in the *Apologia* of Apuleius', *Phoenix*, 51: 203–23.

Bremmer, J. N. (1999). 'The Birth of the Term "Magic"', *ZPE*, 126: 1–12.

Brunt, P. A. (1988). *The Fall of the Roman Republic and Related Essays*. Oxford: Clarendon Press.

Castello, C. (1990). 'Cenni sulla repressione del reato di magia dagli inizi del principato fino a Constanzo II', *Atti dell'Accademia Romanistica Constantiniana: VIII Convegno Internazionale*. Naples: Edizioni Scientifiche Italiane, 665–93.

Champlin, E. (1980). *Fronto and Antonine Rome*. Cambridge, Mass., and London: Harvard University Press.

Cloud, J. D. (1968). 'How did Sulla Style his Law *de sicariis?*', *Classical Review*, n.s. 18: 140–3.

——(1969). 'The Primary Purpose of the Lex Cornelia de sicariis', *Zeitschrift für Religions- und Geistesgeschichte*, 86: 258–86.

Collins, D. (2008). *Magic in the Ancient Greek World*. Oxford and Malden, MA: Blackwell Publishing.

Corcoran, S. (1996). *The Empire of the Tetrarchs: Imperial Pronouncements and Government, AD 284–324*. Oxford and New York: Clarendon Press.

Des Places, E. (1973). *Numenius: Fragments*. Paris: Les Belles Lettres.

Dickie, M. W. (2001). *Magic and Magicians in the Greco–Roman World*. London and New York: Routledge.

Eck, W., Caballos, A., and Fernández, F. (1996). *Das Senatus Consultum de Cn. Pisone Patre*. Munich: Beck.

Evans-Pritchard, E. E. (1937). *Witchcraft, Oracles and Magic among the Azande*. Oxford: Clarendon Press.

Ferrary, J.-L. (1991). 'Lex Cornelia de sicariis et veneficis', *Athenaeum*, 79: 417–34.

——(1996). in M. H. Crawford (ed.), *Roman Statutes*. London: Institute of Classical Studies, ii. 749–53.

Fögen, M.-T. (1993). *Die Enteignung der Wahrsager: Studien zum kaiserlichen Wissensmonopol in der Spätantike*. Frankfurt: Suhrkamp.

Francis, J. A. (1995). *Subversive Virtue: Asceticism and Authority in the Second-Century Pagan World*. University Park, PA.: Pennsylvania State University Press.

Frazer, J. G. (1922). *The Golden Bough*. Abridged edition. London and New York: Macmillan.

Gager, J. G. (1992). *Curse Tablets and Binding Spells from the Ancient World*. Oxford and New York: Oxford University Press.

Gaide, F. (1993). 'Apulée de Madaure a-t-il prononcé le *De magia* devant le proconsul d'Afrique?', *Les Études Classiques*, 61: 227–31.

——(2005). 'Le *De magia* d'Apulée: entre *genus iudiciale* et *genus demonstrativum*', *Pallas*, 69: 97–106.

Garnsey, P. (1970). *Social Status and Legal Privilege in the Roman Empire*. Oxford: Clarendon Press.

Garosi, R. (1976). 'Indagine sulla formazione del concetto di magia nella cultura romana', in P. Xella (ed.), *Magia: Studi di storia delle religione in memoria di Raffaela Garosi*. Rome: Bulzoni, 13–93.

Gordon, R. L. (1999). 'Imagining Greek and Roman Magic', in Ankarloo and Clark 1999: 161–269.

Graf, F. (1997). *Magic in the Ancient World*. Trans. F. Philip. Cambridge, MA: London: Harvard University Press.

——(1999). 'Magic and Divination', in D. R. Jordan, H. Montgomery, and E. Thomassen (eds.), *The World of Ancient Magic*. Bergen: Norwegian Institute at Athens, 183–98.

Harris, M. (1979). *Cultural Materialism: The Struggle for a Science of Culture*. New York and Toronto: Random House.

Harrison, S. J. (2000). *Apuleius: A Latin Sophist*. Oxford: Oxford University Press.

Hunink, V. (1997). *Apuleius of Madauros: pro se de Magia (Apologia)*, 2 vols. Amsterdam: Gieben.

Janowitz, N. (2001). *Magic in the Roman World: Pagans, Jews and Christians*. London: Routledge.

Kippenberg, H. G. (1997). 'Magic in Roman Civil Discourse: Why Rituals Could Be Illegal', in P. Schäfer and H. G. Kippenberg (eds.), *Envisioning Magic: A Princeton Seminar and Symposium*. Leiden: Brill, 137–63.

Kluckhohn, C. (1944/1967). *Navaho Witchcraft*. Boston: Beacon Press.

Krüger, P., Mommsen, T., and Studemund, G. (1878–1927). *Collectio librorum iuris anteiustiniani*. 3 vols. Berlin: Weidmann.

Kunkel, W. (1973). *An Introduction to Roman Legal and Constitutional History.* 2nd edn. Oxford: Clarendon Press, translated from *Römische Rechtsgeschichte.* 6th edn. Cologne: Böhlau-Verlag (1971).

Lamberti, F. (2002). '*De Magia* als rechtsgeschichtliches Dokument', in J. Hammerstaedt, P. Habermehl, F. Lamberti, A. M. Ritter, and P. Schenk, *Apuleius, Über die Magie*, SAPERE 5. Darmstadt: Wissenschaftliche Buchgesellschaft, 331–50.

Levy, E. (1930). 'Paulus und der Sentenzenverfasser', *Stimmen der Zeit*, 50: 272–94, reprinted in his *Gesammelte Schriften*. Cologne: Böhlau-Verlag (1963), 99–114.

——(1943). 'Vulgarization of Roman Law in the Early Middle Ages as Illustrated by Successive Versions of *The Opinions of Paulus*', *Medievalia et Humanistica*, 1: 14–40, reprinted in *Bullettino dell'Istituto del Diritto Romano*, 55–56 suppl. 1951: 222–58 and in his *Gesammelte Schriften*. Cologne: Böhlau-Verlag (1963), 220–47.

Liebs, D. (1993). *Römische Jurisprudenz in Africa, mit Studien zu den pseudopaulinischen Sentenzen.* Berlin: Duncker and Humblot.

——(1997). 'Strafprozesse wegen Zauberei: Magie und politisches Kalkül in der römischen Geschichte', in V. Manthe and J. von Ungern-Sternberg (eds.), *Große Prozesse der römischen Antike*. Munich: Beck, 146–58 and 210–13.

MacMullen, R. (1966). *Enemies of the Roman Order.* Cambridge, MA: Harvard University Press.

——(1986). 'Judicial Savagery in the Roman Empire', *Chiron*, 16: 147–66, reprinted in his *Changes in the Roman Empire*. Princeton: Princeton University Press (1990), 204–17.

Marco Simón, F. (2001). 'Sobre la emergencia de la magia como sistema de alteridad en la Roma del siglo I d. C.', *Mene*, 1: 105–32.

Massonneau, E. (1934). *La Magie dans l'antiquité romaine.* Paris: Librairie du Recueil Sirey.

Mommsen, T. (1899). *Römisches Strafrecht.* Leipzig: Duncker and Humblot.

Müller, C. (ed.) (1885). *Fragmenta Historicorum Graecorum iv.* Paris: Firmin-Didot.

Needham, R. (1975). 'Polythetic Classification: Convergence and Consequences', *Man*, n.s. 10: 349–69.

Nock, A. D. (1933). 'Paul and the Magus', in K. Lake and H. J. Cadbury (eds.), *The Beginnings of Christianity, Part I: The Acts of the Apostles*, vol. v: *Additional Notes to the Commentary*. London: Macmillan, 164–88, reprinted in his *Essays on Religion and the Ancient World* (ed. Z. Stewart). Oxford: Clarendon Press (1972), i. 308–30.

Ogden, D. (1999). 'Binding Spells: Curse Tablets and Voodoo Dolls in the Greek and Roman Worlds', in Ankarloo and Clark 1999: 1–90.

Peachin, M. (1996). *Iudex vice Caesaris: Deputy Emperors and the Administration of Justice during the Principate*. Stuttgart: Steiner.

Pharr, C. (1932). 'The Interdiction of Magic in Roman Law', *Transactions of the American Philological Association*, 63: 269–95.

Phillips, C. R. (1986). 'The Sociology of Religious Knowledge in the Roman Empire to A.D. 284', *ANRW*, 2.16.3: 2677–773.

——(1991). '*Nullum Crimen sine Lege*: Socioreligious Sanctions on Magic', in C. A. Faraone and D. Obbink (eds.), *Magika Hiera: Ancient Greek Magic and Religion*. New York and Oxford: Oxford University Press, 260–76.

——(1994). 'Seek and Go Hide: Literary Source Problems and Graeco–Roman Magic', *Helios*, 21.2: 107–14.

Puccini-Delbey, G. (2004). *De Magia d'Apulée*. Neuilly-sur-Seine: Atlande.

Remus, H. (1999). 'Magic, Method, Madness', *Method and Theory in the Study of Religion*, 11: 258–98.

Riccobono, S., Baviera, J., and Arangio-Ruiz, V. (1940–43). *Fontes Iuris Romani Antejustiniani*. 2nd edn. 3 vols. Florence: Barbera.

Riemer, U. (2006). 'Apuleius, *De Magia*: Zur Historizität der Rede'. *Historia*, 55: 178–90.

Rives, J. B. (2002). 'Magic in the XII Tables Revisited', *Classical Quarterly*, 52: 270–90.

——(2006). 'Magic, Religion, and Law: The Case of the *Lex Cornelia de sicariis et veneficiis*', in C. Ando and J. Rüpke (eds.), *Religion and Law in Classical and Christian Rome*. Stuttgart: Steiner, 47–67.

——(2008). 'Legal Strategy and Learned Display in Apuleius' *Apology*', in W. Riess (ed.), *Paideia at Play: Learning and Wit in Apuleius*. Groningen: Barkhuis, 17–49.

——(2010). '*Magus* and its Cognates in Classical Latin', in R. L. Gordon and F. Marco Simón (eds.), *Magical Practice in the Latin West*. Leiden: Brill.

Robinson, O. F. (1997). *The Sources of Roman Law: Problems and Methods for Ancient Historians*. London and New York: Routledge.

Smith, J. Z. (1975). 'Good News is No News: Aretalogy and Gospel', in J. Neusner (ed.), *Christianity, Judaism and other Graeco–Roman Cults: Studies for Morton Smith at Sixty*. Leiden: Brill, i. 21–38, reprinted in his *Map is not Territory: Studies in the History of Religions*. Leiden: Brill (1978), 190–207.

——(1980). 'Fences and Neighbors: Some Contours of Early Judaism', in W. S. Green (ed.), *Approaches to Ancient Judaism: Theory and Practice*. Missoula, Mont.: Scholars Press, ii. 1–25, reprinted in his *Imagining*

Religion: From Babylon to Jonestown. Chicago: University of Chicago Press (1982), 1–18.

——(1995). 'Trading Places', in M. Meyer and P. Mirecki (eds.), *Ancient Magic and Ritual Power.* Leiden: Brill, 13–27.

Smith, M. (1956). 'Palestinian Judaism in the First Century', in M. Davis (ed.), *Israel: Its Role in Civilization.* New York: Harper and Brothers, 67–81, reprinted in his *Studies in the Cult of Yahweh* (ed. S. J. D. Cohen). Leiden: Brill (1996), i. 104–15.

——(1977). *Jesus the Magician.* New York: Harper and Row.

Speyer, W. (1981). *Büchervernichtung und Zensur des Geistes bei Heiden, Juden und Christen.* Stuttgart: Anton Hiersemann.

Swoboda, A. (1889). *P. Nigidii Figuli Operum Reliquiae.* Vienna, reprinted Amsterdam: Hakkert (1964).

Talbert, R. J. A. (1984). *The Senate of Imperial Rome.* Princeton: Princeton University Press.

Thomasson, B. E. (1996). *Fasti Africani: Senatorische und ritterliche Amtsträger in den römischen Provinzen Nordafrikas von Augustus bis Diocletian.* Stockholm: Jonsered.

Vallette, P. (ed.) (1924). *Apuleius: Apologie, Florides.* Paris: Les Belles Lettres.

Versnel, H. S. (1991). 'Some Reflections on the Relationship Magic–Religion', *Numen*, 38: 177–97.

Woolf, G. (2000). 'The Religious History of the Northwest Provinces', *JRA*, 13: 615–30.

4

New Combinations and New Statuses

The Indigenous Gods in the Pantheons of the Cities of Roman Gaul

William Van Andringa

Coexistence, borrowing, fusion: it is in these terms that religious changes in the Roman provinces of Gaul are very often defined. Generally speaking, ever since the work of Jullian, we have been left with an image of harmony between the indigenous and the Roman gods, the fruit of a religious tolerance that was characteristic of the conquerors. And it was Toutain who observed, in his study of *Pagan Cults in the Roman Empire*, that this Roman tolerance goes hand in hand with the favourable welcome given to the Roman gods by the provincials (Jullian 1993; Toutain 1907–20). Among the evidence cited, we find at the top of the list the Pillar of the Boatmen, still seen recently as a 'pictorial catechism', as well as the large number of divine triads and the crouching or horned gods whose presence is recorded here and there in the sanctuaries, alongside deities of classical appearance. The judgement formed, then, from such evidence, is that the 'indigenous gods continued to live for the duration of the Empire in a coexistence born of syncretism and tolerance'.

This reading of religious phenomena poses a number of problems, predicated as it is upon the firm belief, forged by Gallo–Roman studies throughout the 20th century, that the two cultures merged to produce hybrid pantheons (Hatt 1989; Duval 1993). Yet this harmony, like the idea of religious permanence, is an illusion. The illusion is kept up in various ways:

1. First, by viewing the images in isolation from their archaeological and historical context. The problem here is not simply a methodological one. No doubt it stems in large part from the kind of sources examined: statuary and bas-reliefs that are nearly always found in a context of reuse, thus discouraging an attempt to take account of the archaeological setting of the monument in question. The blocks that make up the Pillar of the Boatmen were discovered in 1711 under the choir of Notre-Dame Cathedral in Paris, inserted into the base of thick walls. This makes it difficult to establish a logical order for them, or to reconstruct the monument in its original surroundings. Did it feature in the headquarters of the association? Was it on public display? In a sanctuary? It is fundamentally impossible to say.

2. Second, the impression of Roman and Gallic cultures existing in harmony is maintained by the conviction that the Gallic gods were unchanging, whereas studies of Greek and Roman religions have for some time now demonstrated the dynamic and evolving nature of ancient polytheistic systems (e.g. Liebeschuetz 1979; Beard et al. 1998; Van Andringa 2009). Moreover, epigraphical and archaeological investigations undertaken over the last fifteen years have shown that it is reductive to assume the presence of indigenous gods throughout Gaul, especially not in every period, and to interpret them more or less superficially so as to conclude that the indigenous divine world was one of utter constancy.

But what then should we make of that Celtic heritage for which there is no lack of evidence? The bas-reliefs of the Pillar of the Boatmen recall the picture of Heracles-Ogmios viewed by Lucian somewhere in Gaul during the second century AD (*Heracles* 1–6); not forgetting the sculptures representing local triads at Nuits-Saint-Georges, Vendœuvres-en-Brenne, and Reims (Fig. 4.1). Nonetheless, questions would still have to be asked about the true number of such depictions, since these are always the monuments that are highlighted in discussions of religion in ancient Gaul, leaving in the background the hundreds of representations of Mercury, Venus, and Jupiter to be found in the volumes published by Espérandieu (1907–81; e.g. Fig. 4.2). And in particular, there would have to be questions about the exact place of these depictions in the sanctuaries

Fig. 4.1. The stele of Reims. Apollo and Mercury flank the god with stag's horns.

and the religion of the cities of the Imperial era. For the problem of the Romanization of cults is clearly less to do with coexistence than with the kind of association maintained between the cults, and thus their hierarchical arrangement; it is less to do with fusion and syncretism than with changes in status and identity.

This point can be shown by re-examining the Pillar of the Boatmen, an artefact from the time of Tiberius that is often invoked to illustrate the balance struck very early on between the two coexisting cultures, Celtic and Roman: do we not indeed find a series of Gallic gods who have been borrowed (Vulcan, Jupiter, Mars, Castor, and Pollux) and indigenous gods who appear to have

Fig. 4.2. A few horned or crouching gods from the dozens of depictions of Mercury derived from the canon of classical models. Statue of Mercury from Auxerre.

retained their identities during the Imperial era (Esus, Tarvos Trigaranus, Cernunnos, Smer[trios]?), in the company of Jupiter and the emperor, both mentioned in the monument's dedication? The reading I wish to put forward here will assess the Romanization of cults and the question of the Celtic heritage.

The Pillar of the Boatmen, discovered in detached pieces, and its inscriptions, have elicited numerous studies, and these can be referred to for in-depth analysis (Duval 1960: nos. 1–26; Lavagne 1984; Adam 1984; Lejeune 1988: nos. 157–76). Needless to say, the monument is well known and there is little point, for current purposes at least, in taking up detailed interpretation of the scenes depicted. This gallery of deities, exhibited in detached pieces, is a familiar display in the Musée de Cluny in Paris. The restoration of the blocks on the same site, along with their morphological characteristics—they are sculpted on all four sides—and the well-known existence of column bases formed from layers of sculpted blocks are all arguments confirming the identification of the blocks as forming a pillar (Adam 1984).[1] From what has been preserved of the monument, it is possible to make out four distinct levels. In the vertical succession of the dadoes, the order is unclear,[2] but the reconstruction proposed by Adam may serve as a guide (Figs. 4.3 and 4.3A).

On level 1, the largest block, pairs of deities are shown. The legends have all but disappeared, hence the problem in identifying the gods:

A. Mars and a goddess without recognizable attributes (Minerva according to Duval) (Fig. 4.4).
B. Mercury (caduceus and petasus) and a goddess, possibly Rosmerta or Maia? (Fig. 4.5).
C. Fortuna and another god (Fig. 4.6).
D. Venus and another deity (Fig. 4.7).

On level 3, a block of medium size, other deities are found:

A. Jupiter depicted in the classic attitude of the Capitoline god, draped, armed with a thunderbolt and accompanied by the eagle (Fig. 4.8). Above the bas-relief, the name of the deity appears to be

---

[1] This section owes much to conversations that I have been able to have with J.-P. Adam and with F. Saragoza, the curator at the Musée de Cluny, whom I wish to thank most warmly. I am also grateful to the participants of the Round Table of Lausanne, in particular P. Le Roux, M. Christol, and C. Goudineau, whose comments and questions led me to re-examine this artefact. Naturally, I bear responsibility for choices made and for possible errors.

[2] The most logical order, however, is given by Lejeune 1988: 159, who places the dado of Jupiter at the top of the monument.

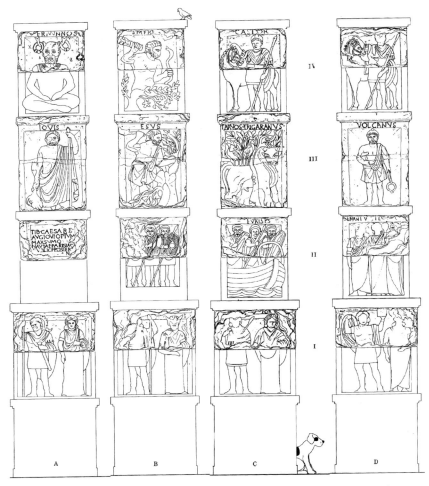

Figs. 4.3 and 4.3A. The four sides of the Pillar of the Boatmen, according to a layout proposed by J.-P. Adam.

engraved in the genitive (IOVIS), unless read as a nominative as with the other gods. Duval and Lejeune are in fact doubtless correct in identifying an old analogical nominative, as was common for Jupiter (Duval 1960: 21; Lejeune 1988: 167; cf. *CIL* xiii. no. 2869).

Fig. 4.4. The Pillar of the Boatmen, Level 1, Face A.

Fig. 4.5. The Pillar of the Boatmen, Level I, Face B.

Fig. 4.6. The Pillar of the Boatmen, Level I, Face C.

Fig. 4.7. The Pillar of the Boatmen, Level I, Face D.

Fig. 4.8. The Pillar of the Boatmen, Level III, Face A, Jupiter.

B. The god Esus with a legend in the nominative (Fig. 4.9). Little is known about this figure from Celtic mythology, other than that he never appears in the epigraphy of the Imperial era. The deity seems to have disappeared, surviving only in a legend that was nonetheless known to the Romans in the first century AD, as it is evoked by Lucan in his *Pharsalia* (lines 441–5).

C. Vulcan (Fig. 4.10), who is also present in the pantheon of the boatmen of the Loire (*CIL* xiii. no. 3105).

Fig. 4.9. The Pillar of the Boatmen, Level III, Face B, Esus.

Fig. 4.10. The Pillar of the Boatmen, Level III, Face D, Volcanus.

   D. Tarvos Trigaranus, the bull with three cranes, a fantastical
   animal from Gallic mythology (Fig. 4.11).

On level 4:

   A. Cernunnos, the god with stag's horns (Fig. 4.12). Other bas-
   reliefs depicting him are known in the Roman era (the relief of
   Reims for example; Fig. 4.1), but here too he does not appear
   on any religious inscription, or in any dedication from the
   Imperial era.

Fig. 4.11. The Pillar of the Boatmen, Level III, Face C, Tarvos Trigaranus.

B. Smert[rios] (Fig. 4.13), in the reading put forward by Duval, following the example of a Mars Smertrius attested in Gaul (*CIL* xiii. no. 11975; 4119).

C and D. Castor and Pollux (Figs. 4.14 and 4.15), Greco–Roman gods who evidently had equivalents in Germania (Tacitus, *Germania* 43. 4–5) and did also probably in Gaul.

Fig. 4.12. The Pillar of the Boatmen, Level IV, Face A, Cernunnos.

Fig. 4.13. The Pillar of the Boatmen, Level IV, Face B, Smertrios.

Fig. 4.14. The Pillar of the Boatmen, Level IV, Face C, Castor.

Fig. 4.15. The Pillar of the Boatmen, Level IV, Face D, Pollux.

Related to this gallery of indigenous and Roman deities is the dedication reconstructed on the second level by Adam (*CIL* xiii. no. 3026):

Tib(erio) Caesare / Aug(usto), Iovi Optumo / Maxsumo s(acrum) / nautae Parisiaci / publice posierun[t].

Under Tib(erius) Caesar Aug(ustus), sacred to Jupiter Best and Greatest, the Parisian boatmen set it up with college funds.

On the other sides of this block, there is a change in register, the gods being replaced by historical scenes in which it is possible to recognize a series of figures wearing togas or bearing arms (Figs. 4.16 and 4.17). For most commentators, these figures armed in the Celtic fashion represent the members forming the corporation of the boatmen, with the classic distinction made for each of the civic groups between *iuvenes* (beardless figures) and *seniores* (bearded figures). Bringing up the procession, the togate figures—the representatives of the cult and thus the corporation—are shown performing a sacrifice before a figure of more significant proportions (Fig. 4.18). In all likelihood, this is a cult statue, depicting a deity or an emperor (*divus*

Fig. 4.16. The Pillar of the Boatmen, Level II, Face B.

Fig. 4.17. The Pillar of the Boatmen, Level II, Face C.

Fig. 4.18. The Pillar of the Boatmen, Level II, Face D.

Augustus or Tiberius). The identity of the heavily disfigured scene is confirmed by the expression SENANT inscribed on the upper frame of the relief, and translated by Lejeune as 'they offer sacrifice' (Lejeune 1988: 176).

But what, then, are we to make of this monument? A rough and ready set of images put together in the interests of religious tolerance? An illustration of successful coexistence between the Gallic and Roman gods? A catechism intended for the faithful, marked out with legends? The monument's dedication here is of prime importance for interpreting the images and their combination (Fig. 4.19). And the inscription is no more concise than any other. Rather than using set phrases, it states what matters, namely the erection of a religious monument by the 'Parisian boatmen', an official college of the city of the Parisii and a powerful corporation whose headquarters was established in Lutetia. And this monument, erected *publice*—'with college funds'[3]—gave clear and precise expression to the status of the corporation. We know that the activities of the boatmen were closely monitored by the Imperial power (Waltzing 1895: 123ff.). There can be little surprise, then, that the Parisian boatmen invoke Tiberius at the head of the dedication. The termination used for CAESAR has created some indecision between a temporal ablative or an archaic dative ending in 'E' (Duval 1960; Lavagne 1984). However, the hypothesis of a temporal ablative seems to be the correct one, to judge by the dedications on other monuments, such as the bridge at Chaves in Portugal. As Duval has observed, this also explains why the living emperor is placed before Jupiter. The mention of Tiberius, though, is not simply a problem of dates: what we have is an explicit reference to the reigning emperor and to the Roman authorities, the sign of an official procedure on the part of the college of the boatmen. Nonetheless, the most important thing is that the monument belongs to Jupiter: it is to the god of the Roman state that the sacrifice offered by the boatmen is addressed. Moreover, the statue to the

---

[3] The word *publice* is attested in a collegial context, as noted by Duval 1960: 10; cf. *CIL* vi. no. 10302; 10409; 10410 for the funerary colleges of Rome; see also *CIL* xiii. nos 2460 and 5874. Though it most frequently relates to the city and public funds, the term occasionally takes the meaning of 'paid for by the community', 'collectively'. The Paris text indeed says: *nautae publice posierunt*, 'the boatmen have collectively had (the monument) erected', in other words with money from college funds.

Fig. 4.19. The Pillar of the Boatmen, Level II, Face A.

father of the gods must have stood at the top of the pillar. This, at least, is the most likely reconstruction, judging by the example of the column at Mainz, which has been preserved in its entirety and which bears at its summit an effigy of the Roman god. The Mainz inscription, in fact, is less ambiguous than the Paris one, establishing as it does that the sacrifice was dedicated to Jupiter 'for the safety of Nero' by the settlers (Bauchhenss and Nölke 1981; Selzer 1988). The Paris text does not imply a sacrifice 'for the safety' of Tiberius, but the living emperor was included on the dedication as guarantor of the imperial system: it is thus possible that this homage involved a small amount of incense and wine poured over the altar flame.

The inscription also makes it possible to situate the monument in its historical context: the pillar was raised during the reign of Tiberius, in other words at least a generation after the organization of the Parisii into a city, at a time when the initial effects of the urbanization of Lutetia must have started to be felt. Thus, in erecting a religious monument to Jupiter and the emperor, in a sanctuary that served as a meeting place for the association or in the headquarters of the college, the boatmen were proclaiming the official existence of their group within the city and the imperial system. In the same period, the butchers of Périgueux, who according to Jullian have just obtained the same status as a corporation, dedicated an altar to Jupiter Best and Greatest, associated with the *genius* of Tiberius (Fig. 4.20; *CIL* xiii. no. 941; Jullian, 1211–3). A little later, other groups who had the recognized status of *vicus* (small town or urban quarter), manifest their attachment to the system of the city in the same way. The Emperor Claudius receives public honours at Marsal, *vicus* Mediomatrici (*CIL* xiii. no. 4565); at Trier, the inhabitants of a neighbourhood of the town constructed an altar and a kitchen dedicated to Jupiter (*CIL* xiii. no. 3650). As a final example—others might be added—at Jouars-Pontchartrain, excavations have recently brought to light the heavily disfigured fragments of a pillar that has some elements in common with the monument of the boatmen (Bacon in Blin 2000: 104–14); Bacon here puts forward the same combination: divine portraits (with perhaps Cernunnos and Minerva), a historical scene depicting the procession of the *vicani*, and a sacrifice. The pillar, which dates from the time of Nerva or Trajan, was connected with a sanctuary of the settlement whose tutelary god appears to have been a major deity. Jupiter most obviously comes to mind, a hypothesis that seems to be supported by the identification of significant traces of the sacrifice of cattle (Blin and Lepetz 2008).

No need to extend the list: in accordance with their status, these groups had precise religious duties that concerned the imperial house and the gods of the Roman state, notably Jupiter. What then to make of the Pillar of the Boatmen's decoration, this gallery of portraits? Many of the deities depicted are of Roman appearance, with Latin names given in the nominative: does this make them Roman gods or are they Gallic gods that have been borrowed? Have these gods become Roman or is it simply a case of repackaging the Celtic deities? Posing the problem in these terms does not yield a clear-cut answer: as Woolf has suggested (1998: 206–15), it comes down to whether the glass is half-full or half-empty. The gods depicted are not Celtic gods in disguise. The adoption of a Roman deity followed an official procedure sanctioned by the authorities of the college or city (Scheid 1991: 46; Van Andringa 2002: 133–58). The gods of the boatmen may in part be borrowed gods, but these deities have changed in appearance, name, and status. They henceforth are patrons of the activities of a college integrated into the city, hence the marked Roman

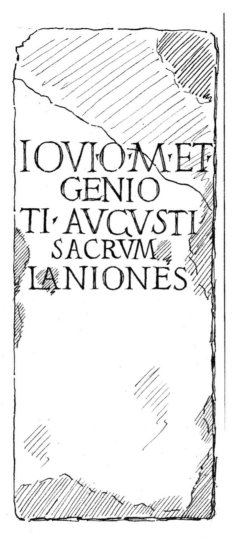

Fig. 4.20. The altar of the butchers of Périgueux.

character of the gods presented. Lavagne is thus doubtless right to identify in this gallery of portraits the pantheon of the boatmen of the Seine (Lavagne 1984: 277): the commercial function of Mercury is perfectly adapted to the activities of the boatmen; in his turn, Vulcan can oversee naval construction. And figuring among these gods, as is fitting, are the ancestral gods who are here the ancient famous deities, easily recognizable to all, even the Romans, judging by the mention of Esus in Lucan's *Pharsalia* (1. 445). In a way, the patronage of the gods, thus defined, sketched out the boundaries of the political and economic territory in which the guild developed. And within this system of patronage, the leading role was assumed by Jupiter Greatest and Best in association with the emperor, thus in effect relegating the Gallic gods or the borrowed gods, their names nonetheless given in the nominative, to second place. More than a coexistence of Roman deities and of indigenous deities who never appear in epigraphy (Cernunnos, Esus, Tarvos Trigaranus), the composition of the Pillar of the Boatmen, crowned by the statue of Jupiter, proclaimed the majesty and the pre-eminence of the great civic god over the ancestral deities of whom we cannot be sure whether they played an active religious role in the official college cult. I am therefore inclined to think that the bas-reliefs do not constitute a catechism, but rather that they ratify the implementation of an established order. And this established order is the power of Rome, which every community integrated into the Empire, city, *vicus*, or college, had to recognize. For the future of provincial communities was thenceforth closely connected to that of the Roman state, as symbolized by the association between the emperor and the father of the gods (Van Andringa 2007a). Rather than an illustration of the coexistence between two cultures or of the tolerance that was characteristic of the Romans, in the end the pillar shows that Jupiter and the emperor stood at the summit of the divine hierarchy, and that they were patrons of the integration of the boatmen into the municipal world and the empire. In short, the issue here is one of hierarchy and of the composition of a pantheon that would be perfectly adapted to the college of the boatmen at the time of Tiberius. Deities protecting commercial and transport activities; gods and mythological references attached to the different geographical areas covered by the boatmen, and serving as a reminder of the corporation's venerable age; divine powers incarnating the local and Roman power: in a way, the divine patronage established for the corporation, one generation after the organization of the Gauls into cities, makes it possible to re-transcribe as accurately as possible the activities of the college of the boatmen, as well as the group's institutional anchorage within the imperial system.

It remains to consider these sculpted monuments in their archaeological context. The discovery of the blocks originally belonging to the monument of the boatmen did not give a firm idea of the pillar's location, no doubt the headquarters of the association or a place of public worship. The case of Jouars-Pontchartrain shows that such monuments could be associated with sanctuaries in which it was clearly not Esus or Taranis who played the leading roles. The same observation can be made about the sculptural dedication of Nuits-Saint-Georges, discovered on the site of a large sanctuary of the *vicus* (Planson and Pommeret 1986; Pommeret 2001; Fig. 4.21). This monument was quickly claimed as 'a perfect example of syncretism in Gaul', and the deities depicted seen as eminently Gallic gods; from left to right a mother goddess, an extension of the ancient cult of the mother goddess, source of fertility, a bisexual Cybele (or a *genius*) and especially the Gallic three-headed horned god, purveyor of riches. This reading stems from a firm belief in the permanence of the old indigenous landscape, a belief nourished by the presence of the horned god. Yet if we take into account the historical and religious context of the discovery, a different reading emerges: the composition is centred on a god with a turreted headdress and the horn of plenty, which to my mind can only be a representation of the *genius* of the settlement or of its inhabitants, the *vicani* (cf. *LIMC* viii. 1997, s.v. *genius* [I. Romeo], 599–607). And the *genius* here is not an indigenous deity, but the religious expression of the urban context, that is to say the *vicus*, which is legally defined as an urban district detached from the administrative centre (cf. *CIL* xiii. nos 1375; 5967; 6433; 7655; 8838). The deity depicted on the right of the *genius* appears to be the goddess Fortuna holding the horn of plenty and a libation bowl in her right hand (cf. *LIMC* viii. 1997, s.v. *Tyché* [L. Villard], 115–25; *ibid.*, s.v. *Tyché/Fortuna* [F. Rausa], 125–41). In the end, the only deity of indigenous appearance is the three-headed god with stag's antlers, who certainly managed to survive, but found

Fig. 4.21. The monument of the Bolards from Nuits-Saint-Georges.

himself associated with gods who expressed new communal realities. It is this association of gods that establishes the religious significance: while the combination adopted left a place for the old ancestral god, as would be only proper, the religious consequence was to bring new realities to the fore and relations with previously unseen deities. We should add that the sculpted dedication was not a cult statue, but that this small-scale monument doubtless commemorated a ceremony celebrated in the great temple of the *vicus*. The sanctuary, which takes on a monumental aspect from the middle of the first century

AD, in conformity with a classical layout, was as the epigraphic documents show doubtless dedicated to Apollo or Mars Segomo, that is to say, in this particular case, the major deities of the nearby city of Augustodunum, the city of the Aedui (Pommeret 2001): the sculpted dedication with its triad of gods was therefore displayed in the sanctuary in a position of secondary importance.

We might as well agree once and for all to abandon this notion of harmonious coexistence between the old Gallic gods and the new arrivals, as it masks what is most important. Instead of coexistence, let us speak rather of new religious combinations. These certainly included ancient ancestral gods or mythological figures—it could not be otherwise in ancient polytheism—but the Pillar of the Boatmen or the stele of Nuits-Saint-George seem to show that within the new combinations formed during the imperial era, these gods changed their appearance or took on less important roles. To form conclusions on the permanence of the gods or cults is merely to make reference to something that existed in accordance with religious piety, something manifest. In contrast, it is essential to specify how these cults were redefined and in what historical context. Was there a reformulation of rites? Was a new altar installed? Are there sources to show the construction of a new sanctuary? Or is there a change in the name and status of the god? Do we see the local or ancestral cult becoming associated with new cults? Finally, were new pantheons formed? There are many possibilities, and evidence of evolution is often hard to come by. We can consider the example, highlighted by Jouin and Méniel (2001), of the sacrifice of horses and dogs in Vertault in eastern France. This was a local practice; but we note that these rituals disappeared in the middle of the first century AD, when the temple was built. Clearly, the form and significance of the cult changed, probably in connection with the development of Vertault, which under the empire becomes a *vicus*. This does not mean that the deity or the cult site disappeared. Horses and dogs are not sacrificed after AD 50, but the site remains a sanctuary and the name of the deity may have stayed the same (why not?). In the end, the problem is more to do with the forms of sacrifice than with the persistence of a sacred site. As for the horses sacrificed at Longueil-Sainte-Marie in northern France, before hearing Gallic echoes, we have to bear in mind the historical context (Gaudefroy and Lepetz

2000): this deposition of about fifty horses seems to date from the second half of the third century AD, and the troubled nature of the period may explain this particular ritual act. Furthermore, the horse corpses had been manipulated, a practice not attested during the Gallic era: the closest example in fact is Vertault, where the deposit dates to the Julio–Claudian period.

To be sure, not all ancestral gods took secondary positions in the pantheons of the cities, as indicated by the various forms of the great Mars in the cities of Gaul: Lenus Mars among the Treveri, Mars Mullo among the Aulerci Cenomani or the Riedoni, Mars Caturix among the Helvetii are examples of great local gods set up as municipal gods (cf. Scheid 1991, 1995; Beard et al. 1998: ii. 313–39; Van Andringa 2002, 141–4). But during the period that concerns us here, these gods are no longer Gallic; they were officially adopted and in the way the cult was organized received perfectly Roman forms, as attested by the *flamines* (Roman-style priests) created at Trier and Rennes, as well as the construction of new sanctuaries (Fig. 4.22). The way that the process unfolds is of decisive importance. There is no fusion or syncretism, or even simple repackaging; these gods have changed their name and their identity. With Mars Caturix, the epithet Caturix served as a reminder that this was an ancient ancestral god, and the special protector of the Helvetii. But with this connection established, it was still Mars who was worshipped, in the same way that a lion is always a lion no matter where, as Paul Veyne has nicely shown (1983; cf also Nock 1972: ii. 752). Between the second and the fourth centuries, visitors to the sanctuary of Uley, in the province of Roman Britain, left lead tablets addressed to Mercury in the form *deus Mercurius, deus sanctus Mercurius*, or *divus Mercurius*. At times, they change their mind, scoring out the tablets, but their corrections relate not to indigenous deities but rather to other gods with Roman names, or combinations of deities such as Mars Mercury or Mars Silvanus (Tomlin in Woodward and Leach 1993). Of course, Mercury may have taken the place of a local god, but once naturalized, he became Mercury. This is by no means unheard of in Graeco–Roman polytheism; quite the contrary, as confirmed by a passage in Livy (42. 3. 9) concerning the sacrilege perpetrated in 173 BC by Quintus Fulvius Flaccus. Quintus was accused of removing the roof from the temple of Juno Lacinia,

Fig. 4.22. A statue base inserted into the ramparts of Rennes. It mentions the offering of a statue to Mars Mullo by the *flamen* of the sanctuary. Mullo has become Mars and has changed status.

goddess of the Brutii, in order to build a sanctuary in Rome. There is no sense in building a temple with the ruins of another temple, Livy points out, for the immortal gods are everywhere the same. Juno, no matter where, is always Juno, just as a lion is always a lion.

By way of reassurance, it is naturally not the intention here to take the gods worshipped in the cities of Gaul and turn them into Roman gods. Indeed, this would make little sense: the Roman gods are first and foremost the gods of the city of Rome. Fundamentally, what is being proposed is to consider these cults in their context and their historical setting, so as to evaluate the new combinations and new statuses established for them, before making a judgment on the nature of the god worshipped. Lenus Mars is not a Gallic god, nor is he an indigenous god, any more than he is Roman or Gallo–Roman.

Rather, he is one of the great gods, if not the main protector and patron god, of the colony of the Treveri; and it is for this reason that his cult was organized according to the normal procedures of the Roman or Latin colonies. Mars Camulus, attested at Reims, is likewise a great god of the city, and it is as such that he is worshipped on the Rhine by the citizens of the Remi—this being the name they give themselves on the inscription—'for the safety of the Emperor Nero'. Likewise, the god Cretus, who for his part kept a local name, is a patron deity of a *pagus* (a territorial subdivision of the city) in the colony of the Treveri (Fig. 4.23). Once more, the god is not alone, but shares in the honours that went to the imperial house and the *genius* of the *pagus*. The Roman state, the religious emanation of a territorial subdivision of the colony and the ancestral god: this is the association

Fig. 4.23. In honour of the divine house, to the god Creto and to the *genius* of a Treverian *pagus*: the divine combination made it possible to anchor local society in the political reality of the time.

that logically adds up, allowing a local community to respond in a precise way to a certain moment in its history; and this connection with reality was symbolized by the assembly of these different gods within the same sanctuary.

Therefore, instead of Gallic, Roman, or Gallo–Roman gods, let us refer, rather, to the gods of the city of the Treveri, the Remi or the Helvetii. Let us understand the gods on the basis not of their past history but of their communal situation at a particular point in time. Let us understand them city by city, in terms of the relations they maintained with one another and the associations they formed. Let us evaluate their new status and their place within the sanctuaries, and instead of looking at the followers, in the general sense of the word, let us look at the communities administering the cults: the college, *vicus, pagus,* or family. And with observations of an essentially archaeological nature, rather than focusing on the meaning of a given artefact or monument—the Gallo–Roman temple naturally comes to mind—let us try to determine the discernible signs of its evolution: it could be the construction or the restoration of a sanctuary, it could be the redesigning of an altar, or it could be the organization of new liturgical and ritual practices (Van Andringa 2007b and 2008; Lepetz and Van Andringa 2008).

The cities of the Roman era set up specific religious systems to cater on the one hand for the new status held by the communities now incorporated into an empire at peace, and on the other for changes and developments taking place within society and faced by individuals as they began to take on Roman citizenship. The question we sought to address concerned the degree to which the old religion survived during the imperial era: the answer is that what survived was integrated into new religious combinations, and that the gods and cults received a new status. This capacity for change and development was characteristic of ancient polytheism, and did not in any way contravene respect for religious tradition. For the gods of polytheism were never timeless entities, shining like stars across the ages. They evolved in the same way as did ancient societies, quite simply because the religious systems in question were human and historical constructions.

BIBLIOGRAPHY

Adam, J.-P. (1984). 'Le pilier des nautes, essai de restitution', in *Lutèce* 1984: 299–307.

Bauchhenss, G. and Nölke, P. (1981). *Die Iupitersaülen in den germanischen Provinzen*, Bonner Jahrbücher Supp. 41. Cologne: Rheinland-Verlag; Bonn: Habelt.

Beard, M., North, J., and Price, S. (1998). *Religions of Rome*, 2 vols. Cambridge: Cambridge University Press.

Blin, O. (2000). 'Un sanctuaire de vicus: Jouars-Ponchartrain', in Van Andringa 2000: 91–118.

——and Lepetz, S. (1998). 'Sacrifice et boucherie dans le sanctuaire de Jouars-Pontchartrain: rituels et vestiges matériels', in Lepetz and Van Andringa 2008: 225–36.

Derks, T. (1998). *Gods, Temples and Ritual Practices. The Transformation of Religious Ideas and Values in Roman Gaul*, Amsterdam Archaeological Studies 2. Amsterdam: Amsterdam University Press.

Duval, P.-M. (1960). *Les inscriptions antiques de Paris*, 2 vols. Paris: Imprimerie nationale.

——(1993). *Les dieux de la Gaule*, 4th edn. Paris: Payot; 1st edn. 1957.

Espérandieu, E., Lantier, R., and Duval, P. M. (1907–81). *Recueil général des bas-reliefs, statues et bustes de la Gaule romaine*, 16 vols. Paris: Imprimerie nationale.

Gaudefroy, S. and Lepetz, S. (2000). 'Le dépôt sacrificiel de Longueil-Sainte-Marie "L'Orméon". Un culte de tradition locale sous l'Empire?', in Van Andringa 2000: 157–92.

Hatt, J.-J. (1989). *Mythes et dieux de la Gaule*, i: *Les grandes divinités masculines*. Paris: Picard.

Jouin, M. and Méniel, P. (2001). 'Les dépôts animaux et le fanum gallo-romains de Vertault (Côte-d'Or)', *Revue Archéologique de l'Est*, 50: 119–216.

Jullian, C. (1993). *Histoire de la Gaule*, 2 vols (8 books). Paris: Hachette; 1st edn. 1920–6.

Lavagne, H. (1984). 'Le pilier des nautes', in *Lutèce* 1984: 275–98.

Lejeune, M. (1988). *Recueil des inscriptions gauloises (R.I.G.)*, ii. 1: *Textes gallo-étrusques, textes gallo-latins sur pierre*, Gallia Supp. 45. Paris: Éditions du C.N.R.S.

Lepetz, S. and Van Andringa, W. (eds.) (2008). *Archéologie du sacrifice animal en Gaule romaine. Rituels et pratiques alimentaires*. Montagnac: Mergoil.

Liebeschuetz, J. H. W. G. (1979). *Continuity and Change in Roman Religion.* Oxford: Clarendon Press.

Lutèce (1984). *Lutèce: Paris de César à Clovis: Musée Carnavalet et Musée national des Thermes et de l'Hôtel de Cluny, 3 mai 1984–printemps 1985.* Paris: Société des amis du Musée Carnavalet.

Nock, A. D. (1972). *Essays on Religion and the Ancient World*, ed. Z. Stewart, 2 vols. Oxford: Clarendon Press.

Planson, E. and Pommeret, C. (1986). *Les Bolards: le site gallo-romain et le musée de Nuits-Saint-Georges (Côte-d'Or)*, Guides Archéologiques de la France 7. Paris: Imprimerie Nationale.

Pommeret, C. (ed.) (2001). *Le sanctuaire antique des Bolards à Nuits-Saint-Georges (Côte-d'Or)*, Revue archéologique de l'Est, Supp. 16. Dijon: Société archéologique de l'Est.

Scheid, J. (1991). 'Sanctuaires et territoire dans la colonia Augusta Treverorum', in J.-L. Brunaux (ed.), *Les sanctuaires celtiques et le monde méditerranéen.* Paris: Éditions Errance, 42–57.

——(1995).'Les temples de l'Altbachtal à Trèves: un "sanctuaire national"?', *Cahiers du Centre Glotz*, 6: 227–43.

Selzer, W. (1988). *Römische Steindenkmäler. Mainz in römischer Zeit.* Mainz: Philipp von Zabern.

Van Andringa, W. (ed.) (2000). *Archéologie des sanctuaires en Gaule romaine.* Saint-Etienne: Publications de l'Université de Saint-Etienne.

——(2002). *La religion en Gaule romaine. Piété et politique (Ier-IIIe siècle ap. J.-C.).* Paris: Errance.

——(2007a). 'Religions and the Integration of Cities in the Empire in the 2nd Century AD: The Creation of a Common Religious Language', in J. Rüpke (ed.), *A Companion to Roman Religion.* Oxford: Blackwell, 83–95.

——(ed.) (2007b). 'Sacrifices, marché de la viande et pratiques alimentaires dans les cités du monde romain', *Food & History*, 5.

——(2008). 'Sanctuaires et genèse urbaine en Gaule romaine', in D. Castella and M.-F. Meylan Krause (ed.), *Topographie sacrée et rituels. Le cas d'Aventicum, capitale des Helvètes*, Antiqua 43. Basel: Archäologie Schweiz, 121–35.

——(2009). *Quotidien des dieux et des hommes. La vie religieuse dans les cités du Vésuve à l'époque romaine*, BEFAR 337. Rome: École française de Rome.

Veyne, P. (1983). '"Titulus praelatus": Offrande, solennisation et publicité dans les ex-voto gréco-romains', *Revue Archéologique*, 1983: 281–300.

Waltzing, J.-P. (1895–1900). *Etude historique sur les corporations profession- nelles chez les Romains*, 4 vols. Brussels-Louvain: Peeters.

Woodward, A. and Leach, P. (1993). *The Uley Shrines. Excavation of a Ritual Complex on West Hill, Uley, Gloucestershire: 1977–79.* London: English Heritage.

Woolf, G. (1998). *Becoming Roman. The Origins of Provincial Civilization in Gaul.* Cambridge: Cambridge University Press.

5

Hypsistos

A Way of Exalting the Gods in Graeco–Roman Polytheism[1]

Nicole Belayche

ὑψίστων μεδέουσα θεῶν, Ἑρμοῦθι ἄνασσα
('ruler of the highest gods, queen Hermouthi')
SB 5. no. 8138. iii. verse 1.

In principle, one might think that there could be no clearer term than ὕψιστος (*hypsistos*, 'highest/most high'), the irregular superlative form of the adverb ὕψι ('on high'),[2] to designate the eminent or pre-eminent position of a deity within the divine edifice as the devotee conceives of it. This edifice may indeed come in different architectural forms: from a single God *Hypsistos*, exclusive of all fellow-deities, to a plurality of divine beings, where one is worshipped as *hypsistos* without *ipso facto* being separated from the others, the plastic structure of the pantheons allowing for different reconstructions to suit particular religious situations.[3] Moreover,

[1] I warmly thank Polymnia Athanassiadi for her kindly and critical reading of this article. Of course, I bear full responsibility for it. I am also indebted to Jake Wadham, who translated the French text in a very intelligent and elegant manner.
[2] Cf. Chantraine 1977: iv.1, 1164: 'ὕψιστος seems analogous with μέγιστος, κύδιστος, the Homeric superlative being ὕπατος'. Also Frisk 1970: ii. 978.
[3] Cf. the seminal work of Vernant 1980: 92–109 and Schmidt 1987.

since antiquity, the superlative—relative or absolute ('the most high/ the highest')—has been subject to various readings,[4] serving to maintain the theological ambiguity of the term.[5]

There is, then, hardly a designation for the divine that has elicited more scholarly debate. There are two main reasons for this: the first reason is that—despite the immediate intelligibility of an authority proclaimed by its epithet as infinitely superior, and thus all-powerful, which along with immortality is the very definition of divinity[6]—it is in practice not so easy to pin down a term which is attested in different regions (the eastern half of the Mediterranean, but stretching to the Iberian peninsula), in different periods (from the second century BC to the fourth century AD), and with different divine names,[7] thus in different religious and cultural environments. The second reason involves a thorny problem concerning the religious evolution of the ancient world. Based on the fact that ὕψιστος ('The Most High') was the translation employed in the Septuagint for one of the names of Yahweh (*Elyon*), historians have foregrounded the Jewish influence upon the pagan use of the epithet[8] at a point in the imperial era when polytheism was moving in a direction

---

[4] Keen to underline the absolute meaning of 'his' Θεὸς ὕψιστος, the Yahweh of the Septuagint, Philo of Alexandria (*Allegorical Interpretation of Genesis* 3. 82 = 1. 103), attaches the circumlocution inspired by Deut.: 'not that there is another God who is not the Highest'. At the end of the first century, the Christian, Clement of Rome (*First Letter to Corinthians* 59. 3) writes in a commentary on Psalm 82 [83]. 19: σε τὸν μόνον ὕψιστον ἐν ὑψίστοις 'you the only highest in the heights'.

[5] Cf. the episode of Paul and Silas at Philippi, Acts 16. 16–18; cf. Trebilco 1989: 51–73.

[6] Cf. for example Libanius (*Oration 30, For the Temples* 4) reconstructing humanity's first experience of the divine and the universal gestures of the orant, with hands (sometimes eyes) raised, cf. Burkert 1996: 85–8. For the question of immortality, cf. below, n. 38 and Robert 1983: 583: 'The gods have by nature been immortal since Homer and literature, theology and devotion' (in translation).

[7] Mitchell 1999: 128–47 gives a useful list of 293 inscriptions (pagan and Jewish) out of more than 360 inscriptions.

[8] Mitchell 1999 makes the Judaizing groups of Hypsistarians in Cappadocia a model for all uses of *hypsistos*. And earlier, in his 1993: ii. 36, 37, 49: 'The influence of Jewish beliefs and cultic organization on the monotheistic strands of paganism in the third century AD, is palpable, above all in the cults of Theos *Hypsistos*'). And with greater nuance: 'In such an environment, contemporaries may have been as hard pressed as modern scholars to ascertain whether a dedication to the highest god was the work of a pagan or a Jew'; and 'The cults of Theos *Hypsistos* [...] occupied the common ground shared by all three [pagan, Jewish, Christian] religious systems.'

commonly interpreted as syncretic.[9] Polytheism of this flavour, in mid-transformation, has long been defined as 'pagan monotheism', and has now been analysed by Athanassiadi, Frede, and a team of other scholars.[10] But given that the definition of monotheism as a concept is itself controversial,[11] this typology, which is based on philosophical texts, runs the risk of obscuring the religious experience conveyed by the epithet.

Without, as it were, a firm hermeneutic footing on which to proceed, I have chosen to approach the question of 'hypsistan' religiosity on several, interrelated fronts, so as not to form conclusions on the basis of evidence pertaining to one particular sphere.[12] I have analysed the possible relations between this designation for the divine and the notion of a cult of 'heights' or 'on the heights', for this dwelling place of the gods is allegedly a feature of Western Semitic conceptions,[13] whose influence upon hypsistan religiosity has been underlined by recent scholarship. I have also examined the theological data to emerge from other epithets directed at deities addressed as ὕψιστος ('most high'), and the deities worshipped with them. Given the polyvalence of the term and the stimulus given to pagan

---

[9] Without giving a full bibliographical survey, cf. the two seminal articles in this debate: Schürer 1897; reinforced by Cumont 1897 and id., *RE* (Pauly-Wissowa) ix. s.v. 'Hypsistos'. Also my unpublished thesis, Belayche 1984.

[10] e.g. Usener 1929: 338; Nilsson 1961: 569–78; Athanassiadi and Frede 1999, especially for Theos *Hypsistos*, Mitchell: 'a form of monotheistic worship'; 'a shared tradition [. . .] of monotheistic worship'; 'this quasi-monotheistic worship' (104, 121, 127). Also in his earlier work, Mitchell 1993: ii. 43–51.

[11] Without going into matters of fundamental theology, cf. Athanassiadi and Frede 1999: 8, n. 10: 'monotheism was perfectly compatible with belief in the existence of a plurality of divine beings', *contra* Vernant 1983: 329 (with different translation): 'The various supernatural powers who together make up divine society as a whole may themselves be apprehended in the singular form of ὁ θεός, *the* divine power, *the* god, without this amounting to monotheism.' See also North, below, Ch. 15.

[12] Mitchell's method is the opposite (1999: 81–97): he starts with the Oenoanda evidence (inscribed oracle + votive) and the groupings of Hypsistarians from the fourth century in order thereby to form the hermeneutic grid for the whole corpus, even though he rightly acknowledges (105–6 and 108) that the majority of dedications 'conformed to the normal pattern of religious activity in the East Roman world', with the exception of aniconism and the absence of animal sacrifices (cf. *infra* for questions relating to ritual). The reservations of Stein 2001 are pertinent here.

[13] Cf. Briquel-Chatonnet 2005 and the historiographical summary of Bonnet 2005.

environments by speculative or biblical approaches, my analysis, inevitably limited by the scope of an article, does not preclude the possibility that (Θεὸς) ὕψιστος ('God Most High') was used to express a monotheistic conception of the divine. But I hope to show that 'hypsistan' religiosity is inscribed within the current of the imperial era polytheism, which 'exalted' deities, without bringing about a theological break by introducing a monotheistic conception of the divine world.

A NUMBER OF GODS ARE DESIGNATED AS ὕψιστος ('MOST HIGH')

Etymologically, those deities designated as *hypsistos* enter into an intensified category of height.[14] The word's semantic field extends across two registers: the physical register of space, and thus remoteness—in the heights—[15] and the abstract, metaphorical register of the intense and the extreme.[16] The Latin equivalents of *hypsistos*[17] reveal a similar panorama, but were not much diffused in cults. At the very most, the triple superlative *exsuperantissimus* ('most highest') was used in the pious dedications offered to the primacy of various forms of Jupiter, such as the Dolichenan or the Roman Jupiter,

---

[14] Usener 1929: 49–50 lists the compounds with ὕψι.

[15] Aeschylus, *Prometheus Bound* 719–20: the Caucasus, ὁρῶν ὕψιστον (the highest of mountains); Sophocles, *Trachiniae* 1191: τὸν Οἴτης Ζηνὸς ὕψιστον πάγον (the highest of Oeta's summits, where Zeus reigns); Diogenes Laertius, *Life of Pythagoras* viii. 31: 'Hermes […] leads the pure [souls] ἐπὶ τὸν ὕψιστον (towards the highest heavens)'. Cf. Ps.-Aristotle, *On the Kosmos* 270b: πάντες τὸν ἀνωτάτω τῷ θείῳ τόπον ἀποδιδόασι 'everyone ascribes the highest place to the divine'.

[16] Pindar, *Pythian* 1. 100 (= 195): στέφανον ὕψιστον 'highest crown' and *Isthmian* 1. 51 (= 74): κέρδος ὕψιστον 'highest prize'; Aeschylus, *Persae* 331κακῶν ὕψιστα, greatest of ills; Lycophron, *Alexandra* 305 (πημάτων ὕψιστον, greatest of troubles); Aristonoos of Corinth in a paean to Pythian Apollo (5. 31–2: ὑψίσταις τίμαις, greatest honours); and Suda, *Lexicon* s.v. 'Nebuchadnezzar': ὁ ὕψιστος τῆς βασιλείας τῶν ἀνθρώπων 'the greatest human kingdom'.

[17] *Altissimus, summus* or *exsuperantissimus*, cf. *Thesaurus Linguae Latinae* i. 1. col. 1772 and 1777 and v. 2. col. 1956. *Altissimus* was used by the philosophers, then by the Christian writers (cf. Blaise 1954: 75 s.v. 'altus'), in competition with *summus*, cf. Battifol 1929: 188–201 and Simon 1972: 381–5.

following its adoption by the emperor Commodus.[18] Its nearest cultic parallel in the Greek world perhaps be a Zeus πανύψιστος ('All Most High'), to whom a devotee makes a vow in imperial Phrygia.[19]

All religious addresses implicitly involve paying homage to the greatness of the gods (cf. Bissinger 1966: i). In every polytheistic cultural tradition of the Roman East, dedications honour the divine majesty, whatever his dwelling place may be.[20] In the Hellenistic era, Poseidon is invoked as ὕψιστε θεῶν ('Most High of the gods') because he is master (πότνιε) of the seas.[21] Likewise, Zeus is 'hypsistos for the assemblies of the blessed',[22] and, in the Roman era, Isis is 'most high (ὑψίσταν) for mortals who are on earth'.[23] The rhetorical emphasis achieved through a ritual acclamation ('Great is/are'), or an epithet of such intensity as hypsistos, brings together a sharpened theological representation and the desire to personalize the inscription with the kind of experience which the devotee has had of the god. The epithet 'hypsistos' translates a certain point of view. In imperial Anatolia, the home of so many attestations of deities named as hypsistos,[24] the

---

[18] At the end of his reign (in AD 191), Commodus bears the title of *Exsuperatorius* (Cassius Dio 73. 15 and Herodian 1. 14. 8). For Jupiter, *CIL* iii. 1, no. 1090 (Apulum, Dacia): 'Iovi summo exsuperantissimo divinarum humanarumque rerum rectori fatorumque arbitro' (to Jupiter, supreme, highest ruler of divine and human affairs, and decider of the fates); cf. Cumont 1906a. For Dolichenian Jupiter, Merlat 1951: no. 251; 1960: 114–15. At Amastris (Pontus), on a bilingual inscription (*ILS* no. 5883), the deified Augustus is ἐπουράνιος θεὸς Σεβαστός 'supracelestial god Sebastos' in Greek and simply *diuus Augustus* in Latin.

[19] Drew-Bear et al. 1999: no. 374, commentary, 49. In the translation of a rescript of Maximin Daia to the inhabitants of Tyre (Eusebius, *Ecclesiastical History* 9. 7. 7) where ὁ ὕψιστος καὶ μέγιστος Ζεύς 'highest and greatest Zeus' translates the *Iupiter summus exsuperantissimus* 'Jupiter supreme, highest' of the chancellery, hypsistos can apply to the two Latin epithets. For the Latin epigraphic version, Mitchell 1988.

[20] In a funerary context, Hecate is depicted on an intaglio engraved with the inscription *Heis theos hypsistos*: Delaporte 1923: 219, no. A 1270 and pl. 108 figs. 17a and b.

[21] Attributed to Arion of Methymna, *Poetae Melici Graeci* no. 939 (D. L. Page). The almightiness of God is characteristic of the Old Testament tradition, cf. Aeschylus the tragic poet, ap. Eusebius, *Preparation for the Gospel* 13. 13. 60: πάντα δύναται γάρ· δόξα δ' ὑψίστου Θεοῦ (for he can do anything; and that is the glory of the Highest God); cf. Capizzi 1964: 1–35.

[22] Aristonoos of Corinth (in a paean to Apollo), Kappel 1992: 384–6, no. 42.

[23] *SEG* 38 (1998), no. 748. In the hymn of Isidoros at Medinet Madi, *SB* v. 8138, i., verses 1–3 (c.AD 80), Isis is 'queen of the gods, almighty sovereign Hermouthis,... Δηοῖ ὑψίστη'; see also iii., verses 1 and 4.

[24] One out of five comes from western Anatolia (Ionia, Caria, Lydia, Phrygia).

acclamation of the 'greatness' of the gods is inscribed in all forms of dedications: votive inscriptions which are either banal or more complex, such as the 'confession steles' which are in fact exaltation steles praising the qualities of the deity (Petzl 1994; cf. Belayche 2006). More or less everywhere, a great god was exalted locally as *hypsistos*, and thus given prime position by his followers. Such is the term applied in a dedication to Apollo Lairbenos, who had his sanctuary at Motella in Phrygia.[25] At Andeda, in Pisidia, it is Mên *ouranios* ('celestial') who is called Theos Hypsistos by his priest (Lane 1971–8: i. 129). Generally, and bearing in mind that the designation Theos/Zeus Hypsistos or simply Hypsistos, may vary within a single place,[26] the divine name is Zeus, whose local representations are infinite. At Tavium in Galatia, Zeus can surely be recognized in the Theos hypsistos of a local merchant who had settled at Ancyra.[27] At Aezani, in northern Phrygia, it must be Zeus whose temple covers the crypt of a Mother of the gods where legends put his birth.[28] At Iconium, the Theos hypsistos to whom thanks are given probably conceals Zeus *megistos* ('greatest'), who is of an agrarian nature to judge by his epithet (*epikarpios*, 'fruitful') and his depiction.[29] In Caria, Zeus Larasios at Tralles, the Zeus of Mylasa (a lease for the grounds of whose sanctuary has been preserved) or the Zeus of Iasos (of whose sanctuary boundary stones remain intact), are *hypsistoi*.[30]

---

[25] The inscription, which has many lacunae, comes from Badinlar, cf. Ramsay 1895–7: i. 154, no. 55. For the sanctuary of Motella, Strobel 1980: 208-18, and Ritti et al. 2000: 3–6.

[26] Cf. on the Pnyx at Athens (below, nn. 103–4), at Stratonicea in Caria (Mitchell 1999: 137–8, nos. 140–56) and at Seleucia on the Calycadnos in Cilicia (*MAMA* iii. nos. 1–4). The same observation also in Mitchell 1999: 99.

[27] Mitchell 1982: ii. 317–18, no. 418. Cf. Strabo, 12. 5. 2 ('where the colossal statue of Zeus and his sacred district are located'). Whether in terms of chronology, onomastics, or epigraphic formulary, there is nothing here to suggest that this is the Jewish Highest God honoured at Ancyra, Mitchell 1982: ii. 177–8, no. 209b.

[28] *MAMA* ix. (1988), no. 59 and P67; *MAMA* x. (1993), no. 261 (with the depiction of an ear of corn); and possibly *MAMA* ix. (1988), no. P68 and Drew-Bear and Naour 1990: 2041, no. 34. Cf. Mitchell 1993: i. 18–19.

[29] *MAMA* viii. (1962), no. 298. Cf. Mitchell 1993: ii. 23. Four Phrygian dedications to Theos *hypsistos* bear ears of corn: *MAMA* v. (1937), nos 186 and 211 and x. (1993), no. 261 and *SEG* 40 (1990), no. 1227.

[30] *IK* 36. 1 (*Tralleis und Nysa*): no. 14; *IK* 34 (*Mylasa* i): nos. 212 and 310; *IK* 28. 2 (*Iasos*): nos. 235 and 236.

At Panamara, an inscription extols the great local gods—Zeus, exalted as *hypsistos*, and Hecate, the great deity of Lagina, as bringing
salvation—and then pays homage to deities of imperial identity:
Capitoline Zeus and the Tyche of the emperor Antoninus Pius (*IK*
22. 1 [*Stratonikeia* i. *Panamara*]: no. 330).

For the worshipper, any deity, also glorified as μέγας ('great')[31] or
μέγιστος ('greatest'),[32] could be at the summit of a divine pyramid,[33]
sometimes in the company of other gods who are no less exalted.[34]
The Isiac hymns, which can serve as a model for the reconstruction of
the pantheon in the imperial era as focused on a single god (so-called
'henotheism'; cf. Versnel 1990 and Merkelbach 1995), amply illustrate this way of exalting a god within a landscape of multiple deities.
At Cyrene, Isis is ὑψίστην θεόν ('most high goddess'), 'the greatest of
all deities in heaven' (πάντων μεγίστην τῶν ἐν οὐρανῶι θεῶν). But in
another praise of the deity, in Egypt (Medinet Madi), Isidoros ac-
claims Isis as both Δηοῖ ὑψίστη ('most high Dêo') and 'thou who

---

[31] At Amastris in Pontus, French 1994: 105, no. N12.3. At Philadelphia in Lydia,
Robert 1969–90: i. 417. For the Near East, Sourdel 1952: 22–4 and *IGLS* vi. nos. 2728–
31. At Tayyibe, the Palmyrean *Mar Olam* is translated as Ζεὺς μέγιστος κεραύνιος
'Zeus greatest of the thunderbolt' (*IGLS* iii. no. 2631 = *CIS* ii. no. 3912). In Egypt (in
the Fayoum), a *Theos megas megas hypsistos* had been classified as Jewish by Frey
1936–52: ii. no. 1532; Horbury and Noy 1992: no. 116, follow this identification
despite their pertinent list of objections (200–1), to which might be added the
theophoric name (Harpocrates) of the husband of the dedicant. The set as a whole
certainly creates doubt. Nonetheless, a Jewish inscription from Alexandria (at the end
of the first century BC): Θεῶι μεγάλωι ἐπηκόωι (Frey 1936–52: ii. no. 1432 = *OGIS* ii.
no. 742) shows the influence of pagan formularies on Jewish epigraphy.
[32] At Thessalonica (Macedonia), a dedication to *Theos hypsistos megistos sôter*
found close to the Serapeum, *IG* x. 2. no. 67 (in 74–5). At Palmyra *OGIS* ii. no. 634
and Seyrig 1933: 276, no. 6. In Syria, Dussaud 1903a: 238–9, no. 2 and *SEG* 37 (1987),
no. 1445. Μέγιστος θεός is the preferred expression of Flavius Josephus for naming
the Jewish God. For a Christian parallel, John Chrysostom, *Commentary on the
Psalms* 143. 3: 'The Highest [. . .], I do not circumscribe him in a place, but I reveal
as much his height (τὸ ὑψηλόν) as the greatness of his nature (μεγαλεῖον αὐτοῦ τῆς
φύσεως)'.
[33] In Thrace, a single dedicant pays homage Δ[ι]ὶ ὑψίστῳ and Κυρίῳ Διί (*IGBulg.*
iii. nos. 965, 966, and 1209 and iv. no. 214); at Anchialos, Zeus *hypsistos* is *despotês*
(*IGBulg.* i. no. 371). Taceva-Hitova 1978: 61 and 69–70 identifies *hypsistos* with a
Thracian solar Apollo-Sabazios.
[34] At Palmyra, in an inscription that cannot be reconstructed with certainty *Zeus
hypsistos kai epêkoos* is honoured together with *Theos megas Zebedouatos* (Müller
1913: 329, no. 177).

reigns as protector of the gods *hypsistoi*.[35] Along with the others, this
account of Isiac religiosity indicates that the quality of *hypsistos*
derives from an intensification of divine figures in a world which
continued to be thought of and experienced as plural. Thus a benefactor from Miletus, Ulpius Carpus, priest/prophet[36] of the most
holy god *hypsistos* the redeemer—in this case Apollo of Didyma—
also worships Serapis, another great god (cf. Robert 1968: 594). This
intensification may equally be observed in the particular homage
paid to the active power of the god: the δύναμις ὑψίστου ('power of
the most high') in a fragmentary text from Galatia,[37] which evokes an
oft-cited Lydian parallel: 'One god in the heavens, great is celestial
Mên, great power of the immortal god (μεγάλη δύναμις τοῦ ἀθανάτου
θεοῦ)'.[38] The exaltation of the gods to the rank of almighty masters,
lords of the territory—even masters of the universe—[39] intimating
their will in personalized epiphanies,[40] was a characteristic feature of
the representation of non-civic pantheons in the Roman era within
the Greek-speaking world. The Isis ὑψίστη παντοκράτειρα ('most
high ruler of all') of Medinet Madi and the Attis *hypsistos* of Rome
(*IGVR* i, no. 129) belong to this trend, as does Helios, twice ὕψιστος
('most high'),[41] but more commonly extolled as celestial, eternal, and
almighty.

[35] Respectively Peek 1930: 129, verses 7–8, and *SB* 5. 8138, i. verse 1 and iii. verse 1
(cf. exergue). On a curse tablet from Hadrumetum (Byzacena), the great god is τὸν
ὑπεράνω τῶν ὑπεράνω θεῶν 'the highest of the highest gods' (Audollent 1904: 374, no.
271, lines 9–10).
[36] Both titles are used, *OGIS* ii. nos. 755 and 756.
[37] Mitchell 1982: ii 127, no. 141 identifies the text as 'typically Jewish', though
Anatolian epigraphy offers many examples of the powers of the gods being acclaimed
(cf. for example Petzl 1994: index, 154 s.v. '*dynamis*'), and of a pagan *Hypsistos*.
[38] *TAM* v. 1 (1981), 75 and the commentary of Robert 1983: 583, n. 1. ('εἷς is the
superlative form of the acclamation [. . .] it does not imply a tendency towards
monotheism') *contra* Mitchell 1999: 104. Cf at Cyrene, Πατρὶ θεῶι Σαμοθρᾶκι
ἀθανάτωι ὑψίσ[τωι], 'To Father god of Samothrace immortal highest', *Bull. Ép.*
(1964), no. 561.
[39] Hermann 1978; κατὰ πρόσταγμα Ὀσείριδος Διὶ τῶν πάντων κρατοῦντι καὶ
Μητρὶ Μεγάληι τῆς πάντων κρατούσηι 'By order of Osiris to Zeus ruling over all
and to the Great Mother ruling over all' (*IG* xi. 4. no. 1234); and Sabazios
πανκοίρανος 'master of all' (Barth and Stauber 1993: no. 1917).
[40] Cf. *TAM* v. 1 (1981), no. 186 (in Lydia): Θεῷ ὑψίστῳ καὶ μεγ[ά]λῳ Θείῳ
ἐπιφανεῖ, cf. below, n. 44.
[41] Fränkel 1895: ii. no. 330 and Marek 1993: no. 1. 156–8.

Θεὸς ὕψιστος ('GOD MOST HIGH')
IN THE PANTHEON

Dedications honouring a deity as *hypsistos* at the same time as other divine companions are not uncommon. There is nothing new within a polytheistic system about the thirty dedications attesting personalized deities (Zeus, Cybele, Serapis, Mithra) described as *hypsistos*, and I will not dwell on them. By contrast, in the case of a Theos *hypsistos* ('God most high'), we enter fully into the theological debate surrounding the divine figure and the significance of his religiosity. Aside from the fact, as already noted, that Theos *hypsistos* often conceals a personalized divine figure of the pantheon, two types of evidence indicate the risks involved in conceiving all devotions to Theos *hypsistos* as the worship of a single deity. First, Theos *hypsistos* is conceived of alongside fellow-deities who are more or less individualized. At Nysa (in Lycia), a collective homage is paid, in the purest, even most formulaic, tradition of Graeco–Roman pantheism: 'to the god *hypsis*[*tos*, to the Mother] of the mountain, following their order, and to all the gods and all [the goddesses]'.[42] It is exactly the same religious atmosphere which inhabits the Anatolian invocations of groups of gods exalted as *megaloi* ('great') or sovereign masters.[43] In Lydia, an inscribed relief dedicated 'to Theos *hypsistos* and the great divine who manifests himself' offers the image— probably after a divine order—of the goddess Larmene (a Mother?) enthroned and holding a sceptre.[44] In two other instances, Theos *hypsistos* is invoked alongside two master gods like him: in Alexandria with Helios and the Nemeseis,[45] and in Phrygia with Zeus and Hosios, the latter being a personification of a divine quality,

---

[42] *TAM* ii. 2 (1930), no. 737 (with Mitchell's correction).
[43] e.g. *TAM* v. 1 (1981), no. 255: 'on the order of Mên Tyrannos, Zeus Ogmenos and the gods who are with him'.
[44] *TAM* v. 1 (1981), no. 186. Cf. Robert 1958.
[45] In an epitaph calling for divine justice: 'to the god *hypsistos* who sees all things, to the Sun and to the Nemeseis' (*SB* i. no. 1323); the likely influence, here, of Judaism upon the conception of the god *hypsistos* does not, all the same, negate the polytheistic framework and its traditionally vengeful deities. Cf. Apuleius, *De mundo* 374 (quoting Plato, *Laws* 715e–716a): 'God is also accompanied, always and everywhere, by vengeful Necessity'.

holiness.[46] This last dedication reveals a second kind of association.
Theos *hypsistos* is invoked on several occasions, either with a personified quality of the divine essence—holiness[47] or benevolence
('the holy refuge'[48])—or with a form of action on the part of the
divine power (his *dynamis*/power or his *nemesis*/judicial power[49]); or
finally just with the divine quality as such (*to Theion*/the Divine).[50]
By contrast, in another dedication also from Carian Stratonicea, the
Divine itself is given the epithets of royal and *hypsistos*.[51]

There are then many different combinations of names, thwarting
any attempt to give a clear account of the image which the devotee
constructs for the 'being-in-the-world' of superior figures. Greek
poetic literature was familiar with the conception of θεῖον
('divine').[52] It is 'the most adequate expression for designating the
divine world freed from anthropomorphic representations' (François
1957: 315, in translation). It was therefore used by philosophers,
speculating both upon the notion of a single divine substance and
upon the multiplicity of the figures which make it up. The majority

[46]   At Nacoleia: 'to Theos Hypsistos and to Hosios and to Zeus' (Ricl 1991: no. 38).
Hypsistos and *Hosios* had enough in common for a stonecutter to have mixed them
up, cf. Malay 1994: no. 181 and Petzl 1998: 22–3.
[47]   The fact that Holiness, treated as an autonomous power, is worshipped in the
form of divine figures who are gendered ('To the god Hosios and Dikaios and to
Hosia and Dikaia', *TAM* v. 1 [1981], no. 247) shows that the theological reflection is
neither abstracted nor released from an anthropomorphic conception of the divine
being. The same conclusion may be drawn from the reliefs depicting the divine
couple with sceptre and scales. Holiness and justice are also qualities of the *Angelos*,
TAM v. 1 (1981), no. 185 (*Angelos Hosios Dikaios*), perhaps because, in this case,
communication with the god benefited from the assistance of the 'prophet Alexan-
dros of Sattai'.
[48]   *Bull. Ép.* (1961), no. 750 (in Pisidia). Scholars rightly detected here the influence
of a Jewish expression, cf. the twenty-odd instances of the expression in the Septuagint (Hatch and Redpath 1897: ii. 748), esp. Psalm 91 (90). 9 (τὸν ὕψιστον ἔθου
κατάφυγήν μου, You have made the Most High my refuge).
[49]   *SB* i. no. 1323 (cited in n. 45). The acclamations clearly bring the *dynamis* into
relation with the god, e.g. Petzl 1994: no. 62.
[50]   *TAM* v. 1 (1981), no. 186 (cited in n. 44 above) and *IK* 22. 1 (*Stratonikeia* ii. 1):
nos. 1113 and 1308.
[51]   *IK* 22. 2 (*Stratonikeia* ii. 2): no. 1309. Mitchell 1999: 138, no. 154, identifies two
distinct figures ('To the royal Divine and to Hypsistos'). If so, it is unique, for (Theos)
Hypsistos is always invoked first when there is more than one addressee.
[52]   Hesiod, *Theogony* 135 and 371; cf. *RE* (Pauly-Wissowa) v. A (1934), 'Theios'
(Ziegler), col. 1611–12.

of inscriptions to a divinity named '*hypsistos*' and to the Divine come from Stratonicea in Caria, the city that was home to the great sanctuaries of Zeus at Panamara and of Hecate at Lagina (Laumonier 1958). They attest both these processes in that they combine the exaltation of the individualized divine figure[53] (at times Theos, but more commonly Zeus *hypsistos*[54]) with a conceptual analysis of its nature. The many facets of the figure are brought out in a number of epithets, and some achieve an autonomous level of representation: 'great', 'royal', 'good',[55] 'angelic/messenger',[56] not to mention *hypsistos*. The deities, or the various active facets of a divinity, receive their equal share of pious homage according to the changing combinations, including the quality of magnitude, which does not make the deity more distant from men. By accentuating the almightiness and justice of the god through various expressions of emphasis, the god remains close to men, for magnitude comprises solicitude, and hence benevolence. As Versnel has subtly observed, 'one of the paradoxes of this religious mentality is that the exalted and omnipotent god owed much of his inaccessible majesty to the fact that he lent an ear to lowly mortals'.[57] It might be less a paradox than an original feature of polytheism in the imperial era, and it represents for sure a notable difference from the philosophical conception, in that it does not promote the assimilation of 'the Divine' with 'the Angel', or the belief that the Divine, as the messenger of the supreme being, occupies relative to Zeus *hypsistos* the position of the inferior beings in the

---

[53] *TAM* v. 1 (1981), no. 246: Stratoneikos Kakoleis, τοῦ Ἑνὸς καὶ Μόνου Θεοῦ ἱερεὺς καὶ τοῦ Ὁσίου καὶ Δικαίου 'priest of the One and Only God, and of the Holy and Just'.

[54] Cf. Mitchell 1999: 137–8 nos. 141–6, 148–50, 152, 155–7. The evidence is not strong enough to identify (as Şahin, *IK* 22. 1 [*Stratonikeia* ii. 1]) the '*Zeus hypsistos und das Göttliche*' of Stratonicea with Isis and Serapis who had a temple there.

[55] Dedications put little emphasis on the moral approach to the divinity. 'Isocrates to Zeus *hypsistos* and to the good Divine' recalls the 'good messenger' of two other inscriptions, *IK* 22. 1 (*Stratonikeia* ii. 1): nos. 1310 and 1117.

[56] The mediatory quality can be that of the great god himself, cf. under Commodus, a dedication offered by the Syrians of Ostia to *I O M angelus Heliopolitanus*, *CIL* xiv. 24. Cf. Sheppard 1980–1 and Ricl 1992: 98–101.

[57] Versnel 1981b: 35. This invocation (Bricault 2005: no. 501/0126) allies supremacy with affectionate assistance: Διὶ Ἡλίῳ μεγάλῳ Σαράπιδι σωτῆρι πλουτοδότῃ ἐπηκόῳ εὐεργέτῃ ἀνεικήτῳ Μίθρᾳ χαριστήριον, 'A thank-offering to Zeus Helios mighty Sarapis saviour, wealth-giver, hearkener, benefactor, unconquerable Mithras.'

system of the philosopher Plotinus (Mitchell 1993: ii. 45–6). The philosophical definition of the supreme god as omnipotent and eternal imposed upon the pantheon a pyramidal structure in which intermediary divine entities allow for communication between the god located in the highest region of the world, beyond the starry sphere—thus essentially and in its essence unattainable[58]—and men.[59] '. . . possessing no name, known by many names, dwelling in fire, this is god. We, his angels, are a small part of god', says Apollo at Claros (Beatrice 2001: i. no. 2; translation Mitchell 1993: ii. 44). In late pagan theologies, the Sun was one of these intermediaries, having the virtue of being a visible image of the god residing in the ethereal spheres.[60] This home of the true god in the ether was capable of taking on a conception, in which the traditional gods of the pantheon became angelic servants of the true god (Mitchell 1993: ii. 43–4 and Petzl 2003: 93–101), and which reached the point where it coincided with the theorized parallelism between divine and human monarchies, both served by messengers and 'workers'.[61]

It is not strictly impossible for the ὕψιστος ('most high') divinity to have attained this degree of transcendence in the mind of some worshippers. Yet in the votive relationship—which is not speculative—the presence of these companions, the Divine or the 'Angel', seems rather to suggest that the worshipper's intention was to double up the address to the god personalized in the form of Zeus *hypsistos* with a homage to the very idea of the god supporting it (a god who communicates with men and listens to them), thereby manifesting the strength of his piety. At Sardis in the second quarter of the second century AD, a public inscription honoured a priestess of Artemis and

---

[58] Cf. Plato, *Symposium* 202d13–203a6; Cicero, *The Republic* 6. 17, and the commentary by Macrobius.

[59] Plato (*Phaedrus* 247c) divides the divine powers into three categories: the supreme god (ὑπερουράνιος/*ultramundanus*), the stars and celestial divinities (*caelicoli*, but *dei medioximi*) and the demons; following on from him, Apuleius, *On Plato* 204–5. The *angelos* may be the representation of the communication established with the god, cf. *TAM* v. 1 (1981), no. 159 and Lane 1971–9: iii. 25–6.

[60] Likewise, in the second to third centuries, the elaboration of the Mithraic doctrine contributed to making the Iranian *Sol Invictus* into a *mésitês*, a mediator of the redemptive power of the god.

[61] The comparison is developed at length by Apuleius, *De mundo* 346ff., who gives as an example the centralized administration of the Persian kingdom.

Athena 'for her pious and holy behaviour towards the divine' (εὐσεβῶς μὲν καὶ ὁσιῶς προσφερομένην πρὸς τὸ θεῖον) (Buckler and Robinson 1932: no. 55, lines 8–10). This 'analytical' way of viewing the world of the gods, magnified by an analysis of its nature, is not new. But while traditional paganism would enumerate in a litany of epithets[62] the gods giving their patronage to the successive stages of an action, here it is the essence of the gods which is dissected. The eagerness to intensify the homage to the greatness of the divine beings expresses itself via an objectification in the ritual address to their mode of being and their means of action (power), which produces a systematic, even minimal, theological utterance. This is what is original. The address to the status of the gods (*Theos hypsistos*), rather than to their person (*Zeus hypsistos*) thus appears to stem less from an abstraction of the divine—which certainly occurred—[63] than from an investigation of their qualities. We might think here of the acclamation of the *dynameis* ('powers') in Lydia and Phrygia, contemporary with dedications to divinities honoured as *hypsistos*.

The divine landscape in which the θεὸς ὕψιστος ('god most high') evolves might make the conception which he incarnates rule out potential acolytes. However, the piety which he arouses did not take on any exclusivist dimension, as attested by fellow-divinities, such as Zeus or Helios, and perhaps precisely because like him they occupied central positions in the ideal structure of the divine world. The fact that 'god most high' is invoked separately in the majority of dedications merely indicates that he was the privileged object of devotion in this particular religious act, as in the majority of dedications preserved from antiquity.

---

[62] Hence the well known sarcastic remarks of Augustine in *City of God* 6. 9. Cf. Scheid 1999.

[63] Cf. Petzl 2005. In the Hermetic tradition, the different names for the divinity, expressed in various mother tongues, are reduced to an impersonal definition of the god: 'I invoke thee, according to the Egyptians [. . .], according to the Jews *Adônaïé Sabaôthu*, according to the Greeks *universal King and only monarch*, according to the great priests *hidden, invisible God, who watches over us all*' (Festugière 1944: i. 298, no. 15).

ὕψιστος ('MOST HIGH') ON HIGH

The Olympians had always been on the heights, even if ancient Greek ritual practice did not designate Zeus as ὕψιστος ('most high'). The ὕπατος Κρονίδης ('highest son of Kronos') of Homer[64] was a celestial god whose adoration on the highest mountains[65] expressed its sovereign statute: 'None is seated above him whom he must worship from below';[66] hence his association with eagles in iconography. Zeus *hypsistos* is represented in anthropomorphic form on only five occasions.[67] His followers (most notably in Macedonia) prefer the eagle for him—this being his animal attribute[68]—as do the followers of Theos *hypsistos*, for whom this is the exclusive representation (Mitchell 1999: 101).

As with any great god who is master of the atmosphere,[69] Zeus *hypsistos* is master of thunder (βρονταῖος)[70] and Theos *hypsistos* of

---

[64] *Iliad* 5. 746. 8. 22 and 32 (cited by Plutarch, *De Is.* 371E) and 17. 339.

[65] Cf. Maximus of Tyre, *Dissertations* 8. 1 (the first men dedicated to Zeus the κορυφὰς ὀρῶν); *RE* (Pauly-Wissowa), Suppl xv. 1978, 'Zeus' (Schwabl), col. 1013 (sections 3 and 4). According to Nonnos (*Dionysiaca* 13. 534), Zeus *hypatos* had a sanctuary high up on mount Sipylos.

[66] Aeschylus, *Suppliants* 595. An altar in Pisidia (with relief) is dedicated to Ζεὺς ὑψίθρον in the second century (Bean 1959: 103, no. 64). Cf. the reference work of Cook 1914–40: i. 100–87, and Rocchi 2005. For the philosophical tradition, Apuleius, *De mundo* 23 [343]: 'he [the supreme god] occupies an eminent and superior abode (*praestantem ac sublimen sedem tenere*); in the eulogies of the poets he receives as epithets titles designating consuls and kings and he has a throne consecrated on the highest summits of heaven (*in arduis arcibus habere solium consecratum*)'.

[67] Rizakis and Touratsoglou 1985: no. 21 (Kozani); Perdrizet 1899: 592–3; *IK* 26. 2 (*Kyzikos*): no. 5; du Mesnil du Buisson 1970: 33 fig. 10, in Byblos; and Dussaud 1903a: 238–9, no. 2 (in the Hauran).

[68] Zeus hypsistos at Palmyra is represented by a winged thunderbolt (Sobernheim 1905: 38–9, no. 31).

[69] Zeus is 'the thunderer' *par excellence*, cf. *RE* (Pauly-Wissowa) xi. 1 (1921), 'Keraunios' (Adler), col. 276, and Cook 1914–40: ii. 1. 722–81, with drawings. At Silandos (Lydia), a dedication to Theos hypsistos (*TAM* v. 1. [1981], no. 52), for which the relief is alas lost, but another to Zeus *Keraunios* displays a thunderbolt (Naour 1983: 117–18, no. 7).

[70] In Mysia, *IK* 26. 2 (*Kyzikos*): no. 5 and pl. iii. fig. 7: Διὶ ὑψίστῳ ... Βρονταίῳ (to Zeus Highest ... Brontaios) depicted with thunderbolt and sceptre by a smoking altar and in the company of Hermes. Other dedications to Zeus displaying a thunderbolt: at Sparta (Woodward et al. 1927–8: 50, no. 72), at Palmyra (*CIS* ii. no. 3994 [a civic offering]) and n. 68 above. For Zeus *Brontôn* in Phrygia, *TAM* v. 1 (1981), nos. 15, 17, 85, 169, 176; a unique case in Lydia (De Hoz 1999: 56). Along more general lines, cf. Cook 1914–40: ii. 1. 833–4.

lightning ($\kappa\epsilon\rho\alpha\acute{\nu}\nu\iota\sigma\varsigma$).[71] This conception in which the seat of the gods is higher than anything available to normal human experience,[72] and so above the clouds, in the ether,[73] was confirmed and given cosmic significance in the celestial and solar speculations of the second century and beyond, in which scholars have seen parallels to Semitic celestial theologies, if not their influence. According to Philo of Byblos, the etymology of the original name of Laodicea of Syria— Ramitha—connected lightning to the god in the heights, who is given the positive, concrete word $\tau\grave{o}$ $\mathring{\upsilon}\psi\sigma\varsigma$ ('the height').[74] However, in the Hellenizing and euhemeristic cosmology which Philo claimed to have taken from Sanchuniathon, he gives as parents of the original couple Ouranos (from his original name $E\pi\acute{\iota}\gamma\epsilon\iota\sigma\varsigma$ $A\mathring{\upsilon}\tau\acute{o}\chi\theta\omega\nu$, 'Earthly Son of the Soil') and Gê: 'a certain Elioum named *Hypsistos* ($\tau\iota\varsigma$ $E\lambda\iota\omicron\hat{\upsilon}\mu$ $\kappa\alpha\lambda\omicron\acute{\upsilon}\mu\epsilon\nu\sigma\varsigma$ $\mathring{\upsilon}\psi\iota\sigma\tau\sigma\varsigma$) and a woman named Berouth, who lived in the vicinity of Byblos'.[75] This Phoenician Elioum/Elyon,[76] Hellenized as *Hypsistos*, owes his primacy to his primordiality, and evolves within an anthropomorphized mythology. Naturally, the gods who are given epithets such as '*hypsistos*' occupy a heavenly domain, which is similar to that of the master-gods of Anatolia[77] and the Near East.[78] Sometimes they are mountain divinities, whose altitude marks out their sovereignty (Herrmann 1978: 415–23 and

---

[71] At Lesbos, *IG* xii. 2. no. 119 ($\Theta\epsilon\hat{\omega}$ $\kappa\epsilon\rho\alpha\nu\nu\acute{\iota}\omega$ $\mathring{\upsilon}\psi\acute{\iota}\sigma\tau\omega$) and 115 (to the same *Theos hypsistos*, with the relief of an eagle).

[72] At the beginning of Hesiod's *Theogony* (lines 1–23), the Muses dance high up on the mountain, but deliver their song to the shepherd 'at the foot of the divine Helicon'.

[73] Cf. Homer, *Odyssey* 7. 42–5 and *TAM* v. 2 (1989), no. 1108.

[74] Philo of Byblos *ap*. Stephanus of Byzantium 17 (= Jacoby 1928–58: iii. C2, 822, no. 790 F 41): 'On being struck by lightning, a shepherd said "Ramanthas", that is, "the god in the heights" ($\mathring{\alpha}\phi'$ $\mathring{\upsilon}\psi\sigma\upsilon\varsigma$ $\acute{o}$ $\theta\epsilon\acute{o}\varsigma$). For *raman* means height ($\tau\grave{o}$ $\mathring{\upsilon}\psi\sigma\varsigma$) and *athas* the god'. Baal Shamîm is a 'master of the heavens' who held power over celestial phenomena and indicated his abode with thunder and lightning, cf. Niehr 2003.

[75] Ap. Eusebius, *Preparation for the Gospel* 1. 10. 14–15 = Baumgarten 1981: 15 [809], lines 14–20.

[76] Cf. Lack 1962: 57, in translation: 'Everything would tend to suggest that Elyôn is nothing else than the epithet for the great god of the time and of the place.'

[77] Cf. Ulpius Carpus, priest of Mên ouranios, invoked as *Theos hypsistos* (n. 36 above).

[78] At Sahin (Syria), a *Theos hypsistos* is *ouranios* (*IGLS* vii. no. 4027), as is a *Zeus hypsistos Saarnaios* near Byblos (*IGR* iii. no. 1060). By contrast, the Jewish God at Ancyra is $\mathring{\epsilon}\pi\omicron\upsilon\rho\acute{\alpha}\nu\iota\sigma\varsigma$, supracelestial (Mitchell: 1982: ii. no. 177–8b), as is the great god of the oracle at Claros (Buresch 1889: 55, no. v): $\mathring{\upsilon}\pi\epsilon\rho\omicron\upsilon\rho\alpha\nu\acute{\iota}\sigma\upsilon$ $\kappa\acute{\upsilon}\tau\epsilon\sigma\varsigma$ $\kappa\alpha\theta\acute{\upsilon}\pi\epsilon\rho\theta\epsilon$ $\lambda\epsilon\lambda\sigma\gamma\chi\acute{\omega}\varsigma$ 'who has the supracelestial vault that is above as his lot'.

Belayche 2005a), and who reply to local names: *Olympios* or *Mater Idaeae* for those cast far and wide from their place of origin,[79] and more generically *Zeus Oreitês* ('Zeus of the Mountain')[80] or *Mater Oreia* ('Mother of the Mountain') in the original rock-cut sanctuaries (Roller 1999 and Thomas 2004), whose sphere of influence was geographically less extensive. Near Kollyda (in Lydia), a *Thea hypsistê* in all probability conceals a local Mother, clearly identified as *Meter Oreia* with Theos *hypsistos* in Lycia.[81] These divine figures, *despoinai*,[82] all-powerful, all-seeing and deliverers of justice (Versnel 1991 and Chaniotis 1997), cry out for being described as most high. They have their parallel at Dura-Europos (Syria) where an exalted sun-god (Zeus Helios Mithra attentive holy *hypsistos*) was *To[ur]masgadès/Mountain of the sanctuary.*[83]

THE '*HYPSISTOS*' DEITIES: A RITUAL BREAK?

Like any divine authority—especially that of a Jupiter-type—a deity designated as *hypsistos* could have his or her earthly seat on a hilltop: a simple and concrete way for people to render his or her sovereign aspect.[84] At Sparta, on the evidence of seven recovered inscriptions, Woodward hypothesized the existence of a sanctuary of Zeus *hypsistos* on the Acropolis.[85] By contrast, at Serdica (modern-day Sofia), where five inscriptions dedicated to Θεὸς ὕψιστος ('God most high')

---

[79] Respectively, Cook 1914–40: i. 113–17, and Borgeaud 1996: 24–5.

[80] Petzl 1994: nos. 6 and 7 (in Lydia). To the east of Sidon, a *Zeus Oreios* (Hajjar 1990: 2667).

[81] Respectively, *TAM* v. 1 (1981), no. 359 and above, n. 42. In Macedonia, a hierodule of the Mother of the gods offers a dedication to *Theos hypsistos*, *SEG* 38 (1988), no. 583.

[82] Esp. in Lydia Katakekaumene (Pleket 1981).

[83] Vermaseren 1956: i. no. 70 (found in the Dolichenum). Cf. Teixidor 1977: 86.

[84] Cf. Vitruvius, *On Architecture* i. 7. 1, for the location of the temples of the Capitoline triad.

[85] Woodward et al. 1923–5: 222–4, nos. 16–18 and 29; 1927–8: 50, nos. 71–3, which has many lacunae (Διὸς ὑψ]ίστ[ου), may have been a boundary stone of a sanctuary, *IG* v. 1. no. 240.

were unearthed,[86] the urban site does not display any specific topo-graphical feature. The cultic objects recovered (altars and votive inscriptions) paint the picture of a standard ritual setting. One of the altars is endowed with three small lamps set on its upper sur-face.[87] Unlike with the evidence from Oenoanda (see below), this is not a strong enough indication to conclude that the sanctuary welcomed *theosebeis* ('godfearers') practising light worship as part of a monotheistic conception of the divine (Mitchell 1999: 120). Offerings of lamps and lights were such elementary gestures of devotion in ancient practice that the imperial law of AD 392 prohib-ited lighting as an element of pagan ritual (*Codex Theodosianus* 16. 10. 12).

On Delos, aside from the Jewish inscriptions in the synagogue bearing the dedication (Θεῷ) ὑψίστῳ ('To (God) Most High'),[88] a sanctuary of Zeus *hypsistos* was situated on Mount Cynthus. Already in the archaic period, this place 'on the heights' was devoted to Zeus *Kynthios* (designated as *keraunios*, 'of the thunderbolt') and Athena *Kynthia*.[89] From the second century BC, its slopes played host to a number of deities who came from Near Eastern shores (Ascalon and Jamnia, for those who have been identified) with their followers (Bruneau 1970: esp. 488–90, and Baslez 1977: 117–20). The layout of the sanctuary of Zeus *hypsistos* recalls other Delian open-air sanctu-aries of Semitic type.[90] The god—neither the Syrian Hadad nor the Zeus *hypsistos*/Palmyrenian Ba'al Shamîm,[91] who each had his own sanctuary—is difficult to identify, as the epithet was applied to a

---

[86]   *IGBulg.* iv. (1966), nos. 1941–4 and 1946, with the mention of a priest. Cf. Taceva-Hitova 1977: 278–81.

[87]   *IGBulg.* iv. (1966), 49, no. 1943 = Tacheva-Hitova 1983: 194–5 no. iv. 7, and pl. lxvi.

[88]   *IDélos* nos 2328 and 2230–2, as well as the two inscriptions from Rhenea (*IDélos* no. 2532), on which the designation of the god is consistent with Jewish formulary (τὸν Θεὸν τὸν ὕψιστον). Cf. Bruneau 1970: 480–93 (484 for the inscriptions) and Bruneau 1982.

[89]   Respectively *IDélos* no. 2477, cf. Plassart 1928: 124–5, and *IDélos* nos. 1532, 1892, 1896, 1897, 2418, and 2425.

[90]   An enclosed space with a small courtyard opening to the East and endowed with a terrace on three sides, Plassart 1928: 288.

[91]   Cf. Kaiser 2002. This is not the place to enter into the debate on the identifica-tion of the *Zeus hypsistos kai epêkoos* (in Greek: 'Zeus Highest and Hearkener')/*He whose name is blessed for eternity* (in Palmyrean).

variety of great gods. On Mount Cynthus, Zeus *hypsistos* did not know the solitude of the Theos *hypsistos* in the synagogue. A dedication offered by a freedman honours both him and at the same time 'the gods to whom altars have been raised'.[92] These are probably the four quadrangular altars discovered at the west of the terrace of the Zeus hypsistos temple (Plassart 1928: 289–91, and fig. 234). Plassart has put the anonymity of these associates' down to an inability to transcribe into Greek names which sounded too barbarous. This seems unlikely, though, once one knows the foreign divine names (or human names) that were transcribed.[93] In any event, Zeus *hypsistos* had close neighbours—perhaps set up earlier, and thus badly identified—to whom his devotee intended to make an equal show of piety. The situation was no different in Rome. The Astarte *hypsistê* venerated on the Via Appia (in the vicinity of the Quintili Villa) shared a sanctuary with Graeco–Roman gods (Jupiter, Hercules, Asclepius, Hygieia, the Dioscuri) and gods of eastern origin (Artemis of Ephesus, Zeus Brontôn, Mithra, and Neotera) (*IGVR* i. no. 136).

At Odessos (in Moesia), a dedication to Zeus *hypsistos* reconstructs the banal topography of the cult site, with a portal,[94] a consecrated area, and properties offered to the deity.[95] The relief above the inscription shows an altar on which a man is scattering incense, while behind him stands a bull (?) with a ritual cloth over its back. Elsewhere, reliefs evoke moments from sacrificial ritual[96] or sculpt

[92] *IDélos* no. 2306: 'Gaius Fabius freed by Gaius, Roman, dedicated the enclosure on the road and the fittings within to Zeus hypsistos and to the gods to whom altars have been raised' (ἐφ' ὁδῶι τὸν περίβολον καὶ τὰ ἐν αὐτῶι χρηστήρια Διὶ ὑψίστωι καὶ θεοῖς οἷς τοὺς βωμοὺς ἱδρύσατο ἀνέθηκεν). For the 'fittings, χρηστήρια', cf. Bruneau 1970: 625, who dates the inscription (p. 241) to the 'Athenian era' (166–69 BC).

[93] For the divine names, cf. e.g. at Rome *Theos Zberthourdos* (*IGVR* i. no. 132) or in Dacia *dei patrii Bebellahamon et Benefal* (*CIL* iii. no. 7954).

[94] In Phrygia, columns with a propylea dedicated to Theos *hypsistos*, *Bull. Ép*, 104 (1991), no. 559.

[95] *IGBulg*. ii. no. 780. Gifts of land also to Zeus *hypsistos*: Rizakis and Touratsoglou 1985: 37–8, no. 22 and at Mylasa (cf. above, n. 30). At Palmyra (cf. above, n. 68), despite the fragmentary condition of the inscription, '...harvests, which this [land produces?]' are probably dedicated to the sanctuary of Zeus *hypsistos*.

[96] A ritual banquet at Panormos (Mysia) beneath the representation of three deities including Zeus, Perdrizet, 1899: 592–3, and pl. iv. 1. At Rome (*IGVR* i. no. 129 = *IG* xiv. no. 1018), the taurobolic altar offered by the pontifex Petronius

the classic motif of the 'sacrificing god'.[97] The sanctuary of $Z\epsilon\dot{v}s$ ὕψιστος ('Zeus most high') on Delos has produced a lamp dedicated to the god along with some magical lead figurines dating from the building of the sanctuary,[98] which complete the attested ritual apparatus. Such evidence suggests that offerings to personalized deities (Zeus, Attis) exalted as '*hypsistos*' were given according to traditional modes of ritual expression, even if Zeus *hypsistos* was also capable of inspiring a form of devotion more given to theological analysis, such as we saw at Stratonicea.

For the inscriptions dedicated to Theos *hypsistos*, Mitchell has identified a ritual break, consistent with the theological break which he also reconstructs.[99] This is a tricky area. A votive foot at Termessos (in Pisidia), a bronze perfume burner at Sibidunda, in Cyprus a cake (?)[100]—to say nothing of the lighting at Oenoanda— these do all seem to point to non-bloody cultic practices. But inscriptions are rarely indicative of offerings,[101] and the remains preserved in the soil are few and far between, especially when the offerings are private. In any case, the appearance of the sanctuaries does not allow anything really specific to be detected. The sanctuary on the Pnyx at Athens is the only archeologically substantial cult site devoted to a ὕψιστος ('most high') deity. Though set up on a hill, it

---

Apollodorus to the universal Mother Rhea, and to Attis *hypsistos* displays the two deities and cultic objects. At Palmyra, burnt offerings and ritual banquets for Zeus *hypsistos* (Milik 1972: 144–9). Banquets for Zeus *hypsistos* at Philadelphia in Egypt, Roberts et al. 1936: 40–2.

[97] Rizakis and Touratsoglu 1985: 89–90, no. 90, and *IK* 26. 2 (*Kyzikos*): no. 5 and pl. iii. fig. 7. For the iconographic type, cf. Veyne 1990 and Patton 1992.

[98] Respectively Bruneau 1965: no. 4380 and 1970: 649–50.

[99] Mitchell 1999: 97–9. It nonetheless remains paradoxical that on the stele of a couple in which the husband is 'priest of the *one and only god*' and which Mitchell (103–4) considers as belonging to 'the monotheistic theology of the Oenoanda oracle', the couple should have asked to be depicted sacrificing on an altar, according to the traditional ritual code, *TAM* v. 1 (1981), no. 246 = Ricl 1991: 3, no. 2, and 55, pl. 1.

[100] Respectively *TAM* iii. 1 (1941), no. 32; *Bull. Ép.* (1961), no. 750; and *SEG* 39 (1989), no. 809.

[101] It is possible that an inscription in Cyprus mentions an 'agent responsible for sacrifices', *SEG* 39 (1989), no. 1555. Cf. also an altar with bucrania offered to the Theos *hypsistos* by a priestess Fabia Primilla (Archaeological museum of Adana [Turkey], inventory no. 919).

does not fit the category of a cult 'of heights'. On the abandoned site of meetings by the assembly of the *polis*, the rear wall of the semicircle carved into the rock was pieced with about fifty rectangular niches in which inscribed stones must have been placed or suspended.[102] One of these niches, which seems contemporary with the reconstruction under Hadrian, is larger than the others, and may have housed a statue of the god, who was therefore personalized despite his frequently anonymous designation. The only cultic attestation preserved comes from votive inscriptions,[103] two-thirds of which carry anatomical reliefs.[104] They suggest that the god of the site, randomly[105] named $\Theta\epsilon\grave{o}s/Z\epsilon\grave{v}s$ $\ddot{v}\psi\iota\sigma\tau os$ ('God/Zeus most high'), or more commonly just $\ddot{v}\psi\iota\sigma\tau os$ ('Most high'), was revered as a healer, principally by women. $\ddot{v}\psi\iota\sigma\tau os$ ('Most high') is not a functional epithet. Naturally, as a deity whose divine essence is qualitatively exalted, its power extends to mastery over the body, similar to other great gods of imperial paganism worshipped as *sôter* ('saviour').[106] Several dedicants give thanks to their god *hypsistos* following physical affliction,[107] or for the deliverance they sought,[108] to say nothing of the more general way in which vows made to the gods sought protection from life's accidents. Here too, the ritual context appears to be traditional.

The evidence is somewhat sparse, but there is no compulsion to identify a ritual break in the dedications offered to the exalted deities, even in the case of Theos *hypsistos*. Chromatis' dedication at

---

[102] Cf. Crow and Clarke 1885–6: 200ff. and map 219; Judeich 1931: 392–3 and map, 390, no. 51; and especially Forsén 1993.

[103] 28 (29?) inscriptions. Cf. Mitchell 1999: 129, nos. 2–23; and *Bull. Ép.* (1955), no. 68; Thompson 1936: 154a, 155 and 155c; *IG* iii, no. 4843; Lajtar 1987; and (?) Meritt 1948: 43, no. 34.

[104] For the catalogue of the 19 'plaques', cf. Forsén 1993: 515–16. Cf. also Van Straten 1981: 117–19 (catalogue).

[105] No distinguishing criteria (gender, illness) are available.

[106] Cf. Mitchell 1999: 106 and the classic formulae *hyper sôterias/hygeias*. For ailments as divine punishments, cf. Chaniotis 1995.

[107] In Phrygia, *MAMA* ix (1988), no. P67: $\dot{\epsilon}\lambda\epsilon\eta\theta\epsilon\grave{\imath}s$ $\dot{a}\pi$' $\ddot{o}\langle\lambda\rangle\omega\nu$ $\tau\hat{\omega}\nu$ $\pi\alpha\theta\eta\mu\acute{a}\tau[\omega]\nu$, $\epsilon\dot{v}\xi\acute{a}\mu\epsilon\nu os$ $\theta\epsilon\hat{\omega}$ $\dot{v}\psi\acute{\iota}\sigma\tau\omega$, 'freed from all illnesses, having prayed to the god most high' ($\pi\alpha\theta\acute{\eta}\mu\alpha\tau\alpha$ has a medical sense, cf. Robert 1969–90: iii. 1521–2). On another side, the Jewish inscription *IDélos* no. 2330 ($\Theta\epsilon\hat{\omega}\iota$ $\dot{v}\psi\acute{\iota}\sigma\tau\omega\iota$ $\sigma\omega\theta\epsilon\hat{\imath}\sigma\alpha$ $\tau\alpha\hat{\imath}s$ $\dot{v}\phi$' $A\dot{v}\tau o\hat{v}$ $\theta\epsilon\rho\alpha\pi\acute{\eta}\alpha\iota s$ $\epsilon\dot{v}\chi\acute{\eta}\nu$, 'a votive offering to God Most High, having been saved by His cures') employs the epigraphic formulations of healing sanctuaries.

[108] At Thessalonica (*IG* x. 2. no. 67); at Gorgippia in the Bosporus (*SEG* 32 [1982], no. 790); near Cyzicus (Barth and Stauber 1993: no. 1917).

Oenoanda, carrying out the ritual injunction given by the oracle of
Apollo of Claros engraved next to it, cannot, therefore, serve as a
model for all testimonies. Moreover, the small number of sanctuaries
known to us are not situated specifically on the heights, nor are their
gods represented as acting from on high, in contrast with their
transcendental homonym, the Jewish God.[109]

HISTORIOGRAPHICAL TRADITION AND HISTORICAL CONFUSION

One final sanctuary 'up on high' might detain us on methodological
grounds. At Neapolis in Samaria (Judaea-Palestine), the civic temple
of the Garizim overlooked the city. The temple, together with the
mountain, was the religious emblem of the city, whose god presided
over almost all aspects of city life.[110] Rebuilt by Hadrian during his
visit of AD 129/130, which he marked by building projects carried out
in honour of Zeus, it was completed by Antoninus Pius and restored
in even more monumental fashion by Caracalla. This vast complex,
which can be pieced together with the help of numismatic and
archaeological evidence,[111] had monumental gateways with Syrian-
style towers, which were themselves located inside a compound
adorned with six outward-facing cisterns. The gateways gave access
to a temple of Greek form (with columns all the way round) on a
raised platform. Although the mountain remained a place of the
highest value for the Samaritans,[112] they did not recover the temple
of theirs destroyed by John Hyrcanus in 112/111 BC.[113] The

[109] Cf. for example Psalm 18. 14 (ἐβρόντησε ἐξ οὐρανοῦ Κύριος / καὶ Ὁ ὕψιστος
ἔδωκε φωνὴν Αὐτοῦ, 'The Lord sent thunder from heaven / and the Most High sent
forth his voice'). In Hellenistic Judaism, 'Heaven' is a frequent metonym for God, cf.
1 Maccabees (2. 21; 3. 18, 19, 40, and 60; 4. 10 and 40; 9. 46; 12. 55) and Daniel 4. 33.
[110] For the pagan cults at Neapolis, cf. Belayche 2001: 199–209.
[111] Cf. BMC Palestine nos. 21–6 (with variants). For archaeological data, Bull 1967
and 1968b; Magen 1993; and 'Gerazim, Mount' in Stern 1993: ii. 488–90.
[112] Cf. the increase in the number of Samaritan synagogues in the surrounding
area in the third century, Segni 1993.
[113] Josephus, Jewish Antiquities 13. 254–7 and Jewish War 1. 63. Cf. Schur 1989:
42–50.

attribution of the sanctuary to Zeus is confirmed by images on coins, depicting the mountain supported by an eagle (e.g. Meshorer 1985: no. 135). Although the temple was refounded by the emperor, this Zeus is no Jupiter Capitolinus.[114] The star, the sun, and the moon depicted on civic coins are not common attributes of the Roman god. Dussaud therefore believed that the Zeus of the Garizim was the Jupiter of Heliopolis represented on the civic coins, whose temple Antoninus Pius had had rebuilt at Heliopolis.[115] It would be surprising that, on this hypothesis, the god of Heliopolis would be one of only two deities to break the Garizim's monopoly in the civic coinage (*British Museum Catalogue, Palestine* no. 27–41, under Marcus Aurelius). As for the lion's head—the animal of Atargatis—discovered in the base of the temple (Bull 1968b: 239), this is too slender a piece of evidence to attribute the sanctuary to Hadad, the male consort of the Syrian goddess Atargatis.

A late literary account further muddies the waters. Marinos (*c.* AD 440, cited by Damascius, AD 458–526) writes that 'on this mountain Argarizon [Al-Garizim], there is a most holy sanctuary to Zeus Most High (ἐν ᾧ Διὸς ὑψίστου ἁγιώτατον ἱερόν), founded by Abraham (ᾧ καθιέρωτο Ἄβραμος), the first ancestor of the Hebrews'.[116] Modern scholars have taken the name 'Zeus Most High' to refer to the temple in the Roman era.[117] However, the two inscriptions found *in situ* are offered ΔΙΙ ΟΛΥΜΠΙΩΙ ('To Olympian Zeus'),[118] of whom a monumental head has been recovered in the ruins of an adjacent building (Bull 1968a: 69–70). Hadrian had placed Olympian

---

[114] At Palmyra, under Diocletian (Gawlikowski 1984: 125, no. 36), a bilingual inscription writes in Greek *Zeus hypsistos* (probably a translation of Baal Shamîm) and in Latin *Iupiter Optimus Maximus*; this unique correspondence expresses the primacy of the two divinities and can also no doubt be explained by the identity of the dedicant, Amathallat son of Sabbitus, a subaltern officer recently Romanized. At Panarama, *Zeus hypsistos* and *Zeus kapetolios* are jointly honoured under Antoninus (above, p. 145).

[115] Dussaud 1903b. Cf. Beaujeu 1955: 262–7 for early misgivings.

[116] Photius, *Library* 242. 345b Bekker, citing Damascius = Athanassiadi 1999: 236, no. 97A.

[117] e.g. Schürer 1973–87: ii. 161, and more recently Niehr 2003: 54–5, who identifies the Hellenistic god as Zeus *Olympios* (even while citing in n. 114 Zeus *Hypsistos*, following Cook!), but making mention of data from the Roman period.

[118] Bull 1968b: 239–40 and xxii a. Their burial could date from the middle of the fourth century.

Zeus at the heart of the grandiose religio–cultural policy which he conducted at Athens, and the coinage of the province of Asia (visited on his way to Syria) immortalized him as Olympian Zeus (Metcalf 1974; cf. Calandra 1996). It is hard to imagine Hadrian, on the eve of founding Aelia Capitolina on the site of Jerusalem, honouring in the land of the Samaritans a Zeus called by an epithet (ὕψιστος, 'Most High') known to be one of the names of the Jewish God in Greek. The Hellenic Zeus who bestrode the mountain was no newcomer to the region. According to Flavius Josephus (citing Dios), Tyre had had a temple of Zeus Olympios from as early as the time of King Hiram, a contemporary of Solomon! (Josephus, *Against Apion* i. 113). In a more historical vein, his cult was imposed by king Antiochus Epiphanes in the temple of Jerusalem. At Gerasa, Zeus was worshipped as *Olympios* (Welles 1938: nos. 2–14), and later, during the Severan dynasty, on the Samarian border (at Mezer), an altar was dedicated Διὶ Ὀλυμπίω(ι) ἐπηκόω(ι) ('To Olympian Zeus the hearer') by a devotee with a Milesian name.[119] In other words, under Antiochus Epiphanes, the Samaritans dedicated a temple to Zeus *Xenios*, whom Flavius Josephus justly calls *Hellenios*,[120] with reference to his cultural heritage, and who becomes *Olympios* under Hadrian.

Marinos' chronological 'compression' is interesting in that in its own way it demonstrates the opacity of the sources mentioning '*hypsistos*' divinities. In the fifth century AD, Palaestina was largely Christianized—especially in its non-Jewish regions like Samaria—and the temple was probably abandoned.[121] Marinos, who doubtless came from a long-standing Graeco–Romanized family of Neapolis, was a Samaritan who had 'converted' to paganism. He therefore knew about the episode of Abraham's stay at Shechem,[122] as he

[119] Applebaum et al. 1978: 136, no. 6.
[120] Respectively, 2 Maccabees 6. 2 (cf. Adler and Séligsohn 1903: 123–46: a temple of '*Saphis*' = Jupiter *Sospes/Xenios* and Josephus, *Jewish Antiquities* 12. 259–61).
[121] Roughly forty years later, under Zeno, a church of Mary Theotokos is erected on the Garizim, cf. Procopius, *Buildings* 5. 7. For the historical context, Maraval 1997: 74–8.
[122] Genesis 12. 6–7. The Septuagint identifies the place as ὑψηλός, i.e. the same name as the place of the sacrifice of Isaac (Genesis 22. 2), whereas, in both verses the Hebrew version gives a place name (Moreh and Moriyyah), cf. Harl 1994: i. 153. In the sixth century, Procopius of Gaza (above, n. 121) also calls the Garizim ὄρος ὑψηλός, 'lofty mountain'.

must have known about the Samaritan traditions which had transferred to the Garizim the founding events located by the Jewish
Pentateuch on Mount Moriah in Jerusalem (Schur 1989: 38). In the
divine epiphany on Mount Sinai, Yahweh, the ὕψιστος ('Most High')
of the Septuagint, places 'the blessing on Mount Garizim' (Deuteronomy 11. 29 and Joshua 8. 33), defined by a Jewish Hellenistic
historian as 'the holy Argarizis, which translates as "mountain of
the Most High"' (ἱερὸν Ἀργαριζιν, ὅ εἶναι μεθερμηνευόμενην ὄρος
ὑψίστου).[123] Moreover, as head of the Neoplatonist philosophical
school, Marinos must have known (directly or indirectly?) the writings of Philo of Alexandria, who frequently calls his God ῾Ο ὕψιστος
('The Most High'), among other times in the episode of Melchizedek
and Abraham (e.g. *Allegorical Interpretation of Genesis* 3. 82–3, citing
Genesis 14. 18; cf. above n. 4). Marinos compressed with even greater
ease the time sequence, for *Olympios* and *Hypsistos* are two epithets of
height. Finally, there is no surprise in seeing under the pen of the
philosopher the divine name Zeus designate the Jewish god. Corre-
spondences between a great pagan god and Yahweh were not new,[124]
and even less so for the current of Neoplatonism which, *via* Porphyry, was nourished by 'the philosophy derived from the oracles'. All
the same, an oracle of Claros, often invoked in modern commentaries, declared 'that Iao is the *greatest* of all the gods (τὸν πάντων
ὕπατον θεόν), in winter Hades, Zeus at the beginning of spring,
Helios in summer, in autumn the splendid Iao (ἁβρὸν Ἰάω)' (Macrobius (citing Cornelius Labeo), *Saturnalia* 1. 18. 20, my emphasis). In
the tradition of initiations and magic (though not in this text), Iao is
Yahweh (Buresch 1889: 48–53), the ὕψιστος ('Most High') of the

---

[123] Eupolemos, *On the Jews of Assyria* (*ap.* Alexander Polyhistor) *ap.* Eusebius,
Preparation for the Gospel 9. 17. 5.
[124] Cf. Origen, *Against Celsus* 5. 45: 'Celsus thinks that there is no difference in
calling Zeus Hypsistos, or Zên or Adonaï or Sabaoth . . .', or John Lydus, *De mensibus*,
iv. 51 (Wünsch, 111): τὸν Διόνυσον, τὸν ὑπό τινων Σαβάζιον ὀνομαζόμενον . . .
Χαλδαῖοι τὸν θεὸν Ἰαὼ λέγουσιν . . . καὶ Σαββαὼθ δὲ πολλαχοῦ λέγεται, 'Dionysos,
called by some Sabazios . . . The Chaldaeans name the god Iao . . . but he is commonly
named Sabbaoth'. The assimilation is carried out either on the basis of lexical
analogies (*Iovem-Yahweh, Iovis-Iao*, [*Dionysos*]*Sabazios-Sabaoth*, Σάβοι σάββατον),
or on that of a set of theological arguments dependent upon a syncretistic philosophical orientation; cf. Cumont 1906b and Simon 1976.

Septuagint, and the name by which the god is known from the oracle of Claros (Beatrice 2001: i. no. 38); cf. Mitchell 1999: 81–92).

CONCLUSION

The body of epigraphic evidence takes us through religious attitudes in which the faithful pay homage to a divinity by means of an epithet which exalts his divine nature without isolating him from his fellow-gods, who may be magnified along with him. The God of the philosophers himself did not abolish the pantheon at the level of daily ritual. The vast majority of pagan dedications offered to deities termed ὕψιστος ('most high') are inscribed within a polytheistic vision of the superhuman world, including a number of great gods who are named explicitly, and others who are identifiable behind the generic heading of *theos*: the Greek Zeus or local equivalents, Sarapis, Sabazios, the Mothers, or a Semitic *Ba'al* (?). Worshippers who chose, in the Greek language, to exalt their divinity through this epithet, may have wished to express the conception which they had of him as occupying a very elevated, celestial position. However, the dedications examined here suggest above all a metaphorical use of the epithet, which had the aim of highlighting the divinity so invoked within a plurality of gods. The use of *hypsistos*, and the aspect of the divine landscape which it constructs, may thus be located within the same religious trend which, through other expressions of emphasis or acclamation, magnified the greatness of the gods. Unlike the epithet *epêkoos*/attentive, which also became more widely used during the imperial era,[125] the devotee who worshipped his god as the 'highest/most high' was not seeking to underline the god's benevolence towards men, but rather his privileged, pre-eminent position at the summit of the divine edifice, which naturally included solicitude for humans, as in the offerings for cures on the Pnyx at Athens. The invocation through the impersonal *Theos*, rather than through the individualized name of the god (Zeus, Apollo, Metêr, etc.), was

---

[125] Weinreich 1912. Zeus *hypsistos* is *epêkoos* in Syria, principally in Palmyra, cf. Mitchell 1999: 145, nos. 272–5 and 277–8.

another way of emphasizing the greatness of his divine nature over his person. This conception of the divinity, 'essentialist'—rather than unique (betraying the idea of a 'One god')—might be what coins the originality of hypsistan religiosity, as far as Graeco–Roman paganism considered superior beings from two points of view: their domain of competence, either local or functionalist, or their modality of action.

Since ὕψιστος ('Most High') equally served as the Greek expression for the Jewish One God,[126] it may have been used by pagan-Jewish groups, the Hypsistarians, and may have been employed in philosophical speculations on the great god, which were fostered by a number of different theological influences, possibly seduced by an epithet unknown to the Greek ritual tradition. However, even Apollo's oracle at Claros, some of whose sayings spread a monotheizing theology, did not make *hypsistos* a privileged name for the great god.

AFTERWORD (2010)

During the last five years, some issues discussed in this paper have continued to be investigated. It is worth mentioning some points, although none of them affects the argument in a substantial way; on the contrary, in my opinion, they actually provide support for it.

1. The methodological line focusing on ritual data in order to grasp conceptions of gods has been supported by recent developments in the archaeology of ritual; see, for example, Scheid 2008. Sadly, it is impossible to apply these developments to this *dossier* of evidence, for they were either found out of context or else come from 'rural' cult places, which have not yet been excavated. Nevertheless, archaeology provides much evidence of the long-time practice of using lamps in cultic places as regular gestures of devotion: Estienne 2008.

---

[126] It is impossible to estimate the debt to Judaism of Theos *hypsistos*, except on late, limited evidence such as the Hypsistarians. There are indeed synagogues in the majority of places where are found dedications to Theos *hypsistos*; but the Jews were spread throughout the Empire. By contrast, cities with strong Jewish communities such as Sardis have not produced dedications to Theos *hypsistos*.

2. The number of testimonies on Zeus or Theos *hypsistos* has increased with newly published inscriptions. However, the most important new discovery is that of a temple of Zeus *hypsistos* in Dion, south of Thessaloniki in Macedonia (Pandermalis 2005, 2006). The temple is of a Graeco–Roman type and the monumental enthroned statue of Zeus *hypsistos* with an eagle at his feet is of a current normal Greek type; this supports my argument, especially the section 'The "*hypsistos*" deities: a ritual break?'.

3. On the ongoing interpretative debate about 'hypsistan' religiosity, see Wischmeyer 2005 and Belayche 2005b. For an attempt at a social-orientated study of *Theos hypsistos*, see Anna Collar's doctoral dissertation, supervised by Stephen Mitchell at the University of Exeter, which ends with a chapter on 'The Cult of the "Most High God". God-fearers and the Redefinition of the Jewish–Gentile Relationship' (2008: 188–240). Relying (unsurprisingly, if somewhat uncritically) on Mitchell's work, she uses the cult as an example of network theory, developing his view that the evidence reveals a unified cult, linked to Jewish monotheism. Unfortunately, some of her own views are unsound. For example, the thesis that Gentile god-fearers became *personae non gratae* among Jews after the events of 70–136 (p. 190: 'the Gentile response to the tightening of boundaries within Judaism') and were compelled to form 'a separate cult, that of *Theos Hypsistos*' (p. 190), 'a sect-like Judaism' (p. 201; see also p. 203), is formulated from an out-of-date historiography of Jewish isolation. This old position is now opposed by numerous studies on the integration achieved by Diaspora Judaism and on the rabbinical casuistic developed in order to allow 'orthodox' Jews to live within a 'pagan' environment (e.g. Schäfer 1998–2002). The hypothesis that 'interactions with Samaritans/Jews on Delos may have been instrumental in the early propagation of the cult' (p. 189; see also p. 210) is opposed by much evidence coming from Macedonia, which has now been convincingly related by Paraskevi Martzavou (2008: ch. 3) to immigrants from Anatolia (Mysia, Bithynia, and the surroundings of Byzantium).

4. About the meaning of '*angelos*' and '*to theion*', see Belayche 2010.

5. About acclamations as a rhetorical pattern for glorifying gods, see Mitchell and Van Nuffelen 2010. This is one of the two

volumes that collect the papers given at the Exeter Conference, 17–20 July 2006, on 'Pagan Monotheism in the Roman Empire (1st–4th Cent. AD)'.

BIBLIOGRAPHY

Adler, E. N. and Séligsohn, M. (1903). 'Une nouvelle chronique samaritaine', *Revue des Études Juives*, 46: 123–46.

Applebaum, S., Isaac, B., and Landau, Y. (1978). 'Varia Epigraphica', *Scripta Classica Israelica*, 4: 133–59.

Athanassiadi, P. (ed.) (1999). Damascius, *The Philosophical History*. Athens: Apamea Cultural Association.

——and Frede, M. (eds.) (1999). *Pagan Monotheism in Late Antiquity*. Oxford: Oxford University Press.

Audollent, A. (1904). *Defixionum Tabellae*. Paris: Fontemoing.

Barth, M. and Stauber, J. (eds.) (1993). *Inschriften Mysia & Troas*. Munich: Leopold Wenger Institut. Universität München [used in CDRom of Ibycus]).

Baslez, M.-F. (1977). *Recherches sur les conditions de pénétration et de diffusion des religions orientales à Délos (IIe–Ier s. avant notre ère)*. Paris: École normale supérieure de jeunes filles.

Battifol, P. (1929). *La paix constantinienne et le catholicisme*, 5th edn. Paris: Gabalda.

Baumgarten, A. I. (1981). *The Phoenician History of Philo of Byblos*, EPRO 89. Leiden: Brill.

Bean, G. E. (1959). 'Notes and Inscriptions from Pisidia', *Anatolian Studies*, 9: 67–117.

Beatrice, P. F. (2001). *Anonymi Monophysitae theosophia. An Attempt at Reconstruction*. Leiden: Brill.

Beaujeu, J. (1955). *La religion romaine à l'apogée de l'Empire*. i. *La politique religieuse des Antonins (96–192)*. Paris: Belles Lettres.

Belayche, N. (1984). *Les divinités ΥΨΙΣΤΟΣ' dans le monde romain impérial*, unpublished dissertation, Paris IV-Sorbonne.

——(2001). *Iudaea-Palaestina. The Pagan Cults in Roman Palestine (Second to Fourth Century)*, Religion der Römischen Provinzen 1. Tübingen: Mohr Siebeck.

——(2005a). '"Au(x) dieu(x) qui règne(nt) sur...": *Basileia* divine et fonctionnement du polythéisme dans l'Anatolie impériale', in A. Bérenger-

Badel, B. Klein, X. Loriot, and A. Vigourt (eds.), *Pouvoir et religion dans le monde romain. En hommage à Jean-Pierre Martin*. Paris: Presses de l'université Paris-Sorbonne, 257–69.

——(2005b). 'De la polysémie des épiclèses. Ὕψιστος dans le monde gréco-romain', in N. Belayche, P. Brulé, G. Freyburger, Y. Lehmann, L. Pernot, and F. Prost (eds.), *Nommer les dieux. Théonymes, épithètes, épiclèses dans l'Antiquité*, Recherches sur les rhétoriques religieuses 5. Turnhout: Brepols; Rennes: Presses universitaires de Rennes, 427–42.

——(2006). 'Les stèles dites de confession: une religiosité originale dans l'Anatolie impériale?', in L. de Blois, P. Funke, and J. Hahn (eds.), *The Impact of Imperial Rome on Religions, Ritual and Religious Life in the Roman Empire*. Leiden: Brill, 66–81.

——(2010). '*Angeloi* in Religious Practices of the Imperial Roman East', *Henoch*, 32. 1: 45–65.

Bissinger, M. (1966). *Das Adjectiv μέγας in der griechischen Dichtung*, Münchener Studien zur Sprachwissenschaft, Supp. K. Munich: Kitzinger.

Bonnet, C. (2005). 'Entre terre et ciel. Parcours historiographique en "hauts-lieux" sur les traces de Franz Cumont et d'autres historiens des religions', *ARG*, 7: 5–10.

Borgeaud, P. (1996). *La Mère des dieux: de Cybèle à la Vierge Marie*. Paris: Seuil.

Bricault, Laurent (2005). *Recueil des inscriptions concernant les cultes isiaques (RICIS)*. Paris: Académie des inscriptions et belles-lettres.

Briquel-Chatonnet, F. (2005). 'Les cités de la côte phénicienne et leurs sanctuaires de montagne', *ARG*, 7: 20–33.

Bruneau, P. (1965). *Les lampes*, Exploration Archéologique de Délos 26. (Paris: de Boccard).

——(1970). *Recherches sur les cultes de Délos à l'époque hellénistique et à l'époque impériale*, BEFAR 217. Paris: de Boccard.

——(1982). '"Les Israélites de Délos" et la juiverie délienne', *BCH*, 106: 486–504.

Buckler, W. H. and Robinson, D. M. (1932). *The Excavations of Sardis*. vii, 1. *Greek and Latin Inscriptions*. Leiden: Brill.

Bull, R. J. (1967). 'A Preliminary Excavation on an Hadrianic Temple at Tell er Ras on Mount Gerizim', *American Journal of Archaeology*, 71: 387–93.

——(1968a). 'The Excavations of Tell er-Ras on Mt Gerizim', *The Biblical Archaeologist*, 31: 58–72.

——(1968b). 'Tell er-Ras (Garizim)', *Revue Biblique*, 75: 238–43.

Buresch, K. (1889). *ΑΠΟΛΛΩΝ ΚΛΑΡΙΟΣ*. Leipzig: Teubner.

Burkert, W. (1996). *Creation of the Sacred. Tracks of Biology in Early Religions*. Cambridge, MA: Harvard University Press.

Calandra, E. (1996). *Oltre la Grecia. Alle origini del filellenismo di Adriano.* Naples: Edizioni scientifiche italiane.

Capizzi, C. (1964). *ΠΑΝΤΟΚΡΑΤΩΡ: saggio d'esegesi letterario-iconografica*, Orientalia Christiana Analecta 170. Rome: Pont. Institutum Orientalium Studiorum.

Chaniotis, A. (1995). 'Illness and Cures in the Greek Propitiatory Inscriptions and Dedications of Lydia and Phrygia', in Ph. J. van der Eijk, H. F. J. Horstmanshoff, and P. H. Schrijvers (eds.), *Ancient Medicine in its Socio-Cultural Context*. Amsterdam: Rodopi, ii. 323–44.

——(1997). '"Tempeljustiz" im kaiserzeitlichen Kleinasien. Rechtliche Aspekte der Sühneinschriften Lydiens und Phrygiens', in G. Thür and J. Velissaropoulos-Karakostas (eds.), *Symposion 1995. Vorträge zur griechischen und hellenistischen Rechtsgeschichte (Korfu, 1995)*. Cologne: Böhlau, 353–84.

Chantraine, P. (1977). *Dictionnaire étymologique de la langue grecque*. Paris: Klincksieck.

Collar, A. C. F. (2008). *Networks and Religious Innovation in the Roman Empire*. University of Exeter: Ph.D. Diss.; I thank the author for informing me that it is available online at: http://hdl.handle.net/10036/55073.

Cook, A. B. (1914–40). *Zeus. A Study in Ancient Religion*. Cambridge: Cambridge University Press.

Crow, J. M. and Clarke, J. T. (1885–6). 'The Athenian Pnyx', *Papers of the American School of Classical Studies*, 4: 205–60.

Cumont, F. (1897). 'Hypsistos', *Revue de l'Instruction Publique en Belgique*, Supp. 40: 1–15.

——(1906a). 'Jupiter Summus Exsuperantissimus', *Archiv für Religionswissenschaft*, 9: 323–36.

——(1906b). 'Les mystères de Sabazios et le judaïsme', *CRAI*, 1906: 63–79.

De Hoz, M. P. (1999). *Die lydischen Kulte im Lichte der griechischen Inschriften*, Asia Minor Studien 36. Bonn: R. Habelt.

Delaporte, L. J. (1923). *Catalogue des cylindres, cachets et pierres gravées de style oriental*, vol. 2. Paris: Musée du Louvre.

Di Segni, L. (1993). 'The Greek Inscriptions in the Samaritan Synagogue at El-Khirbe', in Manns and Alliata 1993: 231–9.

Drew-Bear, T. and Naour, Chr. (1990). 'Divinités de Phrygie', *ANRW*, 2. 18. 3: 1907–2044, 2777–81.

Drew-Bear, T., Thomas, C. M., and Yildizturan, M. (1999). *Phrygian Votive Steles, The Museum of Anatolian Civilizations*. Ankara: Turkish Republic Ministry of Culture.

Dussaud, R. (1903a). *Mission dans les régions désertiques de la Syrie moyenne*. Paris: Imprimerie Nationale.

——(1903b). 'Notes de mythologie syrienne', *Revue Archéologique*, 1903: 347–68.

Estienne, S. (2008). 'Lampes et candélabres dans les sanctuaires de l'Occident romain: une approche archéologique des rituels', *Mythos*, n.s. 2: 45–60.

Festugière, A. J. (1944). *La Révélation d'Hermès Trismégiste*. Paris: Lecoffre, i.

Forsén, B. (1993). 'The Sanctuary of Zeus Hypsistos and the Assembly Place on the Pnyx', *Hesperia*, 62: 507–21.

Fränkel, M. (1895). *Die Inschriften von Pergamon*. Berlin: Spemann.

François, G. (1957). *Le polythéisme et l'emploi au singulier des mots ΘΕΟΣ, ΔΑΙΜΩΝ . . .* Paris: Belles lettres.

French, D. H. (1994). 'Sinopean Notes 4. Cults and Divinities: The Epigraphic Evidence', *EA*, 23: 99–108.

Frey, J.-B. (1936–52). *Corpus inscriptionum Judaicarum*, 2 vols. Vatican: Pontificio istituto di archeologia cristiana; repr. as *Corpus of Jewish Inscriptions*, New York: Ktav, 1975.

Frisk, H. (1970). *Griechisches etymologisches Wörterbuch*. Heidelberg: Winter.

Gawlikowski, M. (1984). *Les principia de Dioclétien: 'Temple des enseignes'*, Palmyre 8. Warsaw: Naukowe.

Hajjar, Y. (1990). 'Divinités oraculaires et rites divinatoires en Syrie et en Phénicie à l'époque gréco-romaine', *ANRW*, 2. 18. 4: 2458–508.

Harl, M. (ed.) (1994). *La Bible d'Alexandrie*. i. *La Genèse*. Paris: Cerf.

Hatch, E. and Redpath, H. A. (1897). *A Concordance to the Septuagint and the Other Greek Versions of the Old Testament*. Oxford: Clarendon Press.

Herrmann, P. (1978). 'Men, Herr von Axiotta', in S. Şahin, E. Schwertheim, and J. Wagner (eds.), *Studien zur Religion und Kultur Kleinasiens. Festschrift für Friedrich Karl Dörner*, EPRO 66. Leiden: Brill, i. 415–23.

Horbury, W. and Noy, D. (1992). *Jewish Inscriptions of Graeco–Roman Egypt*. Cambridge: Cambridge University Press.

Jacoby, F. (1923–58). *Die Fragmente der griechischen Historiker*. Leiden: Brill.

Judeich, W. (1931). *Topographie von Athens*. Munich: Beck.

Käppel, L. (1992). *Paian. Studien zur Geschichte einer Gattung*. Berlin: de Gruyter.

Kaiser, T. (2002). *The Religious Life of Palmyra*, Oriens et Occidens 4. Stuttgart: Steiner.

Lack, R. (1962). 'Les origines de Elyon, le Très-Haut, dans la tradition cultuelle d'Israël', *Catholic Biblical Quarterly*, 24: 44–64.

Laftar, A. (1987). 'An Athenian Vow to Zeus Hypsistos', *ZPE*, 70: 165–6.

Lane, E. N. (1971–8). *Corpus Monumentorum Religionis Dei Menis*, 4 vols., EPRO 19. Leiden: Brill.

Laumonier, A. (1958). *Les cultes indigènes en Carie*. Paris: de Boccard.

Magen, Y. (1993). 'Mount Gerizim and the Samaritans', in Manns and Alliata 1993: 91–148.

Malay, H. (1994). *Greek and Latin Inscriptions in the Manisa Museum, TAM* Supp. 19. Vienna: Österreichischen Akademie der Wissenschaften.

Manns, F. and Alliata, E. (eds.) (1993). *Early Christianity in Context. Monuments and Documents*, Studium Biblicum Franciscanum, Coll. Maior 38. Jerusalem: Franciscan Printing Press.

Maraval, P. (1997). *Le christianisme de Constantin à la conquête arabe*. Paris: Presses universitaires de France.

Marek, C. (1993). *Stadt, Ära und Territorium in Pontus-Bithynia*. Tübingen: Wasmuth.

Martzavou, P. (2008). *Recherches sur les communautés festives dans la "vieille Grèce" (IIe siècle a.C. – IIIe siècle p. C.). Contribution à l'étude du contexte historique et sociologique des cultes dans la Grèce ancienne*. Paris, École Pratique des Hautes Études: Ph.D. Dissertation.

Meritt, B. D. (1948). 'Greek Inscriptions', *Hesperia*, 17: 1–53.

Merkelbach, R. (1995). *Isis Regina—Zeus Sarapis. Die griechisch-ägyptische Religion nach den Quellen dargestellt*. Stuttgart: Teubner.

Merlat, P. (1951). *Répertoire des inscriptions et monuments figurés du culte de Jupiter Dolichenus*. Paris: Geuthner.

——(1960). *Jupiter Dolichenus. Essai d'interprétation et de synthèse*. Paris: Presses universitaires de France.

Meshorer, Y. (1985). *City-coins of Eretz Israel and the Decapolis in the Roman Period*. Jerusalem: The Israel Museum.

Mesnil du Buisson, R. du (1970). *Études sur les dieux phéniciens hérités par l'Empire romain*, EPRO 14. Leiden: Brill.

Metcalf, W. E. (1974). 'Hadrian, *Iovis Olympius*', *Mnemosyne*, n.s. 27: 59–66.

Milik, J. T. (1972). *Dédicaces faites par des dieux (Palmyre, Hatra, Tyr) et des thiases à l'époque romaine*. Paris: Geuthner.

Mitchell, S. (1982). *The Ankara District. The Inscriptions of North Galatia*, Regional Epigraphic Catalogues of Asia Minor 2. Oxford: British Archaeological Reports.

——(1988). 'Maximinus and the Christians in AD 312: A New Latin Inscription', *JRS*, 78: 105–24.

——(1993). *Anatolia. Land, Men and Gods in Asia Minor*, 2 vols. Oxford: Oxford University Press.

——(1999). 'The Cult of Theos Hypsistos between Pagans, Jews and Christians', in Athanassiadi and Frede 1999: 81–148.

——and Van Nuffelen, P. (eds.) (2010). *One God. Pagan Monotheism in the Roman Empire*. Cambridge: Cambridge University Press.

Müller, B. (1913). *Μέγας θεός*, Diss. Halle 21.1. Halle: Karras.

Naour, C. (1983). 'Nouvelles inscriptions du Moyen Hermos', *EA*, 2: 107–41.

Niehr, H. (2003). *Ba'alsämem. Studien zu Herkunft, Geschichte und Rezeptionsgeschichte eines phönischen Gottes*, Orientalia Lovaniensia Analecta 123, Studia Phoenicia 17. Leuven: Peeters.

Nilsson, M. P. (1961). *Geschichte der griechischen Religion*, 2nd edn. Munich: Beck, ii.

Pandermalis, D. (2005). '*Δίον* 2005: *ανασκαφές, έργα αναδείξης και disjecta membra*', *To Arkhaiologiko Ergo sti Makedonia kai sti Thraki*, 19: 373–9.

——(2006). '*Δίον* 2006', *To Arkhaiologiko Ergo sti Makedonia kai sti Thraki*, 20: 567–75.

Patton, K. C. (1992). *When the High Gods Pour Out Wine. A Paradox of Ancient Greek Iconography in Comparative Context*, Ph.D. thesis. Harvard.

Peek, W. (1930). *Der Isishymnus von Andros.* Berlin: Weidmann.

Perdrizet, P. (1899). 'Reliefs mysiens', *BCH*, 23: 592–9.

Petzl, G. (1994). *Die Beichtinschriften Westkleinasiens*, *EA*, 22.

——(1998). *Die Beichtinschriften im römischen Kleinasien und der Fromme und der Gerechte Gott*, Nordrhein-Westfälische Akademie der Wissenschaften, Vorträge G 355. Opladen: Westdeutscher Verlag.

——(2003). 'Zum religiösen Leben im westlichen Kleinasien: Einflüsse und Wechselwirkungen', in E. Schwertheim and E. Winter (eds.), *Religion und Region. Götter und Kulte aus dem östlichen Mittelmeerraum*, Asia Minor Studien 45. Bonn: R. Habelt, 93–101.

——(2005). 'Sur des noms de dieux dans l'épigraphie de l'Asie Mineure', in N. Belayche, P. Brulé, et al. (eds.), *Nommer les dieux: théonymes, épithètes, épiclèses dans l'antiquité.* Turnhout: Brepols; Rennes: Presses universitaires de Rennes, 69–77.

Plassart, A. (1928). *Les sanctuaires et les cultes du Mont Cynthe*, Exploration Archéologique de Délos 11. Paris: de Boccard.

Pleket, H. W. (1981). 'Religious History as the History of Mentality: The "Believer" as Servant of the Deity in the Greek World', in Versnel 1981a: 152–92.

Ramsay, W. M. (1895–7). *The Cities and Bishoprics of Phrygia.* Oxford: Clarendon Press.

Ricl, M. (1991). 'Hosios kai Dikaios. i. Catalogue des inscriptions', *EA*, 18: 1–70

——(1992). 'Hosios kai Dikaios. ii. Analyse', *EA*, 19: 71–103.

Ritti, T., Şimşek, C., and Yıldız, H. (2000). 'Dediche e *καταγραφαί* dal santuario frigio di Apollo Lairbenos', *EA*, 32: 1–88.

Rizakis, T. and Touratsoglou, G. (1985). *Επιγραφές Άνω Μακεδονίας.* Athens: Ekdosē Tameiou Archaiologikōn Porōn kai Apallotriōseōn, i.

Robert, L. (1958). 'Reliefs votifs et cultes d'Anatolie', *Anatolia*, 3: 112–23, repr. in his 1969–90: i. 402–35.

——(1968). 'Trois oracles de la Théosophie et un prophète d'Apollon', *CRAI*, 1968: 568–99, repr. in his 1969–90: v. 584–615.

——(1969–90). *Opera minora selecta*, 7 vols. Amsterdam: Hakkert.

——(1983). 'Documents d'Asie Mineure', *BCH*, 107: 497–599, repr. in his 1987.

——(1987). *Documents d'Asie Mineure*, Bibliothèque des Écoles françaises d'Athènes et de Rome 239b. Athens: École française d'Athènes.

Roberts, C., Skeat, Th., and Nock, A. D. (1936). 'The Guild of Zeus Hypsistos', *HTR*, 29: 39–88; Nock's part repr. in his *Essays on Religion and the Ancient World*, ed. Z. Stewart, 2 vols. Oxford: Clarendon Press (1972), i. 414–43.

Rocchi, M. (2005). 'Culti sui monti della Grecia. Osservazioni da una lettura di Pausania', *ARG*, 7: 56–61.

Roller, L. J. (1999). *In Search of God the Mother: The Cult of Anatolian Cybele*. Berkeley: University of California Press.

Schäfer, P. (ed.) (1998–2002). *The Talmud Yerushalmi and Graeco–Roman Culture*, 3 vols., Texte und Studien zum antiken Judentum 71, 79, 93. Tübingen: Mohr Siebeck.

Scheid, J. (1999). 'Hiérarchie et structure dans le polythéisme romain. Façons romaines de penser l'action', *ARG*, 1: 184–203, translated as 'Hierarchy and Structure in Roman Polytheism: Roman Methods of Conceiving Action', in C. Ando (ed.), *Roman Religion*. Edinburgh: Edinburgh University Press (2003), 164–89.

——(ed.) (2008). *Pour une archéologie du rite. Nouvelles perspectives de l'archéologie funéraire*, Collection de l'École française de Rome 407. Rome: École française de Rome.

Schmidt, F. (ed.) (1987). *The Inconceivable Polytheism: Studies in Religious Historiography*, History and Anthropology 3. Chur and Paris: Harwood Academic.

Schürer, E. (1897). 'Die Juden in Bosporanischen Reich und die Genossenschaften der σεβόμενοι θεὸν ὕψιστον ebendaselbst', *Sitzungb. d. Akad. Berlin*, 11: 200–25.

——(1973–87). *The History of the Jewish People in the Age of Jesus Christ*, revised by G. Vermes, F. Millar, and M. Goodman, 3 vols. Edinburgh: T. and T. Clark.

Schur, N. (1989). *History of the Samaritans*. Frankfurt: Lang.

Seyrig, H. (1933). 'Antiquités syriennes', *Syria*, 14: 368–80.

Sheppard, A. R. R. (1980–1). 'Pagan Cults of Angels in Roman Asia Minor', *Talanta*, 12–13: 77–101.

Simon, M. (1972). 'Theos Hypsistos', in J. Bergman, K. Drynjeff, and H. Ringgren (eds.), *Ex orbe religionum: studia Geo Widengren*. Leiden: Brill, i. 372–85.

——(1976). 'Jupiter-Yahvé', *Numen*, 23: 40–66.

Sobernheim, M. (1905). *Palmyrenische Inschriften*, Mitteilungen der Vorderasiatischen Gesellschaft 10. Berlin.

Sourdel, D. (1952). *Les cultes du Hauran à l'époque romaine*. Paris: Imprimerie nationale.

Stein, M. (2001). 'Die Verehrung des Theos Hypsistos: ein allumfassender pagan-jüdischer Synkretismus?', *EA*, 33: 119–25.

Stern, E. (ed.) (1993). *The New Encyclopedia of Archaeological Excavations in the Holy Land*. Jerusalem: Israel Exploration Society.

Strobel, A. (1980). *Das heilige Land der Montanisten. Eine religionsgeographische Untersuchung*. Berlin: de Gruyter.

Taceva-Hitova, M. (1977). 'Dem Hypsistos geweihte Denkmäler in Thrakien', *Thracia*, 4: 278–81.

——(1978). 'Dem Hypsistos geweihte Denkmäler in den Balkanländern', *Balkan Studies*, 19: 59–75.

——(1983). *Eastern Cults in Moesia inferior and Thracia*, EPRO 95. Leiden: Brill.

Teixidor, J. (1977). *The Pagan God. Popular Religion in the Greco–Roman Near-East*. Princeton: Princeton University Press.

Thomas, Chr. M. (2004). 'The "Mountain Mother": The Other Anatolian Goddess at Ephesos', in G. Labarre (ed.), *Les cultes locaux dans les mondes grec et romain*. Paris: de Boccard, 249–62.

Thompson, H. A. (1936). 'Pnyx and Thesmophorion', *Hesperia*, 5: 151–200.

Trebilco, P. (1989). 'Paul and Silas—"Servants of the Most High God"', *Journal for the Study of the New Testament*, 36: 51–73.

Usener, H. (1929). *Götternamen*, 2nd edn. Bonn: Cohen.

Van Straten, F. T. (1981). 'Gifts for the Gods', in Versnel 1981a: 65–151.

Vernant, J.-P. (1980). *Myth and Society in Ancient Greece*. Brighton: Harvester; Atlantic Highlands, NJ: Humanities (French original, 1974).

——(1983). *Myth and Thought among the Greeks*. London and Boston: Routledge and Kegan Paul (French original, 1965).

Vermaseren, M. J. (1956). *Corpus Inscriptionum et Monumentorum Religionis Mithrae*. Leiden: Brill.

Versnel, H. S. (ed.) (1981a). *Faith, Hope and Worship. Aspects of Religious Mentality in the Ancient World*. Leiden: Brill.

——(1981b). 'Religious Mentality in Ancient Prayer', in Versnel 1981a: 1–64.

Versnel, H. S. (1990). *Inconsistencies in Greek and Roman Religion* i. Ter Unus. *Isis, Dionysos, Hermes. Three Studies in Henotheism*, Studies in Greek and Roman Religion 6. Leiden: Brill.

——(1991). 'Beyond Cursing: The Appeal to Justice in Judicial Prayers', in C. A. Faraone and D. Obbink (eds.), *Magika Hiera. Ancient Greek Magic and Religion.* New York: Oxford University Press, 60–95.

Veyne, P. (1990). 'Images de divinités tenant une phiale ou patère. La libation comme "rite de passage" et non pas offrande', *Métis*, 5: 17–28.

Weinreich, O. (1912). '*Θεοὶ Ἐπήκοοι*', *Athenische Mitteilungen*, 37: 1–68, repr. in his *Ausgewählte Schriften.* Amsterdam: Grüner, 1969–79, i. 131–95.

Welles, C. B. (1938). 'The Inscriptions', in C. H. Kraeling (ed.), *Gerasa, City of the Decapolis.* New Haven CT: American School of Oriental Research, 355–494.

Wischmeyer, W. (2005). 'Theos Hypsistos. Neues zu einer alten Debatte', *Zeitschrift für Antikes Christentum*, 9: 149–68.

Woodward, A. M. and Hobling, M. B. (1923–5). 'Excavations at Sparta, 1924–25', *Annual of the British School at Athens*, 26: 116–310.

——Robert, L., and Woodward, J. M. (1927-8). 'Excavations at Sparta, 1924–28', *Annual of the British School at Athens*, 29: 1–107.

6

On the Uses and Disadvantages of Divination

Oracles and their Literary Representations in the Time of the Second Sophistic[1]

Andreas Bendlin

ON SPEAKING GODS AND SILENT ORACLES:
AN INTRODUCTION

Opramoas of Rhodiapolis in southeast Lycia was a rich and pious man. The inscription adorning his tomb dates from the second third of the second century CE and is an impressive collage of texts from provincial and local decrees, of letters by proconsuls and emperors. It

---

[1] The phrase 'Uses and disadvantages of divination' translates the original title's 'Vom Nutzen und Nachteil der Divination', which is an allusion to Nietzsche's second 'Unzeitgemäße Betrachtung', *Vom Nutzen und Nachtheil der Historie für das Leben* (Leipzig 1874). That allusion's purpose is not primarily to draw attention to, or even endorse, Nietzsche's somewhat crude attack on contemporary historicism. I was rather thinking of Michel Foucault's creative reception of Nietzsche's essay (in, e.g., Foucault 1977) in an attempt to explore the interdiscursive relation between historical practice and discourse, and to demonstrate how tradition, knowledge, or power influence the formation of this relation. Earlier versions of this paper were presented in Eisenach in November 2003 and in Leipzig in June 2004. I would like to thank the participants on those occasions for the active discussion and their comments; also, Jörg Rüpke and Katharina Waldner for their support. For this version, I would like to thank Henry Heitmann-Gordon for the difficult task of translation and Richard Gordon for corrections, suggestions, and advice.

elaborates on his honours, offices, and euergetic philanthropy for the *poleis* of the Lycian alliance, whose Lyciarch and high priest—and thus also the provincial priest of the imperial cult—Opramoas was, at some time between 125 and 141 CE.[2] After his term of office had ended, Opramoas remained a benefactor of the Lycian *poleis*. In the coastal town of Patara alone, which is one of the most prominent towns of the Lycian alliance and where he was granted citizenship, he financed the *panegyris* (festival) for Apollo Patroös—the god whom the ancestors had already worshipped above all others—and the emperor in his function as agonothete, once his obligations towards the Lycian *koinon* had come to an end.[3]

Shortly after that, probably in the year 141 CE, a strong earthquake shook the area and again Opramoas donated copious amounts of money: in Patara alone he paid the total costs of 40,000 denarii for a double stoa at the harbour (Kokkinia 2000: No. 60, XVII E 13–F 14; No. 64, XVIII G 3–6; Balland 1981: nos. 67, 12–14; see pp. 185f., 191f.). But he evidently did even more: in the context of this earthquake, 'forefatherly' Apollo suddenly started giving prophecies again, the oracular shrine having been largely inactive for some time.[4] The inhabitants seized the opportunity and asked Opramoas for more demonstrative proof of his previously displayed piety by renewing (ἀνανεῶσαι) the time-honoured oracle in the town (the text calls it an

---

[2] In the following, the Opramoas inscription will be cited using the edition by Kokkinia 2000. Other euergetic deeds by Opramoas not listed in this inscription can be found in Balland 1981: 173–224. Lyciarchy and priesthood (ἀρχιερωσύνη/ ἀρχιερεὺς τῶν Σεβαστῶν) of Opramoas date between 125 and 141 CE: for the text, see Kokkinia 2000: No. 31, VIII B–IX B with Wörrle 1988: 35–43 (dating the honours to 136 or 137 CE); Kokkinia 2000: 206–11, 214–17 (without a date).

[3] Kokkinia 2000: No. 31, VIII F 2f., IX B 12f. (*agonothesia*); No. 54 XIII C 6–12; No. 60, XVII B 1f.; No. 64 XVIII F 9–12. It has repeatedly been suggested that the sanctuary of Apollo Patroös in Patara was of particular relevance to the Lycian *koinon* (cf. Wörrle 1988: 187–90), which might explain the attachment the former high functionary of the alliance felt towards the god and his oracular shrine.

[4] One can deduce a connection between the earthquake and the revival of the oracle's activity from Kokkinia 2000: No. 64 XVIII F 13–G 3 (Kokkinia's commentary on this passage does not yield much information): The sum of 20,000 denarii which is listed here as given to the town of Patara after the earthquake exactly corresponds to the amount of money Opramoas gave for the oracle and a *panegyris*. The oracle of Apollo in Patara was still active in the first half of the first century CE: *TAM* II no. 420; Robert 1980: 402f.; Parke 1985: 85–193, especially 189–93.

ἀρχαῖον μαντεῖον) and the traditional (πατρική) *panegyris*. Opramoas proceeded to donate another 20,000 denarii. It is remarkable how often the texts of the Opramoas inscription link his beneficial deeds for Patara after the earthquake and the moment the god and his oracle began to speak again to the people.[5]

The Apolline *logos* (response) of the year 141 is not reported by the Opramoas inscription. Did the oracle provide the people of Patara with an answer, when they asked about the reasons for this natural catastrophe? Or did the god volunteer this information of his own accord, without even having been asked? And what were the contents of his statement? Might he have reprimanded the town for neglecting his cult and insisted on being treated with all due respect? Was the *panegyris* intended to mollify Apollo and prevent further catastrophes like the earthquake of 141?

Apollo's oracles were often consulted after earthquakes. After an earthquake in Tralleis in the Meander valley in the early third century CE, the town dedicated an altar in a grove to Poseidon Seisichthon the 'Earth-shaker'. On being asked by the local priest of Zeus, the Delphic Apollo explained the earthquake by a long-standing grudge that Zeus held against the town. The god recommends the priest to perform un-bloody sacrifices, prayers, and hymns for Poseidon and choruses for the Earth-shaker and Zeus in order to appease the angry god. There was also an altar for Poseidon Seisichthon in Didyma. Could

---

[5] The texts are: Kokkinia 2000: No. 56, XIV E 6–F 2:... πάλιν ἀρξ[αμέ]νου μετὰ πολὺν [σιωπ]ῆς χρόνον θεσπ[ίζει]ν τοῦ θεοῦ τάχα κα[τά τε] τὴν εὐσέβειαν [τοῦ ἀ]νδρὸς ἡδομ[ένη τε] τῷ καιρῷ ἐπεδ[εήθη ἡ] Παταρέων [πόλις τὸ] μαντεῖ[ον καὶ τὴν] πατρικ[ὴν πανήγυρι]ν [ἀνανεῶσαι... (At the time the god was beginning to prophesy after a long silence, quickly, through this man's piety and through their pleasure at the event, the city of Patara was required to renew the oracle and their traditional festival.); No. 54, XIII C 13–D 1: εἴς τε τὴν τῶν Σεβαστῶν εὐσέ[βειαν] (...and to the piety of the *Augusti*) [These are probably taxes payable to Rome: Kokkinia 2000: 121] καὶ ἐπὶ [τὸ ἀ]ρχαῖον αὐτῶν καὶ ἀψευδὲς [μαντεῖ]ον (and to their time-honoured and undeceiving oracle...); also see No. 60, XVII E 10–13; No. 64, XVIII G 1–6. On dating the earthquake, see Kokkinia 2000, 168f. The *panegyris* mentioned above cannot be the one financed by Opramoas immediately after his Lyciarchy, but must be a different one; this is evident from No. 56 XIV E 15; 54 XIII D 1f. (Kokkinia's commentary does not elaborate on this). Cf. Balland 1981: no. 67, 15; see p. 186: this inscription lists later euergetic deeds by Opramoas and thus also higher sums of money. It lists an expense of 22,000 denarii for a *panegyris*, but is probably referring to the second agonothesy that became necessary due to the oracle.

its construction be due to a local oracle given by Apollo after an earthquake? Already after a minor quake in the second century BCE, Apollo urged Didyma to placate Poseidon Asphaleios the 'Securer' with bull-sacrifices and prayers in order to prevent a heavier earthquake.[6]

Even the honorary decrees that adorn Opramoas' tomb reflect how important for his contemporaries was the moment when the Apollo of Patara began to speak again. These decrees represent the political elite of Lycia. Thus, they express an evaluation of the matter representative of the political public: for them, the oracle of Patara is an undoubted source of divination. In the inscription, the authority of the oracle's prophecies bases itself on the great age of the shrine, which was merely being renewed in the middle of the second century.

Another point is that, according to the inscription, the oracle explicitly speaks 'without lies and deception': it is $\dot{a}\psi\epsilon\upsilon\delta\acute{\epsilon}\varsigma$. This adjective is already used in Greek literature from the archaic and early classical periods to legitimate the authority of oracles and of their god Apollo. Also in imperial times, the worshippers accept Apollo's prophecies as $\dot{a}\psi\epsilon\upsilon\delta\acute{\epsilon}\varsigma$: for example, the people of Rhodes dedicated a statue of their own Rhodian Apollo to the oracle-giving god of Didyma, because he had given them truthful prophecies from his 'deceit-free tripod' in the past.[7]

Did all members of the provincial upper class in Lycia share this opinion? The Lycian town of Oenoanda, which is about seventy kilometres northeast and inland of Patara, also benefitted from Opramoas' donations. Our sources suggest that an inhabitant of Oenoanda called Diogenes was probably a contemporary of Opromoas. This man had an inscription put up on the wall of a portico (F 3 Smith)—the southern stoa of the old agora, which the archaeologists call the esplanade, in the

---

[6] *IK* 36. 1 (Tralleis): No. 1 = Merkelbach and Stauber 1998–2002: i. 201, no. 02/02/01; Didyma: *IDidyma* No. 133 and No. 132 = Merkelbach and Stauber 1998–2002: i. 78f., no. 01/19/02; Parke 1985: 66f.; Fontenrose 1988: 145f., 189–91. Another example from Kos dates from the beginning of the second century BCE: *IKosS*, ED 178a (A), lines 31–5. On Poseidon's epithets *asphaleios* and *seisichthon* in the context of earthquakes, see Mylonopoulos 2003: 376f., 385, 391–5.

[7] $\dot{A}\psi\epsilon\upsilon\delta\grave{\epsilon}\varsigma$ [$\mu\alpha\nu\tau\epsilon\hat{\iota}$]$o\nu$: Kokkinia 2000: No. 54, XIII D 1. Didyma: *IDidyma* No. 83 = Merkelbach and Stauber 1998–2000: i. 94, 01/19/20: . . . $\dot{a}\psi\epsilon\acute{\upsilon}\sigma\tau\omega\nu$ . . . $\dot{\epsilon}\kappa$ $\tau\rho\iota\pi\acute{o}\delta\omega\nu$. Cf. LSJ s. v. $\dot{a}\psi\epsilon\upsilon\delta\acute{\eta}\varsigma$.

northern part of the town. This inscription promotes Epicurean philosophy as a remedy for salvation: with this philosophical text (γραφή) Diogenes wants to confront his contemporaries with the perversity of their previously held views and supply means of attaining perfect happiness (εὐδαιμονία), which he calls the true *telos* (goal) of human nature.[8]

It is most certainly not a coincidence that Diogenes chose for his plan precisely that kind of building—namely a stoa—from which derives the name of the philosophical school that was vehemently opposed to the Epicureans. The public presentation of the text on the walls of a portico on the old agora also implies that it was addressed to the political public of the town. But the inscription itself does not address the entire public assembled on the agora: the primary addressees are those who are 'well prepared' (εὐσύγκριτοι), those who are capable of engaging themselves in philosophy, not only as far as their intellectual abilities are concerned, but also their natural dispositions.[9]

Whether Diogenes also financed the building of this stoa, or whether another member of his family was responsible for its construction must remain unclear. Diogenes' inscription misses out the passage, so common in public inscriptions, about the relation to the institutions of the town of the text and the monument bearing it—even though he was part of one of the politically most influential families in Oenoanda. Was the author identical to Diogenes the third, great grandson of Moles, who was part of an embassy from Oenoanda to the Roman governor in 125 and applied for the release of the serving agonothete from his (other) duties and for the exemption of the market from taxation during the musical (and also gymnastic) contests founded by C. Iulius Demosthenes? Or was he only a close relative of this envoy? This cannot be ascertained, but the inscription detailing Demosthenes' agonistic foundation and Diogenes' Epicurean inscription are so similar in form

[8] Edited, translated, and commented by Smith 1993. On the intentions behind the inscription, see Diogenes F 3–2; 29–30 Smith (Smith 2003: 64 shows that F 2 belongs after F 3).

[9] Scholz 2003: 213–18 doubts the significance of this statement on the basis of a comparison with Diogenes F 30 Smith (... τοῖς στόμα κόσμιοις) and reduces the number of the inscription's addressees to 'those who had enjoyed the necessary education', as if education was the essential criterion here.

and workmanship that one can probably date the former also to the first half of the second century CE.

What we can say for sure, is that the author of the Epicurean inscription describes himself as an old and ailing man who, in accordance with Epicurean doctrine, does not participate in public political life—or has ceased to do so. We can infer that he must have had the necessary financial means as well as the political influence to have a monumental inscription put up in the most public space in Oenoanda. The original length and size of this inscription must have surpassed not only Demosthenes' foundation inscription but also the inscription on Opramoas' tomb in Rhodiapolis.[10]

Diogenes' original epitome of Epicurean philosophy may have been subdivided into seven parts: the first part was a summary of Epicurean physics, which was situated roughly at eye-level of the reader. Below this summary, there was an account of ethics. Above these two passages of text was—probably still legible for the reader—a third passage containing two philosophical letters from Diogenes to his friends, which imitated the style of Epicurus' letters of teaching. Even higher up, written upwards and in larger letters, was a fourth part which listed Epicurean maxims, a fifth with instructions for families and friends and a sixth with more of Diogenes' and (allegedly) Epicurus' writings. At the top of the inscription and probably hard to read despite the large lettering, a seventh and final part concluded the inscription, which dealt with the Epicurean view of old age—appropriate to the life situation of its author.[11]

---

[10] Smith (1993: 35–48 and 2003: 48–50) discusses the dating of the Diogenes-inscription and the identity of its author. The dating to the time of Demosthenes' inscription is also accepted in his edition by Wörrle 1988: 72, n. 131. On topographical context and the original size of the inscription, see especially Smith 1993: 54–6, 76–108. Due to its nature as an exclusively Epicurean discourse, the Diogenes inscription does not list any public offices held by its author. However we cannot exclude that he had held public offices or religious positions in his life—although the inscription does explicitly state that Diogenes was not politically active at the time the inscription was set up.

[11] See for example Smith 1993: 76–108. The new discoveries we can expect might contribute to a modification of minor details or substantial parts of this reconstruction, as only a small part of this text has been found so far; cf. Smith 2003: 45, 157. P. Gordon (1996: 66–93) hypothesises that the letter 'to his mother', which is part of the sixth group under Epicurus' name, dates from the first or second century CE and might have been written by Diogenes himself.

Criticism of mantic practices appears both in the passage about physics and in the one on ethics. Diogenes deals with two areas of divination: dreams and oracles. The tract on physics deals with dreams (ὄνειροι), in the context of the status of the mental reception of sensations, and states that they were neither sent by gods, nor fulfilled warning, affirming, or instructing functions. Diogenes attacks Democritus for his opinion that the objects that appear in our visions are capable of their own sensations, possess reason, or have the ability to speak (προσλαλεῖν) to human beings. Accordingly, the gods, whom the objects in our dreams represent, are not capable of communicating with humans about the future through dreams. The Epicurean view acknowledges the ability of the human imagination to create a mental image of the gods in dreams—one that may even be representative of an external divine reality. But the construction of this mental image is neither intended by the gods nor controlled by them in order to aid mantic communication, but is rather an accidental by-product of the fact that all things, even the gods, generate images, εἴδωλα, which the soul can pick up (Diogenes F 9–10; 43; 125 Smith, with Smith 1993: 446–51; P. Gordon 1996: 116–22).

Beyond the arguments in philosophical circles, this criticism also addresses the contemporary and widely accepted idea that dreams were a preferred medium of divine communication, which simply had to be interpreted by way of oneiromantics. The Epicurean criticism problematizes the epistemic basis of this idea: according to their doctrine, the interpretation of dreams is based on the false assumption that dreams mediate divine messages, even though in reality the dreamer merely receives images of the objects. Even if dreams seem to suggest 'meaningfulness' beyond the plain presentation of their objects—(underlying messages that the dream interpreter claims to be able to interpret), this suggestive power only proves how constructed meaning is in the material world. So dreams—and this must have been the unsettling message for the contemporary readers—are definitely not media for the gods' communication with humans.[12]

---

[12] Incapability of oneiromantics to interpret dreams correctly: Diogenes F 24 Smith. Cf. also P. Gordon 1996: 122–4; Smith 2003: 85–7. On the great importance of dreams as media of divine communication and the importance of dream interpretation for Diogenes' contemporaries, see Lane Fox 1986: 149–67; Harris 2003: 31–3.

The same must be true of oracles: their ambiguity (ἀμφιβολία) and obscurity especially, which Diogenes emphasizes, allow us to recognize that they cannot be directly communicated messages from a divine object existing outside the world. This ambiguity leads human beings into calamity, as Diogenes illustrates with an example drawn from popular legend. But the basic principles of Epicurean philosophy state that such an outcome is neither intended nor caused by the gods, because they live outside the material world without influencing or directing it in the sense that divine providence (πρόνοια) suggests. As a consequence, the gods cannot be, nor want to be, the source of oracular *logoi*.[13]

This position is elaborated on in the passage on Epicurean ethics: the accidental fulfilment of a prophecy cannot prove the validity of the divination itself, because this supposed argument is disproved by the fact that other prophecies derived from mantic practices are not fulfilled. So Diogenes' refutation of divination starts by deconstructing mantic practice as a false interpretation of mentally perceived images of the divine. This leads to the general Epicurean criticism of divine providence—a concept allegedly manifested in these images and one that other philosophical schools supported. The criticism of divination in the Diogenes-inscription ends by stating that it has freed humanity from believing in predetermined action and fear of god: 'If divination can be excluded, what other proof for fate (εἱμαρμένη) remains?'[14]

This deconstruction of divination does not exhaust itself in internal philosophical propaedeutics, but becomes part of a larger social discourse, whose author, as a true Epicurean, repudiates public political activity yet at the same time uses the public space for this inscription (Diogenes F 3 Smith; cf. F 30).

...Although I, my fellow citizens, am not politically active (οὐ πολ-
[ει]τευόμενος), I say things in this inscription like someone who takes

---

[13] Ambiguity of oracles: Diogenes F 23 Smith. On Diogenes' image of god, see also F 15–22 and NF 126–7 (= Smith 2003: 74–84).

[14] Diogenes F 53–4 Smith. This argument is supported by the disproval of divine providence in NF 126–7 Smith on the basis of the theodicy-argument, meaning that the gods could not prevent evil, let alone determine the world positively.

political action (καθάπερ πρ[άτ]των),[15] in order to try and show that what is useful for our nature, namely the absence of confusion (ἀταραξία), is the same for each and every one of us. (...) I wanted...to aid those well prepared (εὐσύγκριτοι). (...) For the majority is mutually afflicted with a false view (ψευδοδοξία) of their actions, like a collective epidemic, and their number is ever increasing (because they imitate each other, they all infect one another like sheep); and it is also justified to help future generations (for they too belong to us, even though they have not been born yet); and it is also philanthropic (φιλάνθρωπον) to assist the foreigners who come to us. Because (only) the medium of the inscription can reach the majority, it was my intention to propagate the remedy that brings salvation publicly by using the stoa.

In its claim to serve as a public political document, the Diogenes-inscription not only addresses the contemporary accusation that the philosophical discourse is unable to produce practical instructions which could be applied to communal social action; it is also in competition, given its place on the old agora, with honorary inscriptions and decrees, with honorary statues for magistrates and priests, for benefactors and winners of athletic and musical competitions, like the one founded by Demosthenes.

But the expectations with which Diogenes' contemporaries approached a public monumental inscription in the stoa are subverted by the form and content of the inscription: it makes no mention whatever either of the magistrates or the council, of other *poleis*, or the provincial *koinon*, of the Roman governor, or of the emperor in Rome. It lists no offices, euergetic gestures, or honours. The only persons who appear in the inscription are Diogenes himself (he does not even mention his family, as we would typically expect), Epicurus, and their philosophical opponents. The world the inscription presents is not the narrow politically defined society of Oenoanda; it is addressed to a cosmopolitan readership—fellow citizens, future generations, and foreigners—which extends significantly beyond that community.

We can assume that Diogenes' claim that the inscription would benefit everyone only reached the contemporary audience in an

---

[15] Πολιτεύεσθαι and πράττειν describe political activity; see Smith 1993: 438. On the central importance of πολιτεύεσθαι for Opramoas' self-perception in his inscription, see Kokkinia 2000, index s.v.

adulterated fashion. On the one hand, he argues that his inscription, even though he is only addressing those well prepared ($\epsilon\dot{v}\sigma\acute{v}\gamma\kappa\rho\iota\tau\iota$), is intended to have a general philanthropic effect. He employs a term that was frequently used in the euergetic culture of the second and third centuries CE in the context of the question concerning the individual's social responsibility: Demosthenes, for example, also claims to exhibit $\phi\iota\lambda\alpha\nu\theta\rho\omega\pi\epsilon\acute{\iota}\alpha$ (philanthropy) in founding his musical contest; Opramoas' contemporaries also valued his beneficial deeds as proof of his philanthropic attitude.[16]

But in spite of his use of these elements of euergetic language and the philanthropic offer of *ataraxia* (serenity) as a form of release from fear of death and god, Diogenes' inscription contains a truly subversive element. By saying that the establishment of theatres, [...][17] and baths, and the distribution of scents and perfumes (probably in the context of bathing) may well give the masses pleasure, but certainly do not provide true delight to the philosopher, Diogenes dismisses the sort of euergetic gestures his contemporaries liked to make and denies the validity of the objects of euergetism so desirable to local society. He dismisses the contemporary system of euergetism of which Opramoas' activity all over Lycia and Demosthenes' in Oenoanda are prime examples. Diogenes also disapproves of divination as a form of communication between gods and humans; he questions the theological validity and justification of the oracles (if not their very existence) from within the public sphere in which contemporary divination operates. Moreover, Diogenes is also implicitly and concretely

---

[16] On $\phi\iota\lambda\alpha\nu\theta\rho\omega\pi\acute{\iota}\alpha$, see the Demosthenes-inscription, l.122 and Wörrle 1988: 244; the Opramoas-inscription: Kokkinia 2000: II D 5. E 13f. XX D 7. F 14–G 1. XIII F 1 and Balland 1981: 223 with n. 379.

[17] This part of the text is incomplete: Diogenes F 2, III 7–14:... $\tau\hat{\eta}[\varsigma\ \tau\hat{\omega}\ \ddot{o}\nu\tau\iota$ $\tau\epsilon\iota]\mu\acute{\iota}\alpha\varsigma\ \chi\alpha\rho\hat{\alpha}[\varsigma...\theta\acute{\epsilon}\alpha]\tau\rho\alpha\ \kappa\alpha\grave{\iota}\ [\ ...\ ]\ \beta\alpha\lambda\alpha\nu\epsilon\hat{\iota}\alpha\ [\kappa\alpha\grave{\iota}\ \mu\acute{v}\rho\alpha]\ \kappa\alpha\grave{\iota}\ \dot{\alpha}\lambda\epsilon\acute{\iota}\mu[\alpha\tau\alpha\ \ddot{\alpha}\ \delta\grave{\eta}$ $\kappa\alpha]\tau\alpha\lambda\epsilon\lambda o\acute{\iota}\pi[\alpha\mu\epsilon\nu\ \tau o\hat{\iota}\varsigma]\ \pi\lambda\acute{\eta}\theta\epsilon\sigma\iota\nu...$ (of pleasure, expensive in reality, [...]theatres and [...] the baths [and perfumes] and unguents, which we have left to the multitude). It is tempting to supply $\dot{\alpha}[\gamma\hat{\omega}\nu\epsilon\varsigma\ \kappa\alpha\grave{\iota}]$ (i.e. competitions and...) after $\theta\acute{\epsilon}\alpha]\tau\rho\alpha\ \kappa\alpha\grave{\iota}$ (theatres and...). The importance of competitions, especially of athletic ones, in the 'culture of the second sophistic' is emphasized by Van Nijf 2005. The critique of this culture of athletic competitions in contemporary literature is far from uncommon (cf. the detailed discussion by Koenig 2005); but the critique's formulation in the communicative medium of a public monumental inscription is exceptional. On the concept of 'the culture of the Second Sophistic' and on the function of these contests, see further below, 216–9.

criticising the oracle of Apollo that existed in Oenoanda itself.[18] If Diogenes' inscription proves that the oracles are really mute, how can the god possibly give prophecies in Delphi, Didyma, Claros, or Oenoanda? And how can he suddenly begin to speak to the people again in Patara?

Nevertheless, the gap between Diogenes' Epicurean criticism on the one hand and the support of the oracles by the political elites on the other can certainly be bridged. At some time in the second or early third century CE a man called Aurelius Belius Philippus was the leader (διάδοχος) of the Epicurean circle in Syrian Apamea and at the same time held a priesthood at the local oracle of Zeus Belos; his theophoric name almost seems to suggest a relation of some kind. At roughly the same time, an Epicurean philosopher called Philidas held the office of *prophētēs* at the oracular temple of Apollo at Didyma on the coast of Asia Minor. As Epicureans, these two men should really have disapproved of the view of divine truth implied by the oracles. How did they behave when, as religious functionaries, they were required to represent in public the oracle's claim to divine truth?[19] What kind of features must the cultural and communicative space of the second and third centuries CE have had to enable deep veneration of oracle-shrines and their gods, such as we find in Opramoas' inscription, to exist side by side with contemporary criticism by a Diogenes? What sort of communicative space was it where men like Aurelius Belius Philippus and Philidas could epitomize the debate about the uses and disadvantages of divination? What are the functions of temple-divination in this communicative space? What are the functions of philosophical discourse concerning such divination? The intention of the following essay is to answer these questions.

---

[18] Cf. *SEG* 50: no. 1354 bis (second or early third century CE) as proof of the existence of a priest of the oracle of Apollo in Oenoanda and the functions of this local oracle.

[19] Aur. Belius Philippus: Smith 1996; Philidas: *IDidyma* no. 285. Smith 1996: 127–30 also mentions Heraclitus of Rhodiapolis and Rhodes, an Epicurean philosopher, doctor, and (not surprisingly for a physician) priest of Asclepius and Hygieia (*TAM* ii. 351 no. 910), as well as T. Claudius Lepidus from Amastris, ἐπιστάτης τῆς πόλεως and ἀρχιερεύς τοῦ Πόντου (i.e. high priest of the provincial assembly [*koinon*] and thus of the local imperial cult): *IGR* 3 no. 88. He is characterized as a leading Epicurean by Lucian, *Alexander* 25.

FATE AND PROVIDENCE: ON A PHILOSOPHICAL DISCOURSE OF THE ROMAN IMERIAL PERIOD

Between 198 and 209 CE, the *Augusti* Septimius Severus and Caracalla appointed Alexander of Aphrodisias to one of the philosophical 'professorships' that Marcus Aurelius had founded in Athens in 176 CE. In this position, Alexander was to represent the Peripatetic (or Aristotelian) school vis-à-vis the representatives of the Platonic, Stoic, and Epicurean philosophy.[20] The newly appointed philosopher dedicated a text to the two *Augusti* in Rome that discusses the Aristotelian position on fate (Περὶ εἱμαρμένης, *On Fate*).

The question of the importance of fate for human life is highly relevant to the plausibility and validity of divination in general and of dreams and oracles in particular; we have already noted this traditional connection in Diogenes' Epicurean epitome. Characteristic of Alexander's Peripatetic position is that he recommends his readers to deal with the prophecies of (self-proclaimed) diviners sensibly—as would ὁ φρόνιμος (Alexander, *On Fate* 29, p. 200, 2–12 Bruns).

...a sensible man does none of the things he chooses to do because he is forced to (κατηναγκασμένως), but rather in such a manner that he is able freely to decide himself not to do some of those things. For in order to show that he is free in his actions, the sensible man may sometimes find it sensible not to do what should be done rationally, if some seer predicts that he will do it because it is necessary (ἐξ ἀνάγκης). Owing to the fact that those men who call themselves seers also suspect this, they do not give any such predictions to those men who could disprove them—avoiding an anticipated refutation—and, in the same way as they take care not to define the point in time when their prophecies shall be fulfilled, because that could be easily refuted, they also take care not to make predictions to those people who are instantly capable of doing the opposite of the prophecy.

---

[20] The dates given are based on Caracalla's installation as Augustus, which took place either in the autumn of 197 or January 198, and that of Geta, which probably took place in the autumn of 209. The assumption of a terminus ante quem of 211 (e.g. Sharples 2001: 513 with n. 3) assumes without justification in the text that Geta would have had to be removed from the list of addressees on his *damnatio memoriae* in December 211. On the foundation and character of the 'professorships' instituted by Marcus Aurelius, see Glucker 1978: 145–58; obviously this was not an institutionalized faculty of philosophy as they exist today.

This postulation of individual freedom of decision is combined with criticism of other philosophers, who were in favour of a more deterministic view: Alexander's polemic was probably directed at a contemporary Stoic position on the subject (Sharples 2001: 517–20). He also attacks divination itself. The primary object of his criticism is the figure of the seer (Greek μάντις, Latin *vates*), who traditionally had a bad press in literary discourse and through his actions openly discredits the principle of necessarily predetermined action. Furthermore, however, Alexander, unlike the Stoics, also attacks mantic practice in general, because it is an instance of this dubious principle. For a prophecy's claim to truth and usefulness is based on the necessity of its fulfilment, meaning that it has to happen on the basis of certain natural preconditions, which exclude the possibility of the opposite happening. But this principle is refuted by the fact that the *phronimos* is able to falsify a prophecy made by a diviner, because he can prove that the prophecy's fulfilment is merely based on contingency—meaning that this prophecy might not fulfil itself as the seer said, but might take a completely different shape.[21]

The Aristotelian background of Alexander's criticism of divination consists of two presuppositions. The first is that all natural events, and thus the course of nature itself, contain an element of contingency. The second is that things that are impossible by nature are also impossible for the gods: even the gods cannot make two times two equal five or turn back the hands of time. But Alexander seems to be the first Peripatetic philosopher to draw the obvious conclusion from these axioms as far as divine providence and the uses and disadvantages of divination are concerned (Alexander, *On Fate* 29–31, p. 199. 25–204. 5 Bruns). If the nature of an action or a thing contains the possibility of it being or not being, meaning that its development is contingent, then it is impossible for the gods to know for sure whether this action or thing will or will not be. In other words: divine as well as human prophecy of an action or a thing in the sense of necessarily predetermined fulfilmentmust presuppose the negation of contingency, the latter being an axiom of Aristotelian philosophy. But maintaining this axiom

---

[21] Alexander, *On Fate* 9, p. 175, 5–7 Bruns; Sharples 2001: 574–7. In Stoic theology the mantic specialist and not the mantic system itself is to blame for the failure of divination: *Stoicorum Veterum Fragmenta* ii. 1210.

makes every prophecy of a necessarily predetermined event impossible. If things do not necessarily come into being, then neither gods nor humans can accomplish the impossible feat of making something necessary that is not necessary. For both groups it becomes impossible to know and predict the future in oracles or dreams, because its concrete realization is contingent, not bound to come into being.

However, Alexander also claims that he disavows neither divine providence nor the practice of divination itself. He discusses the question of the use and disadvantage of divination by using the traditional example of the Delphic oracle, whose prophecy not only destroyed the mythical king Laius, his wife Jocasta, and their son Oedipus, but also plunged the whole city of Thebes into chaos. Confronted with such an example, would it not be more pious to deny divine providence in the manner of the Epicureans than to accept a misunderstood Stoic view of providence which implies that the gods, who are responsible for good, must also cause evil?[22] Alexander's solution to this dilemma, which is of course central to theodicy, consists of the assumption of a limited, biologistic 'natural teleology' according to which not everything that comes into being, and thus contains the possibility of causing further events, necessarily realizes this capacity; it can also perish without using its potential.[23] Alexander's text *On Providence* also defends the Peripatetic position against the (Middle-)Platonists by arguing that providence is only concerned with the preservation of the species in the sublunar world, but does not influence events in the lives of individuals.[24] On these

---

[22] Alexander, *On Fate* 31, p. 202. 5–204. 5 Bruns. The Laius-oracle that Alexander chooses as his example is discussed again and again in this philosophical debate about fate in the Imperial period, ever since the Stoic philosopher Chrysippus used it in the third century BCE as an example for the unresolved tension between the necessity of a prophecy to be fulfilled and Laius' subjective responsibility: *Stoicorum Veterum Fragmenta* ii. 937, 943f., 956f.; Zierl 1995: 214–18. Later philosophers criticized Chrysippus' analysis as insufficient.

[23] Alexander, *On Fate* 23, p. 193. 4–21 Bruns; cf. Alexander, *On Fate* 6, p. 171. 7–11 Bruns. This argument reappears in Alexander, *Mantissa* p. 185. 33–186 Bruns in a different form to support the advantages of divination: the mantic practice predicts a probable outcome and allows the human to take certain preventive measures, without giving a full guarantee for the fulfilment of the prophecy.

[24] Alexander, *On Providence* p. 57. 11–67. 13 Ruland. The Middle-Platonist position postulates that three areas are affected by providence: the first is the supralunar world and the other two are located in the sublunar world, where providence

assumptions, believing in the effectiveness of divination brings no disadvantages, even for the *phronimos*; there is even a degree of utility (χρήσιμόν τι) in divination in general and dreams and oracles in particular, because they communicate a hitherto unrecognized possibility of avoiding evil and attaining good. So the oracle only has the status of a conditional prophecy[25] that expresses the possibility of a future event, which is however subject to contingency.

On Fate and *On Providence* thus formulate an intermediate position. On the one hand they soften the Stoic (and Middle-Platonist) account of regulative providence by exempting the actions of individuals from its influence on the sublunar world, on the other they disavow the Epicureans' and Cynics' radical rejection of providence. But why was this issue (which Aristotle himself only discussed in a diffuse and rather inconsistent manner) interesting for Alexander, the 'professor' of Aristotelian philosophy? A partial answer to this question can be found in the desire of the Peripatetic school to offer the people a programme that could answer questions of ethical and political relevance for the individual outside academic discourse (Alexander, *On Fate* 39, p. 212. 5–18 Bruns):

... If we cultivate our opinions on the basis of [Aristotle's doctrine], we will demonstrate our piety to the gods by thanking them for the good things that we have already received and pray for further blessings on the assumption that they are free in their decision whether to give or not to give. We will be grateful to you and rulers similar to you, because you do for us what your own decisions tell you, because your decisions are based on choosing the better thing to do and evaluating it sensibly and not on the basis of preformed principles, which you are compelled to obey wherever they may lead you. But we will also strive for virtue, because we can decide freely whether we want to become better or worse; only the individual can decide freely about what he is able to do or not do ...

Believing in gods whose actions are subject to limits is not true piety. The gods can freely decide whether to execute their actions or not.

---

conditions the species and also individual action: [Plutarch], *On Fate* 572F; Apuleius, *On Plato* 96. 9f. Cf. Sharples 2002: 30–6.

[25]   The argument of an anonymous Middle-Platonist philosopher in [Plutarch] *On Fate* 11. 574E goes in a similar direction, when he says that prophecies only express a probable future.

But Alexander does not consider the possibility that they are free to do ill. In principle, humans have the same freedom, they are 'masters' of their decisions, just like the gods (Alexander uses the term κύριοι for both groups, humans and gods alike). The only difference is that they have the possibility to choose evil over good.

But what about the two *Augusti*? They also make their decisions freely and choose good deeds just like the gods, because they are themselves gods already. Accordingly, Alexander dedicates this pre-liminary offering (ἀπαρχή), the text *On Fate*, to them as a votive (ἀνάθημα), because he is not able to go to Rome himself to sacrifice in person in order to thank the two *Augusti* as gods (θεοί) for the good they have done him.[26] On the one hand, this metaphorical imagery of preliminary offerings and votives constructs a relationship of giving and taking, an unequal and asymmetrical relationship. The metaphor gains further relevance if we consider the political back-ground of the time: it is no longer the formerly glorious city of Athens that receives gifts from its tributary allies. On the contrary, these gifts are now being sent from Athens to Rome.

On the other hand, *On Fate* is a kind of imperial *speculum regis* that thematises the constantly discussed relationship between philosopher and ruler (or on a more abstract level, the relationship between 'intel-lect' and 'power') and insists upon the independence of philosophical discourse from the political system and its right to free speech (παρρησία).[27] But the *Augusti* are not only addressed as well-educated amateurs of philosophical disputation. By placing the good emperors on the same level as gods—at least as far as their free decision to choose good deeds is concerned—Alexander also establishes a standard for an emperor's behaviour, because if an emperor were freely to choose evil,

---

[26] Alexander, *On Fate* 1, p. 164. 3–13 Bruns. Plutarch already applies this meta-phorical concept of the preliminary offering to his gift of several of his Πύθιοι λόγοι to the Athenian poet and Stoic philosopher Sarapion: Plutarch, *The E at Delphi* 1. 384E.

[27] For the conceptual dichotomy of 'intellect' and 'power', see Haake (2003: 94f. 97f. 100), whose German formulation of '*Geist und Macht*' does not intend to carry any philosophical connotation; also see below, pp. 195ff. On the discourse of (not only) the Roman imperial period about the relationship between philosopher and ruler and on the importance of philosophical παρρησία, see Hahn 1989: 182–91; Whitmarsh 2001: 144f.; Haake 2003: 94, 130–2; Flinterman 2004: 361–4.

he would immediately lose his status as a god. If the philosopher defines the emperors' actions as good in terms of the Peripatetic ethics of *On Fate*, he is claiming the right to define what is good and what is bad and thus presents himself to his imperial audience as an authority in moral matters: should the emperor's actions not meet the standard, he can warn and even reproach him. This claim by philosophers actually to be able to instruct and correct emperors of course contains much potential for conflict: Alexander and his contemporaries knew that Septimius Severus' legitimacy was also based on the fact that he had often publicly declared that the gods had sent him visions of his future reign in his dreams.[28]

But according to the Peripatetic school, the freedom to choose between good or bad also contains the moral postulate that one should choose the good thing on the basis of moral standards. If need be, these standards have to be followed even against restrictions imposed by a political system, because those rules do not *necessarily* have to be obeyed. This discourse about the relationship of 'intellect' and 'power' is characteristic of the period between the first and the third centuries CE. Even Diogenes of Oenoanda places his project of Epicurean enlightenment—which says that the aim of philosophical study is perfect happiness, which cannot be found in the public political sphere—in contrast with philosophy that uses those with power to attain riches and political success easily (Diogenes F 29 Smith).

This opposition between intellect and power partly explains the choice of topics in *On Fate* and *On Providence*. Another reason is Alexander's need to make the Aristotelian doctrine more concrete and systematic in comparison with other philosophical schools. In his function as the official representative of the Aristotelian tradition, he may have deemed it necessary to defend the Peripatetic position against contemporary criticisms by Middle Platonists on Aristotle (*On Providence*) and to distinguish it more clearly from the deterministic system of the Stoics (*On Fate*).[29]

---

[28] Dio Cassius even wrote a whole book about the dreams and omens with which the gods allegedly communicated Septimius Severus' reign: Dio Cassius 73. 23. 1. On Septimius Severus' opinion of divination, see Lane Fox 1986: 228f.; Harris 2003: 32.

[29] Sharples 2002: 36f. For a Middle-Platonist attack on the Aristotelian position on providence in the second half of the second century CE, which may have been one

Although such an explanation may answer the concrete question as to why Alexander chose these topics, it immediately generates another question, namely why the Middle Platonists were interested in this topic. We can trace their involvement back to Plutarch's Περὶ εἱμαρμένης (*On Fate*), which probably dates from the early second century CE, or even to his so-called *Pythian Dialogues*.

But the period when the philosophical discourse about fate, providence, and divination was formed was between the third and the first centuries BCE. In the imperial period, we have texts Περὶ εἱμαρμένης or *On Fate* by an anonymous Platonist philosopher (Pseudo-Plutarch), the Epicurean Diogenianus and the Peripatetic philosopher Alexander; but already in the Hellenistic period we find texts by Epicurus, Chrysippus, Boethus of Sidon, Poseidonius, and Cicero on the subject. Chrysippus, Panaitius, Philo (and maybe also Philodemus) all wrote texts Περὶ προνοίας or *On Providence* long before Seneca, Alexander, the Stoic Claudius Aelianus, or the neo-Platonist Hierokles of Alexandria. The same is true of texts on divination (i.e. Περὶ μαντικῆς and *De divinatione*), since Diogenes of Seleuceia, Antipater of Tarsos, Poseidonius, and Cicero (and possibly Panaitius too) published on the subject long before Plutarch rediscovered the topic in his *Pythian Dialogues*. Of course this list is not complete; but it shows quite impressively that the Hellenistic discourses were being rediscovered by Stoics, Platonists, Peripatetics, and Epicureans from the late first century CE and being adapted in ever more artful variations on a classic theme. The next question is, why were these discourses suddenly revived?

It is not merely its dedication to Septimius Severus and Caracalla that suggests that Alexander's text *On Fate* was written in a specific cultural context in the Empire, when Peripatetic discourse was characterized by a dual frame of reference. In the first place, as far as form and content were concerned, it returned to a classical, i.e. Aristotelian, interpretative tradition, while its philosophical aims were those typical of the Hellenistic period. Historically speaking, of course, these perspectives were irrelevant to the Empire, but were nevertheless transferred to the contemporary situation. The second reference-point is the

reason for Alexander's riposte in *De providentia*, see Atticus F 3 ll. 52–7, 71–4, 81–5 Des Places.

relationship between intellect and power, which I have referred to already. This dual frame of reference is not only obviously characteristic of Peripatetic discourse, or of a Diogenes of Oenoanda, but also occupies a prominent role in the literary texts produced in the period called the Second Sophistic, that is the time from the second half of the first century CE (the *floruit* of figures like Dio of Prusa) to the middle of the third. It is this link to the literature of the imperial period that makes these discussions of wider interest than simply to historians of philosophy.

However, as a name for an entire period of literary and cultural history, the term Second Sophistic is not without its problems. It is based on a certain *style* of rhetoric and declamation, which Philostratus traces back to Aeschines, the Attic orator of the fourth century BCE, and calls ἡ δευτέρα σοφιστική in his *Lives of the Sophists* written in 237/8 CE. Omitting earlier orators, Philostratus goes on to analyse orators and sophists of the imperial period up to his own day, beginning with Niketes of Smyrna in the mid- to late first century CE. So, to link the style of writers of rhetorical-declamatory and epideictic literature of the imperial period with the rhetoric of the fourth century BCE is to construct a continuity which in this form is certainly fanciful. It was Erwin Rohde in his work on the Greek novel and its predecessors (Rohde 1876/1914) who transformed this vague stylistic concept into a settled term for a literary period and thus started a debate about its use and the quality of the literature generally so known.[30]

Philostratus' account is obviously an attempt at constructing a literary tradition in order to legitimate contemporary rhetorical literature as the successor to the Greek rhetoric of past centuries. However, it is not only the rhetoric of the imperial period but the entire literary (and non-literary) culture between the second half of the first century CE and the middle of the third that has certain common features, especially as regards the aesthetics governing their production and reception and the associated social contexts, which make a common periodization appear attractive (Swain 1996: 1–7; Schmitz

---

[30] Philostratus, *Lives of the Sophists* I *praef.*, 481. 18, 507–19, 512 Kayser. On the history of the term Second Sophistic, ranging from Philostratus to Rohde and twentieth-century debates, see Whitmarsh 2001: 41–5.

1997: 1–18). As a consequence, the pragmatic decision to include not only Philostratus' orators and sophists of the imperial period in what we decide to call the Second Sophistic, but also other forms and phenomena of cultural communication in this time frame is now widely accepted in the field. Thus, the 'period of the Second Sophistic' has also, indeed primarily, come to denote a broad cultural milieu that includes Opramoas of Rhodiapolis and Julius Demosthenes of Oenoanda as well as his fellow-citizen Diogenes or Alexander of Aphrodisias.[31]

This paradigm-shift assumes the dual reference-points mentioned above: a certain understanding of education (*paideia*), based on the language, literature, and cultural traditions of an explicitly Greek past, now becomes the criterion for inclusion in imperial cultural communication. The interlocutors in this communication are those competent to take part in the discourse regarding this concept of education, the educated (*pepaideumenoi*).[32] This second pragmatic extension of the concept Second Sophistic has significant consequences: if such a concept of education becomes the criterion of inclusion in the communicative structures of the Second Sophistic, we are entitled not only to include a much wider range of literary activity than just rhetorical texts but also to extend the phenomenon of the Second Sophistic to many other, non-literary forms of communication via the notion of *paideia*, even those found in epigraphy, numismatics, or material culture.[33]

On the other hand, this contemporary discourse among the authors of the so-called Second Sophistic about education and culture also reflects the social, political, and cultural contexts of its own formation, because it obviously emerged in the imperial period, and

---

[31] On the euergete Opramoas as a product and representative of the 'period of the Second Sophistic', cf. Balland 1981: 223f. Wörrle (1988: 115f.) emphasizes the relevance of the Hellenistic understanding of culture and education for Opramoas' and Demosthenes' foundations. P. Gordon (1996: 4–6, 8–42) discusses whether Diogenes can be seen as an author of the Second Sophistic.

[32] On the importance of *paideia* in the Second Sophistic, see e.g. Schmitz 1997: 44–66, 83–91, 101–10; Whitmarsh 2001: 90–130, 178. On the concept and function of the *pepaideumenos* in this process, see Anderson 1998: esp. 1123f.; Scholz 2000: 110–18.

[33] On this expansion of the frame of reference, see for example Alcock 2001; Galli 2001; van Nijf 2001; Scholz 2003; as well as the contributions in Borg 2004.

is thus temporally very far removed from the 'flowering', whether imaginary or real, of the educational tradition of the Classical period to which it keeps referring. However, the question of how to interpret this double focus of the system of cultural communication is still disputed. Some scholars see it as a result of the tension between the Greek concept of *paideia* and Roman rule, and thus as a (re-) constructed 'Greek cultural identity' in contrast to Rome.[34]

Given this background, I see two advantages in viewing the philosophical discourses about fate, providence, and divination under the Empire in the context of the communicative structures of the Second Sophistic. First, because it allows us to evaluate these discourses in their social and cultural environment, in which philosophers like Diogenes and Alexander played an active part. Second, because the choice of these topics cannot be explained solely by arguing that traditional models of interpretation are being picked up again within a purely autonomous philosophical discourse. We need to explain why those models should have been relevant for intellectuals in the communicative structures of the literature of the imperial period.

INTELLECT AND POWER: THE INTELLECTUAL IN THE SECOND SOPHISTIC

Plutarch's work on fate, providence, and divination takes us to the beginning of the period of the Second Sophistic. Plutarch was born into the local aristocracy of Chaeronea in Boeotia and also held the citizenships of Athens, Rome, and Delphi. He had extensive political and philosophical contacts in Greece and the highest circles of Roman politics and aristocracy. We have evidence for his having held the office of Epimelete in the Delphic Amphictyony in the reign of Hadrian. He was also a ἱερεύς (or 'priest'—a modern term of convenience rather than a satisfactory translation of the Greek

---

[34] See for example Swain 1996: 411 and Goldhill 2001a. Bowie (1970) already viewed the literary production of the Second Sophistic as a process of cultural escapism and implicit resistance against Rome. For some criticism of this paradigm, see pp. 204–6 below.

title) at Delphi from some time in the 90s until the time of Hadrian. Through his academy for Platonic philosophy in Chaeronea, he maintained a network of Platonic philosophers, but also conferred with Peripatetics, Stoics, Pythagoreans, and Epicureans. He called himself a 'philosopher'.[35]

As a *functionary and priest*, Plutarch represented the shrine vis-à-vis the Greek cities and Rome at a time when Delphi was especially important for Greeks and Romans not only in its contemporary role as an oracle but also as a site of cultural remembrance. Plutarch's priesthood coincided not only with a regular boom in imperial building activity at the shrine—a boom contemporaries were well aware of—but with a renewal of intensive dedication by ordinary Greeks and Romans.[36] The fact that Plutarch was so highly praised by his contemporaries reflects a feature of contemporary religious and cultural history that also shines through in his Pythian dialogues, namely the importance of divination for people in the first and second centuries CE.[37]

These dialogues also allow us some insight into the process of creating a literary discourse about this religious practice: as a *philosopher* who writes about divine providence and inspiration as well as divination, Plutarch formed part of a communicative network that connected the intellectual centres of the Roman Empire. This field of discourse was quite open as far as statements about religious truths are concerned and consisted of competing philosophical schools and intellectuals.

[35] For the details, see Ziegler 1951: 639–96; Jones 1971: 3–64. On his self-description, cf. Plutarch, *Table-talk* 617F; *Precepts of Statecraft* 798A–C. Ἐπιμελέτης and ἱερεύς: SIG 829a = CIDelphes iv. no. 150 (from the time of Hadrian); cf. also the posthumous honorific statue erected by Delphi and Chaeronea: SIG 843 = CIDelphes iv. no. 151.

[36] Cf. Stadter 2004 on the possibility that Plutarch may already have been representing Delphi at Rome in the time of the Flavians, and then again under Trajan and Hadrian. On Delphi as a site of remembrance for Greeks and Romans, which the imperial building activity and the rising number of dedications suggest, see Jacquemin 1991; Galli 2004: 320–8; Weir 2004.

[37] The 'Pythian dialogues' is the modern name given to the three dialogues in Plutarch's *Moralia* that deal specifically with Delphi and divination, namely *The E at Delphi, The Obsolescence of Oracles*, and *The Oracles at Delphi*. The name is based on Plutarch's own reference to his 'Pythian Dialogues' in *The E at Delphi* 1.

When Plutarch uses the shrine at Delphi—including its function as a space of cultural and religious remembrance—as the location of the intellectual discussions in his Pythian Dialogues, he employs a form of literary construction that was very popular in the Second Sophistic.[38] But readers of the Dialogues who expect a literary exhibition of this site of remembrance whereby the author and priest is identified with the shrine will be disappointed. In the *De Pythiae oraculis* (*The Oracles at Delphi*), the commentary (*periegēsis)* by the official tour-guides of the monuments and their inscriptions, which constitute that site as a space of remembrance, is not met with enthusiasm by the educated (*pepaideumenoi*) whose philosophical discussion will dominate the remainder of the dialogue. While the bored guides are giving explanations and telling anecdotes that bore their intellectual audience, the *pepaideumenoi* in the audience begin a parallel discourse which already introduces the topic of the text: they discuss what underlying significance the monuments and inscriptions have beyond their material and aesthetically appreciable appearance, and whether they manifest any divine truth. In doing so, the philosophically-interested *pepaideumenoi* also criticize a form of *paideia* based on the unreflective application of aesthetic criteria. The discrepancy between the mediation of traditional knowledge about Delphi, represented by the official *periegēsis*, which talks about the totality of visible things, and the philosophical discourse that investigates the invisible content of selected monuments and inscriptions becomes ever more marked: the *pepaideumenoi* keep asking questions to which the guides are increasingly unable to give adequate answers, and Plutarch's construction of two different levels of discourse and two different types of knowledge ensures that they cannot even theoretically be answered, which results in the feeling of relief that both parties (and the reader) experience when the official tour ends prematurely.[39]

---

[38] On shrines as places of intellectual communication in the Second Sophistic, see Galli 2001: 43–9.

[39] Plutarch, *The Oracles at Delphi* 2. 395D–17. 402B. On the opposition between outward appearance and internal condition in this passage, see Hirsch-Luipold 2002: 86–98. Interestingly enough, Plutarch chooses the monuments discussed in the philosophical arguments of *The Oracles at Delphi*—and in *The Obsolescence of Oracles*—from among the pre-Hellenistic monuments at Delphi, thus suppressing openly visible traces of the site's Hellenistic and Roman past: McInerney 2004: 44–51.

But the most important discourse about divination, the discussion about whether everything is predetermined, is also merely touched upon. In this case it concerns the argument that the prophecies uttered by the oracle at Delphi sufficiently prove divine providence—an argument attacked by the would-be Epicurean Boethus and defended by the Stoic Sarapion. But the real question at stake in *The Oracles at Delphi* is why the Pythia no longer (or hardly ever) utters her prophecies in verse, as she (supposedly) used to do in the distant past,[40] but in prose, which does not meet the aesthetic and stylistic standards of the *pepaideumenoi*.

Thus the real question is whether these prophecies whose presentation is so unsatisfactory can be inspired by something as perfect as divine providence; indeed, whether Delphic Apollo is even present in them at all. Theon, the main speaker of the dialogue, who represents Plutarch's own Platonism, in particular denies this possible negative conclusion. In support of his argument, he employs the distinction I mentioned in the discussion of the relevance of Delphi's monuments and inscriptions: he claims that the outward appearance of the material world does not allow us to draw any conclusions about its internal true reality, for doing so would mean relying on merely aesthetic and stylistic criteria. In fact, the oracle is not uttered by the god, but by the Pythia. She is not the direct spokeswoman of a divine prophetic utterance, whose lines are fed her by a higher power, just like a prompter in the theatre. For, although her utterances are inspired by the god, they are only the splintered reflection of a more complex process of mediation. The god only stimulates the movement (κίνησις); every Pythia is then moved (κινεῖσθαι) differently depending on her natural abilities:[41]

---

[40] We have no means of determining how many of Pythia's prophecies were ever in verse: cf. Fontenrose 1978: 193–5.

[41] Plutarch, *The Oracles at Delphi* 7. 397C (my translation). On the image of a stimulus, see ibid. 7. 397B–C. For the image of a divine prompter: ibid. 20. 404B. On the inconsistencies that result from this argument later in the dialogue, see ibid. 21. 404F and Schröder 1990: 25–29, 46f., as well as the elaborate account in Vernière 1990: Besides his favourite model that distinguishes between the divine stimulus and the natural movement of Pythia's soul, Plutarch also uses a model that interprets mantic inspiration as a blend of the two movements.

For neither the voice nor what is said, neither the elocution nor the metre comes from a god; they are produced by the woman. He merely provides the images (φαντασίαι) and enlightens the soul about the future. For that is exactly what this inspiration (ἐνθουσιασμός) is.

The god (ὁ θεός) in the Pythian Dialogues is Delphic Apollo. At the same time, he is identified with the 'highest god' of Platonism, who differs from, e.g., the Stoic equivalent insofar as he is to an even higher degree thought to be immaterial and transcendent. Plutarch's teacher Ammonius of Alexandria (though he lived in Athens), elaborates on this in another of the Pythian Dialogues, *De E apud Delphos* (*The E at Delphi*):[42]

The god exists... and he does not exist in (limited) time, but in infinity, which is immobile, time-less and invariable, where there is no before or after, no future and no past, no older or younger. But he, being a single entity, fills eternity with a single present; and existence is only real existence if it is akin to him: neither past nor in the future, without beginning and end.

This unchanging Apollo is separate from the material world and neither ought nor desires to care about change and the changing material world. Instead, there is a secondary subordinate deity for dealing with the limited and transient material world. Plutarch postulates a state of chaos that preceded the world, and makes this chaos responsible for the existence of evil. Apollo himself, eternal and good, cannot be responsible for the changeability and evil of the world, whereas matter is passive. As a consequence, Plutarch has to construct a third subordinate level, as transient as the world itself, to be responsible for evil in the sublunar world. By using this limited 'dualistic' construction, Plutarch avoids the accusation implied in the concept of theodicy that the Stoics had to deal with, namely that their highest god also must be responsible for evil.

Although this god is not interested in the changeable material world, he is still concerned for human beings, because their souls at

---

[42] Plutarch, *The E at Delphi* 20. 393A–B (my translation). Cf. ibid. 20. 393C–D on the identification of the highest god with Apollo and the ascription to him of qualities such as 'indestructable', 'unmixed', and 'pure'. On the limited dualistic construction of god by Plutarch in the context of the antithetic dualism Apollo-Dionysus, which I outline further below, see Chlup 2000; also cf. Dillon 2002a.

least are, like god, immortal.[43] This Platonic idea is necessary for the defence of divine providence that Plutarch, unlike Diogenes of Oenoanda or Alexander of Aphrodisias, offers, namely that it is the φαντασίαι sent by Apollo that affect the Pythia's soul. The god uses her soul as a kind of instrument (ὄργανον), and she in turn uses her mouth and voice, so they are not directly the god's instruments. The nature of the instrument obviously also conditions the way the divine is represented. This conditioning of the divine by the material world is also illustrated by the fact that the Pythias of ancient times had been able to transform divine inspiration into verse; nowadays a Pythia from a more humble background can no longer do this, but has to resort to mere prose, because mouth and voice are instruments of the soul. This conditioning is also evident if we recall that the divine inspiration that transmits an impulse to the Pythia's soul only produces a movement inside this instrument, which, being a human soul subject to the impressions of the material world, unable to pass it on in its pure and unadulterated form.[44]

In the context of this theory of representation, it is hardly a coincidence that the traditional possibility of direct inspiration by the divine spirit (Πνεῦμα), allegedly rising up from a crack in the ground in Delphi, which appears in many ancient texts from the first century BCE and also in the Pythian Dialogues, only plays a minor role at the beginning of *De Pythiae oraculis* and never appears again in the dialogue after that.[45]

---

[43] In another dialogue, *On the Delays of Divine Vengeance*, also set in Delphi, Plutarch tries to counter the anti-deterministic argument that many evil-doers obviously escape the punishment they 'deserve'. His counter-argument is based on the Platonic model of the soul and claims that divine providence acts beyond the limits of the criminal's life and is still punishing his immortal soul when his body has long since decayed.

[44] For this line of argument, cf. in particular Plutarch, *The Oracles at Delphi* 19. 404B–C; *The Obsolescence of Oracles* 40. 432C. The argument that the mouth and voice of the Pythia are not instruments of the god appears at *The Obsolescence of Oracles* 9. 414E. On Plutarch's conception of the soul as an ὄργανον, see Schröder 1990: 25–52, esp. 24–43; Hirsch-Luipold 2002: 92–8.

[45] Plutarch, *The Oracles at Delphi* 17. 402B–C. By contrast, at *The Obsolescence of Oracles* 51. 438A Plutarch mentions the harmonic conditioning of the φανταστικὴ καὶ μαντικὴ δύναμις in relation to the πνεῦμα as a necessary requirement for prophetic inspiration. On this issue, see further Vernière 1990; Zagdoun 1995: 589f.

Divine will is changed by human representation in two ways. The first is that it is not the god who speaks through the Pythia, but it is she who speaks in her own person. Second, even if her utterances are due to divine inspiration, her soul is not able to reproduce the divine images directly and without distortion. This theory does not question the claim by the oracle and other divinatory practices at Delphi to mediate divine truth; on the contrary, vague though the analogy may be, the relation between the Pythia's soul and Apollo is that of a tool to its user.

This line of argumentation illustrates the discursive strategy used in the Pythian Dialogues: As priest *and* philosopher, Plutarch deals with the contemporary criticism of the workings of the Delphic oracle and of divinatory practice in general by employing a 'positive theology' based on a Middle-Platonist position. This theology does not see itself as a deconstruction of traditional religious knowledge but rather as a defence of it; according to the Pythian Dialogues, the aim of philosophical discourse among the *pepaideumenoi* is to try and gain a better understanding of divinity, and thereby assert the validity of divination against contemporary unease.[46]

But in his search for the truth in these dialogues, Plutarch also uses the sceptical-dialectical method, which signals to his contemporary readers accustomed to the literary conventions of philosophical dialogues that even those statements about religion and mantic practice inspired by Platonism, inasmuch as they arise in the course of the development of a dialogic discourse, have to be seen as merely probable.[47] Indeed, Plutarch's own contemporaries saw in his Platonism underlying doubts concerning the divine inspiration of oracles: we can at any rate see that in his text Περὶ μαντικῆς (*On prophecy*)—which does not survive—he evidently felt impelled to defend the compatibility of mantic and oracular practice with the Middle-Platonic idea of an Apollo who can only influence the material world indirectly. But this happens in the context of a Platonist conception

---

[46] e.g. Plutarch, *The Obsolescence of Oracles* 16. 418D; 47. 435E; *The Oracles at Delphi* 18. 402E; θειότητος ὄρεξις: *De Iside* 2. 351E.

[47] On the Platonic search for religious 'truth' and its conditioning by the sceptical-dialectical method in Plutarch, cf. Opsomer 1996, who also focuses on mantic practice.

of God, whose theology constructs 'god' as a perfect being who exists in an entirely unattainable, because supra-lunar, world—and postulates this difference between the divine and the material even for the moment of divine inspiration.

In fact, the theological statements made in the Pythian dialogues are quite surprising considering that the author was a priest at Delphi and thus a representative of the traditional religious knowledge of the shrine. For all the knowledge that Plutarch presents to his readers in the shape of the shrine's official representatives and priests is implicitly undermined by the philosophical discourse. For the traditional religious view is that prophecies are direct statements by the god. The idea is that Apollo himself speaks; this belief is massively supported by an uncountable number of literary texts and inscriptions from all over the Mediterranean area, not just at Delphi, Didyma, Patara, or Oenoanda. And no one could know this better than Plutarch, who participated in the process of giving oracles in his function as a ἱερεύς at Delphi.[48] But the god (ὁ θεός) is also present at Delphi independently of divinatory practice. Represented by his statue, he functions together with the assembled ἱερεῖς as a witness to legal procedures undertaken in the shrine.[49]

It is precisely these traditional religious expectations that form the context of, and a contrast to, the discussions in the Pythian Dialogues: the *pepaideumenoi* who are no longer interested in traditional knowledge but thrive on its philosophical analysis, disassociate themselves from the expectations with which a public that is not primarily interested in a particular philosophy (i.e. Platonism) comes to Delphi and its god. The discursive achievement of these 'theological' texts is evidently the differentiation between traditional

---

[48] On the prophecies from Delphi that present Apollo as the speaker, cf. Fontenrose 1978: 93–5, 212f. *passim*. The administrative and cultic duties of the ἱερεύς and προφήτης during the divinatory sessions at Delphi (and their interaction with the Pythia) are discussed by Fontenrose 1978: 218f.; cf. note 85 below. For Didyma, see the formulaic phrases θεὸς ἔπεν or ὁ θεὸς ἔχρησε(ν) in the prophecies: Fontenrose 1988: 180, 182f., 188–90, 193f., 196–9, 202–06 etc. According to one text, the god who gives the oracles at Claros breathes on the petitioner with his voice: Merkelbach and Stauber 1998–2002: i. p. 262, no 02/12/02 lines 1f.

[49] See the text edited by Mulliez in: *BCH* 125 (2001) 289–303 = *Bulletin Épigraphique* 2002: 213, and the correct interpretation in Rigsby 2004.

religious knowledge and an anthropocentric perspective that under-stands God as the end-point of a philosophical search for perfection. As we can see by the way the *pepaideumenoi* treated the Delphic *periegetes*, this discursive construction also presupposes that it differs from that kind of traditional religious knowledge. Something similar happens in *The E at Delphi*, when the interpretation of the golden letter E attached to the temple-wall causes a conflict between the official interpretation and Plutarch's explanation: the periegetes and the shrine's official representatives (οἱ ἀφ' ἱεροῦ), in this case the priest Nicander, interpret the letter as the first letter of the traditional question to the oracle (εἰ, whether); the Platonist Ammonius how-ever explains it as an apostrophe—εἶ, you are—of the one, eternal and truly existing god of Platonic philosophy (Plutarch, *The E at Delphi* 4. 386B–D).

By employing this kind of device, Plutarch is also playing a vari-ation on a popular literary strategy. The affirmation of one's own religious tradition against philosophy is an essential part of, for example, Cicero's dialogues *De natura deorum* (*On the nature of the Gods*) and *De divinatione* (*On divination*). Such a clear affirmation of traditional values against one's own philosophy, in Cicero's case the Academy (i.e. scepticism), can only be found in a weak form in the Pythian Dialogues, where the attempt to downplay the critical im-plications of Plutarch's own, i.e. Platonist, position vis-à-vis religious tradition plays a significantly less important role; hence, the conflict with the priest Nicander is inevitable.[50]

The theological discourse among the *pepaideumenoi* thus reflects a conflict between heterodoxies: the texts include a double 'differential' which always denotes the difference between one's own reflection and that of the interlocutor. Through the medium of the literary

[50] Cf. e.g. Plutarch, *The Oracles at Delphi*, 18. 402E: the argument here (and interestingly enough the speaker here is the traditionalist Stoic Sarapion) is that philosophical discourse allows a better defence of εὐσεβὴς καὶ πάτριος πίστις, hearty traditional faith. The argument of the main Platonist speaker, Theon, on the other hand, is significantly more dialectical and implicitly more negative, without showing much regard for religious tradition. This kind of affirmation of traditional values is also thematized (with a certain amount of irony) in *The Dialogue on Love* 13. 156A–B, where Plutarch's *father* Autoboulos tellingly believes that the necessity of faith in the gods has already been proved by tradition.

dialogue, the texts set out a system of theology and in so doing refer, explicitly or implicitly, to other alternative systems. They also show up the difference between such discourses and traditional religious knowledge: Plutarch's creation of a literary discourse about this knowledge among people like the *pepaideumenoi* undermines the simplification of his work that scholars have often undertaken by explaining the statements made in Plutarch's texts by appeal to his function as an active representative of religion, as if the Pythian dialogues had to be a kind of 'Delphic theology' simply because they were written by a religious specialist at Delphi. Actually the opposite is the case: the co-existence of a variety of representatives of different discursive and performative contexts is characteristic of the reflection upon religious meanings within many different religious and theological discourses all over the Empire in the period of the Second Sophistic. The doubling of social roles (in the case of Plutarch: priest and philosopher) also seems to be characteristic of literary production in this period (and others). It is thus important to distinguish analytically between the social, or the representational, role on the one hand and the 'person' on the other.[51]

The concepts *paideia* and *pepaideumenos* have become, as we have already seen, central terms of reference for any research on the Second Sophistic. But in fact they fail to describe this doubling of roles adequately: as terms, they construct an opposition between (Greek) 'education' or 'intellect' and (Roman) 'politics' or 'power' which at first glance seems to be applicable to the Roman imperial period. But such a contrast completely ignores the differentiation of the discursive contexts of literature implied by the analytical distinction between speaking-role and the actual person, for the sake of substantive ascriptions of meaning and the construction of hierarchies of value. Several scholars have remarked on the fact that the reification of the opposition between Greek culture and Roman rule was undermined in the imperial period by many other ways of constructing identity—regional and local, political and economic, cultural and religious—which may have been very much more

---

[51] The function of ancient theological texts as 'differentials' in Niklas Luhmann's sense is discussed in Bendlin 2005: 218–20; 227f. On the importance of distinguishing between 'social role' and 'person', cf. Haake 2003: 97.

important for the actual individual. Plutarch's work paradigmatically reflects the many identities available to the provincial upper classes in the Roman Empire, ranging from identification with the local *polis* to references to Hellenic traditions or the Roman imperial context.[52]

Moreover, in the literary production of the Second Sophistic, *paideia* cannot be uncritically subsumed under 'Greek cultural identity'. Already in the pre-Hellenistic period 'education' was used as a central plank in the construction of upper-class identity throughout the Mediterranean area (for an elaborate account, see Hall 2002: 172–228). Moreover, in Greek literature *paideia* certainly represents an indigenous (i.e. 'emic') category of cultural identity. But to transfer the term to modern analytical language is unsatisfactory, because it cannot adequately describe the dynamics of the literary discourse of the imperial period in relation to 'education', with all its differentiations, repudiations, and contradictions, beyond the mere opposition between (Greek) education and (Roman) rule. The example of Plutarch's Pythian Dialogues shows how the participants in these discourses construct, compare, and contrast quite different concepts and understandings of *paideia*, all of which go far beyond the mere assertion of its possession. It also shows that as a concept 'education' constantly takes on different meanings in the various discursive and performative contexts.[53]

The traditional emphasis on education fails adequately to register the dynamic inherent in the various speaker-roles with their individual social and performative contexts. In combination with the concept of the 'role of the intellectual', however, the relationship between 'intellect' and 'power', to which I have already alluded more than once, allows a more adequate analysis. The characteristic social feature that Alexander of Aphrodisias, Diogenes of Oenoanda, and Plutarch of Chaeronea have in common is that they all belong to the socio-political upper class; sophists and more especially

---

[52] 'Hellenic identity always possessed multiple levels': Alcock 2001: 345. The 'multiple identities' of the provincial upper classes in the imperial period are also highlighted by Jones 2004. Cf. also Alcock 2002: 86–98, who suggests replacing the term 'Graeco–Roman' with the concept of 'hybrid memories'.

[53] Cf. Alcock 2001: 344–6 on the 'elasticity of [Hellenic] identity, its ability to zoom in and out, as it were'; more fully in Alcock 2002: 36–98. On the constructed quality of ascriptions of cultural identity in the period of the Second Sophistic, see also Whitmarsh 2001: 178–80, 298–301.

philosophers are economically, politically or socially integrated into the society of the imperial period.[54] Discourse among intellectuals takes place within the political, social or economic context in which the author often himself plays an active role as social actor. Moreover, in order to achieve the *paideia* constructed in the Second Sophistic and the rational-philosophical lifestyle associated with it, the intellectual discourse simply presupposes the contemporary political order as the basically acceptable basis of human co-existence, despite individual grumbles and criticisms.

Such a view puts the opposition between (Greek) 'intellect' and (Roman) 'power' into perspective. But there is more to be said here. If we are to understand how embedded the literary production of the Second Sophistic is in its period, it is essential to cease viewing 'power' just as an externally-constructed category, i.e. as a category focused exclusively on Roman rule or the emperor. 'Power' and domination are equally characteristic of the socio-political structures at the provincial and local levels, and imply a social context in which the individual intellectual is usually himself active. As a philosopher, Plutarch is not an exception to this rule, given that he played a prominent part in his political community, whether at the level of the *polis* or the provincial *koinon*, and/or acted as a religious functionary. 'Education' is a privileged form of symbolic capital that the members of the imperial upper classes used in the struggle for power and legitimacy.[55] Seen in this light, the fact that even Diogenes, Aurelius Belius Philippus, or Philidas could use their (potentially subversive) Epicurean philosophical education as symbolic capital becomes less puzzling. But can we provide a full explanation for it?

---

[54] Cf. the general account by Sirago 1989. On the integration of philosophers into contemporary imperial society, see also Hahn 1989 and Dillon 2002b.

[55] The role of education among the strategies for legitimating and confirming power in the Second Sophistic is discussed in relation to rhetoric by Schmitz 1997: 44–50, 101–40. Dillon (2002b: 37f.) lists additional examples of the overlapping of philosophical role and public (religious) office, namely Ammonius of Athens, Favorinus of Arles, and L. Vibius Eumenes of Phocaea (on the latter, cf. *SEG* 40: no. 950). The list could easily be extended, e.g. L. Flavius Hermokrates, philosopher and ἀρχιερεὺς Ἀσίας, who was venerated by the people of Pergamon due to an oracle given by Asclepius after his death: *IPergamon* 3 no. 34 = Merkelbach and Stauber 1998–2002: i. p. 583, no. 06/02/03. For examples of Epicureans as priests, see note 19 above.

If the intellectual of the imperial period drew upon his experience as a member of the upper class and if his intellectualism was a constitutive element in the political discourse of the imperial period, this did not prevent him from criticising contemporary society in literary discourse. The intellectual sphere, and so the role of the intellectual speaker, were dissociated from other social spheres and roles: they were to a degree autonomous.[56] Alexander, Diogenes and Plutarch, and no doubt Aurelius Belius Philippus and Philidas too, exemplify the perception that philosophical discourse is grounded in freedom of speech ($\pi\alpha\rho\rho\eta\sigma\acute{\iota}\alpha$); this literary strategy marks out a distinctive cultural space, manifested in the freedom of the Peripatetic Alexander to address the emperors as well as in Diogenes' attempt to dissociate the public site where he could publish his philosophical inscription from the political public of Oenoanda. But it is also to be found in the $\pi\alpha\rho\rho\eta\sigma\acute{\iota}\alpha$ of the speakers in the Pythian Dialogues: the Platonist Theon insists on his right to employ the dialectical method after the priest Nicander has dogmatically presented the official Delphic interpretation of the letter E as the only valid one.[57] Here again we encounter a conflict between quite different kinds of knowledge and contrasting notions of education.

Integration *and* autonomy: it may be that only the dialectical interplay of these two mutually conditioning parameters can explain the high esteem in which philosophers (and that includes all philosophical schools) were held in the imperial period. It may also explain why the philosopher is represented as a visual image in various different media of the Roman Empire: he appears in literary and epigraphic texts as well as in three-dimensional representations. The iconographic depiction of philosophers in the second century CE (and later, after a decent gap, in keeping with senatorial conceptions of the rules of self-representation, on sarcophagi) expresses the desire of the imperial elites to stylize themselves in terms of this philosophical ideal of the rational life.[58]

---

[56] Cf. Haake 2003: 97–100, esp. 100 with additional literature on the concept of autonomy.

[57] Plutarch, *The E at Delphi* 6. 386D–E: . . . ἤρετο . . . εἰ διαλεκτικῇ παρρησίας μέτεστιν (. . . he asked . . . whether dialectic has a share in freedom of speech, . . .). On the intellectual ideal of παρρησία, see note 27 above.

[58] On this process of self-stylization, cf. Ewald 1999: esp. 131f.; 2003: 568f. The perception of the philosophical role as autonomous can possibly also be traced in the

Many ancient literary texts construct a gap between philosophical discourse and the day-to-day reality of living and acting, which is held to be incompatible with the maxims and rules of the discourse. Modern research has often simply taken over this image of the philosopher. In the context of the literature of the Second Sophistic, however, it requires some nuancing. Philosophical discourse and social-political activities were complementary and equally 'real' spheres in the daily lives of the upper classes of the Roman Empire. One thought might be that the use of the image of the philosopher in the medium of representational art merely reflects the high valuation of philosophical *paideia*. Yet perhaps it was rather the autonomy of the intellectual role of the philosopher, the implied model of a double life, the almost dialectical possibility of combining roles representing the two realms 'intellect' and 'power', that a contemporary audience of politically well-integrated Greek and Roman members of the upper class, people like Opramoas and Demosthenes, found so fascinating about Plutarch, Diogenes, and Alexander?

DIVINATION AND DIVINATORY SPECIALISTS IN THE SECOND SOPHISTIC

It is an obvious assumption that the philosophical and literary discourses of the high Principate about the uses and disadvantages of divination are somehow connected to contemporary practice. But what kind of relationship was there between contemporary religious practices and the discourse concerning them in the literature of the Second Sophistic? Could changes in the wider context between the first and the third centuries have resulted in a change in religious behaviour that also affected contemporary divinatory practice? Is it

chronological development of the art on senatorial sarcophagi: here the philosopher only becomes an image in the late second century, when the number of mythological and military themes starts to decrease. This singular development can probably be explained by the senatorial behaviour when it came to self-representation: it took a while before this social group switched from an imperial to a civil iconography; Wrede 2001.

this altered religious behaviour that surfaces in a new form of literary reflection about divination in the Empire?

In the same generation as Alexander of Aphrodisias (on the cusp of the third century), and metonymically substituting shrine for deity, Clement of Alexandria declared that the oracles of Delphi and Didyma are now fallen silent, and the other oracles too are dead. Clement's claim is not based on empirical reality, but stems rather from this Christian philosopher's teleological wishful thinking—it was not only his Apologist successors who long found themselves confronted by all too active oracles. In fact Clement is using a topos widely familiar in his day: already in the first century CE we find the poet Lucan proclaiming the alleged failure of mantic inspiration at Delphi. But the literary topos does have a basis in fact: not only Delphi but also other traditional oracles seem to have been involved from the Hellenistic period in some kind of development that affected their reputation, a development that later writers saw as decline.[59]

The reasons for this process are not to be found at the level of the psychology of religion. The actual demand for divinatory specialists and mantic techniques was unbroken: the oracle at Delphi was visited by the same kinds of individuals and groups in late Hellenistic times as earlier, and the questions concerned the same topics, namely ailments of various kinds and personal or family problems. In this respect, they do not differ from the cases brought before the Delphic god in Plutarch's day. As a consequence, oracles like Delphi, which from the point of view of literary texts were the 'high' forms of divination, were competing in the religious market-place with numerous 'low' forms of mantic services. We find Cicero already complaining about this competition from the perspective of a mid-first-century BC upper-class augur and philosopher, because official divination was being undermined by the public presence of fortune-tellers and specialists who read the entrails of sacrificed animals, of psycho- and necromancers, of augurs and haruspices, of astrologers and prophets, of *Isiaci coniectores* and other dream-interpreters.

---

[59] Clement of Alexandria, *Protrepticus* 2. 11. 1; Lucan, *Civil War* 5. 67–236 esp. 111–16. The contemporary view that the oracles were in decline can already be found in Cicero, *On divination* 1. 37f., 2. 116f.; Strabo, *Geography* 7. 6. 9, 16. 2. 38, 17. 1. 43, and later in Juvenal, *Satire* 6. 554–6; Orosius 6. 15. 11f.

This attack on the authority of mantic specialists who operate independently of the political structures of ancient cities is reflected in the complaint by the Platonist Theon in Plutarch's *The Oracle at Delphi* about the unofficial interpreters of oracles who offer their services outside the shrine's sacred area and thereby compete with the official temple-personnel. This criticism that Plutarch puts into the mouth of his Platonist speaker culminates in a tirade against the various representatives of contemporary 'low' mantic practices: unlike the Delphic oracle, which claims to be free of deceit (ἀψευδές), these mantic specialists are allegedly frauds (γόητες) and pseudo-prophets (ψευδομάντεις).[60]

However the primary reasons for this process of change affecting the traditional oracles have nothing to do with this competition between the traditional oracles and the alternative providers of divinatory practices; this was probably already the case in Classical times. The real reasons are to be found on a completely different level. In his dialogue *The Obsolescence of Oracles* (*De defectu oraculorum*) Plutarch poses the question as to why most of the old oracles have vanished from the religious map of Greece, and why even Delphi, where oracular practice continued, had had to reduce its number of prophetesses from up to three to one. Plutarch answers this question by blaming the decline on the political, military, and demographic decline of Greece since the Hellenistic period, which caused the depopulation of the land and the decay of many rural, extra-urban areas, which is where many traditional oracles obtained their clientele. But this answer is itself actually a familiar literary topos in Plutarch's day: the shortage of men (ὀλιγοανδρία) and the resulting depopulation of previously heavily-settled areas become part of a model of decadence in the works of Plutarch, Dio of Prusa, and Pausanias that contrasts the former glory of Greece with its allegedly diminishing contemporary political and moral importance.[61]

[60] Cicero, *On Divination* 1. 132; Plutarch, *The Oracles at Delphi* 25. 407B–C. On the denunciation of the independent mantic specialist as γόης καὶ ψευδόμαντις in Greek literature, cf. Hammerstaedt 1988: 38–40; Schröder 1990: 398–401; see further my remarks at pp. 228–41 below.
[61] Plutarch *The Obsolescence of Oracles* 5. 411D–412D, 8. 413F–414B. On the topicality of such statements, cf. Alcock 1993: 24–32 and Zagdoun 1995: 587f.

Despite their inherent topicality, however, such statements also express a general perception in the late first and early second centuries CE, namely that Greece had in the past been subject to significant political, demographic, and economic changes. Plutarch offers a political explanation: owing to the different political situation in the late Hellenistic period, the traditional extra-urban oracles (including the panhellenic ones) were visited by far fewer embassies from *poleis* all over the Mediterranean world to request answers to politically-important questions than they had in the late Archaic and Classical periods. This is certainly an important point: altered political circumstances reduced the number of potential clients and undermined the oracles financially, because both the form and the extent of classical political euergetism had changed.[62]

But we have to be careful with statements about the extent of this process of change in the late Hellenistic and early imperial periods: the archaeological and epigraphic evidence for building- and dedication-activities at Delphi and (especially) at Didyma seems indeed to be less substantial than the evidence for earlier periods or (and I shall come back to this) for the period of the Second Sophistic; but it is certainly too substantial to allow us to conclude that these two oracles experienced a dramatic cultic and material decline. In fact the oracle of Apollo at Claros seems, not least thanks to Roman investment, actually to have grown considerably in importance from the late Hellenistic period.[63] So we cannot speak of a *general* decline of materially-impoverished oracles from late Hellenistic times. The perception of later generations that the oracles had been 'silent' in this period needs to be modified in more than one respect.

An explanation of these *ex eventu* constructions requires a model capable of taking account of the demographic and economic changes of the late-Hellenistic and early-imperial periods without drawing upon this ancient model of decadence. Beginning in the late

---

[62] Cf. Plutarch, *The Obsolescence of Oracles* 7. 413A–B; *Pyth.* 26f., 407C–408C, with Levin 1989: 1607f., 1612.

[63] On Claros, cf. Parke 1985: 125–41; Levin 1989: 1629f. Ferrary 2000 discusses the honorary inscriptions for Romans from the Republican and imperial periods. The literary, epigraphic and archaeological evidence for this general process of change is collected in Wolff 1854: 1f. and *passim*; Parke 1985: 44–68 (Didyma); Fontenrose 1988: 15–20; Levin 1989: 1599–605 (Delphi); 1620–2, 1607f. (Didyma).

Hellenistic period, we can make out a tendency in some regions of Greece gradually to give up small rural settlements and form larger agricultural units, which of course resulted in an increasing concentration of the population in urban centres. Another result of this process was probably a slow shift of financial and religious resources into the towns and an increased dependence of extra-urban or rural oracles on the organizational and financial structures of towns. In other words, such oracles probably became increasingly dependent on urban elites and their euergetic activities in public, political, religious, and cultural life. Such a model has the advantage that it can incorporate the ancient view of this change, which allegedly led to the abandonment of extra-urban oracular and other shrines or at least to a reduction in prosperity at a panhellenic shrine such as Delphi, without having to invoke the idea of decadence that underpins this view.[64]

The texts from the imperial period are therefore particularly interesting because of their perception of their own recent past in the context of the present. Plutarch states in *The Oracles at Delphi* that the Delphic oracle had been neglected and impoverished in the past, but that this process of decline had been arrested in more recent times by generous benefactors. The identity of the guide ($\kappa\alpha\theta\eta\gamma\epsilon\mu\acute{\omega}\nu$) to whom Plutarch refers here, and whom he credits with having brought about this new prosperity, of course with the god's help, is however uncertain.[65] We also find this notion of a religious revival in Opramoas' inscription at Oenoanda: the primary credit is given to the god for reactivating the shrine after its long period of silence, but of course this example of an oracle's 'renaissance' in the middle of the second century CE would have been impossible without funding by a euergete.

Archaeology and epigraphy suggest that this impression given by the literary sources of a 'renaissance' of the oracles is far more than a mere literary fantasy. We have evidence for intensified imperial

---

[64] The model is outlined by Alcock 1993: 72–85, 96–118, 180f., 189–91, 200–12, cf. Alcock 2002: 44–51.

[65] Plutarch, *The Oracles at Delphi* 29. 409A–C. For the discussion about the identity of the $\kappa\alpha\theta\eta\gamma\epsilon\mu\acute{\omega}\nu$ (Domitian, Trajan, Hadrian, some unknown local benefactor, Apollo, even Plutarch himself have all been proposed), see Levin 1989: 1613f.; Schröder 1990: 15–22; Stadter 2004: 26 with n. 38.

building activity already from the reign of Nero onwards, and in Plutarch's day the oracle was already flourishing again; the emperors Trajan and Hadrian were also among the major benefactors of the oracles at Didyma, and others besides. The same goes for Claros. The oracular shrines in Greece and Asia Minor, and many others, prospered during the second and third centuries. *Poleis* resume their despatch of festive embassies to Delphi, Didyma, Claros, and other venerable oracles.[66] The contemporary texts also emphasize the importance for the shrines at this time of upper-class euergetic activity, which is also part of the Second Sophistic. This sudden interest in oracles among members of the upper classes, and its implications for and connections with contemporary cultural trends, is certainly in need of explanation.

Opramoas' inscription mentions an earthquake as a concrete reason for reviving the oracle at Patara. But is this a sufficient answer? Does the need to consult oracles after earthquakes and epidemics express an increasing desire at this period, born of fear, for mantic reassurance (e.g. Lane Fox 1986: 231, 252)? Or is the 'renaissance' of the oracles a symptom of the 'Age of anxiety' that E. R. Dodds claimed to be able to make out between the year 161, the beginning of Marcus Aurelius' reign, and Constantine's conversion to Christianity in the fourth century?[67] Dodds took the phrase 'Age of anxiety' from W. H. Auden's poem of the same name, where it was used as a label for the social situation of the 1930s. For Dodds, this 'Age of anxiety' stood for a feeling of material and moral insecurity, resulting in an increase in emotional religiosity that finds its primary expression in philosophical discourse.[68]

The theory of an 'Age of anxiety' represents a thorough-going attempt at explaining pagan and Christian antiquity by appeal to a psychologizing history of mentality for which Dodds drew upon the psychoanalytic issues of his own time. For Dodds, this

[66] The evidence for such a 'renaissance' is cited in Wolff 1854: 4–43; Parke 1985: 171–97; Lane Fox 1986: 168–261; Marek 2003: 113. Delphi: Jacquemin 1991; Galli 2004: 320–8; Stadter 2004; Weir 2004. Didyma: Parke 1985: 69–92. Claros: Robert 1980: 404 and *passim*; Parke 1985: 142–70.

[67] Dodds 1965: 57: '(...) No doubt much of the increasing demand for oracles simply reflects the increasing insecurity of the times...'.

[68] Dodds 1965: 3.

psychological-anthropological notion of *Angst* was of central importance. It lives on as a catchword in many more recent publications on the religious history of the Roman Empire, whether with a reference to Dodds or completely straight without the historical context of the original paradigm being recognized. But others too have argued, without invoking *Angst*, that the popularity of oracles and other forms of divination in the second and third centuries CE was part of a process marked by more intensive forms of pagan religiosity, even including irrational tendencies, ending in a thorough change in mentality in Late Antiquity.[69]

Are these psychological explanations with their roots in religious evolutionism really satisfying? The material insecurity that for Dodds underpinned his 'Age of anxiety' certainly cannot be traced in the evidence for the second century, or the first half of the third. And the fact that the discourses of this period are characterized both by the popularity of mantic practices and a critique in contemporary literary sources is not sufficient proof of the existence either of an increased religious irrationality on the part of the masses or of a new scepticism on the part of the rational intellectual elites. The fact that we find such clear evidence for these phenomena is owing to the survival of a much larger corpus of epigraphic and literary evidence. The evidence may thus simply attest to cognitive and emotional dispositions that had been in existence for some time.[70] In other words, the communicative shift of the second and third centuries visible in our sources need not mean that the religious habitus actually changed significantly at this time.

There is not even much evidence for the assumption that it was fear of earthquakes, epidemics, invasions and other catastrophes that generated or at any rate heightened contemporary interest in oracles. Of course oracles were consulted in such cases: after an epidemic in the middle of the second century that may have affected wide

---

[69] See for example Veyne 1986; Harris (2003: 31) tentatively approves.
[70] Cf. especially Strobel 1993: 63–74, especially 65f., 72. The problematic presuppositions of an 'Age of anxiety' have been exposed by Gager 1984; cf. also Cambiano 1991, on the influence of contemporary psychology on Dodds. R. Gordon (1972) comments on the uncritical use of psychological explanations for events in religious history in general; Lane Fox 1986: 64–6 also criticizes the idea of an altered and irrational religiosity in the Roman Empire.

swathes of the Empire, the oracle of Apollo at Claros gave the town Hierapolis instructions to make sacrifices for Mother Earth, the Aithēr (Upper Air), the gods in heaven and the gods below the earth, Demeter and the deceased as well as Apollo Kareios, but also to send choruses of boys and girls to Colophon, and, at sacred points outside all the gates of Hierapolis, to erect statues of Clarian Apollo with strung bow, so that he would shoot the plague away. Apollo also advised a town on the river Hermos in the second century to erect in her temple a gold-plated statue of Artemis of Ephesus wearing a quiver, and to burn the wax figurines that represent the spell that had allegedly caused the plague. Around the same time, Clarian Apollo advised Pergamum to have four choirs of ephebes sing hymns to Zeus, Athena, Dionysus, and Asclepius, make sacrifices and pray for salvation, so that the plague might leave Pergamon and move on into the lands of other peoples. The same Apollo also gave the town Odessus in modern Bulgaria an oracle with instructions to aid their struggle against the plague. The oracle also recommends that a statue of Hygieia be put up in Vasada in Isauria to combat the plague. A hexameter line inscribed on an altar from Antioch-on-the-Orontes in Syria reassures passers-by that Apollo will keep the plague away: simple kinds of apotropaic invocation like this are easily reproduced and can be found all over the Greek-speaking east of the Roman Empire; it can hardly be identified as a divine *logos* from a specific oracle.[71] A failed harvest could certainly have been the occasion of the question posed by Nicomedea about how to attain good harvests

[71] Hierapolis: Merkelbach and Stauber 1998–2002: i. pp. 259–60, no. 02/12/01. Apollo at Klaros also advised the people of Caesarea Troketta to combat the plague with a statue of Apollo firing an arrow (Merkelbach and Stauber 1998–2002: i. pp. 396–9, no. 04/01/01); the same is true of Kallipolis (*IK* 19: no. 11). Hermos: Merkelbach and Stauber 1998–2002: i. pp. 296f., no. 03/02/01. Pergamum: Merkelbach and Stauber 1998–2002: i. pp. 575–79, no. 06/02/01. Vasada: Merkelbach and Stauber 1996: 27 no. 12. Odessus: Merkelbach and Stauber 1996: 32f. no. 18. Antioch-on-the-Orontes in Syria: Merkelbach and Stauber 1998–2002: iv. p. 242, no. 20/03/01. Lucian, *Alexander* 36 cites this as an (alleged, see p. 237 below) oracle of Glycon, but owing to its multifunctionality it is obvious that it is not bound to a specific oracle, as comparisons make clear: cf. *Epigrammata graeca* 375 Kaibel (from Aezani in Phrygia); Martianus Capella 1. 18. On the general theme, see also Lane Fox 1986: 231–4, Faraone 1992: 61–6 and Várhelyi 2001: 15f., 17f., who is not the first to try to find connections between the inscriptions and the Antonine Plague. For a more detailed analysis of the various methods of healing and warding off the plague recommended

in the future: Apollo advised sacrifices for Helios, Selene, the winds, and Demeter. At Cius in Bithynia Apollo ordered the population to make sacrifices and stage a procession in honour of a female deity, during which women should follow the *kalathos* barefoot and wearing clean clothes; the occasion of this oracle is unknown, but again a plague or a bad harvest are likely candidates.[72]

Such consultations however do not belong solely to the second century CE. The oracle given by the Apollo of Gryneion that advised the town of Caunus in Caria to worship Phoebus Apollo and Zeus in order to overcome a bad harvest probably dates from the early Hellenistic period. We also have two oracles given by Clarian Apollo in the first century BCE which advise Iconion in Lycaonia and Syedra in Pamphylia to erect in the town-centres a statue of Ares being chained up by Hermes and judged by Dike, as a protection against Cilician pirates.[73]

So plagues, bad harvests, and other similar problems are by no means a privilege of the high Principate. That such enquiries are prominent in second-century evidence is also due to the fact that these sources survive very selectively. And even if the *poleis* really did consult oracles more frequently in cases of catastrophe during the high empire, this cannot be the reason for the 'renaissance' of the oracles: for it does not explain the real problem, which is why oracles should once again have been accepted as valid sources of divine truth; rather the reverse—the frequency of their consultations already presupposes that they had been so accepted.

The answer to this question offered here proceeds in a different direction. I reconsider a model that I offered some years ago, interpreting the alteration in the 'epigraphic habit', i.e. the increase in the quantitative indicators of the epigraphic culture of commemoration

in the oracles, see Várhelyi 2001 (with a questionable classification into 'magical' and 'non-magical' rituals).

[72] Nicomedea: *TAM* iv.1 no. 92 = Merkelbach and Stauber 1998–2002: ii. pp. 200–02, no. 09/06/01. Cius: *IK* 29: no. 19 = Merkelbach and Stauber 1998–2002, ii. p. 134, no. 09/01/01.

[73] Caunus: Merkelbach and Stauber 1998–2002: i. pp. 27, no. 01/09/01. Syedra: Merkelbach and Stauber 1998–2002: iv. pp. 168f., no. 18/19/01. Iconium: Merkelbach and Stauber 1998–2002: iii. p. 99, no. 14/07/01. For another oracle concerning a plague of the first century BCE, cf. *SEG* 50: no. 1352 bis.

in the Roman Empire between the first and the third centuries CE, as a reflection of a shift in the communicative and representative behaviour of the imperial elites. I also attempted to deduce changes in cultural perception from the way in which those elites communicate about religion.[74] It is obvious that any model can only inadequately convey the complexity of historical change; this reservation applies to my model insofar as it can hardly encompass the (potentially infinite) chronological and local variation in the actual developments in the Roman Empire between the first and the third centuries. But this methodological problem does not affect the fact that urban communicative and representative behaviour changed significantly between the first and the second centuries. As evidence for this we can cite (among other things) the monumental representative culture focused on the imperial cult typical of cities in the first century, and still in the second, and the self-representation of the urban elites in the form of honorific statues and inscriptions. The number of such inscriptions, previously the preferred medium of representation, dwindles considerably in the course of the second century, because new media take their place, such as funding building projects (for example public baths), grand religious festivals, athletic and musical competitions, animal-baiting and gladiatorial games. Especially in the Greek East of the Empire we also find a growing public presence of traditional indigenous deities on coins, inscriptions, and in new religious festivals; and we observe the revival on a regional level of ancient city-federations, and of Archaic and Classical traditions in the form of local stories and myths, and even the establishment of cults in honour of an Archaic founder-figure.

These processes cannot be dismissed as mere coincidence resulting from the random selection of surviving sources: the evidence is simply too overwhelming for that. In fact the opposite is the case: these phenomena reflect a general change of mentality at this time. It is no coincidence that the process coincides with the revival of

---

[74] Bendlin 1997: 54–61. This model needs to be extended, especially as far as the representative behaviour of the elites in the third and fourth centuries CE is concerned (this was not the focal point of that article); cf. Borg and Witschel 2001: 87–90, who *a propos* the shift in the 'epigraphic habit' observe 'that it is essentially a cultural phenomenon largely independent of economic factors' (p. 49 n. 4).

Classical forms in architecture and art (especially religious art) in the
second and third centuries. These cultural processes are not an
epigonic imitation of the Classical Greek past but a productive
appropriation and creative transformation of a (frequently re-)
'invented tradition'.[75]

This is the cultural location of the Second Sophistic. Diogenes of
Oenoanda takes the theatre and the public baths, two of the representative media of contemporary euergetic practises, as his targets.
Already in the late first century, under the altered political circumstances of the Roman Empire, Dio of Prusa defines sacrifices to the
gods and festivals as now the privileged forms of representation in
urban self-presentation. And even in the late third century a text for
teaching rhetoric alludes to such themes in an imaginary speech to
the people of Alexandria Troas, near which there was an oracle of
Apollo Smintheus:[76]

Since we [the orator is speaking here] have always experienced the providence (πρόνοια) and the benevolence [of Apollo Smintheus], we do not tire
of worshipping him. He always gives us harvests without losses and saves us
from dangers: thus we propitiate him with hymns. This is the reason why we
host our excellent sacred competition, organize festivals (πανηγύρεις) and
make sacrifices in order to express our gratitude for the blessings we have
received. And you will describe the panegyric [the author of the text now
addresses the reader of his manual], what kind it is, and how grand, how
many visitors attend it; and that some men demonstrate their talents
through speeches or physical prowess, and others are spectators and
listeners.

[75] Cf. Bendlin 1997: 58f. The changes in monumental representative culture in the
second and third centuries are described in Borg and Witschel 2001: 50–78. Games:
Mitchell 1990; Leschhorn 1998; Borg and Witschel 2001: 93–104; Van Nijf 2001;
Koenig 2005: *passim*. On myths being re-discovered as traditional material that towns
would draw upon, from the second half of the first century, see Weiss 2004: 186–96
(on the basis of numismatic evidence). 'Classicism': Alcock 2001: 338–44: 'The
memorial landscape was not so much concerned to preserve the past as to redeploy
it...'; Alcock 2002: 36–98 esp. 40–4, 51–64, 72f. Also Schörner 2003: 206–09: 'The
Greeks of the second century CE did not only see themselves as epigones...'.
[76] Menander Rhetor, p. 444. 12–24 Russell-Wilson; Dio Chrys., *Oration* 31.
162: ... τὸ τοῖς θεοῖς θῦσαι καὶ τὸ ἄγειν ἑορτήν (... sacrificing to the gods and holding
a festival ...).

Games, festivals, and religious rituals: these are the preferred media of the euergetic practices of people like Demosthenes of Oenoanda or Opramoas of Rhodiapolis in the second century CE. But the rhetorical handbook also refers to another important aspect: the prestige of the euergete, but also that of the city as a whole, is increased by the fact that visitors attend the festivals. Demosthenes' inscription is not the only one to give instructions for embassies and delegations from other *poleis* who participate in the religious rituals organized by the city during the period of the festivities. The sources emphasize a feeling of concord (ὁμόνοια) between the *poleis* that was not limited to joint sacrifices (συνθυσίαι), and in so doing gloss over the actual rivalry between them, attested by the number of competing festivals all over the Greek East.[77]

This theme of rivalry does not appear in the euergetic texts. Opramoas' and Demosthenes' inscriptions both emphasize their demonstrative love for their city and refer to its traditions: their own acts are cross-referenced with the deeds of the ancestors (their own and those of the whole city), traditional customs, which are projected back into Hellenistic times, and the cultural and religious traditions of the town. Demosthenes' musical competition at Oinoanda even cites the value of Hellenic education.[78] As a religious festival, his foundation is dedicated to the emperor and the city's own Apollo Patroös. Opramoas' 'ancestral' *panegyris*, organized for the re-inauguration of the oracle at Patara, is likewise dedicated to the local Apollo Patroös. This prominence of a semantic field in the epigraphical evidence of the second and third centuries that values cultural, social, and religious tradition, which I would like to call 'the rhetoric of tradition', reflects a particular contemporary situation: one prominent feature of the various literary and non-literary products of 'the culture of the Second Sophistic' is their repeated invocation of the authority of traditional cultural and religious knowledge.

---

[77] See the elaborate account in Wörrle 1988: 198–203; Weiss 1998; Van Nijf 2001, especially 311f.

[78] Opramoas: Kokkinia 2000: 213: Index s.v. προγονικός, πρόγονος. Demosthenes: Wörrle 1988: 116f., 188–90. On pp. 257f. he emphasizes how 'the festival [. . . seems] to have combined Greek tradition and imperial cult with unforced naturalness'. Polis-patriotism: Wörrle 1988: 51f. and n. 37.

Without being at all exclusive, I want to stress the link between the 'renaissance' of the oracles and this contemporary rhetoric of tradition. Such an account allows us to take cognisance of the rough correlation between the renewed prominence of the oracles from the late first century CE and the 'epigraphic habit', which is a material index of the wider processes of cultural change between the first and the second century. It also allows us to view the 'renaissance' of the oracles as an integral component of the communicative and representative behaviour of the contemporary elites without having to invoke the traditional psychological explanations.

It was in this cultural and political climate, strongly influenced by the rhetoric of tradition, that the traditional oracles became central to communication about religion. Of course this tradition had never completely died out; but in the eyes of contemporaries these oracles now more than ever symbolized a long religious tradition reaching back to Archaic and Classical times, which, as Opramoas' inscription says, was now to be re-discovered and renewed. Already in Nero's day a man called Tib. Claudius Damas left witness to his extraordinary commitment to the oracle at Didyma: as a very old man, after a successful political career, he held the office of *prophētēs* for a second time (perhaps there was no other candidate). He repeatedly boasts that he had re-inaugurated cult practices, rituals, and choral performances in order to maintain or re-create tradition. The text of this inscription was probably also intended to urge his contemporaries to rediscover for themselves what Damas had wanted to make them become aware of, namely πάτρια ἔθη (traditional customs). His successors after the late first century seem to have taken this warning seriously: from now on holding the office of *prophētēs* and at the same time discharging political functions in Miletus was no longer unusual.[79]

The oracles themselves invoke this rhetoric of tradition now employed by contemporaries, and thus the conservative religious stance

---

[79] Damas' renewal of the πάτρια ἔθη: *IDidyma* no. 237, 268, 272; also Robert 1967: 38–52; Weiss 2004: 188. On the not uncommon practice, after the late first century CE, of simultaneously accumulating political and religious offices, cf. the discussions of Fontenrose 1988: 48–55 and esp. Busine 2006. I would like to thank A. Busine for allowing me to see her manuscript in advance of publication.

it implies. Clarian Apollo advises Hierapolis to maintain the customs of the ancestors and of Nature; at Didyma, in answer to a question as to how a cult should be practised he replies that one should prefer ancestral customs and practices.[80] The oracles settle local conflicts, and in so doing represent cultic continuity. In the city of Aizanoi in Phrygia, the priest of the cult of the *ktistēs* (city-founder) is confirmed in his office by Apollo's oracle; Apollo of Didyma lays down the procedure for appointing the priest of Athena Latmia at Heraclea-on-Latmos by appealing to the traditional rules. An orator cites the tradition that virgins from his home-city are chosen as as priestesses of Artemis in the neighbouring town of Sidyma, a tradition based on an oracle given by Apollo from the first century, as an example of the unity and concord of the Lycian cities. At Ulpia Anchialos in modern Bulgaria, the four city-tribes erected statues of the gods because Apollo told them to.[81] Apollo at Didyma declares that we ought to worship *all* gods; another oracle affirms that the immortal gods welcome all forms of worship by humans. Although the circumstances are unknown to us, the oracle at Claros asserts that we should worship *all the gods*; all we know is that this oracle resulted in a wave of inscriptions mostly from the Western part of the Roman Empire dedicated to the *di deaeque* (the dedications themselves however are always to local deities). Finally, in the minds of contemporaries, the oracles also represent the successful export of Greek culture. The rhetorical handbook I have already mentioned sees Apollo's divinatory prowess and his oracles as his greatest achievements, because they alone made the colonization of the *oikoumene* (the inhabited world) possible. As far as the appeal to tradition is concerned, Apollo and Damas are thus at one with Demosthenes and Opramoas.[82]

---

[80] Hierapolis: Merkelbach and Stauber 1998–2002: i. p. 262, no. 02/12/02. Didyma: *IDidyma* no. 499.

[81] Aezani: Merkelbach and Stauber 1998–2002: iii. pp. 202f., no. 16/23/01. Herakleia: Merkelbach and Stauber 1998–2002: iii. pp. 174f., 01/23/02. Sidyma: *SEG* 50: 1356 ll. 71–112. Ulpia Anchialos: *IGBulg* 12 no. 370 = Merkelbach and Stauber 1996: 25 no. 10.

[82] Menander Rhetor, p. 442. 9–24 Russell-Wilson. Didyma: *IDidyma* no. 499. The gods' pleasure in being worshipped and honoured: Merkelbach and Stauber 1998–2002: i. p. 121, no. 01/20/04. According to Paci 2000, there are ten known

This need not surprise us: the official representatives of this religious conservatism in the shrines, the *hiereis*, prophets and *thespiō-dai*, were recruited from the same social groups, shared the same political and social positions and opinions, and came from the same cultural and educational background as the euergetes and political leaders of the time.[83]

But these religious functionaries are also representative of our period in another sense, in their dialectical combination of 'intellect' and 'power'. Plutarch, the Platonist, is a priest of Apollo at Delphi, the Epicurean Aurelius Belius Philippus is a religious official at Apamea in Syria, and at Didyma we have evidence of a Stoic, Aelius Aelianus, a Platonist, Phanias, and an Epicurean, Philidas, holding the office of *prophētēs* (Aelius Aelianus: *IDidyma* no. 310; Phanias: *IDidyma* no. 150). So it is not really surprising that the typical themes of the religio-philosophical debate are manifest in the oracles themselves in the second and third centuries CE. In the reign of Hadrian, the oracle of Zeus Ammon in the Siwa oasis tells a group of worshippers of the god from Cyzicus that in order to please him they should not give gold or sacrifice a bull, but rather burn incense, and send a festive embassy to the oracle at Claros. At Didyma, Apollo stops requiring hecatombs or expensive gifts in the middle of the third century and asks for pious hymns instead, especially if they be very ancient.[84]

examples of the type 'dis deabusque secundum interpretationem oraculi Clari Apol-linis' (to the gods and goddesses according to the interpretation of the Oracle of Clarian Apollo) in the western part of the Roman Empire (only one Greek example, from Melli in Pisidia, is extant). Paci also discusses the possible political context of these inscriptions (including the possibility that they should be dated to the aftermath of the Antonine Plague from the mid-160s onwards).

[83] Busine 2006 emphasizes the fact that the functionaries of the oracles belonged to the contemporary elites and used the religious authority of their offices, and demonstrates the point for Didyma and Claros.

[84] Siwa: Merkelbach and Stauber 1998–2002: ii. pp. 7–9, no. 08/01/01. Didyma: *IDidyma* no. 217 = Merkelbach and Stauber 1998–2002: i. pp. 76f., no. 01/19/01. Despite the claims made by Bradbury 1995: 336 (based on Louis Robert), there is no strictly epigraphic reason to date this inscription to the late third century, nor to interpret it as expressing a late-antique 'spiritualization' such as we find in the philosophical schools of the late third and fourth century, esp. in Porphyry and Iamblichus. Didyma: *IDidyma* no. 217 = Merkelbach and Stauber 1998–2002: i. pp. 76f., no. 01/19/01.

Even a naive observer might suspect that the philosophical and theological interests of the religious functionaries at Delphi, Didyma, Claros, Apamea, and elsewhere could have affected the oracular responses—after all, we can assume that the *prophētēs* at Didyma and the *prophētēs* or *thespiōdes* at Claros were responsible for turning the prophetic messages into intelligible literary texts. Unfortunately, the *prophētēs* of the year in which Apollo at Didyma suddenly decided to demand hymns instead of blood-sacrifices cannot be identified, so we cannot determine the religio-philosophical background to this change of mind. But not long before 250 CE and thus maybe around the time that this oracle was delivered, another *prophētēs* at Didyma, T. Flavius Ulpianus, records an oracle in which the god praises his piety (εὐσέβεια) and also the fact that he had arranged for the blood-sacrifices on the altars in accordance with the old rules (θεσμοί) and oracles (λόγοι). Is it possible that Ulpianus, as the official responsible for the sacrifices, had asked the god how he wanted them to be conducted, and whether he would welcome blood-sacrifice? The *prophētēs* adds a second query concerning the location of the table for the temple-offerings (τράπεζα). Might this give us a glimpse of a religio-philosophical debate about the right sacrifice between the *prophētai* at Didyma?[85]

The oracles did involve themselves in a debate about the nature of divinity that was certainly as important philosophically as the one in Plutarch's Pythian dialogues. Thus Apollo advises a petitioner from Amastris in Paphlagonia to construct an altar for the 'highest god'

[85] *IDidyma* no. 227 = Merkelbach and Stauber 1998–2002: i. pp. 89–91, no. 01/19/10. Lane Fox (1986: 220–4) interpreted this text and *IDidyma* no. 217 (see above n. 84) as evidence of a contemporary debate about the form of sacrifice that would please the god at Didyma. This is debatable, because neither the date nor the prosopography of *IDidyma* no. 217 can be established with any certainty (*pace* Lane Fox). On the probable role of the *prophētēs* at Didyma at sacrifices, see Fontenrose 1988: 51f.; on his possible involvement in the transformation of the oral oracle into verse, see Fontenrose 1988: 52, 103 and Parke 1985: 210–19 who addresses the central issue on p. 218: 'It is better not to attempt to discuss the insoluble question how far the oracular responses were ... the composition of the *prophetes* and his staff...' On the functions of the Delphic ἱερεύς/προφήτης in the process of transforming the oracle into verse and producing a written version, see Fontenrose 1978: 212–24 esp. 218f. The question whether the literary form of the oracles given in Claros was the work of a *prophētēs* or a *thespiōdes*, cannot be solved; for discussion and a *non liquet*, see Busine 2006. I incline towards the first option, as does Louis Robert.

(θεὸς ὕψιστος) who exists in everything and is invisible, but who can see the things that people fear, and can thus protect them from harm. While the philosophical language of this oracle could also be found in a Platonic or Stoic discussion on theodicy, not unlike the one discussed above, the terminology of another oracle borders on the language of the mysteries. The god at Claros advises the construction of an altar to himself. This altar 'faces the beams of far-sighted Helios'; each month 'pure actions' are to be performed at it, so 'that I' (the god speaks in the persona of Apollo-Helios) 'can help to harness the team. For I offer fruits to the mortals [...], whom I wish to save and to whom I know how to bring fame.' Through his philosophical reading, Plutarch was familiar with the idea that Apollo might bear fruits, and with his identification as Helios (which may have a Stoic origin), because he disregards it when developing his own Platonic conception of divinity. Dio of Prusa also thematizes the equivalence of Apollo, Helios, and Dionysus.[86]

In the late second or early third century, the text of an oracle was inscribed on a relief in the form of a stylized altar in the eastern city-wall of Oenoanda. The theological problem that the god was asked to solve was: 'Who is god, and what is his nature?' The answer falls into two parts, the divine response being followed by a theological exegesis:

'Self-created, untaught, motherless, steadfast, ineffable, fire-dwelling, that is God. We messengers (ἄγγελοι) are only a small part of God.' For those who ask about God, and how he is: He declared that the all-seeing Aether is God; you shall look on him and pray to him early in the morning, looking to the East.

Below the text of the oracle's response, a second, smaller altar is chiselled into the wall, commissioned, as the inscription states, by a woman called Chromatis: 'To the highest god (θεὸς ὕψιστος), the lamp and the prayer.' The two reliefs are positioned in such a way that it is possible to pray while facing East when the first ray of sunlight touches the wall. But the relation between the two texts is not entirely clear. Did Chromatis add to the theological statement of

---

[86] Amastris: Marek 2000: 135–7. Apollo-Helios: Merkelbach and Stauber 1998–2002: iii. p. 225, no. 16/31/01; Dio Chrysostom, *Oration* 31. 11. For the philosophical importance of the identity of Apollo and Helios, and Plutarch's rejection of it, see Zagdoun 1995: 590f.; Dillon 2002a: 224; Hirsch-Luipold 2002: 90–2, 165–8. On the dualism of Apollo-Dionysus implied in Dio Chrysostom, *Oration* 31. 11, see also note 42 above.

the oracle-text by honouring the 'highest god' with a lamp, given that he is 'the all-seeing Aether', to be venerated as the source of all light in the morning, as the oracle-text says? Did she do so in order to affirm the oracle's theological assumptions, or did she want to supplement that text (which does not itself mention a 'highest god') by means of a further and possibly later exegesis?[87]

These well-known texts raise other problems too. Is the answer to the question a specific response by the oracle at Claros or a text that circulated freely as part of a collection of oracles and was simply being recycled at Oenoanda? Was this an official exegesis by a functionary of the shrine or simply a commentary that was added at some point in the process of transforming the oral oracle into a literary text?[88] Do Chromatis' dedication to the 'highest god' and the oracle's theological statement allow us to conclude that this is an implicit or explicit anticipation of, or even a form of, monotheism?[89] This is by no means necessary: addressing a god as θεὸς ὕψιστος certainly does not prove a quasi-monotheistic religious environment influenced by Judaism or Christianity. An appeal to a 'highest god' is also part of the vocabulary of pagan religious traditions in the second and third centuries, and the idea of a single super-ordinate god is far older. In isolation, at any rate, the text of the oracle can be explained as a speculative theological collage of Stoic and Platonist motifs from the imperial period.[90]

---

[87] Texts: *SEG* 27: no. 933 = Merkelbach and Stauber 1998–2002: iv. pp. 16–19, no. 17/06/01. *Pace* Mitchell 1999, it is methodologically unsound to take the text as evidence for the cult of θεὸς ὕψιστος.

[88] The classification of the text as an official oracle given at Claros is solely based on the identification of the god as Clarian Apollo by Lactantius, *Divine Institutes* 1. 7. 1. It is accepted by Robert 1971; Lane Fox 1986: 168–71; Mitchell 1999: 86f.; Merkelbach and Stauber 1998–2002: iv. p. 19; Bendlin 2005: 226f. Fowden (1988: 178f.) disagrees; cf. note 104.

[89] Cf. Merkelbach and Stauber 1998–2002: iv. p. 19: The text of the oracle is 'massive propaganda for monotheism'; Mitchell 1999: 91: '...the crucial device by which Hellenic paganism could be reconciled with a monotheistic system of belief'; Barnes 2001: 143: '...most thinking men in late antiquity who reflected at all on what this worship meant were in a very real sense monotheists'.

[90] The identification of the highest god as Aether, who lives in fire, shows Stoic ideas, the dualistic structure of the text is based on Platonic ideas. On the philosophical requirements, cf. e.g. Diogenes Laertius 7. 135; Dio Chrys., *Oration* 31. 11; Robert 1971: 610–14; Lane Fox 1986: 170. For θεὸς ὕψιστος in a pagan context, see Marek 2000: 146; on the interchangeability of divine attributes; Stein 2001 (no 'pagan–Jewish syncretism', against Mitchell 1999). The so-called 'theological oracles' as a part of

The producers of such oracles were of course no longer merely following the rhetoric of tradition but sought to enrich that trope by means of an intellectual discourse that oscillates between tradition and reflection. They thus prove beyond any doubt that Apollo and his functionaries too were perfectly at home in the intellectual climate of the Second Sophistic.

Γόητες AND ψευδομάντεις: DISPUTES OVER THE AUTHORITY OF ORACLES

The first three lines of the Oenoanda oracle-text also appear in a slightly different form as part of a longer text by Lactantius and also in the so-called Tübingen Theosophy, a late fifth century Christian text 'about the true faith'. Neither text cites the passage from autopsy but rather uses existing literary collections of religio-philosophical and 'theological' oracle-texts which circulated as florilegia in the Mediterranean area. The Chaldean Oracles, which were published already in the late second century CE, are of singular philosophical quality and indebted to contemporary Platonism. Two Platonizing texts, *On the oracles given by Apollo of Claros* by Cornelius Labeo, and *On philosophy from oracles* by Porphyry, fit into the cultural environment of the late third century. These texts too contain authentic and fictional oracles side by side.[91] The insight offered by the oracle, and its mode of communication, are thus divorced from a physical location and the ritual involved in consulting the god in the shrine. By entering a literary discourse, the oracle, as a literary text, has become autonomous.

pagan religious thinking: Lane Fox 1986: 256–61. On the general issue of *Hypsistos*, see also Belayche, this volume 139–74.

[91] Lactantius, *Institutes* 1. 7. 1; 'Tübingen Theosophy': *Theosophorum Graecorum Fragmenta* 13 Erbse; cf. Merkelbach and Stauber 1996: 42–5. Livrea 1998 postulates that the text from Oenoanda (which the author wrongly dates to the late third century), the quotation in Lactantius, and the Tübingen theosophy are all based on the Chaldaean Oracles, and claims that the text was transmitted to Lactantius and the Theosophy via Porphyry and an anonymous Christian author. On the cultural background to the transformation of oracles into literary texts in the second and third centuries, cf. Fowden 1988: 179; Barnes 2001: 155–9.

Freeing the oracle-text to turn it into literature is typical of the period of the Second Sophistic. But it is certainly not a new phenomenon: already in the late sixth century BCE an Athenian chresmologist (peddler of oracles) called Onomacritus is said to have collected and edited the legendary oracles of Musaeus, but he was then caught red-handed trying to pass off his own texts as genuine oracles by Musaeus. As a chresmologist, Onomacritus' collection is just one example of many collections of genuine and fictitious oracles, and their re-use in literature, in chresmology, in (local) historiography, in poetry and philosophy. In the Second Sophistic oracles that have become absorbed into a literary discourse are a standard part of the 'encyclopaedia' of the educated man (*pepaideumenos*), the knowedge at hand; it is also the period of prophetic texts and books on divination. Contemporaries were of course aware of the fact that not all texts that claimed to be real oracular responses (λόγοι) could possibly be authentic or verbatim representations. But if an oracle-text is or is at any rate believed to be authentic, then as soon as it becomes a literary text it also legitimates its author. For example, Apollonius of Tyana is said to have discussed with the oracle of the god Trophonius in Boeotian Lebadeia the question of the most complete and pure philosophy. The philosopher collected in a booklet the answers received from the god by consultation, which were in complete agreement with his Pythagorean position. On the other hand, contemporaries also recognized that the absorption of such oracular texts into a literary context always meant that it might not be authentic, which in turn undercut the authority of the author. In the case of Apollonius (who at least during the lifetime of his biographer was venerated as a hero in his birth-place Tyana), Philostratus attempts to forestall such doubts by claiming that the booklet containing Trophonius' quasi-Pythagorean responses was still kept in the library of the imperial palace in Antium.[92]

---

[92] Onomacritus: Herodotus 6. 7. 3f. Ancient texts of divination: Strobel 1993: 59–61, 67f., 71f. Apollonius: Philostratus, *Life of Apollonius* 8. 19f. Heroisation: Cassius Dio 77. 18. 4; *IK* 55 (*Tyana*): no. 112. See the elaborate account of the 'ancient writers who collected oracles of the gods' (*scriptores veteres qui oracula deorum collegerint*) in Wolff 1856: 43–68; Fontenrose 1978: 145–65.

Literary strategies like the one employed by Philostratus operate inside a cultural communicative space where the authenticity and authority of oracles, at least in their textual form, is hard to verify. Of course some oracles, like the one at Didyma, had an archive called the *chresmograph(e)ion*, where oracíes were collected and preserved for later consultation and re-use by the religious officials. We also know of some cases of openly-accessible documentation of oracles in the towns they applied to. But as texts oracles can be copied and reproduced, because they are often so vaguely phrased that they can be re-used in a variety of contexts. These re-cyclings and modifications cannot be traced or controlled; a πεπαιδευμένος would not find it hard to come upon 'authentic' oracles in daily life and in literature, or even to create his own divine *logoi*.

The competition offered by oracles that had become autonomous thanks to their absorption into a literary tradition slowly became a problem for the authority of the mantic specialists. Plutarch complains about the independent 'seers', 'prophets', 'chresmologists', and 'poets' who produce oracles in prose or verse either out of their own heads or on the basis of collections of written oracles, which their clients take home as real *logoi*.[93] By what authority can the official oracles and their functionaries at Delphi, Didyma, Claros and other places be distinguished from these false prophets (ψευδομάντεις)? Is it their piety (εὐσέβεια), which is emphasized again and again in the texts to indicate that they have been chosen by the god? Or is their authority based on their office's exclusive claim to truth (ἀλήθεια), and their exclusive right to communicate the *logoi* 'without lies and deceit'?[94]

In the light of this competition, the texts of the period of the Second Sophistic about fate, providence, and divination cannot be read solely as contributions to a discourse about divination only interested in either affirming or denying oracles. They also fulfil a

[93] *Chrēsmograph(e)ion*: *IDidyma* nos. 31–2. Public presentation in a local context: *SEG* 50: 1356 ll. 71–98. Reproducibility: e.g. Merkelbach and Stauber 1998–2002: i. p. 84, iii. pp. 302f., iv. p. 19. The re-use of an oracle is also complained about in Oenomaus fr. 14 Hammerstaedt. Independent providers: Strabo 9. 3. 5; Plutarch, *The Oracles at Delphi*. 25 407B–C; see also note 60 above.

[94] Piety: e.g. *IDidyma* nos. 191f., 219f., 223 A 229 II 260, 277, 282, 594; Merkelbach and Stauber 1998–2002: i. p. 101, no. 01/19/28, i. p. 363, no. 03/05/02; Parke 1985: 87f.; Lane Fox 1986: 224f. Truth: *SEG* 43: 943B (313/14 CE).

performative function: they discuss the problem of the nature of traditional (religious) authority. Plutarch re-defines the relationship between the traditional authority of the oracles and the material world, and thus raises the issue of the authenticity of the divine component in the process of rendering oracles. Alexander of Aphrodisias declares that traditional mantic practice is probabilistic and contingent, and thus reduces the authority of the mantic specialists. Diogenes of Oenoanda denies the relevance of the gods for this world, and thus questions the authority of divination in general. The texts also react to the contemporary rhetoric of tradition invoked by the religious and political elites to legitimate themselves via the traditional authority of the oracles. In this dialogue with the rhetoric of tradition, the relationship between intellectual formation and such traditional authority, on which the literature of the Second Sophistic is dependent for its very identity, becomes critical. This problem is most clearly revealed in certain texts by Oenomaus of Gadara and Lucian of Samosata.

In Oenomaus' text *The Exposure of Frauds* (γοήτων φώρα), written in the first half of the second century CE, we encounter the traditional elements and motifs of philosophical, in this case Cynic, criticism of divination. The ambiguity of oracles is discussed using examples from myth: Apollo gave the Heracleidae several ambiguous oracles when they were planning to invade the Peloponnese. The ambiguity (ἀμφιβολία) of Delphic responses is illustrated by reference to the examples of Croesus, the enquiries by the Spartans and Athenians during the Persian wars, the Cnidians, the Messenians and again the Spartans. Even this critical text shows the influence of the contemporary rhetoric of tradition, as many of Oenomaus' examples are taken from the Greek past and from reading Herodotus. And according to the narrator, a contemporary investigation confirms this criticism of oracles from the past: he himself visited the shrine at Claros and Apollo gave him two incomprehensible answers; the third the god also gave to another person.[95] We have no way of deciding

[95] Text and commentary: Hammerstaedt 1988. Cf. Hammerstaedt 1990, 2835–9 (author and dates), 2844–60, 2853–62. Heracleidae: Oenomaus fr. 4 Hammerstaedt. Croesus: fr. 5. The other historical examples: fr. 6–9. Claros: fr. 14, 15. 1–19 = Merkelbach and Stauber 1996: 36–9.

whether Oenomaus really visited Claros or whether the supposed visit is merely a literary topos intended to support the authority of the narrative.

However that may be, in the Second Sophistic such criticism of the incomprehensibility of the oracles can be used to criticize the consultants and clients of the oracles or as proof of the impossibility of communication between gods and humans. But Oenomaus chooses a different strategy: such failures either mean that the seer did not understand the oracle's implications (which may also entail the oracle's inability to provide true answers) or that the god who gave the oracle can be malicious or play nasty games with the client. Doing so allows the narrator to indulge in further Cynic criticism: the contents of oracles are often so immoral that they do not fulfil the narrator's own moral principles. It would be better to make the philosopher Socrates the standard of one's decisions rather than the oracles of Apollo.[96] The radical postulate of freedom of will (ἐξουσία) that the Cynics elevated above everything else as the essence of a responsible and good life that can even master the most dire necessities (αὐτοκράτωρ τῶν ἀναγκαιοτάτων), prompts the narrator to deny divine providence, and the idea that human action is determined by fate. Apollo is incapable of making valid statements about the future because the freedom of the will makes the course of future actions unpredictable; the god himself is not free so long as he is forced constantly to give oracles.[97]

But *The Exposure of Frauds* is more than 'merely philosophical' criticism of divination. The narrator of this text denies Plutarch's earlier distinction between the divine authority of the traditional oracles, which as far as the great majority of his contemporaries was concerned were 'without lies and deceit', and the human frauds (γόητες) and pseudo-prophets (ψευδομάντεις). For him even the religious functionaries in the shrines at Delphi or Claros are frauds.

---

[96] Ignorance or malice: Oenomaus fr. 5. 21–30 Hammerstaedt. The question of moral lifestyle is dicussed extensively in the extant fragments; cf. F1–3. 9.17–26. F 10–12. Socrates: F 11A.17–29.

[97] Oenomaus fr. 16. 1–222 Hammerstaedt. The fragment's anti-determinism is examined by Brancacci 2001.

But he goes further still: the oracular god that appears in the text is no longer a divine instance, but a human object of criticism which the narrator can confront in a dialogue. Both the narrator and Apollo are presented as humans: the one is a fraud (γόης) and the other exposes him with all the skill of uncompromising Cynic freedom of speech (παρρησία).[98] To expose Apollo in this anthropological perspective as a sophist and all too human γόης is to unmask current ideas about divine authority and divinity in general; for, according to the Cynics, human notions of religion stem from a wrong image of the gods. Oenomaus' narrator states that whoever dares to doubt the validity of the Cynic position should be beaten, be he a human sophist or a god. Whether the Apollo of this text really is a god or only has this status in the minds of mystified humans, remains ambivalent throughout the text.[99] Instead, Oenomaus argues in terms of moral philosophy: the Apollo presented in *The Exposure of Frauds*—whether he really is a god or only an image we have of the god is unimportant—loses the right to represent traditional mantic authority. The deconstruction of this authority is part of the Cynic denial of any form of social, political, or intellectual authority. The individual is left with role models like Socrates, who represents a Cynic lifestyle through upholding the freedom of the will.

Lucian must have known *The Exposure of Frauds*. The numerous parallels between Oenomaus' text and Lucian's criticism of oracles were already recognized by nineteenth-century scholars:[100] a character called *Kyniskos*, a Cynic, even manages to refute Zeus himself by arguing that the oracles are not sensible forms of communication between god and human and that human fate is not necessarily predetermined by some kind of divine providence. Hera complains to Leto about the ambiguous answers of her son Apollo's oracles: they

---

[98] Oenomaus fr. 16. 47–63; 223–31 with Hammerstaedt 1988: 38–40.

[99] Oenomaus fr. 16. 223–31. On Oenomaus' construction of divinity, cf. Hammerstaedt 1990: 2849.

[100] The passages cited in the following paragraph are: Lucian, *Zeus catechized* 12–14, 18; *Dialogues of the Gods* 16; *Dialogues of the Dead* 10. 2, 12. 5; *Zeus rants*. 20. 28. 30f. These passages and their references to Oenomaus were already discussed in Bruns 1889. On the close thematic connection between the two authors, see also Hammerstaedt 1990: 2860–2; Pozzi 2003: 133f.

are safe and financially profitable for him as they cannot be proven wrong, but potentially perilous for clients. While Leto argues that the gods will just have to endure this false prophet (ψευδόμαντις), she does not even attempt to defend her son at the level of actual content. Like Apollo, the oracle-god Trophonius is also accused of fraud; Ammon at the oasis of Siwa is presented as a *goes* and *pseudomantis*. Momus asked the oracle to resolve the discussion between the Stoic Timocles and the Epicurean Damis, but the result is so incomprehensible that he uses it as proof of the charlatanry of the *goes* Apollo. The discussion ends in *aporia*; there is no divine resolution of this moral-philosophical problem, or at least none that one could trust. The only possibility left is for human philosophers to continue the search. Apollo has been exposed as a fraud and purveyor of oracles that are far from being 'without lies and deceit'—or rather, the image we have of god, and the traditional authority of the oracles, are based on false conceptions.

   In the Lucianic corpus criticizing divination is an anthropological endeavour, but the literary characters who present this criticism, figures like Kyniskos and Momus, are often entirely fictional. At first sight, Lucian's text about the false prophet (*pseudomantis*) Alexander seems to be cut from a different cloth. Alexander invented an oracular cult of the snake god Glycon, the so-called new Asclepius, and introduced it, legitimated by a fake oracle by the Apollo of Calchedon, in his home-town of Abonouteichos/Ionopolis in Paphlagonia. Alexander then made himself the *prophētēs* of the shrine and used this position for criminal schemes. Erasmus of Rotterdam and Christoph Martin Wieland already interpreted Lucian's *Alexander* as an educational text by the 'real' Lucian about religious superstition and beliefs which simply employs the example of a historical second-century oracular cult from the eastern part of the Roman Empire. And indeed, the first-person narrator of the text, who claims to have witnessed Alexander's schemes first hand, calls himself *Loukianos*. He mentions people and events which—apart from Alexander himself obviously—can be historically verified and even allow us to reconstruct a chronology of the events: the narrator must have visited the oracle of Glycon shortly after the late summer of 161 CE. He also states in the foreword of the biography of this anti-hero that he will try to present Alexander's life as accurately as possible (πρὸς τὸ ὁμοιότατον).[101]

In spite of the literary exaggerations it contains, the text is generally taken by many modern scholars (notwithstanding a few exceptions) as a basically historical document about a contemporary oracular shrine of the second century CE and its founder, whose historicity seems undisputable. The oracular cult of the snake god Glycon has also been reconstructed from Lucian's text, at least in its broad outlines, and the fact that archaeological investigation of Abonouteichos/Ionopolis has not produced any proof of its existence yet has not seriously hampered scholarly confidence.[102] We also lack any kind of independent literary evidence that would support Lucian's *Alexander*.

Indirect confirmation of Lucian's narrative about the oracle of Glycon, the influence of which, according to the narrator, extended all the way to Rome, has been sought from numismatic, archaeological, and epigraphic evidence.[103] On early second-century coins from Abonouteichos/Ionopolis we find images of a snake with a human head labelled ΓΛΥΚΩΝ. Another quite similar coin-type that appears elsewhere has also been associated with the oracular cult of Glycon, although it lacks the name-tag. Some sculptures (with or without a head) from Tomis in Moesia Inferior, Amastris in Pontus-Bithynia, Gadara in Palestine, and other cities represent a coiled-up snake which scholars have also identified as Glycon. Two Latin inscriptions from Alba Iulia and Apulum in Dacia are addressed to a god called Glycon.[104] But at best these pieces of evidence provide

---

[101] On the modern reception of this text, see Baumbach 2002: 33f., 92f., 107f., 170, 198. Chronology of the dramatic date of the text: Flinterman 1997. Alleged historical accuracy: Lucian, *Alexander* 3.

[102] The absence of any archaeological material at the site is noted by Marek 2003: 117. Fundamental doubts about the narrative of the *Alexander* are expressed by Branham 1989 and esp. Pozzi 2003 (I only came to know of this important article that complements my own reflections some time after I finished the manuscript of this paper).

[103] See e.g. Robert 1980: 393–421; Lane Fox 1986: 241–50; Marek 1993: 114f.; Miron 1996; Victor 1997; Sfameni Gasparro 1999; Chaniotis 2002; Marek 2003: 111–17.

[104] This and further material has been collected and linked to the oracle of Glycon by Robert 1980: 393–9; 406–08; Miron 1996; Victor 1997: 1–3 and *passim*; Marek 2003: 114–17. For instance, Robert 1980: 405–8 attempts to connect the epigraphic

merely indirect confirmation of the statements made in Lucian's *Alexander*, and only then on the assumption that the text is historically accurate. These few scraps of evidence may prove the existence of a cult of a snake-god called Glycon in Abonouteichos; they do not prove any of the religious details which according to the narrator made the oracular shrine so special.

The fact that the unimportant coastal city of Abonouteichos managed to have its name changed to Ionopolis, the town of Ion, the progenitor of all Ionians, shows the extent and the success of its ambitions, so it would theoretically be possible that its inhabitants also felt the need to found an oracular shrine to complement their claims of pre-eminence. But the gap between this possibility (which cannot be verified archaeologically) and the alleged historical reality described by Lucian is significant—and probably too large to be bridged. In Lucian's text the founder of the cult, Alexander, and his oracle embody a multitude of religious and intellectual characteristics of their time: the *prophētēs* is allegedly interested in philosophy, especially the (neo-)Pythagorean school, believes in the rebirth of the soul and hates Epicureans and Christians. The shrine offers various mantic techniques, elaborate religious festivals, healing, a mystery-cult based on the Eleusinian model as well as institutions for the musical education of young men. One or more of these also feature at other oracles of the time: Didyma and Claros both had initiations

material with the information given in Lucian's narrative: according to him, a man called Meiletos, priest of Apollo in Caesarea Troketta in Lydia and 'son of Glycon, the Paphlagonian' (*IGR* iv. 1498), was a son of the snake-god and indicates that the oracle gained a supra-regional reputation. This widely-accepted theory is mostly based on Lucian's claim that Alexander made female clients of the oracle pregnant (Lucian, *Alexander* 42). This theory could be made more plausible by assuming (though this is not, *pace* Victor 1997: 4f., supported by the text itself) that these female clients had gone to Abonouteichos/Ionopolis because they were infertile and wanted to undergo a ritual of incubation (like those at Epidaurus). But even if we seriously consider that the snake-god could be meant by the name Glycon, which was after all a very common name, would we really expect the highly unusual nomenclature 'son of Glycon the *Paphlagonian*', which goes against all onomastic conventions? To take another example of the modern attempt to verify the Lucianic narrative by adducing non-literary 'parallels': Jones 1998 proposes that we should identify Neiketes, son of Glycon and a doctor in Tieion, who is attested epigraphically (*SEG* 18: no. 519), as a son of the snake-god (or of his prophet), because Lucian, *Alexander* 43 refers to an alleged consultation of the oracle by a priest from Tieion called Sacerdos.

and 'mystery-cults' which we do not know much about. But are scholars right to present the oracle of Glycon at Abonouteichos/ Ionopolis as a shrine of such religious, theological, and cultural multifunctionality that its innovativeness surpassed even Delphi, Didyma, and Claros, just on the say-so of a single text by Lucian?[105]

Doubts about the dominant interpretation are certainly justified, because the narrator of *Alexander* can often be falsified. He claims that on the occasion of Abonouteichos' change of name, Alexander managed, by petitioning the emperor, to have new coins struck: one side showed Glycon and the other—and this is truly unusual— Alexander himself. This statement is definitely false, because all known coins with the legend *IONOΠOΛEITΩN* only bear the image of Glycon.[106]

Here the reader encounters a strategy typical of the Lucianic corpus, namely covertly adding historically falsifiable information; the same occurs in the text *De dea Syria* which can certainly also be ascribed to Lucian. To readers of the *Alexander* this literary strategy indicates that the narrator may not be very reliable: what would a contemporary reader's reaction be if he found that Alexander's plan to gain riches and glory by founding an oracle was based on his own experience? For, according to the narrator, Alexander realized that Delphi, Delos, Claros, and Didyma had become rich and famous because people flocked to these oracles in great numbers, offered hecatombs and expensive gifts, simply to acquire a glimpse into the future. As we have seen, Delphi, Claros, and Didyma were indeed the most important oracles in the time of the Second Sophistic and thus could have provided Lucian's aspiring oracle-founder Alexander with plenty of material. But in the time of the Second Sophistic (nor, for

---

[105] Pythagoreanism: Sfameni Gasparro 1999: 292–4. Mystery-cults: ibid. 303f. Innovative multifunctionality: Chaniotis 2002. As far as Abonouteichos/Ionopolis is concerned, note the interesting contrast between Marek 1993: 83: 'the otherwise obscure marginality of this coastal area...' and Marek 2003: 114: '[the] reputation [of the new oracle] was hardly inferior to those of the great oracles of Asia Minor...'.

[106] Lucian, *Alexander* 58. Note here the unconvincing and confused attempt at harmonizing the text's claim that coins were struck with Alexander's image with the absence of numismatic examples by Miron 1996: 173 with n. 128: 'the type of coin Lucian describes has not been found, we must doubt its existence'; (173) '...obviously also the quasi-autonomous special issue was declined'—phrased as it is, this is pure speculation.

that matter, either before or after) Delos had no comparable divin-atory competence, nor did it have the infrastructure required for a financially-successful oracle; so Alexander would have been acquiring his information in the wrong place.[107]

But the reader has already been warned in the introduction. The narrator claims that he is going to describe the life of the fraud (*goes*) Alexander to an Epicurean called Celsus in the form of a historical biography, and claims that this task is just as difficult as narrating the life of Alexander the Great: just as a biography of Alexander the Great would have to focus on virtue, an account of Alexander of Abonou-teichos would have to focus on moral worthlessness. According to the rules of historical biography, which Lucian's contemporary read-ers undoubtedly knew, characterization has to consist of both posi-tive and negative aspects: in the case of Alexander of Abonouteichos, however, the narrator focuses almost exclusively on the negative rather than on the integration of these two kinds of aspects. He describes himself as an Epicurean writing for another Epicurean, and his intention is to avenge Epicurus and the Epicureans who play an important part in the story as opponents of the *pseudomantis*. Thus the narrator has a deep personal aversion against his subject, the prophet Alexander. In order to legitimate his enterprise, the narrator refers to Arrian (*Alexander* 1):

... Epictetus' pupil Arrian, who was one of the most important Romans and dedicated his whole life to learning, (...) thought it worth his while to compose the Life of the thief Tillorobos. But we will preserve the memory of a far crueller villain, one who did not rob out in the country, but inside towns, who did not only roam Mysia and the mountain-range of Ida and other remote areas of Asia, but exploited the whole Roman Empire with his villainy.

We have no evidence that Arrian wrote a biography of someone called Tillorobos. Even if we assume that it existed, then Lucian's reference to a text of such marginal importance is actually an ironical undercutting of the narrator's claim to publish a work equal to the biography of Alexander the Great. On the other hand, the thief Tilloboros might also be Lucian's own invention: the fact that

---

[107] Lucian, *Alexander* 8. Pozzi (2003: 142) also notes the author's strategy of questioning the competence of his own narrator.

τιλλόροβος is the Pisidian word 'thief' makes such an assumption quite plausible.[108]

But if the narrator invokes Arrian's biography of Tillorobos, and thus the authority of a largely unknown or even fictitious text, then this literary strategy once again casts doubt on the narrator's reliability and competence to report the historically accurate. Once the narrator contrasts the moral worthlessness of his 'protagonist' with the virtue of Alexander the Great, the reader can question the claim by means of the intertextual reference to Arrian's *Anabasis*: the life of Alexander the Great was by no means all sweetness and light, nor does Arrian depict it as such, since as a historical biographer, he obeys the rules of the genre and shows both the positive and negative character-traits of his subject.

In the narrator's opinion, Alexander of Abonouteichos, in 'inventing' the oracle there, was exploiting the weakness of people's minds. He maintains that the lives of human beings are controlled by two powerful forces, hope and fear, and that the success of the oracle was founded on this weakness:[109]

During the plague he sent an oracle to all nations. It consisted of one line only: 'Phoebus, the longhaired, disperses the cloud of the plague.' This phrase could be seen written on door-frames all over the place as a form of protection against the plague. In most cases it had the opposite effect— due to some coincidence, those houses on which the legend was written were most affected. But you must not suppose that I mean that they died because of it—no, that happened by mere coincidence. But maybe the majority put their trust in the phrase and lived carelessly, and did not help the oracle against the plague, as though these words were fighting on their behalf, and long-haired Phoebus were shooting down the plague with his arrows.

Part of the one-liner was found on the base of an altar at Antioch-on-the-Orontes in Syria, restored from Lucian's text—ΓΦοῖβος ἀκειρεκόμης λοιοῦ νε]φέλην ἀπερύκει—and used as an argument for the supra-regional importance of the Glycon-oracle.[110] But is this kind of restoration legitimate? As we have seen, the literary

---

[108] Lucian, *Alexander* 1f. The same position is taken by Pozzi 2003: 136–40; cf. already Tonnet 1988: 73, who quite plausibly suspects that 'Tillorobos' might be a name for Alexander the Great, 'un nom plaisant donné à Alexandre par Lucien. Alexandre n'est-il pas, dans la tradition hostile, "le brigand des nations"?'.

[109] Lucian, *Alexander* 36; cf. also 8.

[110] See e.g. Robert 1980: 404; Merkelbach and Stauber 1998–2002: iv. p. 242, no. 20/03/01. For doubts about this interpretation, see note 71 above.

transformation of oracles makes them autonomous; they are no longer bound to a shrine or the occasion of oracular consultation. As a consequence, if there is no independent evidence to confirm it, none of the texts the narrator cites need actually have come from the oracle at Abonouteichos/Ionopolis. Another question is whether this one-liner is really an oracle at all. As we saw earlier, the oracles given at Claros advised in convoluted language the erection of statues of Apollo and the performance of elaborate rituals to avert the plague. The Glycon-oracle by contrast consists of just one line (its brevity is even emphasized in Lucian's text), and we can assume that it was a standard-formula that was widely known and utilized for its apotropaic efficacy, and not associated with a specific site.

This oracle, allegedly given by Glycon during an epidemic, is ridiculed by the Epicurean narrator in the course of his diatribe about the pointlessness of hoping for the fulfilment of prophecies; for, as one might expect, he claims that all events are caused by mere coincidence (τύχη). The narrator contrasts people's fear of the epidemic and their (pointless) hope for salvation through the oracles with Epicurean serenity (ἀταραξία), the state that truly frees human beings from hope and fear. The account of Alexander's death also exemplifies this Epicurean concept, since it is most pitiful and painful and full of emotion, and very far from embodying the ἀταραξία that only philosophy can provide. It is as if the reader were watching a play that begins with Alexander's entrance in Abonouteichos and ends with his death. The use of theatre-imagery in the text invites the readers to 'view' the text as a dramatic performance of a tragic story; Alexander's death marks the end of this performance (τραγῳδία), the *dénoument* (καταστροφή) of the drama. One might think that this ending was pre-determined, had the narrator not presented it as a coincidence (τύχη). What cannot be coincidental is that, in a text about divination and its criticism, the word foresight (πρόνοια) appears only once, namely at this point immediately before the conclusion.[111]

Like Oenomaus', this text actually presents a truly anthropological endeavour: it provides a moral-philosophical discussion of the proper mode of human life, while pretending to criticize oracles

---

[111] Lucian, *Alexander* 60. On the use of theatre-imagery in the *Alexander*, see Chaniotis 2002: 80f.

and the culture of divination. Alexander, the *pseudomantis* who in dying fails to observe his own philosophical maxims, not only reminds us of Apollo and Ammon whom in some of his other work Lucian disavows as *goetes* and *pseudomanteis*, but also of the alleged 'holy man' Peregrinus in Lucian's text of the same name, and of the *goes* Apollonios of Tyana, whose pupil at one remove Alexander allegedly was. The text problematizes a would-be Pythagorean's philosophy of education and life-style as well as the Stoic and Platonic view of divination.

Nevertheless it is not an Epicurean text. The narrator, who claims to possess Epicurean ἀταραξία, is himself disavowed and 'Lucian' exposed as a would-be Epicurean. His account of the false prophet is itself so laden with aggressive emotions and his personal hatred of Alexander that he finally loses control during a visit in Abonouteichos/Ionopolis and bites Alexander's proffered hand. An analysis of the text that sees it as an equivalent of Diogenes' Epicurean criticism of divination or Oenomaus' Cynic attack is thus too simple. As author, Lucian ironically deconstructs the moral message of this quasi-Epicurean text (taken as a serious Epicurean diatribe, it would simply be bad), and thus the seemingly privileged position of his narrator 'Lucian'.[112]

After all this analysis of Lucian's text we still do not really know anything about the historical reality of Alexander and the Glycon oracle. Whether the author, who repeatedly distances himself from the narrator 'Lucian', really visited Abonouteichos/Ionopolis during his lifetime, and what there was to see there, remains obscure. Nor can we finally decide whether the actions of the historical persons are accurately reported or are simply part of a literary characterization. This is due to the fact that the narrator's manoeuvres undermine his claim that he is going to provide an accurate account of the cult on the basis of the literary genre of the historical biography. An educated

---

[112] Lucian, *Alexander* 55 with Branham 1989: 204–07; Pozzi 2003: 133–5. For the remarkable, even exaggerated, prominence of Epicureans and Epicurean philosophy in the narrative of the Epicurean narrator, see *Alexander* 17, 25, 43–7, 61. Cf. also Von Möllendorff 2000: 563 on the 'tension between self-affirmation and ironic self-destruction which we can also see in Lucian's other work'; but on the next page he implies that, in spite of all the irony, the invective against Alexander should be read as a statement by the 'real' Lucian.

reader at the time of the Second Sophistic would probably also have realized that the oracle of Glycon is meant to be read as a literary construction because it, together with its prophet, is situated in a 'utopian' space somewhere in Paphlagonia. Abonouteichos' exaggerated old-fashioned ambition to be the 'city of Ion' was counterbalanced by its no doubt in reality slight importance as the site of the shrine of a(n oracular?) god named Glycon. Lucian's *Alexander* thus becomes part of the discourse about the authority of contemporary oracles and their gods at the period of the Second Sophistic. It was much easier to conduct this discourse by adducing the example not of Delphi, Didyma, or Claros and their religious functionaries but of this small and unimportant Paphlagonian coastal-town and its preposterous, and probably fictitious, cult founder.

But the text also raises the question of the authority of the elites that support these shrines, because Lucian's Abonouteichos/Ionopolis is construed as a place that is not only visited by uneducated (ἀπαίδευτοι) locals—many clients come long distances, for example from Bithynia, Galatia, Thrace, Cilicia, and Ionia, and some are members of the political elites, among them the brother of a senator. Supporters come from all parts of the Empire, even from the highest political circles: P. Mummius Sisenna Rutilianus (*cos. suff.* 146) supposedly married Alexander's daughter; M. Sedatius Severianus (*cos. suff.* 153) was taken in by the false oracles of the false prophet; and the provincial governor, L. Hedius Rufus Lollianus Avitus (*cos. ord.* 144), allegedly supported Alexander against the powerless narrator's attacks. The elite families of Paphlagonia and Pontus entrust Alexander with the musical education of their sons—the various foundations of Demosthenes of Oenoanda and Opramoas of Rhodiapolis have a quite similar 'educational' function; and the provincial elites supposedly meet in the shrine.[113] Lucian's *Alexander* is an additional indication that intellectual freedom of speech (παρρησία) was the characteristic ideal of the Second Sophistic: contemporary readers probably read this text too as a satirical commentary on the

---

[113] Lucian, *Alexander* 17f., 24f., 27, 30f., 33, 35–7, 41, 45, 55, 57. Flinterman 1997 lists the historical persons; Pozzi 2003: 242f.; 251–3 advises caution regarding the historicity of the actions attributed to these people. On the educational foundations of Demosthenes and Opramoas see the literature cited in note 31 above.

relationship between intellect and power, as a critical discussion of the importance of education in times of corrupt political and moral authority.

But the authorial deconstruction of the narrator's claim to be telling the truth, and the irony underlying his deconstruction of divinatory practices, also imply that criticism of the false prophet Alexander by 'Lucian' cannot be the final word. Is the narrator not himself shown up? In good dialectical fashion, the author allows his readers to choose which side they want to be on: whether they want to apply 'Lucian' the narrator's account of the Paphlagonian oracle to contemporary oracular practice in general, or whether they want to believe that, despite this wretched example of Glycon and his false prophet in far-off Paphlagionia, oracles can indeed speak 'without lies and deceit'. Fate, providence, and divination: the discussion simply goes on and on and on.

AFTERWORD (2009)

Two detailed studies, Busine 2005 and Oesterheld 2008, re-examine the pragmatics of consultation at Claros and Didyma and the oracular texts themselves. Graf (2007) has revisited some of the texts from Claros. Jones (2005; 2006) tentatively links many of the examples that mention a plague to the so-called Antonine Plague from the mid-160s CE onward, and wishes to see the mostly Latin dedications to 'all gods and goddesses' as a response to that calamity, but the effects of the Antonine Plague, particularly in the West, must remain a matter of speculation.

I continue to believe psychological interpretations of the imperial resurgence of oracular activity to be wrong-headed, when they suggest that the imperial acme of oracular consultations indicates an increasing desire for mantic reassurance in times of change, crisis, and anxiety (e.g. Nollé 2007). Such explanatory models substitute crude psychologizing for historical analysis, but fail to address the real question, which is why oracular shrines should again become socially and culturally acceptable sources of divine authority for people in times of prosperity so that they would turn to them for help in moments of calamity and fear.

Hence my attempt to explain the resurgence of mantic practice at the oracular shrines in the Eastern Mediterranean between the late first and the mid-third century CE as one aspect of wider behavioural and communicative changes among the provincial elites. These changes suggest a close relation between two phenomena, as the new flourishing of oracles appears to coincide with the existence of the so-called 'Second Sophistic'—a phenomenon that ought to be understood as denoting a much broader cultural milieu than that of Philostratus' sophists. However, the almost arbitrary use of the term 'Second Sophistic' and its wide ahistorical application strongly suggest to me now that we either agree on a more stringent definition or indeed develop a more comprehensive and possibly more neutral terminology. I hope to be able to return to this issue in due course.

The period's intellectual climate is brought out in exemplary fashion by the Epicurean inscription authored by Diogenes of Oenoanda (on which see, most recently, the surveys by Smith and Hammerstaedt (2007; 2008)). Meanwhile, Milner and Eilers (2006: 61, 63) have doubted, on solid architectural and archaeological grounds, the identification of the stoa mentioned as the location of Diogenes' inscription (F 3 Smith) with the south stoa of the Upper Agora. As Milner kindly confirms by letter, the south stoa was indeed built partly using the stones that carry Diogenes' inscription, but they are all in re-use and not in their original position. Recent investigations have also unearthed an inscription mentioning Theos Hypsistos on Oenonada's southern city-wall, together with inlets in the stone to hold oil-lamps, which provides a parallel to the well-known dedication to the 'highest god' from the eastern city-wall (p. 224 above) by a certain Chromatis (who need not be a woman: see Jones 2005: 295 n. 5).

The concluding part of my essay also argues that Lucian's 'false prophet' Alexander of Abonouteichos may be a fictitious character. Many would agree that Lucian's narrative is not a reliable historical document but a text given to satirical exaggeration and partial falsification. Yet just as many maintain that it depicts some historical reality and allows the scholar to reconstruct some kind of historical ritual and oracular practice at least in broad outline. There is nothing wrong with using literary texts in order to reconstruct sentiments and social practices of the time of their composition.

However, the 'New Historicism' represented in these approaches adduces the widest possible range of supposed literary and non-literary parallels to Lucian's narrative in order to explain and thus reify the supposed historical information provided by the literary text. The problem with such an approach is not just that it elides the differences between text and context; even more problematically, it is the historian who selects the contexts s/he finds relevant to elucidate the text's historical core. Some, such as Gerlach (2005), have resisted the temptation of the New Historicism to do justice to the literary strategies of Lucian's *Alexander*. Even they do not, however, deny the historicity of Alexander, which I continue to doubt.

BIBLIOGRAPHY

Alcock, S. E. (1993). *Graecia Capta: The Landscapes of Roman Greece*. Cambridge: Cambridge University Press.

——(2001). 'The Reconfiguration of Memory in the Eastern Roman Empire', in S. E. Alcock, T. N. D'Altroy, K. D. Morrison, and C. M Sinopoli (eds.), *Empires: Perspectives from Archaeology and History*. Cambridge: Cambridge University Press, 323–50.

——(2002). *Archaeologies of the Greek Past: Landscape, Monuments, and Memories*. Cambridge: Cambridge University Press.

Anderson, G. (1998). 'L'intellettuale e il primo impero romano', in S. Settis (ed.), *I Greci: storia, cultura, arte, società II.3*. Turin: Einaudi, 1123–46.

Balland, A. (1981). *Fouilles de Xanthos. Tome VII: Inscriptions d'époque impériale du Létoon*. Paris: Klincksieck.

Barnes, T. D. (2001). 'Monotheists All?' *Phoenix*, 55: 142–62.

Baumbach, M. (2002). *Lukian in Deutschland: Eine forschungs- und rezeptionsgeschichtliche Analyse vom Humanismus bis zur Gegenwart*. Munich: Fink.

Bendlin, A. (1997). 'Peripheral Centres — Central Peripheries: Religious Communication in the Roman Empire', in H. Cancik and J. Rüpke (eds.), *Römische Reichsreligion und Provinzialreligion*. Tübingen: Mohr Siebeck, 35–68.

——(2005). 'Wer braucht Heilige Schriften? Die Textbezogenheit der Religionsgeschichte und das "Reden über die Götter" in der griechisch-römischen Antike', in C. Bultmann, C. P. März, and V. N. Makrides (eds.),

Heilige Schriften: Ursprung, Geltung und Gebrauch. Münster: Aschendorff, 205–28, 251–4.

Borg, B. E. (ed.) (2004). *Paideia: The World of the Second Sophistic.* Millennium-Studien 2. Berlin; New York: De Gruyter.

——and Witschel, C. (2001). 'Veränderungen im Repräsentationsverhalten der römischen Eliten während des 3. Jh. n. Chr.', in G. Alföldy and S. Panciera (eds.), *Inschriftliche Denkmäler als Medien der Selbstdarstellung in der römischen Welt*, HABES 36. Stuttgart: F. Steiner, 47–120.

Bowie, E. L. (1970). 'The Greeks and their Past in the Second Sophistic', *Past & Present*, 46: 3–41.

Bradbury, S. (1995). 'Julian's Pagan Revival and the Decline of Blood Sacrifice', *Phoenix*, 49: 331–56.

Brancacci, A. (2001). 'La polemica antifatalistica di Enomao di Gadara', in A. Brancacci (ed.), *Antichi e moderni nella filosofia di età imperiale*. Naples: Bibliopolis, 71–110.

Branham, R. B. (1989). *Unruly Eloquence: Lucian and the Comedy of Traditions.* Cambridge, MA: Harvard University Press.

Bruns, I. (1889). 'Lucian und Oenomaus', *Rheinisches Museum*, 44: 374–96.

Busine, A. (2006). 'The Officials of Oracular Sanctuaries in Roman Asia minor', *ARG*, 8: 275–316.

Cambiano, G. (1991). 'Eric R. Dodds entre psychoanalyse et parapsychologie', *Revue de l'histoire des religions*, 208: 3–26.

Chaniotis, A. (2002). 'Old Wine in a New Skin. Tradition and Innovation in the Cult Foundation of Alexander of Abonouteichos', in E. Dabrowa (ed.), *Tradition and Innovation in the Ancient World*, Electrum 6. Krakau: Jagiellonian University Press, 67–85.

Chlup, R. (2000). 'Plutarch's Dualism and the Delphic Cult', *Phronesis*, 45: 138–58.

de Blois, L., Bons, J., Kessels, T. and Schenkefeld, D. M. (eds.) (2004). *The Statesman in Plutarch's Works. I: Plutarch's Statesman and his Aftermath: Political, Philosophical and Literary Aspects.* Leiden: Brill.

Dillon, J. M. (2002a). 'Plutarch and God: Theodicy and Cosmogony in the Thought of Plutarch', in Frede and Laks 2002: 223–37.

—— (2002b). 'The Social Role of the Philosopher in the Second Century C. E.: Some Remarks', in P. A. Stadter and L. van der Stockt (eds.), *Sage and Emperor: Plutarch, Greek Intellectuals, and Roman Power in the Time of Trajan.* Leuven: Leuven University Press, 29–40.

Dodds, E. R. (1965). *Pagan and Christian in an Age of Anxiety: Some Aspects of Religious Experience from Marcus Aurelius to Constantine.* Cambridge: Cambridge University Press.

Elm, D. (2003). '"Alexander oder der Lügenprophet"– ein religiöser Spezialist und ein Text zwischen Tradition und Innovation: Ein Beispiel für die Darstellung, Legitimierung und Plausibilisierung von Religion im lokalen und reichsweiten Kontext', in H. Cancik and J. Rüpke (eds.), *Römische Reichsreligion und Provinzialreligion. Globalisierungs- und Regionalisierungsprozesse in der antiken Religionsgeschichte.* Erfurt: SPP 1080, Religionswiss., Philos. Fak., Univ., 34–46.

Ewald, B. C. (1999). *Der Philosoph als Leitbild*, RM Ergänzungshefte. Mainz: von Zabern.

——(2003). 'Sarcophagi and Senators: The Social History of Roman Funerary Art and its Limits', *JRA*, 16: 561–71.

Faraone, C. A. (1992). *Talismans and Trojan Horses: Guardian Statues in Ancient Greek Myth and Ritual.* New York and Oxford: Oxford University Press.

Ferrary, J.-L. (2000). 'Les inscriptions du sanctuaire de Claros en l'honneur de Romains', *BCH*, 124: 331–76.

Flinterman, J.-J. (1997). 'The Date of Lucian's Visit to Abonouteichos', *ZPE*, 119: 280–2.

——(2004). 'Sophists and Emperors: A Reconnaisance of Sophistic Attitudes', in Borg 2004: 359–76.

Fontenrose, J. E. (1978). *The Delphic Oracle: Its Responses and Operations with a Catalogue of Responses.* Berkeley: University of California Press.

——(1988). *Didyma: Apollo's Oracle, Cult, and Companions.* Berkeley: University of California Press.

Foucault, M. (1977). 'Nietzsche, Genealogy, History', in his *Language, Counter-memory Practice: Selected Essays and Interviews.* Ithaka: Cornell University Press, 139–64.

Fowden, G. (1988). 'Between Pagans and Christians', *JRS*, 78: 173–82.

Frede, D. and Laks, A. (eds.) (2002). *Traditions of Theology: Studies in Hellenistic Theology, its Background and Aftermath*, Philosophia Antiqua 89. Leiden: Brill.

Gager, J. G. (1984). 'The Dodds Hypothesis', in R. C. Smith and J. Lounibos (eds.), *Pagan and Christian Anxiety: A Response to E. R. Dodds.* Lanham, MD: University Press of America, 1–12.

Galli, M. (2001). 'Pepaideumenoi am Ort des Heiligen: Kommunikationsformen und euergetische Initiativen in griechischen Heiligtümern zur Zeit der Zweiten Sophistik', in C. Reusser (ed.), *Griechenland in der Kaiserzeit: Neue Funde und Forschungen zu Skulptur, Architektur und Topographie.* Bern: Institut für Klassische Archäologie der Universität Bern, 43–71.

——'"Creating religious identities": paideia e religione nella Seconda Sofistica', in Borg 2004: 315–56.

Glucker, J. (1978). *Antiochus and the Late Academy*, Hypomnemata 56. Göttingen: Vanderhoeck and Ruprecht.

Goldhill, S. (ed.) (2001). *Being Greek under Rome: Cultural Identity, the Second Sophistic and the Development of Empire*. Cambridge: Cambridge University Press.

——(2001a). 'Introduction. Setting an Agenda: "Everything is Greece to the Wise"', in Goldhill 2001: 1–25.

Gordon, P. (1996). *Epicurus in Lycia: The Second-Century World of Diogenes of Oenoanda*. Ann Arbor, MI: University of Michigan Press.

Gordon, R. (1972). 'Fear of Freedom?', *Didaskalos*, 4: 48–60.

Haake, M. (2003). 'Warum und zu welchem Ende schreibt man Perí basileías? Überlegungen zum historischen Kontext einer literarischen Gattung im Hellenismus', in Piepenbrink 2003: 83–138.

Hahn, J. (1989). *Der Philosoph und die Gesellschaft: Selbstverständnis, öffentliches Auftreten und populäre Erwartungen in der Hohen Kaiserzeit*, Heidelberger althistorische Beiträge und epigraphische Studien. 7. Stuttgart: F. Steiner Verlag.

Hall, J. M. (2002). *Hellenicity: Between Ethnicity and Culture*. Chicago and London: University of Chicago Press.

Hammerstaedt, J. (1988). *Die Orakelkritik des Kynikers Oenomaus*, Beiträge zur Klassischen Philologie 188. Frankfurt am Main: Athenäum.

——(1990). 'Der Kyniker Oenomaos von Gadara', in *ANRW*, 2. 36. 4: 2834–65.

Harris, W. V. (2003). 'Roman Opinions about the Truthfulness of Dreams', *JRS*, 93: 18–34.

Hirsch-Luipold, R. (2002). *Plutarchs Denken in Bildern: Studien zur literarischen, philosophischen und religiösen Funktion des Bildhaften*, Studien und Texte zu Antike und Christentum 14. Tübingen: Mohr Siebeck.

Jacquemin, A. (1991). 'Delphes au IIᵉ siècle après J.-C.', in S. Said (ed.), *Hellenismos: quelques jalons pour une histoire de l'identité grecque*. Leiden: Brill, 217–31.

Jones, C. P. (1971). *Plutarch and Rome*. Oxford: Clarendon Press.

——(1998). 'A Follower of the God Glykon?', *EA*, 30: 107–9.

——(2004). 'Multiple Identities in the Age of the Second Sophistic', in Borg 2004: 13–21.

Kokkinia, C. (2000). *Die Opramoas-Inschrift von Rhodiapolis: Euergetismus und soziale Elite in Lykien*, Antiquitas 3, 40. Bonn: Habelt.

Lane Fox, R. (1986). *Pagans and Christians in the Mediterranean World from the Second century A.D. to the Conversion of Constantine*. London and New York: Penguin.

Leschhorn, W. (1998). 'Die Verbreitung von Agonen in den östlichen Provinzen des römischen Reiches', *Stadion*, 24. 1: 31–57.

Levin, S. (1989). 'The Old Greek Oracles in Decline', in *ANRW*, 2. 18. 2: 1599–649.

Livrea, E. (1998). 'Sull'iscrizione teosofica di Enoanda', *ZPE*, 122: 90–6.

Marek, C. (1993). *Stadt, Ära und Territorium in Pontus-Bithynia und Nord-Galatia*, Istanbuler Forschungen 39. Tübingen: E. Wasmuth.

——(2000). 'Der beste, höchste, größte, allmächtige Gott: Inschriften aus Nordkleinasien', *EA*, 32: 129–46.

——(2003). *Pontus et Bithynia: Die römischen Provinzen im Norden Kleinasiens*. Mainz: von Zabern.

McInerney, J. (2004). '"Do you see what I see?" Plutarch and Pausanias at Delphi', in de Blois et al. 2004: 43–55.

Merkelbach, R. and Josef, J. (1996). 'Die Orakel des Apollon von Klaros', *EA*, 27: 1–54.

——and Stauber, J. (1998–2002). *Steinepigramme aus dem griechischen Osten* (4 vols). Munich and Leipzig: Saur.

Miron, A. V. B. (1996). 'Alexander von Abonuteichos: zur Geschichte des Orakels des Neos Asklepios Glykon', in W. Leschhorn, A. V. B. Miron, and A. Miron (eds.), *Hellas und der griechische Osten: Studien zur Geschichte und Numismatik der griechischen Welt*. Saarbrücken: SVD Saarbrücker Druckerei und Verlag, 153–88.

Mitchell, S. (1990). 'Festivals, Games and Civic Life in Roman Asia Minor', *JRS*, 80: 183–93.

——(1999). 'The Cult of Theos Hypsistos between Pagans, Jews, and Christians', in P. Athanassiadi and M. Frede (eds.), *Pagan Monotheism in Late Antiquity*. Oxford: Clarendon Press, 81–148.

Myonopoulos, J. (2003). *Πελοπόννησος οἰκτήριον Ποσειδῶνος: Heiligtümer und Kulte des Poseidon auf der Peloponnes*, Kernos Supplément 13. Liège: Centre Internationale d'étude de la religion grecque antique.

Opsomer, J. (1996). 'Divination and Academic "Scepticism" according to Plutarch', in L. van der Stockt (ed.), *Plutarchea Lovaniensia: A Miscellany of Essays on Plutarch*. Leuven: Catholic University of Leuven, 165–94.

Paci, G. (2000). 'L'oracolo dell'Apollo Clario a Cosa', in G. Paci (ed.), *ΕΠΙΓΡΑΦΑΙ: Miscellanea epigrafica in onore di Lidio Gasperini*. Tivoli (Rome): Tipigraf, ii. 661–70.

Parke, H. W. (1985). *The Oracles of Apollo in Asia Minor*. London: Croom Helm.

Piepenbrink, K. (ed.) (2003). *Philosophie und Lebenswelt in der Antike*. Darmstadt: Wissenschaftliche Buchgesellschaft.

Pozzi, S. (2003). 'Sull attendibilità del narratore nell'Alexander di Luciano', *Prometheus*, 29: 129–50; 241–58.

Rigsby, K. J. (2004). 'Claudius at Delphi', *ZPE*, 146: 99–100.

Robert, L. (1967). *Monnaies grecques: types, légendes, magistrats monétaires et géographie*. Genf and Paris: Droz.

——(1971). 'Un oracle gravé à Oenoanda', *CRAI*, 597–619, repr. in Robert, *Opera Minora Selecta: épigraphie et antiquités grecques*. Amsterdam: Hakkert, 1989, v. 617–39.

——(1980). *À travers l'Asie mineure: poètes et prosateurs, grecques, voyageurs et géographie*, Bibliotèque des écoles françaises d'Athènes et de Rome 239. Athens: École française d'Athènes.

Rohde, E. (1876). *Der griechische Roman und seine Vorläufer*. Leipzig: Breitkopf and Härtel. [Third edn., with additions, 1914].

Schmitz, T. (1997). *Bildung und Macht: Zur sozialen und politischen Funktion der zweiten Sophistik in der griechischen Welt der Kaiserzeit*, Zetemata 97. Munich: Beck.

Schörner, G. (2003). *Votive im römischen Griechenland: Untersuchungen zur späthellenistischen und kaiserzeitlichen Kunst- und Religionsgeschichte*, Altertumswissenschaftliches Kolloquium 7. Stuttgart: Steiner.

Scholz, P. (2000). 'Zur Bedeutung von Rede und Rhetorik in der hellenistischen paideia und Politik', in C. Neumeister and W. Raeck (eds.), *Rede und Redner: Bewertung und Darstellung in den antiken Kulturen*. Möhnesee: Bibliopolis, 95–118.

——(2003). 'Ein römischer Epikureer in der Provinz: Der Adressatenkreis der Inschrift des Diogenes von Oinoanda — Bemerkungen zur Verbreitung von Literalität und Bildung im kaiserzeitlichen Kleinasien', in Piepenbrink 2003: 208–27.

Schröder, S. (1990). *Plutarchs Schrift De Pythiae oraculis. Text, Einleitung und Kommentar*, Beiträge zur Altertumskunde 8. Stuttgart: Teubner.

Sfameni Gasparro, G. (1999). 'Alessandro di Abonutico, lo "pseudo-profeta" ovvero come costruirsi un'identità religiosa. II. L'oracolo e i misteri', in C. Bonnet and A. Motte (eds.), *Les syncrétismes religieux dans le monde méditérranéen antique*. Brussels and Rome: Institut Historique Belge de Rome, 275–305.

Sharples, R. W. (2001). 'Schriften und Problemkomplexe zur Ethik', in P. Moraux and J. Wiesner (eds.), *Der Aristotelismus bei den Griechen. III: Alexander von Aphrodisias*. Berlin and New York: De Gruyter, 511–616.

——(2002). 'Aristotelian Theology after Aristotle', in Frede and Laks 2002: 1–40.

Sirago, V. A. (1989). 'La seconda sofistica come espressione culturale della classe dirigente del II sec.', in *ANRW*, 2. 33. 1: 36–78.

Smith, M. F. (1993). *Diogenes of Oinoanda: The Epicurean Inscription*, La Scuola di Epicuro Supplement 1. Naples: Bibliopolis.

——(1996). 'An Epicurean Priest from Apamea in Syria', *ZPE*, 112: 120–30.

——(2003). *Supplement to Diogenes of Oinoanda: The Epicurean Inscription*, La Scuola di Epicuro Supplement 3. Naples: Bibliopolis.

Stadter, P. A. (2004). 'Plutarch: Diplomat for Delphi?', in de Blois et al. 2004: 19–31.

Stein, M. (2001). 'Die Verehrung des Theos Hypsistos: Ein allumfassender pagan-jüdischer Synkretismus?', *EA*, 33: 119–25.

Strobel, K. (1993). *Das Imperium Romanum im 3. Jahrhundert': Modell einer historischen Krise?* Historia Einzelschriften 75. Stuttgart.

Swain, S. (1996). *Hellenism and Empire: Language, Classicism, and Power in the Greek World. AD 50–250.* Oxford: Clarendon Press.

Tonnet, H. (1988). *Recherches sur Arrien: sa personnalité et ses écrits atticistes.* Amsterdam: A. M. Hakkert.

van Nijf, O. (2001). 'Local Heroes: Athletics, Festivals and Elite Self–Fashioning in the Roman East', in Goldhill 2001: 306–34.

Várhelyi, Z. (2001). 'Magic, Religion, and Syncretism at the Oracle of Claros', in S. R. Asirvatham, C. O. Pache, and J. Watrous (eds.), *Between Magic and Religion. Interdisciplinary Studies in Ancient Mediterranean Religion and Society.* Lanham, MD, and Oxford: Rowman & Littlefield, 13–31.

Vernière, Y. (1990). 'La théorie de l'inspiration prophétique dans les Dialogues Pythiques de Plutarque', *Kernos*, 3: 359–66.

Veyne, P. (1986). 'Une évolution du paganisme gréco-romain: injustice et piété des dieux, leurs ordres ou "oracles"', *Latomus*, 45: 259–83.

Victor, U. (1997). *Lukian von Samosata, Alexander oder der Lügenprophet.* Leiden: Brill.

von Möllendorff, P. (2000). *Auf der Suche nach der verlogenen Wahrheit: Lukians 'Wahre Geschichten'*, Classica Monacensia 21. Tübingen: G. Narr.

Weir, R. G. A. (2004). *Roman Delphi and its Pythian Games*, British Archaeological Reports, International Series 1306. Oxford: John and Erica Hedges.

Weiss, P. (1998). 'Festgesandtschaften, städtisches Prestige und Homonoia-prägungen', in *Stadion*, 24.1: 59–70.

——(2004). 'Städtische Münzprägung und zweite Sophistik', in Borg 2004: 179–200.

Whitmarsh, T. (2001). *Greek Literature and the Roman Empire: The Politics of Imitation.* Oxford: Oxford University Press.

Wörrle, M. (1988). *Stadt und Fest im kaiserzeitlichen Kleinasien: Studien zu einer agonistischen Stiftung aus Oinoanda*, Vestigia 39. Munich: Beck.

Wolff, G. (1854). *De novissima oraculorum aetate.* Berlin.

———(ed.) (1856). *Porphyrii de philosophia ex oraculis haurienda librorum reliquiae.* Berlin (reprinted Hildesheim 1983).

Wrede, H. (2001). *Senatorische Sarkophage Roms. Der Beitrag des Senatorenstands zur Kunst der hohen und späten Kaiserzeit.* Mainz: von Zabern.

Zagdoun, M.-A. (1995). 'Plutarque à Delphes', in *Revue des Études Grecques*, 108: 586–92.

Ziegler, K. (1951). 'Plutarchos (2)', in *RE*, 21. 1: 636–962 (= K. Ziegler, *Plutarchos von Chaironeia*, 2nd edn. 1964. Stuttgart: Waldsee).

Zierl, A. (1995). *Alexander von Aphrodisias: Über das Schicksal.* Berlin: Akademie Verlag.

II

Elective Cults

7

Homogeneity and Diversity in the Religions of Rome

Simon Price

The city of Rome used to be a great black hole in our understanding of Roman imperial history: we knew more about the provinces than the capital.[1] One aspect of our ignorance concerned the religious life of Rome during the principate. Many histories of Roman religion used to peter out with the reign of Augustus. Attention shifted to 'Oriental cults', and to Judaism and the triumph of Christianity. Wissowa was less guilty of this than some of his successors: in handling Roman official cults in his *Religion und Kultus der Römer* (*Religion and Cult of the Romans*) he did include a section on 'the religion of the imperial age', and he prolonged the accounts of individual topics through that period. Wissowa also included a section on *sacra peregrina*, foreign cults mainly of the imperial period (1912: 73–102, 348–79).

The challenges facing us now are both to argue for the importance of official cults of Rome under the empire, and also to integrate into a general picture material on the various cults of Rome. The post-Wissowa segregation of official Roman cults and *sacra peregrina* into separate books (which is the legacy of Franz Cumont) is regrettable. But one should not simply return to Wissowa's position in *Religion*

---

[1] A different version of the ideas of this article will be found in Beard et al. 1998: i. ch. 6; fuller documentation of the data will also be found there and in the accompanying volume of sources.

und Kultus. We need to go further even than Wissowa and analyse at the same time Jewish and Christian material alongside the evidence for other religious cults of the period. We also need to be as inclusive as possible in the types of evidence exploited for religious history: not just texts, but also physical evidence (both iconography and buildings). The illustrations to this article are exemplary reminders of the importance of the physical evidence, and their inclusion here indicates that in the analysis of material evidence we must go beyond what Wissowa sought to do.

My general objective is to reconstruct the religious life of imperial Rome. This article is limited to one aspect of it, which raises questions of approach, that is, the problem of religious identities at Rome. People usually talk of the cults of this period as if they were homogeneous entities that were exclusive of each other. I want us to think again about these terms. What follows is structured round three questions: (1) Is it right to think of religious groups at Rome as homogeneous? (2) Were they exclusive at the theological level? (3) Were individual allegiances to these groups exclusive?

WERE RELIGIOUS GROUPS AT ROME HOMOGENEOUS?

The official cults of Rome continued to be important throughout the imperial period. They were headed by the emperor, but they also impacted on the population of Rome as a whole. Here we see on a sarcophagus of the mid-fourth century elephants pulling a divine/ imperial image, and an image of Mater Magna carried on a litter, through the streets of Rome on the way to games in the Circus Maximus (Fig. 7.1). The official system was not simply a sop for the senatorial class. The people, both citizen and non-citizen, were deeply involved in the official cults of imperial Rome. In addition to the official cults, there were other cults in Rome which had an ethnic basis: Jews, for example, or the immigrants to Rome from Palmyra in Syria who established a sanctuary to Palmyrene gods in Trastevere, on the west bank of the Tiber; there they made dedications to 'their

Fig. 7.1. Sarcophagus of *c.* AD 350 from Rome.

ancestral deities' in a combination of languages, Latin, Greek, and Palmytene, the common language of the near east (Schneider 1987; Chausson 1995). We cannot hope to understand imperial Rome without thinking also about the Roman Empire. Rome comes to symbolize the empire; it is also the place to which inhabitants of the empire were drawn, and in which they practised their ancestral cults.

There also developed religious choices outside the framework of both official and ethnic cults, which offered possibilities for new religious identities. It is possible to map the locations of some of those cults—the ones originating allegedly in Egypt, Syria, and Asia Minor (Fig. 7.2). At Rome such choices existed from at least the early second century BC onwards, and were well established by the imperial period. There is also evidence for some twenty-five Mithraic sanctuaries in Rome. I would emphasize the *coexistence* of the official or ethnic cults and these religious groups, and also the novelty of the new groups: with their demands of personal commitment, they offered a new sort of identity. Religion was not just one of a bundle of characteristics defining ethnic or civic identity, it was *the* defining characteristic. The cults offered, in short, *religious* identity to their members.

The interesting issue is to see how these identities related to one another, and to ethnic or civic identities. Here it is crucial to be as comprehensive as possible. We shall never make progress if we remain locked into particular specialisms: historians of Isis, of Mithras, of Judaism, of Christianity. To exclude any of these at the

Map 2. Sanctuaries of Magna Mater, Syrian-Phoenician gods, and Egyptian gods in Rome. The sites are numbered from east to west in three main groupings.

Magna Mater
1 'Basilica' Hilariana
2 Shrine of Magna Mater in Via Sacra
3 Temple of Magna Mater on Palatine (= Map 1 no 13.)
4 Image of Magna Mater in Circus Maximus (cf. no.27)
5 Cult of Magna Mater and Navisalvia 'Ship Saver'
6 Phrygianum in Vatican (cf. Map 3 no.40)

Syrian-Phoenician Cults
7 Jupiter Dolichenus in Cavalry Camp (cf Map 3 no 10)
8 Jupiter Dolichenus on Esquiline
9 Temple of Sol built by Aurelian
10 Cult of Caelestis and Jupiter Africanus on Capitoline
11 Temple of Elagabalus
12 Jupiter Dolichenus on Aventine (cf. Map 3 no.35)
13 Syrian cults near Wholesale Market
14 Palmyrene sanctuary in Trastevere
15 Syrian cults of Trastevere
16 Syrian sanctuary on Janiculum

Egyptian Cults
17 Isis in Praetorian Camp (cf. Map 3 no.21)
18 Isis and Serapis
19 Iseum Metellinum
20 Isis Athenodoria
21 Shrine near S Martino in Monti (in some house as Map 3 no.5)
22 Isis Patricia
23 Sanctuary in Sallustian Gardens
24 Serapis on Quirinal (cf. Map 3 no.12)
25 Isis on Capitolium
26 Isis and Serapis in Campus Martius
27 Isis in Circus Maximus (cf. no.4)
28 Isis below Santa Sabina
29 Isis in Trastevere
30 Isis in Vatican

31 Underground Basilica

▲ Magna Mater
■ Syrian-Phoenician cults
● Egyptian cults
+ Underground Basilica
····· pomerium after Vespasian
A symbol in outline indicates uncertain location

Fig. 7.2. Map of sanctuaries of 'Oriental cults' at Rome.

outset is to prejudge the issues: in particular, it is important to have Judaism and Christianity in the picture, otherwise one is liable to uphold *a priori* a dichotomy between 'paganism' and 'Christianity', and to exclude Jews from the picture altogether, which is deeply unhelpful.

In examining such connections, we need to avoid the conventional category 'Oriental religions'. In the hands of the brilliant Franz Cumont, the category seemed to be the key to understanding the religious history of the period. But in fact the category conflates things that need to be kept separate and is founded on arbitrary premises. Even though several of the cults proclaimed an eastern 'origin' for their wisdom, the 'origins' were quite different (Egypt, Syria, Persia) and do not constitute a homogeneous 'Orient'. Some of the cults (Mater Magna, Isis) began as public cults and only later acquired private mysteries, which were quite distinct. Some of these mysteries, even if they claimed an eastern origin, were in fact descended from earlier Greek initiation cults. Nor can one assume a common preoccupation with 'salvation', which made the 'Oriental cults' precursors of and rivals to Christianity. For there is no real body of evidence to show this, and the assumption is implicitly Christianizing.

In the past scholars have assumed that ancient religious groups, especially Judaism and Christianity, were homogeneous and exclusive entities. That is, their theological and practical positions each had a normative core, consistent across place and time; round that core were a number of awkward heretical or deviant groups which could be treated as simply marginal. They were exclusive of each other and of other religious groups of the time. The current trend in the study of Judaism and Christianity is firmly against the normative assumptions of the old picture. In fact, scholars have realized that the two religions in question sought only much later to define and protect orthodoxy.[2] This claim entails that we should not seek for this period a clear core of Judaism and of Christianity, which would be homogeneous across the whole empire. It is much better and less anachronistic to talk for each cult in terms of clusters of ideas and of people rather than of core and

---

[2] See, for example, the papers of a Princeton–Oxford conference: Becker and Reed 2003. Emphasis on varieties of Christianity goes back to Bauer 1934.

periphery. At the general level, there is a good formulation of this idea by the anthropologist Rodney Needham (1975): he defines the classification in terms of family resemblances, talking of 'polythetic classification'. In relation to Christianity, this approach helps us to avoid falling into the traditional, crypto-Protestant project of deciding how far the core of primitive Christianity was affected by its Jewish and Graeco–Roman environment. This trend in the study of Judaism and Christianity has led to questions about how far one should rethink the old model for understanding other cults of the period. This paper deals primarily with the Mater Magna, Jupiter Dolichenus, Jupiter Heliopolitanus, Isis, and Mithras, though it will also touch on Jews and Christians.

The background to the issue of homogeneity is the wide geographical spread of these cults, though the precise distribution pattern varies greatly from cult to cult. Mithras was common in Italy (especially Rome and Ostia) and along the Rhine-Danube frontier zone, but appears hardly at all in Greece, Asia Minor, Syria, Egypt, North Africa, or Spain. The cult of Isis is found in the Hellenistic period in Greece, but its expansion under the empire was largely western, in Italy, Africa, Spain and Gaul. Jupiter Dolichenus proclaimed its origin at Doliche in North Syria, and some seventeen sanctuaries of the cult have been found, ranging from Dura Europus on the Euphrates to Germany. There were three sanctuaries in Rome: on the Aventine, the Caelian and the Esquiline. Despite being quite widespread each cult was relatively uniform. Dedications to Jupiter Dolichenus from various parts of the empire employ a very similar iconography.[3] The cults of Mithras also display a striking degree of uniformity. Shrines excavated in Britain or Germany are much the same as those in Rome or even at Dura Europus: a long cave-like building with benches along the side and a relief or painting at the far end of Mithras slaying the bull (Fig. 7.3).

All that is obvious enough, but how far did such homogeneity go? How indeed are we to assess degrees of homogeneity? The inevitably fragmentary and disparate nature of our evidence makes it almost

---

[3] Hörig and Schwertheim 1987: nos. 5 (Doliche, Syria), 103 (Iasen, Moesia Superior), 201 (Lussonium, Pannonia Inferior), 371 (Aventine, Rome), 512 (Heddernheim, Germania Superior).

Fig. 7.3. The sanctuary of Mithras below S. Prisca at Rome. The benches along the walls lead up to the cult image of Mithras slaying the bull. In front, uniquely, is an image of the river Tiber.

inevitable that those seeking to interpret the cults should set up clear and unitary models within which the individual items of evidence can fit. The assumption of homogeneity is almost a necessary heuristic device. But for how long should one maintain it?

The best example for exploring the issue of homogeneity is the cult of Mithras, one of the most complex, and most complexly documented, cults of the Roman empire. This cult, allegedly originating in Persia in the remote past, in fact developed in the Latin west in the late first/early second century AD. Though the bull-slaying scene was an easily recognizable icon wherever the cult existed, the extent of iconographical uniformity should not be exaggerated (Fig. 7.4). The side scenes round the representation of Mithras and the bull do not appear in a fixed sequence; there seem to be two major groupings, found primarily in the Rhine and in the Danube areas, but Italy was

Fig. 7.4. The Mithraic relief from Aequiculi. Cf. Beard et al. 1998: ii. 307–8, with full commentary.

different and even within the two areas there was much diversity (Gordon 1980). Such diversity might be taken as regional variations, drawing on a common repertoire of images, but more worrying are the sequences of planetary gods. Some studies bravely try to make the maximum degree of order out of these sequences, but the evidence just does not fit together as neatly as they imagine (Beck 1988, with review by Price 1990).[4] In fact there are different sequences in different contexts, and it is not possible to reduce them to a central normative core with peripheral elaborations.[5]

If one does not start from the assumption that there is a core of 'real' Mithraic doctrines and a penumbra of divergences or misunderstandings, a possible solution would be to say that the mysteries of Mithras consist of a cluster of overlapping readings, offering different (and sometimes incompatible) systems. If that is the correct interpretation of some rather thorny aspects of Mithraism, it suggests that one should return to the so-called 'Mithras liturgy', preserved as part of a long sequence of magical texts. This amazing text gives instructions about the gaining of divine revelation from Helios Mithras. Early in the twentieth century it was argued that it was an actual text of the Mithraic mysteries (hence its common name, the 'Mithras liturgy') (Dieterich 1923). This idea was so roundly criticized that the text practically dropped out of discussions of Mithraism. In fact one should not try to decide if it was 'really' Mithraic (as was originally argued); it is more useful to look at the way that it employs Mithraic themes. Or one can consider, at a different level, the issue of women in the cult. They were not initiated into the cult, and indeed Porphyry says that they were classified as noxious hyenas. But the place of women in the cult is more complex than the image of the hyena might suggest. Take the excavations of the S. Prisca Mithraic sanctuary in Rome. The sculpture included the portrait bust of an old lady.[6] She was not necessarily initiated, but hardly a hyena. Perhaps she was

---

[4] For 'local jargons' in Mithraism see Gordon 1994.

[5] Beck 2000: 171–2, accepts that orthodoxy/heresy are not helpful poles, but wishes to push the notion of 'norms' in Mithraism, and in Christianity (though he does note the current usage of 'Christianities'). He seems to overplay uniformity, and marginalize regional or other diversities.

[6] Vermaseren and Van Essen 1965: 454, no. 11. On this sanctuary, see further Beard et al. 1998: ii. **12.5h** = pp. 316–19; Steinby 1993–9: iii. 268–9.

the mistress of the house in which the sanctuary was located. Or take another find from a Mithraic sanctuary in Rome: the inscribed version of a prayer to Mithras by a woman, one Cascellia Elegans (Mussies 1982). 'Not really Mithraic', some experts claim, but there is nothing in it that is impossible in a Mithraic context. The ideology of the cult was perhaps not as homogeneous as modern theory would like, and there are indeed cases where women make dedications to Mithras. So I submit that a cluster model does seem helpful, and in general provides a better initial starting point.

THEOLOGICAL EXCLUSIVITY

Now for the second of my three questions: were the religious cults exclusive at the theological level? It is easy to assume that the peculiarities of each cult left no place for the ordinary Graeco–Roman pantheon, and that if any ordinary gods do appear in the cult they have to have peculiar interpretations placed on them. In fact, this assumption needs to be rejected. Consider, for example, the sanctuary of Mater Magna at Ostia (Vermaseren 1977–89: iii. 107–19). Within it there were not only temples of Mater Magna and of Attis, but also of Bellona, all of Antonine date. What is Bellona doing here? Scholars sometimes say that she is here seen as an aspect of Mater Magna, but is this a necessary assumption? Then there are statues of other gods dedicated in the sanctuary: Pan (twice), Dionysus, Venus (five times) and perhaps Ceres. They certainly do not play a fixed part in the cult of Mater Magna, and there is surely no reason to deny that these gods carry with them all or most of the evocations they have in other contemporary contexts. But, one might argue, Mater Magna was an institutionalized if marginal cult, whose official acceptance at Rome makes it unsurprising to find other gods in her sanctuary.

What about Jupiter Dolichenus, whose cult was not institutionalized? The sanctuary on the Aventine in Rome (frequented by civilians) is perhaps the best known of his sanctuaries in the empire (Fig. 7.5; for its location, see Fig. 7.2, no. 12; Hörig and Schwertheim 1987: 221–35; Bellelli and Bianchi 1997; Beard et al. 1998: ii. 295–7; Steinby 1993–9: iii. 133–4, v. 270). The adherents formed a tightly

Fig. 7.5. A model of the Dolocenum on the Aventine.

knit group, with a complex hierarchy: a 'father of candidates', priests, and 'patrons' presided over a series of candidates. Jupiter Dolichenus was here described as 'protector of the whole world', and is often called Optimus Maximus and his female partner Juno Regina, the technical names for the first two members of the Capitoline triad. So the cult borrowed elements of the Capitoline triad, but did so in order to assert the overarching position of *this* deity. In addition, all sorts of other gods were represented in this sanctuary. First, the ordinary Graeco–Roman gods, for example, Apollo; it is striking that the statue of Apollo was put up 'on the order of Jupiter Optimus Maximus Dolichenus'. Second, there were images related to the Egyptian gods Isis and Sarapis. Third, there were some Mithraic reliefs. Presumably the implication of these dedications is that Jupiter Optimus Maximus Dolichenus was the new head of the old pantheon, superior both to the gods like Apollo, and to the Egyptian and Persian gods. This sort of cosmology would have had no need to be exclusivist: indeed incorporation would have reinforced its strength.

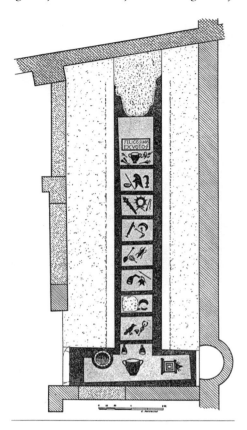

Fig. 7.6. Sanctuary of Felicissimus at Ostia. Mosaic floor with symbols of the seven grades. Cf. Beard et al. 1998: ii. 305–6, with full commentary, and also below, Ch. 9, Fig. 9.1.

Mithras is more of a problem (Fig. 7.6). Mithraic cosmology was radically novel and allowed no place for the ordinary gods of the pantheon. What mattered was the ascent of the initiate through the seven grades; as each grade was correlated with a different planet (e.g. Lion with Jupiter, Father with Saturn), the soul of the initiate was probably conceived to rise during his lifetime further and further away from the Earth, finally achieving *apogenesis*, or birth away from the material world. (For further discussion of the grades, see Gordon, this volume pp. 327–36). Does that mean that for the Mithraic initiate (at least in certain contexts) the traditional Graeco–Roman gods had no role? Scholars sometimes give the impression that this is the case, but again the finds from the S. Prisca sanctuary show that the matter is more complex than theory would suggest. The excavations revealed, along with all the Mithraic material, representations of various Olympian gods (Vermaseren and Van Essen 1965). The text of the final report mentions only three stucco heads of Serapis, Venus, and perhaps Mars; the rest are buried in the catalogue of finds and the problems they raise for the issue of Mithraic exclusivity have been little discussed.

There are however parallels for this range of dedications from other Mithraic sanctuaries. The Walbrook sanctuary in London contained, in addition to Mithraic images, images of ordinary Olympian gods: Minerva, Serapis, Mercury, the Dioscuri, and Mother-goddesses associated with river deities (Toynbee 1986; Shepherd 1998). And reliefs in Gaul and Germany sometimes represent an assembly of gods; for example the great relief of Osterburken includes Jupiter, Apollo, Mars, Hercules, Juno, Minerva, Venus, and others.[7] Mithraic sanctuaries were, at least from time to time, quite hospitable to other gods.[8] Toynbee argued that the gods represented in the Walbrook sanctuary cohered with the basic ideology of the cult, in that all were concerned with salvation. That is a possible interpretation, though one has to press Minerva rather hard to make her fit, and it does not seem to account for the range of deities found at S. Prisca or Osterburken. Instead, one might suggest that the current interpretations of the cult, which privilege the arcane and astronomical aspects of the cult, have to be seen as coexisting, rather messily no doubt, with all sorts of gods familiar to the initiates from the rest of their lives. Presumably they were not structured, as in the cult of Jupiter Dolichenus, into a new pantheon (that was hardly possible with the overall Persian ideology of the cult), but individuals did think from time to time that particular Graeco–Roman gods had

[7] Vermaseren 1956: 966 (Saarburg); 1292 (Osterburken). Cf. Clauss 2000: 155–67.
[8] For example, a Mother Goddess at Carrawburgh on Hadrian's Wall (Richmond and Gilliam 1951; Coulston and Phillips 1988: no. 164) or Mercury at Stockstadt in Germany (Vermaseren 1956: 1176, 1178, 1179; Schwertheim 1974: 140, no. 116, p, r, s).

their place in a Mithraic sanctuary. Thus the cult of Mithras, which is often alleged to have been exclusive, in fact turns out not to have been so.

Isis is also surprising, but perhaps for exactly the opposite reasons. According to the ideology of the cult, Isis was all-encompassing. For example, in a surviving cult hymn from Kyme, Isis is made to say, 'I taught humans to honour images of the gods, I founded sanctuaries of the gods'.[9] So Isis, though of firmly Egyptian origin, was responsible for the apparatus of the ordinary Graeco–Roman pantheon. She was also worshipped under various names throughout the world. This cosmology is very inclusive, but we need to see what the actual sanctuaries of Isis were like. Those in Italy do *look* resolutely Egyptian in tone. The great sanctuary of Isis and Serapis on the Campus Martius in Rome had a large obelisk, a Serapeum modelled on that at Alexandria, and a sanctuary of Isis with a processional route lined with Egyptian statues.[10] The sanctuary of Isis at Beneventum had an obelisk, images of Isis, Apis bulls, lions, sphinxes, statues of priests or worshippers, and even images of Domitian represented as Pharaoh (Müller 1969). The iconography could hardly be more resolutely Egyptian than that, but there and elsewhere we do also find images of ordinary, non-Egyptian gods.

The proclamation of one, supreme god was characteristic of the new cults. Jupiter Dolichenus was described in the Aventine sanctuary as 'protector of the whole world'. Isis was believed to be the supreme power in the universe and the origin of civilization. The cult of Mithras focused on the exploits of Mithras. Judaism and Christianity both stressed the might of one god. But this does not mean, as scholars have sometimes claimed, that there was a general move towards 'monotheism'. As we have seen, the cosmologies of the various cults were quite different, and describing them all as 'monotheistic' blurs profound differences between them. Indeed the label may in fact be inapplicable even for Judaism and Christianity. In Judaism god was generally seen as the head of a number of divine beings, who were not always under his control, and in Christianity

---

[9] *Inschriften von Kyme* 41 (trans. in Beard et al. 1998: ii. 297–8).
[10] Lembke 1994; Steinby 1993–9: iii. 107–9. For other sanctuaries of Isis at Rome, see Steinby 1993–9: iii. 110–16, v. 269.

the supreme god was related, in different ways and by different groups, to the Son and Holy Spirit. Nor was the claim of supremacy for one god wholly new: that position in the official cults of Rome was traditionally held by Jupiter Optimus Maximus. However, the claim to a new, though not necessarily exclusive, supremacy was an important part of the appeal of the elective cults.

Where does this brief account of Mater Magna, Jupiter Dolichenus, Mithras and Isis leave us? The cosmologies of all four are quite different, three inclusivist, and one (Mithras) exclusivist. And yet at the level of sanctuary dedications, Mater Magna, Jupiter Dolichenus, and even Mithras accommodated the ordinary Graeco–Roman gods; only Isis may have excluded them, perhaps to maintain the Egyptian allure of her sanctuaries, but perhaps also because (as we shall see) the level of allegiance to her was very high.

EXCLUSIVITY OF ALLEGIANCE

That brings us to our third main question: how far did these cults claim exclusivity of allegiance from individuals? If one was initiated into one cult, did that preclude membership of others? Or did they serve different functions for the same people at different times? The second alternative (different functions for different people) is certainly what one would expect in the ordinary Graeco–Roman pantheon. The various gods of the Roman calendar had particular functions to serve; individuals, families, and other groups would turn to one or another deity depending on the circumstances. On the other hand, exclusivity of allegiance is what one would expect to follow from the profound differences between the cosmologies of the different cults. Whereas the gods of the Roman calendar were perceived as belonging together in one pantheon, Isis and Mithras proclaimed that they were responsible for different and incompatible cosmologies. It is hard to imagine reconciling the two, but could individuals live with such inconsistencies?

There is some evidence that this was indeed possible. A fine Mithraic relief from central Italy has an inscription on the bottom: 'Apronianus the civic treasurer made it at his own expense' (*ILS* 4190;

Vermaseren 1956: 650; above, Fig. 7.4). It so happens that we have another inscription from the same town in which Apronianus the civic treasurer proclaims that he paid for the erection of statues of Serapis and Isis.[11] This suggestion of multiple allegiances (whether serial or contemporary) is reinforced by the terminology of the cults themselves. It seems that the initiates of most of the cults did not generally use any particular term of self-description to define themselves as potentially exclusive adherents of the cult concerned. Modern scholars may talk of 'Mithraists', but there is no corresponding term in the ancient sources; while the grades of initiation were precisely that—not terms regularly used outside a specifically cultic context. The most we can detect are some much vaguer terms of self-description (*syndexios*—'he who has performed the ritual hand-shake', or *sacratus*—'devotee').

In some cults there is a difference between those whose religious, and maybe social, identity had come to depend on the worship of their particular deity (and who were rarely involved in more than one of the new cults) and those nearer the margins (who were much less likely to be so exclusive). In the cult of Mater Magna, for example, the castrated cult servants, the *galli* are not found playing other religious roles. This exclusivity is predictable, insofar as their castration marked them out in perpetuity as belonging to this one deity; for the *galli*, that is, this religious role was their principal role, their claim to status and self-definition—as is suggested by the fact that some chose to have themselves represented on their tombstones in the costume of, and with the symbols of, their religious office (Strong 1920; Vermaseren 1977–89: iii. 140–2, 152–3, the latter in Beard et al. 1998: ii. 211).

With the cult of Isis too there were some overachievers whose physical appearance was crucial. Those who had shaved their heads as priests of Isis also sought to display to the world that they belonged to Isis. And Lucius in Apuleius' novel is presented as having no time for any deity other than Isis. Lucius says to Isis before leaving her sanctuary in Corinth, 'I shall make sure I do all the things a religious but poor person can: I shall for ever guard your sacred appearance

---

[11] *ILS* 4381 = Vidman 1969: no. 477.

and most holy divine power in the depth of my heart and gaze upon it'. When he went from Corinth to Rome, on the instruction of Isis, he was again initiated into her mysteries there. The story presupposes and evokes the idea that some people were exclusively attached to the cult of Isis (even if the story is in the end critical of such fanaticism). Funerary inscriptions with Isiac language or decoration again help to confirm this impression about allegiance. Some begin with the traditional formula 'Dis Manibus' ('To the Spirits of the Dead') and continue with references to attachment to Isis. But what is particularly striking about the texts is the range of positions that was commemorated on the tombstones. Unlike Mater Magna, where only the *galli* commemorate themselves, all sorts of Isiac offices are mentioned. In Rome, for example, a wife was commemorated in a long verse epigram as 'chaste and attentive worshipper of the Pharian goddess [i.e. Isis], with whom I spent thirty years of happiness'.[12]

No other cult, it seems, generated such an extensive public display in funerary monuments. One might say that this is because of the connection between Isis and the after-life. There certainly was such a link. For example, some funerary inscriptions from Rome hope that Osiris will grant the deceased refreshment in the afterlife. So tombstones were at least an appropriate context in which to commemorate Isiac attachments, but they do not read like a form of Pascal's wager, to maximize the chances of the deceased. Rather, they pick out Isiac attachments as crucial attributes of the *living*. And the cult offered an extremely wide range of positions in which people could feel proud. Unlike the cult of Mater Magna, there were many ways in the cult of Isis of marking one's primary if not exclusive allegiance to the cult.

The argument as presented so far has implications for our understanding of the exclusivity of Jews and Christians in this period. There are certainly monuments peculiar to each of the groups: for example, catacombs containing images of the Jewish *menorah*; or the memorial to Peter below St Peter's. However, the exclusivity of Judaism and Christianity is difficult to assess because of the dominance of later orthodoxy which sought to exclude overlapping

[12] Vidman 1969: no. 451.

involvements and which has been retrojected back onto our period. Jews in some places simply kept apart and (so far as we know) did not produce treatises on the nature of the debarred cults; in contrast 'godfearers' may not have expected to reject all of their own religious heritage. Some strands in Christianity did, however, seek to explain how Christianity was superior both to Judaism and to the traditional cults. The relationship between Judaism and Christianity, a crucial issue from the earliest days of the Christian church, was articulated in various ways. Some, like Marcion, who taught in Rome in the mid second century AD, rejected both the Old Testament and the god of the Jews. Marcion was a controversial figure, condemned by self-styled 'orthodox' writers, but the founder of long-lived Marcionite communities. This 'hard line' rejection of Judaism was, however, only one strand in second-century Christianity. Some Christians practised circumcision and followed an obviously 'Jewish' way of life. Others who rejected Judaism as a system nonetheless borrowed much from Jewish thought. For example, images in the Via Latina Catacomb in Rome use images from the Old Testament as precursors of Christ's actions, e.g., Samson smiting the Philistines with an ass's jawbone (Fig. 7.7).

If one accepts the suggestion about the relative *lack* of homogeneity and exclusivity among at least some of the traditional cults, it perhaps becomes easier to understand the behaviour of some Jewish and Christian groups. That is, the 'cluster' or 'polythetic' approach to the two religions, which formed our starting point and which is normally applied *within* the context of Judaism and Christianity, can be extended to the relations between Jews and Christians and between them both and traditional cults. If the experience of the cults of, for example, Jupiter Dolichenus or Mithras, let alone of the ordinary civic cults, was of a kind of inclusivity, it is perhaps easier to see how some individuals could be led to at least the fringes of Judaism or Christianity. Jewish 'God-fearers' or their Christian equivalents might expect not to have to reject the whole of their own religious heritage, however much hard-liners might denounce the whole apparatus of 'paganism'.

In the second and third centuries there were debates about how much traditional thought should be taken over by Christians. Some Christians even felt that they could participate in traditional cults.

Fig. 7.7. Via Latina Catacomb. Wall-painting of Samson smiting the Philistines with an ass's jawbone (Judges 15. 15–17).

Some of these were said to eat sacrificial meat and gather at pagan festivals, imagining that they were beyond pollution. Others held that traditional cults preserved part of the truth. The Naassenes were said to hold that performances of the mysteries of Attis were under the guidance of providence. Without themselves being castrated, they would attend the mysteries of Mater Magna 'considering that they can actually observe their own mystery in those rites'.[13] Hippolytus, who reports their actions, is horrified, and most church historians have not really escaped from his perspective, but the attitude of the Naassenes should perhaps be seen as predictable, and perhaps even normal, in the religious life of the Roman empire.

One further aspect of some of these cults is gender participation. Did women and men have different religious identities at this period? In terms of ethnic and civic identities the picture remained much as

---

[13] Hippolytus, *Refutation of All Heresies* 5. 6–9 (trans. in Beard et al. 1998: ii. 341–2).

it had been in the classical period. The religious systems of Rome and of individual cities in the empire drew on women so far as was necessary for cults of a peculiarly 'female' nature, and permitted their attendance at public ceremonials (Scheid 1992).[14] Were women short-changed, and ready for new roles? Upper class men feared any activity by women outside these closely defined roles, and operated with a stereotype of extensive female participation in some elective cults. But the extent of female participation was in fact not as great as feared in the stereotype. Though women did take part in the cult of Isis, they did not predominate numerically, and the principal offices were held by men (Mora 1990: ii. 1–29). Lower class women generally could not join the occupational or burial associations formed by slaves, ex-slaves and free poor; only in the purely domestic associations of the great households were women normally members. It was the *mixed* membership of *some* of the cults (Isis, Judaism, Christianity) that differentiated them from the traditional cults of Greece and Rome, where the norm was segregated participation. Such freely mixed participation in elective cults was extremely radical.

In conclusion, I have tried to show something of the pluralism of religious life in imperial Rome. The cults about which I have been talking were recognizable all over the Roman empire, but their identities, I have suggested, should not be seen in this period as monolithic. By the fourth century boundaries had become harder, and more policed, by traditionalists, Jews, and Christians. But in the first three centuries of our era religious identities were more fluid and variously defined. The evidence on the ground shows that the cults which are often seen as both homogeneous and exclusive are neither. The hypothetical creator of a cult such as Mithraism might have expected both homogeneity and exclusivity for his new vision of the world, but the worshippers had quite different expectations, derived from ordinary polytheism. The worshippers did not treat the cults as homogeneous: the cults of any given Graeco–Roman god were not homogeneous. Nor did they treat them as exclusive, any more than the traditional cults were exclusive. But the cults do have a recognizable degree of cluster or polythetic cohesion. And, with the exceptions of Judaism,

----

[14] For a critique, see Flemming 2007.

Christianity, and Manichaeism, they are found only within the bounds of the Roman empire. Their adherents desired cults that were not limited to one town, but transcended particular places or regions. These cults offered new religious identities within the framework of the Roman empire. As was said in the cult of Mithras, 'Hail to the Fathers from East to West'. I wonder what Wissowa would have made of all this. As Wissowa was aware of the provisional status of his handbook, he might have seen these ideas as a possible development of his own interest in *sacra romana* and *sacra peregrina*.

BIBLIOGRAPHY

Bauer, W. (1934). *Rechtgläubigkeit und Ketzerei im ältesten Christentum.* Tübingen: Mohr. Eng. trans.: *Orthodoxy and Heresy in Earliest Christianity.* Philadelphia: Fortress Press (1971); London: SCM Press (1972).

Beard, M., North J., and Price S. (1998). *Religions of Rome,* 2 vols. Cambridge: Cambridge University Press.

Beck, R. (1988). *Planetary Gods and Planetary Orders in the Mysteries of Mithras,* EPRO 109. Leiden: Brill.

——(2000). 'Ritual, Myth, Doctrine, and Initiation in the Mysteries of Mithras: New Evidence from a Cult Vessel', *JRS,* 90: 145–80, repr. in his *Beck on Mithraism: Collected Works with New Essays.* Aldershot: Ashgate (2004), ch. 4.

Becker, A. H. and Reed, A. Y. (eds.) (2003). *The Ways that Never Parted: Jews and Christians in Late Antiquity and the Early Middle Ages.* Tübingen: Mohr Siebeck.

Bellelli, G. M. and Bianchi, U. (eds.) (1997). *Orientalia Sacra Urbis Romae: Dolichena et Heliopolitana. Receuil d'études archéologiques et historico-religieuses sur les cultes cosmopolites d'origine commagénienne et syrienne.* Rome: 'L'Erma' di Bretschneider.

Chausson, F. (1995). '*Vel Iovi vel Soli*: Quatre études autour de la Vigna Barberini (191–354)', *Mélanges de l'École française de Rome, Antiquité,* 107: 661–765.

Clauss, M. (2000). *The Roman Cult of Mithras.* Edinburgh: Edinburgh University Press (German original 1990).

Coulston, J. C. N. and Phillips, E. J. (1988). *Corpus Signorum Imperii Romani, Great Britain i. 6.* Oxford: Oxford University Press.

Dieterich, A. (1923). *Eine Mithrasliturgie* (3rd edn.). Leipzig: Teubner (first edn. 1903).

Flemming, R. (2007). 'Festus and the Role of Women in Roman Religion', in F. Glinister and C. Woods (eds.), *Verrius, Festus, and Paul: Lexicography, Scholarship and Society*, Bulletin of the Institute of Classical Studies, Supp. 93. London: Institute of Classical Studies, 87–108, repr. in J. North and S. Price (eds.), *Oxford Readings in Roman Republican Religion: Rome and Italy*. Oxford: Oxford University Press.

Gordon, R. L. (1980). 'Panelled Complications', *Journal of Mithraic Studies*, 3: 200–27, reprinted in his, *Image and Value in the Graeco–Roman World*. Aldershot, Hampshire and Brookfield, VA (1996).

——(1994). 'Mystery, Metaphor and Doctrine in the Mysteries of Mithras', in J. R. Hinnells (ed.), *Studies in Mithraism*. Rome: 'L'Erma' di Bretschneider, 103–24.

Hörig, M. and Schwertheim, E. (1987). *Corpus cultus Iovis Dolicheni*, EPRO 106. Leiden: Brill.

Lembke, K. (1994). *Das Iseum Campense in Rom*, Archäologie und Geschichte, 3. Heidelberg: Verlag Archäologie und Geschichte.

Mora, F. (1990). *Prosopografia Isiaca*, 2 vols, EPRO 113. Leiden: Brill.

Müller, H. W. (1969). *Der Isiskult im antiken Benevent*, Münchner ägyptologische Studien, 16. Berlin: B. Hessling.

Mussies, G. (1982). 'Cascelia's Prayer', in U. Bianchi and M. J. Vermaseren (eds.), *La soteriologia dei culti orientali nell'impero romano*, EPRO 92. Leiden: Brill, 156–67.

Needham, R. (1975). 'Polythetic Classification: Convergence and Consequences', *Man*, n.s. 10: 349–69.

Price, S. R. F. (1990). *Phoenix*, 44: 194–6 [Review of Beck 1988].

Richmond, I. A. and Gilliam J. P. (1951). *The Temple of Mithras at Carrawburgh*. Newcastle upon Tyne: Society of Antiquaries of Newcastle upon Tyne.

Scheid, J. (1992). 'The Religious Roles of Roman Women', in P. Schmitt Pantel (ed.), *A History of Women: From Ancient Goddesses to Christian Saints*. Cambridge, MA and London: Belknap Press, 377–408.

Schneider, E. E. (1987). 'Il santuario di Bel e delle divinità di Palmira. Comunità e tradizioni religiose dei Palmireni a Roma', *Dialoghi di Archeologia*, 3rd ser., 5: 69–85.

Schwertheim, E. (1974). *Die Denkmäler orientalische Gottheiten im römischen Deutschland*, EPRO 40. Leiden: Brill.

Shepherd, J. D. (1998). *The Temple of Mithras, London: Excavations by W. F. Grimes and A. Williams at the Walbrook*, Archaeological Report, English Heritage, 12. London: English Heritage.

Steinby, E. M. (1993–9). *Lexicon Topographicum Urbis Romae*, 6 vols. Rome: Quasar.

Strong, A. (1920). 'Sepulchral Relief of a Priest of Bellona', *Papers of the British School at Rome*, 9: 205–13.

Toynbee, J. M. C. (1986). *The Roman Art Treasures from the Temple of Mithras [London]*. London: London and Middlesex Archaeological Society.

Vermaseren, M. J. (1956). *Corpus Inscriptionum et Monumentorum Religionis Mithrae*. Leiden: Brill.

——(1977–89). *Corpus cultus Cybelae Attidisque*, 7 vols, EPRO 50. Leiden: Brill.

——and Van Essen, C. C. (1965). *The Excavations in the Mithraeum of the Church of Santa Prisca in Rome*. Leiden: Brill.

Vidman, L. (1969). *Sylloge inscriptionum religionis Isiacae et Sarapiacae*, Religionsgeschichtliche Versuche und Vorarbeiten, 28. Berlin: Walter de Gruyter.

Wissowa, G. (1912). *Religion und Kultus der Römer*. 2nd edn. Munich: Beck.

8

Mysteries and Oriental Cults

A Problem in the History of Religions

Giulia Sfameni Gasparro

QUESTIONS OF METHOD

The advent of a third age of research into 'Oriental religions', for which Jean-Marie Pailler (1989) already indicated some major lines of enquiry, is now clearly becoming a reality: since Franz Cumont's brilliant invention of the subject and the construction of a rich body of documents through research on a mostly regional scale (though some fairly wide-ranging thematic overviews have also been attempted) under the direction of Vermaseren in the prestigious series *Études préliminaires aux religions orientales dans l'Empire romain*, scholars have come to realize that it is necessary to survey this wide field from new vantage points and with more up-to-date methodologies.[1] This does not mean, in my opinion, that this process of review of a historical problem such as that posed by Cumont's research and pursued by scholars of considerable stature can be carried out solely through a programme of criticism or even an overhauling of traditional positions. There is no place for iconoclastic struggles in the advancement of historical knowledge, in this as in all fields. What is needed instead is patient research aimed at verifying our working hypotheses on the available documentary evidence. It is a matter of

---

[1] See the comments by Rousselle 1989, and especially the formulation of some criteria for research in Belayche 2000.

asking new questions of the evidence; these can, on occasion, shake the foundations of ancient theoretical edifices, but at the same time they must allow us to progress towards a correct interpretation of the phenomena while respecting the historical data, rather than simply construct new theories—or, worse still, new ideologies—no less impermanent and open to criticism than those they supplant.

The subject of this article is a privileged testing ground for such an enquiry, but it also presents remarkable difficulties, because it calls into question two terms which are both very broad and intrinsically problematic. The term 'Oriental cults' refers to the entire spectrum of phenomena which we are accustomed to include under a single heading, following Cumont's formulation, but which we want to free from this formulation in order to situate them in a new perspective, one yet to be defined. The term 'mysteries' refers to an equally large category, which also needs to be redefined. The fundamental problem, then, in relation to both these terms, is the following. There is a need, both legitimate and methodologically correct, to avoid generic definitions, which tend in any case to be all-inclusive. There is also a need to pursue a programme (already anticipated by Cumont himself and continued by the entire tradition which has given us the materials and problems relating to each of the 'Oriental cults') of reconstructing and differentiating the various 'Oriental' mythic-cultic structures on the one hand, and the 'category' of mysteries on the other. These actions do not necessarily involve the dismemberment of Cumont's programmatically unified picture, whose unity is deemed to be based on common features shared to some degree by the various contexts, and essentially accepted in subsequent formulations. In other words, the question is whether it is possible to re-establish on new foundations, while also taking into account some principles of the original system, a more articulated but still sufficiently homogeneous historical picture for which we can continue to use— *mutatis mutandis*—a single category of classification.

With regard to 'Oriental cults', such a category—within Cumont's perspective—aims to include all the mythic-cultic systems relating to a single deity, or, more often, to a group of interconnected deities, which arose in specific historical and cultural territories in the Mediterranean basin east of Greece as far as Iran, and which, especially from Hellenistic times, are to be found (in various

circumstances which it is the task of historical research to explain)
both in Greece itself and further westward, beyond the ideal watershed represented by Greece. In Cumont's vision, this ideal watershed
dividing the Mediterranean world was in large measure determined
by the presumed existence of a series of specific religious connotations
connected with 'Oriental cults' as opposed to 'Graeco–Roman paganism'; this paganism in turn was considered as a substantially homogeneous entity onto which 'Oriental cults' were gradually grafted,
causing some substantial modifications. But recent research has to a
large extent corrected this manner of framing of the question by the
creation of documentary corpora of considerable size which trace
the history of one or more deities outside their original country in
the whole Mediterranean region. Suffice it to mention Vermaseren's
monumental *Corpus cultus Cybelae Attidisque*, only whose first volume is devoted to the documents pertaining to this cult in its original
home of Asia Minor (Vermaseren 1977–89); or Bricault's invaluable
Atlas de la diffusion des cultes isiaques, which provides us with a
comprehensive map of these cults outside Egypt.[2]

This shift of perspective has also substantially modified our
approach to religious–historical exegesis: the problematic presence
of an Oriental cult outside its country of origin is no longer interpreted along an East–West axis but rather within the broader context
of the entire Mediterranean world, which is better suited to throw
light on the motivations and the historical and cultural circumstances of the general phenomenon by which many mythic-cultic
systems spread outside their local centres. There is no need to
emphasize how such a phenomenon finds a basis (certainly not a
necessary cause but a favourable objective condition) in the common
polytheistic religious structure to which belong, in different ways and
with connotations peculiar to each case, the various local religious
traditions, with the exception of the Judaic. To this picture, then,
properly belongs the equally significant question of the 'Oriental
diffusion' of Western deities and ritual practices—Greek, in the
first instance, but later, with the gradual rise of Rome, Roman, too,
and in imperial times also of other Western peoples.

---

[2] Bricault 2001. The epigraphic evidence for this widespread diffusion can now be
found in the rich corpus carefully assembled by Bricault 2005.

The traditional chronological boundaries of the question under consideration, are once again determined by Cumont's formulation and are generally constituted by conquests—Alexander the Great's on the one hand and the end of the Roman empire on the other. The latter was preceded by the gradual rise and diffusion of the new Christian religious identity and, later, by Constantine's momentous reform and the gradual but not painless transformation of the socio-cultural and religious structures of the whole of the Mediterranean world, with all the problems of influences and transformations occasioned by the encounter and confrontation between the two opposed forces.[3]

There is no need to insist on the antiquity of the circulation and migration of mythic-cultic structures within the Mediterranean area. These go back to the historically traceable origins of the various cultures gravitating in the vast Mediterranean area and the Near East and worked in both directions; their reciprocal influence is often hard to reconstruct with our tools of historical research, but is detectable through significant clues.[4] Nevertheless, it cannot be denied that the phenomenon of religious 'interference' between East and West displays some specific characteristics during the Hellenistic and Roman imperial periods, which render it a unique historical event. This can be situated in a dialectic of 'globalization' and 'localization': on the one hand, it reflects a sum of cultural and religious circumstances largely, if not universally, shared by the various peoples of the Mediterranean world; on the other, it displays a strong tendency to recover and value the qualifying elements of the various ethnic identities.[5] For this reason I hold that it is legitimate, in a religious–historical perspective, to continue delimiting our

---

[3] This subject is notoriously complex and the object of intense historiographical debate. Since it is not possible to give a full account here, the reader is referred to some stimulating, if at times questionable, contributions by MacMullen (1981, 1984, 1997).

[4] Suffice it here to mention one of the most recent interventions by the scholar who more than any other has contributed to the progress of research in this area (Burkert 1999) and the updates in Ribichini, Rocchi, and Xella 2001.

[5] Cf. Sfameni Gasparro 2004 and, at greater length, the various essays edited by Martin and Pachis 2004.

subject-matter according to the traditional chronological parameters just outlined.

The distinction between 'West' and 'East' in the geographical and cultural landscape in question is increasingly recognized as in large measure culturally determined: it reflects a long historiographical tradition that has at times turned it into a conventional stereotype far from historical reality. The manner in which the two strongest 'identities' in this scenario—the Greek and the Roman—distanced themselves from the 'Other' did not normally express itself in terms of East against West. On the other hand, it is precisely the compactness of the Greek and Roman identities and their undoubted capability to make a decisive impact on both the cultural and political dimensions of that geo-cultural landscape that allow us to continue framing the question in these terms, while striving for the flexibility indispensable to historical and comparative research. It is a case of investigating the meaning and the modalities of a process which, with the intensification of relations between different cultures and peoples in this period and geographical context, brought about a series of religious transformations both of these two 'identities' and of the distinguishing features of the numerous ethnic groups which converged in this context, resulting in the emergence of new and peculiar religious realities.

It seems to me necessary, therefore, to maintain in our research a readiness to continue asking questions about a possible thematic 'specificity' of this phenomenon on the basis of detailed enquiries on all aspects and elements recurring with varying degrees of frequency in the various Oriental mythic-cultic systems occurring outside their national boundaries. All this is in the context of an inevitable review of the entire spectrum of questions presented, using all the tools of a historical methodology sensitive to the specific and the individual, and founded on a comparative approach aimed more at distinguishing than at assimilating phenomena, while at the same time able to identify analogies. These are intended in the Aristotelian sense of *analoga*, that is of things which are neither identical nor disparate, as employed by Bianchi, arguing for the notion, derived from Pettazzoni but reinterpreted, of 'historical typology'. This notion of 'historical typology' is to be understood not in a horizontal, static sense, but rather vertically and dynamically as applied to historical processes reconstructed on the basis of the evidence and comparable on the grounds of specific similarities, without however overlooking their equally significant and peculiar differences.[6]

MYSTERIA: A GREEK EXPERIENCE

A first contribution to this project may result precisely from an examination of the question of 'Mysteries and oriental cults'. Such an examination, now that the notion of an almost automatic overlap of the two terms[7] has been abandoned, and eschewing the equally outdated definition of 'mystery religions', must face without prejudice the question of the religious–historical character of those ritual systems which the Greeks called *mysteria* (μυστήρια), with their divine referents and corresponding mythic foundations. In fact, as the historiography of the question makes clear, it is not legitimate to speak ahistorically of 'mysteries' outside the cultural and religious context from which this term derives and the religious reality that it encompasses. I beg the reader's leave to take as read my earlier analyses of the problem,[8] as well as the rich bibliography on the subject, which is now for the most part accessible, together with a rich collection of the principal sources, in the two valuable volumes by my colleague Paolo Scarpi.[9] Here I shall simply offer some observations suggested by renewed examination of the evidence and fresh consideration of the subject.

The most ancient testimony for the term *mysteria* and its religious content is found in a fragment of Heraclitus dating from the end of

---

[6] Among the many formulations of this notion, see Bianchi 1979a. A critical evaluation of Bianchi's scientific approach can be found in the collection of essays edited by Casadio 2002.

[7] This overlap, evident in the title, persists in the recent monograph by Álvar 2008, who appears to equate 'Oriental cults' with 'mysteries'.

[8] It is not possible here to list the extensive evidence and accompany it with the necessary critical analysis; the reader is referred to Sfameni Gasparro 1971, 1984, 1985, 1986, 1994, 2003a.

[9] Scarpi 2002a, 2002b: an extensive collection of sources on the mysteries. Cf. also the collection of texts concerning the various Oriental cults in Sanzi 2003.

the sixth or the beginning of the fifth century BC and originating from the highly Hellenized Asiatic city of Ephesus. As in all cases in which a fairly short citation of an ancient author is transmitted indirectly, and especially those in which the source is a Christian polemical source, it is necessary to examine critically the wider context of the fragment. Clement of Alexandria quotes Heraclitus in the context of a harsh attack on that area of polytheistic religious experience which he considers as a vast yet homogeneous and special 'category', that is to say ta *mysteria* (τὰ μυστήρια). 'But what if I were to recount the mysteries for you?', he asks, and immediately adds that he does not wish to 'burlesque them'[10] as Alcibiades did, clearly alluding to the latter's sacrilegious parody in fifth-century-BC Athens of the Eleusinian mysteries (which he has already established as the model mystery *par excellence*). Instead Clement will uncover their deceit, bringing to light the vanity 'of your gods, whose rites (τελεταί) are mystic (μυστικαί)' (*Protr.* 2. 12. 1). With this last formula the author supplies an alternative definition of *mysteria* that shows how, even in the second century AD, in order to associate *teletai* with mysteries it was necessary to add the adjective *mystikai*, that is to say it was necessary to evoke μυστήρια explicitly.

It is not possible here to analyse in detail the passage of Clement, though both in terminology and content it is extremely informative and valuable to our enquiry. Turning to the text of Heraclitus, we must note how it is employed by the Christian polemicist at the conclusion of a long passage in which the Eleusinian mysteries, in their mythical and ritual form, act as the chief referent; but weaved into them are significant strands of reports on Orphic rituals and exegesis (in turn thickly woven with Eleusinian themes), on Diony-siac contexts (these too presented in an Orphic guise), as well as reports on the mysteries of Cybele, Attis, and the Corybantes. The Eleusinian mysteries' essential impropriety in Clement's eyes induced him to conclude his argument with a citation from Heraclitus which seems to imply an allusion, as a contrast, to the eschatological hopes we know to have been connected with such practices: 'They will

---

[10] Note that the verb used is ἐξορχήσομαι, which vividly expresses the spectacular, almost 'theatrical' character of the rites in question.

meet, after death, an unexpected destiny!' (μένει τελευτήσαντας ἄσσα οὐδὲ ἔλπονται).[11] He continues: 'For whom, then, is Heraclitus of Ephesus prophesying? For people who go about at night, *magoi*, bacchants, *lēnai, mystai*. These are those he threatens with what follows death, these are those to whom he foretells fire: 'For they have the impiety to be initiated into rites which are considered mysteries among people' (or else 'because they are impiously initiated in what are considered mysteries among people').[12]

There is no way of knowing in what sequence these fragments appeared in the original text and how they were connected. In the first fragment, as we have seen, there is a reference to a destiny met '... after death', which is contrary to expectation, and which does not fail to evoke by an ironic inversion the 'good hope' of many Eleusinian testimonies. In the second passage, which many scholars have argued not to belong to the quotation from Heraclitus,[13] are mentioned a series of behaviours (wandering by night) and categories— *magoi* (the earliest use of the term without reference, so it seems, to the Persian magi, but rather with the new Greek meaning of practitioner of 'magical' rites),[14] bacchants, both male and female, and *mystai*, that is to say participants in the *mysteria*. This definition leaves open the question whether Heraclitus intended to refer also to Bacchic followers (which would then also be 'initiates', participants in the *mysteria*) or to a different category, that is to say the category of those who 'undergo an unholy initiation into what people deem mysteries' (τὰ γὰρ νομιζόμενα κατὰ ἀνθρώπους μυστήρια ἀνιερωστὶ μυοῦνται).

The Heraclitean passage, at any rate, shows awareness of the two decisive terms of the question under consideration—*mysteria* (μυστήρια) and *myein* (μυεῖν)—and perhaps also the related substantive *mystes* (μύστης). In all subsequent evidence, these terms

[11] *Vors.* 22 B 27 Diels–Kranz = fr. 113 Diano and Serra 1993.
[12] *Protr.* 2. 22, 1–2 Τίσι δὴ μαντεύεται Ἡράκλειτος ὁ Ἐφέσιος; "Νυκτιπόλοις, μάγοις, βάκχοις, λήναις, μύσταις", τούτοις ἀπειλεῖ τὰ μετὰ θάνατον, τούτοις μαντεύεται τὸ πῦρ· "τὰ γὰρ νομιζόμενα κατὰ ἀνθρώπους μυστήρια ἀνιερωστὶ μυοῦνται."
[13] In the edition of Diano and Serra (1993) only the sentence τὰ γὰρ νομιζόμενα κατὰ ἀνθρώπους μυστήρια ἀνιερωστὶ μυοῦνται is recorded as fr. 122.
[14] Cf. Bremmer 1999.

designate Greek systems of festivals, first among them the Eleusinian—often referred to simply as 'the mysteries' (τὰ μυστήρια) without further specification. Such festivals were characterized by a rigorous esoterism and by a special personal involvement on the part of the followers. This was expressed specifically by the verb *myein* (μυεῖν), which renders one a *mystes* (μύστης), implying therefore a change of status, whose essence and effects must be defined. As Scarpi noted in a recent article (Scarpi 2002b), Heraclitus' formula 'rites which are considered mysteries among people' (τὰ γὰρ νομιζόμενα κατὰ ἀνθρώπους μυστήρια) is undoubtedly generalizing, even though the mention of 'people'—within a Hellenocentric perspective—is understood as being limited to the philosopher's cultural environment. It seems legitimate, then, to conclude that in the context of Greek religious experience of the late sixth/early fifth century BC there was a familiar category of ritual practices of a particular kind and definable with the terminology in question, and that, therefore, the scientific impulse to investigate the nature, origin, and extent of such a category has a precise historical foundation, is indeed imposed by the comparative vocation of religious–historical research.

Herodotus' testimony, as we all know, adds detail and broadens this picture, throwing light on a series of aspects also illuminated by later documentation, progressively wider and more varied (literary, epigraphic, monumental, and iconographic). For our purposes, it suffices to focus on some familiar elements of this picture that may be likened to a guiding thread for an investigation that aims to proceed on the basis of solid documentary evidence and at the same time to elaborate a sufficiently homogeneous while still articulated historical typology of the phenomena called by the Greeks μυστήρια, both within their cultural context and also, perhaps, in relation to other people's. We must not forget that the problem of the existence and nature of 'mysteries' outside Greece, and specifically in one or other 'Oriental' religious context, arises in the first place from the definition of certain non-Greek mythic and cultic systems in Greek authors, or at any rate authors of Greek language and culture. It is the 'Greek gaze' which first turns us to this question and to an extent 'creates' our object—'mysteries'—engaging us to ask whether and in what measure the phenomenon thus defined—especially

when it belongs to a non-Greek historical and cultural context—
presents characteristics that make it structurally comparable with
those mythic-cultic complexes which the most ancient Greek sources
called μυστήρια and considered to be distinguished by esotericism
and initiation. The latter (which within this semantic sphere is
indicated, besides the verb 'to initiate' (μυεῖν), also by the substantive
'initiation' (μύησις)) is understood in the sense of a ritual practice
aimed at the person of the believer and aimed at procuring him a
specific religious status that distinguishes him from those who have
not undergone such an experience.

This sense of the verb 'to initiate' (μυεῖν) appears evident from a
Herodotean passage that vividly expresses the religious reality of the
Eleusinian ceremonial system. Already in epigraphic documents
dating to the middle of the fifth century (*IG* i³. no. 6), this is
presented as the 'mysteries' *par excellence*. It is defined by Herodotus
as a 'festival' (ὁρτή) that 'the Athenians celebrate each year for the
Mother and the Daughter, and those among them who wish it . . . are
initiated'.[15] It is, then, a civic festival dedicated to two great divinities
of the state pantheon; it does not imply any tension within general
religious practice but is rather perfectly integrated in it. Its singularity
derives from the esoteric character of an essential component of the
ritual and the individual's personal decision to take part.

This esoteric texture, which later sources show to have been so
marked that it even affected the identity of the cult divinities,[16]
comes to the fore in the other Greek cultic system—albeit at the
periphery of the Greek world, on the island of Samothrace—designated
as μυστήρια by Herodotus.[17] The picture is broadened by the mention of a 'sacred speech' known only to initiates, and complicated by
the parallel definition as *orgia* of the cult of Samothrace, which the
historian, like the long tradition which followed, attributed to the
Cabiri (with a mention also of an ithyphallic Hermes) (Hemberg
1950). Leaving aside for the moment the important question of

---

[15] Herodotus, *Histories* 8. 65: τὴν . . . ὁρτὴν ταύτην ἄγουσιν Ἀθηναῖοι ἀνὰ πάντα ἔτεα
τῇ Μητρὶ καὶ τῇ Κόρῃ καὶ αὐτῶν τε ὁ βουλόμενος καὶ τῶν ἄλλων Ἑλλήνων μυεῖται.

[16] See the sources in Scarpi 2002a: ii. E 3–4, 6–8, 11, 14–17, etc. Cf. also Lewis 1958.

[17] *Histories* 2. 51. 1–3. Among the most recent contributions see Cole 1984, 1989;
Burkert 1993; Mari 2001; Goceva 2002.

this terminology, which is used also of the Eleusinian cult in the earliest surviving literary evidence (if the dating of the *Homeric Hymn to Demeter* to around 600 BC is accepted),[18] we note that the aspects common to the two systems of Eleusis and Samothrace turn out now to be the initiatory-esoteric character, the nature of cults offered to gods of the Greek pantheon, the peculiar position of their followers, who are personally involved in the ritual practice to the extent that their religious status changes, and the specific localization in contexts that present themselves as the only sites of a ritual practice carried out according to the sources within the sanctuary by specialized personnel. In addition there is the 'sacred speech' reserved for the initiates; this is mentioned by Herodotus only in connection with Samothrace, but we know from other sources that the Eleusinian cult, too, involved a sacred speech, side by side with the 'vulgate' myth illustrated by the *Hymn to Demeter* and echoed, with many variants, in all the later tradition.

One last analogy between the two contexts in question cannot pass unmentioned, even though it is not evoked in our source. This is, of course, the component, present in both contexts in very different forms, of the 'hopes' offered to the followers by the initiatory-esoteric cults of Eleusis and Samothrace. For the latter we are only aware of a specialization in terms of protection from the perils of the sea and of the conferment of a state of purity and 'justice'[19] (though there are grounds for suspecting a more general guarantee against the risks of life, especially for those who were most dramatically open to them, such as sailors, tradesmen, soldiers). The promises of the Eleusinian mysteries, on the other hand, concerned both the earthly life, with a wealth of blessings for the individual as well as for the Athenian community as a whole, and the otherworldly life, with a guarantee of a privileged survival in the underworld, often expressed in terms of enjoyment of light and a 'life' contrasted with the vacuity of the shadowy survival generally vouchsafed to the uninitiated.[20]

---

[18] Among the most recent contributions to the problem, I refer the reader only to Simms 1990, Motte and Pirenne-Delforge 1992.

[19] Cf. Diodorus Siculus 5. 49. 5–6 = Scarpi 2002a: ii, F. 1.

[20] On the subject of 'soteriology' in mystery cults, as well as the proceedings of the conference in Rome organized by Ugo Bianchi (Bianchi and Vermaseren 1982), I take the liberty of citing my own recent restatement of the problem of 'salvation' in the

On the basis of these testimonies, it seems to me possible to reassert that our two key requirements, that is to say an individualizing approach, which is sensitive to the specificity of individual historical phenomena, and a generalizing one, aimed at comprehending—on the basis of the comparative analysis of religious–historical research—similarities and differences between the phenomena, are both anticipated and to some extent imposed by the Greek sources. Heraclitus, in Ephesus, a Greek city on Asiatic soil, is aware in the late sixth to early fifth century of 'rites which are considered mysteries among people' (τὰ ... νομιζόμενα κατὰ ἀνθρώπους μυστήρια), to which are also impiously 'initiated' individuals probably belonging to various religious communities. He outlines an 'ecumenical' perspective ('among people', κατὰ ἀνθρώπους), though in all probability one Hellenocentrically limited to the Greek cultic environment, of which a large area of 'Oriental' Asia Minor had for centuries been a vital part. In the fifth century, Herodotus, in defining as μυστήρια the cult of Demeter and Kore at Eleusis and of the Cabiri of Samothrace, confirms the followers' personal involvement. This is expressed by the verb 'to be initiated' (μυεῖν in the passive voice), which makes of each follower an 'initiate' (μύστης), terms rendered by the verb and noun 'initiate' in English and by comparable forms in other modern languages. At the same time he insists on these cults' peculiar exclusivity by highlighting their esoteric character in relation both to ritual practice and to some of its mythic and theological contents.

An important element of Herodotus' picture is the relation of the Eleusinian and Samothracian μυστήρια to a specific cultic site, which the documentary evidence shows to have been entrusted to specialized personnel, especially in the case of Eleusis. Initiation and esoterism, localization at a permanent sacred site, a form of cult directed at divinities from the common Greek pantheon, but with a call for a personal decision on the part of the individual, who

ancient world (Sfameni Gasparro 2006). This is of course a fundamental question, the object of differing interpretations and stances, among which one must not overlook the balanced view of Burkert 1987. See the perceptive observations of Smith 1990, articulated around the distinction between a 'locative' and a 'utopian' soteriological perspective.

opens himself up to an intense and involving experience capable of transforming his religious identity—these, then, appear to have been the constitutive characters of the mythic-ritual complexes of Eleusis and Samothrace. These aspects, distinctive with respect to the general charateristics of Greek religion yet common to both contexts, allow us to discuss the typology of mysteries on a historical basis, one that is not predetermined or indeed normative.

A first essential difference between the two contexts lies in the nature of the promises each offered to their followers. These are otherworldly and eschatological in the case of the Eleusinian mysteries, where the 'locative' interest for life and worldly wellbeing, particularly in the sense of agrarian abundance for the individual initiate as well as for the whole civic community, guaranteeing the periodic celebration of the Two Goddesses' cult, is combined with an equally marked 'utopian' tendency, that is to say a search for guarantees beyond life, represented variously in different sources and at different times, but in any case oriented towards the underworld. The Samothracian mysteries, on the other hand, appear to know only the first kind of promise: protection from the perils of the sea and more generally from the various dangers of life, and the attainment of a peculiar condition of purity and justice are the benefits due to the pious *mystes* of the Great Gods of Samothrace. This state of affairs makes it impossible to regard an eschatological perspective as essential to μυστήρια. Rather it suggests the necessity of operating in a flexible manner, without forcing the meaning of our source, in order to identify in each case the nature and qualities of the benefits offered by initiatory-esoteric cults, whether they are Greek or belonging to an 'Oriental' context.

The question of the presence of religious phenomena similar to Greek μυστήρια such as Eleusis and Samothrace in other cultural contexts is, of course, suggested already by Herodotus' statement that the secret rites in the temple of Athena (= Neith) at Sais are called μυστήρια by the Egyptians.[21] These are said to involve 'repre-

---

[21] *Histories* 2. 171. 1: Ἐν δὲ τῇ λίμνῃ ταύτῃ τὰ δείκηλα τῶν παθέων Αὐτοῦ νυκτὸς ποιεῦσι, τὰ καλέουσι μυστήρια Αἰγύπτιοι.

sentations of his sufferings', that is to say of Osiris, left unnamed by the historian in a manner which evokes implicitly the typical 'unutterable' (*arrheton*) of mysteries. It is not possible to discuss here at length the exegetical problem posed by this famous passage. The extensive Egyptian documentary evidence allows us to conclude without great difficulty that the Osiric rites, as they were still celebrated in the fifth century BC, did not display the element of initiation that was a distinctive trait of contemporary Greek 'mysteries'.[22] In this case, then, we can be certain that it is Herodotus' Greek gaze that creates its object. Still, we must enquire about the reasons for such a construction. For the question cannot be resolved by an appeal to simple assimilation to Greek norms or to Greek ethnocentrism: some elements of the picture outlined by the historian and of the underlying, authentic, 'foreign' religious reality lend scope for comparison between the Greek and Egyptian contexts. One might indeed add that it is precisely the historian's cultural sensibility—for he was knowledgeable on the Greek phenomenon of μυστήρια—that allows him to discern with quick perception the similarities between some aspects of Greek cult and the Osiric mythic-cultic system. The nighttime setting, as well as the secrecy of the ritual practice and its mythic foundations,[23] and, most of all, the deep connection between myth and cult—these are the elements that prompted Herodotus' comparative assessment. The 'sufferings' (πάθη) of the god and their ritual representation (τὰ δείκηλα) evoke to Herodotus' mind a qualifying dimension of reality familiar to him from the Eleusinian and Samothracian μυστήρια, the only ones he mentions elsewhere in his work. This calls into question an important aspect of the problems under consideration, that is to say the historical legitimacy of a specific typology of deities culted in μυστήρια.

---

[22] Cf. Nagel 1944, whose conclusions remain valid today. Some relevant observations also in Dunand 1975.

[23] It is well known that the Egyptian texts never narrate in detail the 'passion' of Osiris. Plutarch (first–second cc. AD) is the only Greek author to have preserved the entire narrative sequence, which the original sources evoke with very great frequency but always in an allusive manner. One example may stand for all: the *Hymn to Osiris* of the Louvre, translated by Moret 1931.

SIGNIFICANCE AND LIMITS OF A TYPOLOGY
OF THE DEITIES OF MYSTERIES

I need not here illustrate in further detail either the now outdated
formula of the 'god who dies and returns',[24] that is to say Frazer's
'fertility god', or the formula, elaborated by Ugo Bianchi and substan-
tiated with precise historical content, of the *dio in vicenda* ('god in
vicissitude'). The latter is certainly connected with the classic themes of
fertility cults, accepted also by Raffaele Pettazzoni (1924), and placed by
both scholars at the root of the historical development of mystery cults.
For Bianchi (1965, 1976, 1979c, 1982), the notion of the *dio in vicenda*,
though more sharply separated from the connection with fertility,
is located in the context of a distinction, likewise aimed at the formulation of historical typologies, between 'mystic' and 'mysteric', terms that
qualify both entire cultic structures and their individual elements, such
as the various divine protagonists of such cults.

For my part, I consider historically legitimate the distinction between
mythic-cultic structures such as those of Eleusis and Samothrace, in
which the components of initiation and esoterism are decisive and
qualifying, and other phenomena of fundamental importance to the
question under consideration, which are often designated in Greek with
the terms *teletai* and *orgia*. Though these phenomena present qualified
similarities with mysteries such as the Eleusinian and Samothracian
(which in turn are often designated with those same terms), they do
not include, at least in their earliest form, the features of initiation and
rigorous esoterism characteristic of mysteries. While fully aware that the
differentiation of 'mystic' and 'mysteric' is a mere convention (after all,
the adjective μυστικός pertains to the sphere of μυστήρια) I have
decided nevertheless to adopt it: I employ 'mysteric' to refer to the
specific initiatory-esoteric component of cults such as Eleusis and Samothrace, while I use the term 'mystic' in a more specialized sense, in
relation to the content of these cults from the point of view of the
divinities which are their object and of the religious experience their
followers find in them. At the same time, 'mystic' lends itself to a more
general use, in defining divine figures and religious experiences within

---

[24] The theme is revisited in the collection of essays edited by Xella 2001.

ritual practices which do not present an initiatory and esoteric structure in the strict sense. This enables us to take into account for the purposes of comparison the whole spectrum of the components of mysteries. At the same time, by keeping fixed the specific connotation of mysteries constituted by the initiatory element, we can broaden our field of comparison to encompass a larger spectrum of religious phenomena which were essential to the Greek religious experience, such as *teletai* and *orgia*, which included the most ancient manifestations of Dionysism,[25] Corybantism,[26] and the rites of Cybele of classical times,[27] to mention only the most famous. Most of all, this allows us to employ a more flexible conception so as to broaden the comparative perspective in the direction of non-Greek historical and cultural contexts. These, too, must have included phenomena similar to the Greek 'mystic' and 'mysteric' phenomena, both in their original distinct characteristics and as they converged with the Greek world, implying varying degrees of Helleniza-tion in general, and in particular the formation of mysteric structures, for which the Greek model appears to have been historically decisive.

What must in my opinion be clearly emphasized is that the terms and distinctions here proposed are drawn from the documentary evidence and used only as heuristic tools rather than as definitions or, worse still, as given and necessary categories. More specifically, the typology of the *dio in vicenda* or 'god in vicissitude' is indeed useful in defining significant aspects of the 'characteriology' of the protag-onists of some mysteric cults (particularly the Eleusinian and, among the 'Oriental cults', that of Isis–Osiris) and in qualifying figures such as the Dionysus of the *bakcheia* and, most of all, the Orphic Diony-sus, who is subject to being torn apart and rebirth,[28] and the Egyp-tian Osiris with his 'sufferings'. But on the other hand I do not

---

[25] For the main items of a bibliography of exceptional proportions and in contin-ual expansion cf. Scarpi 2002a: i. lxxi–lxxvi, to which must be added Casadio 1981, 1983, 1994, and 1999.

[26] Cf. Poerner 1913; Linforth 1946; Pretini 1999; Voutiras 1996; Ustinova 1996b.

[27] Sfameni Gasparro 1985: 9–19.

[28] Among the more or less important titles on a classic theme of religious–historical study of the ancient and late-antique world (cf. Scarpi 2002a: i. lxxvi–lxxxii), I limit myself here to citing Borgeaud 1991; Masaracchia 1993; Brisson 1995; Tortorelli Ghidini, Storchi Marino, Visconti 2000. The valuable collection of frag-ments and testimonia on Orphism edited by Bernabé (2004–5) also provides a virtually complete bibliographical update.

believe that this typology should be taken as an *a priori* condition in a historical enquiry into mysteries, either Greek or Oriental. In other words, precisely on account of the programmatically historical character of any religious–historical typology, the one in question is the result of specific investigations on individual contexts: it will, in differing degrees in each case, reflect certain of their qualifying aspects and elements, without presuming to exhaust all their scope of meaning. At the same time, this approach does not stipulate any kind of necessary relation between the type of the 'mystic god' and the mysteric form. It recognizes the existence, at different times and in differing cultural environments whose peculiar identities must be defined on a case by case basis, of mysteric phenomena (or at least of phenomena defined as such in the sources) dedicated to various deities whom we cannot, given the state of our evidence, assimilate to superhuman beings definable as *dèi in vicenda*. They experience, in the adventures told of them in myth and evoked in ritual, forms of 'suffering' and 'labour' that go beyond the limits of the divine condition as they were commonly drawn in ancient polytheisms in order to share in certain features of human life, with crises and disappearances, if only temporary, until the final threshold of death.

The flexibility of the typology in question can be essayed by testing the possibilities and limits of its applicability to the figure of the 'mysteric' god *par excellence*: the 'Roman' Mithras. Mithras is the recipient of the only initiatory-esoteric cult to which the formula of 'mystery cult' can be applied, yet he is in no way 'suffering' but rather 'unconquered' (*invictus*). Previous analysis[29] has shown how, by fully recognizing this essential difference and the combativeness and this-worldly involvement of Mithraic religiosity, it is possible, precisely by reference to our typology, to perceive some reasons for the deep transformation undergone by the ancient Iranian god of justice and oaths to become—probably by an act, or series of acts, of religious

---

[29] I refer to the collection of essays now edited by Sfameni Gasparro 2003a: 119–210, written for the 1978 international conference on 'La specificità storico-religiosa dei Misteri di Mithra . . .', and originally published in Bianchi 1979b: 299–384, 397–408. See also the observations formulated at that conference by Cerutti 1979, aimed at limiting the applicability of the 'model' in question to the 'Unconquered Mithras'.

'creation'[30]—the recipient of an esoteric cult by initiation, as well as the protagonist of a complex cosmic story that, though untouched by hopelessness and death, yet knows exhaustion, commitment, crises, and struggles, before ending victoriously with an ascension to a higher, celestial and divine, plane.

The peculiar connotations of a *dio in vicenda*, in the sense described above, are probably precisely what seemed to Herodotus (and perhaps also to his Egyptian informants, who were aware of Greek matters) to legitimate the definition of the Osiric rites of Sais as *mysteria*. At any rate, after roughly nine centuries marked by evolutions and deep transformations, these connotations figure clearly in the scenario evoked by Firmicus Maternus around the 'idol' whose body is reconstituted and 'carried out' from his burial place to be offered to the worship of the faithful. These are addressed by the priest who anoints their throat with the reassuring announcement: 'Take heart, initiates of the saved god: for us too there will be delivery from hardship.'[31] If, as all the elements of the picture lead

---

[30] See in particular the statements of Beck 1998 (whose exegesis of Mithraism is now more amply illustrated by Beck 2004), and Gordon 2001. Some of the many earlier contributions by this scholar are collected in Gordon 1996.

[31] *On the Error of Profane Religions* 22. 1–3: *Aliud etiam symbolum proferimus, ut contaminatae cogitationis scelera revelentur. Cuius totus ordo dicendus est ut apud omnes constet divinae dispositionis legem perversa diaboli esse imitatione corruptam. Nocte quadam simulacrum in lectica supinum ponitur et per numeros digestis fletibus plangitur. Deinde, cum se ficta lamentatione satiaverint, lumen infertur. Tunc a sacerdote omnium qui flebant fauces unguentur, quibus perunctis sacerdos hoc lento murmure susurrat:* θαρρεῖτε μύσται τοῦ θεοῦ σεσωσμένου· ἔσται γὰρ ἡμῖν ἐκ πόνων σωτηρία . . . *Idolum sepelis, idolum plangis, idolum de sepultura proferis et, miser, cum haec feceris gaudes. Tu deum tuum liberas, tu iacentia lapidis membra componis, tu insensibile corrigis saxum. Tibi agat gratias deus tuus, te paribus remuneret donis, te sui uelit esse participem. Sic moriaris ut moritur; sic vivas ut vivit.* 'We mention yet another symbol, in order to reveal the wickednesses of an impure way of thinking. We must discuss its whole ritual to make clear to everyone that the law of the divine order has been corrupted by a perverse imitation of the Devil. On a particular night, an image of the god is laid on its back in a litter, and is mourned with lamentations set to music. Next, when they are sated with bogus tears, a torch is brought in. Then, the throats of all those who were weeping are anointed by the priest. After this anointing, the priest slowly murmurs and whispers as follows in Greek: "Be of good cheer, initiates of the god who is saved: we will have salvation from our troubles". . . It is an idol that you bury, an idol that you mourn, an idol that you bring forth from the tomb, and, wretched one, you rejoice in having done this. It is you that frees your god, you that puts together his inert limbs of stone, you that sets straight the

us to conclude, the anonymous 'saved god' (θεὸς σεσωσμένος) is Osiris,[32] then we have here evidence for a process of continuity but also of profound transformation of a religious context: in the course of a long historical development involving among other things the crossing of its national boundaries, it appears to have assumed—in socio-cultural conditions and in geographical areas which historical research is not able to define precisely—the typical initiatory-esoteric structure of Greek *mysteria*, while still maintaining the distinctive character of its original Egyptian identity.

EXAMPLES OF 'ORIENTAL' MYSTERIES

General questions

There is no need to emphasize that the religious–historical evaluation of the Osiris cult and the problems of changes within it and its extension beyond its native home directly call into question the figure of Isis, who is usually the focal point for the diffusion beyond Egypt of 'Egyptian cults', and in particular for the question of the 'mysteries' pertaining to them.[33] The question is a complex one, and I can only here offer some brief observations. Initiatory-esoteric aspects in the cult of Isis are attested late–first century AD[34] at the earliest, not counting some allusions in the aretalogic texts of the first century BC, and the strongly 'Eleusinian' image of the Isis of Maronea of the second to first centuries BC (Grandjean 1975). This late date tells against the tendency to overestimate the role of the mysteric

---

insensate rock. Your god could thank you, could recompense you with equivalent gifts, could wish you to share in himself. One way, you would die as he dies; the other way, you would live as he lives.'

[32] It has been convincingly argued that the character in question should be identified with Osiris rather than Attis, as previously hypothesized; see Podeman Sørensen 1989.

[33] For an update of research see the three International Colloquia of Isis Studies organized by Laurent Bricault (Bricault 2000, 2004; Bricault et al. 2007). A recent contribution by Michel Malaise is aimed at defining the 'classifying' language most appropriate to this mythic-cultic complex (Malaise 2005).

[34] Cf. Dunand 1975; Bianchi 1980; Malaise 1981, 1986; Bergman 1982.

form in Oriental cults in general and the cult of Isis in particular, even indeed to make it coextensive with the span of their diffusion. This, moreover, suggests a fairly deep influence of the Eleusinian 'model' in the process of institution of mysteric practice in the cult of Isis, rather than a fully independent 'evolution' of the cult. A further contradictory factor lies in the notorious rarity of positive attestations of 'initiates' and mysteric practices, in contrast with the exceptional wealth and scope of the evidence for Isiac presence throughout the Mediterranean basin starting in the fourth century BC.[35]

Finally, the substantial differences between the images of the mysteries of Isis offered by our two witnesses, Plutarch and Apuleius, must act as a warning of the difficulty, if not the impossibility, of reconstructing a compact and monolithic reality for the mysteries of Isis, and, more generally, for the mysteries of other Oriental deities, without taking into account two fundamental factors. The first is the quality of the source, especially when this is literary, since then the degree of elaboration of any objective information is likely to be higher, and personal interests and points of view play a greater part. The second factor is the variety of times, places, and socio-cultural environments to which the phenomena evoked by the source belong. The mysteries of Isis and Osiris,[36] like the mysteries of Cybele, sometimes associated with Attis, and finally those of Mithras, do not appear to be tied to a single cultic centre. In this they differ from the *mysteria* of Eleusis and Samothrace, as well as the many other instances of similar phenomena which emerge gradually on the Greek scene (e.g. Andania in the Peloponnese; Thebes with its mysteries of the Cabiri, present also on Lemnos; and the many instances of mysteries of Demeter in the Hellenistic world).[37] These are too

---

[35] The attestation of 'mysteries' of the 'new' god Serapis (Borgeaud and Volokhine 2000; Sfameni Gasparro 2003b) in an unusual rock sanctuary brought to light at Panoia (Portugal) is exceptional. Cf. Alföldi 1997.

[36] Also those of Serapis in one case—at Panoia in Portugal.

[37] Since it is not possible here to offer even a brief review of this diverse scene, I mention only the contributions edited by Cosmopoulos 2003, which examine some of the mysteries mentioned. See esp. Graf 2003, who aptly emphasizes the significance of the extraordinary flourishing of the phenomenon in Hellenistic and Roman times. The question of the 'mysteries' occasionally attested in the context of Imperial cult calls for renewed examination. Cf. Nilsson 1957; Robert 1960: 316–24; Pleket 1965; Price 1984: 190–1. There is also a pressing need to examine the religious–historical

little known to us, but receive significant mention in our sources, especially during the imperial period and in the variously Hellenized Anatolian region, as well in Sardis,[38] Ephesus (mysteries of Artemis),[39] Panamara (mysteries of Zeus),[40] Lagina (mysteries of Hecate),[41] Didyma and Claros, where singular initiatory practices are connected with their respective oracles of Apollo.[42] Like the Dionysiac phenomenon, with its wide dissemination even when the ancient structure of the *bakcheia* is joined, in different times and ways, by the initiatory-esoteric structure of the *mysteria*, so too the mysteries of Oriental deities display a typical mobility and wide diffusion, for which it is necessary to evaluate the dialectic between unchanged constants and local traits with their corresponding diversifications. In this picture, Mithraism is a case unto itself: despite undoubted local connotations and the extraordinary breadth of its expansion in the Mediterranean world, the monumental and figurative evidence suggests an essentially homogeneous and stable character. This character leads us to hypothesize a unitary centre for its formation and in all likelihood it presupposes, as recent research has suggested, an actual 'act of foundation' aimed at creating a religious reality around an ancient deity on the basis of a traditional religious heritage of Iranian origin. Moreover, both these elements were originally revisited in the light of clearly Hellenistic notions (for instance the strong astral component and the dense network of cosmic references) and in a historical context strongly anchored in a social and cultural sense to the structures of the Roman Empire, as is evident from the

significance of the use of mysteric terminology in this and in similar cases in which it is difficult to perceive the content of the cultic reality encompassed by such terminology.

[38] Herrmann 1996.

[39] Picard 1922: 287–302; Horsley 1992; Rogers 1999. Cf. Oster 1990.

[40] Oppermann 1924; Roussel 1927; Laumonier 1958: 221–343.

[41] Laumonier 1938; 1958: 344–425. Mysteries are attested also at Stratonicea, in relation to the local cult of Apollo and Artemis (Laumonier 1958: 193–220).

[42] Picard 1922: 303–11. The phenomenon of the connection between oracles and mysteric cults is well exemplified by the unusual religious creation of the prophet Alexander, who founded in his birthplace of Abonouteichus in Paphlagonia a successful oracle of the 'new Asclepius' in the form of a snake, Glycon, and cleverly associated to it a mysteric structure clearly modelled on Eleusis. Cf. Sfameni Gasparro 2003: 149–202.

cult's prevalent appeal to the military and administrative classes. It has even been suggested that the 'creation' of Mithraism in an Oriental, Anatolian milieu should be ascribed to individuals who migrated to Rome and were in close contact with the centres of power (Beck 1998). At any rate, the Western cult of Mithras, as it is portrayed in our sources from the first century AD, is set apart by its strong 'theological' and ritual compactness, and its wholly initiatory-esoteric character, which is devoid of any of the public manifestations that characterized most worship of Isis and Cybele. Mithraism alone among the Oriental cults justifies the phrase 'mystery religion'. Its complexity must be reconstructed through patient and cautious exegesis of a complex iconography that is to an unusual extent richly evocative and dynamically performative rather than statically declarative. It displays to the highest degree the traits of that alternation between 'innovation' and 'tradition' which renders 'Oriental cults' in general, and any mysteric dimension to them, essentially dynamic and creative phenomena.

The Isiac mysteries

To return to the reports on the mysteries of Isis found in Plutarch[43] and Apuleius,[44] we may draw attention to some elements that, within the common cultural–historical and religious referent, set out two incompatible scenarios; this goes to show how our object of observation reveals different aspects and meanings when we shift our point of view. Plutarch addresses himself to the priestess Clea, who is located in a religious space identified as Delphi, with its sanctuary of Apollo (which seems to have an Isiac appearance, perhaps specifically associated with initiation), and in a contemporary historical dimension. Yet he elaborates a highly directed and Platonizing exegesis of the Egyptian mythic-cultic complex, and proposes a reading of what appears to be its mysteric dimension that privileges the 'pathetic' aspect of the divine story and the relation of *sympatheia* between it and the general human condition. After the narrative of

---

[43] Plutarch, *On Isis* 27; see the edition with commentary by Griffiths 1970.
[44] Apuleius, *Metamorphoses* 11. Cf. Griffiths 1975.

the adventures of Osiris and her faithful spouse Isis, the author suggests a direct link between them and the cultic reality lived by the devotees: 'The sister and wife of Osiris, however, as his helper quenched and stopped Typhon's mad frenzy, nor did she allow the contest and struggles which she had undertaken, her wanderings and her many deeds of wisdom and bravery, to be engulfed in oblivion and silence, but into the most sacred rites she infused images, suggestions, and representations of her experiences at that time, and so she consecrated at once a pattern of piety and an encouragement to men and women overtaken by similar misfortunes.'[45]

The 'most holy rites' (ἁγιώταται τελεταί) instituted by Isis are a 'life lesson' (εὐσεβείας ... δίδαγμα), in conformity with the laws of respect for men and gods, since the *eusebeia* mentioned here refers to the behaviour of the 'good *daimones*' Osiris and Isis and of the other characters of their circle, in contrast with the blind and destructive violence of Seth-Typhon and of his acolytes. They are also a 'paramyth' (παραμύθιον), a reassurance that man can ultimately overcome the more or less painful and dramatic vicissitudes of his existence. There is no mention in this passage, nor in the rest of Plutarch's treatise, of any soteriological perspective in an eschatological framework connected with the Isiac cult and in particular with its mysteric dimension.

These perspectives are instead presented as an important component of that kind of Isiac message that Apuleius puts in the goddess's mouth at the moment of her lunar epiphany. This has a clear henotheistic and densely cosmosophic appearance: the protagonist's deliverance from his asinine form must be the beginning of a religious journey of complete devotion to the foreseeing and benevolent *Fortuna* who appeals to Lucius. Isis guarantees at last for Lucius *precaria salus* (*Met.* 11. 21), 'salvation obtained by an act of grace', configured especially as liberation from the tyrannical power of the blind Fortuna (with strong astral connotations) who has dominated

---

[45] *On Isis* 27, 361 C–D: ἡ δὲ τιμωρὸς 'Οσίριδος ἀδελφὴ καὶ γυνὴ τὴν Τυφῶνος σβέσασα καὶ καταπαύσασα μανίαν καὶ λύσσαν οὐ περιεῖδε τοὺς ἄθλους καὶ τοὺς ἀγῶνας, οὓς ἀνέτλη, καὶ πλάνας αὑτῆς καὶ πολλὰ μὲν ἔργα σοφίας πολλὰ δ' ἀνδρείας ἀμνηστίαν ὑπολαβοῦσαν καὶ σιωπήν, ἀλλὰ ταῖς ἁγιωτάταις ἀναμίξασα τελεταῖς εἰκόνας καὶ ὑπονοίας καὶ μιμήματα τῶν τότε παθημάτων εὐσεβείας ὁμοῦ δίδαγμα καὶ παραμύθιον ἀνδράσι καὶ γυναιξὶν ὑπὸ συμφορῶν ἐχομένοις ὁμοίων καθωσίωσεν (transl. Griffiths 1970: 159).

his life up to that point, and she even suggests the possibility of extending his lifespan beyond the limits imposed by fate. Moreover, Isis promises Lucius a *post mortem* privilege consistent with the general canons of Egyptian tradition, that is to say the enjoyment of contemplation of the divine image in the underworld, in a context of light.[46] Participation in the Isiac 'mystery', configured in the pregnant and allusive terms of a cosmic journey and a liminal experience between death and access to the divine level,[47] becomes a solar and cosmic exaltation of the initiate, without further mention of hopes beyond life (*Met.* 11. 23–4). The second initiation, accomplished by order and with the patronage of the 'sovereign' Osiris, does not appear to have any purpose other than that of increasing the religious zeal of Lucius and giving him reassurance for his 'sojourn in a foreign country' and success in his profession (*Met.* 11. 27). Finally, when Lucius moves from Corinth, the seat of Isiac mysteries, to Rome, the call to a third initiatory experience is motivated somewhat banally by the necessity of acquiring new sacred garments to take the

---

[46] *Metamorphoses* 11. 6: *Vives autem beatus, vives in mea tutela gloriosus, et cum spatium saeculi tui permensus ad inferos demearis, ibi quoque in ipso subterraneo semirutundo me, quam vides, Acherontis tenebris interlucentem Stygiisque penetralibus regnantem, campos Elysios incolens ipse, tibi propitiam frequens adorabis. Quodsi sedulis obsequiis et religiosis ministeriis et tenacibus castimoniis numen nostrum promerueris, scies ultra statuta fato tuo spatia vitam quoque tibi prorogare mihi tantum licere.* 'You shall live a blessed life, you shall live under my protection a life of glory, and when you have reached the end of your time and go down into the underworld, there too you will often worship me (who will be favourable to you) in the semicircular space beneath the earth, seeing me shining in the darkness of Acheron and ruling in the Stygian depths, when you yourself are living in the Elysian fields. But if by diligent attention, devout service and continuing purity you will be worthy of our divine power, you will know that I alone can extend your life beyond the span laid down by fate.' (trans. Beard et al. 1998: ii. 299)

[47] *Metamorphoses* 11. 23 *Accessi confinium mortis et calcato Proserpinae limine per omnia vectus elementa remeavi, nocte media vidi solem candido coruscantem lumine, deos inferos et deos superos accessi coram et adoravi de proximo. Ecce tibi rettuli, quae, quamvis audita, ignores tamen necesse est. Ergo quod solum potest sine piaculo ad profanorum intellegentias enuntiari, referam.* 'Having reached the boundary of death and having stood on the threshold of Proserpina, I was borne through all the elements and returned. In the middle of the night I saw the sun shining with a brilliant light. I approached the gods below and the gods above and worshipped them close to. There, I have reported to you things which, even though you have heard them, you must fail to understand. So I shall tell you only what can be reported without sin to the minds of the uninitiated.' (trans. Beard et al. 1998: ii. 299–300)

place of the ones left behind in Greece. The benefits of the initiation are very prosaic: a prestigious status within the sacred hierarchy through admission 'into the college of the *pastophori* and even into the quinquennial *decuriones*', and success as a legal advocate and high earnings. There is an exclusive insistence on the locative dimension of the mysteric phenomenon and an apparently complete obscuring of the utopian dimension projected beyond everyday life (*Met.* 11. 30).

Cybele: Anatolian roots and a Greek appearance

The third cultural–historical context which is traditionally considered to play an essential part in the question of 'Oriental cults and mysteries' is the Anatolian, and more especially Phrygian, context. This revolves around the figure of the 'mountain' Mother with her many toponymic appellations, preeminent among them that of Cybele, derived from Mt. Cybelon. To Cybele are attached, in a complex network of mythic and ritual relationships variously configured according to time, place, and historical circumstances, other characters such as the Corybantes, Sabazius,[48] and, above all, Attis. Since it is not possible here to delve into detail, I shall merely flag for critical attention some aspects that stand out as structurally essential to our question and help direct us towards a correct religious–historical exegesis.

A first distinctive element of this religious horizon acts as a guiding thread from its earliest manifestations in Archaic and Classical Greece to its last in Late Antiquity, when in Rome, now ruled by Christian emperors, the cult of Cybele—introduced by the Republican state as a guarantee and seal of its national identity[49]—was the instrument of ultimate affirmation of the traditional 'pagan' religious physiognomy of large swathes of the senatorial aristocracy. I am referring to the dimension of 'madness' (μανία) and 'religious

---

[48] See e.g. Strabo on the various epichoric names of the goddess in Asia Minor, particularly in Phrygia, and the network of divine and 'daemonic' associations centred around her (10. 3. 12).

[49] As well as the now outdated but still useful work of Aurigemma 1900, see Lambrechts 1951. For the tradition on the mode of introduction of this cult in Rome cf. Köves 1963; Bömer 1964; Bremmer 1979.

enthusiasm' (ὀργιασμός) as peculiar connotations of the recipients of cult and of the behaviour of their followers, who were usually united in communities such as *thiasoi* and *orgeones*.[50] This scenario also includes a strong cathartic component, at times dialectically related to the punitive and destructive force of the 'madness' itself, which is the mirror counterpart of its positive capability to instaurate a strong relationship of 'communication' between the divine and the human level. There is also an aspect of peculiar reserve and a strong sense of belonging to a religious community, as expressed in Euripides' inspired phrase θιασεύειν ψυχάν, 'to become a member of the *thiasos* of the soul', which is almost untranslatable and in which the bacchants are associated to those who celebrate the *orgia* of Cybele and of the Corybants.[51]

These distinctive traits stand out vividly in the image of the *thiasos* of Aeschines and his mother painted in polemical tones by Demosthenes in his *De corona* (259–60). Lane has brought some significant arguments to bear against the most common interpretation (based on the interpretations of ancient scholiasts and lexicographers) of the ritual cry *euoi saboi* as evoking Sabazius, whom many of the testimonies link with the Great Mother Cybele.[52] Still, it does not seem to me that the common interpretation can be definitively ruled out when we consider that the 'exotic' (Anatolian, Phrygian) atmosphere in which the two characters operate ritually is reinforced by the second ritual cry attributed to the female members of the *thiasos*: ὑῆς ἄττης, ἄττης ὑῆς (cf. also Kraemer 1981). This is widely regarded as being, together with a passage of the comic poet Theopompus,[53] one of the most ancient traces in Greece of the figure of

[50] Cf. Foucart 1873; Ferguson 1944, 1949, and, most recently, Ustinova 1996a.

[51] Eur. *Bacch.* 72–82, with Dodds' invaluable commentary (Dodds 1960). Cf. also Coche de la Ferté 1980. An analysis of the *parodos* in Festugière 1956. On the 'blessings of madness' which characterize the religious character of *orgia* of Dionysus, Cybele, and the Corybantes, still essential is the suggestive exegesis by Dodds 1951: 64–101.

[52] Lane 1985: 52 (*testimonium* placed among the *Testimonia antiqua dubia*); 1989: 49–60. For some remarkable correspondence between the ritual described by Demosthenes and that attested at Erythrae by an inscription dated to the second half of the fourth c. BC, with a *lex sacra* pertaining to the cult of the Corybants, see the observations in Wankel 1979.

[53] Fr. ii. 801 Meineke = 28. 2 Kassel–Austin, in Hepding 1903: 6.

Attis, at once closest to the Great Goddess and most problematic from a religious–historical point of view.

The relationship of the Phrygian goddess with Sabazius, whom the Greek literary sources usually identify with Dionysus—in contrast with the epigraphic and iconographic evidence, which is especially rich in his Anatolian homeland and assimilates him to Zeus[54]—is configured under the cultic category of *mysteria* in an exceptional epigraphic text from the imperial period (second c. AD). This refers to and quotes from a decree promulgated by the Persian governor of Sardis during the reign of King Artaxerxes II (*c.*365 BC). The dedication of a statue of Zeus (of) Baradates, clearly a Hellenized version of the Iranian god Ahura Mazda, is accompanied by the prohibition to his followers, and particularly to the templewardens admitted to the inner sanctuary of the god, to 'take part in the mysteries of Sabazius, of those who carry the candelabra [or the sacrificial victims] and of Agdistis and Ma'.[55]

If the decree, in the Greek version believed by Robert to be contemporary with the original Aramaic text, indicates by the term μυστήρια the specific religious reality of the initiatory-esoteric ritual familiar from the Greek world, then it offers the most ancient evidence for a mysteric dimension of the cults mentioned, while at the same time appearing to connect them with each other, though the precise terms of such a connection escape us. It is worth noting that this testimony comes from the homeland of the Great Goddess—here referred to by her other, peculiarly Phrygian, name of Agdistis[56]—and of Sabazius; the latter is the recipient of μυστήρια also at Pergamum at the time of Attalus II (*c.*135/4 BC) (Lane 1985: 12 n. 27) and in third-century AD Lydia (Lane 1985: 19 n. 43), and these initiatory practices are known also from the literary sources.[57]

---

[54] See Lane 1980 and the ample demonstration, based on a rich collection of evidence, in Lane 1989.

[55] Johnson 1967; Robert 1975; Sokolowski 1979; Lane 1985: 14 n. 15; Vermaseren 1977–89: i. 133, no. 456; Herrmann 1996: 330–5.

[56] Cf. Gusmani 1959.

[57] Clement of Alexandria, *Protrepticus* 2. 16. 2: Σαβαζίων γοῦν μυστηρίων σύμβολον τοῖς μυουμένοις ὁ διὰ κόλπου θεός· δράκων δέ ἐστιν οὗτος, διελκόμενος τοῦ κόλπου τῶν τελουμένων, ἔλεγχος ἀκρασίας Διός. 'At any rate, in the Sabazian mysteries the sign given to those who are initiated is "The god over the breast"; this is a

The mention of the goddess Ma of Comana in Cappadocia, who is moreover also connected, by the peculiar 'orgiastic' connotations of her cult, to the Phrygian Cybele/Agdistis, enriches a complex picture in which the unifying theme is precisely the 'mystic-orgiastic' dimension of their respective rituals. The transcription of the decree after a spell of five or six centuries is a clear indication not only of the persistence of the originally Iranian cult in the Lydian mother city Sardis, which is confirmed by other documents between the first century BC and the first to second centuries AD, but also of the *mysteria* in which the worshippers of Zeus-Ahura Mazda are forbidden to participate. Further epigraphic documents confirm that in Roman imperial times there was a high density of mysteric cults in the city: we find attestations of some '*mystai* of Apollo' (Herrmann 1996: 318–21), a society of *mystai* without any indication of the deity to which their cult was offered (Herrmann 1996: 317–18), *mystai* and worshippers of Zeus (Herrmann 1996: 321–9), and a community whose *mysterion* (a meeting-room for mysteries) was dedicated to Attis.[58]

We cannot tell whether this *mysterion* of Attis was connected with the mysteries of Agdistis mentioned in the decree, and if any such

serpent drawn over the breast of the votaries, a proof of the licentiousness of Zeus' (trans. Loeb, p. 35). Arnobius, *Against the Nations* 5. 21: *Ipsa novissime sacra et ritus initiatione ipsius, quibus Sebadiis nomen est, testimonio esse poterunt veritati: in quibus aureus coluber in sinum demittitur consecratis et eximitur rursus ab inferioribus partibus atque imis.* 'Lastly, the sacred rites themselves and the actual ceremony of initiation, named Sebadia, might attest the truth; for in them a golden snake is let down into the bosom of the initiated, and taken away again from the lowest parts.' Firmicus Maternus, *On the Error of Profane Religions* 10. 2: *Sebazium* (= *Sabazium*) *colentes Iovem anguem cum initiant per sinum ducunt.* 'The worshippers of Jupiter Sabazius, when they perform initiations, make a snake glide over their breast'. Detailed re-examination of the problem seems necessary in view of interpretations—now superseded—attributing great importance to a Jewish 'syncretism'. Cf. Cumont 1906; Jamar 1906; Oesterley 1935.

[58] Vermaseren 1977–89: i. no. 464; Herrmann 1996: 316–17. On the pantheon of Sardis cf. Hanfmann 1983. At Pessinus, two inscriptions from the first c. AD mention a community of *Attabokaoi*, who define themselves as οἱ τῶν τῆς θεοῦ μυστηρίων μύσται (the initiates of the mysteries of the goddess) or συμμύσται (fellow-initiates), Hepding 1903: 79, nos. 7–8; Vermaseren 1977–89: i. 25–6, nos. 59–60. As a parallel to the use of μυστήριον as a room in which the esoteric rites of Attis were celebrated, see the ὀργαστήριον of Attis known to Hermesianax (Hepding 1903: 8) and the ἀναδυτήριον of the sanctuary of Cybele of the caves of Yuvadya, which was the seat of a *thiasos* (Moretti 1923–4a, 1923–4b; Vermaseren 1977–89: i. 227–8, nos. 750–4).

connection can be projected back in time on the religious realities
underlying the document's original composition. In imperial times,
the mythic–cultic relation between the two characters is an established reality dating back in Greece, especially in Athens, at least to
the fourth century BC; it is documented by the fine relief at the
Piraeus, datable to around 300 BC (Vermaseren 1977–89: ii. 92–3
no. 308), and by the whole religious physiognomy of the local
orgeones, which in the second century BC celebrated the festival of
Attis, involving the preparation of two banquets and festive spring
meetings, under the direction of a body of priestesses.[59] These rites,
moreover, do not display initiatory-esoteric traits, but rather are
characterized by a sense of reservedness and apartness which belongs
properly to the private cults of individual religious associations.
Some attestations of the mysteries at Troezen (middle of the third
c. BC), Argos (date uncertain) and Minoa on the island of Amorgos
(first c. BC), as well as the scene depicted on a Hellenistic relief from
Lebadeia interpretable as a male or female initiate of the goddess,
suggest that the *Meter* (Mother, or Cybele) was the sole recipient of
this esoteric cult.[60]

It would appear, then, that in the Greek world the cults of Cybele
developed in a mysteric direction along two lines, moving from two
different if related aspects of 'mysticism' (understood in the sense
explained above). These appear to have been inherent in various ways
at different times, and only a patient critical analysis can hope to
throw light on the details. On the one hand, we have a typically
'enthusiastic–orgiastic' element, in which forms of contact between
the human and divine level are sought through 'madness' ($\mu\alpha\nu\acute{\iota}\alpha$)
sacrally induced by specific ritual procedures (dances, the use of
musical instruments such as tympana, auloi, and cymbals) with
cathartic content; this results in an interference and deep 'sympathy'
($\sigma\upsilon\mu\pi\acute{\alpha}\theta\epsilon\iota\alpha$) between human and divine, and the achievement of an
exciting religious experience such as is also a notable feature of
$\mu\upsilon\sigma\tau\acute{\eta}\rho\iota\alpha$, particularly the Eleusinian mysteries, which are those

---

[59] Foucart 1873: 191–7, nos. 4–8; Hepding 1903: 79–81, nos. 9–11. On the
religious situation of the Piraeus see Garland 1987.
[60] For a fuller discussion of the problem of mysteries in the cult of Cybele, cf.
Sfameni Gasparro 1985: 20–5, 64–83.

best known to us. In this sense, that is to say on account of its qualified connection with μυστήρια, this form of cult and its corresponding religious experience can be termed 'mystic', though it does not present an initiatory-esoteric component in the strict sense, or, in our terminology, a 'mysteric' component. This mystic experience appears in fact to be the most typical and pervasive feature of the religious context of Cybele and can also be open to a mysteric connection, though this latter dimension is only sporadically attested.

Furthermore, it is difficult to evaluate the relative significance in this picture of the Greek element and its original Oriental, particularly Phrygian, dimension. The Anatolian identity of the goddess is guaranteed by all the most ancient evidence from the territory of Asia Minor and the Near East,[61] and emerges clearly in the eighth century BC, from the well-known Phrygian rock monuments and the unusual sanctuary of Agdistis (third c. BC–third c. AD) in the so-called 'City of Midas' (seventh–sixth centuries BC).[62] Still, in the formation, around the mid-sixth century, of the iconographical scheme that would identify her throughout her historical development, that is to say the goddess seated on a throne, often inside a shrine, accompanied by a lion (sometimes crouching on her lap, sometimes in heraldic position at the side of the throne), and usually endowed with attributes (patera, sceptre, and tympanon, in various compositions), we perceive the inextricable interconnection of the two dimensions of deity and cult. This iconography almost takes on the role of a foundation act of the goddess's identity when she becomes involved in a movement of westward expansion encompassing first mainland Greece, then also Southern Italy and Sicily, and reaching as far as the Phocaean colony of Marseille.[63] It is defined in the work of artists from Ionia, a Greek context already for centuries rooted on Asiatic

---

[61] Cf. esp. the relationship with the Syrian Kubaba, 'queen of Kargamish'. Cf. Laroche 1960.

[62] Vermaseren 1977–89: i. 51–60, nos. 148–60. For archaeological evidence and iconography in Asia Minor see Albright 1928–9; Akurgal 1961; Hanfmann and Waldbaum 1969; Helck 1971; Haspels 1971; Naumann 1983; Işık 1986–7, 1987; Rein 1996.

[63] Reservations on whether the shrines with a seated female figure from Marseille pertain to the cult of Cybele are advanced by Hermary 2000a. On the 'ambiguity of the Greek archaic iconography' see Hermary 2000b.

soil or, to put it the other way round, in a cultural and religious territory of Asia Minor densely imbued with Hellenic culture.[64]

The question of Attis: ancient exegeses and modern interpretations

The second 'mystical' dimension in the sphere of Cybele centres on the figure of Attis and the modalities of his relation with Cybele/ Agdistis. This, too, contributes towards a development in a mysteric direction, and is equally deeply marked by a component of 'madness' ($\mu\alpha\nu\acute{\iota}\alpha$) and 'religious enthusiasm' ($\dot{o}\rho\gamma\iota\alpha\sigma\mu\acute{o}s$).[65] The debate on the 'origins' of Attis is not new; it can be traced as far back as the ancient tradition in which he figures as 'devotee' of the goddess and proto- type of the eunuch Gallus. The same ancient tradition puts him at the centre of a very complex story involving an extraordinary birth connected with a primordial androgynous entity with chthonic roots, some kind of relation with a nymph, either mother or wife *manquée*, a brief and intense life set in a naturalistic wild and mountainous landscape, in close familiarity with the goddess,[66] culminating in the crisis of a violent death as a result of external aggression or self-mutilation under the impulse of 'madness' ($\mu\alpha\nu\acute{\iota}\alpha$). This death is redeemed by a tacit form of survival, expressed by the image of physical incorruptibility; above all, it is religiously

---

[64] It is not possible to tackle directly the question of the 'Hellenization' of the goddess or, as some interpreters would have it, of the 'creation' in Greece of a new identity with an Oriental appearance superimposed in some way on the Greek 'Mother of the Gods'. I shall merely repeat here that, in my opinion, the evidence allows us to maintain the historical identity of a Cybele originally from Asia Minor who is present in the Greek religious horizon from Archaic times, though she is to some extent associated to Greek divine figures such as Rhea, mother of the Olympian gods, and even Demeter (cf. Will 1960). For the various stances on this subject see, as well as Borgeaud 1996; Robertson 1996; Roller 1996; Blomart 2002.

[65] A stimulating exegesis of the myth already in Borgeaud 1988, who returns to the problem in Borgeaud 1996. See also his essay of 2001.

[66] In the version of the myth related by Arnobius (*Against the Nations* 5. 5–7), the divine figure is split between the solemn *Meter Megale* and the hermaphrodite Agdistis, reduced to his female state as a result of self-mutilation. The main sources, after Hepding 1903, in Scarpi 2002a: ii. 264–347. Fundamental among them, for the mythical story, is the testimony of Pausanias 7. 17. 9–12.

consecrated when Attis becomes the recipient of cultic honours together with the goddess. Only in late Christian sources, in which it is likely that we should see an implicit Christian interpretation of the cult rather than a sign that Christian belief in resurrection had influenced the mystery rites of Cybele,[67] do we hear that Attis returns to life. This is in any case coherent with the notion—essential in this context—of his 'presence' or 'subsistence' in death, which I continue to regard as the most appropriate means of characterizing his religious identity.

The hypothesis of a human origin of Cybele's partner has recently been defended anew by Roller (1994, 1999), who argues that the iconography and even the concept of Attis as a god evolved in Greece, specifically in Athens, in the fourth century BC. According to Roller, it results from Greek ignorance of Phrygian religious customs, in which Attis was supposedly the name of the ancient Phrygian regal dynasty of the eighth and seventh centuries before becoming, in consequence of its members' supposed cultic duties, a priestly title. The well-known relief from the Piraeus with a dedication to Attis and Agdistis depicting the latter handing the youth what Roller interprets as a ritual vessel would then be a visualization of this process of 'promotion' and 'consecration': 'Attis' is promoted from a priestly title and a 'common name' among the most widespread in Phrygian onomastics to the name of a deity.

It is not possible here to discuss this interpretative formula with the detail required to justify its acceptance or rejection. I shall merely point out that this reconstruction, though it is not lacking in stimulating observations, is weakened by the serious gaps in our knowledge of eighth–seventh-century Phrygia, which prevents us from

---

[67] Bremmer 2002: 50–5 interprets to this effect the report in Firmicus Maternus, *On the Error of Profane Religions* 3. 1–2, which also uses allusive expressions in a strongly polemical context and in relation to a physicalist interpretation of the myth (*. . . quem paulo ante sepelierant revixisse iactarunt . . . Mortem ipsius dicunt quod semina collecta conduntur, vitam rursus quod iacta semina annuis vicibus reconduntur.* 'They proclaim the resurrection of the one whom they just buried . . . They claim his death, when they bury the grain that had been gathered, and his rebirth, when in the annual cycle they rebury the grain that is sown.') The passage of Hippolytus, *Refutation* 5. 8. 22–4, which according to Bremmer confirms the notion of Attis' 'resurrection' must be read in the light of the mysteriosophic and dualistic interpretation of the Naassene gnostics. Cf. Sfameni Gasparro 2004: 249–90.

reaching any firm conclusions.[68] Above all, it is based at too many points on hypotheses that quickly, by a conceptual slide, become statements and are in turn used as grounds for further conclusions; in short, it cannot offer a solution to our complex problematics.

On the other hand, if the mythic-cultic complex revolving around Attis were an entirely Greek 'creation', we would have to acknowledge an unusual instance of 'reflux'—from West to East—of a Western cult which spreads in the East after taking on the fictitious mask of 'Orientalism', and becomes established in what is thought of as its original territory in Anatolia, especially in Phrygia and Lydia, coherently with the two main mythic clusters. In late Hellenistic and Imperial times, the mythic-cultic system of Cybele in its Phrygian guise becomes widespread throughout the Mediterranean. This movement of 'reflux' from Greece to the East must be supposed to have been playing itself out already in early Hellenistic times if, as our sources tell us, the Roman cult of *Magna Mater*, combined with an official, fully Romanized dimension an Oriental and specifically Phrygian[69] aspect. As Romanelli's excavation in the sanctuary on the Palatine revealed (Romanelli 1963), this included the youth Attis, whose presence is attested by figured terracottas dating from the second to first centuries BC. The cult at Pessinus or Pergamum, from which Republican Rome drew directly—that is to say without

---

[68] See the discovery of three palaeo-Phrygian inscriptions (seventh–sixth cc. BC) in an area very likely to have had sacred connotations; these might attest the presence of an *Atas* interpretable as divine 'Father' and evocative of the (Attis/Zeus) Papas of later sources (Brixhe and Drew-Bear 1982: 83; cf. Drew-Bear and Naour 1990: 2018–22). The extreme uncertainty of our readings of such inscriptions counsels prudence, such as is expressed also by the editors of the texts in their conclusion. After reasserting 'the religious character of the texts' and the impossibility of deciding with certainty the meaning of the term *Agomoi* in the first inscription, they declare, that 'il pourrait s'agir d'une épiclèse du dieu désigné par *Atas* en III, lequel est susceptible de correspondre à Attis' (ibid. 87). Varinlioğlu 1992 is more willing to make a positive statement by recognizing Attis in the names *Atas* and *Ata* inscribed on numerous votive objects (small silver cauldrons, ladles, small bowls, etc.) found in a funerary mound in the Anatolian locality of Bayındır, considered contemporary with the so-called Tomb of Midas at Gordion. Though the present state of the evidence does not allow us to reach conclusions on this question, we cannot however overlook the valuable clues represented by these frequent occurances of the name in cultic and funerary contexts.

[69] Cf. Dionysius of Halicarnassus, *Roman Antiquities* 2. 19. 4–5.

any Greek mediation—the 'ancient Mother' connected with the Trojan origins of Rome as a guarantee of the survival and success of the State, would then have received and in turn contributed to spread a Greek, more specifically Athenian, religious creation. Were, then, these Anatolian environments in the third century BC also ignorant of the cultic practices in which Attis was no more than a royal and priestly title when they accepted the new divine guise created in the West? This question demands an answer, which I do not believe can come from a simple transferral to the Eastern context of Pessinus of such a guise invented merely for the sake of the Galli, the 'eunuch priests'[70] whose descent from a hypothetical Phrygian royal funerary tradition is improbable. This is the substance of a recent interpretation dependent on Roller's, but to a yet greater extent based on unverifiable hypotheses and conjectures.[71]

At any rate it must be noted that the character of Attis, such as it emerges from the 'Phrygian' mythic-cultic cycle, displays some peculiar traits of the superhuman being *in vicenda* ('in vicissitude'), who suffers crises and disappearance, in our case even death, but is also rescued from death and given a strong presence on a ritual level. Even though the chthonic-vegetation elements of this figure and his mythical story must be scaled down, they cannot be completely dismissed as the mere product of naturalistic and physicalist exegeses in Late-Antique learned circles. The March ceremonies celebrated from the first and second centuries AD at Rome and in various other cities of the Empire are the conclusion of a long historical process of elaboration which our sources suggest was controlled from the capital. Yet they show that those 'vegetation connections' were not simply the expression of learned speculation without any foundation in the identity of the character and in the larger context of Cybele of the

---

[70] As has now been amply demonstrated, the Galli did not have a 'priestly' status. Among the many contributions on this category of devotees of Cybele, with its complex sacral characteristics, I mention here only those of Carcopino 1942: 76–171; Sanders 1972; Giammarco Razzano 1982; Pachis 1996; Lane 1996b; Baslez 2004. For the situation of the sanctuary of Pessinus in Hellenistic times and role of the highest religious offices of the 'Attis' and the 'Battakes', cf. Virgilio 1981; Boffo 1985: 34–41 and *passim*.
[71] Lancellotti 2002. A series of objections to this interpretative model in Bremmer 2004, who still privileges Attis' 'Greek' dimension.

time, but were also perceived and celebrated at the popular level. Though the documentary evidence does not clearly testify to a rooting of this chthonic-vegetation dimension and even of the physiognomy of Attis as a superhuman, suffering figure in the more ancient Phrygian context that was the source of the complex of Cybele, a minimal and provisional conclusion is that such a character of the cult was elaborated at a time and in an environment that we cannot, on the basis of our scanty evidence, define with any certainty. However, this ritual feature was elaborated along the lines of a sufficiently coherent historical model aimed at depicting the divine suffering of the Great Goddess and at the same time of her companion, contextually translated into a series of ritual practices involving the faithful in an equally suffering and highly participatory religious experience. This experience is achieved above all in the public forms of the March festival cycle, established in all likelihood in the first centuries of the Empire and later modified, but not disconnected from the original Anatolian context.[72] The existence of a mysteric structure receives sporadic attestation in seldom explicit epigraphic sources, and the well-known testimony of the Christian polemicists: Clement of Alexandria, in a context difficult to interpret on account of the strong Demeter-Orpheus connotations of the overall picture, into which the cults of Cybele appear to have been brought because of the similarities between the two mysteries;[73] and

---

[72] Attributed by Carcopino 1942: 49–75 to a single intervention by the emperor Claudius, the Phrygian ritual seems rather the result of later reforms, culminating with the constitution of the entire ceremonial cycle during the reign of Antoninus Pius. Cf. Lambrechts 1952a, 1952b; Beaujeau 1955: 279–330; Fishwick 1966.

[73] *Protrepticus* 2. 15. 1–3 Δηοῦς δὲ μυστήρια [καὶ] Διὸς πρὸς μητέρα Δήμητρα ἀφροδίσιοι συμπλοκαὶ καὶ μῆνις (οὐκ οἶδ' ὅ τι φῶ λοιπὸν μητρὸς ἢ γυναικός) τῆς Δηοῦς, ἧς δὴ χάριν Βριμὼ προσαγορευθῆναι λέγεται, <καὶ> ἱκετηρίαι Διὸς καὶ πόμα χολῆς καὶ καρδιουλκίαι καὶ ἀρρητουργίαι· ταῦτα οἱ Φρύγες τελίσκουσιν Ἄττιδι καὶ Κυβέλῃ καὶ Κορύβασιν. τεθρυλήκασιν δὲ ὡς ἄρα ἀποσπάσας ὁ Ζεὺς τοῦ κριοῦ τοὺς διδύμους φέρων ἐν μέσοις ἔρριψε τοῖς κόλποις τῆς Δηοῦς, τιμωρίαν ψευδῆ τῆς βιαίας συμπλοκῆς ἐκτιννύων, ὡς ἑαυτὸν δῆθεν ἐκτεμών. τὰ σύμβολα τῆς μυήσεως ταύτης ἐκ περιουσίας παρατεθέντα οἶδ' ὅτι κινήσει γέλωτα καὶ μὴ γελασείουσιν ὑμῖν διὰ τοὺς ἐλέγχους· "Ἐκ τυμπάνου ἔφαγον· ἐκ κυμβάλου ἔπιον· ἐκιρνοφόρησα· ὑπὸ τὸν παστὸν ὑπέδυν." 'The mysteries of Demeter commemorate the amorous embraces of Zeus with his mother Demeter, and the wrath of Demeter (I do not know what to call her for the future, mother or wife) on account of which she is said to have received the name Brimo; also the supplications of Zeus, the drink of bile, the tearing out of the heart of victims, and unspeakable obscenities. The same rites are performed in honour of Attis and Cybele and the Corybantes by the Phrygians, who have spread

Firmicus Maternus.[74] These authors transmit only the initiatory formula, which evokes the eating and drinking of the sacred instruments (tympanon and cymbal) and, respectively, the bearing of sacred vessels (*kernophoria*) and the acceptance of the initiate in the chamber (*pastos*), or rather a declaration of his affiliation to the person of Attis ('I have become a *mystes* of Attis').

As a matter of fact, despite the different interpretation of Philippe Borgeaud (1998), which can also be situated in a solid research tradition, I persist in my conviction that it is wrong to assimilate to the mysteries of Cybele the complex rite of the sacrifice of a bull (*taurobolium*) and the related sacrifice of a ram (*criobolium*). In its most ancient forms, this appears unequivocally to be a public sacrificial act, accomplished for the wellbeing (*salus*) of the emperor and his family and for the benefit of whole civic communities[75] as well as

---

it abroad how that Zeus tore off the testicles of a ram, and then brought and flung them into the midst of Demeter's lap, thus paying a sham penalty for his violent embrace by pretending that he had mutilated himself. If I go on further to quote the symbols of initiation into this mystery they will, I know, move you to laughter, even though they are in no laughing humour when your rites are being exposed. "I ate from the drum; I drank from the cymbal; I carried the sacred dish; I stole into the bridal chamber." ' (trans. Loeb, 35)

[74] *On the Error of Profane Religions* 18. 1: *In quodam templo, ut in interioribus partibus homo moriturus possit admitti, dicit 'De tympano manducaui, de cymbalo bibi et religionis secreta perdidici', quod Graeco sermone dicitur ἐκ τυμπάνου βέβρωκα, ἐκ κυμβάλου πέπωκα, γέγονα μύστης Ἄττεως.* 'There is a temple where, to be admitted to the most secret parts, the candidate vowed to death declares: "I have eaten from the drum; I have drunk from the cymbal; I am fully instructed in the secrets of the religion", which in Greek runs: "I have eaten from the drum; I have drunk from the cymbal; I have become an initiate of Attis." '

[75] The earliest epigraphic attestation of the rite (AD 160) comes from Lyon and reads: *Taurobolio Matris d(eum) m(agnae) I(daeae) / quod factum est ex imperio Matris deum / pro salute Imperatoris Caes(aris) T(iti) Aeli / Hadriani Antonini Aug (usti) Pii p(atris) p(atriae) / liberorum eius / et status coloniae Lugudun(ensium) / L (ucius) Aemilius Carpus IIIIIIvir Aug(ustalis) item / dendrophorus / uires excepit et a Vaticano trans/tulit ara(m) et bucranium / suo inpendio consacrauit / sacerdote / Q (uinto) Sammio Secundo ab XVuiris / occabo et corona exornato / cui sanctissimus ordo Lugudunens(ium) / perpetuitatem sacerdoti(i) decreuit/ App(io) Annio Atilio Bradua T (ito) Clod(io) Vibio / Varo co(n)s(ulibus)* (CIL xiii. no. 1751= *ILS* no. 4131 = Vermaseren 1977–89: v. no. 386, 1–19; Scarpi 2002a: ii. 320 C 27). 'In the *taurobolium* of The Great Idaean Mother of the Gods, which was performed on the instruction of the Mother of the Gods, for the well-being of the emperor Caesar Titus Aelius Hadrianus Antoninus Augustus Pius [i.e. Antoninus Pius], father of his country, and of his children, and [for the well-being] of the condition of the *colonia* of

of single individuals.[76] I stand, therefore, by my earlier conclusion that:

> the *taurobolium* . . . , in all likelihood introduced [into the cult of Cybele] by an act of religious politics aimed at increasing the 'national' relevance of the cult of the Great Mother of the Gods, gradually transforms itself as it succumbs to the general change in religious values, in the context of a progressive emergence of exotic cults increasingly embraced by the populations of the Empire. The *taurobolium* evolved from the sacrificial rite which it appears to have been originally and acquired a new individual dimension; it assumed cathartic connotations and later gathered around itself a complex set of religious and ethical values. Thus the *taurobolium*, in its final cathartic form of sprinkling of blood, presents itself in some areas of the Late-Antique world as a cultic act capable of conferring an initiatory sacral qualification and of procuring a feeling of spiritual renewal, and on this account, it becomes, to the mind of the last defenders of the traditional values of paganism, the final defensive enclave against the victorious pressure of the new Christian message.[77]

In conclusion, the varied landscape of 'Oriental cults', observed from the standpoint of its mysteric component, is confirmed as being a privileged ground of enquiry for a religious–historical research that aims at perceiving similarities and differences, the complexity of distinct historical processes that are yet in various ways interlocked in a network of contacts and reciprocal influences. In this way such research is capable of reconstructing a set of religious worlds which are distinct while also shot through with analogies, in the common dialectic of traditional continuity and creative invention.

Lugdunum, Lucius Aemilius Carpus, *sevir Augustalis* and at the same time *dendrophorus* received the "powers" and transferred them from the Vaticanum, and consecrated an altar adorned with an ox-head at his own expense. The priest, Quintus Sammius Secundus, was honoured with an armlet and garland by the *quindecimviri*, and the most holy town-council of Lugdunum decreed him a lifelong priesthood. In the consulship of Appius Annius Atilius Bradua and Titus Clodius Vibius Varus [AD 160].' (trans. Beard et al. 1998: ii. 162)

[76] A suggested reconstruction of the history and transformation of the rite in Duthoy 1969.

[77] Sfameni Gasparro 2003a: 327. A more articulated discussion of the problem, with the related documentation, on pp. 291–327, and 29–32 with reference to the positions of McLynn 1996 and Borgeaud 1998.

BIBLIOGRAPHY

Akurgal, E. (1961). *Die Kunst Anatoliens von Homer bis Alexander.* Berlin: de Gruyter.

Albright, W. F. (1928–9). 'The Anatolian Goddess Kubaba', *Archiv für Orientforschung*, 5: 229–31.

Alföldi, G. (1997). 'Die Mysterien von Panóias (Vita Real, Portugal)', *Mitteilungen des Deutschen Archäologische Instituts, Madrider Mitteilungen*, 38: 176–246, plates 15–41.

Álvar, J. (2008). *Romanising Oriental Gods: Myth, Salvation and Ethics in the Cults of Cybele, Isis and Mithras*, RGRW 165. Leiden: Brill. (Spanish original 2001).

Aurigemma, S. (1900). 'La protezione speciale della gran Madre Idea per la nobiltà romana e le leggende dell'origine troiana di Roma', *Bullettino della Commissione Comunale di Roma*, 31–65.

Baslez, M.-F. (2004). 'Les Galles d'Anatolie: images et réalités', *Res Antiquae*, 1: 233–45.

Beaujeu, J. (1955). *La religion romaine à l'apogée de l'Empire.* i. *La politique religieuse des Antonins (96–192).* Paris: Belles Lettres.

Beard, M., North, J. and Price, S. (1998). *Religions of Rome*, 2 vols. Cambridge: Cambridge University Press.

Beck, R. (1998). 'The Mysteries of Mithras: A New Account of their Genesis', *JRS*, 88: 115–28.

——(2004). *Beck on Mithraism. Collected Works with New Essays.* Aldershot: Ashgate.

Belayche, N. (2000). 'L'Oronte et le Tibre: l' "Orient" des cultes "orientaux" de l'Empire Romain', in M. A. Amir-Moezzi and J. Scheid (eds.), *L'Orient dans l'histoire religieuse de l'Europe.* Turnhout: Brepols, 1–35.

Bergman, J. (1982). 'Per omnia vectus elementa remeavi. Réflexions sur l'arrière-plan égyptien du voyage de salut d'un myste isiaque', in Bianchi and Vermaseren 1982: 671–708, figs. 1–8.

Bernabé, A. (2004–5) (ed.), *Poetae Epici Graeci Testimonia et Fragmenta*, Pars II: *Orphicorum et Orphicis similium Testimonia et Fragmenta*, Fasciculi 1–2. Munich: Sauer.

Bianchi, U. (1965). 'Initiation, mystères, gnose (Pour l'histoire de la mystique dans le paganisme gréco-oriental)', in C. J. Bleeker (ed.), *Initiation.* Leiden: Brill, 154–71.

——(1976). *The Greek Mysteries*, Iconography of Religions, 17/3. Leiden: Brill.

——(1979a). 'The History of Religions and the "Religio-Anthropological Approach"', in L. Honko (ed.), *Science of Religion: Studies in Methodology.*

The Hague: Mouton, 299–321; repr. in his *Saggi di metodologia della Storia delle religioni*, Nuovi Saggi 75. Rome: Ateneo and Bizzarri (1979), 123–51.

——(1979b) (ed.), *Mysteria Mithrae: Atti del Seminario Internazionale su 'La specificità storico-religiosa dei Misteri di Mithra, con particolare riferimento alle fonti documentarie di Roma e Ostia'*, EPRO 80. Leiden: Brill.

——(1979c). 'Prolegomena. The Religio-Historical Question of the Mysteries of Mithras I–III', in Bianchi 1979b: 3–66.

——(1980). 'Iside dea misterica: quando?', in *Perennitas: Studi in onore di Angelo Brelich*. Rome: Ateneo, 9–36.

——(1982). 'Lo studio delle religioni di mistero: l'intenzione del Colloquio', in Bianchi and Vermaseren 1982: 1–16; 'Epilegomena', ibid, 917–29.

——and Vermaseren, M. J. (1982) (eds.), *La soteriologia dei culti orientali nell'Impero romano*, EPRO 92. Leiden: Brill.

Blomart, A. (2002). 'La Phrygienne et l'Athénien: quand la Mère des dieux et Apollon Patrôos se rencontrent sur l'agorà d'Athènes', in *Religions méditerranéennes et orientales de l'Antiquité*, Bibliothèque d'Étude 135. Cairo: Institut francais d'archéologie orientale, 21–34.

Bömer, F. (1964). 'Kybele in Rom: Die Geschichte ihres Kults als politisches Phänomen', *Mitteilungen des Deutschen Archäologische Instituts, Römische Abteilung*, 71: 130–51.

Boffo, L. (1985). *I re ellenistici e i centri religiosi dell'Asia Minore*. Florence: La Nuova Italia.

Borgeaud, P. (1988). 'L'écriture d'Attis: le récit dans l'histoire', in C. Calame (ed.), *Métamorphoses du mythe en Grèce antique*. Geneva: Labor et Fides, 87–103.

——(1991) (ed.), *Orphisme et Orphée en l'honneur de Jean Rudhardt*. Geneva: Droz.

——(1996). *La Mère des dieux: de Cybèle à la Vierge Marie*. Paris: Seuil.

——(1998). 'Taurobolion', in F. Graf (ed.), *Ansichten griechischer Rituale: Geburtstags-Symposium für Walter Burkert*. Stuttgart: Teubner, 183–98.

——(2001). 'Itinéraires proche-orientaux de la Mère', in Ribichini, Rocchi, and Xella 2001: 117–28.

——and Volokhine, Y. (2000). 'La formation de la légende de Sarapis: une approche transculturelle', *ARG*, 2: 37–76.

Bremmer, J. N. (1979). 'The Legend of Cybele's Arrival in Rome', in M. J. Vermaseren (ed.), *Studies in Hellenistic Religions*, EPRO 78. Leiden: Brill, 9–22; repr. as 'Slow Cybele's Arrival', in Bremmer and N. M. Horsfall, *Roman Myth and Mythography*, Bulletin of Classical Studies London, Suppl. 52. London: 1987, 105–11.

——(1999). 'The Birth of the Term "Magic"', *ZPE*, 126, 1–12; repr. in Bremmer and J. R. Veenstra (eds.), *The Metamorphosis of Magic from Late Antiquity to the Early Modern Period*. Leuven: Peeters, 2002, 1–11.

——(2002). *The Rise and Fall of the Afterlife*. London and New York: Routledge.

——(2004). 'Attis: A Greek God in Anatolian Pessinous and Catullan Rome', *Mnemosyne*, 4th ser., 57: 534–73.

Bricault, L. (2000). *De Memphis à Rome*. Leiden: Brill.

——(2001). *Atlas de la diffusion des cultes isiaques (IVᵉ s. av. J.-C.–IVᵉ s. apr. J.-C.)*. Paris: de Boccard.

——(2004). *Isis en Occident: Actes du IIᵉᵐᵉ Colloque international sur les études isiaques*. Leiden: Brill.

——(2005). *Recueil des inscriptions concernant les cultes isiaques (RICIS)*. Paris: Académie des inscriptions et belles-lettres.

——Versluys, M. J., and Meyboom, P. G. P. (2007) (eds.), *Nile into Tiber: Egypt in the Roman World*. Leiden: Brill.

Brisson, L. (1995). *Orphée et l'Orphisme dans l'Antiquité gréco-romaine*. Aldershot: Ashgate.

Brixhe, C., and Drew-Bear, T. (1982). 'Trois nouvelles inscriptions paléo-phrygiennes de Cepni', *Kadmos*, 21: 64–87.

Burkert, W. (1987). *Ancient Mystery Cults*. Cambridge, MA, and London: Harvard University Press.

——(1993). 'Concordia Discors: The Literary and the Archaeological Evidence on the Sanctuary of Samothrace', in N. Marinatos and R. Hägg (eds.), *Greek Sanctuaries. New Approaches*. London and New York: Routledge, 178–91.

——(1999). *Da Omero ai Magi; la tradizione orientale nella cultura greca*. Venice: Marsilio.

Carcopino, J. (1942). *Aspects mystiques de la Rome païenne*, 6th edn. Paris: Artisan du Livre.

Casadio, G. (1981). 'Per un'indagine storico-religiosa sui culti di Dioniso in relazione alla fenomenologia dei misteri I', *Studi Storico–Religiosi*, 6: 209–34.

——(1983). 'Per un'indagine storico-religiosa sui culti di Dioniso in relazione alla fenomenologia dei misteri II', *Studi e Materiali di Storia delle Religioni*, 49 (n. s. 7): 123–49.

——(1994). *Storia del culto di Dioniso in Argolide*. Rome: Gruppo editoriale internazionale.

——(1999). *Il vino dell'anima: storia del culto di Dioniso a Corinto, Sicione, Trezene*. Rome: Il Calamo.

——(2002) (ed.). *Ugo Bianchi: una vita per la Storia delle religioni*. Rome: Il Calamo.

Cerutti, M. V. (1979). 'Mithra "dio mistico" e "dio in vicenda"?', in Bianchi 1979b: 389–95.

Coche de la Ferté, É. (1980). 'Penthée et Dionysos: nouvel essai d'interprétation des "Bacchantes" d'Euripide', in R. Bloch (ed.), *Recherches sur les religions de l'antiquité classique*. Geneva: Droz; Paris: Champion, 105–257.

Cole, S. G. (1984). *Theoi Megaloi: The Cult of the Great Gods at Samothrace*, EPRO 96. Leiden: Brill.

——(1987). 'The Mysteries of Samothrace during the Roman Period', in *ANRW*, 2. 18. 2: 1564–98.

Cosmopoulos, M. B. (ed.) (2003). *Greek Mysteries: The Archaeology and Ritual of Ancient Greek Secret Cults*. London and New York: Routledge.

Cumont, F. (1906). 'Les mystères de Sabazius et le judaïsme', *CRAI*, 63–79.

Diano, C., and Serra, G. (1993). *Eraclito: i frammenti e le testimonianze*. Milan: Mondadori.

Dodds, E. R. (1951). *The Greeks and the Irrational*. Berkeley, CA: California University Press.

——(1960). *Euripides Bacchae*, 2nd edn. Oxford: Clarendon Press.

Drew-Bear, T. and Naour, C. (1990). 'Divinités de Phrygie', *ANRW*, 2. 18. 3: 1907–2044, 2777–81.

Dunand, F. (1975). 'Les mystères égyptiens aux époques hellénistique et romaine', in Dunand et al., *Mystères et syncrétismes*. Paris: Geuthner, 11–62.

Duthoy, R. (1969). *The Taurobolium: Its Evolution and Terminology*, EPRO 10. Leiden: Brill.

Ferguson, W. S. (1944). 'The Attic Orgeones', *Harvard Theological Review*, 37: 61–140.

——(1949). 'Orgeonika', *Commemorative Studies in Honor of Theodore Leslie Shear, Hesperia*, Suppl. 8 (Princeton), 130–63.

Festugière, A. J. (1956). 'La signification religieuse de la parodos des Bacchantes', *Eranos*, 54: 72–86; repr. in his *Études de religion grecque et hellénistique*. Paris: Vrin, 1972, 66–80.

Fishwick, D. (1966). 'The *Cannophori* and the March Festival of Magna Mater', *Transactions and Proceedings of the American Philological Association*, 97: 193–202.

Foucart, P. F. (1873). *Des associations religieuses chez les grecs: thiases, éranes, orgéons*. Paris: Klincksieck.

Garland, R. (1987). *The Piraeus from the Fifth to the First Century B.C.* London: Duckworth; Ithaca, NY: Cornell University Press.

Giammarco Razzano, M. C. (1982). 'I "Galli di Cibele" nel culto di età ellenistica', *Miscellanea Greca e Romana*, 8: 227–66.

Goceva, Z. (2002). 'Le culte des Grandes Dieux de Samothrace à la periode hellénistique', *Kernos*, 15: 309–15.

Gordon, R. L. (1996). *Image and Value in the Graeco–Roman World: Studies in Mithraism and Religious Art.* Aldershot: Ashgate.

——(2001). '"Persaei sub rupibus antri": Überlegungen zur Entstehung der Mithrasmysterien', in M. Vomer-Gojkovič, *Ptuj im römischen Reich/Mithraskult und seine Zeit*, Archaeologia Poetovionensis, 2, 289–301.

Graf, F. (2003). 'Lesser Mysteries—Not Less Mysterious', in Cosmopoulos 2003: 241–62.

Grandjean, Y. (1975). *Une nouvelle arétalogie d'Isis à Maronée*, EPRO 49. Leiden: Brill.

Griffiths, J. G. (1970) (ed.), *Plutarch's De Iside et Osiride.* Cardiff: University of Wales Press.

——(1975) (ed.), *Apuleius of Madauros: The Isis-Book (Metamorphoses, Book XI)*, EPRO 39. Leiden: Brill.

Gusmani, R. (1959). 'ΑΓΔΙΣΤΙΣ', *La Parola del passato*, 14: 202–11

Hanfmann, G. M. A. (1983). 'On the Gods of Lydian Sardis', in R. M. Boehmer and H. Hauptmann (eds.), *Beitrage zur Altertumskunde Kleinasiens. Festschrift für Kurt Bittel.* Mainz am Rhein: Von Zabern, 219–321.

——and Waldbaum, J. C. (1969). 'Kybebe and Artemis. Two Anatolian Goddesses at Sardis', *Archaeology*, 22: 264–9.

Haspels, C. H. E. (1971). *The Highlands of Phrygia. Sites and Monuments*, 2 vols. Princeton, NJ: Princeton University Press.

Helck, W. (1971). *Betrachtungen zur Großen Göttin und den ihr verbundenen Gottheiten.* Munich and Vienna: Oldenbourg.

Hemberg, B. (1950). *Die Kabiren.* Uppsala: Almqvist and Wilksells.

Hepding, H. (1903). *Attis: Seine Mythen und sein Kult.* Giessen: Ricker; repr. Berlin: Töpelmann, 1967.

Hermary, A. (2000a). 'Les naïskoi votifs de Marseille', in Hermary and H. Tréziny (eds.), *Les Cultes des cités phocéennes.* Aix-en-Provence: Edisud, 119–33.

——(2000b). 'De la Mère des dieux à Cybèle et Artémis; les ambiguïtés de l'iconographie grecque archaïque', in *Agathòs Daimon: Études d'iconographie en l'honneur de Lilly Kahil*, BCH suppl. 38. Paris: École française d'Athènes, 193–203.

Herrmann, P. (1996). 'Mystenvereine in Sardeis', *Chiron*, 26: 315–48.

Horsley, G. H. R. (1992). 'The Mysteries of Artemis Ephesia in Pisidia: A New Inscribed Relief', *Anatolian Studies*, 42: 119–50.

Işık, F. (1986–7). 'Die Entstehung der frühen Kybelebilder Phrygiens und ihre Einwirkung auf die ionische Plastik', *Jahreshefte des Österreichischen Archäologischen Institutes in Wien*, 57: 41–108.

——(1987). 'Zur Entstehung der phrygischen Felsdenkmäler', *Anatolian Studies*, 37: 163–78.

Jamar, A. (1909). 'Les mystères de Sabazius et le judaïsme', *Le Musée Belge*, 13: 227–52.

Johnson, S. E. (1967). 'Sabazius Inscription from Sardis', in J. Neusner (ed.), *Religions in Antiquity. Essays in Memory of Erwin Ramsdell Goodenough*. Leiden: Brill, 542–50.

Köves, T. (1963). 'Zum Empfang der Magna Mater in Rom', *Historia*, 12: 321–47.

Kraemer, R. S. (1981). '"Euoi Saboi" in Demosthenes *De Corona*: In Whose Honor were the Women's Rites?', *Society for Biblical Literature, Seminar Papers*, 20: 229–36.

Lambrechts, P. (1951). 'Cybèle, divinité étrangère ou nationale?', *Bulletin de la Société royale belge d'anthropologie et préhistoire*, 62: 44–60.

——(1952a). 'Les fêtes "phrygiennes" de Cybèle et d'Attis', *Bulletin de l'Institut historique belge de Rome*, 27: 141–70.

——(1952b). 'Attis à Rome', in *Mélanges Georges Smets*. Brussels: Université Libre de Bruxelles, 461–71.

Lancellotti, M. G. (2002). *Attis. Between Myth and History: King, Priest and God*, RGRW 149. Leiden: Brill.

Lane, E. N. (1980). 'Towards a Definition of the Iconography of Sabazius', *Numen*, 27: 9–33.

——(1985, 1989). *Corpus Cultus Iovis Sabazii (CCIS)*, ii: *The Other Monuments and Literary Evidence*; iii: *Conclusions*, EPRO 100. Leiden: Brill.

——(1996a). *Cybele, Attis and Related Cults: Essays in Memory of M. J. Vermaseren*, RGRW 131. Leiden: Brill.

——(1996b). 'The Name of Cybele's Priests the "Galloi"', in Lane 1996a: 117–33.

Laroche, E. (1960). 'Koubaba, déesse anatolienne, et le problème des origines de Cybèle', in *Éléments orientaux dans la religion grecque ancienne*. Paris: Presses universitaires de France, 113–28.

Laumonier, A. (1938). 'Recherches sur la chronologie des prêtres de Lagine', *BCH*, 62: 251–84.

——(1958). *Les Cultes indigènes en Carie*, BEFAR 188. Paris: de Boccard.

Lewis, N. (1958). *Samothrace I. The Ancient Literary Sources*. London: Routledge and Kegan Paul.

Linforth, I. M. (1946). 'The Corybantic Rites in Plato', *University of California Publications in Classical Philology*, 13/5: 121–62.

MacMullen, R. (1981). *Paganism in the Roman Empire*. New Haven and London: Yale University Press.

——(1984). *Christianizing the Roman Empire* A.D. *100–400*. New Haven and London: Yale University Press.

——(1997). *Christianity and Paganism in the Fourth to Eighth Centuries*. New Haven and London: Yale University Press.

Malaise, M. (1981). 'Contenu et effets de l'initiation isiaque', *L'Antiquité classique*, 50: 483–98.

——(1986). 'Les caractéristiques et la question des antécédents de l'initiation isiaque', in J. Ries and H. Limet (eds.), *Les Rites d'initiation*, Homo religiosus 13. Louvain-la-Neuve: Centre d'histoire des religions, 355–62.

——(2005). *Pour une terminologie et une analyse des cultes isiaques*. Brussels: Académie Royale de Belgique.

Mari, M. (2001). 'Gli studi sul santuario e i culti di Samotracia: prospettive e problemi', in Ribichini, Rocchi, and Xella 2001: 155–67.

Martin, L. H. and Pachis, P. (eds.) (2004). *Hellenisation, Empire and Globalisation: Lessons from Antiquity*. Thessaloniki: Vanias.

Masaracchia, A. (ed.) (1993). *Orfeo e l'Orfismo*. Rome: Gruppo editoriale internazionale.

McLynn, N. (1996). 'The Fourth-Century *Taurobolium*', *Phoenix*, 50: 312–30.

Moret, A. (1931). 'La légende d'Osiris à l'époque thébaine d'après l'Hymne à Osiris du Louvre', *Bulletin de l'Institut Français d'Archéologie Orientale*, 30: 725–50.

Moretti, G. (1923–4a). 'In-Daghindà Qogia-in: la grande caverna nelle montagne delle caverne', *Annuario della R. Scuola Archeologica di Atene e delle Missioni Italiane in Oriente*, 6–7: 509–46.

——(1923–4b). 'Le grotte sacre di Iuvadjà', *Annuario della R. Scuola Archeologica di Atene e delle Missioni Italiane in Oriente*, 6–7: 547–54.

Motte, A. and Pirenne-Delforge, V. (1992). 'Le mot et les rites: aperçu des significations de ὄργια et de quelques dérivés', *Kernos*, 5: 119–40.

Nagel, G. (1944). 'Les "mystères" d'Osiris dans l'ancienne Égypte', *Eranos Jahrbuch*, 11: 145–66.

Naumann, F. (1983). *Die Ikonografie des Kybele in des phrygischen und des griechischen Kunst*, Istanbuler Mitteilungen Supp. 28. Tübingen: Wasmuth.

Nilsson, M. P. (1957). 'Royal Mysteries in Egypt', *Harvard Theological Review*, 50: 65–6.

Oesterley, W. O. E. (1935). 'The Cult of Sabazios', in S. H. Hooke (ed.), *The Labyrinth: Further Studies in the Relation between Myth and Ritual in the Ancient World*. London: SPCK, 115–58.

Oppermann, H. (1924). *Zeus Panamaros*, Religionsgeschichtliche Versuche und Vorarbeiten, 3. Giessen: Töpelmann.

Oster, R. E. (1990). 'Ephesus as a Religious Center under the Principate, I. Paganism before Constantine', in *ANRW* 2. 18. 3: 1662–1728.

Pachis, P. (1996). '"Γαλλαῖον Κυβέλης ὀλόλυγμα" (Anthol. Palat. VI, 173). L'élément orgiastique dans le culte de Cybèle', in Lane 1996a: 193–222.

Pailler, J.-M. (1989). 'Les religions orientales, troisième époque', *Pallas*, 35: 95–113.

Pettazzoni, R. (1924). *I misteri: saggio di una teoria storico-religiosa.* Bologna: Zanichelli; repr. Cosenza: Giordano, 1997.

Picard, C. (1922). *Éphèse et Claros. Recherches sur les sanctuaires et les cultes de l'Ionie du nord.* Paris: de Boccard.

Pleket, H. W. (1965). 'An Aspect of the Emperor Cult: Imperial Mysteries', *Harvard Theological Review*, 58: 331–47.

Podeman Sørensen, J. (1989). 'Attis or Osiris? Firmicus Maternus, De errore 22', in P. Sørensen (ed.), *Rethinking Religion. Studies in the Hellenistic Process.* Copenhagen: Museum Tusculanum, 73–86.

Poerner, I. (1913). *De Curetibus et Corybantibus*, Diss. Halensis, 22/2. Bonn: Niemeyer.

Pretini, R. (1999). 'Il coribantismo nelle testimonianze degli autori antichi: una proposta di lettura', *Studi e Materiali di Storia delle Religioni*, 65 (n. s. 23): 283–308.

Price, S. R. F. (1984). *Rituals and Power: The Roman Imperial Cult in Asia Minor.* Cambridge: Cambridge University Press.

Rein, M. J. (1996). 'Phrygian Matar: Emergence of an Iconographic Type', in Lane 1996a: 223–37.

Ribichini, S., Rocchi, M., and Xella, P. (2001) (eds.), *La questione delle influenze vicino-orientali sulla religione Greca. Stato degli studi e prospettive della ricerca.* Rome: Consiglio nazionale delle ricerche.

Robert, L. (1960). 'Recherches épigraphiques', *Revue des Études Anciennes*, 62: 276–361; repr. in Robert 1969–90: ii. 792–877.

——(1969–90). *Opera minora selecta*, 7 vols. Amsterdam: Hakkert.

——(1975). 'Une nouvelle inscription grecque de Sardes: règlement de l'autorité perse relatif à un culte de Zeus', *CRAI* 306–30, repr. in Robert 1969–90: v. 485–509.

Robertson, N. (1996). 'The Ancient Mother of the Gods: A Missing Chapter in The History of Greek Religion', in Lane 1996a: 239–304.

Rogers, G. M. (1999). 'The Mysteries of Artemis of Ephesos', in H. Friesinger and F. Krinziger (eds.), *100 Jahre Österreichische Forschungen in Ephesos.* Vienna: Österreichischen Akademie der Wissenschaften, 241–50.

Roller, L. E. (1994). 'Attis on Greek Votive Monuments: Greek God or Phrygian?', *Hesperia*, 63: 245–62, pls. 55–6.

——(1996). 'Reflections of the Mother of the Gods in Attic Tragedy', in Lane 1996a: 305–21.

——(1999). *In Search of God the Mother. The Cult of Anatolian Cybele.* Berkeley: University of California Press.

Romanelli, P. (1963). 'Lo scavo al Tempio della Magna Mater sul Palatino e nelle sue adiacenze', *Monumenti antichi pubblicati dall'Accademia Nazionale dei Lincei,* 46: 201–330.

Roussel, P. (1927). 'Les mystères de Panamara', *BCH,* 51: 123–35.

Rousselle, A. (1989). 'La transmission décalée. Nouveaux objects ou nouveaux concepts?', *Annales ESC,* 44.1: 161–71.

Sanders, G. M. (1972). s.v. 'Gallos', in Theodor Klauser et al. (eds), *Reallexikon für Antike und Christentum* (Stuttgart: Hiersemann), viii. 984–1034.

Sanzi, E. (2003). *I culti orientali nell'Impero romano: un'antologia di fonti.* Cosenza: Giordano.

Scarpi, P. (ed.) (2002a). *Le religioni dei misteri,* i: *Eleusi, Dionisismo, Orfismo;* ii: *Samotracia, Andania, Iside, Cibele e Attis, Mitraismo.* Milan: Mondadori.

——(2002b). 'Alle origini della comparazione storico-religiosa in Italia: i misteri tra modello tipologico e specifico storico-culturale', *Storiografia,* 6: 49–71.

Sfameni Gasparro, G. (1971). 'Le religioni orientali nel mondo ellenistico-romano', in G. Castellani (ed.), *Storia delle religioni.* Turin: Unione Tipografico-Editrice, iii. 423–564.

——(1984). 'Dai misteri alla mistica: semantica di una parola', in E. Ancilli and M. Paparozzi (eds.), *La mistica: fenomenologia e riflessione teologica.* Rome: Città nuova, i. 73–113; repr. in Sfameni Gasparro 2003a: 49–98.

——(1985). *Soteriology and Mystic Aspects in the Cult of Cybele and Attis,* EPRO 103. Leiden: Brill.

——(1986). *Misteri e culti mistici di Demetra.* Rome: 'L'Erma' di Bretschneider.

——(1994). 'Le religioni del mondo ellenistico', in G. Filoramo (ed.), *Storia delle religioni,* i, *Le religioni antiche.* Rome: Laterza, 409–52.

——(2003a). *Misteri e teologie: per la storia dei culti mistici e misterici nel mondo antico.* Cosenza: Giordano.

——(2003b). 'Nuovi dèi per uomini nuovi: Serapide e il sogno di Tolemeo', in N. Bonacasa, A. M. Donadoni Roveri, S. Aiosa, and P. Minà (eds.), *Faraoni come dei, Tolemei come Faraoni.* Turin and Palermo, 133–47.

——(2004). 'The Globalisation and Localisation of Religion: From Hellenism to Late Antiquity. Assessing a Category in the History of Religions', in Martin and Pachis 2004: 41–83.

——(2006). 'Strategie di salvezza nel mondo ellenistico-romano: per una tassonomia storico-religiosa', *Pagani e cristiani alla ricerca della salvezza, secoli I–III*, Studia Ephemeridis 'Augustinianum' 96. Rome: Institutum patristicum Augustinianum, 21–53.

Simms, R. M. (1990). '*Myesis, Telete*, and *Mysteria*', *Greek, Roman and Byzantine Studies*, 31: 183–95.

Smith, J. Z. (1990). *Drudgery Divine: On the Comparison of Early Christianities and the Religions of Late Antiquity*. Chicago: Chicago University Press.

Sokolowski, F. (1979). '*TA EMΠYPA*: On the Mysteries in the Lydian and Phrygian Cults', *ZPE*, 34: 65–9.

Tortorelli Ghidini, M., Storchi Marino, A., and Visconti, A. (eds.) (2000). *Tra Orfeo e Pitagora: origini e incontri di culture nell'antichità*. Naples: Bibliopolis.

Ustinova, Y. (1996a). 'Orgeones in Phratries: A Mechanism of Social Integration in Attica', *Kernos*, 6: 227–42.

——(1996b). 'Corybantism: The Nature and Role of an Ecstatic Cult in the Greek Polis', *Horos*, 10–12: 503–20.

Varinlioğlu, E. (1992). 'The Phrygian Inscriptions from Bayındır', *Kadmos*, 31: 10–20.

Vermaseren, M. J. (1977–89). *Corpus Cultus Cybelae Attidisque (CCCA)*, 7 vols., EPRO 50. Leiden: Brill.

Virgilio, B. (1981). *Il 'tempio stato' di Pessinunte fra Pergamo e Roma nel II–I secolo a.C. (C. B. Welles, Royal Corr., 55–61)*. Pisa: Giardini.

Voutiras, E. (1996). 'Un culte domestique des Corybantes', *Kernos*, 9: 243–56.

Wankel, H. (1979). 'I. Erythrai 206, 6–12 und Demosth. 18, 259', *ZPE*, 34: 79–80.

Will, E. (1960). 'Aspects du culte et de la légende de la Grande Mère dans le monde grec', in *Éléments Orientaux dans la religion grecque ancienne*. Paris: PUF, 95–111.

Xella, P. (2001) (ed.), *Quando un dio muore: morti e assenze divine nelle antiche tradizioni mediterranee*. Verona: Essedue.

Supplementary Bibliography (2009), arranged Thematically:
General works

Various authors (2006). *Les 'religions orientales': approaches historiographiques. Die 'orientalische Religionen' im Lichte der Forschungsgeschichte*, *ARG*, 8: 151–272.

Álvar, J. (2008). *Romanising Oriental Gods: Myth, Salvation and Ethics in the Cults of Cybele, Isis and Mithras*, RGRW 165. Leiden: Brill. (Spanish original 2001, corrected and expanded by Richard Gordon).

Auffarth, Chr. (2006). '"Licht vom Osten": Die antiken Mysterienkulte als Vorläufer, Gegenmodell oder katholisches Gift zum Christentum', *ARG*, 8: 206–26.

Bonnet, C. (2006). 'Les "Religions orientales" au laboratoire de l'Hellénisme. 2. Franz Cumont', in *ARG*, 8: 181–205.

Bonnet, C., Pirenne-Delforge, V., and Praet, D. (eds.) (2009). *Les religions orientales dans le monde grec et romain: centans après Cumont (1906–2006)*. Rome: Institut Historique Belge de Rome.

Bonnet, C., Ribichini, S., and Steuernagel, D. (eds.) (2007 [2008]). *Religioni in contatto nel Mediterraneo antico. Modalità di diffusione e processi di interferenza*, Mediterranea 4. Pisa: Serra.

Bonnet, C., Rüpke, J., and Scarpi, P. (eds.) (2006). *Religions Orientales-culti misterici: Neue Perspektiven — nouvelles perspectives — prospettive nuove*, Postdamer Altertumswissenschaftliche Beiträge, 16. Stuttgart: Steiner.

Borgeaud, P. (2006). 'L'Orient des religions. Réflexions sur la construction d'une polarité, de Creuzer à Bachofen', *ARG*, 8: 153–62.0.

Casadio. G. and Johnston, P. A. (eds.) (2009), *Mystic Cults in Magna Graecia*. Austin, TX: University of Texas Press.

Payen, P. (2006). 'Les "Religions orientales" au laboratoire de l'Hellénisme. 1. Johan Gustav Droysen', in *ARG*, 8: 163–80.

Peducci, G. (2009). *Cibele frigia e la Sicilia. I santuari rupestri nel culto della dea*. Rome: L'Erma di Bretschneider.

Sfameni Gasparro, G. (2009). *Problemi di religione ellenistica. Dèi, dèmoni, uomini: tra antiche e nuove identità*, Hierà 12. Cosenza: Giordano.

Isiac studies

Bricault L. (ed.) (2008). *Sylloge Nummorum Religionis Isiacae et Sarapiacae (SNRIS)*, with the collaboration of R. Ashton, F. Delrieux, W. Leschhorn, U. Peter, C. Sfameni, and G. Sfameni Gasparro, Mémoires de l'Académie des Inscriptions et Belles-Lettres, 38. Paris: De Boccard.

——Versluys, M. J., and Meyboom, P. G. P. (eds.) (2007). *Nile into Tiber. Egypt in the Roman World*. Leiden: Brill.

Periodical: *Bibliotheca Isiaca*, 1 (2008), edited by Laurent Bricault. Bordeaux: Ausonius.

Orphica - Dionysiaca

Bernabé, A., and Casadesús, F. (eds.) (2008). *Orfeo y la tradición órfica. Un reencuentro*, 2 vols, Akal universitaria. Serie Religiones y mitos, 280–1. Tres Cantos: Akal.

——and Jiménez San Cristóbal, A. I. (2007). *Instructions for the Netherworld. The Orphic Gold Tablets*, RGRW 162. Leiden: Brill.

Graf, F. and Johnston, S. I. (2007). *Ritual Texts for the Afterlife. Orpheus and the Bacchic Gold Tablets.* London: Routledge.

Jaccottet, A.-F. (2003). *Choisir Dionysos. Les associations dionysiaques, ou, la face caché du dionysisme,* 2 vols. Kilchberg: Akanthvs.

Tortorelli, G. M. (2006). *Figli della Terra e del Cielo stellato. Testi orfici con traduzione e commento.* Naples: M. D'Auria.

Varia

Borgeaud, Ph. (2007). 'Rites et émotions. Considérations sur les mystères', in J. Scheid (ed.), *Rites et croyances dans les religions du monde romain,* Entretiens sur l'Antiquité classique, 53. Geneva: Fondation Hardt, 189–222, with discussion 223–9.

Rüpke, J. with Fabricius, F. (2006). 'Roman Imperial and Provincial Religion: An Interim Report', *ARG,* 8: 327–42.

9

Ritual and Hierarchy in the Mysteries of Mithras

Richard Gordon

The general subject of the relation between religion and the maintenance of political and social power in the ancient world has not until
recently received the attention it deserves. It has in fact traditionally
been taken for granted, particularly in relation to the most obviously
relevant case, the cult of Hellenistic kings and Roman emperors: it
was only in the 1980s that the issues of the subjects' attitudes to such
cults, and the relationship between ruler cult and other religious cult,
were seriously raised (Price 1980: 28–43; 1984; Fishwick 1987–92;
Turcan 1996; Clauss 1999). At about the same time, attempts were
made to problematize the nature of religious authority in the classical
city state and at Rome, and contrast them with the patterns found in
the complex states and empires of the ancient Near East (Garland
1982; Beard 1989; Beard and North 1990). There have also been
attempts, initially inspired by the Besançon group of ancient historians (Clavel-Lévêque 1972; Février 1976), but more recently by the
realization that religion needs to be 'written back into the heart of all
our narratives' of the emergence of imperial culture (Woolf 2000), to
examine the relation between religious institutions and colonial
power in the Latin West. One account of this has indeed argued
that the religious choices of the élite were always decisive in the
construction of 'civic religion' itself, a notion which never represented more than a highly selective version of the true cult activity
of the city population, let alone that of its dependent territory
(Bendlin 1998; 2000).

There has been less interest in the question of how exactly religious practice contributes to the maintenance and legitimation of socio-political hierarchy. This is partly a matter of our sheer ignorance, for it would be reasonable to suppose that an important, perhaps a crucial, aspect of this problem might be provided by a semiotic or other account of ritual; but it is precisely ritual action in the ancient world about which we know least. Moreover, the ritual aspects of civic sacrifice, insofar as they are known to us, do not suggest that, even if we knew many more details, they would contribute to a greater understanding of how religious practice legitimates social hierarchy. The way in which other aspects of ritual, for example, festivals and processions, concretize and legitimate social hierarchy, has however been studied with profit,[1] as have imperial funerary rituals.[2] All this, though, remains rather impressionistic. But in a recent book, Jaime Alvar has suggested that examination of the 'oriental cults' of the Roman Empire, precisely because they were not so embedded in the other socio-political institutions of the ancient world, may be valuable here, partly because their rituals, being 'strange', are more reported, and partly because myth plays a more direct role in legitimating these rituals than is commonly the case in civic ritual (Alvar 2001/2008). He has profitably examined the myths of the cults of Isis, Cybele-Attis, and Mithras from this point of view.

In this chapter I would like to suggest some further ways in which the cult of Mithras simultaneously drew upon wider conceptions of hierarchy and gave individual initiates a concrete, personal, experience of the necessity of social asymmetry.

---

[1] Quet 1981; Rice 1983; Price 1984: 101–14, 128f. (on Dio Chrysostom, *Oration.* 35. 10); Fishwick 1987–92: 2.1: 475–590; Schmitt Pantel 1992; Lozano 1995: 139–53; Gascó 1995: 165–70. There was a good deal of interest in civic ritual in the historiography of early-modern Europe in the late 1970s, e.g. Muir 1981; 1997. It must be confessed, however, that in ancient history evocations of festivals, crowds, and processions often serve a merely descriptive, non-analytic end, e.g. MacMullen 1981; Lane Fox 1986: 66–8.

[2] Gesche 1978: 374–90; Kierdorf 1986: 43–69; Price 1987: 56–105. On late-antique imperial funerals: MacCormack 1981: 93–158; Rebenich 2000: 300–24; with the remarks of Brown 1992: 3–15.

PATRONAGE AND DEFERENCE

Although so much about the mystery cult of Mithras remains obscure, it seems clear that the internal organization was ranked into a hierarchy of holders of different initiatory grades. The traditional view that there were seven of these, which was based upon the explicit listing of the names by St Jerome in relation to an incident at Rome involving the Urban Prefect Furius Maecius Gracchus in 376/7,[3] seemed to be satisfactorily confirmed by the discovery at Ostia in the course of the Fascist excavations (1938–42) of a mosaic floor representing seven grade-symbols in a line stretching from the entrance to the cult-niche (Fig. 9.1) (Becatti 1954: 105–12 = Vermaseren 1956–60: no. 29). This in turn seemed to be confirmed by the paintings on the right-hand wall of the S. Prisca mithraeum on the Aventine, discovered in 1935 and first published in 1940, which include a series of acclamations to all seven of the grades listed by Jerome (Ferrua 1940; Vermaseren and van Essen 1965: 155–60 (upper layer); 167–9 (lower layer)).

The inference has however recently been denied on two different grounds. Manfred Clauss has argued that the grades were in fact ranks within the priesthood, and that most members of the cult were not members of grades, they were initiated once and that was all. The main argument in favour of this hypothesis, which is based on the analogy of other mystery cults, is the highly uneven epigraphic evidence for the grades, which are far more common in Rome and more generally in Italy, than they are on the Rhine-Danube area, from where most of the archaeological evidence for the cult derives (Clauss 1990a; 2000: 131–3 (= 1990b 138–40)). Only about 14% of the *c.*1050 epigraphically-attested Mithraists mention their grade.

---

[3] *(Gracchus) specum Mithrae et omnia portentosa simulacra quibus Corax, Nymphus, Miles, Leo, Perses, Heliodromus, Pater imitantur subvertit . . .*, (Gracchus) 'destroyed a "cave" of Mithras and all the amazing images by which Raven, Nymph, Soldier, Lion, Persian, Sun-messenger, Father are imitated (i.e. represented?)': Jerome, *Letter* 107. 2. *Imitantur*, the reading of all the main manuscripts, has been rejected in favour of *initiantur* by Vallarsi and many later editors. This would make better sense, but *imitantur* seems to allude to a tradition similar to that known by Ambrosiaster (see below).

Fig. 9.1. The mosaic ladder of the grades in the Mitreo di Felicissimo, Ostia (*c*.AD 250). Each grade is associated with the symbols of a planet, from the lowest (Mercury) to the highest (Saturn). Cf. above, Ch. 7, Fig. 7.6.

There are four good arguments against this view. First, a recently-discovered *album*, or membership-list, from Virunum, clearly implies that there was a specific notion of membership in the Mithraic community: over an 18-year period, following the initial list relating to the year 183/4 AD, several new names were added annually by the *scrutator* or *scriba*, never less than one (in AD 186, 190, 194, 196 and 201), never more than eight (184, after the losses caused by the plague (*AE* 1994: no. 1334, with Piccottini 1994: 24–8). The document seems to exclude the idea that there were many initiates who never became full members of the cult (or 'priests' in Clauss' terminology). Second, the small size of most Mithraic temples, and their resemblance to *triclinia*, dining-halls, tends to confirm the idea that the notion of membership was well-developed in this cult. This suggests that Clauss' distinction between simple initiates and a special élite of 'priests' is inappropriate, especially since the epigraphical evidence tends to support the view that *sacerdos* normally implied the grade *Pater*—a *Pater* need not have been a priest, but a *sacerdos* usually required to have achieved the grade *Pater*.[4] If all the grade-members had been priests, it would have been nonsensical to create a special title of this kind for certain *Patres*. Third, the casual manner in which Tertullian refers to the initiation-rite for Miles, to the allegorical significance of Mithraic Lions, and to Fathers, strongly suggests that he thought of these grades as membership grades and not as a qualification open only to a small minority of members.[5] Finally, the dozens of graffiti on the columns of the North side of the mithraeum at Dura-Europos, which Clauss does not allude to at all, strongly support the assumption that to be an ordinary member of a Mithraic congregation involved membership of one of the seven grades.[6] Here too there are acclamations to individuals, for example Mareos and Maximinus, both wall-painters, and another individual who was a professional scribe, who are given no grade.[7] In each of these cases,

[4] Mitthof 1992. Although his material so clearly suggests that Clauss is wrong, Mitthof concludes his article by agreeing with his view.
[5] *On the Crown* 15 (*Miles*); *Against Marcion* 1. 13. 4 (*Leo*); *To the Nations* 1. 7. 23; *apologeticus* 8. 7 (*Pater sacrorum*).
[6] Rostovtzeff et al. 1939: nos. 848, 855, 857–8, with p.123f. (= Vermaseren 1956–60: nos. 54, 57, 59–60). Others are mentioned by Francis 1975.
[7] Rostovtzeff et al. 1939: nos. 853, 860, 854 = Vermaseren 1956–60: nos. 46, 62, 56.

however, it seems reasonable to suppose that these acclamations are to be taken as an expression of gratitude for services provided, and have no significance for the issue of grades. However until these graffiti are fully published—an event we have now been awaiting for half a century—any statement about the case at Dura must remain provisional.

Clauss however does not dispute that the system of seven grades did apply widely through the Empire, albeit only to 'priests'. It is precisely this that Robert Turcan has now questioned, on the grounds that the complete system of seven is only attested for Rome and Ostia, and then only from the Severan period—the Mitreo di Felicissimo in Ostia is even later (mid-third c. AD).[8] He stresses that several grades, for example Perses and Nymphus, are never attested epigraphically outside Rome and Dura, and Heliodromus does not occur even at Dura, being apparently substituted by *Stereôtes*.[9] Porphyry mentions only *Patres, Persai, Leones*, and *Korakes*; and there are only two grades, not seven, represented in the well-known Feast-scene from Konjic, Dalmatia (Vermaseren 1956–60: no. 1896.3). He argues that only the grades *Leo* and *Korax/Corvus* are original to the cult of Mithras, and that the full system of seven is a late, and purely local, expansion whose intention was to correlate the grade system with that of the planets, a typical strategy of occultism.

Salutary as this criticism of the conventional position is, it should not be allowed too much weight. For one thing, there is no good reason to expect votive inscriptions to mention grade-membership. Grade-membership was, on the conventional understanding, merely a phase in a religious progression; an inscribed votive on the other hand is an intentionally permanent, or near-permanent, record of a quasi-contractual relation with the god. One ought in fact to consider the mention of a grade on a votive the exception rather than the rule, a function of the loosening of the generic rules for different types of epigraphic composition, and of the tendency, very marked in

[8] Turcan 1999; but MacMullen (1981: 124) had much earlier stressed the discrepancies in the epigraphic evidence for the grades, as well as the existence at Dura-Europos of other titles (such as *magos* and *sophistês*) which could not be fitted into the conventional scheme, though in his subsequent remarks he negligently confuses cult-positions with initiatory grades.

[9] On *stereôtes*, see Francis 1975: 441; Gordon 1994: 112f.

the cult of Mithras, for later documents to be more revealing, more 'garrulous', than earlier ones. Second, although it appears from the indices of Vermaseren's *Corpus* that *Patres* are attested far more often than other grades, almost half of these attestations occur as a form of context-specific dating, 'during the Fathership of X', and have a distorting effect upon the figures. And there is anyway a well-known general tendency in epigraphy for senior functions to be over-represented (e.g. Forbis 1996: 96–102). Third, the only grade listed in the Virunum bronze album mentioned above, which is the most important document we possess for the history of recruitment to a Mithraic community, is that of Father. The inference is not that no other grades existed, but that grades below Father were not listed because they were merely temporary achievements. There must have existed other documents in the community which recorded the progress of individuals through the grade ladder but which were not considered worth recording in bronze.[10]

It is not at all surprising therefore to find that the two sites where evidence for grades is most plentiful are Santa Prisca and Dura. In neither temple is there a single votive inscription which mentions a grade. All the evidence occurs in the form of dipinti, a non-monu-mental and relatively informal type of commemoration. Moreover, the existence at Dura of technical terms for those desirous of rising to the next grade, *melleôn*, for example, and *petitor*, terms that are unrecorded elsewhere, suggests that at any rate there the notion of ascending a graduated scale of grades was well-established.[11] Equally, there is no reason to think that this was a peculiarity of Dura. The cult of Mithras was re-introduced into the city at the time of

[10]   Francis (1975: 440f.) notes one or two cases of rare names that recur at Dura in association with different grades, which permit the inference that these are the same individuals rising through the system. But most names recur too often to allow this sort of conclusion.

[11]   *Melleôn*, 'aspirant Lion': Rostovtzeff et al., 1939: 124 (no inscription cited); *petitôr* is a simple transcription of the military Latin word for an aspirant to a higher post, and may in this case mean 'aspirant to the grade of *Pater*': Rostovtzeff et al., 1939: no. 848 = Vermaseren 1956–60: no. 54. The case of *antipatros* is unclear. It seems to be inspired by bureaucratic/military coinages such as *antigraphon*, a copy of a document, and *antistratêgos, antitamias* in Roman usage, and should therefore mean 'substitute Father': Rostovtzeff et al., 1939: no. 855 = Vermaseren 1956–60: no. 57.

its re-occupation shortly before the death of Septimius Severus in 211, by vexillations from IV Scythica and XVI Flavia. Both of these units were stationed in Syria at the time, where vexillations are found in widely different commissions; yet it has always been accepted that the general form of phase II at Dura implies that its inspiration was both from the Danube frontier area and from Italy.[12]

Then again, although it may be true that Porphyry does not mention all seven grades, there is no reason, given the nature of his arguments, why he should: he mentions grades invariably in relation to a particular point, for example, to explain the names taken from the animal kingdom (Lion, Raven), not as part of a concern with the Mysteries for their own sake. And the notion of a regular seven-fold Mithraic hierarchy based upon the scheme of planets is taken for granted by Celsus, writing in the 160s, although his sources, which have been thought to be Alexandrian, elaborate upon the scheme for their own, again occultist, ends, correlating the scheme with metals.[13]

Finally, Turcan developed his point in ignorance of some important new evidence which suggests that the grade system, though not necessarily in its sevenfold form, was known in Germany in the first half of the second century AD., and probably earlier than *c.*140. This is the evidence of the Wetterau-ware cult-vessel (*Schlangengefäß*) discovered in Mainz in 1976, but first published in 1994, and which has now been the subject of an important article by Roger Beck (Horn 1994; Beck 2000). One face of the vessel undoubtedly represents a *Pater* sitting down and taking aim with an armed bow at an initiand (Fig. 9.14). The other face represents a sort of Mithraic procession of four individuals walking to the left. The third figure in the procession (Fig. 9.2) holds the whip that is Sol's usual attribute in the iconography, and possibly a radiate crown seen from the side, at any rate with a curious elongation extending from the front.[14] Beck identifies this scene as a procession of *Heliodromus*, the Sun-Runner, the second

---

[12] Rostovtzeff et al. 1939: 82; cf. the telling comparison of Roll (1977: 59–62) between Duran and Italian Mithraic iconography.

[13] Celsus, *ap.* Origen, *Against Celsus* 6. 22; cf. Turcan 1975: 44–61; Couliano 1994.

[14] On the iconography of Helios and Sol, see Letto 1988; Yalouris 1990. Helios' 'radiate crown' emerges in the early fifth century BC, apparently as an allusion to the head-gear worn by participants in the *lampadedromiai*, the boys' torch-races at Athens: Parisinou 2000: 36–44.

Fig. 9.2. Heliodromus, from the procession on the Mainz cult-vessel.

highest grade, a procession intended to evoke the Sun's annual journey along the ecliptic. That solar journey is punctuated by two opposed pairs of astronomical events, the solstices and the equinoxes, and he takes these opposed astronomical pairs to be connoted by the rods held by the figures immediately in front of and behind Heliodromus, the first with rod held downwards, the hindmost figure with his rod held erect (2000: 156–8). The procession would thus connote one of the central themes of the Mysteries. Whether this be the case or not,[15] it is undeniable that we have here indubitable, and early, evidence for a grade, Heliodromus, Runner of the Sun, not mentioned in a single epigraphic text on stone anywhere in the Empire, which again suggests something of the bias of that epigraphic evidence. The figure leading the procession wears a cuirass (Fig. 9.3), and it is natural to identify him as an emblematic *Miles*, Soldier. But the Mainz cult-vessel apparently makes no allusion either to *Leo*, Lion, or to *Corvus*, Raven, though representations of both are found in evidence widely scattered over the Empire.[16] Its silences too therefore cannot be pressed to provide evidence in favour of Turcan's claim, but its positive evidence shows that at least three of the grades known from Rome *c.*200 AD already were known in Germany sixty or seventy years earlier. To deny the general existence within the mysteries of Mithras of a graduated hierarchy of initiatory grades, even if not of all seven in the standard list, is beginning to look perverse.

These considerations suggest that we are justified in continuing to claim that the cult of Mithras was from its early expansion in the Roman Empire at the end of the first century AD a mystery cult deliberately constructed around the idea of repeated, and indeed progressive, initiation. Whatever other celebrations took place in Mithraic temples, initiations were evidently of primary importance, even if not necessarily the most common or everyday events: successive initiation provided a structure to each Mithraist's membership of the group. At Dura-Europos it was regular practice to acclaim each initiate on reaching a new grade, for example: Νάμα Κα[μ]ερίῳ στρατιώτῃ ἀκερίῳ, 'Hail to Kamerios, an unsullied *Miles*', or Νάμα ἐλπίσι Ἀντωνείνῳ [σ]τερεώτῃ ἀγαθῷ συνδεξίῳ τῷ εὐσεβεῖ, 'Hail, with good hopes (for the future), to Antoninus the *Stereôtês*, a

---

[15] It seems to me that the second, grandly dressed, figure must represent a Father (see Fig. 9.9 below), but for Beck's argument it is necessary that his staff complement that of the small hindmost figure, and he does not identify him.

[16] *Leo*, representations on pottery: two late Antonine terra-sigillata sherds from the potteries at Ittenwiller or Rheinzabern, showing figures dressed in a tunic and apparently wearing lion-masks: (1) Forrer 1915: 116 fig. 84 = Clauss 2000: 117 fig. 74; (2) Petry and Kern 1978: 27, fig. 6D. The only other straightforwardly recognizable representation of a *Leo* occurs on the reverse of the Konjic relief: Vermaseren 1956–60: no. 1896.3d (4th cent. AD). *Corvus*: Vermaseren 1956–60: no. 42.13 (Dura, final phase); no. 397 rev (Castra Praetoria, Rome); no. 1896.3a (Konjic).

Fig. 9.3. Miles, leading the procession on the Mainz cult-vessel.

good Mithraist, and reverent'.[17] Together with words like *melloleôn* and *petitor*, noted above (n. 11), acclamations such as these,

---

[17] Rostovtzeff et al. 1939: 120 nos. 857, 859 = Vermaseren 1956–60: nos. 59; 60. The *Report* apparently considers the 'hopes' to relate to military promotion; in my view, it is a military metaphor now applied to initiation (cf. Francis 1975: 439 with n. 75). *Nama*-acclamations of a similar type are known from S. Prisca in Rome, and

invariably prefaced by a self-conscious allusion to the Persian character of the cult (*Nama* is an authentic Old Persian word), underline the importance of going through the sequence of grades: each successive rise is collectively acknowledged by the whole congregation, and fixed in writing on the walls of the temple. It is worth stressing that these graffiti are often beautifully written, and in several colours of ink (Rostovtzeff et al. 1939: 118), they were private honorific texts, quite different from the majority of the graffiti at Pompeii or in the *ludus magnus* in Rome.

It is evident from the language of the Duran acclamations that promotion in the Mysteries was at least partly justified in religio-moral terms: the achievement of a higher grade was legitimated by a candidate's fulfilment of certain moral expectations. What these were we can vaguely infer from the rather stereotyped adjectives that describe many of the grades at Dura, such as *agathos, akeraios, dikaios, eusebês, hieros* (good, unsullied, just, pious, holy); less clearly from the commonest adjective there for the Lions, *ABPOΣ*, (*h*)*abros*, which in Greek means 'delicate, luxurious, graceful', even 'soft',[18] but which has been understood as a neologism based on the word ἄβρα, common in later Greek, meaning 'personal maid'.[19] If we are prepared to consider Semitic loan-words at Dura, however, there are two other possibilities which offer at least as good a sense as 'companion (*syndexios*)': אבר, in Hebrew *abir*, 'strong, noble', and בר in Hebrew *bar*, 'pure, clean'.[20] However that may be, what needs to be stressed in the present context is that a hierarchical system which applies rational criteria in the selection of those to be promoted concentrates authority in the hands of those qualified to apply

from one or two inscriptions, all from mid-Italy: Vermaseren 1956–60: nos. 214 (Tibur); 308 (Ostia); 416 (perhaps a forgery); 591 (Rome).

[18] Rostovtzeff et al. 1939: 124. The interest of this word was first noted by Cumont 1975: 199f., suggesting that it was a poetic word derived from a ritual hymn.

[19] Francis 1975: 444, with *LSJ* Supplement *s.v.* This word is identical to Aramaic הכרה, *hab.ra*, 'female companion'. Such a coinage might parallel the Mithraic neologism *nymphos* from *nymphê* (f.), 'bride'.

[20] In the latter case, since in Semitic languages the definite article is attached both to the noun and to the adjective, the word would normally occur, when used of a man, as הכר, in Hebrew *hâbăr*. The hypothesis is only plausible if in Palmyrene or Nabatean, the local languages at Dura, the *ă* were pronounced quiescently, as a vocal šewa. If *ABPOΣ* is related to בר, its force would be the same as ἀκέραιος, 'pure'.

the criteria, in the Mithraic case, the Fathers of the community, just as it makes willing subordinates of those who strive to be promoted, who must internalize the values of the system. That is, the type of initiation practised by the cult of Mithras led directly to a social pattern in which authority was complemented by deference.[21] Deference is the tool with which the weak prise advantages from their superiors; social capital is the reward of those superiors for playing the game more or less according to the rules.

We should, at any rate, be aware of the issues of power and patronage within the microcosm of the Mithraic congregation even if we are scarcely in a position to point to evidence that concretely illuminates them. If individual Fathers felt impelled to provide cult furniture at their own expense, *de sua pecunia*, and did so gladly,[22] their reward did not simply lie, as they piously claimed, in heaven. The Fathers must have been in many ways the driving forces within Mithraic congregations: their knowledge and enthusiasm was crucial to the continued existence of such small religious groups not guaranteed by the casual weight of the divine system inscribed in the civic calendar. Gifts of cult-furniture, above all of the cult-relief, which was the essential minimum requirement for carrying on the collective worship, signalled a claim to the knowledge that underlay the cult's claims (cf. Clauss 2000: 43). But more than anything else, such gifts established the Father as a benefactor, whose gifts create a permanently asymmetrical relation between giver and receiver, a relation in which the receivers have no hope of reciprocating, and so cancelling out, the value of the gift (Bailey 1971: 238–41; Sahlins 1974: 249f.; cf. Schmitt Pantel 1992: 408–20). In return for that outlay of time, knowledge, expense, and effort, the Fathers as a group expected deference, loyalty, submission. This theme of asymmetrical social relations is deployed far more insistently in the Mysteries of Mithras than in other analogous cults of the Empire.

---

[21] We shall see later that the rituals themselves emphasized the same point.

[22] *Sua pecunia* vel sim.: 1956–60: no. 233; *ILS* no. 4212 = Vermaseren 1956–60: no. 312f. (Ostia); Vermaseren 1956-60: no. 626 (relief plus temple decoration); *ILS* no. 4224 = Vermaseren 1956–60: no. 706 (restoration after fire, Mediolanum); Vermaseren 1956–60: no. 1243 = Schwertheim 1974: #108c (altar, Bingium).

Fig. 9.4. Altar of Diocles, Ostia, Mitreo di Lucrezio Menandro (Vermaseren 1956–60: no. 225), first half of the third c. AD.

At Ostia, for example, one Diocles dedicated his brick altar faced in marble to Mithras (Fig. 9.4) *ob honorem C. Lucreti Menandri patris*, as a mark of respect to the Father (Becatti 1954 = Vermaseren 1956–60: no. 225, probably from *c.*210–220 AD). An unknown dedicator at the mithraeum *degli Animali* in the same town made a gift of some kind to the temple; he expresses his undertaking as a gift to M. C(a)erellius Hieronymus, *patri et sacerdoti suo*, and it was Hieronymus, in his capacity as *antistes templi*, the supervisor of the mithraeum, who actually dedicated it to the god.[23] Another man, on recording his restoration of two statues of the torchbearers,

---

[23] Vermaseren 1956–60: no. 282 = *CIL* XIV 70 (late Antonine or Severan). The text reads: ... *]d(onum)d(edit) /M.·Cerellio/Hieronymo patri/et·sacerdoti·suo/ eosque antistes·s(upra)·s(criptus)·/deo libens dicavit. Eos* must refer to the gift, i.e. no doubt *fratres*, statues of Cautes and Cautopates, as in the inscription mentioned in the next note; and *antistes* refers back to Hieronymus. Although a fictional gift to the Father is unique in Mithraic epigraphy, it is consistent with the other evidence adduced here, and is preferable to assuming a writer's error, in an otherwise literate text, e.g. *eiusque antistiti*. The two last lines were apparently added later as an afterthought.

prefaced his inscription with the characteristic Mithraic greeting to his Father: *na]ma Victori patri.*[24] At Rome, the lateral face of a pair of small altars from the mithraeum of the Castra Peregrina beneath S. Stefano Rotondo on the Celimontana, is inscribed simply *Leo vivas cum Caedicio patre,* 'Long may you live, Lion, together with the Father Caedicius Priscianus'.[25] At Dura, Marinus an aspirant (*petitor*) to an unnamed grade, hailed first Mithras, then the two presiding Fathers of the Fathers, and himself only third.[26] An instructive *symbolon,* a secret utterance belonging to the sacred 'property' of an initiation cult, addresses the Mithraic initiate as συνδέξιος πατρὸς ἀγανοῦ, 'hand-shaker (i.e. initiate) of an illustrious Father'.[27] Whatever the actual routes by which new members were introduced to a Mithraic congregation, symbolically the initiate owed his new existence to the Father, who is given the Homeric epithet 'illustrious'.

We may profitably think of this relationship as a specialized instance of a much wider form of social relation in the Roman Empire, that of patronage. It is familiar that Roman society was articulated not merely by legal, economic, cultural, and geographic differentia but also by placement within patronage networks (Alföldy 1975: 89f.; Millar 1977; Roniger 1983; Garnsey and Saller 1987: 148–59; Wallace-Hadrill 1989). If the key central patron was the emperor, who found his own moral and political justification in the exercise of differential patronage, his very capacity to act as patron within the Empire as a whole, and at the level of hundreds of individual cases, was brokered by individual senators and equestrians. The standing of any individual in these orders was at least partly a function of his ability to obtain constructive favours for communities and individuals who looked to him, whether formally

---

[24] Vermaseren 1956–60: no. 308 (see n. 17 above); the inscription is poorly recut over an earlier one. Probably mid- to late third century AD.

[25] *AE* 1980: 49b, 50b (late Antonine). 'Lion' refers to Baebius Quintianus, one of the dedicators of the statues of the torchbearers mentioned in the main texts.

[26] Rostovtzeff et al. 1939: 87 no.848 = Vermaseren 1956–60: no. 54 (*c.*211–12 AD) (cited n. 11 above). A similar honorific allusion to Fathers before the dedicant's own name in Vermaseren 1956–60: no. 57 = Rostovtzeff et al. 1939: 119 no. 855, listing two *patres paterôn* before the lower initiates (though in this case it is possible that all have just been promoted).

[27] Firmicus Maternus, *On the Error of Pagan Religions* 5. 2 (p. 46.11 Ziegler). The initiand owes his new status to the initiator, in a sense he belongs to him.

or informally, as patron, just as the standing of the emperor was a function of his ability to exercise patronage according to the tacit rules of fairness, appropriateness, measure, disinterestedness, consistency. 'Grand' patronage was thus the indispensable grease that oiled the machinery of a society of legally-differentiated orders. As a mode of social interaction, it simultaneously confirmed the necessity and propriety of the unequal distribution of power and wealth in such a society, and, because it was a temporary, and within an order often reversible, relation, gave the impression that the distribution of those social goods was subject to the intervention of rational good-will. It has thus an important masking effect (Merquior 1979: 1–38). At the same time, it offered a powerful model for social interaction throughout the society, down to the slave-*familia* itself.

We can trace the descent of patronage networks down through the structures of local city government to the micro-level of the *patroni* of professional corporations. But the operation of patronage as a system is quite independent of the existence of formal titles. Anyone in a position to accord or withhold favours, distribute rewards or sanctions, can act in the manner of a patron at the micro-level. In so doing, he asserts his (temporary) social power, fulfils the possibilities of his social position, and acquires that 'profit par excellence' which consists in the feeling both that one's existence is justified and that one is *comme il faut* (Bourdieu 1979: 252f.). An initiator in a mystery cult such as Mithraism possessed a body of esoteric lore, relating both to the elementary symbols of the temple, and to their deeper meanings and exegetical possibilities. He possessed, quite simply, the power that his knowledge grants him (Fig. 9.5). The ambition to acquire that knowledge must have been one of the most powerful inducements for individuals to continue through the successive stages of initiation—not perhaps that all, or even most, actually did so. If the ideal description of the senior Mithraic initiate is *sophistês*, the one who knows, the condition of the beginner is suggested by the Hermupolis catechism: ἀπορεῖ, 'he is/you are at a loss, do not know the answer'.[28]

---

[28] *Sophistês*: Rostovtzeff et al. 1939: 123; Cumont 1975: 202f. (but the unpublished text there referred to in n. 284 perhaps suggests that not all *sophistai* held a high rank); Hermupolis catechism: Brashear 1992: 18; 20f. This text is generally considered not to be Mithraic in the narrow sense, however, but to emanate from an unknown esoteric group in the fourth century AD.

Fig. 9.5. One of the 'Magi' from the front of the arcosolium, Dura phase 3 (Vermaseren 1956–60: no. 22b). The scroll (in his left hand, faded) and staff (in his right hand) denote the Fathers' claim to status and authority based on literate knowledge.

The analogy between patronage in the outer world of political and social relations and the relation of the Mithraic Father to the rest of the congregation was exploited unselfconsciously within the Mysteries. For example, in the procession of the grades on the right wall of both layers of paintings at S. Prisca in Rome (Fig. 9.6), the Father is represented as sitting alone on a throne or chair, his hand raised in a gesture of acknowledgement of the offerings brought him by the Lions (Vermaseren and van Essen 1965: 155f. with pl. LIX (upper layer); 168 no.1 (lower layer)), in a manner reminiscent of the emperor receiving honour from military commanders (Fig. 9.7), or

Fig. 9.6. A seated Father, dressed to recall Mithras, receiving the offerings of the Mithraic Lions. S. Prisca, right wall, upper layer, *c*.AD 220.

Fig. 9.7. Tiberius and Drusus presenting Augustus with olive branches, to mark peace after their conquest of Raetia. Denarius of Augustus, 15–13 BC, reverse.

gifts from foreign clients (Fig. 9.8).[29] The main figure of the procession of the Mainz cult-vessel, who in my view is the Father, is represented as walking majestically forward, in a flowing robe and holding a staff (Fig. 9.9). All this, deportment, bearing, and staff, suggest the dignity and authority of the person of high standing. The same claim is made in a summary or symbolic manner by the staff in the Father-frame in the floor-mosaic of the Mitreo di Felicissimo in Ostia (Fig. 9.1), and indeed by the Phrygian cap with ear-flaps next to it, which links the Father directly with the god.[30]

[29] Rightly noted by Vermaseren and van Essen 1965: 158f., though the iconographic model has a much longer history in imperial art than they suggest. It is also worth noting that the Father, at least in the upper layer, is dressed in a red robe, red, because of its expense, connoting high status.
[30] On the different (Graeco–)Persian types of tiara, Nollé 1992: 45–7.

Fig. 9.8. Augustus receiving a child from a German client, referring to the re-settlement of German peoples within the Empire. Denarius, 8 BC, reverse.

We may suggest that Mithraic social organization borrowed from the outside world the model of the patron–client relationship; but transformed it into an ideal form. What remained was the desirable essence, generous altruism, philanthropy, service of the other world: what is given to the initiate is solely for his own true good; the return for the initiator is the satisfaction derived from the performance of a holy duty. The religious act decently masks its contribution to, and naturalization of, the reproduction of social relations of inequality. It is moreover in the context of such private religious structures, which represent a fully moralized and rationalized conception of religion, that we can see the emergence of a characteristically Graeco–Roman kind of religious specialist, not full-time or supported by the state apparatus, as in the complex pre-industrial states of the Fertile Crescent, nor an itinerant purifier and wonder-worker as in the Archaic world, but a kind of petty bureaucrat of the holy, a mediator of routinized religious experience.

Fig. 9.9. The Father in the Heliodromus procession on the cult-vessel from Mainz, *c.*AD 120–40.

PATTERNS OF RITUAL

In the second part of the paper, I wish to go further and suggest how such patterns of deference were conveyed in and through ritual performance, and thus experienced physically and directly, not merely as abstract thoughts or ideals. We of course know extremely little about Mithraic ritual, as we do about ritual in all ancient religion. Moreover, it may very well be that different Mithraic communities constructed their own particular rituals in keeping with their understanding of the requirements. There would then be not one Mithraic ritual system but many, each presenting slightly different value commitments. Nor is it always clear what kind of events we are dealing with: Mithraic rituals seem consistently to ignore the boundaries usually suggested for the study of ritual. With these important reservations in mind, I propose to look at three rituals, or groups of rituals, of which we know something (which of course really means 'hardly anything') and read them as means of inscribing the value of hierarchy and subordination into the unmediated experience of the initiate. I do not thereby mean to suggest that there are no other equally legitimate ways of reading them.

'Liberation'

The late fourth-century commentator Ambrosiaster denounces Mithraic initiation in his *Quaestiones veteris et novi testamenti*. The initiates, he claims, are blind-folded and some have to flap their arms as though they were birds, and others roar as if they were lions, but others *ligatis manibus intestinis pullinis proiciuntur super foveas aqua plenas, accedente quodam cum gladio et inrumpente intestina supra dicta qui se liberatorem appellet.*[31]

This text's gross misrepresentation of the terms *Leo* and *Corax* suggest that its value is not to be over-estimated.[32] Moreover, as usual, we cannot tell what significance such a ritual incident might have taken on when set, as it surely must have been, into the context of a longer ceremony. But the account is interesting because it bears a

---

[31] '...have their hands tied with chicken's guts and are then pushed across a pit full of water; and then someone comes up with a sword and cuts through the guts, saying that he is their liberator', *Quaestiones veteris et novi testamenti* 114 (CSEL 50). See also Vermaseren 1963: 133f.

[32] Both Euboulus and Pallas however attest considerable interest in the fact that these grades are named after animals (ap. Porphyry, *On Abstinence* 4. 6. 3 Patillon-Segonds), so that Ambrosiaster's scorn surely picks up a well-known theme. Pits that could represent *foveae* are not quite unknown: Schatzmann 2004: 18f.

very general similarity to some of the panels from the mithraeum beneath S. Maria Capua Vetere discussed below. Here I want to note just three points.

a) The initiate is subjected to restriction upon his free movement and humiliation—also pain—by being pushed about with his hands bound behind his back. Such treatment recalls that of prisoners-of-war and condemned persons, for example on Antonine battle-sarcophagi, or the column of M. Aurelius (AD 180–92).[33] And, as ritual action, it is characteristic of 'transition' or 'liminal' rites (Van Gennep), which effect the initiand's symbolic transition from one status to another.

b) The bonds used, chicken-guts, are evidently 'symbolic': they are slimy and disgusting, but not really painful. The 'make-believe' aspect of ritual performance is clearly evident here, as is the challenge to common-sense ('Why chicken-guts?'), which impels subjective interpretation of meaning. This aspect of the ritual points away from actual experience towards the construction of primary meaning by the initiate. The significance of the ritual is hinted at in the liberator's announcement of his function or identity: *Ego sum liberator tuus.* Retrospectively, the pit becomes the Styx; the chicken-guts represent the toils of the Underworld or mortality (the cock being associated with Persephone and the Underworld);[34] the 'liberation' is freedom from the power of death; humiliation is a necessary precondition to salvation, just as this world is to another.

c) Although the violence is merely enacted, the implicit message of the ritual is that the asymmetry between 'liberator' and initiand has an exemplary, privileged status. The 'liberator' is in a position to bring the initiand into contact with the transcendent world, from which he (the initiand) can 'borrow' life. The 'liberator' can bestow this gift in the measure that he is empowered to subject the initiand to the violence of bondage and humiliation

---

[33] e.g. Neoptolemus sarcophagus from Via Collatina, Museo naz. delle Terme, c.162–65 AD; Column: Bianchi Bandinelli 1970: fig. 365 (barbarian prisoners being beheaded). Vermaseren (1971: 31) aptly cites panels on the Trajanic Adamklissi monument.

[34] Porphyry, *On Abstinence* 4. 16. 6 Patillon-Segonds.

(Bloch 1986: 188f.). All this the initiand can perceive and accept. But the most important wider achievement of ritual is not perceptible to the participants or actors, 'the way in which the hegemonic social order is appropriated as a redemptive process and reproduced' (Bell 1992: 110). The other rituals/ritual clusters I wish to discuss here may contribute to this issue.

Rituals of abasement

The mithraeum beneath the church of S.Maria Capua Vetere (not far from Naples) is unique in having relatively well-preserved frescoes depicting initiation on the fascias of the lateral podia, dating from the first half of the third century AD.[35] These frescoes, which consist of six panels on the right-hand podium (of which four are reasonably well-preserved), and seven on the left (only three of which are preserved), do not carry explanatory graffiti, and their role or intention is quite unclear. It is possible that they were intended as a sort of visual priestly book, that is, as a prescriptive account of rituals to be carried out, although without the corresponding verbal *symbola* they can have been of little use. Or they may be a commemoration for some reason of a particular initiation-series, perhaps of the donor.[36] But it is undecidable even whether the panels represent a sequence of rituals relating to a single grade, or an ideal series of moments from initiations for different grades. They certainly bear no close relation to any ritual transmitted to us by a literary source.[37] Vermaseren believed that they provide a sort of narrative sequence, moving from the right podium to the left, and from entrance to cult-niche, but this is extremely doubtful, as are many of his readings of what can be

[35] The original publication is Minto 1924. The most detailed, but not always satisfactory, account is Vermaseren 1971: 26–48. Because the frescoes cannot be reproduced in black and white, the relevant scenes are here shown in rough tracings based on Vermaseren's colour plates.

[36] There seems no doubt that these panels are somewhat later than the rest of the paintings in the mithraeum, which are mainly late Antonine. The podia themselves were enlarged in the Severan period.

[37] Horn 1994: 27f.; Clauss 2000: 102f. The late literary tradition, stemming from Gregory of Nazianzen in the fourth century (*oration* 4. 70), speaks of 'tests' involving cold, heat, fasting etc., but is in detail completely worthless.

made out on each panel. It is anyway not my intention here to discuss the possible content of the panels (which now seems a hopeless undertaking), but to explore the general structure of some of the moments of ritual. In each of the panels, the initiate is represented naked, again a characteristic feature of 'transition' or 'liminal' rituals.

Two of the four readable scenes on the right podium have structural analogies with Ambrosiaster's account, although there is no point in comparing them closely. In one, the initiand is stumbling forward, blind-folded, with his arms stretched out before him; a much taller figure, a mystagogue, stands behind him to guide him forward (Fig. 9.10).[38] In the next, the initiand is represented as

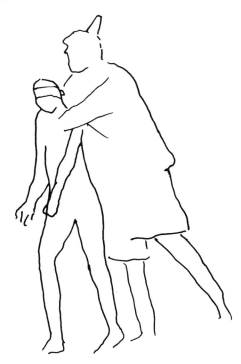

Fig. 9.10. Blindfolded, naked initiand being pushed forward by a mystagogue (right-hand podium, panel 1, S. Maria Capua Vetere mithraeum).

[38] Vermaseren 1971: 26f., panel I (Right), pl. XXI = Vermaseren 1956–60: no. 187.

Fig. 9.11. A Father approaching a blindfolded initiand with a lighted torch (right hand podium, panel 2, S. Maria Capua Vetere mithraeum).

kneeling, again blind-folded, with his hands bound behind his back (Fig. 9.11). An assistant, in a white tunic and short red cape, stands behind him with his right hand on his neck holding him firm while a larger, bearded, figure, splendidly dressed in cloak, mantle and Phrygian cap, presumably the Father, approaches threateningly with a lighted torch.[39]

All three readable panels on the left podium are similar in intent. In one, the initiand lies prostrate on the ground, surrounded by several indeterminate objects, of which only a scorpion can be made out for certain (Fig. 9.12). At least two figures surround the initiand, both doing something to him (the one on the right perhaps pointing a staff towards him) (Vermaseren 1971: 43f., Panel II (Left), pl. XXVI = Vermaseren 1956–60: no. 193). In the second, the initiand kneels on the ground with his hands outstretched, again with an assistant supporting or holding him, and the initiator, in a red cloak and a Phrygian cap, extends two ?torches towards him (Vermaseren

---

[39] Vermaseren 1971: 28–34, Panel II (Right), pl. XXII = Vermaseren 1956–60: no. 188. Vermaseren (1971: 28) expressly denies that the initiator is wearing a Phrygian cap, and claims to be able to see a helmet. He identifies the scene as a fire-test.

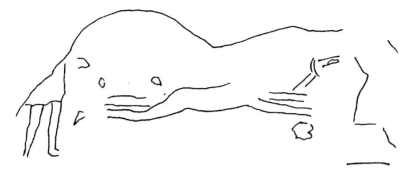

Fig. 9.12. An initiand lying prostrate on the ground, with mystagogues at his head and foot (left hand podium, panel 2, S. Maria Capua Vetere mithraeum).

1971: 44f., Panel III (Left), pl. XXVII = Vermaseren 1956–60: no. 195). In the last, the initiand kneels with his hands (?tied) behind his head, apparently held there by the assistant (Fig. 9.13). To the right, the Father seems to be indicating with his staff a round object lying on the ground.[40] The remaining two panels in which scenes can be made out may have a different, 'celebratory' character.[41]

The third ritual I wish to adduce here is similar in principle to those depicted on the podia of the Capua mithraeum. I have already invoked one face of the new cult-vessel from Mainz (p. 332). On the other, a Father, sitting on a chair, aims an armed bow (Fig. 9.14) at a naked young man, evidently an initiand, whose wrists seem to be bound, and who is evidently turning away in fear (Fig. 9.15). Behind the initiand is an assistant, who raises his right hand in a gesture which suggests that he is uttering a *symbolon* that links this enactment to the established body of Mithraic meanings. The similarity between this enactment and the well-known narrative scene in which

[40] Vermaseren 1971: 45–47, Panel IV (Left), pl. XXVIII = Vermaseren 1956–60: no. 194. Vermaseren's account of this scene is quite different and, I believe, largely fanciful. He claims that with one hand the initiand is offering a *rhyton* (drinking-cup) to the assistant behind him, while holding the other across his chest; and that the assistant is meanwhile pouring liquid from a little cup into the *rhyton*.

[41] Vermaseren 1971: Panel IV (Right), pl. XXIII = Vermaseren 1956–60: no. 190, ?ritual embrace; Panel V (Right), pl. XXV = Vermaseren 1956–60: no. 191, bestowal of victor's crown.

Fig. 9.13. A Father pointing with his staff at a ?loaf of bread lying beside a kneeling initiand (left hand podium, panel 4, S. Maria Capua Vetere mithraeum).

Mithras fires an arrow at a rock-face to release water, strongly suggests that the *symbolon* implied by the Mainz cult-vessel referred to that mythical event.[42] But in the present connection, the point to be emphasized is the sharp contrast between the Father and assistant on the one hand, and the anxious, naked initiand on the other.

*

The panels at Capua and the Mainz vessel do not depict rituals in any direct or unmediated sense. They depict arrested, perhaps idealized, moments within rituals, moments which could be claimed to have some special significance either for the donor or for the Mithraic

---

[42] Horn 1994: 23; 27f.; better: Beck 2000: 149–54; 167–71, on the bow itself as a symbol of harmony through opposites. Although Mithras is almost invariably on German monuments shown standing to shoot his bow, in the depictions of the scene on the Danube he generally sits on a rock. This fact, which I take to be a naturalistic representation of the Father's seated position in the ritual, suggests that the latter was not practised solely in Mainz, but also widely in the Danube area, and that the connection between myth and ritual was explicit; cf. Gordon 1998: 250.

Fig. 9.14. A Father seated and aiming his bow at an initiand on the Mainz cult-vessel.

community at large. As such, we may argue that they have done for us the work of sifting the oppositions which construct the actual rituals. Oppositions at any rate there certainly are. There is first the contrast between the sizes of the participants: the initiand is consistently presented as smaller than the assistants, who are in turn smaller and less magnificent than the officiants. Although the initiand is at the centre of each scene, the other, in this context more powerful, figures are visually dominant. The nakedness of the initiand is stressed by the tone of brick-red or brown used, contrasting with the 'purple' and white of the mystagogues. Then again, the officiants are bearded (as on the Mainz vessel), the initiand beardless, signalling a contrast between the

Fig. 9.15. The initiand, holding up his arms to protect himself.

ideal dignity of maturity and the prescriptive inferiority of the initiand's status (youth = socially less significant). We may also note the contrasts between kneeling, prostration, or (in the case of the Mainz vessel) shrinking away, and standing upright, which is often underlined by the bonds which confine the initiand's free movement. These contrasts are reinforced by the fact that the initiand is, at least in some panels, blindfolded and cannot see where he is going, a contrast that alludes to that between knowledge and ignorance. The Mainz vessel makes explicit another contrast which is not so evident at Capua, between self-command and anguish, fear or anxiety. These contrasts can be summarized as that between purposive agency and passive submission, between the free action of an agent and the enforced re-action of a subject.

These contrasts serve the same purpose as the rhetorical tropes of emphasis, such as anaphora, epizeuxis or ploche, and can be listed like Aristotle's list of Pythagorean contrasts:

full-sized	small
clothed	naked
bearded	beardless
standing	kneeling/prostrate/shrinking back
freely moving	bound
sighted	blind
self-controlled	anxious
knowledge	ignorance
purposive agency	passive reaction

The sheer number of these correlated oppositions gives the initi- and a loose sense of totality, as though these were the significant terms of which the world is constructed, above all, in terms of domination and subordination.

The anthropologist Catherine Bell has recently attempted in her *Ritual Theory, Ritual Practice* to escape from what she sees as the unhelpful opposition between thought and action characteristic of traditional views of ritual, which see the latter as conveying by symbolic means a specific idea.[43] She prefers to concentrate on the notion of ritualization, a social strategy for privileging valued dis- tinctions: 'Acting ritually is first and foremost a matter of nuanced contrasts and the evocation of strategic, value-laden distinctions' (p. 90). These evocations are primarily conveyed by the role of the body in ritual: the implicit end of ritualization is production of a 'ritualized body'. Ritual practices construct an environment in space and time that is organized according to schemes of privileged oppos- itions. Although in the course of a ritual performance many such oppositions may be evoked, a few come tacitly to dominate. These

---

[43] Bell 1992: 88–117. Her work is extremely dense, and I can here only render it in a very superficial manner. See also her textbook (Bell 1997).

oppositions are internalized through performance of ritual into the ritualized body. 'Through the orchestration in time of loosely and effectively homologized oppositions in which some gradually come to dominate others, the social body reproduces itself in the image of the symbolically schematized environment that has been simultaneously established' (p. 110).

The Mithraic representations show very clearly the way in which a number of correlated oppositions can be made to provide the skeleton of an entire ritual complex which impresses itself upon the social body of the subject. Bell rightly insists that the body is central. 'Kneeling does not merely *communicate* subordination to the kneeler. For all intents and purposes, kneeling produces a subordinate kneeler in and through the act itself.'[44] This point should motivate us to look at the Mithraic images with special attention, noting their insistence on the overwhelming authority and power accorded the mystagogues, and the implied dependence and humiliation of the initiand.[45] These rituals impressed onto the initiand's body the experience of insignificance, confinement, helplessness, fear, in such a way that they became for the subject not a mere charade, which is generally how such ritual events in antiquity are regarded, nor a purely private memory, but part of his social body. The subject enacts subordination in its most abject form, just as the initiators enact domination in a free and untrammelled form.

But Bell is equally concerned to suggest how ideological commitments implicit in the religious sphere might be effective also in the world outside, how the realm of the sacred leaks into the profane. Drawing on Bourdieu and Foucault, therefore, she argues further that, because the ritualized body is also the individual's social body, the oppositions once imposed can be transposed into other sociocultural situations beyond that of the ritual itself. The schemes implicit in the movement of bodies in ritual are reabsorbed, taken on, by the participants as real, and defining (Bell 1992: 99; Blacking 1987). It is the individual's social body which on the one hand projects the organizing oppositions onto the space-time environment,

---

[44] Bell 1992: 100; cf. Rappaport 1999: 276: 'When an actor performs a liturgical order he participates in it, which is to say he becomes part of it...'.
[45] Particularly if Vermaseren (1971) is correct to see a scorpion beside the prostrate initiand in panel 2 Left (Fig. 12).

but also re-absorbs them as the 'nature of reality', as natural givens. Once absorbed, the structured oppositions condition both the day-to-day behaviour of those who have passed through the rituals, and feeds back into their conception of how ritual ought to look if it is to be effective. A pattern of value and behaviour thus comes into being, which re-deploys the patterns once acquired in ritual experience in other contexts. This is a theoretical, and necessarily very general, non-specific, account of how the make-believe, or enacted, world of ritual comes to have an effect in the world of daily behaviour and existential value.

This emphasis on the role of the body as mediating between the world of ritual and the world of everyday life makes Bell's account attractive to anyone who is compelled to discuss ritual behaviour exclusively on the basis of iconography or brief accounts by hostile or tendentious sources, as we are in the case of the Mysteries of Mithras. For these sources provide us with distortions of the reality they report. Whatever the precise history of their origin, which is likely to remain indefinitely a matter of dispute,[46] the Mysteries emerged in a world already steeply stratified and hierarchized. They developed a more complex and explicit account of the cosmos than the other 'oriental cults', and to this complexity there corresponded a system of initiation, which, as far as the majority of initiates were concerned, deferred the revelation of a central 'secret' indefinitely. No other mystery cult, so far as we know, deferred revelation in this way.[47] Correlated with deferred revelation was the grade-system, which was the organizational expression of this restrictive attitude towards knowledge (and doubtless salvation). By means of this organizational structure, the Mysteries were able to turn what in other mystery cults was a single idea or claim into a diffuse, ramified system of ideas centred on a number of key cosmological oppositions. This oppositional structure was repeated in the cult's ethical teaching, which, at least in the case of the Lions, sharply contrasted negative and positive moral values,[48] and in its social teaching, above all in its exclusion of women (Gordon 1980: 42–64).

---

[46] For some recent theories, see Beck 1998: Gordon 2001.

[47] The case at Eleusis cannot be understood as a genuine deferral in this sense: Dowden 1980.

[48] The clearest case is Porphyry, *On the Cave of the Nymphs* 15; cf. now Álvar 2008: 194–9, who also discusses the implications of the late fourth-century frescoes in the

The stress of Mithraic initiations upon a set of oppositions exemplifying domination and subordination is thus perfectly consonant with a whole pattern of contrasts within the cult. Within the cult, these initiations were linked to the promise of well-being, salvation, knowledge, transcendence. The bodily experience of humiliation and subjugation was inextricably bound up with the promise of redemption, just as the power of the initiators was perceived as redemptive. The connection between humiliation, deference, and redemption is neatly expressed in one of the panels at Capua which I have not discussed here, in which the kneeling, naked initiand, whose hands are no longer bound, receives a crown(?) from a mystagogue standing behind him and whom he cannot see.[49]

But this elective association in the Mysteries in fact reproduces in its own idiom the much wider and more abstract claim made by the Roman state to be responsible, in the person of the sacrificial emperor, for the well-being, the redemption, of the entire population of the Empire. The Mithraic ritual, we might say, reproduces in miniature the grand alchemy whereby the repressive apparatus of the Roman state, with its infliction of large-scale violence, both military and in relation to criminal justice, both in the amphitheatre and in the slave *familia*, is justified by the emperor's key role in the maintenance of the *pax deorum* (Gordon 1990).

What the initiand subjectively feels is that this social order based upon deference and subjugation of the inferior is right and proper, indeed redemptive; and he responds by dedicating his votive in honour of Mithras thankfully *in honorem domus divinae, devotus numini maiestatique eius, pro salute d.n.imp....., pro sal. Augg. nn.,* or *num. aug.*[50] Religious crisis occurs when this type of deference and self-humiliation begin to lose their redemptive value. Redemption

---

mithraeum at Hawarte, near Apamea in Syria. For a report on, and good colour photos of, these, see Gawlikowski 2007.

[49] Vermaseren 1971: Panel V (Right), pl. XXV, cited n. 41 above.

[50] 'To the glory of the Imperial House', 'dedicated to his godhead and majesty', 'for the protection by the gods of Our Lord the Emperor', 'for the protection by the gods of our Augusti', '(To the) divine power of the emperor(s)'. See the list in Clauss 1990b: 441–50.

must then be sought elsewhere, in the repression of desire, or in the radical rejection of this world.

AFTERWORD 2009

I have discussed the same theme with more exclusive focus on the initiation-scenes of the podium-frescoes at S. Maria Capua Vetere in a paper originally delivered at a conference on religious cult in Magna Graecia held in 2002 at the Villa Vergiliana at Cuma near Naples, whose proceedings have now appeared (Gordon 2009). In that version, which also revisits the Capuan frescoes in some archaeological detail, I explore the Mithraic themes of humiliation and suffering in terms of M. Foucault's work (1975) on punishment and some suggestions by Brent Shaw (1996) on the place of endurance under suffering in early Christianity. Otherwise, despite the major interest in the Christian body, little interest has been shown in this specific topic: the lure of the riddles of Mithraic theology is irresistible.

Since this paper was written, there has been some further discussion of the exclusion of women from the cult, which certainly has implications for the Mithraic understanding of the body. Almost all the archaeological 'evidence' cited in a very poor article by David (2000), has rightly been dismissed by Griffith (2006), but her arguments simply reinforce the point that women were not admitted into the cult, whatever marginal place might be found for female deities in cult (or rather iconography). The traditional view of exclusion, which I support, has been very competently re-affirmed by Aleš Chalupa (2005). Note also the remarks of Alvar (2008), who rightly stresses the album from Virunum in Noricum (*AE* 1994: no. 1334), which lists the names of 99 members of a Mithraic group in that town admitted between AD 183 and 201, among which there is not a single female name. I would also highlight his conclusion (p. 202):

Part of the cult's appeal was its masculine exclusiveness, which favoured the development of a specifically male ethic of aesceticism, an ethic fitted for those for whom the sentimentalization of marriage held no attraction.

BIBLIOGRAPHY

Alföldy, G. (1975). *Römische Sozialgeschichte*. Wiesbaden: Steiner.

Alvar, J. (2001/2008). *Los Misterios: religiones 'orientales' en el imperio romano* (Barcelona: Crítica), now in a revised English translation (2008): *Romanising Oriental Gods: Myth, Salvation and Ethics in the Cults of Cybele, Isis and Mithras*, RGRW 165. Leiden: Brill.

——Blánquez, C. and Wagner C. G. (eds.) (1995). *Ritual y conciencia civica en el Mundo antiguo: Homenaje a F. Gascó*, ARYS 7. Madrid.

Bailey, F. G. (1971). *Gifts and Poison: The Politics of Reputation*. Oxford: Blackwell.

Beard, M. (1989). 'Accia Larentia Gains a Son: Myths and Priesthood at Rome', in M. M. MacKenzie and C. Roueché (eds.), *Images of Authority: Papers for Joyce Reynolds*, Cambridge Philological Society, Supplement 16. Cambridge: Cambridge Philological Society, 41–61.

Beard, M. and North, J. A. (eds.) (1990). *Pagan Priests*. London: Duckworth.

Becatti, G. (1954). *Scavi di Ostia, 2: I Mitrei*. Rome: Libreria del Stato.

Beck, R. L. (1998). 'The Mysteries of Mithras: A New Account of their Genesis', *JRS*, 88: 115–28.

——(2000). 'Ritual, Myth, Doctrine and Initiation in the Mysteries of Mithras: New Evidence from a Cult-vessel', *JRS*, 90: 145–80.

Bell, C. (1992). *Ritual Theory, Ritual Practice*. New York and Oxford: Oxford University Press.

——(1997). *Ritual: Perspectives and Dimensions*. New York and London: Oxford University Press.

Bendlin, A. (1998). 'Peripheral Centres—Central Peripheries: Religious Communication in the Roman Empire', in H. Cancik and J. Rüpke (eds.), *Römische Reichsreligion und Provinzialreligion*. Tübingen: Mohr Siebeck, 35–68.

——(2000). 'Looking Beyond the Civic Compromise: Religious Pluralism in Late-Republican Rome', in E. Bispham and C. Smith (eds.), *Religion in Archaic and Republican Rome and Italy*. Edinburgh: Edinburgh University Press, 115–35.

Bianchi Bandinelli, R. (1970). *Rome the Centre of Power*. London: Thames and Hudson.

Blacking, J. (1987). 'Towards an Anthropology of the Body', in J. Blacking (ed.), *The Anthropology of the Body*. London: Academic Press, 1–28.

Bloch, M. (1986). *From Blessing to Violence: History and Ideology in the Circumcision Ritual of the Merina of Madagascar*. Cambridge; New York: Cambridge University Press.

Bourdieu, P. (1979). *La distinction: critique sociale du jugement.* Paris: Les Éditions de Minuit.

Brashear, W. (1992). *A Mithraic Catechism from Egypt*, Tyche Supplement-band 1. Vienna: Holzhausens Nfg.

Brown, P. R. L. (1992). *Power and Persuasion in Late Antiquity: Towards a Christian Empire.* Madison, Wis.: University of Wisconsin Press.

Chalupa, A. (2005). 'Hyenas or Lionesses? Mithraism and Women in the Religious World of Late Antiquity', *Religio* (Brno), 2: 199–230.

Clauss, M. (1990a). 'Die Sieben Grade des Mithras-Kultes', *ZPE*, 82: 183–94.

——(1990b). 'Sol invictus Mithras', *Athenaeum*, 78: 423–50.

——(1999). *Kaiser und Gott: Herrscherkult im römischen Reich.* Stuttgart and Leipzig: Teubner.

——(2000). *The Roman Cult of Mithras: The God and his Mysteries.* Edinburgh: Edinburgh University Press. = Eng, trans. of *Mithras: Kult und Mysterien.* Munich: Beck.

Clavel-Lévêque, M. (1972). 'Le syncrétisme gallo-romaine, structures et finalités', in F. Sartori (ed.), *Praelectiones Patavinae*, Università Padova, Pubbl. Ist. di Storia antica, 9. Rome: 'L'Erma' di Bretschneider, 51–134.

Couliano I. P. [sic], (1994). 'The Mithraic Ladder Revisited', in Hinnells 1994: 75–91.

Cumont, F. (1975). 'The Dura Mithraeum', in Hinnells 1975: i. 151–214.

David, J. (2000). 'The Exclusion of Women in the Mithraic Mysteries: Ancient or Modern?', *Numen*, 47: 121–41.

Dowden, K. (1980). 'Grades in the Eleusinian Mysteries', *Revue de l'histoire des religions*, 197: 409–27.

Ferrua, A. (1940). 'Il mitreo sotto la chiesa di S. Prisca', *Bullettino della Commissione archeologica comunale di Roma*, 68: 59–70.

Février, P.-A. (1976). 'Religion et domination dans l'Afrique romaine', *Dialogues d'histoire ancienne*, 2: 305–63.

Fishwick, D. (1987–92). *The Imperial Cult in the Latin West: Studies in the Ruler Cult in the Western Provinces of the Roman Empire*, EPRO 108. Leiden: Brill.

Forbis, E. P. (1996). *Municipal Virtues in the Roman Empire: The Evidence of Roman Honorary Inscriptions*, Beiträge zur Altertumskunde 79. Stuttgart and Leipzig: Teubner.

Forrer, R. (1915). *Das Mithra-Heiligtum von Königshoffen bei Straßburg.* Stuttgart: Kohlhammer.

Foucault M. (1975/7). *Surveiller et punir: Naissance de la prison.* Paris: Gallimard. = Eng. trans. (1977) *Discipline and Punish: The Birth of the Prison.* London: Allen Lane.

Francis, D. (1975). 'Mithraic Grafffiti from Dura-Europos', in Hinnells 1975: ii. 406–45.

Garland, R. L. (1982). 'Religious Authority in Archaic and Classical Greece', *Annual of the British School at Athens*, 77: 125–76.

Garnsey, P. D. A. and Saller, R. P. (1987). *The Roman Empire: Economy, Society and Culture*. London: Duckworth.

Gascó, F. (1995). 'Evérgetas, fiestas y conciencia cívica en las ciudades griegas de época Imperial', in Alvar et al. 1995: 165–70.

Gawlikowski, M. (2007). 'The Mithraeum at Hawarte and its Paintings', *JRA*, 20: 337–61.

Gesche, H. (1978). 'Die Divinisierung der römischen Kaiser in ihrer Funktion als Herrschaftslegitimation', *Chiron*, 8: 374–90.

Gordon, R. L. (1980). 'Reality, Evocation and Boundary in the Mysteries of Mithras', *Journal of Mithraic Studies*, 3: 19–99, reprinted in R. L. Gordon, *Image and Value in the Graeco–Roman World: Studies in Mithraism and Religious Art*. Aldershot: Variorum (1996).

——(1990). 'The Veil of Power: Emperors, Sacrificers and Benefactors', in Beard and North 1990: 201–31.

——(1994). 'Mystery, Metaphor and Doctrine in the Mysteries of Mithras', in Hinnells 1994: 103–24.

——(1998). 'Viewing Mithraic Art: The Altar from Burginatium (Kalkar), Germania Inferior', *ARYS*, 1: 27–58.

——(2001). '*Persei sub rupibus antri*: Überlegungen zur Entstehung der Mithrasmysterien', in *Ptuj im römischen Reich/Mithraskult und seine Zeit*. Archaeologia Poetovionensis 2 (Ptuj), 289–301.

——(2009). 'The Mithraic Body: The Example of the Capua Mithraeum', in P. A. Johnston and G. Casadio (eds.), *The Cults of Magna Graecia*. Austin, TX: Texas University Press, 290–313.

Griffith, A. (2006). 'Completing the Picture: Women and the Female Principle in the Mithraic Cult', *Numen*, 53: 48–77.

Hinnells, J. R. (ed.) (1975). *Mithraic Studies*. Manchester: Manchester University Press.

——(ed.) (1994). *Studies in Mithraism*, Storia delle Religioni 9. Rome: 'L'Erma' di Bretschneider.

Horn, G. (1994). 'Der Mainzer Kultgefäß', *Mainzer Archäologische Zeitschrift*, 1: 21–66.

Kierdorf, W. (1986). '"Funus" und "consecratio". Zur Terminologie und Ablauf der kaiserlichen Apotheose', *Chiron*, 16: 43–69.

Lane Fox, R. (1986). *Pagans and Christians*. London: Viking.

Letto, C. (1988). *s.v.* 'Helios/Sol', in *LIMC*, 4: 592–625.

Lozano, A. (1995). 'Vida política y fiestas religiosas en Estratonicea de Caria', in Alvar et al. 1995: 139–53.

MacCormack, S. G. (1981). *Art and Ceremony in Late Antiquity.* Berkeley, CA: University of California Press.

MacMullen, R. (1981). *Paganism in the Roman Empire.* New Haven, CT: Yale University Press.

Merquior, J. G. (1979). *The Veil and the Mask: Essays on Culture and Ideology.* London: Routledge and Kegan Paul.

Millar, F. (1977). *The Emperor in the Roman World.* London: Duckworth.

Minto, A. (1924). 'S. Maria Capua Vetere, scoperta di una cripta mitriaca', *Notizie dei Scavi*, Ser. 5. 21: 353–74.

Mitthof, F. (1992). 'Der Vorstand der Kultgemeinden des Mithras: eine Sammlung und Untersuchung der inschriftlichen Zeugnisse', *Klio*, 74: 275–90.

Muir, E. (1981). *Civic Ritual in Renaissance Venice.* Princeton, NJ: Princeton University Press.

——(1997). *Ritual in Early Modern Europe.* Cambridge and New York: Cambridge University Press.

Nollé, M. (1992). *Denkmäler vom Satrapensitz Daskyleion.* Berlin: Akademie Verlag.

Parisinou, E. (2000). *The Light of the Gods: The Role of Light in Archaic and Classical Greek Cult.* London: Duckworth.

Petry, F. and Kern, E. (1978). 'Un mithraeum à Biesheim (Haut-Rhein)', *Cahiers Alsaciens d'Archéologie et d'Histoire*, 21: 4–32.

Piccottini, G. (1994). *Mithrastempel in Virunum.* Klagenfurt: Verlag des Geschichtsvereines für Kärnten.

Price, S. R. F. (1980). 'Between Man and God: Sacrifice in the Roman Imperial Cult', *JRS*, 70: 28–43.

——(1984). *Rituals and Power: The Roman Imperial Cult in Asia Minor.* Cambridge: Cambridge University Press.

——(1987). 'From Noble Funerals to Divine Consecration', in D. Cannadine and S. R. F. Price (eds.), *Rituals of Royalty: Power and Ceremonial in Traditional Societies.* Cambridge: Cambridge University Press, 56–105.

Quet, M.-H. (1981). 'Remarques sur la place de la fête dans les discours des moralistes grecs et dans l'éloge des cités et des évergètes aux premiers siècles de l'Empire', in *La fête: pratique et discours.* Paris: Presses universitaires de Franche-comté, 41–84.

Rappaport, R. (1999). *Ritual and Religion in the Making of Humanity.* Cambridge: Cambridge University Press.

Rebenich, S. (2000). 'Vom dreizehnten Gott zum dreizehnsten Apostel?: Der tote Kaiser in der Spätantike', *Zeitschrift für Antikes Christentum*, 4: 300–24.

Rice, E. E. (1983). *The Grand Procession of Ptolemy Philadelphus*. Oxford: Oxford University Press.

Roll, I. (1977). 'The Mysteries of Mithras in the Roman Orient', *Journal of Mithraic Studies*, 2.1: 53–68.

Roniger, L. (1983). 'Modern Patron-Client Relations and Historical Clientelism: Some Clues from Ancient Republican Rome', *Archives européennes de Sociologie*, 24: 63–95.

Rostovtzeff, M. I., Brown, F. E., and Welles, C. B. (1939). *The Excavations at Dura-Europos: Preliminary Report of the Seventh and Eighth Seasons, 1933–4, 1934–5*. New Haven, CT: Yale University Press.

Sahlins, M. (1974). *Stone-Age Economics*. London: Tavistock Publications.

Schatzmann, A. (2004). 'Möglichkeiten und Grenzen einer funktionellen Typographie von Mithrasheiligtümern', in M. Martens and G. de Boe (eds.), *Roman Mithraism: The Evidence of the Small Finds*, Archeologie in Vlaanderen, Monografie 4. Brussels: Instituut voor het Archeologisch Patrimonium/Museum het Toreke, 1–24.

Schmitt Pantel, P. (1992). *La cité au banquet: histoire des repas publics dans les cités grecques*, Collection de l'École française de Rome 157. Rome: École française de Rome.

Schwertheim, E. (1974). *Die Denkmäler orientalischer Gottheiten im römischen Deutschland*, EPRO 40. Leiden: Brill.

Shaw, B. (1996). 'Body/Power/Identity: The Passion of the Martyrs', *Journal of Early Christian Studies*, 4.3: 269–312.

Small, A. (ed.) (1996). *Subject and Ruler: The Cult of the Ruling Power in Classical Antiquity*, JRA Supplement 17. Ann Arbor, MI: Journal of Roman Archaeology.

Turcan, R. (1975). *Mithras platonicus: recherches sur l'hellénisation philosophique de Mithra*, EPRO 47. Leiden: Brill.

——(1996). 'La promotion du sujet par le culte du souverain', in Small 1996: 51–62.

——(1999). 'Hiérarchie sacerdotale et astrologie dans les mystères de Mithra', in *La science des cieux: sages, mages astrologues*, Res orientales 12. Bures-sur-Yvette: Groupe pour l'étude de la civilisation du Moyen-Orient (GECMO), 249–61.

Vermaseren, M. J. (1956–60). *Corpus Inscriptionum et Monumentorum Religionis Mithriacae*. 2 vols. The Hague: Nijhoff.

——(1963). *Mithras, the Secret God*. London: Chatto and Windus.

——(1971). *Mithriaca 1: the Mithraeum at S. Maria Capua Vetere.* EPRO 16.1. Leiden: Brill.

——and van Essen, C. C. (1965). *The Excavations in the Mithraeum of the Church of Santa Prisca, Rome.* Leiden: Brill.

Wallace-Hadrill, A. (ed.) (1989). *Patronage in Ancient Society.* London and New York: Routledge.

Woolf, G. (2000). 'The Religious History of the Northwestern Provinces', *JRA*, 13: 615–30 [review of T. Derks, *Gods, Temples and Religious Practices: The Transformation of Religious Ideas and Values in Roman Gaul.* Amsterdam Archaeological Studies 2. Amsterdam: Amsterdam University Press (1998)].

Yalouris, N. (1990). *s.v.* 'Helios', in *LIMC* 5: 1005–34.

10

Community and Community

Reflections on Some Ambiguities Based on the Thiasoi *of Roman Egypt*

John Scheid

In his dissertation, the young Theodor Mommsen made a distinction between two kinds of association in the Roman world, professional colleges and religious associations.[1] The second category concerned associations of lowly people (*collegia tenuiorum*) who organized themselves under the patronage of a deity, either for charitable ends or in order to guarantee their members a burial, a funeral, and a funerary cult. Frequently taken up since and developed by specialists of the colleges, this conception has recently been called into question, notably by the work of Ausbüttel (1982: 22–33). One outcome of this reassessment is that the *collegia tenuiorum* correspond, in the language of the Early Empire jurists, to colleges of *humiliores*, as opposed to *honestiores*. Another is that the distinction established on the basis of line 12 of the constitution of the college of Diana and Antinous (*ILS* no. 7212) between professional colleges and funerary colleges, precisely these colleges of the poor, does not hold. For as shown some time ago now by Joyce and Arthur Gordon (1964: 61–8), the lacunae at the beginning of the lines are more important than had been thought, and on line 12 we should read

---

[1] Mommsen 1843: 87–106. In a similar vein, see Boissier 1906: 238–304; and with slight differences, Waltzing 1885–1900: i, 141–60. See also the comments of Kloppenborg 1996: 21–3. The study by Bowersock 1999 is also useful.

C]RA (*sac]ra*), instead of ERA (*fun]era*).[2] In fact, all colleges had attachments to deities and religious duties, regardless of whether they were professional, functional, or otherwise. Independently of this fact, some of these colleges would carry out the last honours of their members.[3]

Yet Mommsen's distinction seems to re-emerge in different apparel through a new conception that would apply particularly to Roman Egypt. In this hub of Christian monasticism, existed, according to Wipszucka (1970) 'groups of people who joined together and accepted a certain form of organization in order to lead a communal religious life, but without breaking their ties with the "world" '. Distinct from monastic brotherhoods, these religious associations have been related to earlier Egyptian associations by Muszynski (1977: 145–74). 'Appearing in the course of the 26th dynasty, these brotherhoods (*shnt*)', are seen as 'an Egyptian creation, perhaps translating the population's desire to affirm its cultural identity in the face of the influx of foreigners, more or less on mass, into the Valley of the Nile, and its bewilderment before an archaistic religion that was unable to provide the answers to its most deeply felt aspirations' (Muszynski 1977: 160–1 and 159).

This dialectical reconstruction, which can be directly traced back to Romantic idealism,[4] is in itself enough to reveal the Christian bias inherent in this kind of approach towards the Egyptian associations. Indeed, questions might be asked about the reality of the supposed bewilderment on the part of the Egyptians before their 'archaistic religion'.[5] The same reaction is attributed by the moderns to the Greeks and Romans of the Classical and Hellenistic periods. However, as with the polytheistic ritualism of Egypt, this negative reaction results essentially from a misunderstanding of ritualism, and from the reduction of all religions to an internalized religion centred on the salvation of the soul. Be that as it may, for Muszynski, the arrival

[2] On lines 11 and 12, according to Ausbüttel 1982: 27, we should therefore read: *qui stipem menstruam conferre uo(lent ad facienda sa'cra*, 'who wish to contribute a monthly sum for the performance of rites'.

[3] Ausbüttel 1982: 27–9. For all these reasons, there is no sense in pursuing the 'Mommsenian' distinction and seeing the early Christians as funerary colleges (29).

[4] Cf. Scheid 1987; Durand and Scheid 1994.

[5] It is useful with regard to this problem to consult Frankfurter 1998: 23–7.

of the Greeks and Ptolemies brought only minor changes. 'Religious associations', thus understood as voluntary associations with religious ends, would have nothing in common with 'professional associations', which for their part would be purely Greek (Muszynski 1977: 161). Here the expression of Egyptian 'spirituality', there the manifestation of Greek ritualism. The proximity of these two types of association is nonetheless seen to have caused 'contamination', and so little by little, between the second century BC and the third century AD, the professional associations took on the guise of brotherhoods (Muszynski 1977: 162). In other words, it is effectively impossible to locate the category defined by Muszynski from among the mass of Graeco–Roman associations. Muszynski skates over this reconstruction and the problems to which it gives rise so as to come to his primary concern, which is to uncover in the religious associations of the later period their monastic predecessors, even if these earlier associations did not in any way involve asceticism, celibacy, communal possessions, or the reclusive life.[6]

There can be no doubt that the question of associations in Roman Egypt needs to be approached differently. First of all, neither in Egypt nor elsewhere in the Roman world can such a distinction be made between religious associations strictly devoted to religious life and professional associations with purely secular ends. This historiographical myth has long since been deconstructed by work as diverse as that of Jean-Pierre Waltzing (1895–1900), Arthur Darby Nock (1972), and the recent volumes published by Onno Van Nijf (1997) and John Kloppenborg and Stephen Wilson (1996). There is little point repeating here what these authors have admirably established. Rather, I shall give a brief summary of current positions, before adding a few words on the 'voluntary' association and on the social consequences arising from the existence of *thiasoi* and colleges.

Gaston Boissier had already observed that 'each time isolated individuals grouped together to form an association, they gathered around the same altar; the deity worshipped there would become the focal point of the new society and its common bond, usually giving it

---

[6] Muszynski 1977: 162–3. The list of associations, however, given by Muszynski in an appendix is most useful.

its name.[7] As in the cities, the deity or deities in question were like members of this community, and part of the activities of the group concerned was to venerate them and invoke their presence through rites, for these deities served, in a way, as the supreme guarantee, reference, and patron for the community. This did not make the city a religious institution, and so to with the *thiasos* or college. The cultic bond of the association, the somewhat banal inscription of every kind of community within a religious framework, the association of one or several deities with every human gathering: all this amply demonstrates that the distinction established by Muszynski does not exist. There are no religious associations as distinct from other associations.[8] Making a distinction between associations that are purely secular or operating under a different 'guise', and 'religious' associations where the deity or deities are supposed to occupy a central place in the group, in order to recognize in these 'religious' communities the direct ancestors of monastic communities, strikes me as entirely artificial.

For everything that is attributed to 'religious' associations could also apply to professional associations, be they domestic or funerary. And the fact that certain groups closely connected with the cult of a deity, like the *pastophori* of the cult of Isis,[9] make up a college is not enough for them to be described as 'religious associations': they form a group in order to be present in communal life, not for religious reasons. The type of organization adopted by the *pastophori* is the same as any organization of citizens or peregrines wishing to be present in communal life. And whatever the 'indigenous' background and historical origin of a certain association—generally impossible to define with any clarity—the form it took was that of the Graeco–Roman associations. This form, and this form alone, is nearly always discernable. It is certainly important not to mistake form for content, or in a judicial sense, procedure for the individual case: colleges or *thiasoi* may well bear deep within them the kind of religious organizations sought by Muszynski, but the sources left behind by such

---

[7] Boissier 1891: 416; Boissier 1906: 266; Waltzing 1895–1990: i. 195–9.
[8] See also Kloppenborg and Wilson 1996: 5–7 and 13 and Bowersock 1999.
[9] Cf. also, for Egypt itself, de Cenival 1969.

organizations do not grant access to this background. The very most one can say here is that the function of the associations can vary in size and scope. An association of cereal traders has other activities besides the cult of Ceres or Vulcan that forms the crux of its organization, whilst the Mithraic association of such and such a place appears only to be dedicated to the cult of Mithra. But this is where one can go wrong. A venerable association of traders, for instance, may well have lost its professional function some time ago and been reduced to a brilliant association of notables.[10] By the same token, a Mithraic association may quite conceivably be a body that in a given area allows the followers of Mithra to exist in law and enjoy effective self-administration. It is nonetheless possible for this association in fact to bring together the local customs officers, like at Vratnik in Dalmatia, for example, the headquarters of the Illyricum customs (Beskov 1980). Likewise, the Isiac *pastophori* of Rome were initially a vehicle for families trading at Delos (Coarelli 1984).

A recent series of inscriptions dating from the time of the Empire and coming from the area around the temple of Hatshepsut at Deir el-Bahri, provides a good example of the everyday character of the associations, even in the cult sites, and of the ambiguity of the sources. Four inscriptions painted into the niche of a chapel of Amenhotep and Imhotep preserve the memory of the cultic gatherings of a 'college of ironworkers from Hermonthis' ($\pi\lambda\hat{\eta}\theta\text{os}$ $\sigma\iota\delta\eta\rho\text{ovp}\gamma\hat{\omega}\nu$ $'E\rho\mu\acute{\omega}\nu\theta\epsilon\text{os}$), which were punctuated by the sacrifice of donkeys and by banquets (Lajtar 1991). The earliest inscription dates from AD 324, but the institution appears to be older. Details concerning the professional activity of the 'ironworkers of Hermonthis' are still unknown; by contrast, their religious activities, and in particular their visits to the temple of Deir el-Bahri are minutely described in the inscriptions. It was during these visits that they sacrificed a donkey. The sacrificer would sometimes be the 'guardian of the donkey' ($\dot{o}\nu\eta\lambda\acute{a}\tau\eta\text{s}$) (in 324; *SEG* 1991: no. 1612, line 8), and sometimes the 'secretary' ($\gamma\rho\alpha\mu\mu\alpha\tau\epsilon[\acute{v}\text{s}]$) of

---

[10] Such is the case for the colleges of *fabri* or of *dendrophori*, for example, whose original purposes are still somewhat unclear.

the association (for example in 333/4 or 347/8; *SEG* 1991: no. 1613, line 9). After the sacrifice, the ironworkers would pay homage to the gods ($\pi\rho o\sigma\kappa\acute{v}\nu\eta\mu a \ldots \acute{\epsilon}\pi o\acute{\iota}[\eta\sigma a\nu]$; *SEG* 1991: no. 1612, line 9). From the citation of a brewer ($\xi\upsilon\tau o\pi(o\iota\acute{o}s)$), it can be deduced that the celebration equally comprised a ritual banquet (*SEG* 1991: no. 1612, line 5). Unlike these 'ironworkers of Hermonthis', whose only known activities relate to their cult, the *thiasos* of Zeus *Hypsistos* at Philadelphia (Nock 1933) is as far as we know not concerned with religious matters. These examples, which are far from isolated, are enough to show that such superficial judgments lead nowhere. It makes no sense to consider the ironworkers of Hermonthis as a professional college and the *thiasos* of Zeus *Hypsistos* as a religious association.

A number of parallel cases could be cited, both in the Greek-speaking world and the Latin West. Let us take another example. If, at a different social and political level, the colleges of Roman public priests are organized *as* colleges, it is not because they aspired to a more elevated communal life, but because all magistrates, quasi-magistrates, and more generally those who carried out a public function, already had this status. The *pontifices* and *flamines* would form a college so as to be able to act collectively within the traditional legal framework, just as the ushers of the pontiffs and *flamines* would be brought together in a college. And the college headquarters stood on public premises, the *regia*, situated at the southernmost limit of the Roman forum, which was also home to the official headquarters of the pontiffs. Subject to a certain number of rules that may recall the life of later monastic communities, and living together in a house, the six Vestal Virgins belonged in equal measure, officially, to the pontifical college, in the same way as the *flamines* (Wissowa 1912: 503–4). Their public organization needs to be distinguished from their cultic community and ritual functions. To see them, however, on the basis of the close attachment to the goddess Vesta that their name attests, as a pious community, like that of nuns, would be a mistake (Schilling 1961). To repeat: whether or not indicated by its name, every college had an attachment to one or more deities and to certain religious duties, and this is not sufficient evidence for these communities to be considered as early monasteries.

The example of ancient Dionysian *thiasoi* might be invoked here as a way of approaching another type of religious community.[11] At the same time, it should be noted that in the period that concerns us, *thiasos* is a term that far exceeds Dionysian 'mysticism'.[12] In particular, the Bacchic *thiasoi* that we know about seem more like associations of members of the elite than individuals in search of a new connection with the deity (Hanoune 1986, Moretti 1986, and Scheid 1986).

A firm resolution must be made, then, to separate the communal structure from the religious phenomenon as such, and there is no point trying to locate the origins of certain Judaeo–Christian religious customs in the *thiasoi* of Graeco–Roman colleges. The real question, rather, concerns the 'temporal' structure of Jewish, Christian and Manichaean communities. We might ask whether they were organized as colleges, and what might have been the consequences of this kind of organization?

The volume edited by John S. Kloppenborg and Stephen G. Wilson replies to these questions at length. The Canadian group under their direction was also interested in the present-day problem of sects and

[11] See the comments of Cazanove 1986: 9–11.

[12] *Oxford Classical Dictionary* 1996, s.v. 'Thiasos'. As a case in point, we know of the *thiasos* of worshippers of Heracles of Tyre, at Delos, in 54/53 BC (Bruneau 1970: 622) (the *thiasos* [θίασος] in question is also called an association [κοινόν]); still at Delos, the members of the association of the worshippers of Poseidon are called members of a *thiasos*, with at their head a 'chief member of the *thiasos*' (Bruneau 1970: 629), and the Dionysian association of the Ἀμειοιχεῦται is called 'association' (σύνοδος) or *thiasos* (θίασος) (Bruneau 1970: 631). In Cyprus, around 250 BC, an association of artillerymen is named *thiasos*, (*SEG* 42 [1992], no. 1312), and in the first century BC, Caesar, affirming the right of Jews to assemble, which have funds and to worship in accordance with their tradition, calls the colleges of Rome *thiasoi* (Josephus, *Jewish Antiquities* 14. 213). In Illyria, in the third century AD, we find a *thiasos* of slaves (*SEG* 38 [1988], no. 546); in Dalmatia, at Narona, a '*thiasus* of the youth' (*thiasus iuuentutis*) erects a funerary inscription (*CIL* iii. no. 1828); at Philippi in Macedonia, the *thiasi Liberi patris Tasibasteni* receive a sum of money to celebrate a funerary cult (*CIL* iii. no. 703–4), and at Pozzuoli, at the beginning of the third century AD, a certain sum would be paid, *introit[us causa]*, to gain entry into the Bacchic *thiasos*, as into other colleges (*CIL* x. no. 1585). From the fourth century BC, the sub-divisions of certain Attic phratries were named *thiasoi* (Andrewes 1961: esp. 9–12; though 'it is not clear that they had religious functions': Parker 1996: 104–5, n. 9). In short, the impression gained is that the term *thiasos* may cover many different situations, and often serves as an equivalent to other terms denoting associations.

the way that sects have been defined by sociologists. As a result, there are some suggestive connections to be found in this work with current religious or sectarian movements, along with analysis of the distinction between 'new religious movement' and sect. The group's aim was to understand the degree to which Jewish and Christian communities were integrated into the framework of Graeco–Roman community life. To distinguish these communities from institutional or familial associations, the term voluntary association is used. It is a problematic notion, though, implying as it does a coded reference to that model of society, attributed by Tocqueville and Weber to the United States, that organizes itself around voluntary associations in order to defend the interests of its members. This type of voluntary association is based on the principles of individual freedom and pluralism. That the model does not fit the ancient context is demonstrated by the rest of the volume, with its emphasis on the fact that all Graeco–Roman associations were subject to a form of social determinism, that they were always local rather than universal, and finally that belonging to a college hardly ever excluded other affiliations. The term is nonetheless employed in the book, including in the title, as it makes it possible to bring together under the category of associations not only the traditional Graeco–Roman colleges, but also the philosophical schools, the mystery cults, the followers of Asclepius, the community of Qumran, the synagogues and the early Christian communities. At the same time, this term, to which in the end the group prefers that of private association, allows them to open up a dialogue with sociologists and current debates. In any event, the Kloppenborg and Wilson volume describes the full spectrum of characteristics belonging to the associations of the Graeco–Roman world. I shall give a brief summary of this here.[13]

A *synodos, thiasos,* or college, or whatever the term used,[14] was an association that allowed a given group to exist and to be integrated within social life, affording it ongoing protection. These associations were officially set up, at least in principle. They all had a religious attachment, including affiliations with one or more deities, and they

---

[13] See, in particular, the synthesis given by Wilson 1996.
[14] See n. 12 above; for a list of all the terminology, see Waltzing 1895–1900: i. 339ff.

thus comprised certain cultic duties. As local rather than translocal associations, they upheld rather than contested the social and political order. Their size varied between 15 to 20 members and 1200, but the majority of colleges had a reduced number of members. The headquarters of the associations was located either in public places such as temples, porticos, and granaries, or in private places: *scholè* (headquarters) or private houses. From its inception, every organization was formally organized, with a 'superior', a fund, and a set of regulations. Membership of an association was more often than not determined by social occupation, place of abode, geographical origins, and family. Entry into the association was subject to a variety of rules, such as an admission fee or the organization of a banquet, but with some groups it also involved more elaborate initiation rites (Mithraic associations, for example). Alongside their role as regulators of collective activities, some associations promoted a particular ethos (synagogues, churches, philosophical schools). These colleges never required exclusive allegiance, not even the philosophical sects or the Jewish and Christian communities. Ordered along strict hierarchical lines, the associations accentuated rather than eased social divisions. If especially attractive to the lower strata of society, they also include members of the elite, and they seek out the patronage of the great and the good, in whose houses they may on occasion assemble. Certain associations, such as the Athenian Iobakkhoi (Moretti 1986), or the patients of Asclepius known to Aelius Aristides (Remus 1996), were composed exclusively of members of the elite. If women are excluded from the majority of colleges, their membership of certain colleges is attested. In all colleges, members celebrated meals, even in the mystery colleges, and generally in connection with sacrifices. Finally, many colleges saw to the funerary rites of their members. The point should also be made that the Greek and Roman terminology used for the associations and for the titles of the associations' dignitaries is numerous and varied, frustrating any attempt to determine what might be specific to any given association.

This inventory of the associations' principal characteristics shows that there is nothing structurally to distinguish them from Jewish and Christian groups. Or rather, it invites the conclusion that when Jews, Christians, philosophers or the followers of

Mani organized themselves, this was the manner in which they did so.[15] Indeed, their collective behaviour corresponded to that of other inhabitants of the Graeco–Roman world. Even so, I do not believe, for example, that the early Christian groups presented themselves straightaway as a new religious movement, organized and autonomous, like the *thiasos* or the ecclesia *of the Christians*. My sense, rather, is of groups belonging to a certain synagogue,[16] or groups of Syrians gathering in a certain place, the inhabitants of a certain district or street, or even persons practising a particular trade. The early communities may have organized themselves within a perfectly lawful, and often non-confessional, framework. As Kloppenborg has suggested,[17] the expression used by Paul, 'the church in their house' (ἡ κατ' οἰκὸν αὐτῶν ἐκκλησία; Romans 16. 5; Colossians 4. 15), could well be taken to imply that certain Pauline churches came into being within domestic colleges. It is not impossible, as has also been highlighted, that Paul began his activities in the association of tent makers at Tarsos.[18]

At the same time, it should be noted that as a rule, such associations were tolerated and even officially recognized. The Roman attitude towards the colleges was both severe and flexible. On the one hand, from the first century BC, the legislation on colleges was repressive, and associations were closely monitored by the authorities.[19] In 64 BC, those colleges deemed a threat to public order had been banned due to the trouble they were always causing for Rome, and thenceforth, despite the return to a more tolerant attitude from

[15] One may refer here, for example, to the articles of Seland 1996 and Hudson McLean 1996.

[16] We should remember that from the time of Caesar on, Jews benefited from the right to assemble, to observe their sacred rites and customs, to collect levies and to celebrate communal meals. See Cotter 1996: 74–89, esp. 76–8, although caution should be observed for the rest of the article, which among other things appears not to know the work of Ausbüttel.

[17] Kloppenborg 1996: 23 cites as a parallel the Roman *collegium quod est in domo Sergiae, L(uci) f(iliae), Paullinae* 'the college which is in the house of Sergia Paullina, daughter of Lucius' (*CIL* vi. no. 9148, 9149, 10260–4), which is known from funerary inscriptions.

[18] For example, the term 'of the same trade' (ὁμότεχνον) (Acts 18. 3) is attested in the context of artisanal colleges (Kloppenborg 1996: 24).

[19] See Jacques and Scheid 1990: 333–6, and the clarifications of Ausbüttel 1982: 22–33; also Cotter 1996.

Augustus onwards, colleges were kept under close supervision. In AD 111, Trajan elected not to follow the recommendation made by his legate in Bithynia, Pliny the Younger, to authorize the creation of a college of *fabri* (building workers) in Nicomedia of around a hundred and fifty men for the purpose of fire-fighting, wary that it might get deflected from this function.[20] The emperor justified his refusal by stating that these colleges risked degenerating into 'hetairiai', political clubs. We should bear in mind that Bithynia was at the time located close to the Parthian front, and that the severity of the emperor was doubtless due to this particular circumstance. It may nonetheless be noted that in the second case outlined by Pliny, namely the creation of a college of *erani* (an association with charitable ends), at Amisos, a grumbling Trajan agrees to the constitution of the college, adding some words of warning (Pliny, *Letters* 10. 92–3). In effect, the free city of Amisos was capable of governing itself in conformity with its institutions, which was not the case with Nicomedia, a provincial capital and above all a simple peregrine city. The situation in which an association found itself was thus dependent on the legal status of the city concerned, and the degree of repression exercised by the governor differed accordingly. Furthermore, the central power and the local authorities were generally quite lenient, and many groups formed associations without really requesting or obtaining public permission. This state of affairs lasted for as long as there were no problems. The story of the fighting that broke out in AD 59 in the amphitheatre of Pompeii perfectly illustrates the policy of the authorities. Besides the prohibition of these types of games for a period of ten years and the exile of the show's organizers, the repressions to which these disturbances gave rise included the dissolution of illegal associations.[21] This means that in Pompeii there were unofficial colleges that had never been formally sanctioned. The authorities generally turned a blind eye, and only reacted when there was trouble. Such might be a summary of the turbulent history of the colleges.

[20] Pliny, *Letters* 10. 33–4. Cotter 1996: 82 makes a slip in giving the location as Nicaea.

[21] Tacitus, *Annals* 14. 17 (*collegiaque quae contra leges instituerant dissoluta*, 'and colleges which they had set up contrary to the laws were dissolved').

Coming back, then, to the question in hand, it is possible to conclude that Jewish, Christian, and Manichaean groups belonged either to lawful associations—synagogues or various kinds of colleges—or to unofficial groups that were tolerated by the authorities or else unknown to them. In both cases, the communities concerned were integrated into the social life of the cities and the districts, and if need be benefited from protection, where the higher the legal status of the association the greater the protection received. However, they also ran a number of risks. As mentioned above, the colleges were always suspected by the authorities of being potentially seditious. Even if the majority of them did not get involved in politics, they regularly had problems with the authorities.

I have cited anecdotes from Pompeii, Nicomedia, and Amisos. Another clear example is given by the second column of Papyrus Giessen 40, whose first column preserves the famous edict of AD 212, conferring Roman citizenship on all free men of the Empire. The second column of the papyrus reproduces another edict of Caracalla, issued at Alexandria in late 215/early 216.[22] In this edict, Caracalla orders all Egyptians living in Alexandria, especially the peasants (ἄγροικοι) to leave the city in order to keep up agricultural production, and because their presence served no purpose other than to ferment disorder, with the exception of the swine merchants, the ferrymen and the purveyors of reeds for the baths, these all being indispensable for daily life and for keeping Alexandria in supplies. The Egyptians are nonetheless authorized to make brief visits to the city in order to participate in an urban festival, to enjoy the pleasures of city life or to conclude a deal (Papyrus Gissensis 40. ii, lines 16–26). The edict goes on to address the specific case of the linen weavers, among whom Egyptians could easily be recognized from their dialect and comportment (Papyrus Gissensis 40. ii, lines 26–9). This section is curious, as it is difficult to see why the emperor targeted the linen weavers in particular. The only explanation would be that the peasants who had settled in Alexandria especially devoted themselves to the weaving of linen, one of the specialities of the city. As Kostas Buraselis (1995: 168–9) has noted, the instructions in the

---

[22] Cf. Kuhlmann 1994: 246–55. See the bibliography in Buraselis 1995; I have been heavily influenced by this work.

edict suggest that the weavers were very well acquainted with the Egyptian 'immigrants' who belonged to their professional associations, but that they did not, it would appear, inform on them,[23] providing another motive for dealing with them severely. This observation offers a fine illustration of the way in which diverse social categories might be wrapped up within existing associations.

However that may be, the point of interest here concerns the disturbances that these 'peasants' are meant to have provoked in Alexandria (ταράσσουσι τὴν πόλιν). The expression is sufficiently strong to suggest serious disturbances, which may be identified as those that marked the visit of Caracalla to Alexandria and that ended in a bloodbath. This most likely comes down to the attitude displayed by artisans working for the state (ἐργολάβοι). Following the massacre of a number of these artisans, Caracalla placed a ban on the shows and the social gatherings (συσσίτια) of the Alexandrians, building walls and towers to keep the population in check and prevent them from assembling (Dio, *Roman History* 77 (78). 23. 3). Drawing on other repressive measures targeting the social gatherings, under both Caracalla and Augustus, Buraselis (1995: 174–80) has been able to show that this term referred in all probability to the colleges. In AD 215/16, the suppression targeted more particularly colleges that were not indispensable to the upkeep of the city.[24] Caracalla reacted very violently to the beginnings of an uprising, suppressing the colleges, and notably those that had played a prominent role in the unrest. And among these associations, those of the linen weavers, whose seditious reputation is attested by other accounts (Buraselis 1995: 182–4), were especially targeted. Given that the city could not do without their industry, the size of the weavers' workforce was reduced, no doubt in order to rein in their power.

The details of this suppression are not of any consequence here. The various accounts illustrate the problems faced by associations in the

---

[23] Dio, *Roman History* 77 (78). 22–3 with the *Excerpta Vaticana* of Petrus Patricius (Bossevain iii. 400); Herodian 4. 8. 6 – 4. 9; Scriptores Historiae Augustae, *Carus* 6. 2–3. According to Kuhlmann 1994: 248–55, the real reason for the repressions was the depopulation of the countryside and the overpopulation of Alexandria.

[24] It is even possible that the ban on shows has to be understood, in fact, as a ban on associations of actors' 'supporters' (Buraselis 1995: 180, n. 75). We also recall the banning of games during the suppression of the disturbances in Pompeii.

Roman world. On the one hand, these welcomed diverse categories of members with whom they felt solidarity. And, at times of social tension and disturbance, it was generally the associations that were hit, since to the extent that they served as a forum for the lower classes, they were in a position to play the role of leader in any uprising.

In other words, the tendency, quite customary in the Roman world, to become organized as a college allowed an official position to be accorded to the group thus constituted. At the same time, this mode of integration involved certain risks. Even if the colleges benefited from long periods of peace, sources regularly evoke the suppression, dissolution, and prohibition of these hotbeds of subversion. The risk was all the more acute when the associations were unlawful, when they were isolated from social life and when they contained a large contingent of foreigners. In such cases, the bad reputation of the colleges could increase the weight of suspicion on the group concerned and attract accusations of plotting against society, on the part of their neighbours as well as the authorities. One can equally imagine the kind of conflicts that could break out in a college that was host to radical Christians or Jews, refusing, for example, to participate in rites and communal banquets: here, it is within the association that quarrels could arise, which risked spilling over the framework of the association and degenerating into pogroms.

I do not wish to claim that the persecutions of Christians and other social groups are due to their membership of colleges. I merely want to draw attention to the fact that within the Roman world, those who constitute themselves as a group do so in the form of an association, or else are assimilated into associations. As a result, they run the risks inherent in Roman associative and community life, and where conflict arose, these risks could include often quite severe cases of dissolution and suppression.

BIBLIOGRAPHY

Andrewes, A. (1961). 'Philochoros on Phratries', *Journal of Hellenic Studies*, 81: 1–15.

Ausbüttel, F. M. (1982). *Untersuchungen zu den Vereinen im Westen des römischen Reiches.* Kallmünz: Lassleben.

Beskov, P. (1980). 'The Portorium and the Mysteries of Mithra', *Journal of Mithraic Studies*, 1–2: 1–18.

Boissier, G. (1891). *La fin du paganisme. Étude sur les dernières lutes religieuses en Occident au IVe siècle*, vol. 1. Paris: Hachette.

——(1906). *La religion romaine d'Auguste aux Antonins*, 6th edn. Paris: Hachette.

Bowersock, G. (1999). 'Les *Euemerioi* et les confréries joyeuses', *CRAI*, 1999: 1241–56.

Bruneau, Ph. (1970). *Recherches sur les cultes de Délos à l'époque hellénistique et à l'époque impériale*, BEFAR 217. Paris: Boccard.

Buraselis, K. (1995). 'Zu Caracallas Strafmassnahmen in Alexandrien (21/16). Die Frage der Leinenweber in P. Giss. 40 II und der *syssitia* in Cass. Dio 77 (78) 23. 3', *ZPE*, 108: 166–88.

De Cazanove, O. (ed.) (1986). *L'association dionysiaque dans les sociétés anciennes*, Collection de l'Ecole française de Rome 89. Rome: Ecole française de Rome.

Coarelli, F. (1984). 'Iside capitolina, Clodio e i mercanti di schiavi', in *Alessandria e il mondo ellenistico-romano: Studi in onore di Achille Adriani*, 3 vols. Rome: L'Erma di Bretschneider, iii. 461–75.

Cotter, W. (1996). 'The Collegia and Roman Law: State Restrictions on Voluntary Associations. 64 BCE–200 CE', in Kloppenborg and Wilson 1996: 74–89.

De Cenival, F. (1969). 'Les associations dans les temples égyptiens d'après les données fournies par les papyrus démotiques', in Ph. Derchain (ed.), *Religions en Égypte hellénistique et romaine*. Paris: Presses universitaires de France, 5–19.

Durand, J.-L. and Scheid, J. (1994). '"Rites" et "religion". Remarques sur certains préjugés des historiens de la religion des Grecs et des Romains', *Archives des sciences sociales des religions*, 85: 23–43.

Jacques, F. and Scheid, J. (1990). *Rome et l'intégration de l'Empire, 44 av. J.-C.–260 ap. J.-C.* Paris: Presses universitaires de France.

Frankfurter, D. (1998). *Religion in Roman Egypt: Assimilation and Resistance*. Princeton: Princeton University Press.

Gordon, J. S. and Gordon, A. E. (1984). *Album of Dated Latin Inscriptions. Rome and the Neighborhood. ii. AD 100–199*. Berkeley: University of California Press.

Hanoune, R. (1986). 'Les associations dionysiaques dans l'Afrique romaine', in De Cazanove 1986: 149–64.

Hudson McLean, B. (1996). 'The Place of Cult in Voluntary Associations and Christian Churches on Delos', in Kloppenborg and Wilson 1996: 186–225.

Kloppenborg, J. S. (1996). 'Collegia and Thiasoi: Issues in Function, Taxonomy, and Membership', in Kloppenborg and Wilson 1996: 16–30.

——and Wilson, S. G. (eds.) (1996). *Voluntary Associations in the Graeco–Roman World*. London: Routledge.

Kuhlmann, P. A. (1994). *Die Giessener literarischen Papyri und die Caracalla-Erlasse. Edition, Übersetzung und Kommentar*. Giessen: Universitätsbibliothek Giessen.

Laitar, A. (1991). 'Proskynema Inscriptions of a Corporation of Iron-workers from Hermontis in the Temple of Hatshepsut in Deir el-Bahari: New Evidence for Pagan Cults in Egypt in the 4th cent. AD', *Journal of Juristic Papyrology*, 21: 53–70.

Mommsen, Th. (1843). *De collegiis et sodaliciis Romanorum*. Kiel: Libraria Schwersiana.

Moretti, L. (1986). 'Il regolamento degli Iobacchi ateniensi', in De Cazanove 1986: 247–59.

Muszynski, M. (1977). 'Les "associations religieuses" en Égypte d'après les sources hiéroglyphiques, démotiques et grecques', *Orientalia Lovaniensia Periodica*, 8: 145–74.

Nock, A. D. (1933). 'The Gild of Zeus Hypsistos', *HTR*, 29: 39–88, repr. in part in Nock 1972: i. 414–43.

——(1972). *Essays on Religion and the Ancient World*, ed. Z. Stewart, 2 vols. Oxford: Clarendon Press.

Parker, R. C. T. (1996). *Athenian Religion: A History*. Oxford: Clarendon Press.

Remus, H. (1996). 'Voluntary Association and Networks: Aelius Aristides at the Asclepieion in Pergamon', in Kloppenborg and Wilson 1996: 146–75.

Scheid, J. (1986). 'Le thiase du Metropolitan Museum (*IGUR* I, 160)', in De Cazanove 1986: 275–90.

——(1987). 'Polytheism Impossible; Or, the Empty Gods: Reasons behind a Void in the History of Roman Religion', in Schmidt 1987: 303–25.

Schilling, R. (1961). 'Vestales et Vierges chrétiennes dans la Rome antique', *Revue des Sciences Religieuses*, 35: 113–29, reprinted in his *Rites, cultes, dieux de Rome*. Paris: Klincksieck, 1979, 166–82.

Schmidt, F. (ed.) (1987). *The Inconceivable Polytheism: Studies in Religious Historiography*, History and Anthropology 3. Chur and Paris: Harwood Academic.

Seland, T. (1996). 'Philo and the Clubs and Associations of Alexandria', in Kloppenborg and Wilson 1996: 110–27.

Van Nijf, O. (1997). *The Civic World of Professional Associations in the Roman East*. Amsterdam: Gieben.

Waltzing, J. P. (1895–1900). *Étude historique sur les corporations profession-elles chez les Romans depuis les origins jusqu'à la chute de l'Empire*, 4 vols. Louvain: Peeters.

Wilson, S. (1996). 'Voluntary Association: An Overview', in Kloppenborg and Wilson 1996: 1–15.

Wipszucka, E. (1970). 'Les confréries dans la vie religieuse de l'Égypte chrétienne', in D. H. Samuel (ed.), *Proceedings of the Twelfth International Congress of Papyrology*. Toronto: Hakkert, 511–25.

Wissowa, G. (1912). *Religion und Kultus der Römer*, 2nd edn. Munich: Beck.

III

Co-existences of Religions,
Old and New

11

Acculturation and Identity in the Diaspora

A Jewish Family and 'Pagan' Guilds at Hierapolis[1]

Philip Harland

INTRODUCTION

Recent studies of the diaspora in the Roman period are beginning to address regional variations among Judaean (Jewish) gatherings and are giving attention to the relationships between these groups and the societies in which they found themselves.[2] The graves of those who had passed on can also further our understanding of cultural interactions among the living.[3] Leonard Victor Rutgers' study of Judaean

---

[1] This paper benefited from discussions at the Canadian Society of Biblical Studies in Winnipeg (2004), at the Hellenistic Judaism section of the Society for Biblical Literature in San Antonio (2004), and at Concordia University, Montreal. Research for this paper, including a trip to Hierapolis, was supported by grants from the Fonds Quebecois de la recherche sur la société et la culture and the Social Sciences and Humanities Research Council of Canada. I would like to thank Prof. Francesco D'Andria, the director of the Italian Archeological Mission at Hierapolis, and the staff at the Hierapolis museum for their permission to examine and photograph monuments.
[2] On Asia Minor, see for example, Trebilco 1991: 167–85; Barclay 1996: 259–81, 320–35; Goodman 1998; Rajak 2002: 335–54, 355–72, 447–62; Harland 2003.
[3] On Judaean burial in the diaspora see, for example, van der Horst 1991; Williams 1994; Strubbe 1994 and 1997; and Noy 1998.

burials at Rome (second-fourth centuries), for instance, demonstrates this well and finds that instead 'of living in splendid isolation or longing to assimilate, the Roman Jews...appear as actively and, above all, as self-consciously responding to developments in contemporary non-Judaean society' (Rutgers 1994: 263). Careful attention to burial customs in other parts of the empire can provide a new vantage point on questions of acculturation and identity among cultural minority groups such as Judaean synagogues.[4]

This paper explores cultural interactions in the ancient context with special attention to Judaean epitaphs from Hierapolis in Asia Minor, some of which are newly published by Elena Miranda (1999; cf. *SEG* 49 [1999], nos. 1814–36). In particular, I focus my attention on the family grave of P. Aelius Glykon and Aurelia Amia (*c.*200 CE), recently re-published by Tullia Ritti (Ritti 1992–3; Frey 1936–52: ii. no. 777). This grave illustrates well the complexity of cultural identities and the potential for interaction between Judaeans (Jews) and their neighbours in the cities of Asia Minor. It involves Glykon's bequest to local guilds of purple-dyers and carpet-weavers in order to regularly perform ceremonies at this family grave on Judaean (Passover and Pentecost) and Roman holidays (Kalends of January).

Few scholars fully explore this family grave within the framework of burial practices among Judaeans in Hierapolis and in relation to guild-life in Asia Minor. In looking at this case, I also work to resolve an ongoing debate regarding the composition of the guilds mentioned in the inscription. While several scholars make known their differing views on the identity of these groups (Judaean, non-Judaean, or mixed), few sufficiently investigate this issue in relation to other evidence for the purple-dyers at Hierapolis. I conclude with

---

[4] My use of the terms 'assimilation' and 'acculturation' are informed by sociological theories which I discuss at length in the final section of this paper. My use of 'identity' is informed by social–psychological studies of social identity, which use the term in reference to a person's self-conception as a group member, and by anthropological studies on the ascriptive (rather than primordial) nature of ethnic identities specifically (which follow the lead of Fredrik Barth). In both cases, these theories emphasize the complexity and shifting multiplicity of social or cultural identities. For an excellent discussion and bibliography in reference to the ancient context see Esler 2003: 19–76. Cf. Abrams and Hogg 1990.

comments on the dynamics of acculturation and assimilation among cultural minority groups in the diaspora.[5]

JUDAEANS AT HIERAPOLIS

Recent discoveries of graves have added to our knowledge of Judaeans at Hierapolis. Miranda's recent publication (1999) includes a total of twenty-three grave-inscriptions (out of a total of over 360 published epitaphs from Hierapolis), including thirteen new inscriptions beyond those previously published by Walther Judeich (in 1898) and by Fabrizio A. Pennacchietti (in 1966–7).[6] The majority of the Judaean inscriptions (Miranda 1999: nos. 1–21) are from the northern necropolis, which was extended from the time of Antoninus Pius (138–161 CE) and whose monuments date mostly from the middle of the second to the third centuries (Pennacchietti 1966–7: 293-4; cf. Ritti 1992–3: 42). Two Judaean tombs were found elsewhere in the area of the eastern burial grounds (Miranda 1999: nos. 22–3). The Judaean inscriptions range in date from the second half of the second to the third or fourth centuries based on onomastics (especially the presence of Aurelius-related names), and on the forms of the lettering in relation to other dated inscriptions. It is difficult to date them with any more certainty, as none expressly supply a date and rarely are named figures known from other sources.

The majority of these inscriptions (eighteen) involves an individual identified as 'Judaean' (*Ioudaios*; traditionally translated 'Jew') making provisions for the burial of him or herself and family

[5] For further discussion of Judaeans within the context of associations and cultural minorities in the Roman empire, see Harland 2009.
[6] Those previously published are: Miranda 1999: no. 5 = Judeich 1898: no. 69 = Frey 1936–52: ii. no. 776; no. 6 = Pennacchietti 1966–7: no. 14; no. 8 = Judeich 1898: no. 72 = Frey 1936–52: ii. no. 778; no. 9 = Judeich 1898: no. 97; no. 10 = Judeich 1898: no. 104; no. 11 = Pennacchietti 1966–7: no. 30; no. 16 = Judeich 1898: no. 212 = *IGR* iv. no. 834 = Frey 1936–52: ii. no. 775; no. 20 = Pennacchietti 1966–7: no. 46; no. 22 = Judeich 1898: no. 295; and no. 23 = Judeich 1898: no. 342 = Frey 1936–52: ii. no. 777. All twenty-three are also now included, with commentary, in Ameling 2004: 187–209.

members, without explicit reference to a Judaean community. Almost all of these identify the owners of the grave and surrounding area and list other family members that were to be buried there. Several go further in following standard forms of burial inscriptions in this part of Asia Minor by warning that no one else should be buried there and by providing for fines in the event that anyone attempted to do so (Miranda 1999: nos. 1, 2, 4, 7, 8, 9, 10, 18, 19, 21). Fines were most often payable to the 'most sacred treasury' (*tamion*) or, in one case, to the civic 'elders' organization' (*gerousia*) (Miranda 1999: nos. 1 (*gerousia*), 2, 4, 7, 8, 9, 10a, 18, 19, 21). Several of those that specify fines also mention that a copy of the inscription was placed in the civic archives, which was another important formal institution in the Greek cities of Asia Minor (Miranda 1999: nos. 1, 2, 5, 8, 10, 18, 19, 21). The act of placing a copy of these stipulations in the civic archives is suggestive of the formal legal procedures that would be followed in the event that provisions for care and protection of the grave were violated in some way.[7]

Several inscriptions (three, or perhaps four, of the twenty-three) use terminology suggestive of a group or association of Judaeans, providing the only information we have about the local synagogue (or perhaps synagogues, over time) at Hierapolis (Miranda 1999: nos. 5, 6, 14b, 16). The epitaph which is inscribed with the plural possessive *Ioudeōn* (sic), '(Grave) of the Judaeans', alongside the depiction of a menorah and lion likely refers to a *family* of Judaeans, rather than an association (see Fig. 11.1). There are three other definite references to an association or group of Judaeans (Miranda 1999: no. 6 = Ameling 2004: no. 187; cf. Miranda 1999: no. 10).

Yet, interestingly enough, each of the three epitaphs uses different terminology for the group. In one, a woman and a man explicitly identify themselves as belonging to the 'people (*laos*) of the Judaeans' and make fines for violation of their grave payable to this group (see Fig. 11.2):

---

[7] On τυμβωρυχία (tomb violation) in Asia Minor see Judeich 1898: nos. 275, 312 (cf. *IK* 28 [*Iasos*]: nos. 376, 392). Judeich 1898: no. 195, which also involves guilds, more directly indicates this legal context in providing a reward (of 800 denaria) for the 'one prosecuting the case (τῷ ἐκδικήσαντι)' for violation. See also Gerner 1941: esp. 250–8, and Strubbe 1991: 48, n. 9. For other Judaean references to the crime see Ameling 2004: nos. 146 (Thyatira), 174 (Akmoneia).

Fig. 11.1. Grave 'of the Judaeans' from Hierapolis, with a menorah and lion (Miranda 1999: no. 6 = Ameling 2004: no. 187).

The grave and the burial ground beneath it together with the base and the place belong to Aurelia Glykonis, daughter of Ammianos, and her husband Marcus Aurelius Alexander Theophilos, also known as Aphelias, of the people of the Judaeans.[8] They will be buried in it, but it is not lawful for

---

[8] The designation *laos* for a group, which seems to be distinctively Judaean in epigraphy (cf. Frey 1936–52: ii. nos. 662, 699–702, 704–708, 720; *IK* 23–4 [*Smyrna*]: no. 296), is also attested nearby at Nysa, where it is taken as a synonym for *synodos*

Fig. 11.2. Grave mentioning the 'people of the Judaeans' at Hierapolis (Miranda 1999: no. 5 = Ameling 2004: no. 206).

anyone else to be buried in it. If this is violated, the guilty one will pay a fine of 1000 denaria to the people of the Judaeans. A copy of this inscription was placed in the archives.

ἡ σορὸς καὶ τὸ ὑπὸ α[ὐτὴν θ]έ[μ]α σὺν τῷ βαθρικῷ [καὶ] | ὁ τόπος Αὐρελίας Γλυ[κω]νίδος Ἀμμειανοῦ καὶ τ[οῦ] | ἀνδρὸς αὐτῆς Μ. Αὐρ. Ἀλεξάν[δρ]ου Θεοφίλου, ἐπίκλην | Ἀφελίου, Ἰουδαίων, ἐν ᾗ κηδευ[θή]σονται αὐτοί, ἑτέρῳ δὲ οὐ|δενὶ ἐξέσται κηδεῦσαι ἐν αὐτῇ τ[ινα]· εἰ δὲ μή, ἀποτείσαι τῷ λαῷ | τῶν Ἰουδαίων προστείμου ὀνό[μ]ατι δηνάρια χείλια. ταύτης τῆς | ἐπιγραφῆς ἁπλοῦν ἀ[ν]τίγραφον ἀπετέθη εἰς τὰ ἀρχῖα.

(Miranda 1999: no. 5 = Ameling 2004: no. 206 = *IGR* iv. no. 835; late-second or third century)[9]

(Lifshitz 1967: no. 31 = Ameling 2004: no. 26, now dated to the first century BCE by Ameling).

[9] Here and in the following inscriptions I follow Miranda's readings of the text. Miranda suggests the second half of the second century or early third based on the

The couple of this epitaph are following the standard form of burial inscriptions at Hierapolis, providing for fines to be paid for violation, in this case to a local association to which they presumably belonged.

A second inscription refers to the 'settlement' (*katoikia*) of Judaeans in Hierapolis:

This grave and the surrounding place belong to Aurelia Augusta, daughter of Zotikos. In it she, her husband, who is called Glykonianos, also known as Hagnos, and their children will be buried. But if anyone else is buried here, the violator will pay a fine of 300 denaria to the settlement of the Judaeans who are settled in Hierapolis and 100 denaria to the one who found out about the violation. A copy of this inscription was placed in the archive of the Judaeans.

ἡ σορὸς καὶ ὁ περὶ αὐτ<ὴ>ν τόπος Αὐρ. Αὐγούστας Ζω|τικοῦ, ἐν ᾗ κηδευθήσεται αὐτὴ καὶ ὁ ἀνὴρ <αὐ>τῆς Γλυκωνιανὸς | ὁ καὶ Ἅγνος καὶ τὰ τέκνα αὐτῶν. εἰ δὲ {ΕΤΕ} ἕτερος κηδευθήσει, δ
ώσει τῇ κατοικίᾳ τῶν ἐν Ἱεραπόλει κατοικούντων Ἰουδαίων προστείμου (δηνάρια) τ' καὶ τῷ ἐκζητή-σαντι (δηνάρια) ρ'. ἀντίγραφον | ἀπετέθη ἐν τῷ ἀρχίῳ τῶν Ἰουδαίων.

(Miranda 1999: no. 16 = Ameling 2004: no. 205 = *IGR* iv. no. 834 = Frey 1936–52: ii. no. 775; mid–late second century CE)[10]

Here the group is described with terminology that is commonly used by groups of foreigners or ethnic-based associations in Asia Minor. This is especially well attested in the case of associations of resident Romans (*hoi katoikountes Romaioi*), such as the 'settlement' of Romans that existed at nearby Phrygian Apameia (north-east of Hierapolis) from the first to at least the third centuries.[11] This suggests that 'Judaeans' or 'those from Judaea' (in an ethno-geographical and cultural sense) is the best way to translate *Ioudaioi* in this case. The seemingly redundant 'settlement of Judaeans who are settled in Hierapolis' also further suggests this sense of settled immigrants originally from elsewhere.[12] This inscription also

---

lettering and the onomastics (presence of Aurelia); Ameling suggests second half of the second century.

[10] This rough date is once again based on the presence of the gentilicium Aurelius.

[11] *IGR* iv. no. 785–86, 788–91, 793–94; *MAMA* vi. nos. 177 (*c*.65–9 CE), 183. Cf. *IDélos* nos. 1619–82 (Athenians on Delos) and *OGIS* no. 595 = *IGR* i. no. 421 (Tyrian merchants at Puteoli).

[12] On debates regarding possible geographical meanings of *Ioudaioi*, which some-times centre on the '*hoi pote Ioudaioi*' ('the former Judaeans') inscription from

includes the common provision for storage of a copy of the inscription, but in this case this is expressly the archives 'of the Judaeans' rather than the civic archives, as was the norm in other Judaean (and non-Judaean) inscriptions. This suggests a well-established group (by the mid–late second century), such that it would begin to maintain its own archives for a time.

One face (side b) of a third inscription, now published for the first time by Miranda, refers to a group of Judaeans as 'the most holy synagogue':

(Side a)
The grave, the burial ground beneath it, and the area around it belong to Nikotimos Lykidas, son of Artemisios. In it he has buried Apphias, his wife. A copy of this inscription was placed into the archive. Judaean.

ἡ σορὸς καὶ τὸ ὑπὸ αὐτὴν θέμα καὶ ὁ περὶ αὐτὴν τόπος | Νεικοτείμου Λυκιδᾶ τοῦ Ἀρτεμισίου, ἐν ᾗ κεκήδευ|ται Ἀπφιάς, ἡ γυνὴ αὐτοῦ. ταύτης ἀντίγραφον ἀπετέθη εἰς τὸ ἀρχεῖον. Ἰουδαηκή.

(Side b)
The grave and the place around it belong to Aur. Heortasios Julianus, Tripolitan, Judaean, now living in Hierapolis. In it he and his wife, Glykonis, will be buried, and let their children be buried here as well. It is not lawful for anyone other to be buried in it. If someone does such things, he will pay two silver coins to the most holy synagogue.

ἡ σορὸς καὶ ὁ περὶ αὐτὴν τόπος Αὐρ. Ἑορτασίου | Ἰουλιανοῦ Τριπολείτου Ἰουδέου, νοῖν οἰκο<υ>ντ[ος] | ἐν Εἰραπόλι, ἐν ᾗ κηδευθήσεται αὐτὸς καὶ ἡ γυνὴ αὐτοῦ Γλυκωνίς, κηδεύωνται δὲ καὶ τὰ | τέκνα αὐτῶν, ἑτέρῳ δὲ οὐδενὶ ἐξέσται κηδευ|θῆναι, ἐπεὶ ὁ παρὰ ταῦτα ποιήσας δώσει τῇ ἁγιωτά|τῃ συναγωγῇ ἀργυροῦ λείτρας δύο.

(Miranda 1999: no. 14 = Ameling 2004: no. 191 = SEG 49: no. 1827; *side a*, late second century CE; *side b*, third or fourth century CE)[13]

Smyrna (*IK* 23–4 [*Smyrna*]: no. 697 = Frey 1936–52: ii. no. 742) see, on the one hand, Williams 1997 (for the non-geographical, apostasy theory) and, on the other, Kraabel 1982: 455; Kraemer 1989; Harland 2009: 150–2 (for the ethno–geographical interpretation).

[13] Miranda's dating (1999: 125) depends primarily on the forms of the lettering in relation to other dated monuments at Hierapolis. Ameling (2004: 408) suggests that side b may date from the fourth century based on the use of *litra*, which Robert (1946: 106) suggested was characteristic of the fourth or fifth centuries.

The earlier of the two sides of the monument (side a) mentions only that the family members buried there were 'Judaean', and does not mention a community. The reverse of the original inscription (side b) pertains to a family of Judaeans whose relation to those buried earlier is unclear. They were previous inhabitants, or perhaps citizens, of nearby Tripolis and they assign any potential fines to 'the most holy synagogue'.[14]

Overall, then, the evidence from Hierapolis indicates that there was a notable number of Judaeans living in the city in the period from the mid-second to third or fourth centuries who openly identified themselves as such on their family tombs. Through the accidents of survival and discovery, we happen to encounter about twenty or so families who felt it was important to express Judaean aspects of their identities in this way (two of them decorating their graves with a menorah or other related symbols). There was at least one ongoing gathering or association of Judaeans, though few families chose to mention such an association on their epitaphs. By the late second century, an association of Judaeans was well-organized enough to have its own archives. Yet many of the known Judaean epitaphs seem to follow local custom in having copies of the inscription placed in, and/or fines for violation payable to, civic institutions of Hierapolis.

THE FAMILY TOMB OF P. AELIUS GLYKON AND AURELIA AMIA

One epitaph at Hierapolis does not explicitly use the term 'Judaean (*Ioudaios*)', nor does it refer to an established Judaean association. Instead, it clearly indicates connections with Judaean culture by

---

[14] The descriptive term 'most holy' (*hagiotat-*) and its synonyms are common self-designations among associations and civic bodies in Asia Minor and in Hierapolis specifically (cf. Judeich 1898: nos. 40–1, 342; Pennacchietti 1966–7: no. 25). Although probably the local Tripolis (cf. Pennacchietti 1966–7: no. 22), there are known cities of the same name in Pontus, in Syria, and in North Africa. Cf. Leon 1995: 153–4, 240, on the Tripolitan synagogue at Rome.

Fig. 11.3. Grave of P. Aelius Glykon and Aurelia Amia, involving guilds of carpet-weavers and purple-dyers (Miranda 1999: no. 23 = Ameling 2004: no. 196).

referring to holy days, or festivals. The family grave of P. Aelius Glykon and Aurelia Amia dates to the late-second or early-third century of our era, based on the wife's family name, Aurelia, and the forms of the lettering (see Fig. 11.3).[15] This is a limestone sarcophagus (with a partially damaged lid) inscribed on its long side (facing north-west), which is located in the south-eastern necropolis of Hierapolis near the remains of the Martyrium of St Philip, with no other surviving graves in its immediate vicinity.[16] Tullia Ritti's re-discovery and thorough new reading of the inscription, which was first inadequately published in 1868, has significantly

---

[15] Cf. Ritti 1992–3: 48; Miranda 1999: 132; Ameling 2004: 416.

[16] Measurements: Bottom: approx. 239 cm long, 93 cm tall, and 135 cm wide. Lid: 74 cm tall at its high-point. Lettering: approx. 4 cm. The sarcophagus is located at the beginning point of the main gap between two hills near where the main walk-way to the Martyrium of St Philip (now) ends and the staircase ascending to the martyrium begins.

filled in previously gaps, including the important reference to the feast of the Kalends in lines 9–10 and to the name of Glykon's wife.[17]

The inscription provides important evidence regarding the complexity of cultural identities and the nature of Judaean interactions with others in the Greek city, and reads as follows:

This grave and the burial ground beneath it together with the surrounding place belong to Publius Aelius Glykon Zeuxianos Aelianus[18] and to Aurelia Amia, daughter of Amianos son of Seleukos. In it he will bury himself, his wife, and his children, but no one else is permitted to be buried here. He left behind 200 denaria for the grave-crowning ceremony to the most holy presidency of the purple-dyers, so that it would produce from the interest enough for each to take a share in the seventh month [i.e. March–April] during the festival of Unleavened Bread. Likewise he also left behind 150 denaria for the grave-crowning ceremony to the association of carpet-weavers, so that the revenues from the interest should be distributed, half during the festival of Kalends on the eighth day of the fourth month [i.e. 1 January] and half during the festival of Pentecost. A copy of this inscription was put into the archives.

[ἡ] σορὸς καὶ τὸ ὑπὸ αὐτὴν θέμα σὺν τῷ βαθρικῷ καὶ τῷ περικειμένῳ τό|πῳ
Ποπλίου Αἰλίου Γλύκωνος Ζευξιανοῦ Αἰλια[νοῦ καὶ Αὐ]ρηλίας Ἀμίας |
Ἀμιανοῦ τοῦ Σελεύκου, ἐν ᾗ κηδευθήσεται αὐτὸς καὶ ἡ γυνὴ αὐτοῦ | καὶ τὰ
τέκνα αὐτῶν, ἑτέρῳ δὲ οὐδενὶ ἐξέσται κηδευθῆναι. κατέλιψεν δὲ [κα]ὶ τῇ
σεμνοτάτῃ προεδρίᾳ τῶν πορφυραβάφων στεφα]νωτικο[ῦ] (δηνάρια) διακόσια,
πρὸς τὸ δίδοσθαι ἀπὸ τῶν τόκων ἑκάστῳ τὸ | αἱροῦν μη. Ζʹ ἐν τῇ ἑορτῇ
τῶν ἀζύμων. ὁμοίως κατέλιπεν καὶ τῷ συνεδρίῳ τῶν ἀκαιροδαπισ<τ>ῶν
στεφανωτικοῦ (δηνάρια) ἑκατὸν πεντήκοντα, ἄτιl(vac.)
να καὶ αὐτοὶ δώσουσι ἐκ τοῦ τόκου | διαμερίσαντες τὸ ἥμισυ ἐν τῇ ἑορτῃ τῶν
καλανδῶν, | μη. δʹ, ηʹ, καὶ τὸ ἥμισυ ἐν τῇ ἑορτῇ τῆς πεντηκοστῆς. | ταύτης τῆς
ἐπιγραφῆς τὸ ἀντίγραφον ἀπε<τέ>θη ἐν τοῖς ἀρχείοις.[19]

---

[17] Previously partial or undocumented were what is now line 1, much of line 2, lines 9–10, part of line 11, and line 13. For a list of publications of the original reading (= Frey 1936–52: ii. no. 777) see Ritti 1992–3 or Miranda 1999: 131–2, no. 23. New reading: Ritti 1992–3; *AE* (1994), no. 1660; *SEG* 46 (1996), no. 1656; Labarre and Dinahet 1996: 102–3, no. 62; Miranda 1999: 131–2, no. 23; Dittmann-Schöne 2000: 226–7, no. V.5.10; Ameling 2004: no. 196.

[18] Or, possibly: 'P Aelius Glykon, son of Zeuxis Aelianus' (cf. Ameling 2004: 416).

[19] Ritti 1992–3 = *AE* (1994), no. 1660 = Miranda 1999: no. 23 = Ameling 2004: no. 196, revising Frey 1936–52: ii. no. 777.

JUDAEAN FACETS OF IDENTITY

The request that customary grave-ceremonies be held on two Judaean holidays clearly points to this family's identification with Judaean cultural practices. Glykon has consciously made a decision that his death (and that of his family members) be commemorated indefinitely on the feasts of Unleavened Bread (in the month of Nisan [March–April]) and on Pentecost (the spring harvest festival), two of the most important Judaean festivals.[20] The inscription nowhere identifies the owner (Glykon) as *Ioudaios*, as do some other Judaean epitaphs at Hierapolis, but this would be unnecessary in light of the explicit mention of Judaean holy days (cf. Ritti 1992–3: 59).

There is the question, then, of whether Glykon and his family were (born) Judaeans or whether they were gentiles who adopted important Judaean practices ('judaizers') and then arranged that others (guilds) also engaged in these practices after their deaths. It seems probable, in my view, that Glykon was Judaean based on the primary concern that Judaean festivals be celebrated in connection with the family grave, as most who discuss the inscription also suggest. As Ritti notes, seemingly 'non-Judaean' elements in the inscription which entail local or Roman practices, including the grave-crowning ceremonies and the celebration of the Roman New Year, can readily be understood within the framework of a Judaean family well-adapted to life in Graeco–Roman Hierapolis (Ritti 1992–3: 59–60).

This is not to discount the possibility that Glykon and his family were gentiles with a significant level of involvement in Judaean practices, along the lines of the 'god-fearers' in Aphrodisias in the fourth century (Ameling 2004: no. 14).[21] In the event that Glykon was a gentile adopting Judaean practices and then arranging for others to participate in some way in the festivals, then we would be witnessing strong signs of acculturation to Judaean ways on the part of a non-Judaean rather than acculturation of Judaeans to local or

---

[20] On Judaean festivals in the diaspora see Barclay 1996: 415–16. Cf. Josephus, *Jewish Antiquities* 14. 256–8 and 16. 45; Reynolds 1977: 244–5, no. 17 (feast of Tabernacles at Berenike, Cyrenaica *c.*24 CE).

[21] On the fourth or fifth century dating, see Chaniotis 2002.

Graeco–Roman ways.[22] The problem is that, unlike the case of the god-fearers at Aphrodisias, nothing in the Glykon inscription itself provides a basis for building a solid case that Glykon or his family was *gentile rather than Judaean*.[23] As we shall see, although there is no clear evidence that Glykon was a gentile, there is indeed corroborating evidence that some members of the purple-dyers' guild mentioned in this inscription were gentiles. The discussion here explores the multiple and intertwined facets of identity in the case of this family and the purple-dyers' guild, returning in the conclusion to the implications for acculturation depending on whether Glykon was a Judaean or a gentile judaizer.

ROMAN FACETS OF IDENTITY AND THE FEAST OF THE KALENDS

Alongside this family's clear identification with Judaean customs are various signs of intertwined Hierapolitan, Hellenistic, and Roman elements, which I explore throughout this paper. As recent studies of the diaspora stress, Judaean identities were by no means incompatible with a sense of belonging within the Graeco–Roman world. Before considering indications of assimilation to local cultural life in Hierapolis, which inevitably also involve intertwined Roman elements, it is important to note some clear signs of this family's *Roman* identity specifically.

First, P. Aelius Glykon's name indicates that he is a Roman citizen. If the inscription pre-dates or immediately follows the universal grant of citizenship in 212 CE (the *Constitutio Antoniniana*), as most suggest, then Glykon's choice to include his three names indicates some sense of pride in possessing the status of Roman

---

[22] On possible cases of gentile Judaizing in Asia Minor and Syria based on Christian literary evidence, see Murray 2004.

[23] On the difficulties of identifying some inscriptions as Judaean, Christian, or pagan, and of finding gentile sympathizers in particular see Kraemer 1989; Williams 1997; Ameling 2004: 16–20. Miranda (1999: 144–5) is attracted by the hypothesis that Glykon was a 'Jewish sympathizer' but admits the difficulties here. Also see the discussion of the purple-dyers and the Aphrodisias material further below.

citizen.[24] It is possible that Glykon or his ancestors were formerly slaves who gained Roman citizenship upon manumission, though there is nothing in the inscription or from other sources relating to Hierapolis that would confirm that. With regard to this man's cognomen, it is worth mentioning that personal names with the root Glyk- ('sweet') are very common in Hierapolis and Phrygia generally, and that this was likewise quite common among Judaeans at Hierapolis.[25] So even this man's name indicates Roman and Hierapolitan dimensions of his identities.

Beyond Roman citizenship, we lack clear indications of Glykon's social–economic status within Hierapolis. Still, it is worth mentioning that for most monuments in which a family provides a foundation to a local association or guild to perform grave ceremonies, the deceased (or deceased-to-be) was a Roman citizen with some degree of wealth (compare section below on the grave-crowning ceremony). Glykon's total amount of 350 denaria (200 plus 150) for the grave-crowning ceremonies (*stephanotikon*) is greater than, yet comparable to, the case of Aurelius Zotikos Epikratos, who gave 150 denaria to the guild of nail-workers (Judeich 1898: no. 133). On the other hand, Glykon's foundation is less than Publius Aelius Hermogenes' substantial grant of 1000 denaria to the guild of dyers (Judeich 1898: no. 195). Tiberius Claudius Kleon, whose position as high-priest (*archiereus*) suggests he is among the civic elites,[26] donated the largest attested amount for the grave-crowning ceremony at Hierapolis, granting the sum of 2500 denaria to the civic elders' organization (*gerousia*; Judeich 1898: no. 234). So Glykon is among many other Roman citizens,

---

[24] Of the twenty-three Judaean epitaphs at Hierapolis, sixteen (including the Glykon inscription) provide a name which suggests Roman citizenship and five of these are dated to the post-212 CE era by Miranda. Eleven are potentially cases of Jews with Roman citizenship before the universal grant (mainly in the late-second or early-third centuries CE).

[25] See Miranda 1999: nos. 5, 11, 14, and 16 (cited earlier). See Miranda's discussion of naming practices among Jews at Hierapolis (1999: 136–40).

[26] Compare the high-priest Tiberius Claudius Zotikos Boa, who also held other important civic offices or liturgies including *strategos*, *agonothetês*, and *presbeutês*. He was honoured by both the 'most sacred guild of wool-cleaners' and the 'most sacred guild of purple-dyers' on two separate monuments (Judeich 1898: nos. 40–1; probably third century).

some of higher and others of lower social-economic or civic status, at Hierapolis, but we do not know whether he was a citizen and, if so, whether we can consider him among the civic elites who assumed important offices.

A second, more significant sign of the adoption of things Roman has been revealed only with the new edition of the epitaph. Glykon chooses to have his family remembered not only on principal Judaean holidays, but also on the feast of the Kalends, the Roman New Year celebration on 1 January. Glykon leaves funds (150 denaria) to the association of carpet-weavers, specifying that half of the proceeds from the foundation be used during the feast of the Kalends (and half during Pentecost).

It is important to say a few words regarding this Roman New Year festival to assess its significance here at Hierapolis. The sparseness of our evidence for the celebration of this particular Roman festival in Asia Minor makes the Glykon inscription all the more relevant to issues of Romanization.[27] Michel Meslin's study of the festival emphasizes two complementary dimensions: the official ('civic') and the unofficial ('private').[28] The official side of the festival was focused on vows for the well-being of Rome and its empire as one year ended and the new began. Pliny the Younger provides some limited evidence that this aspect of the festival was celebrated in northern Asia Minor by the early second century (Pliny, *Letters* 10. 35–6, 100–1; cf. Suetonius, *Nero* 46. 4). The Glykon inscription now confirms the continuing adoption of this festival in another area of Asia Minor a number of decades later.

There were also unofficial dimensions to the Roman New Year festival, which would likely be of greater relevance to the situation within a local guild at Hierapolis. These informal celebrations were

---

[27] While evidence for the celebration of the Roman New Year festival (in January) in Asia Minor is partial at best, we do know that, beginning in about 9 BCE and continuing at least into the second century, New Year's celebrations were held in the province of Roman Asia on the birthday of Augustus (23 September), and associations were sometimes involved in those celebrations (Fränkel 1890–5: no. 374 = *IGR* iv. no. 353, trans Beard et al. 1998: ii. 255–6; and *IK* 11–17 [*Ephesos*]: no. 3801). See Price 1984: 54–5; Harland 2003: 94–5, 102.

[28] For the following see: Meslin 1970: 23–50 and Nilsson 1916–19: 54–5, who also notes the involvement of *collegia* in the celebrations.

'anchored in the collective psyche of the Romans' and charged with social and religious significance, as Meslin puts it (1970: 23, trans. mine). Although the festival originally focused its attention on the old Italian god Janus (two-faced protector of doors), its significance expanded beyond this focus. Ovid's famous poetic tribute to the Roman festivals (the *Fasti*), written in honour of Augustus, emphasizes the exchanges of 'good wishes' and gifts which accompanied the celebration, including 'sweet' gifts (e.g. dates, figs, honey), as well as cash, indicating an omen of a sweet year to come (*Fasti* 1. 171–94). Ovid also alludes to the common practice of workers dedicating their occupational activities in connection with the commencement of the new year (*Fasti* 1. 169–70), which may be of relevance to workers such as the carpet-weavers at Hierapolis. A statement by Herodian, a third-century Greek historian, confirms the importance of 'exchanging friendly greetings and giving each other the pleasure of interchanging gifts' (*History* 1. 16. 2). If Tertullian's negative assessment of Christians' participation in New Year's gift-giving as 'idolatry' is any indication, the exchange of gifts (*strenae*) specifically remained prominent as the festival made its way into the provinces, at least in regions like North Africa around the turn of the third century.[29]

It is likely these social aspects of celebrating the end of the old year and the beginning of the new, exchanging positive wishes and gifts, remained the focus of attention in many contexts, including this case at Hierapolis. Not surprisingly, diaspora Judaean attitudes and practices in relation to such festivals could extend beyond the views expressed in rabbinic sources (in the *Abodah Zarah* tractates), which simply assume that Judaeans should distance themselves from any relation to major gentile festivals, including the Kalends specifically.[30]

---

[29] Tertullian, *On Idolatry* 10 and 14; cf. *On Military Crowns* 12. 3; *Apology* 35. 7. On gifts (*strenae*) see Suetonius, *Augustus* 57, *Tiberius* 34, *Caligula* 42.

[30] Cf. Hadas-Lebel 1979. Translation in Beard et al. 1998: ii. 328–9. Some debates about contact with gentiles are reflected in a story of a gentile Roman official (quaestor) who, in celebration of the Roman New Year, honoured Yudan the patriarch with a gift of a chest of coins. The rabbi accepted only one of the coins and sent back the chest (presumably to avoid offence and to recognize the generosity of the gift-giver), but another rabbi was of the opinion that it was prohibited to benefit from even that one coin (*Jerusalem Talmud Abodah Zarah* 1. 1). A tradition in both Talmuds suggests that Adam founded the festival of Kalends and observed eight

FUNERARY PRACTICES AND ASSOCIATIONS
IN ROMAN ASIA

The nature of this family's participation in local cultural practices can be better understood in relation to other Judaeans in the city and in relation to other (non-Judaean) Hierapolitans who involved guilds in funerary provisions. Glykon's choice to include guilds in funerary commemorations on Judaean and Roman festivals excluded— whether incidentally or not—the local Judaean association from any direct relation to the burial and upkeep of the family grave. Glykon was certainly not alone in failing to even mention the local synagogue on his epitaph, however, as many other known Judaean and non-Judaean epitaphs make no mention of any local group or synagogue with which the family was affiliated.

A discussion of funerary involvements among associations (including Judaean groups) in western Asia Minor will provide important context here, pointing towards common burial customs shared by Judaeans (or possibly gentile Judaizers) such as Glykon and his family.[31] There were three main ways in which guilds and other associations participated in grave-related activities. First, associations could play a role in the burial of their members, sometimes collecting ongoing fees for later use in funerary related expenses (actual burial or funerary banquets, for instance) (cf. Artemidoros, *Dream Book* 5. 82). Local custom varied in the details and in the importance of this role, however. There is limited evidence that associations in some regions of Asia Minor might also have had their own group burial plot or collective tomb for this purpose. This was the case with the guild of flax-workers at Smyrna, who received a vault as a donation, and the guild of bed-builders at Ephesos, who dedicated a common burial plot.[32] As with associations generally, it seems that collective burial by association was

---

days of festivities, but he did so for the 'sake of heaven' while the pagans established a corresponding festival for 'idolatry' (*Babylonian Talmud Abodah Zarah* 1. 3).

[31] On funerary practices in Asia Minor generally see, most recently: Strubbe 1991, 1994 and 1997. On the role of associations in the Greek East see, for example, van Nijf 1997: 31–69 and Dittmann-Schöne 2000: 82–93.

[32] *IK* 23–4 [*Smyrna*]: no. 218; *IK* 11–17 [*Ephesos*]: no. 2213; cf. *IK* 11–17 [*Ephesos*]: no. 2213; Bean and Mitford 1970: 190–202; Paton and Hicks 1890: nos. 155–9; Fraser 1977: 58–70. Also see van Nijf 1997: 43–9.

not the norm among synagogues in the diaspora; instead, the shared *family* tomb was standard among both Judaeans and non-Judaeans (including those who happened to belong to an association). Still, there is one clear example from Tlos (in Lycia) in which a man named Ptolemais adopts this (local, Tlosian) practice by preparing a common burial area (*hērōon*) for his son and for 'all the Judaeans' (first century CE).[33] Having noted this role of associations in the burial of individual members and a few cases of common burial by association, it is important to point out that there are many epitaphs that simply do not refer to such groups at all. So the Judaeans at Hierapolis who failed to mention any affiliation with a Judaean association or who did not involve a local guild in funerary arrangements there are not out of the ordinary in this respect.

A second funerary role involves associations being named as recipients of fines for any violation of the grave alongside other civic institutions (e.g., civic treasury, council, people, elders' organization), or alone. Several guilds at Kyzikos are designated as recipients of any fines for violation of the grave, for instance, and a similar picture emerges at Smyrna, where two different families chose an association of porters who worked in the harbour.[34] So in some ways the 'head of the synagogue' at Smyrna in the second or third century (a woman named Rufina) was following local custom when she made fines for violation of her household's grave payable to the 'most sacred treasury' of Smyrna (1500 denaria) and to an association

[33] Ameling 2004: no. 223 = Frey 1936–52: ii. no. 757 = *TAM* ii. no. 612. This inscription from Tlos plays a role in a recent debate regarding how common were such collective 'Jewish cemeteries' in the first two centuries (before the catacombs of Rome). Strubbe (1994: 101–2) draws on the clear Tlos case to argue for the commonality of collective Judaean grave plots in Asia Minor (using other less certain evidence along the way). On the other hand, David Noy (1998: 81) argues that 'the existence of separate Jewish burial areas before the catacombs seems on the whole fairly unlikely'. I would suggest that forms of Judaean burial would be dependent on variations in local practice among associations, and, in fact, at least two epitaphs from Tlos appear to confirm this point. Like the Judaean epitaph, they involve a collective burial area (*hērōon*). Each lists names (with no mention of familial relation among the names) of those who are to be buried within it, likely the members of associations (*TAM* ii. nos. 604 and 615).

[34] *IK* 18 (*Kyzikos*): nos. 97, 211, 291 (marble-workers, clothing-cleaners, and porters); *IK* 23–4 (*Smyrna*): nos. 204–5; cf. *IK* 53 (*Alexandreia Troas*): no. 122 (coppersmiths, second c. CE), 151–2 (porters).

(1000 denaria), in this case the *ethnos* (kin-group) of the Judaeans of which she was a leader or benefactor.[35]

A third area of funerary involvement on the part of associations in Asia Minor entails groups being designated recipients of a foundation that made them responsible for visiting and maintaining the grave, including yearly (or more frequent) ceremonies at the site.[36] It was not necessarily the case that the owner of the grave was a member of the association in question.[37] It seems that the more important factor in decision-making (on the part of the deceased-to-be or family members of the deceased) concerned choosing a group that could indeed be trusted to help protect the grave and fulfill other obligations, and sometimes this was a group to which a family member belonged.

Several inscriptions from Ephesos illustrate this function of associations, for instance. In one first-century epitaph, a silversmith and his wife designate the association (*synedrion*) of silversmiths as recipient for any fines, but they also leave behind specific funds so that the group can 'take care of' (*kedetai*) the grave-site (*IK* 11–17 [*Ephesos*]: no. 2212).[38] In another, a physician and his wife leave behind an endowment for the 'association (*synedrion*) of physicians in Ephesos who meet in the "museum" (*mouseion*)' to take care of the grave (*IK* 11–17 [*Ephesos*]: no. 2304). Especially interesting for our present purposes is the family epitaph of a chief-physician at Ephesos (named Julius), who asked that 'the Judaeans in Ephesos' (not the *synedrion* of physicians) maintain the tomb.[39] It is unclear as to whether Julius was a Judaean or not, but either way we are seeing Judaeans participating in local customs in places like Ephesos.

---

[35] *IK* 23–4 (*Smyrna*): no. 295 = Ameling 2004: 43 = Frey 1936–52: ii. no. 741. Cf. Ameling 2004: 154, 157 (Nikomedia, third c. CE).

[36] On grave visitation, see Garland 2001: 104–20. On Roman burial practices, see Toynbee 1971: 61–4. On crowns, see Goodenough 1953–68: vii. 148–71.

[37] Thus, for instance, Aurelius Zotikos Epikratos made arrangements for the guild of nail-workers to perform the grave-crowning ceremony. The fact that the deceased was not a member of that guild is suggested by the fact that two other guilds (coppersmiths and purple-dyers) are listed as back-ups if the nail-workers failed to fulfill their obligations (Judeich 1898: no. 133; cf. Judeich 1898: no. 227).

[38] Cf. *IK* 11–17 (*Ephesos*): nos. 2402 (potters), 2446 (linen-workers).

[39] *IK* 11–17 (*Ephesos*): no. 1677 = Ameling 2004: 32 = Frey 1936–52: ii. no. 745; second c. CE. See Noy 2003–5: i. no. 76 from Venosa for another Judaean chief-physician.

Along similar lines, a devotee of the Judaean God (either a Judaean or a Christian) in third-century Akmoneia donated several tools to 'the neighbourhood of those near the first gateway' (Ameling 2004: no. 171).[40] He did so on the condition that this neighbourhood-association yearly decorated his wife's grave with roses (*rodisai*), performing the Roman ceremony of *rosalia*, which would have most likely included a banquet.[41] This offers an interesting parallel to Glykon's request to have grave-crowning ceremonies held on the Roman New Year, led by the carpet-weavers' association.[42] In both cases a traditionally Roman festival is adapted to local custom (involving associations) by families devoted to the Judaean God, presumably omitting practices that would evoke honours for Graeco–Roman deities (namely, sacrifice).

GUILDS AT HIERAPOLIS AND THE IDENTITIES OF THE PURPLE-DYERS

Turning to Hierapolis specifically, it is important to give some sense of what role the guilds played in funerary practices there, which will

---

[40] The inscription uses the so-called Eumeneian formula, which stipulates that if someone violates arrangements on the epitaph they will have 'to reckon with the justice of God' (*estai auto pros ton theon*). Ramsay and others felt that the inscription was Christian, assuming the Eumeneian formula was exclusively Christian, which is now known to be used also by Judaeans (Ramsay 1895–7: ii. 520). Robert (1960a) thought that the owner of the grave was probably Judaean, based on the 'Semitic' name of the man (Math(i)os) who sold the plot to Aur. Aristeas (assuming that they were 'co-religionists') and on the absence of other evidence of Christians in third-century Akmoneia (cf. Trebilco 1991: 78–80; Strubbe 1994: 72–3). The arguments for Judaean identity are less than certain, and either option (Judaean or Christian) remains a possibility here. For Judaeans at Akmoneia see Ameling 2004: 168–78. For Christians see *MAMA* vi. no. 336.

[41] On associations and the *rosalia* festival in the Greek East, see *IG* x. 2 no. 260; Dimitsas 1896: no. 920; *CIL* iii. nos. 703, 704, 707 (from Macedonia); Fränkel 1890–5: no. 374B; *IK* 31 (*Klaudiupolis*): no. 115; *IK* 9–10 (*Nikaia*): nos. 62, 95, 1283, 1422; *SEG* 49 [1999], nos. 1790 and 2508 (from Asia Minor). Cf. Perdrizet 1900; Robert 1960c: 342; Trebilco 1991: 80–1. On *collegia* in the Latin West see Toynbee 1971: 61–4; Lattimore 1962: 137–41 (cf. *CIL* v. nos. 2090, 2176, 2315, 4015, 4017, 4448).

[42] On the use of crown symbolism in Judaean art, architecture, and literature, see Goodenough 1953–68: vii. 149–52. For Judaean adaptation of granting crowns as a form of honour for living benefactors see Ameling 2004: 36 (Phokaia or Kyme; third c. CE) and Bruneau 1982; Horsley 1981– : viii. 12 (Samaritans on Delos; *c.* second–first c. BCE).

then shed more light on the significance of Glykon's decision to include guilds (and the purple-dyers in particular) in his bequest. Of the sixteen extant inscriptions that refer to occupational associations at Hierapolis, ten are epitaphs, and six of these expressly involve a guild or guilds in some ongoing grave ceremonies or superintendence of the grave (including the Glykon inscription). Most of these (four) involve the local practice of providing 'funds for the grave-crowning' (*stephanōtikon*), which in this form of expression seems peculiar to the Lycos valley, primarily Hierapolis.[43] Another refers to the responsibility of a guild (purple-dyers or, if they fail, the livestock-dealers) in 'burning the incense (*papoi*) on the customary day' (Judeich 1898: no. 227b; *c*.190–250 CE). Furthermore, five of the ten epitaphs also mention guilds as recipients of any fines for violation of the grave (Judeich 1898: no. 218; Pennacchietti 1966–7: nos. 7, 23, 25, 45).

Since there are cases where several guilds are involved on one epitaph, in all there are a total of ten guilds mentioned in connection with funerary arrangements in the extant monuments of Hierapolis: dyers, nail-workers, copper-smiths, purple-dyers, livestock-dealers, water-mill engineers, farmers, wool-cleaners, carpet-weavers, and an unknown 'guild'. The association of purple-dyers, in particular, stand out prominently as a favourite in the funerary monuments that have survived to us, appearing as recipients of fines or bequests for visitation ceremonies on nearly half (four out of ten) of the grave-inscriptions involving guilds, including the Glykon family grave itself.[44]

The fact that a family devoted to the Judaean God specifically chose to call on the services of the purple-dyers, as well as the carpet-weavers (known only from the Glykon inscription), begs a question regarding the composition or ethnic identities of the membership of these guilds. This issue is important in evaluating the possibilities regarding dynamics of assimilation or interaction that we are witnessing. Scholarly discussions of this inscription, including many based on the earlier reading which lacked the reference to the

[43] Judeich 1898: nos. 50, 195; Pennacchietti 1966–7: no. 45; Miranda 1999: no. 23 = Judeich 1898: no. 342. On this local ceremony see Judeich's 1898 notes to no. 195, as well as nos. 133, 153, 209, 234, 270, 278, 293, 310, 336 (cf. Robert 1969: nos. 84–5, Laodikeia).

[44] Judeich 1898: nos. 133, 227; Pennacchietti 1966–7: no. 23, and Miranda 1999: no. 23 = Judeich 1898: no. 342.

Kalends, address the question of whether the guilds were (1) solely
Judaean, (2) solely gentile ('pagan'), or (3) a mixture of both, but
seldom with reference to other epigraphical evidence for the purple-
dyers. Such evidence shows that, for the purple-dyers, at least, the
first option is untenable, the second plausible, and the third most
likely.

Erich Ziebarth was among the first to suggest that these two guilds
were solely Judaean in membership, and other scholars have followed
suit, including William Ramsay and Shimon Applebaum.[45] Most
recently, Miranda (1999: 140–5) suggests that the purple-dyers, at
least, were solely Judaean, based on the fact that Glykon chose to have
the purple-dyers provide their services only on a Judaean holiday,
whereas the bequest to the carpet-weavers involves both a Roman
and a Judaean holiday, reflecting Glykon's choice of separate holidays
for the gentile and Judaean members of that mixed group, in her
view. However, the Glykon inscription does not give any clear indication that either of these guilds were distinctively Judaean, nor that
they stood out from other such groups in Hierapolis.

More importantly, numerous inscriptions (seven in all)
concerning purple-dyers in this period (mid-second to early-third
centuries) show that, rather than being distinctively Judaean, this
guild consisted principally of gentiles (at the points we have any
evidence for them) and were viewed as a typical guild in the city.[46]
Thus, for instance, the purple-dyers joined with the *polis* in about
209 CE to dedicate a portion of the theatre (two levels of the archi-
trave) to Apollo Archegetes ('the Founder'), to other gods of the
homeland, and to the emperors Septimius Severus and Caracalla
(Ritti 1985: 108–13). And beyond the Glykon inscription, none of

[45] Ziebarth 1896: 129; Ramsay 1900: 81 and 1902; Applebaum 1974: 480–3.
[46] Cf. Judeich 1898: 174; Ritti 1992–3: 66–7. There are slight variations in the
terminology used in reference to the purple-dyers, but it would be problematic to
argue that more than one guild of purple-dyers existed at one time based on such
slight changes, since such variations (rather than strict titles) were common among
other associations and terms such as 'most holy' or 'most sacred' often appear when
the group in question (rather than someone else) was in charge of having the
monument inscribed (cf. n. 13). The purple-dyers are to be distinguished from the
'dyers' (*bapheis*), however, who formed a separate guild (Judeich 1898: nos. 50 and
195).

the other four families who included the purple-dyers (or its leader-ship, 'the board of presidency of the purple-dyers') in funerary arrangements expressly indicate any Judaean connections regarding either the family who owned the grave or the guild in question.[47]

When the 'sacred guild (*ergasia*) of purple-dyers' set up its own honorary monuments for civic and imperial officials, once again there is no indication that they were distinctively Judaean in compos-ition.[48] It is certainly possible, however, that the guild included Judaeans in its membership when such honorary activities took place (the membership would no doubt change over generations), especially in light of evidence from elsewhere concerning Judaeans' interactions with imperial-connected individuals who were not Ju-daean (see Harland 2003: 219–28). So, although we cannot necessar-ily assume that the purple-dyers were solely gentile, we do know that they were *not* solely Judaean during the era of the Glykon inscription.

In light of this, there are two main possibilities regarding the composition of these guilds. In either case we have evidence not only for the participation and integration of Judaeans in civic life but also for Judaean affiliations with, or even memberships in, local occupational associations at Hierapolis. On the one hand, if the guild was composed exclusively of gentiles, as Judeich and Cichorius suggested early on, we have a Judaean following burial conventions of non-Judaeans in Hierapolis (and Asia generally) by including guilds in funerary provisions (Humann et al. 1898: 46, 51, 174). In this case, the reason for Glykon's asking these guilds (instead of a Judaean group, for instance) to perform the grave rituals would presumably relate to the fact that he had contacts with purple-dyers

---

[47] Judeich 1898: no. 133; Judeich 1898: no. 227b (a legacy to τῷ συνεδρίῳ τῆς προεδρίας τῶν πορφυραβάφων 'the board of presidency of the purple-dyers'); Pen-nacchietti 1966–7: no. 23 (referring to the προεδρία τῶν πορφυραβάφων, 'the pre-sidents of the purple-dyers'. Cf. Judeich 1898: no. 156; Pennacchietti 1966–7: no. 37 (each involving a purple-*dealer* with no Judaean connection involved).

[48] Judeich 1898: no. 42; Judeich 1898: no. 41= *IGR* iv. no. 822 (probably third c. CE). The use of 'most sacred' is typical of associations, organizations, and civic bodies when they express their own identities, namely, when they are having the monument inscribed (see n. 13; cf. Judeich 1898: nos. 36, 40). Other inscriptions relating to the purple-dyers at Hierapolis were inscribed under the auspices of the *polis* or by families in connection with burial, where less praising language is used.

and carpet-weavers in the context of commercial networks, perhaps as a regular customer or benefactor of the groups.[49]

What seems even more likely is that, although consisting principally of gentiles, at Glykon's time these two guilds included individual devotees of the Judaean God (Judaeans, or perhaps gentile sympathizers or Judaizing Christians),[50] who happened to be purple-dyers or carpet-weavers. Paul R. Trebilco is among those who mention this third possibility, yet he is hesitant to take a stand on which of the three options seems most or least likely.[51] Suggesting the presence of devotees of the Judaean God in the guilds would have the advantage of better accounting for Glykon's request that gentile guilds perform the customary grave-ceremony on Judaean holidays, and we know that Judaeans sometimes did engage in clothing and other related occupations (cf. Frey 1936–52: ii. nos. 787, 873, 929, 931; Acts 16. 14–15; 18. 2–3).

If this is indeed the case, then we can begin to imagine processes whereby ordinary gentiles might become gentile sympathizers or god-fearers (such as those at Aphrodisias in the fourth century), since the Glykon family's choice to corporately involve these guilds in celebrating Judaean festivals would involve some gentiles who had little or no previous involvement in Judaean practices per se. Social network connections based on common occupation could become the basis of new adherences, in this case perhaps leading to an increase in the number of gentiles with some level of attachment to the Judaean God or community.[52]

[49] It is unlikely that Glykon is himself a member in one of the guilds in question since he does not identify his occupation (as one would expect). It was common for wealthier individuals to call on the funerary-related services of a guild to which they did *not* belong (see the earlier discussion of socio–economic status and n. 36).

[50] On Christians at Hierapolis, see n. 58 below.

[51] Trebilco 1991: 178–9. Kraabel (1968: 134–5) was among the first to mention this option. Ritti 1992–3 further explores this possibility and is less hesitant in suggesting that this may be a mixed guild. Miranda (1999: 141–4) discusses evidence of Judaean occupational organizations (in Palestine and Alexandria) at some length, and suggests that the purple-dyers were likely Judaean and that the carpet-weavers may have been mixed. The new edition of Schürer's work (1973–87: iii. 27) states that 'the members of the guilds must also have been influenced by Judaism'. Cf. *AE* (1994), no. 1660 on the possibility of *theosebeis*.

[52] Compare the situation in fourth century Aphrodisias, where several Jews and god-fearers came from occupations related to clothing production or sale (rag-dealer,

If there were Judaeans (or sympathizers) as members of these guilds at Hierapolis, as I argue, Glykon's reasons for choosing these two guilds (rather than other known guilds) would involve a combination of factors, including his contacts (for commercial and/or benefaction purposes) with both Judaeans and gentiles *and* his ethno-cultural affiliations with fellow-Judaeans (or at least gentile devotees of the Judaean God) in Hierapolis. It is this combination of attachments which makes this third option concerning the mixed composition of the guild most effective in making sense of our evidence. The theory that Judaeans at Hierapolis maintained affiliations with or memberships in other groups or associations within the city is also consistent with Judaean evidence from other areas.[53] In cases where we know the occupation of Judaeans there is a range of activity comparable to the known guilds, and the fact that occupations are mentioned at all on Judaean monuments suggests that this was an important component in their identities.[54] So it is not too surprising to find Judaeans affiliating with their fellow-workers within occupational networks and guilds.

CONCLUSION: DYNAMICS OF ACCULTURATION AND INTERACTION IN THE DIASPORA

Throughout this discussion we have encountered members of cultural minority groups, namely Judaeans at Hierapolis, adopting and adapting to local cultural practices and interacting with their Greek

---

fuller, boot-maker, linen-worker, and purple-dyer) and where, in at least one case, the occupation of a named Judaean (a bronzesmith) matches that of two god-fearers, who are also bronzesmiths (Ameling 2004: no. 14b, lines 25, 46, 53; cf. Reynolds and Tannenbaum 1987: 116–23). Rajak and Noy (1993) have shown that even those who were designated *archisynagogoi* may have been non-Judaean benefactors of Judaean groups, for instance; cf. Rajak 2002: 373–91.

[53] See Harland 2003: 200–10. For Judaeans in age-based, gymnastic organizations, for instance, see Robert 1946: 100–1 (ephebes at Iasos; second–third c. CE); Robert 1960b (elders at Eumeneia; second–third c. CE); Lüderitz 1983: 11–21, nos. 6–7 (ephebes at Cyrene; late first c. BCE–early first c. CE).

[54] See van der Horst 1991: 99–101; Cohen 1993: 10; Reynolds and Tannenbaum 1987: 116–23.

or Roman neighbours. The case of Hierapolis demonstrates well some dynamics of cultural and structural assimilation in the ancient context, and it is worthwhile placing this evidence within a broader social scientific framework here.[55]

J. Milton Yinger's sociological study defines assimilation as 'a process of boundary reduction that can occur when members of two or more societies or of smaller cultural groups meet' (Yinger 1981: 249). Yinger and others distinguish between sub-processes of assimilation, the most important here being (1) cultural assimilation, or acculturation, and (2) structural assimilation (cf. Yinger 1981; Marger 1991: 116–29). First, *acculturation* refers to processes which occur when individuals or groups of differing cultural backgrounds come into first-hand contact with one another, with resulting transformations in the cultural patterns of one or both groups (cf. Redfield et al. 1936: 149). Acculturation can involve the selection, adoption, and adaptation of a variety of cultural traits including language, dress, religion, funerary practices, and other cultural conventions, beliefs, and values of a particular cultural group. This process is selective and transformative as 'the patterns and values of the receiving culture seem to function as selective screens in a manner that results in the enthusiastic acceptance of some elements, the firm rejection of other elements'; furthermore, 'the elements which are transmitted undergo transformations' in the process (Barnett 1954).

It is important to emphasize that in this theoretical framework acculturation can progress significantly without the disintegration of a group's boundaries in relation to a larger cultural entity. Cultural adaptation can be a two-fold process entailing the 'maintenance of cultural integrity as well as the movement to become an integral part of a larger societal framework', as John W. Berry (1980: 13) points out.

The second main sub-process of assimilation, *structural assimilation*, entails both informal and formal levels. At the *informal* level, individual members of a given ethnic or cultural group can interact with persons from other cultural groups through personal, social network connections, including memberships in neighbourhoods,

---

[55] For others who have drawn on such social scientific insights in studying religious and immigrant groups in the ancient context see Balch 1986; Barclay 1996; Noy 2000.

clubs, and associations (cf. Yinger 1981: 254; Marger 1991: 118). The *formal* level of structural assimilation involves members of a particular cultural minority group participating in political, legal, social, or economic institutions of society.

These concepts about processes of assimilation provide a framework in which to make better sense of the ancient evidence—albeit fragmentary—for Judaean or other immigrant groups within the cities of the Roman empire. Moreover, both the form and content of the Judaean epitaphs at Hierapolis illustrate both cultural and structural assimilation. First of all, we have seen that the *form* of Judaean grave-inscriptions indicates acculturation to patterns of other non-Judaean graves from the same locale.[56] Moving beyond the form of epitaphs to the content and its implications, we should notice important, though subtle, evidence of *formal structural* assimilation in relation to important institutions of the *polis*. The inclusion of formal institutions, usually the civic ('most sacred') treasury, as recipients of fines in many (nine) Judaean inscriptions at Hierapolis (and on Judaean epitaphs elsewhere) implied some level of civic responsibility for preservation or maintenance of the family tomb.[57] Violators would have to answer not only to the descendants of the family, if any, but also to the city of Hierapolis itself, so to speak. Including local associations, alongside civic institutions or alone, was thought to further bolster this insurance that the family grave would remain intact and undisturbed.

There are other signs of formal structural assimilation among Judaeans here. Like their non-Judaean counterparts, nearly half (ten) of the Judaean epitaphs from Hierapolis (the Glykon grave included) also clearly mention that a copy of the epitaph was placed in the archives. This, too, has a structural significance beyond its seemingly incidental mention. For placing a copy in the civic archives further ensured that, if anyone should fail to obey the will of the deceased or actually modify

---

[56] Among these standard inscriptional patterns (including the common vocabulary used) are: (1) identification of the owner(s) of the tomb and surrounding area; (2) stipulations that no one else, beyond those designated, is to be buried on the site; (3) preventative measures of setting fines should the instructions be violated; (4) arrangements for payment of such fines to civic institutions (treasury or elders' organization) and/or local associations (e.g. Judaean synagogues, guilds); and (5) deposit of a copy of the inscription in the civic archives.

[57] Cf. Ameling 2004: nos. 172 (Akmoneia), 216 (Termessos), 233, 238 (Korykos).

(or remove) the original inscription from the tomb, legal action could follow. This expectation of justice from relevant civic institutions is a significant indication of structural integration in local society.

It is within this context of interaction and acculturation that we can better understand the Glykon family grave itself. If, on the one hand, Glykon and his family were gentile sympathizers (or Judaizing Christians, for instance)[58] who had adopted important Judaean practices, which is possible though difficult to establish, then this provides an interesting case of gentile acculturation to the ways of local Judaeans while also continuing in burial customs characteristic of Hierapolis and Asia Minor. Furthermore, the involvement of a guild which did include gentiles in its number (the purple-dyers) is suggestive of at least some level of acculturation to Judaean practices on the part of these gentile guild-members at Hierapolis; yet here it is the family, not the gentiles in the guilds, who have chosen to have the guilds participate on Judaean holy days and on a Roman festival. Unlike the case of the god-fearers at Aphrodisias, we have no clear indication that the gentile guild-members were members in the synagogue or in an association devoted solely to the Judaean God.

If, on the other hand, Glykon and his family were Judaeans, this inscription provides further evidence of both cultural and structural assimilation among Judaean families at Hierapolis. We have found that the fabric of this family's identity consisted of intertwined Judaean, Roman, and Hierapolitan strands. Most prominently in setting this family apart as Judaean is the concern to have the grave visited on the festivals of Passover and Pentecost. While many Judaean families did assert their identity (in relation to non-Judaeans) by using the designation *Ioudaios*, the Glykon inscription

---

[58] Literary evidence shows that followers of Jesus lived at Hierapolis already in the first century (Colossians 4. 13). The prophetic daughters of Philip, bishop Papias, and bishop Apollinarius are also associated with Hierapolis in the second century (cf. Eusebius, *Ecclesiastical History* 3. 31. 3, 3. 36. 1–2, 4. 26. 1). The earliest openly Christian inscriptions from Hierapolis date to Byzantine times, when the martyrium associated with Philip was established (cf. Judeich 1898: nos. 22, 24; fifth century or later). Attempts by those such as Ramsay to identify other inscriptions as Christian based only on the inscription's use of 'unusual' language are problematic at best (e.g. Judeich 1898: no. 227 with notes by Judeich refuting Ramsay's suggestion of Christianity here; see Ramsay 1895–7: i. 118–19, no. 28).

stands out among the epitaphs of Hierapolis, and even Asia Minor or the empire, in its special concern to carry on Judaean *observances* even after death, thereby continuing to express this aspect of identity within Hierapolis indefinitely.

At the same time, Glykon felt himself to be Roman, both in proudly indicating his status as Roman citizen and by choosing to include the Roman New Year festival as a time when the family would be remembered by a guild in Hierapolis. In fact, the rarity of epigraphic evidence concerning the celebration of this Roman festival in the provinces draws further attention to its significance here as a sign of Romanization among Judaeans.

Alongside these Judaean and Roman facets of identity, the family also belonged specifically within the community of Hierapolis in many respects. At the formal structural level, this family, like other Judaeans, deposited a copy of the inscription in the civic archives, indicating an expectation of some level of justice from local legal procedures and institutions. Furthermore, these Judaeans were acculturated to Hierapolitan practice in leaving 'grave-crowning funds' and followed regional custom in entrusting their final bequest to occupational associations. Not only that, but the family also chose one of the most popular and, it seems, widely trusted local guilds to fulfil this duty.

Both Glykon and the devotees of the Judaean God who belonged to the guilds of purple-dyers and carpet-weavers illustrate the potential for multiple affiliations with sub-groups of local society. This is an important factor in the process of informal structural assimilation. Moreover, information concerning the Glykon family, as well as other Judaeans at Hierapolis, points toward significant levels of integration within the society of Graeco–Roman Hierapolis alongside a continued sense of being Judaean.

BIBLIOGRAPHY

Abrams, D. and Hogg, M. A. (1990). 'An Introduction to the Social Identity Approach', in Abrams and Hogg (eds.), *Social Identity Theory: Constructive and Critical Advances*. New York: Harvester Wheatsheaf, 1–5.

Ameling, W. (2004). *Inscriptiones Judaicae Orientis: ii. Kleinasien.* Tübingen: Mohr Siebeck.

Applebaum, S. (1974). 'The Organization of the Jewish Communities in the Diaspora', in S. Safrai and M. Stern (eds.), *The Jewish People in the First Century: Historical Geography, Political History, Social, Cultural and Religious Life and Institutions*, 2 vols. Assen: Van Gorcum, i. 464–503.

Balch, D. L. (1986). 'Hellenization/Acculturation in 1 Peter', in C. H. Talbert (ed.), *Perspectives on First Peter.* Macon: Mercer University Press, 79–101.

Barclay, J. M. G. (1996). *Jews in the Mediterranean Diaspora from Alexander to Trajan (323 BCE–117 CE).* Edinburgh: T. and T. Clark.

Barnett, H. W., Broom, L., Siegel, B. J., and Vogt, E. Z. (1954). 'Acculturation: An Exploratory Formulation', *American Anthropology*, 56: 973–1002.

Bean, G. E. and Mitford, T. B. (1970). *Journeys in Rough Cilicia, 1964–1968*, Ergänzungsbände zu den Tituli Asiae Minoris 3, Denkschriften (Österreichische Akademie der Wissenschaften. Philosophisch-Historische Klasse) 102. Vienna: Böhlau.

Beard, M., North, J., and Price, S. (1998). *Religions of Rome*, 2 vols. Cambridge: Cambridge University Press.

Berry, John W. (1980). 'Acculturation as Varieties of Adaptation', in A. M. Padilla (ed.), *Acculturation: Theory, Models and Some New Findings*, AAAS Selected Symposium 39. Boulder, Colorado: Westview, 9–26.

Bruneau, P. (1982). '"Les Israélites de Délos" et la juiverie délienne', *BCH*, 106: 465–504.

Chaniotis, A. (2002). 'The Jews of Aphrodisias: New Evidence and Old Problems', *Scripta Classica Israelica*, 21: 209–42.

Cohen, S. J. D. (1993). '"Those Who Say They Are Jews and Are Not": How Do You Know a Jew in Antiquity When You See One?', in Cohen and E. S. Frerichs (eds.), *Diasporas in Antiquity.* Atlanta: Scholars Press, 4–8.

Dimitsas, M. G. (1896). Ἡ Μακεδονία ἐν λίθοις φθεγγομένοις καὶ μνημείοις σωζομένοις, 2 vols. Athens: Adelphōn Perrē, repr. as *Sylloge inscriptionum graecarum et latinarum Macedoniae*, Chicago: Ares, 1980.

Dittmann-Schöne, I. (2000). *Die Berufsvereine in den Städten des kaiserzeitlichen Kleinasiens*, Theorie und Forschung 690. Regensburg: Roderer.

Esler, P. S. (2003). *Conflict and Identity in Romans: The Social Setting of Paul's Letter.* Minneapolis: Fortress.

Fränkel, E. (1890–5). *Die Inschriften von Pergamon*, 2 vols. Berlin: Spemann.

Fraser, P. M. (1977). *Rhodian Funerary Monuments.* Oxford: Clarendon.

Frey, J.-B. (1936–52). *Corpvs inscriptionvm ivdaicarvm*, 2 vols. Vatican: Pontificio istituto di archeologia cristiana, repr. as *Corpus of Jewish Inscriptions*, New York: Ktav, 1975.

Garland, R. (2001). *The Greek Way of Death*, 2nd edn. Ithaca: Cornell University Press.

Gerner, E. (1941). 'Tymborychia', *Zeitschrift der Savigny-Stiftung für Rechtsgeschichte, Romanistische Abteilung*, 16: 230–75.

Goodenough, E. R. (1953–68). *Jewish Symbols in the Greco–Roman Period*. New York: Pantheon Books.

Goodman, M. (ed.) (1988). *Jews in the Graeco–Roman World*. Oxford: Clarendon.

Hadas-Lebel, M. (1979). 'Le paganisme à travers les sources rabbiniques des IIe et IIIe siècles. Contribution a l'étude du syncrétisme dans l'empire romain', *ANRW*, 2. 19. 2: 426–41.

Harland, P. A. (2003). *Associations, Synagogues, and Congregations: Claiming a Place in Ancient Mediterranean Society*. Minneapolis: Fortress.

——(2009). *Dynamics of Identity in the World of the Early Christians: Associations, Judeans, and Cultural Minorities*. New York and London: T. and T. Clark.

Horsley, G. H. R. (1981–). *New Documents Illustrating Early Christianity*. North Ryde, N.S.W.: Ancient History Documentary Research Centre, Macquarie University.

Horst, P. W. van der (1991). *Ancient Jewish Epitaphs: An Introductory Survey of a Millennium of Jewish Funerary Epigraphy (300 BCE–700 CE)*, Contributions to Biblical Exegesis and Theology 2. Kampen: Kok Pharos.

Humann, C., Cichorius, C., and Judeich, W. (1898). *Altertümer von Hierapolis*, Jahrbuch des Kaiserlich Deutschen Archäologischen Instituts, Ergänzungsheft 4. Berlin: Reimer.

Judeich, W. (1898). 'Inschriften', in Humann et al. 1898: 67–181.

Kraabel, A. T. (1968). *Judaism in Western Asia Minor under the Roman Empire, with a Preliminary Study of the Jewish Community at Sardis, Lydia*. Unpublished dissertation, Harvard University.

——(1982). 'The Roman Diaspora: Six Questionable Assumptions', *Journal of Jewish Studies*, 33: 445–64.

Kraemer, R. S. (1989). 'On the Meaning of the Term "Jew" in Greco–Roman Inscriptions', *HTR*, 82: 35–53.

Labarre, G. and Le Dinahet, M.-Th. (1996). 'Les métiers du textile en Asie Mineure de l'époque hellénistique a l'époque imperiale', in *Aspects de l'artisanat due textile dans le monde Mediterranéen (Egypte, Grèce, monde romain)*, Collection de l'Institut d'Archéologie et d'Histoire de l'Antiquité, Université Lumière-Lyon 2. Paris: De Boccard, 49–116.

Lattimore, R. A. (1962). *Themes in Greek and Latin Epitaphs*. Urbana: University of Illinois Press.

Leon, H. J. (1995). *The Jews of Ancient Rome*, 2nd edn. Peabody: Hendrickson (1st edn. 1960).

Lifshitz, B. (1967). *Donateurs et fondateurs dans les synagogues juives*. Paris: Gabalda.

Lüderitz, G. (1983). *Corpus jüdischer Zeugnisse aus der Cyrenaika*, Beihefte zum Tübinger Atlas des Vorderen Orients. Wiesbaden: Reichert.

Marger, M. N. (1991). *Race and Ethnic Relations: American and Global Perspectives*, 2nd edn. Belmont, CA: Wadsworth.

Meslin, M. (1970). *La fête des kalendes de janvier dans l'empire romain: étude d'un rituel de Nouvel An*, Collection Latomus 115. Brussels: Latomus.

Miranda, E. (1999). 'La comunità giudaica di Hierapolis di Frigia', *EA*, 31: 109–55.

Murray, M. (2004). *Playing a Jewish Game: Gentile Judaizing in the First and Second Centuries CE*. Waterloo: Wilfrid Laurier University Press.

Nijf, O. M. van (1997). *The Civic World of Professional Associations in the Roman East*. Dutch Monographs on Ancient History and Archaeology 17. Amsterdam: Gieben.

Nilsson, M. P. (1916–19). 'Studien zur Vorgeschichte des Weihnachtsfestes', *Archiv für Religionswissenschaft* 19: 50–150, repr. in his *Opuscula selecta linguis Anglica, Francogallica, Germanica conscripta*, 3 vols. Lund: Gleerup (1951–60), i. 214–310.

Noy, D. (1998). 'Where Were the Jews of the Diaspora Buried?', in Goodman 1998: 75–89.

——(2000). *Foreigners at Rome: Citizens and Strangers*. London: Duckworth.

——(2003–5). *Jewish Inscriptions of Western Europe*, 2 vols. Cambridge: Cambridge University Press.

Paton, W. R. and Hicks, E. L. (1890). *The Inscriptions of Cos*. Oxford: Clarendon.

Pennacchietti, F. A. (1966–7). 'Nuove iscrizioni di Hierapolis Frigia', *Atti della Accademia delle Scienze di Torino: II classe di scienze morall storiche e filologiche*, 101: 287–328.

Perdrizet, P. (1900). 'Inscriptions de Philippes', *BCH*, 24: 299–323.

Price, S. R. F. (1984). *Rituals and Power: The Roman Imperial Cult in Asia Minor*. Cambridge: Cambridge University Press.

Rajak, T. (2002). *The Jewish Dialogue with Greece and Rome: Studies in Cultural and Social Interaction*. Leiden: Brill.

——and Noy, D. (1993). '*Archisynagogoi*: Office, Title and Social Status in the Greco–Jewish Synagogue', *JRS*, 83: 75–93.

Ramsay, W. M. (1895–7). *The Cities and Bishoprics of Phrygia*, 2 vols. Oxford: Clarendon.

——(1900). 'Antiquities of Hierapolis (Humann, Cichorius, Judeich, Winter)', *Classical Review*, 14: 79–85.

——(1902). 'The Jews in the Graeco–Asiatic Cities', *Expositor*, 5: 98–101.

Redfield, R., Linton, R., and Herskovits, M. J. (1936). 'Memorandum for the Study of Acculturation', *American Anthropologist*, 38: 149–52.

Reynolds, J. (1977). 'Inscriptions', in J. A. Lloyd (ed.), *Excavations at Sidi Khrebish Benghazi (Berenice). i: Buildings, Coins, Inscriptions, Architectural Decoration*, Supplements to Libya Antiqua 5. Libya: Department of Antiquities, Ministry of Teaching and Education, 233–54.

——and Tannenbaum, R. (1987). *Jews and God-fearers at Aphrodisias: Greek Inscriptions with Commentary*, Cambridge Philological Society, Supp. 12. Cambridge: Cambridge Philological Society.

Ritti, T. (1985). *Fonti letterarie ed epigrafiche*, Hierapolis Scavi e Ricerche 1. Rome: Bretschneider.

——(1992–3). 'Nuovi dati su una nota epigrafe sepolcrale con stefanotico da Hierapolis di Frigia', *Scienze dell'antichità. Storia archeologia antropologia*, 6–7: 41–68.

Robert, L. (1946). 'Un corpus des inscriptions juives', *Hellenica*, 3: 90–108.

——(1960a). 'Épitaphes juives d'Éphèse et de Nicomédie', *Hellenica*, 11–12: 409–12.

——(1960b). 'Épitaphes d'Eumeneia de Phrygie', *Hellenica*, 11–12: 436–9.

——(1960c). 'Recherches épigraphiques', *Revue des Etudes Anciennes*, 62: 276–361, repr. in his 1969–90: ii. 792–877.

——(1969). 'Les inscriptions', in J. Des Gagniers (ed.), *Laodicée du Lycos: Le nymphée*. Québec: Presses de l'Université Laval; Paris: de Boccard, 247–389.

——(1969–90). *Opera minora selecta*, 7 vols. Amsterdam: Hakkert.

Rutgers, L. V. (1994). *The Jews in Late Ancient Rome: Evidence of Cultural Interaction in the Roman Diaspora*. Leiden: Brill.

Schürer, E. (1973–87). *The History of the Jewish People in the Age of Jesus Christ*, revised by G. Vermes, F. Millar and M. Goodman, 3 vols. Edinburgh: T. and T. Clark.

Strubbe, J. H. M. (1991). '"Cursed be He That Moves My Bones"', in C. A. Faraone and D. Obbink (eds.), *Magika Hiera: Ancient Greek Magic and Religion*. Oxford: Oxford University Press, 33–59.

——(1994). 'Curses Against Violation of the Grave in Jewish Epitaphs of Asia Minor', in J. W. van Henten and P. W. van der Horst (ed.), *Studies in Early Jewish Epigraphy*. Leiden: Brill, 70–128.

——(1997). *ΑΡΑΙ ΕΠΙΤΥΜΒΙΟΙ: Imprecations Against Desecrators of the Grave in the Greek Epitaphs of Asia Minor. A Catalogue*, IK 52. Bonn: Habelt.

Toynbee, J. M. C. (1971). *Death and Burial in the Roman World.* London: Thames and Hudson.

Trebilco, P. R. (1991). *Jewish Communities in Asia Minor.* Cambridge: Cambridge University Press.

Williams, M. H. (1994). 'The Organization of Jewish Burials in Ancient Rome in the Light of Evidence from Palestine and the Diaspora', *ZPE,* 101: 165–82.

——(1997). 'The Meaning and Function of *Ioudaios* in Graeco–Roman Inscriptions', *ZPE,* 116: 249–62.

Yinger, J. M. (1981).'Toward a Theory of Assimilation and Dissimilation', *Ethnic and Racial Studies,* 4: 249–64.

Ziebarth, E. (1896). *Das griechische Vereinswesen.* Stuttgart: Hirzel.

12

Josephus and Variety in First-Century Judaism

Martin Goodman

It is a commonplace that Judaism before 70 CE included a number of distinct varieties. The question to be tackled in this paper is the extent of such variety. It will be my contention that a proper awareness of the necessary limitations of the surviving evidence should encourage scholars to expect greater variety than is always acknowledged.[1]

Scholarship on late Second Temple Judaism is voluminous, and the constant stream of studies over the past century and a half shows no sign of abating, but there is no sign of a consensus on this central issue. In essence scholars divide into two camps. Those temperamentally inclined to harmonisze the evidence take parallels to indicate probable identity, so that, for instance, the Dead Sea sectarians are judged to have been Essenes (or Sadducees, or Jewish Christians), or Beth Shammai are identified with the Zealots.[2] On the other side,

---

[1] This is a modified version of a lecture presented to the Academy in April 1998 in the course of a visit arranged under the exchange scheme with the British Academy. I am grateful to the Academy for its hospitality and to a number of colleagues for their helpful comments after the lecture. Since the subject of the lecture deals with general issues of historical method and does not attempt to introduce readers to previously unnoticed evidence, I have preserved the lecture format in the published text rather than presenting numerous examples or citations of modern scholarship to reinforce the points made. I hope that as a result the argument may emerge more clearly.

[2] Examples are too numerous to list, but for the Dead Sea sectarians as Essenes see, e.g., Vermes in Schürer (1973–87), ii. 583–5; as Sadducees, North 1955, and much

those temperamentally inclined to distinguish between groups may be accused of producing a veritable hubbub of varieties of Judaism, and some scholars have even taken to referring to Judaisms in the plural.[3] When trying to justify their approach (which they do only rarely), both sides in this historiographical conflict have tended to resort to appeals to instinct or taste or (at best) to the simplicity of their explanation of the evidence, as if it can be taken for granted that the explanation should be simple. My intention in this paper is to provide a rationale for preferring one approach over the other, so that in future investigations of the evidence scholars may have a better idea of what the significance of the similarities between groups they discover is likely to be. I shall try to demonstrate that it is better to distinguish rather than harmonize. I shall do so through an investigation of the main source of evidence for Second Temple Judaism, the writings of Flavius Josephus.

Josephus does not of course provide the only evidence for first-century Judaism, but his writings have a special significance for two reasons. First, most of the other evidence was written either by those within a particular branch of Judaism for fellow insiders (for example, the Dead Sea Scrolls and rabbinic texts), thus showing no interest in discussion of other types of Judaism except when they impinged upon their own type, or by outsiders for outsiders (for example, the pagan writings collected and edited by Menahem Stern [1974–84]), thus all too readily falling into caricature. Only Philo, in some of his extant writings, and Josephus in (probably) all of his, were insiders who set out to explain Jews and Judaism

recent scholarship based on 4QMMT; as Jewish Christians, Eisenman 1996. On Beth Shammai and the Zealots, see Ben-Shalom 1993.

[3] On Judaisms in the plural, see, e.g., Neusner et al. 1987. I should state clearly at the outset that the extreme form of this view, that there was no common core at all in late Second Temple Judaism, seems to me demonstrably incorrect, since all pious Jews shared at least the beliefs that they worshipped the God whose Temple was in Jerusalem and that they had a common history in which a covenant between God and Israel was enshrined in the Torah which all Jews knew they had to observe. It is important also to clarify that the varieties I am investigating constituted self-aware groups (what Josephus and others called *haireseis*). It is unwarranted and misleading to treat each text or author as if it or he constituted a separate Judaism. For a brief but acute analysis of the external impulses which lead scholars either to conflate or to divide, see Schwartz 1996: 72.

to outsiders.[4] Second, and more crucially, only in Josephus' works is an extensive description of the different types of first-century Judaism provided.

Thus, if Josephus' writings did not survive it would be hard to reconstruct the picture of variety that he presents in the *Jewish War*, the *Jewish Antiquities*, and the *Life*. Philo referred to the Essenes, Therapeutae, and unnamed extreme allegorists, but not to Pharisees, Sadducees, the Fourth Philosophy, Zealots, Christians, or *hakhamim*. In the New Testament there is mention of Pharisees and Sadducees and of course Jewish Christians, but nothing about Essenes. Tannaitic texts are similarly silent about Essenes. By contrast surviving pagan writings from the first two centuries CE on Jews and Judaism appear completely unaware that Judaism was in any way divided: both Pliny and Dio Chrysostom referred to the Essenes, and Tacitus mentioned Christians, but, although these authors were aware that these groups originated in Judaea, they did not describe them as types of Jews.[5]

Thus the only ancient source to refer even to all three of the Jewish philosophies specially singled out by Josephus on numerous occasions as characteristic of Judaism, let alone the numerous other types of Judaism to which he referred in passing such as the Fourth Philosophy, ascetics such as Bannus and John the Baptist, and so on, was Josephus himself. So the crucial question is how full a picture Josephus intended to give of first-century Judaism.

The first common misapprehension to clear away is the widespread belief that Josephus' division of Judaism into three *haireseis* (schools or sects) should be taken seriously as evidence that only three types of Judaism existed in his day (e.g. Broshi 1998). It is true enough that Josephus made frequent mention of this division,[6] often referring the reader back to his full discussion of the Pharisees, Sadducees, and Essenes in *Jewish War* 2. 119–61, but his insistence on this three-fold division is bizarre when the whole point of

---

[4] On the readers of Philo's works, see Schürer 1973–87: iii. 814, 817–18, 840, 853–4, 878, 889; on the readers of Josephus' historical writings, see Bilde 1988: 75–8, 102–3.

[5] Pliny, *Natural History* 5. 73; Dio ap. Synesius, *Vita Dionis* (= Stern 1974–84: i. 539); Tacitus, *Annals* 15. 44. 2–8.

[6] *Jewish War* 2. 119; *Jewish Antiquities* 13. 171–3, 18. 11; *Life* 10: the *haireseis* are three in number 'as I have often said'.

describing the three philosophies in that context was to introduce to readers a novel Fourth Philosophy, on which he laid the blame for the outbreak of war against Rome. Thus in all references to Judaism after 6 CE, such as at *Life* 10, Josephus ought, if he was consistent, to have referred to the four philosophies in Judaism—but he never did; it will not do to argue that he referred only to the three philosophies of which he approved, and omitted the fourth philosophy for that reason, since he seems also to have disapproved of the Sadducees, who are described unfavourably in all the passages which refer to them in any detail. Hence the appearance of a similar three-fold division of Judaism in *Pesher Nahum*, where Israel is divided into Judah, Ephraim, and Menasseh, should be taken as evidence not that Josephus was pedantically accurate in his assertion that there were three philosophies, but as evidence that Jews liked to divide up their society in this way, perhaps in imitation of a *topos* familiar elsewhere in the Hellenistic world (Flusser 1970: 159). Similarly, patristic writers from Justin Martyr to Epiphanius liked to list seven Jewish *haireseis*, although the names on their lists varied tremendously.[7]

Second, it is not even the case that Josephus consistently stressed that there were different varieties of Judaism. On the contrary, the main message of Josephus' only deliberate presentation of the theology of Judaism, in *Against Apion* 2. 179–210, specifically stressed the unity and uniformity of Jewish beliefs and practices. Doubtless this emphasis on uniformity was occasioned in part by apologetic concerns, since Josephus was intent in this passage on comparing Jews to the fickle and variegated Greeks, and quite possibly Josephus took at least some of his description of Judaism from an Alexandrian predecessor, but it is hard to see why he should have copied down from an earlier text a description of Judaism which he did not himself believe to be true, and it is difficult to understand how he could have hoped to convince about the unity of Jews his gentile readers, some of whom he expected to have read his earlier works, if he thought those earlier works painted a clear picture of Jewish heterogeneity (Goodman 1999a).

---

[7] On the patristic texts, see Lieu 1988.

The probable conclusion is that Josephus did not believe that he had drawn up a proper picture of Judaism at all in his earlier works. He did indeed intend (so he said) to write a description of the nature of Jewish customs, but the project was apparently never completed.[8] His aim in the works he did write was entirely different. The *Life* constituted an apologetic autobiography, in which Josephus defended himself against attacks on his behaviour in the revolt against Rome; apart from his protestations about his personal piety, religion was hardly relevant (see Bilde 1988: 104–13). The *Jewish War* and the *Antiquities* concentrated on political and military history in imitation of Thucydides and Polybius (in the case of the *War*) and (probably) Dionysius of Halicarnassus (in the case of the *Antiquities*), so there was no need to refer to any variety of Judaism except when it had an impact on political events (Bilde 1988: 65–104). Impact on political events was indeed the explicit reason for the description of the three *haireseis* in *War* Book 2 and *Antiquities* Book 18 as a contrast to the Fourth Philosophy, which, so Josephus claimed, caused the uprising against Rome in 6 CE. Similarly Philo, 'not inexperienced in philosophy', was mentioned only because he was at the head of the Jewish delegation which went from Alexandria to Italy to bring a complaint before the emperor Gaius Caligula (*Jewish Antiquities* 18. 259).

Hence it is entirely probable that Josephus may have failed to mention those religious groups and tendencies which had no political impact of the type that interested him, even if such groups were influential in other ways or such varieties of Judaism were commonly espoused. Only a miniscule proportion of Josephus' writings has anything at all to say about any variety of Judaism. It is quite wrong, for example, to view *Antiquities* 13–18 as an apologia for Pharisees since they hardly feature in the narrative.[9]

What should follow from all this is a radical disinclination, when confronted with evidence from other sources which does not

[8] On this uncompleted project to compose four books on Jewish theology and practice, see *Jewish Antiquities* 20. 268 and elsewhere; see the brief and not wholly convincing discussion by Altschuler 1978–9.
[9] Williams 1993: 39, notes that only 0.0109% of *Jewish Antiquities* books 13–18 refers to Pharisees either individually or collectively.

explicitly tie up with the evidence in Josephus, to use subtle arguments to make the evidence appear so to conform. Such arguments are of course perfectly possible and are often deployed: distinctions are made between the views of a Jewish group from inside and from outside; discrepancies are explained as the result of the development of a group over time, or as evidence that different strands of a group co-existed; as a last resort, the sources of the evidence which contradicts Josephus are sometimes dismissed as ignorant. My point is simply that the deployment of such arguments itself presupposes a degree of thoroughness in Josephus' treatment of varieties of Judaism in his day for which there is no warrant.

In the study of two groups in particular the tendency of scholars to conflate evidence seems to me to have been particularly misleading: the Dead Sea sectarians, whose close relationship with the Essenes in Josephus is still only doubted by a minority of scholars, and the *hakhamim* ('the wise') found in tannaitic texts, whose close relationship to the Pharisees in Josephus is almost universally taken for granted.

In the half century since the first scrolls were found by the Dead Sea, the group behind the sectarian documents has been identified variously with Pharisees, Sadducees, Jewish Christians, Zealots, and, most commonly, Essenes.[10] In each case it is possible to point to parallels between specific aspects of sectarian behaviour or theology as revealed by the scrolls and similar traits attributed to one or other group in the Greek and Latin descriptions, but it is self-evident from the multiplicity of hypotheses that the total set of parallels is not sufficient in any one case to establish identity. Thus the leading Essene hypothesis has to cope with serious discrepancies, such as the contradiction between the strong insistence of the classical sources on the Essenes' devotion to the common ownership of property and the assumption in some scrolls (e.g. *Damascus Rule* 9. 10–16) that sectarians might own their own goods. It seems to me (as to some others) better to treat the Dead Sea sect as a previously unknown Jewish group (see Talmon 1994). The whole value of the chance find of these new documents was not to fill in the gaps in an

---

[10] For the argument which follows, see in greater detail Goodman 1995.

obscure corner of an already fairly complete picture of late Second Temple Judaism but, far more importantly, to reveal a type of Judaism not previously attested.

Far less has been written about the relationship between the *hakhamim* and the Pharisees. There is a consensus that it is wrong simply to equate the two groups but also that in some way the *hakhamim* 'emerged' from the Pharisees. Thus, for example, rabbinic stories about the Houses of Hillel and Shammai have been characterised as 'Rabbinic Traditions about the Pharisees before 70' (Neusner 1971).

This quasi-unanimity is rather curious, because there are quite powerful arguments against identification.[11] Most important of these is the fact that the tannaim never referred to themselves or their predecessors before CE 70 as 'Pharisees': there is absolutely no explicit evidence that Hillel or Shammai considered themselves to be Pharisees. It is hard to see how this can have been accidental, or simply a contrast between 'insider' and 'outsider' literature. *Pharisaios* in Greek was a self-designation used by both Josephus and St Paul.[12] Whatever its derivation, it was evidently a Semitic term in origin, translatable into Hebrew as *perush* (cf. Baumgarten 1983), for the tannaim did refer occasionally to *perushim* as opponents of Sadducees on halakhic issues, but without identifying themselves with such *perushim*. Thus the tannaim knew that there was a group of Jews called Pharisees but they did not consider them connected to their own circle.[13] The distinction is clear in *Mishnah Yadaim* 4. 6: 'The Sadducees say, 'We cry out against you, O Pharisees, for you say "The Holy Writings make the hands unclean", but the writings of Hamiram do not make the hands unclean!' Rabban Yohanan b. Zakkai said, 'Have we nothing against the Pharisees save this!...' It is clear from this passage that Yohanan b. Zakkai at least did not identify himself as a Pharisee, or at least he was not so identified by the

---

[11] See Schäfer 1991; see also, more briefly, S. Cohen 1984.

[12] Josephus, *Life* 12 (despite the cautionary remarks of Mason 1991: chs. 14–15); Paul in Philippians 3. 5.

[13] The only explicit texts are *Mishnah Yadaim* 4. 6, 7; and *Tosefta Hag.* 3. 35. Other relevant texts are conveniently collected in Bowker 1973, along with those passages in which the term *perushim* appears to have been used in a purely negative sense of 'separatists' (e.g. *Mishnah Sotah* 3. 4).

compiler of the Mishnah. Ingenious arguments can of course be devised to explain these phenomena and conflate the evidence, but I would suggest that it is not justifiable to seek to do so when conflation is in itself deemed implausible.

I suggest, then, that Pharisees and *hakhamim* were two quite separate, self-aware groups which flourished both before and after 70 CE. I make this suggestion in full awareness that the hypothesis raises three difficulties, which will need to be discussed separately.

The first problem, and the easiest to deal with, is the fact that on all issues on which rabbinic texts state that Pharisees took a particular stance against others, their stance was identical to that taken by the *hakhamim* themselves when the stance of the *hakhamim* happens to be recorded in later texts.[14] From this it can be deduced only that Pharisees and *hakhamim* had in some respects similar views, not that their groups were identical. In the late Second Temple there seems to have been a series of issues on which all Jews, and each group of Jews, might be expected independently to take a stand, such as purity rules (for example, the requisite dimensions of a *mikveh*), controversial elements of the Temple cult (for instance, the sacrifice of the red heifer, the date of the *omer* offering, and the calendar), life after death, eschatology, or messianism.[15] It was perfectly possible for two groups to agree on one issue but disagree on another: thus the Dead Sea sectarians followed the same hala-kha as the Sadducees in some cases, but there is no reason to suppose that they did so *qua* Sadducees; on the contrary, the author of 4QMMT was explicit that the 'we' and the 'you' in the text—clearly separate groups—could agree in specific instances against 'them' (see Sussmann 5750). In the same way, different groups might adopt the same slogans and concepts but adapt them to their own use: quite different Jews might appeal to the notion of 'zeal' as shown in the distant past by Pinchas, or to the name Zadok, or to separation or separateness as desirable (Baumgarten 1997: 56). The identification of common themes and slogans is an important part of the study of Judaism in this period, but it is a

---

[14] e.g. *Mishnah Yadaim* 4. 7, on details of purity law and on the law of damages.
[15] A similar point is made by Baumgarten 1997: 55–7.

quite separate exercise from the identification of distinct groups or tendencies.

The second problem is the later rabbinic construction of Jewish history in Second Temple times, in which actions attributed by Josephus to Pharisees are sometimes attributed directly in amoraic sources to rabbinic-type sages, such as the hostile relationship of the Pharisees as a group to Alexander Jannaeus and their amicable relations with his widow, Shelomzion.[16] The best explanation seems to me to lie in the rabbinization of history. One of the most striking features of the earliest stratum of rabbinic literature is its apparent vagueness about the rabbinic past before the time of Hillel and Shammai: the chain of tradition in *Mishnah Abot* chapter 1 is as significant for what it does not say as for what it does. By the amoraic period, the need to understand all of Jewish religious leadership since Moses as rabbinic led to the description of even a figure such as Ezra as a *talmid hakham*, Torah scholar.[17] It was comparatively easy to claim for the rabbinic movement a figure from the early first century BCE such as Shimon b. Shetah.

The third and final factor has probably been the most influential in the common tendency to treat Pharisees and *hakhamim* as part of a single movement, and that is the extent to which both Pharisees and *hakhamim* were closely related to the common Judaism of ordinary Jews. Here there has been much confusion, and a longer discussion is necessary.

Pharisees were, according to Josephus, influential with the masses (*Antiquities* 13. 298), although they were themselves quite a small group—the number given for the Pharisees who refused to take an oath of loyalty to the emperor in the time of Herod was six thousand (*Antiquities* 17. 42). The explanation of their influence must therefore lie in their teachings but, despite Josephus' assertion at *Antiquities* 18. 15, it is hard to accept that the teachings which gave them prestige were their idiosyncratic views on

---

[16] Compare Josephus, *Antiquities* 13. 288–98 to *Babylonian Talmud Kiddushin* 66a (cf. Geller 1979) and see the traditions about Shimon b. Shetah and Yannai in *Genesis Rabbah* 91. 3 and parallels, and about Shimon b. Shetah and Shelomzion in *Babylonian Talmud Taanith* 23 a. See in general S. Cohen 1986.

[17] For the stories about Ezra, see Ginzberg 1909–38: iv. 354–9, vi. 441–7.

fate and on the after-life. It is more plausible that their popularity stemmed from their attitude to ancestral tradition.[18]

Josephus stated in various places that, unlike the Sadducees, the Pharisees accepted the regulations handed down by ancestral tradition (*Antiquities* 13. 297, 408). This terminology does not imply that this tradition was particularly Pharisaic: Josephus used the same terms to refer to the traditions by which Josiah had been guided long ago (*Antiquities* 10. 51), and here the ancestors in question were evidently those of all Jews. What distinguished this ancestral tradition was that it was not written down, which was why the Sadducees rejected it (*Antiquities* 13. 297), but there is no reason to suppose that it was therefore preserved orally, let alone that it should be identified with what rabbis described from the amoraic period on as the Oral Torah. It is far more likely that the *paradosis*, or transmission, accepted by Pharisees from previous generations was transmitted not by words but through behaviour, as Philo assumed in praising ancient ancestral customs in a commentary on Deuteronomy 19. 4:

Another commandment of general value is 'Thou shalt not remove thy neighbour's landmarks which thy forerunners have set up'. Now this law, we may consider, applies not merely to allotments and boundaries of land in order to eliminate covetousness but also to the safeguarding of ancient customs. For customs are unwritten laws, the decisions approved by men of old, not inscribed on monuments nor on leaves of paper which the moth destroys, but on the souls of those who are partners in the same citizenship. For children ought to inherit from their parents, besides their property, ancestral customs which they were reared in and have lived with even from the cradle, and not despise them because they have been handed down without written record. Praise cannot be duly given to one who obeys the written laws, since he acts under the admonition of restraint and the fear of punishment. But he who faithfully observes the unwritten deserves commendation, since the virtue which he displays is freely willed.

(*On Special Laws* 4. 149–50, Loeb translation)

---

[18] For a slightly more detailed version of this argument, see Goodman 1999.

As Philo suggested (rightly), religion is usually caught, not taught.[19]

The Pharisees not only accepted for themselves the validity of customary interpretation of halakha, but added authority to such customs by asserting that their acceptance was not arbitrary—on the contrary, they prided themselves on the accuracy of their interpretation of the Torah (*Antiquities* 17. 41; *Life* 191, etc.).[20] It is unsurprising that Pharisees were popular when they supported ordinary Jews in their customary behaviour, giving to those Jews the comforting knowledge that they had the approval of pietists who were 'unrivalled experts' in the law (*Life* 191). In any particular case, it may have been hard to tell whether a custom was carried out just because it was customary or because it had the approval of the Pharisees or for both reasons. There were doubtless cases, such as the attack by the Sadducee Jonathan on the Pharisees in the time of John Hyrcanus which, according to *Antiquities* 13. 296, led Hyrcanus to abrogate all the *nomima*, customs, established by the Pharisees for the people and to punish all those who observed such regulations, when the enemies of the Pharisees clearly implied that these were *Pharisaic* rules, but this is the stuff of polemic. Usually, perhaps, it was unnecessary to ask whether ancestral tradition or Pharisaic concurrence with such tradition mattered most.

It is probable that the relation of the rabbinic *hakhamim* to ordinary customs was similar. The best evidence can be culled from the marriage contracts, divorce documents, deeds of sale, renunciations of claim and other legal documents of the Bar Kochba period which have been discovered in the Judaean Desert.[21] The documents were certainly written by or for Jews and in some cases refer explicitly to 'the law of Moses and Israel' but, as has long been noted, although the law in use is essentially similar to that found in tannaitic texts, there is no evidence that any rabbi was involved either in the preparation or the enforcement of the agreements, and there are

---

[19] On the Pharisaic *nomima*, see the survey of scholarship in Mason 1991: 230–45. On the Philo text, see N. Cohen 1993: 258–72, but note that she too takes unwritten law to be oral (p. 281).

[20] On the Pharisees' claim to *akribeia* (accuracy), see Baumgarten 1983: 413–17.

[21] The bulk of the documents are now published in the series Discoveries in the Judaean Desert 1955– : ii and xxvii, and Yadin 1989.

also numerous variations from tannaitic law, some minor, others of greater import.[22] One way to explain these differences is to dismiss the Jews who produced the documents as marginal to Jewish society, and the claim that this was so is undisprovable. However it is equally possible that the Judaean Desert documents simply reflect one strand in a general common Jewish law, and that what the tannaim did was to put into order existing legal customs by subjecting them to analysis on the basis of legal principles, logic, and biblical proof texts.[23] That this was indeed the case at least to some extent is clear from the internal evidence of the Mishnah that, for instance, quite substantial differences in marriage customs in Galilee and Judaea were both acknowledged and accepted by the tannaim (cf. e.g. *Mishnah Ketuboth* 4. 12). That is to say, rabbinic Judaism was not a special variety of Judaism created by the decrees and decision of innumerable *hakhamim* through the ages; rather, it was ordinary, customary Judaism as interpreted and approved by the *hakhamim* in the first two centuries CE.

If this analysis is correct, it will be seen that the Judaism of the Pharisees and the Judaism of the *hakhamim* must have been in some respects very similar, since both accepted the validity of ancestral custom, but this does not at all reinforce the notion that the two movements were in some way connected. It is entirely possible for two groups to co-exist in one period and place with almost identical interests but clearly separate identities—an outsider viewing varieties of orthodox Judaism in the contemporary world could not easily see the differences which divide one hasidic group from another, but it would be a big mistake to ignore the strong sense of group identity within each type of hasidism. It is often by the little differences— 'little' as perceived by outsiders—that people and groups establish their identity against others. Modern scholars may be unable to find a specific identifiable difference in theology or practice between the *hakhamim* and the Pharisees, but this may simply reflect our ignorance of, in particular, the theology and practices of the Pharisees. In any case it may be otiose to look for any such difference: as with contemporary hasidim, it may be mainly or only the names and the

---

[22] See the summary by Cotton in Cotton and Yardeni 1997: 154–7.
[23] This was the argument of Goodman 1983: 160–1.

allegiances of the members of two groups that differentiate one from another.

It is of course true that in the period while the Temple still stood two sages are specifically attested as belonging both to the Pharisees and to the *hakhamim*: Rabban Gamaliel and his son, Simon.[24] These two are the only *hakhamim* described in extant Greek sources as Pharisees, although, since the family was both prominent and rich, there is no particular reason to attribute their evident influence in Judaean politics to their membership of either group (see Schäfer 1991: 172). It is naturally possible that the fact that these two individuals are ascribed in one source to the *hakhamim* and in another source to the Pharisees is explained by the basic identity of these two groups, as is usually assumed, but it is no less possible that an enthusiastic Jew could, if he so wished, belong to more than one group at a time. There is indeed evidence that just as it was possible to migrate from one variety of Judaism to another, as Josephus did according to his autobiography (*Life* 10–12), so it was possible to hold combined membership of two groups. Not all groups were tolerant of each other—thus it was presumably impossible to be both a Pharisee and a Sadducee—but other combinations, such as Pharisaism and the Fourth Philosophy, were less obviously contradictory (cf. Josephus, *Antiquities* 18. 4, 23). It may be best to envisage the varieties of Judaism as a series of overlapping circles, much as some eclectic Roman thinkers in the early empire found it possible to align themselves with a number of different philosophies at the same time. The notion of choice underlies the term *hairesis* used of all these varieties of Judaism not only by Josephus but also by Philo and the author of the Acts of the Apostles.[25] Thus what made each group distinct was simply the fact that some individual Jews chose to adopt their ideas and practices.

My intention has been to show how partial our knowledge of Jewish history in this period really is. If we relied, as for other

---

[24] On Gamaliel, see Acts 5. 34–9; 22. 3; *Mishnah Orlah* 2. 12; *Mishnah Rosh Hashanah* 2. 5; *Mishnah Yebamoth* 16. 7; *Mishnah Sotah* 9. 15; *Mishnah Gittin* 4. 2–3; *Mishnah Aboth* 1. 16; on Simon b. Gamaliel, see Josephus, *Life* 191; *Mishnah Aboth* 1. 17; *Mishnah Kerithoth* 1. 7.

[25] See the examples gathered by Baumgarten 1997: 3.

religions in the Roman Empire, on the evidence of pagan authors and archaeology and inscriptions, we would be unaware of any variety within Judaism at all (see Goodman 1998). Hence our picture of the different types of Judaism relies wholly on the sources preserved, for religious purposes, by later Jewish and Christian tradition. Since much of the material found in each of these traditions is lacking in the other, it is obvious that both traditions have been highly selective, and it was always likely that there existed further material which had been ignored by both. The Dead Sea scrolls provided historians with precisely such material, and their significance should not be weakened by forcing what they tell us into the straitjacket of what was already known from other sources.

Hence the number of varieties of Judaism at the end of the Second Temple period must be judged even greater than emerges from simply reading Josephus. According to *Jerusalem Talmud Sanhedrin* 29c, Rabbi Yohanan stated that 'Israel did not go into exile until there were twenty-four sects of *minim*'. It is not clear precisely what constituted a 'sect of *minim* [heretics]', but it is likely that Rabbi Yohanan reckoned that there were at least twenty-five types of Judaism before the destruction of the Temple in 70 CE—one acceptable variety, and twenty-four others. I would not advocate reliance on Rabbi Yohanan's mathematics, but I would suggest that in essence he was just about right.

BIBLIOGRAPHY

Altschuler, D. (1978–9). 'The Treatise "On Customs and Causes" by Flavius Josephus', *Jewish Quarterly Review*, 69: 226–32.

Baumgarten, A. I. (1983). 'The Name of the Pharisees', *Journal of Biblical Literature*, 102: 411–28.

——(1997). *The Flourishing of Jewish Sects in the Maccabean Era*. Leiden: Brill.

Ben-Shalom, I. (1993). *The School of Shammai and the Zealots' Struggle against Rome*. Jerusalem: Yad Izhak Ben-Zvi Press and Ben Gurion University of the Negev Press (in Hebrew).

Bilde, P. (1988). *Flavius Josephus, between Jerusalem and Rome: His Life, his Works and their Importance*. Sheffield: JSOT Press.

Bowker, J. (1973). *Jesus and the Pharisees*. Cambridge: Cambridge University Press.

Broshi, M. (1998). 'Ptolas and the Archelaus Massacre (4Q468g = 4Q Historical Text B', *Journal of Jewish Studies*, 49: 341–5.

Cohen, N. G. (1993). *Philo Judaeus: His Universe of Discourse*. Frankfurt: P. Lang.

Cohen, S. (1984). 'The Significance of Yavneh', *Hebrew Union College Annual*, 55: 36–42.

——(1986). 'Parallel Historical Traditions in Josephus and Rabbinic Literature', in *Proceedings of the Ninth World Congress of Jewish Studies*. Jerusalem: World Union of Jewish Studies, i. 7–14.

Cotton, H. M. and Yardeni, A. (eds.) (1997). *Aramaic, Hebrew and Greek Documents. Texts from Nahal Hever and Other Sites*, Discoveries in the Judaean Desert, 27. Oxford: Clarendon Press.

Discoveries in the Judaean Desert (1955–). *Discoveries in the Judaean Desert*. Oxford: Clarendon.

Eisenman, R. H. (1996). *The Dead Sea Scrolls and the First Christians*. Shaftesbury: Element.

Flusser, D. (1970). 'Pharisees, Sadducees and Essenes in Pesher Nahum', in M. Dorman, S. Safrai, and M. Stern (eds.), *Essays in Jewish History and Philology in Memory of Gedaliahu Alon*. Jerusalem: Hakibbutz Hameuchad, 133–68 (in Hebrew), translated into English by A. Yadin as 'Pharisees, Saducees, and Essenes in Pesher Nahum', in D. Flusser, *Judaism of the Second Temple Period*. Grand Rapids, Michigan, and Cambridge: Eerdmans; and Jerusalem: Magnes Press and Jerusalem Perspective (2007), i. 214–57.

Geller, M. J. (1979). 'Alexander Jannaeus and the Pharisee Rift', *Journal of Jewish Studies*, 30: 202–11.

Ginzberg, L. (1909–38). *Legends of the Jews*, 7 vols. Philadelphia: Jewish Publication Society of America.

Goodman, M. D. (1983). *State and Society in Roman Galilee*, A.D. *132–212*, Totowa, N.J.: Rowman and Allanheld.

——(1995). 'A Note on the Qumran Sectarians, the Essenes and Josephus', *Journal of Jewish Studies*, 46: 161–6, repr. in his *Judaism in the Roman World: Collected Essays*. Leiden: Brill (2007), 137–43.

——(1998). 'Jews, Greeks and Romans' in M. Goodman (ed.), *Jews in a Graeco–Roman World*. Oxford: Oxford University Press, 3–14.

——(1999a). 'Josephus' Treatise Against Apion', in M. Edwards, M. Goodman, and S. Price (eds.), *Apologetic in the Roman Empire: Pagans, Jews, and Christians*. Oxford: Oxford University Press, 45–58.

——(1999b). 'A Note on Josephus, the Pharisees and Ancestral Tradition', *Journal of Jewish Studies*, 50: 17–20, repr. in his *Judaism in the Roman World: Collected Essays*. Leiden: Brill (2007), 117–21.

Lieu, J. M. (1988). 'Epiphanius on the Scribes and Pharisees', *Journal of Theological Studies*, 39: 509–24.

Mason, S. (1991). *Flavius Josephus on the Pharisees: A Composition-Critical Study*. Leiden: Brill.

Neusner, J. (1971). *Rabbinic Traditions about the Pharisees before 70*, 3 vols. Leiden: Brill.

——Frerichs, E., and Green, W. S. (eds.) (1987). *Judaisms and their Messiahs*. Cambridge: Cambridge University Press.

North, R. (1955). 'The Qumran "Sadducees"', *Catholic Biblical Quarterly*, 17: 164–88.

Schäfer, P. (1991). 'Der vorrabbinische Pharisäismus', in M. Hengel und U. Heckel (eds.), *Paulus und das antike Judentum*. Tübingen: Mohr, 125–75.

Schürer, E. (1973–87). *The History of the Jewish People in the Age of Jesus Christ*, rev. G. Vermes, F. Millar, and M. Goodman, 3 vols. Edinburgh: T. and T. Clark.

Schwartz, D. R. (1996). 'MMT, Josephus and the Pharisees', in J. Kampen and M. J. Bernstein (eds.), *Reading 4QMMT: New Perspectives on Qumran Law and History*. Atlanta: Scholars Press, 67–80.

Stern, M. (1974–84). *Greek and Latin Authors on Jews and Judaism*, 3 vols. Jerusalem: Israel Academy of Sciences and Humanities.

Sussmann, Y. (5750 [= 1990]). 'The History of Halacha and the Dead Sea Scrolls: Preliminary Observations on *Miqsat Ma'ase ha-Torah* (4QMMT)', *Tarbiz*, 59: 11–76 (in Hebrew).

Talmon, S. (1994). 'The Community of the Renewed Covenant between Judaism and Christianity', in E. Ulrich and J. Vanderkam (eds), *The Community of the Renewed Covenant*. Notre Dame, Ind.: University of Notre Dame Press, 5–10.

Williams, D. S. (1993). 'Morton Smith on the Pharisees in Josephus', *Jewish Quarterly Review*, 84. 1: 29–42.

Yadin, Y. (1989). *The Finds from the Bar-Kokhba Period in the Cave of Letters: ii. Greek Papyri*, ed. N. Lewis, Jerusalem: Israel Exploration Society.

13

The Forging of Christian Identity and the *Letter To Diognetus*

Judith Lieu

To speak of 'the forging of Christian identity' is to choose a deliberate ambiguity. 'Forging' sounds both more decisive and more creative than 'formation' or 'development'. Yet 'forging' also suggests other possibilities, and, if one were to abstract any moral judgement implied, it would be interesting to explore the role of pseudonymity, of the preservation and multiplication of favourable imperial rescripts and other documents, and of the late (re-)appearance of 'apostolic' records, bishop lists, and the like in the early Christian discovery of its own history. That is not the task of this paper, although 'forging' will offer a reminder of the often derivative and imitative character of early Christian identity-formation.

This, the creation, at least rhetorically, of a self-conscious and distinctive identity is a remarkable characteristic of early Christianity from our earliest sources; indeed it is inseparable from the appearance of those sources and from Christianity's equally characteristic literary creativity.[1] This itself creates a problem which will provide a thread through this paper. For our period, the first two centuries CE,

---

[1] See Cameron 1991: 21: 'But if ever there was a case of the construction of reality through text, such a case is provided by early Christianity...Christians built themselves a new world. They did so partly through practice—the evolution of a mode of living and a communal discipline that carefully distinguished them from their pagan and Jewish neighbours—and partly through a discourse that was itself constantly brought under control and disciplined'; and p. 32: 'As Christ "was" the Word, so Christianity *was* its discourse or discourses.'

material remains are not available as markers of Christian identity, or/and, if available, they would not be or perhaps are not distinguishable (Kraemer 1991: 141–62). What is the relationship between an analysis of identity or ethnicity based on material remains and that based on internal literary sources? How far should literary sources, particularly by a single author, be seen as evidence of a pre-existing identity, how far are they constructive of identity, but only once they become internalized and authorized within the community?

Historical studies have long paid attention to the development of Christian identity, defined traditionally in terms of ecclesiastical authority and of doctrinal formulation, often seeing in it little cause for surprise; more recent emphasis, however, on social history in its various forms has produced an unabating flood of analyses of the formation of Christian identity and its 'difference'. Since the vast majority of those working on 'early Christianity' are trained as and continue to identify themselves as New Testament specialists, the focus has inevitably settled on the New Testament texts.

Three distinct, if overlapping, approaches may be detected in the scholarly literature. Perhaps the first was the observable or external identity of early Christian communities. Eschewing the assumption that 'the church', the *ekklesia*, was *sui generis*, best interpreted through theological categories, what were the models of collective organization known in the Graeco–Roman world to which it most closely conformed? In terms of what known categories would observers, and perhaps adherents, interpret its common life and organization? Initially, Graeco–Roman 'voluntary associations', *collegia* and *thiasoi*, were set over against the Jewish synagogue; cults, particularly mystery cults, and philosophical schools were also brought into the comparison (Wilken 1972, 1984; Meeks 1983: 74–84); broadening the range may have served only to demonstrate the limitations of the enterprise as a means of differentiation: for example, synagogues may have been treated as a form of *collegium*, and also may have presented themselves as centres of philosophy (Kloppenborg and Wilson 1996). It may be doubted whether more can be achieved along these lines, and there are problems: the apparently dispassionate exercise could, of course, mask or provoke theological concern. Barton and Horsley's oft-quoted analysis of the cult-group founded by Dionysius (*SIG* 985) is a case in point: the final paragraph, entitled 'Salvation: Present or Future', claims 'The consequence of this [i.e. Christian belief in the inbreaking of a new age] for their morality (as a response to "grace") and their corporate activity (as sharing of a common experience of "grace") ... lies at the basis of the differences separating them from a group like Dionysius', and in so saying moves beyond the espoused realm of description.[2] For Meeks a decisive distinguishing characteristic of the church, at least in its Pauline manifestation, was its universal or translocal form, something not so easily explained within his descriptive framework (Meeks 1983: 107). Yet, on the one hand, such a universal self-awareness may not have been unique to Christianity, while, on the other, when and how it developed is an important but problematic question: even in the case of the Pauline churches it may have been mediated more through Paul's own person as founder and traveller than fixed in any primary community consciousness (so rightly, Ascough 1997). As important for our purposes is the tension between self-identity and perceived identity. It is arguable that early Christianity as portrayed by Luke-Acts may be described in the language of 'school', yet the terminology that the author prefers is the anomalous ἐκκλησία, primarily of the local community, perhaps germinally of the community of communities, constructing a harmonious unity that was more ideal than real.[3]

An apparently more comprehensive key to Christian identity-formation has been offered by recent exploration of the separation between Christianity and Judaism, an exploration inspired by two primary factors: first, the rediscovery of the multi-faceted richness of first- and second-century Judaism, of which the earliest 'Jesus movement' was a part; second, the timely recognition of the shameful heritage of the unreflected repetition of the rhetoric of identity and

---

[2] Barton and Horsley 1981; Kloppenborg 1996 is more cautious, warning against an idealism that treats rhetoric as descriptive.

[3] On early Christianity as a school see Alexander 1993: esp. 32–9; Barrett 1989 emphasizes Luke's own preference for the language of ἐκκλησία. See Wilken 1972: 269: 'We would expect the self-understanding of the Christians to differ from the impression of them which was held by outsiders. Yet on many points we have, quite uncritically, accepted the Christian view of things and dismissed the views of their contemporaries.'

destiny, both of self and 'other', which accompanied that separation. Contemporary preoccupation with a child's discovery of identity through painful separation from the parent, and the Biblical adoption of the folk-loric or mythical theme of sibling rivalry, have provided congenial models for understanding the development of Christian identity through distancing from and conflict with Judaism (Cf. Segal 1986). Christians claimed to be the true heirs of the inheritance, to be 'Israel', children of Abraham and heirs of the promise made to him; to rightly represent the original intention of the founder, of God or of Moses, in the giving of the Law; to possess the proper interpretation of the definitive texts, the Scriptures; all these claims, incessantly repeated in early Christian literature, not only in that directed against the Jews but also in apologetics for outsiders, as well as in paraenesis and exegesis for insiders, could readily be paralleled, *mutatis mutandis*, in other sectarian, reformist, and break away movements. Novelty, particularly but not only in the ancient world, offers only an insecure identity: even gnostic groups, who largely rejected an identity founded on historical continuity with Israel's past, discovered for themselves a new 'history' through the 'myths' of cosmic fall and redemption.

The reverse side of the coin may seem to have a certain inevitability. The 'failure' of most of the Jews to recognize in Jesus and the early Christian movement the true goal of the promises and dynamic of past experience threatened the credibility of Christian claims, both in the eyes of outsiders and also in those of insiders. The solution was to discredit the Jews, not only for their present unbelief, but for a history of wilful disobedience and obtuseness stretching back to the beginning, a history that was authenticated by a re-reading of the shared Scriptures. Thus Jewish identity, negatively constructed, came to constitute the necessary foil for the construction of Christian identity. The terms that have been used in the last few sentences, 'inevitability', 'necessary', have come to provoke searching analysis: can Christian identity tolerate the dissolving of the demonized identity of the Jews which accompanied its formation? Was the latter really an integral element or merely a contingent ancillary throughout the process? Recognition of the function of vituperation in ancient rhetoric has given a historical context for the vigour of the polemic; yet it has not wholly stifled the sometimes anguished debate as to whether the responsibility of the historian is to remain distanced from the past or to acknowledge its post-history and continuing power.[4]

Various forms of sociological analysis have refined or at least given a quasi-scientific veneer to the generalized account given above. By applying conflict analysis or by comparing the strategies adopted by groups in the face of the apparent disconfirmation of the core values or principles of their identity, scholars have sought to side-step the long tradition which gave an automatic theological affirmation to the past tradition. Sociological analysis has also been applied to the Christian communities themselves as represented by the surviving literature. Particularly influential has been the emphasis on the symbolic universe by which people organize, make sense of, and rationalize their experience.[5] Thus the subjects of 'theology' become the structural components of a social world; the reversal of values or of status epitomized by Jesus' humiliation in incarnation and death becomes the norm for Christian social experience and its value system. Ritual, specifically baptism and eucharist, legitimates this social world by establishing new patterns of belonging, effecting dramatic separation from past experience, embodying a unity which transcends real difference. Equally important has been the analysis of sectarian formation, definition, legitimation, and development. Not only can Christianity's separation from Judaism be explored in terms of sect formation, but the different patterns of relationship towards 'the world' which have been used to categorize nineteenth- and twentieth-century sects can be or have been applied to early Christian communities as accessible through the literature.[6]

Such approaches have become commonplace and need not be further described here. Some features require special emphasis: first, emphasis on internal rhetoric inevitably leads to a strong sense of self-identity, often at odds with other evidence that early Christian groups were more amorphous. Inevitably, the moment of

---

[4] On the issues in this paragraph see further Lieu 1996.
[5] The influence of P. Berger (e.g. Berger 1966) has been paramount.
[6] Here Wilson 1967 has been most influential.

separation provokes much more vigorous rhetoric, enhancing this sense of otherness, which may be less visible to outsiders; the rhetoric of difference may become less urgent precisely when a clearer separate identity becomes more visible to outsiders.

Second, a consequence of the concentration on the textual rhetoric of identity has been the increasing difficulty of talking about '*Christian* identity'. In part this is in recognition that such terminological precision is lacking in the first century, and that the concept is self-evidently anachronistic. Paul, the Gospel according to Matthew, or the Gospel according to John, each presents a different model of the relationship between Judaism and Christianity, reflects a different social context, and betrays a different potential both for existing relationships and for future development. The Pauline Epistles have been particularly receptive to the sociological analysis of community formation, if only because in Paul's letters we have open address to a number of such communities (Meeks 1983; Theissen 1982, 1993). The communities behind the various Gospels, although at times viewed as more accessible to scholarly reconstruction than the so-called historical Jesus, are necessarily more opaque. Yet despite such opacity, each produces a different model of identity and structure. New Testament scholars have found it easier to talk about Pauline, Johannine, or Matthaean Christianity than about first-century Christianity. This is, perhaps, an inevitable consequence of the work of W. Bauer, who, more than sixty years ago, exploded the 'myth' of a pristine Christian 'unity' and 'orthodoxy'; in so doing he paved the way for an emphasis on diversity, free of the value judgements favouring an orthodoxy that was now perceived as the result of political processes (Bauer 1934/71). The result is that the questions of cohesive or integrating identity, and of the path to the development of such an identity in the second century are ever more problematic.[7] One answer has been to distinguish 'identity', which is 'what one's allegiance makes one to be', and which has an atemporal quality, from 'self-definition', which is 'identity culturally

---

[7] See Meyer (1986), who finds sociological approaches such as that of Meeks inadequate in answering questions as to why the early Christian diversity did not lead to schism.

and historically conditioned'.[8] Another answer would be to come to a better understanding of the still inadequately explained mechanisms of cohesion in the second century: in literary terms, the development of the concept of a fourfold Gospel (Stanton 1997), and the rapid development of the letter genre, used even for martyrdom accounts which themselves serve to create identity.

Third, these sociological models operate with an oppositional model, leading to a tendency to see early Christian formation exclusively in opposition to Graeco–Roman society: where Christianity adopted contemporary social patterns it is frequently said to have reversed or inverted them. This is surely tendentious: the correlation between social change and religious change may be disputed; yet whereas earlier studies saw Christianity's success as a response to and evidence for Graeco–Roman religion's failure, it might be better to see it rather as a symptom of and a participant in contemporary social change and potential for change.[9]

In this paper it is argued, first, that the construction of Christian identity is much more fragile than much of this contemporary analysis presupposes. Further, that there are a number of variables in the formation of Christian identity, the interplay between which invites exploration. Most obvious are, the second major theme, those inner tensions provided by the Jewish origins of Christianity. Here, it is often said that Judaism represents an ethnic or a particularist identity, Christianity a universalist one. This has been rightly criticized in recent debate, but the comparison continues to require clearer analysis (cf. Levenson 1996; Barclay 1996). Yet, third, equally clear are the tensions between a discrete local and a common 'universal' identity, and between the language of differentiation from the trends of society and that of reflection of them. Seen within a wider framework, these have been recurrent and perhaps inherent tensions

---

[8] Meyer 1986: 174; 1992; Wimbush speaks of 'discursive and rhetorical formations ever productive of new social formations' (1997: 34).

[9] So Theissen, 'Christology and Social Experience', in Theissen 1993: 187–201, who argues that the plausibility structures of Christian christological convictions, particularly about the self-humiliation and subsequent exaltation of Christ as a model for all believers, and about the body as a symbol of unity in society, are rooted in social change and ideology of the early Empire; see also Cameron 1991: 31. See also Lieu 2002: 97–9.

in Christian history: Christian missions have played their part in the articulation of local identities, for example in the development of scripts and the recording of local languages, or in the identification of particular forms of Christianity with particular national groups such as the Arian Goths; yet they have also provoked intense debate about the integrity of indigenous articulations of Christian identity in a post-colonial age and their relationship to any universal identity. Martin Luther's search for an identity established before and by God alone, i.e. theoretically independent of local or institutional control, has been seen as resulting both in 'a strong sense of group identity which is closely linked, though not identical with various German regional identities', and in a dualistic negation of other cultures (Riches 1996: esp. 435–6).

In this context two quotations may set the theme for this discussion:

This conviction that they were a *people*—i.e., the transference of all the prerogatives and claims of the Jewish people to the new community viewed as a new creation which exhibited and put into force whatever was old and original in religion—this at once furnished adherents of the new faith with a *political and historical* self-consciousness. Nothing more comprehensive or complete or impressive than this consciousness can be conceived . . . This estimate of themselves rendered Christians impregnable against all attacks and movements of polemical criticism, while it further enabled them to advance in every direction for a war of conquest

(von Harnack 1904–5: 300–01).

We may contrast with this the claims of the *Epistle to Diognetus*, a perhaps late-second-century apologetic writing whose original authorship, context, and audience is now lost to us:

For Christians are distinguished from the rest of humankind not by land nor by language nor by customs. For they do not live in their own cities nor use any corrupted dialect, nor do they practise a distinctive life . . . . Dwelling in both Greek and barbarian cities, as allotted to each, and following the native customs in clothing and life-style and the rest of life . . . (*Epistle to Diognetus* 5. 1–2. 4).

The contrast between the two estimates might be seen as the internal self-identity, clearly defined and separate, as represented by Harnack, *versus* the external, observed identity—a lack of visible differentiation—at least as conceived and portrayed by the apologist. It may also be seen as two sides of a common coin: both in effect express the sublimation of any particularist identity in order to claim a highly articulated meta-identity. This claim is already there in the *Epistle to Diognetus*: to complete the last sentence:

Dwelling in both Greek and barbarian cities...and following native customs...they demonstrate that the constitution of their own citizenship (πολιτεία) is both marvellous and self-evidently strange (παράδοξος)...To put it shortly, what the soul is for the body so are Christians in the world. (5. 4; 6. 1)

Although translated 'citizenship', πολιτεία would provide a good equivalent or foundation for 'identity', at least in the present context and in that of the search for and maintenance of identity in Graeco–Roman cities.[10] Yet here it implies a complete relativization of any local loyalty or identity: 'They inhabit their own native lands, but as sojourners; they share everything as citizens, and endure everything as foreigners' (5.5). The language of sojourning and foreignness is already well established in the first century in a variety of New Testament contexts (1 Peter 1. 1, 17; 2. 11; Ephesians 2. 19; Hebrews 11. 13); it is, of course, rooted in the Jewish tradition (cf. Genesis 23. 4; Psalm 39. 12), a tradition ignored by this author.[11] When its correlative is a citizenship of heaven (cf. Philippians 3. 20) it can justify an immunity to social values or pressures. So, here, 'They pass their time on earth, but exercise a citizenship in heaven' (5. 9) leads into a celebration of the abuse, persecution, and rejection they endure: 'They are dishonoured and are glorified in the dishonour' (5. 14). In this way such an ethos serves an internal purpose of reinforcing group solidarity and identity—their heavenly citizenship explains the abuse, abuse is a confirmation of that citizenship. Yet its external apologetic value would be ambivalent, as, too, would its effectiveness in shaping an alternative social identity.

---

[10] On πολιτεία and πολιτεύομαι in the Jewish claim for identity see below nn. 13–15.

[11] Meecham 1949: 109 refers to Philo, *On the Confusion of Tongues* 17 [77f.]. Yet, as noted below, the charge of being 'aliens' in a civic sense is sharply rejected by Josephus when speaking of the Jews of Alexandria (*Against Apion* 2. 6 [71]). On the Jewish tradition and its re-use in the New Testament see Feldmeier 1996.

This is particularly clear when we contrast the use in second-Temple Jewish literature of πολιτεία for a distinctive and ancient way of life. Josephus, rewriting Moses' farewell to the Jews in Deuteronomy, and reinterpreting the significance of the Torah, has him say, 'I have compiled for you, under God's dictation, laws and a πολιτεία, and if you observe it in due fashion, you would be considered by all to be the most fortunate of people'.[12] He also, I would suggest deliberately, uses the same term for the political status guaranteed from the beginning to the Jews in Alexandria and in the cities of Asia Minor, where he likewise vigourously opposes their treatment as 'aliens': Josephus too could say that the Jews have a πολιτεία in other cities but his meaning is very different![13] More particularly, πολιτεία denotes the distinctive Jewish way of life when threatened by suppression: in 2 Maccabees 13. 14 Judas Maccabeus urges his fellow combatants to fight to the death 'for the laws, the Temple, the city, their native land, and the πολιτεία'.[14] Similarly, Jewish texts speak of their πατρίοι νόμοι (ancestral laws) for which they die and by which they are to govern themselves—if this is, as it surely must be, the Torah, it is viewed not as divine revelation but as national tradition: the despotic Antiochus inveigles them, 'Have confidence then and you will receive governing rule over my affairs, once you have denied the ancestral ordinances (θεσμός) of your πολιτεία' (4 Maccabees 8. 7).[15] Not surprisingly, this phrase is nowhere used by the early Christians.

---

[12] *Jewish Antiquities* 4. 8. 2 [193]. Bartlett (1985: 161–2) sees Josephus as setting the Mosaic Law in a new context here.

[13] *Against Apion* 1. 22 [189]; 2. 4 [39], 6 [71]; *Jewish Antiquities* 12. 3. 1–2 [119–128].

[14] 2 Maccabees 4. 11; 8. 17; 3 Maccabees 3. 21, 23; 4 Maccabees 3. 20; 8. 7; 17. 9; cf. Josephus, *Jewish Antiquities* 12. 6. 3 [280], 13. 1. 1 [2]. Philo uses *politeia* of Jewish life (*On Special Laws* 1. 9 [51], 11 [63], 57 [314], 59 [319], 2. 25 [123] etc.); in *On Special Laws* (2. 17 [74]) he implies the potential universalization of *politeia* in 'the *politeia* which is wholly on virtues and laws which alone propound the common good'. Yet the characterization by common laws remains its chief characteristic: *On Special Laws* 3. 9 [51], 'the *politeia* according to Moses does not permit any harlot…'.

[15] Cf. Josephus, *Jewish Antiquities* 12. 5. 1 [240]; 2 Maccabees 6. 1; 7. 2, 8, 24, 27, 37; 4 Maccabees 4. 23; 5. 33; 9. 1; 16. 16. However, see van der Klaauw 1989, esp. at 222, for debate as to whether the reference is to the Torah.

This difference is underlined by the *Letter to Diognetus* when the author adds to his New Testament models, 'Every foreign country is their native land, and every native land foreign' (5. 5). This may point to a 'citizenship of the world', and might suggest the adoption of the ideals of some contemporary thought; Epictetus spoke of the world as a city, and held up the example of Heracles 'who had the power to live happily in every place', for all are citizens of Zeus.[16] Philo, perhaps more realistically, sees the world as a 'megalopolis', governed by a single πολιτεία which is reason, although it is constituted by individual cities with their own, additional laws, necessitated by the inability of Greeks and barbarians, and divisions within these, to get on with each other.[17] The dilemma Christian identity faced in claiming to incarnate such an ideal may be seen in Lucian's *Hermotimus*, more or less contemporary with the *Letter to Diognetus*. Hermotimus, an adherent of Stoicism, is slowly and insidiously weaned from his philosophical commitment by Lycinus, who starts by purportedly sharing his friend's idealism. An old man had once told him about a city where 'all were aliens and foreigners, and no one was a native, but even many barbarians and slaves and cripples and dwarfs and impoverished were citizens...There neither was nor was named in the city inferior or superior, noble or ignoble, slave or free.' Yet citizenship of such a city would mean abandoning native country, children, and parents. At the end of the dialogue Lycinus persuades Hermotimus to abandon his quest and to join the common life, 'and share in citizenship with others'.[18]

So does such an apparent disinterest towards specific loyalty invite the charge of disloyalty—a charge, ironically, which might also be laid against Jewish communities: so Tacitus, 'Those who convert to their customs observe the same practice. The first thing they learn is to scorn the gods, to cast off their native country, to hold cheap fathers, children, brothers (*Histories* 5. 5). The answer given by the *Letter to Diognetus* is emphatic: 'They obey the ordained laws, and in

---

[16] Epictetus, *Discourses* 3. 24. 9–21.

[17] *On Joseph* 6 [29–31]; but see *On the Creation of the World* 49–50 [142–4] for citizens of the world. Celsus wishes, but gives up on the wish, 'that it were possible to unite under one Law inhabitants of Asia, Europe, and Libya, both Greeks and barbarians, even at the farthest limits.' (Origen, *Against Celsus* 8. 72).

[18] Lucian, *Hermotimus* 22–4, 84. The parallel is noted by Meecham 1949: 108.

their own lives surpass the laws' (5. 10). Yet any practical content to this is surprisingly thin and hardly able to create an alternative community: 'They marry as do all, they have children, but they do not expose their offspring. They provide a shared table, but not a shared bed' (5. 7). Other apologists will add to these values, but barely trespass beyond their bounds; they are, ironically, the values already established by Jewish communities in the Diaspora and by Jewish apologetic writings.[19]

Earlier, the author of 1 Peter had taken a different track but only to reach a similar impasse; it has been argued that the 'sojourners' to whom that letter is addressed—'Peter, apostle of Jesus Christ to the elect sojourners of the diaspora of Pontus, Galatia, Cappadocia, Asia and Bithynia' (1 Peter 1. 1)—are not those exiled from heaven, as assumed by most modern translations, but those who socio-politically had no secure place in the city structures. Within the Christian community such alienation might continue to be their lot but it would be compensated for by a new belonging and identity within the household of God (so Elliott 1982). Yet when the author of 1 Peter comes to articulate the rules of the new household he says little that would shock contemporary moralists—'Be subject to every human institution . . . whether the Emperor . . . or governors . . . Slaves be subject in all fear to your masters, not only to the good and gentle but also to the harsh . . . Likewise, let wives be subject to their own husbands' (1 Peter 2. 13–14, 18; 3. 1). Reassurance may, of course, have been part of his intention, and was an important part of early apologetic—Christians do not subvert the established *mores*, indeed they surpass them;[20] the need for such reassurance may betray the existence of very different patterns of behaviour and principle in early communities—and some recent studies have preferred to focus on that implied world, a world of egalitarian freedom from social convention, rather than on the constructed world of the

---

[19] On the coherence between Christian and Jewish apologetic values see Aristides, *Apology*, and Lieu 1996: 173–5.

[20] See Balch 1981; Theissen 1993: 257–87 ('Some Ideas about a Sociological Theory of Early Christianity'); see esp. p. 285: 'Where rules of conduct and values were shared with the world around the difference took the form of an outbidding of the consensus. Christians were not merely citizens like everyone else; they were "better citizens".'

exhortation. But for the moment we may stay with that constructed identity, even while viewing it with due suspicion.

If identity-formation is a process of differentiation, the social identity of the Christians here appears remarkably opaque. To return to the *Letter to Diognetus*, the analogy the author develops between Christians in the world and the soul within the body (6) only reinforces this opacity: it implies symbiosis and invisibility, not differentiation. This is surely deliberate. One of the anomolies of the *Letter to Diognetus* is its silence about the Jewish heritage of Christianity and about the need to respond to contemporary Judaism's claim to that heritage. Yet when the author says that Christians are not distinguished by land, language, or customs, we may wonder whether there is an implied apologetic contrast with the Jews who, notoriously, were, at least in popular polemic, so distinguished.[21] Although Jews were scattered around the then known world, Josephus could assert 'Our race is one and the same everywhere . . . why should you be surprised if those who came to Alexandria from elsewhere remained within the laws established from the beginning' (*Against Apion* 2. 6 [66–7]).[22] Tacitus expresses the view from the other side: 'With them all is profane that among us is sacred. Again, acts with them are permissible that for us are incestuous' (*Histories* 5. 5). The Christian apologist Justin Martyr's Jewish dialogue partner, Trypho, sees the Christian 'difference' from another—Jewish—point of view: 'although you claim to be pious and consider yourselves different from other people, you do not separate yourselves from them at all, neither do you distinguish your way of life from that of the gentiles' (*Dialogue* 10. 3); although Trypho speaks only with Justin's permission and through his pen, his objection is never seriously addressed. Social separation is not a Christian characteristic.

---

[21] So also Meecham 1949: 108. Cassius Dio interprets the recent Bar Kochba revolt as inspired by Jewish rejection of 'another people' or 'alien rites' being established in their city (*Roman History* 69. 12). This would be particularly significant if the *Letter to Diognetus* was written while this was still a vivid memory.

[22] Cf. Philo, *Embassy* 29 [194] which contrasts the *politeia* of the Jews throughout the world with being Alexandrians.

In contrast to this 'invisibility', the opening chapter of the *Letter to Diognetus* introduces a further model which will be equally problematic—rhetorically effective but practically tenuous:

Since I see, most excellent Diognetus, that you are particularly enthusiastic to learn about the piety ($\theta\epsilon o\sigma\acute{\epsilon}\beta\epsilon\iota a$) of the Christians and are clearly and diligently inquiring about them.... and why this '*genos*' or practice has entered life as a new thing now and not before... (1).

Here the Christians represent a new '*genos*' and practice ($\grave{\epsilon}\pi\iota\tau\acute{\eta}\delta\epsilon\nu\mu a$) in contrast to the Greeks and the Jews. *Genos* is ambiguous; in other writers, including the apologist Aristides, perhaps writing earlier than the *Letter to Diognetus*, it may be translated 'race' and is explicitly prefixed 'third', as contrasted with Jews and Greeks.[23] There is some debate as to whether that idea originates in the polemic of observers, for which we may recall Suetonius' description of the Christians as a '*genus* of men given to a new and wicked superstition' (*Nero* 16. 2) as well as Tertullian's cameo of the 'peoples of the nations' crying out 'Whence the third race?' (*Scorpiace* 10. 10);[24] or whether its source is Christian self-consciousness, for which we may appeal already to Paul in the middle of the first century, 'There is neither Greek nor Jew, circumcision nor uncircumcision' (Colossians 3. 11). The alternatives illustrate the ambivalence of the claim: on the one hand a 'fifth column', subverting the proper and accepted structuring of the world which underlies the organization of all society—so Celsus who speaks of the Christians as a 'people who... wall themselves off and break away from the rest of humankind' (Origen, *Against Celsus* 8. 2; see Schneider 1968: 187–91); on the other, a new category, superseding and embracing within it the existing dichotomies (Smith 1980, esp. 12–13).

The latter—a new inclusive category—is Paul's theoretical construct and so he speaks of a new $\check{a}\nu\theta\rho\omega\pi o\varsigma$ (human being), whose ultimate pattern and goal is 'the image of the creator' (Colossians 3. 10), i.e. humankind as first created before the various forms of

---

[23] Aristides, *Apology* 2; the Syriac speaks of four races and has some claim to originality, see Lieu 1996: 65–9.

[24] See also *To the Nations* 1. 8 where Tertullian objects that every race has its Christians, and then admits that as third '*genus*' it is a matter of religion (*superstitio*) and not of nation (*natio*); 20. 4.

polarization and opposition which, according to this reading of the Genesis narrative, eventuated. This is not the place to explore the theological roots and ramifications of Paul's concept, but his letters bear eloquent testimony to the practical context, the creation of new communities both out of individuals and out of existing networks or households of both Jewish and non-Jewish background without, theoretically, giving priority to either.[25] The fragility of the construct, both practically and theoretically, is equally clear. Thus Paul's letters also bear eloquent testimony to what has been seen as a tension between identity and ethos, understanding ethos as that which ensures the continuity of a social system, particularly when it is a minority within a wider culture (Wolter 1997). In practice, what we see in the Pauline communities is a spectrum of ethos, even to the point of potential conflict, between those whose background was Jewish and those who were Gentile, or between those who favoured affirmation of or continuity with the majority society, and those who rejected it, for example in the heated debate as to the permissibility of continuing to participate in meals which might involve eating 'meat offered to idols' (1 Corinthians 8; 10. 14–33).

Such tensions were not, of course, new with Christian communities. Jewish communities, which also espoused a degree of exclusive self-identity, faced similar dilemmas in balancing the equation between identity and integration. Indeed, it is arguable that the sharpening rhetoric of self-identity characteristic of the late Second-Temple period is as much a function of internal conflicts over the issue as of external attempts to suppress identity.[26] Philo condemns those who, on the grounds of an allegorical interpretation of circumcision and sabbath which he shares, treat their literal observance lightly: 'As if they were living alone by themselves in a desert land or had become disembodied souls and knew neither city, nor village, nor house, nor any form of human association'; for Philo due observance is an expression of recognition of our bodily existence and the careful concern for the πάτριος πολιτεία (*On the Migration of*

---

[25] On the importance of networks in the spread of early Christianity see White 1992.

[26] As is well illustrated by the debate over the interpretation of the Maccabean revolt and the question of Hellenism.

Abraham 16 [88–93]). Yet while recognizing that Jewish communities maintained a sufficiently separate identity over the centuries both to survive and to be recognized and reviled for the distinctiveness by observers, recent attempts to describe the core of that identity have found themselves speaking of Judaisms, and asking 'Who was a Jew?' or 'How would you know a Jew' (Neusner et al. 1987; Goodman 1989; Cohen 1993). We may summarize the problem as 'How broad a range or spectrum is possible without fracturing identity?'

In proclaiming a new identity in which the contrasted identities of Jew and Greek, itself a Jewish polarity, had no place, Paul was not solving but compounding the Jewish dilemma. John Barclay has recently attempted to analyse different Jewish patterns of response to the majority society along three scales, accommodation, acculturation, and assimilation (Barclay 1995a; 1995b). However useful that may prove, it cannot be applied to early Christianity. If the problem about the 'Judaism and Hellenism' debate is that we do not have the evidence to describe Judaism before Hellenism (Momigliano 1969)—we cannot measure acculturation if we do not know what is being acculturated—there is no Christianity to be described prior to its interaction with the majority society. Jew and Greek remained as much as did slave and free, male and female (Galatians 3. 28)—or if they did not so remain what did they become?[27]

The practical problem, therefore, is what is a third race without an identity? Again, Christian self-designation as a race, which in the second century we also find in the *Martyrdom of Polycarp* and in Melito of Sardis, as well as in the *Preaching of Peter* excerpted by Clement of Alexandria, is paralleled by and perhaps dependent on the Jewish self-ascription common in the Maccabean literature (Lieu 1996: 166–9; 1995). Yet this only underscores the contrast and the dilemma, for what constitutes a 'race'? Is an identity which subsumes and so obviates the identity of Jew or Greek a possibility?

---

[27] In this context Pauline Christianity cannot only be seen in relation to its 'separation' from Judaism. Thus L. Michael White distinguishes the Matthaean sectarian (= separatist/revolutionary) pattern from the Pauline 'cult' pattern which represents the attempt to import 'an essentially novel world view into a dominant culture': White 1988, esp. p. 23.

The theoretical problem is closely related. Identity, so we are told, is constructed by opposition; it involves self-awareness in relation to the other: 'us' demands 'them'. It is the assertion of a collective self and the simultaneous negation of collective others (Porton 1988: 288–9). Indeed, if such a binary mode of thought is fundamental to human thinking and identity, this is why 'third race' is perceived as subversive. In practice this is also how the rhetoric of the third or new race or kind works in early Christian writers; it is characterized not by its inclusiveness of earlier dichotomies but by its exclusiveness. Christians share in the errors of neither Greeks not Jews. In practice for Diognetus this can be limited to the nature and worship of God: 'they do not reckon the gods so-considered by the Greeks, neither do they observe the superstition of the Jews' (1). Both Greeks and Jews are thus identified not by a broad spectrum of social and cultural practice, but purely by what is now a conventional exposé of idolatry and of Jewish praxis, both drawn more from a polemical tradition than from any genuine social experience: he even treats the Jerusalem sacrificial system as still in place. This is not to deny the enormous and fundamental consequences of Christian rejection of what is so blithely described as the worship of wood, stone, and metal work (2.2); it is to wonder, rather, at the failure to exploit this for identity: how can the author still say that Christians live in Greek and barbarian cities and follow local customs; even that the Christian θεοσέβεια (piety) remains invisible (6. 4)?

Again dependence on Jewish models is both self-evident and paradoxical; Jewish Hellenistic texts abound in the condemnation of idolatry, and in isolating it as the characteristic marker of non-Jewish versus Jewish identity.[28] For the *Letter of Aristeas* the rest of humankind think there are many gods and this is why God 'hedged us in to prevent our being perverted by contact with others or by mixing with bad influences' (§§ 134; 142); yet such Jewish texts seem to see avoidance of idolatry as a virtue available to all people (Collins 1983: 167–8; 180–1). For Christian writers it is a matter of exclusive

---

[28] See Collins 1983; e.g. *III Sibylline* lines 545–55; *V Sibylline* lines 75–85, 353–60, 403–5; *Joseph & Asenath* 8. 5. Even in Rabbinic Judaism the Gentile as 'Other' is the Gentile as idolater, cf. Porton 1988. Christians took over this definition of Gentile otherness from the beginning, cf. 1 Thessalonians 4. 3f.

self-definition, and when they extend the differentiation to include the Jews as 'other', Jewish worship of God and observance of the law are brought under the same rubric of idolatry: for the *Letter to Diognetus* 'they seem to me to differ not at all from those who show the same honour to what are deaf' (3. 5).[29] In practice, however, Christian avoidance of involvement in idolatry differed from Jewish by being less marked—although it is only at the beginning of the third century that we find this seriously discussed.[30]

The persistence of a binary model of self-identity is thus self-evident in this as in all early Christian writings, including those which speak of a third race or kind. It is also there when this author speaks of the soul and the world: 'the world hates the Christians although it has not been wronged by them' (6. 5). Such an affirmation sits oddly with the more integrative comments a little earlier. It is the use of 'the world' which makes this possible. Although it has its roots in the Jewish eschatological contrast between 'this world' and 'the world to come', this opposition to 'the world' is characteristically, although not exclusively, Christian.[31] Within the New Testament it is most developed in the Johannine literature where it has often been dubbed 'sectarian', yet in principle it may become a fundamental organizing point for Christian self-identity, capable of multiple expressions (Wimbush 1997: 32–4). This is the language of internal identity-formation, not of external visible perception. Its effectiveness in maintaining cohesion, in legitimating ascetic life-styles, and in explaining hostility, is self-evident: the latter is no longer rejection by former family and friends, or by the state to which one claimed loyalty, but by a universalized and impersonalized opposition.

Thus, while a binary opposition may be endemic to all identity-formation, it is particularly attractive in a context of persecution. The interplay between persecution and identity for both Jews and Christians is not unexpected, and the development of 'citizenship' language in this context has already been noted above. Similarly, it

---

[29] On the presentation of the Jews as idolatrous see Lieu 1996: 145.

[30] The practical ambiguities are illustrated by Tertullian, *On Idolatry*, who describes idolatry as 'the chief crime of the human race' (1. 1) but carefully has to allow for Christians in general and for slaves to participate in family festivals involving idolatry so long as they do not share in the act itself (16–17).

[31] A rare Jewish example is *Testament of Job* 48–9.

is also in the literature associated with the persecution and ensuing revolt under the Maccabees in the early second century BCE that Hellenistic Jewish literature develops the language of 'race' as well as the term 'Judaism'. 'Christianity'/ 'Christianismos' and 'Christian' also seem first to seed and flower in that context (Lieu 1996: 29–31, 85–6). Paradigmatically, towards the end of the second century CE (?) in Pergamum, the 'martyr' responds to the question, 'What is your name?', 'My first and most distinctive name is Christian, but if you seek that in the world, Carpus.'[32] It is a reflection of the ambiguities which this paper has explored that Jewish literature does not develop the opposition from or to 'the world' in the persecution context.[33] Christian self-identity, however, because of, or in spite of, its non-differentiation, demanded the alternative identity of 'the world' so that, as Celsus perceptively commented, 'If all men could be Christians, the Christians would no longer want them' (*Against Celsus* 3. 9).

Finally, there is one further route to self-identity: the discovery of a past. It is a common argument that a major component of identity is a common history, ancestry or descent, which may but need not be conceived in biological terms (Porton 1988: 291–3). Such a history might seem intrinsically problematic for a third or new race, as also for a *politeia* without a native land. Yet while in terms of individual history, at least initially, Christian literature spoke of a separation from the past, a model that was to become paradigmatic, in terms of corporate history it found a history either in the Scriptures—as when Christians called Abraham 'our father' (*1 Clement* 31)—or in the Christian story—as when the *Martyrdom of Polycarp* becomes a literary mimesis of the Gospel narrative (19. 1). The *Letter to Diognetus* is unusual in the second century in not finding any such history;[34] consistent this may be, yet ultimately it was to prove

---

[32] See the *Martyrdom of Carpus, Papylus, and Agathonice* 2–3 in Musurillo 1972: xv–xvi; 22–37. See further below.

[33] Ctr. 4 Maccabees 17. 14, 'Eleazar was the first contestant, the mother of the seven sons entered the contest, and the brothers contended. The tyrant was the antagonist; the world and the life of humankind were watching.'

[34] It mentions nothing of Israel's history, shows no knowledge of the Hebrew Scriptures, and little of the 'Jesus' story; it knows only the past 'time of unrighteousness' now overtaken by the 'time of righteousness' (9. 1).

unsatisfactory, and the denial of history, as implied by Marcion's rejection of the Creator God of the Jews, was excluded as heretical. This may bring us back to the beginning and the 'forging' of Christian identity—'Without [that] historical continuity any answer to the identity question can only be invented rather than discovered' (Novak 1995: 2).

AFTERWORD (2009)

This paper was written in 1998 at the beginning of what was to prove a much more extensive exploration of the way a distinctive sense of 'being Christian' was shaped during the second century CE (Lieu 2004). That continuing exploration was able to interact with the emerging rich body of secondary literature on aspects of identity in the ancient world. The result was a much stronger sense of the degree to which early Christian strategies of self-definition paralleled, and indeed consciously mimicked, those of their contemporaries, even while loudly proclaiming difference. The consequence is that— something already implicit here—despite early Christian claims to transcend the boundaries of race, as of gender and status, they do indeed use ethnic categories (see Buell 2005). An immediate objection is that the language of race and ethnicity is a modern development inappropriate to the ancient world. This objection could be extended: the concept of 'identity' itself is a modern one, shaped in particular by nineteenth and twentieth century experience, and has no semantic expression in the language of antiquity. This is even more true of an awareness of individual identity, although that is not primarily in view here.[35] More broadly, although barely developed in this essay, the studies and book that followed it, like the similar works about antiquity already mentioned, make heavy use of recent models of the way identity is constructed and maintained; again, many would object that social scientific models developed within the modern world cannot properly be applied to the ancient

---

[35] This often causes misunderstanding, particularly in languages other than English. How the individual's sense of self relates to social identity is another debate.

world with its different social structures and where direct observation and testing are not possible. An answer would be that such models are heuristic, being used to display and interpret patterns of behaviour that *we* discern in our sources, and are not being treated as prescriptive. Hence, in subsequent work a range of contemporary models has been used eclectically, without rigid adherence to any one 'school'. In addition, it is now widely contended that all identity is constructed, not primordially or essentially 'given'—and this includes 'ethnicity'; if they are constructed then there is no reason to restrict such concepts to their self-conscious and explicit use. Within this context a stronger emphasis on 'construction' would perhaps now mollify (or complement) the deliberate ambiguity of the 'forging' of the title as well as the false alternative of the closing quotation: is not *invenire* to discover?

This emphasis on 'construction' coheres with the emphasis here on a particular written text that cannot be located or even dated with any certainty.[36] Our primary access to early Christianity is through its literary heritage, and it is suggested here that this is not just a matter of the necessities of survival but reflects the key role played by the production and dissemination of texts in its self-fashioning. It should be added that one text does not speak for them all; the *Letter to Diognetus* belongs to what is loosely called 'apologetic', and other literary genres construct identities in different ways. The second century is marked not only by the emergence of a self-conscious literary culture among Christians but also by its diversity.

If being written now there is much that would be different, including some of the issues touched on above. What should also be added would be a greater emphasis that the porosity of boundaries, which might seem to contribute to the 'fragility' of identity, is of course true of all boundaries, and is, perhaps, their intention. Further, subsequent debate about identity has drawn more attention to the multiple identities that individuals and groups inhabit, and to the strategies of negotiation and hierarchy between them that can be employed.

---

[36] Although conventionally dated to the second century, the *Letter to Diognetus* has been placed in the fourth century by some, although the lack of Christological development makes this unlikely.

It is not the task of this chapter to determine how far the 'identity' constructed here mirrors that actually experienced or lived out by those who called themselves 'Christian'—something that in this period cannot easily be answered, although hints and shadows can be grasped at. In particular, what many would expect to be at the heart of that self-designation, patterns of belief about Jesus Christ and, even more, something that modern adherents would identify as 'faith in Jesus' or as 'religious experience' are not a primary theme here. An answer would have to be that although not absent, the former in particular, from the literature of the period,[37] they do not belong to the primary level of discourse. Why that is so, is another question.

BIBLIOGRAPHY

Alexander, L. (1993). 'Acts and Ancient Intellectual Biography', in B. W. Winter and A. D. Clarke (eds.), *The Book of Acts in its Ancient Literary Setting*. Grand Rapid, MI: Eerdmans/Carlisle: Paternoster Press, 31–63.

Ascough, R. (1997). 'Translocal Relationships among Voluntary Associations and Early Christianity', *Journal of Early Christian Studies*, 5: 223–41.

Balch, D. (1981). *Let Wives be Submissive. The Domestic Code in 1 Peter*, Society of Biblical Literature. Monograph Series 26. Chico, CA: Scholars Press.

Barclay, J. (1995a). *Jews in the Mediterranean Diaspora*. Edinburgh: T. & T. Clark.

——(1995b). 'Paul among Diaspora Jews: Anomaly or Apostate', *Journal for the Study of the New Testament*, 60: 89–120.

——(1996). '"Neither Jew nor Greek": Multiculturalism and the New Perspective on Paul', in Brett 1996: 197–214.

Barrett, C. K. (1989). 'School, Conventicle, and Church in the New Testament', in K. Aland and S. Meurer (eds.), *Wissenschaft und Kirche. Festschrift für Eduard Lohse*. Bielefeld: Luther-Verlag, 96–110.

Bartlett, J. R. (1985). *Jews in the Hellenistic World. Josephus, Aristeas, The Sibylline Oracles, Eupolemus*, Cambridge Commentaries on the Writings

---

[37] A concern with faith about Jesus tends to be strongest in polemical literature directed against other 'insiders', or intended to define them as 'outsiders'.

of the Jewish & Christian World 200BC to AD200. Cambridge: Cambridge University Press.

Barton S. C. and Horsley, G. R. (1981). 'A Hellenistic Cult Group and the New Testament Churches', *Jahrbuch fur Antike und Christentum*, 24: 7–41.

Bauer, W. (1934/1971). *Rechtglaubigkeit und Ketzerei im altesten Christentum*. Tübingen: Mohr. English trans. 1971: *Orthodoxy and Heresy in Earliest Christianity*. Philadelphia, PA: Fortress.

Berger P. (1966). *The Social Construction of Reality*. Garden City, NY: Doubleday.

Brett, M. (ed.) (1996). *Ethnicity and the Bible*, Biblical Interpretation Series 19. Leiden: Brill.

Buell, D. K. (2005). *Why this New Race? Ethnic Reasoning in Early Christianity*. New York: Columbia University Press.

Cameron, A. (1991). *Christianity and the Rhetoric of Empire: The Development of Christian Discourse*, Sather Classical Lectures 45. Berkeley, CA: Univ. of California Press.

Cohen, S. (1993). 'Those who say they are Jews and are not', in S. Cohen and E. Frerichs (eds.), *Diasporas in Antiquity*, Brown Judaic Studies 288. Atlanta, CA: Scholars Press, 1–47.

Collins, J. J. (1983). *Between Athens and Jerusalem: Jewish Identity in the Hellenistic Diaspora*. New York: Crossroad.

Elliott, J. H. (1982). *A Home for the Homeless. A Sociological Exegesis of 1 PETER, Its Situation and Strategy*. London: SCM Press.

Feldmeier, R. (1996). 'The "Nation" of Strangers: Social Contempt and Its Theological Interpretation in Ancient Judaism and Early Christianity', in Brett 1996: 240–70.

Goodman, M. (1989). *Who was a Jew?*. Oxford: Yarnton Trust for Oxford Centre for Postgraduate Hebrew Studies.

Kloppenborg, J. (1996). 'Egalitarianism in the Myth and Rhetoric of Pauline Churches', in E. A. Castelli and H. Taussig (eds.), *Reimagining Christian Origins: A Colloquium Honoring Burton L. Mack*. Valley Forge: Trinity Press International, 247–63.

——and Wilson, S. G. (eds.) (1996). *Voluntary Associations in the Graeco–Roman World*. London: Routledge.

Kraemer, R. (1991). 'Jewish Tuna and Christian Fish: Identifying Religious Affiliation in Epigraphic Sources', *Harvard Theological Review*, 84: 141–62.

Levenson, J. D. (1996). 'The Universal Horizon of Biblical Particularism', in Brett 1996: 143–69.

Lieu, J. M. (1995). 'The Race of the Godfearers', *Journal of Theological Studies*, 46: 483–501, reprinted in Lieu 2002: 49–68.

——(1996). *Image and Reality. The Jews in the World of the Christians in the Second Century.* Edinburgh: T. & T. Clark.

——(2002). *Neither Jew nor Greek?* London; New York: T. & T. Clark.

——(2004). *Christian Identity in the Jewish and Graeco–Roman World.* Oxford: Oxford University Press.

Meecham, H. (1949). *The Epistle to Diognetus. The Greek Text with Introduction, Translation and Notes.* Manchester: Manchester University Press.

Meeks, W. (1983). *The First Urban Christians.* New Haven, CT, and London: Yale University Press.

Meyer, B. (1986). *The Early Christians. Their World Mission and Self-Discovery.* Wilmington, DE: Michael Glazier.

——(1992). 'The Church in Earliest Christianity: Identity and Self-Definition', in *Christus Faber: The Master Builder and the House of God.* Allison Park, PA: Pickwick Publications, 149–69.

Momigliano, A. D. (1970). Review of M. Hengel, *Judentum und Hellenismus: Studien zu ihrer Begegnung unter besondere Berüksichtung' Palästinas bis zur Mitte des 2. Jh. v. Chr.* (Tübingen: Mohr, 1969), *Journal of Theological Studies* 21: 149–153, reprinted in his *Quinto contributo alla storia degli studi classici e del mondo antico.* ii. Roma: Edizioni di storia e letteratura (1975), 931–6.

Musurillo, H. (1972). *The Acts of the Christian Martyrs.* Oxford Early Christian Texts. Oxford: Clarendon Press.

Neusner, J. W., Green, S., and Frerichs, E. S. (eds.) (1987). *Judaisms and their Messiahs at the Turn of the Christian Era.* Cambridge: Cambridge University Press.

Novak, D. (1995). *The Election of Israel. The Idea of the Chosen People.* Cambridge: Cambridge University Press.

Porton, G. (1988). *GOYIM. Gentiles and Israelites in Mishnah-Tosefta*, Brown Judaic Studies 155. Atlanta, GA: Scholars Press.

Riches, J. (1996). 'Cultural Bias in European and North American Biblical Scholarship', in Brett 1996: 431–48.

Schneider, A. (1968). *Le Premier Livre Ad Nationes de Tertullien.* Neuchâtel: Inst. Suisse de Rome.

Segal, A. (1986). *Rebecca's Children: Judaism and Christianity in the Roman World.* Cambridge, MA., and London: Harvard University Press.

Smith, J. Z. (1980). 'Fences and Neighbours: Some Contours of Early Judaism', in W. S. Green (ed.) *Approaches to Ancient Judaism ii.* Brown Judaic Studies 9. Chico, CA: Scholars Press, 1–26.

Stanton, G. N. (1997). 'The Fourfold Gospel', *New Testament Studies*, 43: 317–46.

Theissen, G. (1982). *The Social Setting of Pauline Christianity.* English trans., Edinburgh: T. & T. Clark.

——(1993). *Social Reality and the Early Christians.* English trans., Edinburgh: T. & T. Clark.

van der Klaauw, J. (1989). 'Diskussion', in J. W. van Henten, B. Dehandschutter, and J. van der Klaauw (eds.), *Die Enstehung der jüdischen Martyrologie.* Studia Post-Biblica 38. Leiden: Brill, 220–61.

von Harnack, A. (1904/5). *The Expansion of Christianity in the First Three Centuries.* Eng. trans., London: Williams & Northgate.

White, L. M. (1988). 'Shifting Sectarian Boundaries in Early Christianity', *Bulletin of the John Rylands Library of Manchester,* 70: 7–24.

——(ed.) (1992). *Social Networks in the Early Christian Movement. Issues and Methods for Social History,* Semeia 56. Atlanta, GA: Scholars Press.

Wilken, R. (1972). 'Collegia, Philosophical Schools and Theology', in S. Benko and J. J. O'Rourke (eds.), *Early Church History: The Roman Empire as the Setting of Primitive Christianity.* London: Oliphants [originally published as *The Catacombs and the Colosseum.* Valley Forge, PA: Judson Press (1971)], 268–91.

——(1984). 'Christianity as a Burial Society', in *The Christians as the Romans Saw Them.* New Haven, CT and London: Yale University Press, 31–47.

Wilson, B. (1967). *Patterns of Sectarianism.* London: Heinemann.

Wimbush, V. (1997). '"...Not of this World...": Early Christianities as Rhetorical and Social Formation', in E. A. Castelli and H. Taussig (eds.), *Re-imagining Christian Origins: A Colloquium Honoring Burton L. Mack.* Valley Forge, PA: Trinity Press International, 23–36.

Wolter, M. (1997). 'Ethos und Identität in Paulinischen Gemeinden', *New Testament Studies,* 43: 430–44.

14

Purification and its Discontents

Mani's Rejection of Baptism

Guy G. Stroumsa

INTRODUCTION

What happens when the means of purification from defilement which had been in use in a given religious system break down, when they are not believed to function anymore? No religious community can survive without easy reach of ways of purification, which alone permit the reintegration within the community of members declared impure, for either cultic or moral reasons. Hence the centrality of means of purification for the very identity of religious communities.[1]

The example of Mani is topical, and will serve us here to understand the central function of conceptions of purity—and hence of purification—in the transformation process of religious beliefs.[2] Mani, who had grown up among a Jewish–Christian baptismal community, the Elkasaites, rejected in his youth the validity of the baptismal ritual, and in particular of their daily purificatory

---

[1] For one of the few attempts to tackle the problem from a different point of view, see *Guilt or Pollution* 1968. From a comparative perspective, see also 'Purification', *Encyclopedia of Religion*, 1st edn., xii. 91ff. [2nd edn., xi. 7503ff.]; 'Reinigungen', *Religion in Geschichte und Gegenwart*, v. 946ff.; and especially 'Pureté et impureté; I. L'histoire des religions', *Supplément au Dictionnaire de la Bible*, ix. 398–430.

[2] Oddly enough, it seems that little has been done on the topic. For a rather general statement of the problem, see the abstract by Ort 1968.

ablutions.[3] The young Mani turned against both the practices and the underlying beliefs of the baptismal sect, and soon offered an alternative to their cultic behaviour as well as to their articles of faith. This alternative did not only take the form of a new cult, but offered a total system of the universe, which integrated cosmogony, cosmology and world history into a complex web of myths: indeed, the very birth of the Manichaean religion can be observed hatching out of a polemics focusing, precisely, upon the concepts of purity, impurity, and purification. An inquiry focusing upon Mani's rejection of baptism should therefore help us to understand more fully the nature of his new approach. Mani offered nothing less than a religious *revolution*, which is sometimes (as in the so-called *Cologne Mani Codex* [=*CMC*]) framed in terms of a radical *reformation* of the cult, advocating a return to the original teaching distorted by mistaken believers.

To a great extent, however, the attempt to dissociate between beliefs and *praxis* is misleading. Mani did not reject the cultic practices of the Elkasaites while retaining their fundamental beliefs— although this is what some of the texts would seem to suggest. He rejected their religious practices precisely because they entailed some anthropological presuppositions that he did not accept. Hence, it is the very validity of the Elkasaites' religious system that the young Mani radically questioned.

THE TEXT

With the discovery and publication of the *CMC*, we are fortunate to possess now a detailed and impressive testimony of the deep crisis into which Mani threw the community when he expressed serious doubts as to the value of Elkasaite 'law'.[4] I propose to reflect here on a

---

[3] See Henrichs 1973. On the Elkasaites, see Cirillo 1984 and Luttikhuizen 1985. Both works, independently, provide detailed analyses of the sources, which catalogued and attacked heresies.

[4] νόμος, e.g., 89. 12. Cf. 'their every ordinance and order according to which they walk (καθ᾽ ἣν πορεύονται)' (80, 3–5; the expression reflects a linguistic calque of Hebrew *halakhah*, i.e., the legal system of religious duties). I quote *CMC* according to

particularly pregnant passage concerning the validity of the washings. The text is here put under the name of Baraies the Teacher, a Manichaean leader of the first generation.

My lord (Mani) said: 'I have had enough debating [with] each one in that Law, rising up and questioning them [concerning the] way of God, [the] commandments of the Saviour, the washing (περὶ τοῦ βαπτίσματος), the vegetables they wash, and their every ordinance and order according to which they walk.

Now I destroyed and [put to nought] their words and their mysteries, demonstrating to them that they had not received these things which they pursue from the commandments of the Saviour; some of them were amazed at me, but others got cross and angrily said: "does he not want to go to the Greeks?" But, when I saw their intent, I said to [them] gently: "[This] washing (τὸ βάπτισμα) by which you wash your food is of [no avail] (οὐδὲν τυγχάνει). For this body is defiled (μιαρόν) and molded from a mold of defilement...' (79. 13–81. 3)

Mani then justifies his statement about the uselessness of the washing of vegetables through the intestinal transformation of food.

Likewise, the loathsomeness and dregs of both [types of food] are seen as not differing from each other, so that what has been washed, which [it (the body) rejected] and sloughed off, is not at all distinguishable from that [other] which is unwashed. (81. 13–24)

Mani goes on and submits the daily washings of the baptists to the same scathing critique:

Now the fact that you wash in water (βαπτίζεσθε ἐν ὕδασιν) each day is of no avail. For having been washed and purified once and for all, why do you wash again each day? So that also by this it is manifest that you are disgusted with yourselves each day and that you must wash yourselves on account of loathsomeness (διὰ τὴν βδελυρότητα βαπτίζεσθαι) before you can become purified. And by this too it is clear most evidently that all the foulness is from the body. And, indeed, [you] have put it (i.e., the body) on.

Therefore, [make an inspection of] yourselves as to [what] your purity (καθαρότης) [really is. For it is] impossible to purify your bodies entirely (ἀδύνατον γὰρ τὰ σώματα ὑμῶν παντελῶς καθαρίσαι)—for each day the

the translation of Cameron and Dewey 1979. See also the first edition and commentary of Koenen and Henrichs 1978 (for *CMC* 72. 8–99. 9). For a critical edition, see Koenen and Römer 1988; their text is used in the on-line *Thesaurus Linguae Graecae*.

body is disturbed and comes to rest through the excretions of faeces from it—so that the action comes about without a commandment from the Saviour. The purity, then, which was spoken about, is that which comes through knowledge (διὰ τῆς γνώσεως) a separation (χωρισμός) of light from darkness, of death from life, of living waters from turbid, so that [you] may know [that] each is [...] one another and [...] the commandments of the Saviour, [so that ...] might redeem the soul from [annihilation] and destruction. This is in truth the genuine purity (ἡ κατ᾿ ἀλήθειαν εὐθυτάτη καθαρότης), which you were commended to do; but you departed from it and began to bathe, and have held on to the purification of the body, (a thing) most defiled and fashioned through foulness; through it [i.e., foulness] it [the body] was coagulated and having been founded came into existence. (82. 23–85. 12)

The text goes on to state that it is precisely these words of the young Mani which sparked the split within the community: while some were deeply impressed and regarded him as 'a prophet and teacher', others became 'filled with jealousy and rage, some of whom were voting for (my) death'. Mani is summoned and accused of destroying 'the washing of our Law and that of the fathers', as well as the commandments of the Saviour. Of course, he denies doing this last thing, claiming on the contrary that he is the real follower of the Saviour, i.e., Jesus (90–1).

To be sure, this extremely rich text should not be understood as quoting Mani's actual words. We deal here with a later reconstruction, written by a Manichaean author, perhaps one generation after Mani, describing the beginning of his teaching. In many ways, indeed, *CMC* can be considered to be an official biography of the prophet. In that sense, we cannot expect our text to reveal the true motives for Mani's break with the baptists. But it does offer us a very important insight into the justification of this break proposed by the first generation of Manichaean teachers, perhaps for the later Mani himself.

ELKASAITE BAPTISM

In order to understand better the nature of Mani's stance, we have to assess with some precision what he rejects. What do we know about Elkasaite baptism? From our sources, mainly a few reports by Church

Fathers who catalogued heresies, we know that the Elkasaites practiced various kinds of purificatory ablutions: side by side with the washing of vegetables, they practiced an initiatory sacramental baptism, which was meant for the remission of sins, as well as daily baths.[5]

Although various features distinguished the Elkasaites from the other baptismal groups swarming in the Near East in the second and third centuries, including the Mandeans, they can quite safely be identified as a rather special branch of Jewish–Christians.[6] Their religious way of life is called *nomos*, 'law', in *CMC*, which refers to the Baptists' 'ancestral traditions'. As pointed out by Gerard P. Luttikhuizen (1985: 164), 'these features suggest that the ritualistic piety of the baptists had developed from Jewish roots'. On the other hand, some Christian elements are clearly present. The practice of daily baths they shared with other Jewish–Christian groups, such as the Hemerobaptists and the Ebionites (who also practised a sacramental baptism). Indeed, one can say, with Luigi Cirillo (1986b: 111), that Elkasaism represents one of the most important manifestations of the baptismal movement stemming from Palestine, and also its most northern branch.

The reference to the purifying role of the various ablutions does not in itself make clear that the various baptismal rites were used as a therapy against both spiritual and physical evils, a fact which emphasizes an important character of their anthropology (which was of course not only their own, but was widely spread amongst many highly diverse religious and cultural groups): there is a continuum between the body and the spirit, and hence there is no hiatus between physical and ethical or spiritual purity.[7]

The development of the 'second repentance', or the second baptism, meant to cleanse the sinner, notoriously one of the most complex questions in early Christianity, cannot be discussed here (see Stroumsa 1999). Such a second baptism, for the forgiveness of sins, was also known to the Elkasaites—an oddity, it would seem,

---

[5] See Henrichs 1973: esp. 46–7, on the concordance between the data of the writers on heresies and of *CMC*.

[6] On the various baptismal groups, see Rudolph 1981. See further Rudolph 1986 and Strecker 1986.

[7] Jean Daniélou (1991: 100) suggests that Elkasaite baptism might also have been an act of reconciliation, which could however have been suppressed later because of the ambiguity with the first, initiatory baptism.

since there was no dearth of opportunities for cleansing ablutions in their religious system. According to Hippolytus, the *Book of Elchasai* mentioned seven witnesses to the second baptism, intended for the remission of sins (*Refutatio* 9. 15. 1–2):

If therefore, children, someone has had intercourse with any animal or with a male or a sister or a daughter, or if he has committed adultery or fornication, and wishes to receive remission of his sins, let him, as soon as he has heard this book, be baptized a second time in the name of the great and most high God and in the name of his Son, the Great King. Let him purify and cleanse himself (καθαρισάσθω καὶ ἁγνευσάτω) and let him call to witness the seven witnesses written in this book: the heaven and the water and the holy spirits and the angels of prayer and the oil and the salt and the earth.

This text reveals clearly that the sins for which one needs to be cleansed through immersion are all of a sexual nature. Epiphanius too mentions Elxai's seven witnesses for oaths.[8] The seven witnesses do not seem to appear elsewhere. From ancient Near Eastern literature, however, we know that heaven and earth can often be called to witness solemn oaths (Delcor 1966). Moreover, the seven witnesses to the baptismal rite recall the five seals (σφραγῖδες) to gnostic baptism as described in the *Apocryphon of John*.[9] In the various literatures of the ancient Near East, 'seal' usually refers to an attestation, an authentication (Stroumsa 1992: 275–88). Hence, one can say that 'seal' and 'witness' perform similar functions at the solemn occasion of an oath or a lustration. One may speculate that the origin of the Manichaean conception of seals *replacing* baptism may find its origin in the witnesses/seals *accompanying* solemn baptism among Elkasaites and various Gnostic groups.

MANI'S REJECTION OF BAPTISM AND ITS GNOSTIC BACKGROUND

It is to the repeated ablutions, as well as the washing of the food, that Mani objects. Our text does not mention the initiatory baptism, but

---

[8] *Panarion* 19. 6, on the Osseans. See Luttikhuizen 1985: 126 and 199–200.
[9] *Nag Hammadi Codices* ii. 31. 11–27; see Sevrin 1986: 31–7.

from Mani's arguments, it is hard to believe that it would have fared better than the other ablutions. According to him (or more precisely to the words put into his mouth by Baraies), these ablutions do not work, since water is incapable of purifying either the food or the body. The reason given is the same in both cases: the digestion process shows the body to be irremediably impure. But Mani does not reject the very notions of purity and impurity, and hence of purification. In that sense, what he proposes appears at first sight more like a reform: going back to the real intentions of the Saviour, which were forgotten by the Baptists' mistaken conceptions. Purification is necessary, and also possible, provided one does not try to purify the body, through water, but rather the soul, through what the text calls *gnosis*, salvific knowledge. Incidentally, Mani's rejection of physical baptism also meant that he denied Jesus's baptism; according to our sources, indeed, such a baptism would have meant his sinfulness.[10]

What is the nature of this *gnosis*? Although our text is not explicit here, it stands to reason to assume that it is the knowledge of Manichaean mythological theology, for which impurity lies in the very mixture of light particles with matter in the physical, created world. Hence, real purification will mean the understanding of the cause of impurity, and the attempt to restore the original separation (χωρισμός) between the elements of light and those of matter. The whole Manichaean religion, indeed, its cult as well as its mythology, is precisely aimed at dismantling the impure mingling (μίξις) through which our world came to be.

In Manichaean doctrine, there are two ways of speaking of impurity. On the one hand, impurity is the very mingling between the two realms, the realm of light and the realm of darkness. In a more basic sense, however, the realm of darkness, by itself, is impure. Purification, therefore, will essentially involve the separation of the two realms, achieved through *gnosis*, i.e. the purification of the light elements. This is not attained though a purely intellectual process of knowledge, but also through Manichaean cultic practices: Manichaeism is a fully-fledged religion, not a philosophical system.

Mani's radical rejection of baptism and its replacement by *gnosis* should be understood within the context of Gnostic traditions. There

---

[10] *Acta Archelai* 60. 11; Augustine, *Contra Faustum* 23. 3; references in Henrichs and Koenen 1978: 143, n. 204.

are indeed some quite striking Gnostic parallels to Mani's rejection of baptism. In the earliest strata of Gnosticism, moreover, there seems to have been an obsession with purity and purification from pollution. The centrality of 'saving knowledge' probably developed at a later stage in the movement (as concluded in Stroumsa 1984).

In a seminal study, Ludwig Koenen was able to show that the theme of the metaphorization of baptism is widespread in various Gnostic texts from Nag Hammadi as well as in traditions in the writings on heresies (Koenen 1981). His analysis also reflects the strong vitality of baptismal rites, even among Gnostic groups. It is precisely with this background of vitality that the movement of reaction can be understood. There is no need to repeat here Koenen's results. Let us only refer to texts such as the *Paraphrase of Shem*, the *Testimony of Truth*, the *Exegesis of the Soul* (which understands in a metaphorical way the Biblical baptism of repentance), as well as the rejection of baptism by the Valentinians, or the reference to 'dark and filthy waters' by Hippolytus's Sethians.

CHRISTIAN ORIGINS OF MANI'S ATTITUDE?

In their detailed commentary to the *CMC*, Henrichs and Koenen state (1978: 142, n. 198; 145, n. 206) that Mani's reinterpretation of baptism into *gnosis* stands at the end of a long historical evolution. According to them, the rejection of baptism by various Gnostic thinkers finds its ultimate origin in Jesus's polemics against the Pharisaic purificatory rites (see further Koenen 1981: 749ff.).

Henrichs and Koenen state that Mani's claim that the daily washings only emphasize the uselessness of the first baptism finds its origin in the Letter to the Hebrews 10. 1–4, esp. 10. 2:

For then would they [i.e., the sacrifices] not have ceased to be offered? because that the worshippers once purged (ἅπαξ κεκαθαρισμένους) should have had no more conscience of sins (συνείδησιν ἁμαρτιῶν).

In Hebrews (9. 12–14), the yearly sacrifices are replaced by the single sacrifice of Christ, whose blood purifies the conscience of the believers (καθαριεῖ τὴν συνείδησιν ἡμῶν), rather than their flesh, of dead works.

There are some other New Testament parallels to Mani's objection to the washings. One may think of Peter's vision of the impure food (Acts 10. 9–16): 'What God has cleansed, that call not thou common (ἃ ὁ θεὸς ἐκαθάρισεν σὺ μὴ κοίνου).' Similarly, Paul states (Romans 14. 14) that 'nothing is in itself impure (κοινόν)'.[11]

Such positions would appear to be in direct relationship with the famous words of Jesus in his polemics against the Pharisees' purity laws (Mark 7. 14–23; Matthew 15. 10–20):

There is nothing from without a man, that entering into him can defile (κοινῶσαι) him: but the things which come out of him, those are they that defile that man. (Mark 7. 15; cf. Mathew 15. 11, 20).

The reason given by Jesus to the lack of food's defiling power of food is based upon the fact of digestion:

And he saith unto them, Are ye so without understanding also? Do ye not perceive, that whatsoever thing from without entereth into the man, it cannot defile him; because it entereth not into his heart, but into the belly, and goeth out into the draught ... (Mark 7. 18–19; cf. Mathew 15. 16–18).

There is indeed a striking similarity between this argument and that buttressing Mani's claim that baptism by water cannot cleanse, since the body remains bound to perform the same activity of defecation, with or without ablutions. It is this similarity that has brought the learned editors of *CMC* to relate to Jesus's words Mani's claim that the body cannot be cleansed by Jesus's words.

What does defile man are the evil thoughts which come out of his heart, as well as 'adulteries, fornications, murders, thefts, covetousness, wickedness, deceit, lasciviousness, and evil eye, blasphemy, pride, foolishness' (Mark 7. 21–2; cf. Mathew 15. 19–20).

Together with its parallel in Matthew, this passage of Mark is usually considered as the *locus classicus* of Jesus's radical rejection of the very foundations of the 'Mosaic Law', of the entire Jewish halakhic system.[12] Similarly, Herbert Braun, as quoted by Kümmel

---

[11] κοινόν renders the Hebrew *hulin*. On Mani and Paul, see Betz 1986.
[12] 'The radical nature of Jesus' relationship to the Torah is shown nowhere more clearly than in debates about purity laws', as stated, for instance, by Klein 1984: 59.

1978, can claim: 'The extremely unJewish nature of this position proves the genuineness of a Jesus utterance like Mark 7. 15.' For the New Testament scholars who share this opinion, the fact that these words can plausibly be considered as Jesus's actual utterances is highly significant, since it emphasizes Jesus's 'basic position in relation to the Torah', in Kümmel's words. Although this reading is fairly common, it is highly inadequate, as we shall see.

The hypothesis according to which the rejection of baptism finds its ultimate origins in Jesus's doctrine seems to have been accepted without questioning. It is however rather puzzling, if not altogether paradoxical: after all, Jesus is at the origin of the exportation of baptismal rites from Judaea to the world at large. Some serious arguments may be adduced against it.

First of all, the hypothesis does not take into account the fact that the critique of Israelite ritual and doubts upon its value when it is not accompanied by the right attitude of mind, is known already from the Hebrew Bible, and is well attested in the Prophets and in the Psalms. Psalm 51, for instance, deals with the impossibility of expiating a sin by the conventional method of sacrifice after the destruction of the Temple (see Caquot 1968). Philo, too, insists upon the need of unity between body and soul with respect to pure intention accompanying sacrifices (Wenschkewitz 1932: ch. 3). The need of moral cleanness going together with ritual purity is emphasized in various Jewish texts from the second Temple period (see, for instance, Brody 1958). Jacob Neusner (1973: esp. 125) has argued convincingly that the most important point for understanding the idea of purity in ancient Judaism is the relationship between physical and moral purity.

The same is true at Qumran, where the scrupulous observance of ritual laws concerning purity and impurity is directly related to the obsession of the members of the sect with the idea of the physical defilement produced by moral fault (see Dupont-Sommer 1968: esp. 79, and further García Martínez 1988). As David Flusser has argued (1979: esp. 87), a similar relationship between ritual and ethical purity is found at Qumran and in John the Baptist. This Jewish traditional attitude is the background of Jesus's attack against the inadequacy of Jewish ritual purity laws:

And the Lord said unto him: 'Now do ye Pharisees make clean the outside of the cup and the platter; but your inward part is full of ravening and wickedness.' (Luke 11. 39; cf. Matthew 23. 25–6).

Obviously, such a text does not deny the legitimacy of the purity rules, but insists that their validity is conditioned upon a complete coherence between inner intention and cultic action. Such a demand is similar to that of the prophets, who 'had nothing to object to sacrifice, provided it was carried out with a clean mind and with due esteem for law and justice'.[13] It may be noted here that a similar trend is found in classical Greece with regard to rituals of purification. As emphasized by Walter Burkert, Plato's statement: 'The impure man is whoever is wicked in his soul',[14] or the inscription over the entrance of the Asklepios sanctuary at Epidauros: 'Purity is to think pious things' 'were regarded not as devaluing the outer forms of piety, which were still rigorously upheld, but as adding a deeper dimension. In the sphere of purification, ritual and ethical reflection could therefore emerge without a break.'

From the prophets onwards this insistence upon inward, moral purity, side by side with the continued development of the ritual washings that have their ultimate roots in Leviticus, is found time and again in Jewish texts.[15] From apocryphal literature, through Philo, and up to Targumic and Rabbinic literature, we can follow a continuous trend 'spiritualizing' the cultic concepts, and insisting upon inward purity as a necessary condition for the legitimacy and functioning of the ritual purity laws.[16]

Moreover, the New Testament texts nowhere allude to a possible rejection of baptism itself. On the contrary, the importance of Jewish baptismal practices is much enhanced in their reinterpretation in

---

[13] Brody 1958: 122. For some reflections on the 'purity of the heart' for Jesus, see Betz 1997.

[14] *Laws* 716e; cf. Euripides, *Orestes* 1604; Aristophanes, *Frogs* 355. These texts are quoted by Burkert 1984: 77.

[15] On the common roots of Jewish and Christian baptism, see Yarbro Collins 1996.

[16] See esp. Wenschkewitz 1932. Let us mention here, at least, Philo, *Life of Moses* 2. 24; see also the references in Strack and Billerbeck 1956–63: i. *s.v.* Matthew 15. 11, pp. 719ff.; esp. Rabbi Meir, in *Mishnah Berakhot* 17a: 'Keep thy mouth from every sin, and purify thyself from all sin and guilt; for I shall be with thee everywhere'; cf. *Mishnah Sanhedrin* 65b, 'spirit of purity, not of impurity'.

early Christian baptism (Yarbro Collins 1996). As we have already seen, what we have in Jesus's polemics with the Pharisees is rather a demand that cultic practices not be disconnected from an interior, ethical, purified mind. One cannot therefore simply speak of a clear, radical opposition to external purification rituals in the New Testament. In the conclusion of a careful study of Jesus and the purity laws, Roger Booth states (1986: 211): 'Jesus did not deny the concept of cultic purity absolutely, but only relatively in comparison with ethical purity.' In other words, Jesus 'did not deny the fact of cultic impurity... but only treated it as of less gravity than moral impurity'. Similarly, analysing the idea of purity of the heart in the Beatitudes, Jacques Dupont (1973: 590) concludes that there is no opposition between ritual and moral purity.[17] Hence, in different ways, and from various points of view, a great number of scholars seem to reject the traditional perception of a Jesus in direct and radical opposition to the Jewish ritual system.

The same tendency to insist upon the internalization of cultic behaviour is found later, in Patristic literature. At the end of the second century, for instance, Tertullian insists that the purification of the soul must be parallel to bodily purification: 'Is it reasonable to pray after having washed one's hands, but with a defiled mind?'[18]

In other words, and in radical contrast with Mani, Jesus does not demand a radical separation of the elements of light from those of darkness, of soul from body. On the contrary, he asks for purification of conscience, i.e., a unification of the person, soul, and body, in order to avoid the disconnection between beliefs and behaviour ($\delta\iota\psi\upsilon\chi\acute{\iota}\alpha$).

Moreover, contrary to the general scholarly view, the idea of ritual impurity was retained in early Christianity, as Marcel Simon (1968) argued convincingly. In early Christian context sexual impropriety ($\pi o\rho\nu\epsilon\acute{\iota}\alpha$) involves a defilement that is ritual rather than moral, in nature. The Christian insistence on the essential unity of the human

---

[17] See also Spicq 1965: 202–3, on the purification of conscience from sin in the New Testament. For an excellent overview of the problem, see Cothenet 1979.

[18] *On Prayer* 13. 1. On interior purification ($\kappa\acute{\alpha}\theta\alpha\rho\sigma\iota\varsigma$), which is identical with repentance ($\mu\epsilon\tau\acute{\alpha}\nuo\iota\alpha$), cf. Clement, *Stromateis* 4. 22. 143. 1. Both texts are quoted in Karpp 1970: 138–9 and 166–77. For Origen's discussion of ritual purity, see Cocchini 1996. On Clement, see further Baumgarten 1984: 12–13.

composite presents a new anthropology, but more within the Graeco–Roman world than in a Jewish context (Stroumsa 1992: 199–223). This new anthropology is reflected also in the new Christian practice of burying the dead within the walls of the settlement.[19] A similar revolution in the attitude to the dead body is reflected in the Christian practice of burial near to the tombs of saints, which represented a radical break with old habits in the various Mediterranean societies.[20]

Mani, on the other side, does not conceive the possibility of unification between soul and body. Since the human composite is an unnatural mingling ($\mu\acute{\iota}\xi\iota\varsigma$), due to evil archons, the only possible salvation entails a complete separation of body from soul. We have here an anthropology established on a quite different basis. The radical encratism reflected in this kind of anthropology is usually explained, genetically, as the end of a radical evolution originally stemming from some elements within the Biblical (Jewish and early Christian) traditions. Yet, it may also reflect an influence from a quite different source.

A BUDDHIST ORIGIN?

I wish here to call here attention to an early Buddhist text, which offers a striking parallel, still unnoticed, to Mani's objections to baptism:

Thus have I heard: On a certain occasion the Exalted One was staying near Gayâ, on Gayâ Head. Now on that occasion a great number of ascetics, on the cold winter between the eighths in time of snowfall,[21] were plunging up and down [in the water] and sprinkling and burning sacrifice, thinking: This way comes purity.

---

[19] See Dagron 1977, who states: 'La levée de l'interdit religieux sur la sépulture *intra muros* vieux d'un millénaire ... est le signe d'une véritable mutation historique' (quoted by Brown 1981: 133, n. 16).

[20] Parker 1983: 71, who refers to Ariès 1981: 30–40, for the origins of burial near saints.

[21] i.e., the eighth day before and after full moon of the months equivalent to January and February.

Now the Exalted One saw that great number of ascetics so doing, and at that time, seeing the meaning of it, gave utterance to this verse of uplift:

Not by water is one pure, tho' many folk bathe here.
In whom is truth and dhamma, he is pure and he's a brâhmin.

This Pali text, which I quote in Woodward's translation, is taken from the *Udâna*, the third of fifteen books of the *Khuddaka-nikaya*, which is the fifth collection of the Pali *Sutta Pitaka*.[22] It is a collection of eighty inspired verses reportedly uttered by the Buddha himself. Each verse is preceded by a short anecdote that more or less sets forth the occasion for the utterance.

In other words, we have here, at least from a phenomenological point of view, a rather precise parallel to Mani's argument against the purifying capacity of water in *CMC*. Like Mani, Buddha rejects the ablutions of the ascetics around him, claiming that water cannot purify the body. It strikes me that this parallel is much closer to Jesus's utterances. None of his words, after all, refers to the cleansing power of water. To be sure, Buddha's utterances in this text can no more be considered his actual utterances than Mani's in *CMC*. But the real question is whether we have here more than a phenomenological parallel, namely a possible source for the early Manichaean rejection of baptism. Although they cannot be dated with precision, the texts of the Pali canon are early. They were certainly in existence before the third century CE, and Mani might well have heard similar arguments when he spent time in Buddhist kingdoms of Northern India. Al-Biruni, who is generally an accurate and well-informed writer, tells us that Mani had gone to India after having been exiled from the Sasanian empire, adding that he learned there, from the Hindus, the doctrine of metempsychosis, the transmigration of souls, which he then adapted into his own system.[23] Al-Biruni mentions the Hindus, but Mani could of course have heard about metempsychosis equally from the Buddhists, in whose system *samsara* plays a major role. Although his trip took place after his break with the community of

---

[22] I quote the translation of Woodward 1948: 7–8. On the *Udâna*, see further Reynolds 1981: 102, and Norman 1983: 60–1. Our passage was already quoted, in a different context, by Scheftelowitz 1914: 369.

[23] References given by Lieu 1985: 56.

his youth, he may have found there also a theoretical justification for his opposition to the baptismal practices of the Elkasaites.

The once fashionable view that Mani's syncretism amalgamated elements taken from Zoroastrianism and Buddhism as well as from Christianity has long ceased to be popular. With good reason, most scholars focus today upon the Jewish–Christian and Gnostic texts, which provide the immediate religious background of Mani. Despite the few mentions of the Buddha in the Coptic *Kephalaia* (Gardner 1995: i. 33 l. 17)—the text being probably written in the first generation after Mani—the scholarly consensus today is that 'Buddhist elements [in Manichaeism] were acquired in the course of mission, and were not fundamental to Manichaeism'.[24]

In itself, the striking parallel on the powerlessness of water is not enough to break this consensus. However, it is worth calling attention to yet another similarity between the earliest stages of Manichaean doctrine and Buddhist traits, side by side, also, with metempsychosis and the denigration of the cleansing power of water. I am referring to the idea and practice of monasticism, and, more specifically, to the monastic community perceived as the real nucleus of the religious community, the *samgha*, while married people are looked upon as supporters, 'fellow travellers', rather than first-class members of the community. Years ago, I argued that, since we know of the existence of Manichaean monasteries in Egypt a few decades before the first appearance of Christian monasticism, the former might well have provided a catalyst for the emergence of the latter. Furthermore, It postulated a Buddhist influence, acquired by Mani himself during his stay in northern India, upon the idea of the elect and the outer circle (Stroumsa 1992: 299–327). There seems, therefore, to be mounting circumstantial evidence, calling for a revision of the consensus denying any serious Buddhist (or perhaps also Jain) influence upon nascent Manichaeism.[25]

The history of religions offers many examples of sects emerging from broad religious traditions. Since Troeltsch, the sociology of

[24] Lieu 1985: 53–4. For a synthetic study of the question, see Klimkeit 1986.
[25] The best study of the topic is Sundermann 1986. See further Sundermann 1997. He remains sceptical as to the possible Buddhist influences upon Mani, and thinks that during his stay in India, Mani taught rather than learned. See also Ries 1986.

religions has learned to analyse the conditions within which sects are born and can grow. What is much less common, however, is the mutation through which out of a sectarian milieu emerges a fully-fledged religion, with ecumenical ambitions. This is exactly what the birth of Manichaeism offers: a very special case study for historians of religions. In her well-known thesis, propounded a generation ago, Mary Douglas (1966) argued that rules of purity and impurity (and hence rituals of purification) develop especially in societies that must avoid contact with the world at large in order to survive. Mani's rejection of Elkasaite baptismal practices tends to sharpen Douglas's underlying thesis. Indeed, rituals of purification seem to be often central in the self-definition of religious groups, and calling the value of these rituals into question may bring a radical transformation of the group's identity.

BIBLIOGRAPHY

Ariès, P. (1981). *The Hour of our Death*. London: Allen Lane.

Baumgarten, A. (1984). 'Josephus and Hippolytus on the Pharisees', *Hebrew Union College Annual*, 55: 1–25.

Betz, H.-D. (1986). 'Paul in Mani's Biography (Codex Manichaicus Coloniensis)', in Cirillo 1986a: 215–34.

——(1997). 'Jesus and the Purity of the Temple (Mark 11. 15–18): A Comparative Religion Approach', *Journal of Biblical Literature*, 116: 455–72.

Booth, R. P. (1986). *Jesus and the Laws of Purity: Tradition History and Legal History in Mark 7*, Journal for the Study of the New Testament, Supp. 13. Sheffield: University of Sheffield Press.

Brody, A. (1958). 'On the Development and Shifting of Motives in the Israelitic–Jewish Conceptions of Clean and Unclean', in D. S. Löwinger, A. Scheiber, and J. Somogyi (eds.), *Ignace Goldziher Memorial Volume*. Jerusalem: Mass, ii. 111–26.

Brown, P. (1981). *The Cult of the Saints: Its Rise and Function in Latin Christianity*. Chicago: Chicago University Press.

Burkert, W. (1984). *Greek Religion: Archaic and Classical*. Cambridge, MA: Harvard University Press.

Cameron, R. and Dewey, A. J. (1979). *The Cologne Mani Codex (P. Colon. inv. nr. 4780) 'Concerning the Origin of his Body'.* Missoula, Mont.: Scholars.

Caquot, A. (1968). 'Ablution et sacrifice selon le Psaume LI', in *Guilt or Pollution* 1968: 75–7.

Cirillo, L. (1984). *Elchasai e gli Elchasaiti: un contributo alla storia delle comunità giudeo-cristiane.* Cosenza: Marra.

——(ed.) (1986a). *Codex Manichaicus Coloniensis: Atti del Simposio Internazionale.* Cosenza: Marra.

——(1986b). 'Elchasaiti e battisti di Mani: i limiti di un confronto delle fonti', in Cirillo 1986a: 97–139.

Cocchini, F. (1996). 'La normativa sul culto e sulla purita rituale nella interpretazione di Origene', *Annali di Storia dell'Esegesi*, 13: 143–58.

Cothenet, E. (1979). 'Pureté et impureté, 3. Nouveau Testament', *Supplément au Dictionnaire de la Bible*, ix. 508–54.

Dagron, G. (1977). 'Le christianisme dans la ville byzantine', *Dumbarton Oaks Papers*, 31: 11–19.

Daniélou, J. (1991). *Théologie du Judéo-Christianisme.* 2nd edn. Paris: Desclée-Cerf.

Delcor, M. (1966). 'Les attaches littéraires, l'origine et la signification de l'expression biblique "prendre à témoin le ciel et la terre"', *Vetus Testamentum*, 16: 8–25.

Douglas, M. (1966). *Purity and Danger: An Analysis of Concepts of Pollution and Taboo.* London: Routledge and Kegan Paul.

Dupont, J. (1973). *Les Béatitudes*, iii, Etudes Bibliques 56. Bruges: Abbaye de Saint-André.

Dupont-Sommer, A. (1968). 'Culpabilité et rites de purification dans la secte juive de Qoumrân', in *Guilt or Pollution* 1968: 78–80, more fully in *Semitica*, 15 (1965), 61–70.

Flusser, D. (1979). 'John's Baptism and the Dead Sea Sect', in Flusser, *Judaism and the Origins of Christianity* (Tel Aviv: Sifriat Poalim), 81–112 (Hebrew).

García Martínez, F. (1988). 'Les limites de la communauté: pureté et impureté à Qumrân et dans le Nouveau Testament', in T. Baarda, A. Hilhorst, G. F. Luttikhuizen, and A. S. van de Woude (eds.), *Text and Testimony: Essays on New Testament and Apocryphal Literature in Honour of A. F. J. Klijn.* Kampen: Kok, 111–22.

Gardner, I. (ed.) (1995). *The Kephalaia of the Teacher.* Leiden: Brill.

Guilt or Pollution (1968). *Guilt or Pollution and Rites of Purification*, Proceedings of the XIth International Congress of the International Association for the History of Religions, ii. Leiden: Brill.

Henrichs, A. (1973). 'Mani and the Babylonian Baptists: A Historical Confrontation', *Harvard Studies in Classical Philology*, 77: 23–59.

——and Koenen, L. (1978). 'Der Kölner Mani-Kodex (P. Colon. Inv. Nr. 4780): Περὶ τῆς γέννης τοῦ σώματος αὐτοῦ. Edition der Seiten 72, 8–99, 9, *ZPE*, 32: 87–199.

Karpp, H. (1970). *La pénitence*. Neuchâtel: Delachaux et Nestlé.

Klein, G. (1984). 'Gesetz. 3. Neues Testament', *Theologische Realenzyklopädie*, xiii. 58–75.

Klimkeit, H.-J. (1986). *Die Begegnung von Christentum, Gnosis und Buddhismus an der Seidenstrasse*. Opladen: Westdeutscher Verlag.

Koenen, L. (1981). 'From Baptism to the Gnosis of Manichaeism', in B. Layton (ed.), *The Rediscovery of Gnosticism, ii: Sethian Gnosticism*. Leiden: Brill, 734–56.

——and Römer, C. (1988). *Der Kölner Mani-Kodex*, Abhandlungen der rheinisch-westfälischen Akademie der Wissenschaften. Opladen: Westdeutscher Verlag.

Kümmel, W. G. (1978). 'Äussere und innere Reinheit des Menschen bei Jesus', reprinted in his *Heilsgeschehen und Geschichte*, Marburger Theologische Studien 16. Marburg: Elwut, ii. 117–129.

Lieu, S. N. C. (1985). *Manichaeism in the Later Roman Empire and Medieval China: A Historical Survey*. Manchester: Manchester University Press.

Luttikhuizen, G. P. (1985). *The Revelation of Elchasaai: Investigations into the Evidence for a Mesopotamian Jewish Apocalypse of the Second Century and its Reception by Judeo–Christian Propagandists*. Tübingen: Mohr [Siebeck].

Neusner, J. (1973). *The Idea of Purity in Ancient Judaism*, Studies in Ancient Judaism 1. Leiden: Brill.

Norman, K. R. (1983). *Pâli Literature*. Wiesbaden: Harrassowitz.

Ort, L. J. R. 'Guilt and Purification in Manichaeism', in *Guilt or Pollution* 1968: 69.

Parker, R. (1983). *Miasma: Pollution and Purification in Early Greek Religion*. Oxford: Clarendon.

Reynolds, F. E. (1981). *A Guide to the Buddhist Religion*. Boston, MA: Hall.

Ries, J. (1986). 'Buddhism and Manichaeism, the Stages of an Inquiry', *Buddhist Studies Review*, 111: 108ff. (= 'Bouddhisme et manichéisme, les étapes d'une recherche', in *Indianisme et bouddhisme, Mélanges Etienne Lamotte* [Louvain la Neuve: Université Catholique de Louvain, Institut Orientaliste, 1980], 281–95).

Rudolph, K. (1981). *Antike Baptisten: zu den Überlieferungen über frühjüdische und christliche Taufsekten*, Sitzungsberichte des sächsischen Akademie der Wissenschaften zu Leipzig, Phil.-hist. Klasse, 121. 4. Berlin: Akademie Verlag.

——(1986). 'Jüdische und christliche Täufertraditionen im Spiegel des CMC', in Cirillo 1986a: 69–80.

Scheftelowitz, I. (1914). 'Die Sündentilgung durch Wasser', *Archiv für Religionswissenschaft*, 17: 353–412.

Sevrin, J.-M. (1986). *Le dossier baptismal séthien: études sur la sacramentaire gnostique*, Bibliothèque copte de Nag Hammadi. Québec: Laval.

Simon, M. (1968). 'Souillure morale et souillure rituelle dans le Christianisme primitif', in *Guilt or Pollution* 1968: 87–8.

Spicq, C. (1965). *Théologie morale du Nouveau Testament*, Etudes Bibliques 51. 1. Paris: Gabalda.

Strack, H. L. and Billerbeck, P. (eds.) (1958–63). *Kommentar zum Neuen Testament aus Talmud und Midrasch*, 2nd unaltered edn. Munich: Beck.

Strecker, G. (1986). 'Das Judenchristentum und der Manikodex', in Cirillo 1986a: 81–96.

Stroumsa, G. (1984). *Another Seed: Studies in Gnostic Mythology*, Nag Hammadi Studies, 24. Leiden: Brill.

——(1992). *Savoir et salut*. Paris: Cerf.

——(1999). 'From Repentance to Penance in Early Christianity: Tertullian's *De paenitentia* in Context', in J. Assmann and G. Stroumsa (eds.), *Transformations of the Inner Self in Ancient Religions*. Leiden: Brill, 167–78.

Sundermann, W. (1986). 'Mani, India and the Manichaean Religion', *South Asian Studies*, 2: 11–19.

——(1997). 'Manichaeism Meets Buddhism: The Problem of Buddhist Influence on Manichaeism', in P. Kiefer-Pülz and J.-U. Hartmann (eds.), *Bauddhavidyāsudhākarah, Studies in Honour of Heinz Bechert* (Swisttal-Odendorf: Indica et Tibetica Verlag), 647–56.

Wenschkewitz, H. (1932). *Die Spiritualiserung der Kultusbegriffe: Tempel, Priester und Opfer im Neuen Testament*, Angelos, 4. Leipzig: Pfeifer.

Woodward, F. L. (1948). *The Minor Anthologies of the Pali Canon, ii: Udâna: Verses of Uplift*. London: Cumberlege.

Yarbro Collins, A. (1996). 'The Origin of Christian Baptism', in her *Cosmology and Eschatology in Jewish and Christian Apocalypticism*, Journal for the Study of Judaism Supp. 50. Leiden: Brill, 218–38.

15

Pagans, Polytheists, and the Pendulum[1]

J. A. North

'It is pleasant to dream of a world without militant faiths, religious or political. Pleasant but idle. Polytheism is too delicate a way of thinking for modern minds.'

(John Gray, *Straw Dogs*, 126)

CURRENT RESEARCH DIRECTIONS

This paper is one of general reflection on the current study of the religious history of the Greeks and Romans; it is focused on the state of that religion in the later third century CE, but reflections on religious history necessarily range backwards and forwards in time. My starting-point is the observation that ideas seem to have been moving recently in a different direction among those who study the religion of the Greeks and Romans in the centuries BCE, compared to those who do so in the early centuries CE and especially in the period when traditional Graeco–Roman worship starts to become marginalized after the reign of Constantine. The former trend has been to say that the strength of the religion has been methodically under-estimated: the systems of behaviour and

[1] This paper was read at Stanford University, as well as at Columbia. I am grateful to colleagues for helpful comments made on both these occasions, but particularly to Alan Cameron for much discussion and ideas on several points. I also have a debt to Keith Hopkins, who spent a few of his last minutes telling me what he thought about the argument.

conception associated with it are so radically different from those familiar to us and its location in society is so alien to our expectations that, when we meet the phenomena in the ancient evidence, we lack any sense of direction or comprehension in dealing with the evidence. Critics have tended to declare that they find a state of arid ritualism, when they have in fact been lost in an alien landscape.[2] The claim (and it is not just my claim) is that we need to make a radical re-adjustment of our ideas if we are to grasp what (e.g.) the multiplicity of deity actually meant to the worshippers in Greek and Roman cities during these centuries. Twenty-first century 'common sense' is in any case a thoroughly bad guide.[3]

In the study of late antiquity on the other hand, while the continuing strength of Graeco–Roman religion has been well recognized, in a way it used not to be, and while religious factors in a broad sense have been given a central importance in the whole conception of late antique society, the alienness of Graeco–Roman religion has not been at all a prominent theme in the discussion.[4] My impression is rather the opposite: just as in wider issues the trend has been away from seeing profound economic, social, or political changes between the early and later periods of the Roman Empire, so there has been a tendency to minimize the distance between Graeco–Roman traditional religion and the new religions of the imperial period. Emphasis is placed on their common features, on their successful co-existence and degree of mutual tolerance; just as the Christians by and large avoid revolutionary politics, so the traditionalists only make erratic and partial gestures of resistance against the new faiths.[5] Non-Christians often tend to slip unnoticed into the role of converts, because the differences between the two religions are seen as less important than the similarities.

Even if I am right about the divergence between these two trends in scholarship, the difference is not, of course, necessarily a problem. It

---

[2] Famously in Mommsen's account (1854: i. 170) describing the whole religious system as *geistlos*. Warde Fowler (1911: 270–313) found much the same characteristics, though he saw them as the product of a longer process of decline. For discussion of the whole tradition, Scheid 1987.

[3] See e.g. Beard et al. 1998: i; Scheid 2001.

[4] For recent surveys of the progress in the study of later antiquity, Averil Cameron 2002; Swain and Edwards 2004. On the influence of Peter Brown and his students in particular see Howard-Johnston and Hayward 1999; Averil Cameron 2002: 166–72.

[5] Well-argued in Drake 1996.

is possible, even quite likely, that the two views are both right at once. But on any view, if both these approaches have validity as interpretations of the 'same' religion, then those who write the history of that religion have a duty to explain how they understand the transition from one state to the other. If the religion of the centuries BCE was something quite alien to our expectations, by what processes and at what date did that same religion become transformed into one that, by the third century CE, was not, after all, so radically different from the new faiths?[6] It is easy enough to say that there had been convergence, but what does that mean?

SOME RECENT SHIFTS OF OPINION

There are two more specific debates about the naming and identity of the religion in question; up to this point I have—self-consciously and more than a little preciously—been using clumsy periphrases in the hope of deferring the issues; but also hoping to show that the people under discussion have to be given some name or it becomes impossible to discuss them rationally at all. Traditionally, we speak of pagans and pagan-ism. Both words are given a small initial 'p', so as to contrast with Christianity, Judaism, and Islam, thus neatly conveying, every time we write the word, our contempt for the whole business. But at least it is a name; should it be changed? If so, should the same name be used for all the non-Judaeo–Christian religions of the ancient world or should we seek to differentiate either in terms of place or of period?

Second, there is the issue of late 'pagan' monotheism. The proposition that pagans were interested by the idea of monotheism is not of course a recent development, indeed, in some ways it is, as we shall see, an obvious truth that has long been recognized. But some interest has focused on this question recently,[7] and potentially it might provide the key to some of the problems of the subject: if it

---

[6] For discussion, see Drake 2000: 136–53; the claim that pagan religion was becoming increasingly 'personal' is very plausible, but it does not follow that this necessarily correlates with the rise of monotheism.

[7] Triggered particularly by the publication of Athanassiadi and Frede 1999.

is true that there is solid evidence to suggest that pagans were progressively becoming monotheistic, abandoning the cultic and sacerdotal specificities of their own tradition and forgetting the complex identities of the powers recorded in their books, then evidently the transition to Christianity for individuals would have become far more straightforward. But is this perception right? What is the relevant evidence? And how does this line of thought relate, if it does at all, to the renaming issue raised above?

Third, and perhaps to be combined with either of, or both of, the above questions, there is the status of the religion of the pagans in itself. It is more or less agreed that to speak of any religious situation as an *-ism* (Hindu-ism, Juda-ism, Catholic-ism) implies a degree of coherence, of self-consciousness and of doctrinal unity among the members of the group being defined by the word. For the situation of pagans before the Common Era to be so described seems therefore to be profoundly misleading. The word is used to describe the religious life and system of all those (except the Jews) who lived in and around the Roman Empire. These peoples certainly had some things in common: they all believed in many deities; they mostly practised some form of animal sacrifice; they tended to have developed ritual systems of worship and consultation. But beyond these basic similarities, it would be impossible to say that they shared any beliefs and still less that they had any substantial sense of belonging to a common faith. They would have assumed themselves that their religion corresponded precisely with the membership of their particular tribe or city or region—that is, assuming that they could have grasped the modern conception of a religion at all.

It is always tempting to dismiss such issues of naming and definition as being too theoretical to be of any value in a historical debate. Well-trained historians should ignore such diversions and get on to the facts, or better still back into the archives. It is indeed common ground that there is no agreed cross-cultural definition even of the word 'religion' itself;[8] not that this situation seems to inhibit continuing debate on the subject. But in the case of the word

---

[8] For a recent 'loose characterization', offered in place of a definition, see Rappaport 1999: 1–22, cf. 23. For the problems that arise in discussing ancient religious life in particular, see Gradel 2002: 4–8.

'pagan', it is far from clear to me that the debate with which this book is concerned can proceed rationally at all without some agreement about the terms we are to use, their meanings and their boundaries. If it is not to be pagan, what is to be the new term?

HISTORICAL META-NARRATIVES

There is another matter of theory to be considered before looking more carefully at the questions raised so far. Notoriously, the history of what I shall, at least for the moment, continue to call 'paganism' has been the object of a classic evolutionary historical meta-narrative.[9] For the most part, of course, such evolutionary narratives have been identified and abandoned; but it is of their nature that they continue to operate subconsciously even when nobody wants to defend them or is even aware of them as such. The effect they then have is to impose teleological assumptions and to shape the selection of evidence to be prioritized in the light of these assumptions. In the case of religious history in this period, there is just such a residual but strongly felt meta-narrative of events.

The classic formulation (though it is only the final concentration of a line of thought with far deeper roots) is that of Hermann Usener (1896). His theory aspired to do two things: first, to provide a clear formulation of how the gods and goddesses of the pagan tradition came into existence in the form we know them; second, to show how that tradition, despite being degenerate and weakened from the archaic period onwards, was nevertheless only destroyed by waves of influence from Eastern religions, 'oriental cults', hammering away generation after generation at the chronically weakened structures of the Greeks, Romans, and of their neighbours. In the end, the out-come was to be Christian monotheism, though Usener in fact only hinted briefly at this consummation.[10] The whole theory is the type of evolutionary staged development so prevalent in the nineteenth

---

[9] For the notion, see Appleby, Hunt and Jacob 1994: 231–7; Fulbrook 2002: 53–73.
[10] Usener 1896: 348: 'Nur von aussen der alten Welt diese klärende offenbarung kommen. Sie kam von Galiläa . . .'.

century and so influential in some quarters through the twentieth. However, the basis of this particular theory has long since been in question and, comprehensive and influential as it was in its day, has fallen apart from beginning to end. The origin of the gods from *Sondergötter* (specialized gods) and *Augenblicksgötter* (momentary gods) has too little to support it and is essentially philosophical speculation;[11] the long agonizing weakness of pagan religion has been shown to be based on misunderstanding and partial readings of the evidence,[12] the role attributed to the rise of Oriental cults was rooted in misconceptions now elaborately taken apart and so on.[13] The effects of the evolutionary theory in the history of the history of Roman religion have been, to say the least, limiting: interest focused for many years above all on the pre-history of the gods and goddesses (the so-called pre-deistic phase); and on their demise, their replacement by 'better' things; the theory also legitimized those who wanted to concentrate on the areas of Greek and Roman life that they found answered to their own 'common sense' (politics, law, engineering), while ignoring the irrational elements, which they could conveniently assume were regarded as superstition by the ancient elite, precisely as it was by themselves.[14] Even today, the view has not disappeared completely that pagan religious belief was a matter for the vulgar masses, while the intellectual elite were to a man and woman scientific proto-monotheists paying lip-service to popular superstitions, which they found in any case a valuable tool to manipulate lower-class credulousness.

Interesting light can be shed on these matters by the thoughts of Martin West in the first chapter of *Pagan Monotheism in Late Antiquity* (West 1999), a book which will play a considerable part in this argument. The chapter is called (perhaps unsurprisingly) 'Towards Monotheism' and provides an introduction to a book dealing with late antiquity by tracing the evolution of the same idea in the later Near Eastern and early Greek worlds. West's collection of data, which covers the period from Sumer to Herodotus, is extremely

---

[11] For the origin of these ideas in Hegel, see Scheid 1987: 316–20.
[12] See e.g. Beard et al. 1998: i. 117–34.
[13] Gordon 1980; Sfameni Gasparro 1985; Smith 1990.
[14] For an overall survey, North 1997.

wide-ranging and impressive: he can show that while at every stage and in every society discussed the basic religion is polytheistic, higher level discussions always show one or other of a series of re-interpretations moving towards monotheism. The Near Eastern and Homeric pattern tends to be towards a council of gods, which West calls a *fable convenue*; the Hesiodic pattern is rather towards the promotion of one god towards a position of supreme ruler, in whose power the whole universe ultimately lies. Other gods and goddesses are assumed to be subordinate to this supreme power. Everywhere the story is the same; you might think that the dominant thought-system is of multiple independent powers, but everywhere poets, philosophers, and historians re-interpret this to their intellectual taste and always in a monotheistic direction.[15]

There are two points to be noted here. First, the general sense of the rest of the book seems to be (broadly, though admittedly not comprehensively) to put forward the possibility that pagan monotheism was growing in late antiquity and to survey its various forms and impact with a view to showing that this tendency is a crucial part of the religious history of the period.[16] To my mind, therefore, West's position, perfectly valid in itself, does not so much reinforce the rest of the book, as cut across its logic. If we are to be persuaded that the various late imperial monotheistic developments are in fact significant ones in the history of religion, we will surely want to be persuaded that something was happening in the third century CE that had *not* happened before. The precise chronology of the change need not be too closely defined: but on West's view the great breakthrough was already trembling on the verge of happening in the archaic Greek world. To quote him:

It was a small step from here to dogmatic monotheism: but there was no pressure or haste to take this step. People are slow to adjust their religion to their philosophy.
(West 1999: 40)

---

[15] West 1999: 22–38, collects evidence from Sumerian and Akkadian texts onwards.
[16] For the variety of the views discussed, see the excellent introduction by the editors Athanassiadi and Frede 1999: 1–20.

'Slow', in this case, means taking approximately a thousand years. Of course, West himself was not responsible for the relationship between his own views and the rest of the book, but there is a real divergence here, not obviously resolved.

The second point is West's own clear commitment to a natural, unavoidable evolution of the kind being discussed. It is pre-supposed in his comments that monotheism is a later stage of human development; that the only open question is not whether it will emerge triumphant, but how long it would be before the next step to be taken; that it is somehow inherent in the logic of the human situation that mankind would first see multiple powers as controlling the world and then evolve to realize that there must have been a single grand designer. In other words, West's view is in complete conformity with the evolutionary meta-narrative of religious history.

HUME'S PENDULUM-SWING

The progressive evolution of religious ideas can, of course, be traced further back than Usener. David Hume, to take one example, offers a version of much the same set of arguments in the *Natural History of Religion*:[17] he argues (in polemic against those who had proposed a primitive monotheism[18]) that polytheism must have evolved first, because harassed and ignorant early mankind would not have had the time or opportunity to reflect on the nature of divine power and would have explained the events of natural life by powers local to the specific phenomena. Only when individual men (it would have been *men*) had acquired the leisure and capacity to think logically about their whole situation did they realize that the nature of the whole natural order implied a single creative intellect that had to have been responsible for the design of the universe. So he too in this argument accepts the chronological evolutionary scheme: it starts from a general state of ignorance, evolves into a version of polytheism and

---

[17] See the edition of Root: Hume 1777/1957; see also Wollheim 1963: 31–98.
[18] For the context of this argument, see Gaskin 1988: 184–7.

hence finally to monotheism, which is of course coincident with the arrival of Judaism, Christianity, and Islam.

Hume's thought on the subject did not stop here. In his later work, he attacked some of the ideas that underpin this pattern of development and in particular the argument from design (Gaskin 1988: 11–51); but even within the *Natural History* itself, he has another theory of some significance for this discussion. He is still concerned with polytheism and monotheism and their mutual relationship: but he describes this as one of 'flux and reflux'.[19] The idea is that neither of the two is ever stable for long, because each is unsatisfactory to one or other section of any population. Polytheism (which is, still on this view, chronologically prior) is unsatisfactory to the intellectuals, who attack it as illogical on the grounds roughly of the argument from design, i.e. they argue that there must have been a single creative intelligence, not a multiplicity of competing powers for the universe to function as it does. As a result of their reforming zeal, polytheism breaks down and monotheism replaces it: this situation, however, is unsatisfactory to the great mass of humanity because it implies a remote single power that can only be imagined at all as operating on a level so remote from everyday human concerns as to be quite useless in their lives. What is needed by the mass of humanity is a deity who will make sure that you have enough to live on and to feed your children. To quote Hume's own words in *Natural History of Religion*:

The feeble apprehensions of men cannot be satisfied with conceiving their deity as a pure spirit and perfect intelligence; and yet their natural terrors keep them from imputing to him the least shadow of limitation and imperfection. They fluctuate between these opposite sentiments. The same infirmity still drags them downwards, from an omnipotent and spiritual deity, to a limited and corporeal one, and from a corporeal and limited deity to a statue or visible representation. The same endeavour at elevation still pushes them upwards, from the statue or material image to the invisible power; and from the invisible power to an infinitely perfect deity, the creator and sovereign of the universe.   (1777/1957: 48)

---

[19] Hume 1777/1957: ch. 8. For recent discussion, see Livingston 1984: 173–4; Badía Cabrera 2001: 107–27.

I am not advocating the use of this pendulum-swing theory in exactly the form that Hume proposed it.[20] It is, as Gellner pointed out (1968: 5–7), and as such theories so often are, cast in overly psychological terms as if religious history was a form of rational debating club. It is dependent also on his sharp division between the ignorant masses on the one hand and the educated elite on the other. Religious divisions are never as clear cut as that, and the notion of a separate popular religiosity has been effectively attacked since Hume's time (Momigliano 1971). Also, it is unhelpful that the theory should operate chronologically, history being divided into phases of polytheism and phases of monotheistic reaction. But the notion of flux and reflux, of the pendulum-swing between polar opposites, does seem to evoke something highly significant about the situation we are seeking to define. It is at least a different model from his own evolution from polytheism to monotheism; indeed these two chapters of the *Natural History* seem at first sight to be in unresolved contradiction of one another.[21] It is perhaps better to see them as complementary elements of Hume's general approach to history: the first model reflects his acceptance of long-term change in human history, the second reflects his view that there were constant elements in human nature, which would always create similar effects even under radically changed social and economic conditions. So in this particular case there is no doubt that pagan religion is replaced as the dominant form by new forms of religious life; but in the new world so created, or even in very much later periods, the same cycle from monotheism to polytheism continues, though translated into the terms of the new religious order of things.[22]

Of these two Humean theories, the first has attracted more attention, no doubt because it anticipated much of what was to be said in the nineteenth century. But the notion of a long-term consistency allowing for rhythmical variations within its boundaries has not perhaps received the attention it deserves. It allows us to open the possibility that the monotheistic element was not a slow progressive

[20] Acute comments in Gellner 1968.
[21] There is at least no attempt to explain their relationship in the text of the *Natural History of Religion* itself. See Badía Cabrera 2001: 117–18.
[22] For this line of thought, Livingston 1984: 214–25; Badía Cabrera 2001: 117–27.

erosion of the nature of paganism, but an essential aspect of the way pagans of all periods thought and acted. At the same time, we should recognize that the regular rhythm of theoretical challenge by monotheism and yet persistence of polytheistic practice in fact demonstrates to us time after time the underlying strength of ancient ritual practice and traditional belief. On this view, these two aspects of pagan religion are not in perpetual conflict, but mutually supportive in the longer run.[23] The existence of monotheistic ideas would not be a source of weakness or decline but of strength and flexibility.

RE-NAMING THE RELIGION OF THE
GRAECO–ROMAN WORLD

The words 'pagan' and 'paganism' took their origins in obscure circumstances. The obvious guess has seemed to be that the terms were intended to be hostile, meaning roughly what Cicero meant when he called ordinary Roman soldiers '*homines agrestes*' or 'ignorant bumpkins'.[24] Alan Cameron, in a forthcoming reconsideration of the whole question (Cameron 2011: 14–25), points out very effectively that the Latin word for bumpkin is always either *rusticus* or *agrestis* and never *paganus*. The rather unclear origin of the term perhaps would not matter too much since other names start as abuse and end up as just names, quite probably including 'Christian' itself. In the circumstances of the third/fourth centuries CE, whatever term the Christians had chosen to designate non-Christians would in time have developed an abusive connotation. But in this case it is true that the term has continued, like heathen, to have a pejorative force when used by Christians or others to refer to those outside the religions of the book; and expressions such as 'little better than pagans' continue to have some currency. I have myself seen a London conference aimed at 16–17 year-olds boycotted by some secondary schools on the grounds that some non-Christian students might think 'pagan'

---

[23] See below pp. 496–9.
[24] For this view, see Zeiller 1917: 29–70; the texts are collected at 71–102.

was a rude word applicable to them, i.e. presumably that it characterizes all forms of polytheism from a monotheist perspective. It is easy to see therefore that those who have recommended abandoning the term and replacing it with a more anodyne (or PC) expression do indeed have a serious point (Fowden 1993; 1998). The trouble is that the term has a very wide range of meaning and replacing it with another term risks creating confusions, even when the new term seems at first sight to indicate the same people, or is intended by the author to indicate the same people. More particularly, to call the pagans polytheists, which has been proposed, is potentially very misleading for the reasons we have already considered.

There are two main problems here: first, the term polytheist is essentially a classification from a Jewish–Christian perspective, not from the point of view of the members of the religion themselves; it is intended to imply that the defining characteristic of the people in question is their belief in many gods and their rejection of monotheism. So it fails to cover all those whom we normally include among the pagans and limits itself to those 'pagans' who are firmly of the polytheistic persuasion. In so far as there were pagan monotheists, as so many historians are seeking to persuade us there were, these are presumably not to be categorized amongst the polytheists at all. And those who retain an attachment to traditional Graeco–Roman rituals, but seek to interpret them within a monotheistic frame, in the manner of Praetextatus' address in Macrobius' *Saturnalia*, are presumably, something in between.[25] Alternatively, of course, we might start making subtler distinctions: distinguishing between polytheistic polytheists, monotheistic polytheists, semi-polytheistic polytheists and semi-monotheistic polytheists and so on.

The second problem is rather more my own business as a historian of the religion of what we used to call *pagan* Rome. If the correct description of an adherent of the religion of the Greeks and Romans is to be polytheist not pagan, then it must be right to start using that term for Augustus, Cicero, Plato, Homer, and all the other pagans of the pre-Christian era. That seems to me to be a gross distortion: however these people might have categorized themselves had they

---

[25] Macrobius, *Saturnalia* 1. 17–23; discussion by Liebeschuetz 1999. For the date, Alan Cameron 1966. On Praetextatus himself, Kahlos 2002.

sought to do so at all, it seems in the very highest degree improbable that they would have done so in terms of the plurality of their deities. All the 'sane' peoples they knew, not to mention all kinds of barbarians, had many gods and goddesses. In fact, for most purposes they believed something even simpler: that all normal people believed in *the* gods and goddesses, i.e. the same gods and goddesses, whose names differed from society to society, but whose essence remained the same. Caesar in Gaul does not ask the question what are these gods? but rather which of these gods is Iuppiter?[26] In these circumstances, it would be paradoxical in the extreme for them to be defined by the one characteristic they all share, and which in their view was to all intents and purposes universal.

There is another possible line that might be taken here, in the light of this criticism: polytheist/polytheism could be the name not for all pagans at whatever period they lived, but only for those who lived in the full awareness of the other views—whether monotheistic, dualistic or henotheistic. It would then follow that the new name should be seen as inappropriate before some agreed date, after which the use of 'pagan' would be banned from the discourse of the learned and 'polytheist' become *de rigueur*. From my own interested viewpoint (North 1992), there is something to be said for this idea. There is a strong case for arguing that the nature of the religion of the pagans did change radically in the course of the second century CE; and the change is closely related to growing awareness of groups that rejected the traditional deities and their worship and hence the identification of the 'pagan' as one amongst a range of options. To change the name used in modern historiography would certainly have the effect of underlining the profound nature of this change.[27] However, this is surely the most impractical of solutions: it flies in the face of the strong convictions of the late imperial pagans that they were precisely

---

[26] Caesar, *Gallic War* 6. 17. The identity of Roman with Gallic deities is simply to be assumed: *Deum maxime Mercurium colunt* (The god they chiefly worship is Mercury); and they hold approximately the same beliefs as others do—e.g. that Apollo drives away diseases. Caesar seems unconcerned by, or did not notice, the circularity of this procedure. See Beard et al. 1998: ii. 54–5.

[27] It would however be a precedent for historians' changing the name of a religion whenever they perceived radical change in its history—a dangerous procedure to start applying to living religions.

operating in the age-old traditions of Greek and Roman culture.[28] It must be the duty of historians of religion to point out when they see profound changes to which the adherents of the religion at the time were insensitive or which they deliberately concealed; but it surely is not their job to provide changes of name that would have been unrecognizable to the contemporaries of the events themselves.

The conception of the history of pagan-ism for which I should argue is that the crucial factor is not some internal change or transformation, still less an evolution according to some pre-determined process, but rather the necessary effects of confrontation and co-existence with the new types of religious groups, Jewish, Christian, and others, with which pagans in all the cities of the Empire had to deal from the first century onwards. The effect was to create a self-consciousness about their own position and a need to define and justify themselves, which had simply not existed before, when there were no alternative systems against which they had to measure themselves. It is in this context that they themselves have to produce a doctrine and an identity and it is their response that justifies the use of the word 'pagan-ism'. It is not necessary for this view that there should have been much, if any, violent conflict between pagans and others; what we have to believe is that there was a steady drift of pagans away from their traditional attachments and a great deal of peaceful co-existence and discussion; but that the survival of pagan practice depended on their success in retaining members, generation by generation. It remains, of course, a serious question why pagans did so drift away from traditional attachments.

CRITERIA FOR RELIGIOUS 'PROGRESS'

Some of the evidence brought forward to illustrate the rise of pagan monotheism might help to indicate the criteria that could help to identify where serious change was happening. The precise question at issue in the debate is not whether there was in the end any

---

[28] For this notion, especially in the East, Bowersock 1990.

convergence between pagan and Christian thought. We know very well that there was: the texts of Gnostics, Chaldaean Oracles, Neo-Platonic thinkers of various kinds show quite clearly that once a sustained debate was established a great deal of common ground could be and was found.[29] Nor is it difficult to concede that although much of this is late in date, much of it goes back to earlier centuries and is well-established in pagan thought. But none of it can show in itself that the religion of the pagans was itself changing in the direction of monotheism, granted that monotheistic thought dates back a thousand years. The problem is the lack of criteria to establish that something has changed.

All scholarly roads, it seems, lead to monotheism. If the gods and goddesses hold a conference and make decisions (as in Homer), that is a step towards monotheism (see West 1999: 22–4); if some of them merge their identities into a single composite deity (as happens e.g. with Isis) through 'syncretism', that is another step towards monotheism;[30] if there is a deity achieving wide pre-eminence (as the Sun apparently did in the third century), that is a step towards monotheism;[31] if a deity has a title implying predominance over the others (as *Hypsistos*), that is a step towards monotheism;[32] if a philosopher or historian treats the divine as a unity (as many of them do from Herodotus onwards),[33] without breaking the unity down into the specific deities, that is a step towards monotheism. Pagan deities in this period cannot stir hand or foot without being interpreted as on their way to some kind of grand universal convergence. But, as we

[29] Frede 1999; but cf. the comments of Edwards 2004: 212–17; Athanassiadi 1999.

[30] As in the so-called Isis Aretalogies, for which see e.g. Grandjean 1975. For the alternative term 'henotheism', to express the assertion of one deity without denying the power of others, see Versnel 1990: esp. 35–8.

[31] The increased importance of the sun-cult, especially in Rome, is a major development, but one whose importance can all too easily be exaggerated: see e.g. Latte 1960: 349–53; Nilsson 1961: 507–19; Dörrie 1974; Halsberghe 1972; Fauth 1995; Liebeschuetz 1999: 187–92. Aurelian's invention of the *pontifices Solis*, to parallel the traditional *pontifices*, is certainly remarkable; but there is no reason to think that it led to the elimination of other deities or other cults. Even in Praetextatus' oration, surely a rhetorical tour de force not a statement of anybody's beliefs, the practice of paganism is not to be discontinued; see above pp. 483–6.

[32] On this see below, pp. 494–6.

[33] See, e.g., Herodotus 1. 32. 9: 'For the god gives many men a glimpse of happiness and then utterly destroys them.'

have seen, it is possible to produce evidence of all these tendencies from early Greece onwards. What are the criteria that will enable us to distinguish when such events signify real change in the nature of pagan religious life rather than the swing of Hume's pendulum?

One potentially very important area of research has been emphasized by Stephen Mitchell, who provides one chapter of the collection on *Pagan Polytheism* (Mitchell 1999). The theme is a deity (for the moment, it can be assumed that it was one deity) called either Zeus *Hypsistos* or Theos *Hypsistos*. The word Zeus is not present in the majority of the inscriptions, but among those who use *Hypsistos* alone or *Theos Hypsistos* some imply a reference to Zeus by the presence of an eagle (Mitchell 1999: 101). The evidence about this cult is largely epigraphic; it is mostly limited in time to the centuries of the Roman Empire and geographically to the Eastern provinces, though very widespread within that area.[34] The dedicants are predominantly not from the high elite class of the different areas, but both from town and country. Modern discussions have adopted a term from the Christian bishops to describe the adherents of the cult as 'Hypsistarii' or 'Hypsistiani'.

There is no doubt (as was made clear many years ago by A. D. Nock [1936: 414–43, esp. 416–30]) that the worshippers of *Hypsistos* must have been situated at the meeting point of various tendencies in the religious atmosphere of their time. The problem is to know how coherent they were as a group and what were their fundamental beliefs. It is quite clear from some of the evidence that there is a strong connection between the *Hypsistos* inscriptions and the Jewish communities of the areas concerned, as has long been recognized (Simon 1972; Trebilco 1991). There seems in fact to be a strong correspondence between the Hypsistarians and the godfearers, also pagans, but specifically attached to Jewish congregations without converting fully to Jewish identity.[35] The economical view of the evidence therefore is that *Theos Hypsistos* is the Jewish god, particularly as seen by pagan adherents. That cannot, however, be the whole story.

[34] The evidence is fully listed by Mitchell 1999: 128–47 and analysed, 97–108; see also Belayche, above Ch. 5.
[35] For god-fearers: Rajak 1992: 19–21; Feldman 1993; Mitchell 1998.

The most direct evidence, assuming that it does reflect their point of view, comes from a famous inscription from Oenoanda:[36]

> Self-born, untaught, motherless, unshakeable,
> Not holding a name, many-named, dwelling in fire,
> This is god. We his angels are a small part of god.

The same text is quoted in later sources as a response by the Clarian Apollo to the question 'are you god? or is some other?'[37] However, both Lactantius and the so-called Theosophy of Tübingen, for whom the verses provide pagan endorsement of monotheism, give a different reading of the second verse, eliminating the word 'many-named', presumably because of its pagan implications.[38] And their accounts do not fit accurately with the Oenoanda version. But assuming that this is a pagan oracle and the speaker a pagan god, then it does provide us with a definite indication of a pagan viewpoint on the cult. The 'highest' god is perceived as the supreme governor, who might or might not be called Zeus and the other pagan deities are perceived agents or angels of this supreme will. It does seem quite legitimate to call this a pagan version of monotheism seeking to preserve a distinctively pagan identity in the context of a monotheistic religion. What is more, this evidence has the great merit that it depends on solid evidence of cultic activity not, like so much of what has been prominent in this debate before, philosophical, or quasi-philosophical, debate, abstracted from worship.

There are, however, problems with this formulation of the facts. First, the evidence does not start in the period we are thinking about: the movement seems rather to go back to the late Hellenistic period and even then we would be making the dangerous assumption that the cult does not long precede the earliest epigraphic evidence for its existence (so, Mitchell 1999: 108–10). Second, whatever you may make of the Hypsistarians, they do seem to be inextricably mixed with a pagan vision of the Jewish god; that surely implies that they

---

[36] First published by Bean 1971: no. 37 and discussed by Robert 1971. See also, Lane Fox 1985: 168–76; Potter 1990: 351–5; Mitchell 1999: 81–92. Translated in Beard et al. 1998: ii. 57.

[37] Discussion in Mitchell 1999: 86–7.

[38] Tübingen Theosophy (= Erbse 1995, §13, ll. 12–16); Lactantius, *Divine Institutes* 1. 7.

should not be used as evidence for an internal development of paganism towards monotheism; they should rather be understood as one of the predictable consequences of the new competitive environment. It may indeed be very probable that the emphasis on the *Theos Hypsistos* is the result of that Jewish influence; but what we cannot know is which feature of contemporary Jewish life was attractive to its pagan adherents. It might have been monotheism that was so attractive; but that is precisely what we are seeking to prove. There are other aspects of Jewish life that might explain the appeal.[39] In other words, this is undoubtedly an important area for further research and it is relevant to the issues we are discussing; but it is not clear yet what light it throws on these particular questions.

There might be some temptation to say at this point that the whole attempt to conceive the conflict between pagans and Christians in terms of polytheists and monotheists is doomed to be un-illuminating. There are, after all, plenty of other factors that can provide part of a complex explanation of the tilt in favour of Christianity and against paganism with which this book is concerned: the Christian emphasis on doctrine; the involvement of intellectuals in religious debates; the creation of an autonomous organizational structure; the group support the Christians offered to their members and so on. There is no shortage of factors that can be shown to have played their part in inducing the conversions on which the expansion of Christian membership depended. How can we ever prove that it was the issue of monotheism that was the most important factor? And, if we cannot, how can this line of research produce serious results?

The situation described above is, after all, a paradoxical one and we must be alive to its contradictions. The terms 'monotheism' and 'polytheism' are not translatable into Greek or Latin and they cannot therefore represent the terms in which ancient pagans themselves thought about these matters. Most of those whom we want to classify as the pagan supporters of monotheistic thinking were not engaged in any open attack on polytheistic practice. Characteristically, they continued to support the separate worship of the traditional gods

---

[39] Such as its moral order, social support, ritual traditions and so on: see in general Rajak 1992, Feldman 1993.

and goddesses, even while arguing for their ultimate unity; this pattern recurs generation after generation from Plato and the Stoics to Cicero and Macrobius' Praetextatus. One might argue that the whole system of classification is an alien imposition, which cannot help us understand the religious life of the ancients. That religious life may be full of inconsistencies, but religions cannot be judged by the standard of twenty-first century everyday rationality. On the basis of this argument we should expel both terms from the religious vocabulary we use.[40]

It would, however, be a mistake to dismiss the area of debate in quite this way. The reason for this is partly that, in many of the Christian texts of the period, the theme of the superiority of recognizing one divine power and the corresponding inconsistencies of having multiple divine powers recurs frequently and powerfully—think of the fierce attacks of Arnobius of Sicca[41] or even of Constantine himself.[42] For them, it is clear that the weaknesses of polytheism as they conceived them constituted at the very least an important weapon for their assault on pagan traditions. Their emphasis may have been wrong and we may still conclude that the real issues lay elsewhere; but we need at least to explain why the emphasis falls on this particular issue.

Still more significantly, the pagan monotheism discussed in this paper could well be seen as a long-established feature of the pagan religion and, before it was placed in confrontation with other religions, as a source of its strength; but as its crucial weakness thereafter. Flux and re-flux may have operated successfully for centuries, so long as there were no alternative religions in the field. But when the same mechanism was transferred into the new conditions of competition and co-existence, the implications would have become completely different. At that point, the strong pagan tradition of sympathy with monotheism must have become a weak point in pagan defences; meanwhile, the concern of ancient contemporary Christians was precisely to define the pagans as polytheists, so creating an easier

---

[40] For the notion of inconsistency in religion, see especially Versnel 1990: 1–35.

[41] Arnobius, *Against the Nations*, especially Books 3 and 4; on the general issues, see Simmons 1995: 174–215.

[42] For his *Oration to the Saints*, see Edwards 2003: 1–62.

target for themselves. Once the Christians had successfully redefined pagans as polytheists, then the strong tradition of philosophic monotheism could be turned back against them. It is, of course, a delusion to think that major changes in the history of religion can be analysed as if they were constructed from rational arguments and counter-arguments. All the same, the converting of pagans to Christianity must at least in part have been a matter of taking part in and winning arguments. If Varro could be turned round against the pagans by using his philosophical thoughts, that was surely a point gained.[43]

It needs to be made very clear, however, to what extent the use of this terminology has a valuable role to play in the analysis of religious history and at what point it fails to illuminate or actually breeds confusion. Polytheism–monotheism is a modern analytic tool that has been imported into the discussion of the religious life of this period. It is obviously a perfectly valid way of classifying some aspects of religious life. It also draws our attention to characteristics that need to be studied and interpreted. Graeco–Roman religious practitioners both acted and thought in terms of a multitude of divine powers; they gave care, thought, money and devotion to the specific requirements and ritual needs of these male and female supernatural beings. In order to do so, they needed skill and knowledge of traditional practices and rules. Frustratingly for us, they did not for the most part attempt to reduce all this complexity to any simplifying formula. Understanding and responding to this divine multiplicity, without much guidance from ancient discussions, is the essential task of those who seek to study the realities of pagan activity.[44] To this extent, it is obviously very helpful to think in terms of polytheism and of polytheistic forms of worship.

There are, no doubt, some dangers in the usage. Monotheism and polytheism work as a pair in our conceptions, the one implying the other as its polar opposite. Automatically, an assumption arises that there must be opposition and conflict between the two. This may be appropriate enough in dealing with the late Empire, though it risks begging important questions even at that date. In earlier periods, it is certain that opposition to monotheism forms no part of the

---

[43] As e.g. by Arnobius, *Against the Nations* 7. 1.
[44] For discussion of these issues: Scheid 1987; 1999.

polytheistic tradition, since there was no monotheistic religion to be opposed. Monotheistic speculation in its turn should not be seen either as hostile to the normal civic religions of the day. Hume's pendulum can provide us with a useful model for thinking through the relations of the two terms, setting them in creative tension, but not creating conflict where none existed; but a tool for creating a model should not be confused with any statement of ancient reality. At least it should be beyond dispute that neither of them can provide the building blocks for an evolutionary theory.

BIBLIOGRAPHY

Appleby, J. O., Hunt, L. A., and Jacob, M. C. (1994). *Telling the Truth about History*. New York and London: Norton.

Athanassiadi, P. (1999). 'The Chaldaean Oracles: Theology and Theurgy', in Athanassiadi and Frede 1999: 149–83.

——and Frede, M. (eds.) (1999). *Pagan Monotheism in Late Antiquity*. Oxford: Clarendon.

Badía Cabrera, M. A. (2001). *Hume's Reflection on Religion*, Archives internationales d'histoire des idées 178. Dordrecht and London: Kluwer Academic.

Bean, G. E. (1971). *Journeys in Northern Lycia 1965–1967*. Vienna: Böhlau.

Beard M., North, J., and Price, S. (1998). *Religions of Rome*, 2 vols. Cambridge: Cambridge University Press.

Bell, M. (1999). 'Hume on Superstition', in D. Z. Phillips and T. Tessin (eds.), *Religion and Hume's Legacy*. Basingstoke and New York: St. Martin's Press, 153–70.

Bowersock, G. W. (1990). *Hellenism in Late Antiquity*. Ann Arbor, MI: University of Michigan Press.

Cameron, A. (2002). 'The "Long" Late Antiquity: A Late Twentieth-Century Model', in T. P. Wiseman (ed.), *Classics in Progress*. Oxford: Oxford University Press, 165–91.

Cameron, Alan (1966). 'The Date and Identity of Macrobius', *JRS*, 56: 25–38.

——(2011). *The Last Pagans of Rome*. Oxford and New York: Oxford University Press.

Drake, H. A. (1996). 'Lambs into Lions: Exploring Early Christian Intolerance', *Past and Present*, 153: 3–36.

——(2000). *Constantine and the Bishops: The Politics of Intolerance*. Baltimore, MD and London: Johns Hopkins University Press.

Dörrie, H. (1974). 'Die Solar-Theologie in der kaiserzeitlichen Antike', in H. Frohnes and U. W. Knorr (eds.), *Die Alte Kirche*. Munich: Kaiser, 283–92.

Edwards, M. (ed.) (2003). *Constantine and Christendom: The Oration to the Saints, etc.* Liverpool: Liverpool University Press.

——(2004). 'Pagan and Christian Monotheism in the Age of Constantine', in Swain and Edwards 2004: 211–34.

Erbse, H. (ed.) (1995). *Theosophorum Graecorum Fragmenta*, 2nd edn. Stuttgart and Leipzig: Teubner.

Fauth, W. (1995). *Helios Megistos*, RGRW 125. Leiden: Brill.

Feldman, L. H. (1993). *Jew and Gentile in the Ancient World: Attitudes and Interactions from Alexander to Justinian.* Princeton, NJ: Princeton University Press.

Fowden, G. (1993). *Empire to Commonwealth: Consequences of Monotheism in Late Antiquity*, Princeton, NJ: Princeton University Press.

——(1998). 'Polytheist Religion and Philosophy', in Averil Cameron and P. Garnsey (eds.), *The Cambridge Ancient History* xiii. *The Late Empire, A.D. 337–425.* Cambridge: Cambridge University Press, 538–60.

Frede, M. (1999). 'Monotheism and Pagan Philosophy in Later Antiquity' in Athanassiadi and Frede 1999: 41–67.

Fulbrook, M. (2002). *Historical Theory*. London: Routledge.

Gaskin, J. C. A. (1988). *Hume's Philosophy of Religion*, 2nd edn. Basingstoke: Macmillan.

Gellner, E. (1968). 'A Pendulum-Swing Theory of Islam', *Annales Marocaines de Sociologie*, 1: 5–14, repr. in R. Robertson (ed.), *Sociology of Religion: Selected Readings*. Harmondsworth: Penguin (1969), 127–38.

Gordon, R. L. (1980). 'Reality, Evocation and Boundary in the Mysteries of Mithras', *Journal of Mithraic Studies*, 3: 19–99, repr. in his *Image and Value in the Graeco–Roman World*. Aldershot: Variorum, 1996.

Gradel, I. (2002). *Emperor Worship and Roman Religion*. Oxford: Clarendon.

Grandjean, Y. (1975). *Une nouvelle arétalogie d'Isis à Maronée*, EPRO 49. Leiden: Brill.

Halsberghe, G. H. (1972). *The Cult of Sol*, EPRO 23. Leiden: Brill.

Howard-Johnston, J. D. and Hayward, P. A. (eds.) (1999). *The Cult of Saints in Late Antiquity and the Early Middle Ages.* Oxford: Oxford University Press.

Hume, D. (1777/1957). *The Natural History of Religion*, ed. H. E. Root. Stanford, CA: Stanford University Press.

Kahlos, M. (2002). *Vettius Agorius Praetextatus: A Senatorial Life in Between.* Rome: Institutum Romanum Finlandiae.

Lane Fox, R. (1985). *Pagans and Christians*. Harmondsworth: Penguin.

Latte, K. (1960). *Römische Religionsgeschichte*, Handbuch der Altertumswissenschaft 5. 4. Munich: Beck.

Liebeschuetz, W. (1999). 'The Significance of the Speech of Praetextatus', in Athanassiadi and Frede 1999: 185–205.

Lieu, J., North, J., and Rajak, T. (eds.) (1992). *The Jews among Pagans and Christians in the Roman Empire*. London and New York: Routledge.

Livingston, D. W. (1984). *Hume's Philosophy of Common Life*. Chicago, IL: University of Chicago Press.

Mitchell, S. (1998). 'Wer waren die Gottesfürchtigen?', *Chiron*, 28: 55–64.

——(1999). 'The Cult of Theos Hypsistos between Pagans, Jews, and Christians', in Athanassiadi and Frede 1999: 81–148.

Momigliano, A. D. (1971). 'Popular Religious Beliefs and the Late Roman Historians', *Studies in Church History*, 8: 1–18, repr. in his *Quinto contributo alla storia degli studi classici e del mondo antico* (Rome: Edizioni di storia e letteratura, 1975), ii. 73–92, and in his *Essays in Ancient and Modern Historiography* (Oxford: Blackwell, 1977), 141–59.

Mommsen, T. (1854). *Römische Geschichte*. Berlin: Weidmann.

Nilsson, M. P. (1961). *Geschichte der griechischen Religion*, 2nd edn., Handbuch der Altertumswissenschaft 5. 2. Munich: Beck, ii.

Nock, A. D. (1936). 'The Gild of Zeus Hypsistos', *HTR*, 29: 39–88 (with C. Roberts and T. C. Skeat). Nock's section repr. in his *Essays on Religion and the Ancient World*, 2 vols (Oxford: Clarendon, 1972), i. 414–43.

North, J. A. (1992). 'The Development of Religious Pluralism', in Lieu et al. 1992: 180–93.

——(1997). 'The Religion of Rome from Monarchy to Principate', in M. Bentley (ed.), *Companion to Historiography*. Edinburgh: Edinburgh University Press, 57–68.

Potter, D. S. (1990). *Prophecy and History in the Crisis of the Roman Empire*. Oxford: Clarendon.

Rajak, T. (1992). 'The Jewish Community and its Boundaries', in Lieu et al. 1992: 9–28, repr. in her *The Jewish Dialogue with Greece and Rome* (Leiden: Brill, 2000), 335–54.

Robert, L. (1971). 'Un oracle gravé à Oinoanda', *CRAI*, 597–619, repr. in his *Opera Minora Selecta* (Amsterdam: Hakkert, 1989), v. 617–39.

Scheid, J. (1987). 'Polytheism Impossible: Or the Empty Gods: Reasons behind a Void in the History of Roman Religion', *History and Anthropology*, 3: 303–25.

——(1999). 'Hiérarchie et structure dans le polythéisme romain: Façons romaines de penser l'action', *ARG*, 1: 184–203, translated as 'Hierarchy and Structure in Roman Polytheism: Roman Methods of Conceiving Action', in C. Ando (ed.), *Roman Religion*. Edinburgh: Edinburgh University Press (2003), 164–89.

——(2001). *Religion et piété à Rome*, 2nd edn. Paris: Albin Michel.

Sfameni Gasparro, G. (1985). *Soteriology and Mystic Aspects in the Cult of Cybele and Attis*, EPRO 91. Leiden: Brill.

Simmons, M. B. (1995). *Arnobius of Sicca*. Oxford: Clarendon.

Simon, M. (1972). 'Theos Hypsistos', in J. Bergman, K. Drynjeff, and H. Ringgren (eds.), *Ex orbe religionum: studia Geo Widengren*. Leiden: Brill, i. 372–85.

Smith, J. Z. (1978). *Map is not Territory: Studies in the History of Religion*. Leiden: Brill.

——(1990). *Drudgery Divine. On the Comparison of Early Christianities and the Religions of Late Antiquity*. London and Chicago: Chicago University Press.

Swain, S. and Edwards, M. J. (eds.) (2004). *Approaching Late Antiquity*. Oxford: Oxford University Press.

Trebilco, P. R. (1991). *Jewish Communities in Asia Minor*. Cambridge: Cambridge University Press.

Usener, H. (1896). *Götternamen: Versuch einer Lehre von der religiösen Begriffsbildung*. Bonn: Cohen.

Versnel, H. S. (1990). *Inconsistencies in Greek and Roman Religion. i. Ter Unus. Isis, Dionysos, Hermes. Three Studies in Henotheism*, Studies in Greek and Roman Religion, 6.1. Leiden: Brill.

West, M. L. (1999). 'Towards Monotheism', in Athanassiadi and Frede 1999: 21–40.

Wollheim, R. (ed.) (1963). *Hume on Religion*. London: Collins.

Zeiller, J. (1917). *Paganus: étude de terminologie historique*, Collectanea Friborgensia n.s. 17. Fribourg: Librairie de l'Université.

IV

Late Antiquity

16

Early Christianity and the Discourse of Female Desire

Averil Cameron

The most cursory reading of early Christian literature demonstrates that the representation of women presented major difficulties. They attracted attention from Christian writers—almost exclusively male—both as members of the Christian community and as the subject of discourse. Much of the latter was negative in character, expressing suspicion of the female and denying women a place equal to that of men in the Christian dispensation. Yet it coexisted not merely with a glorification of female virgins in general, and especially of the virgin mother of Jesus, but also with the description of the relation of the soul and God in explicitly sexual and bridal imagery. This chapter explores some of these tensions within the context of early Christian texts and asks what they mean in relation to early Christian attitudes to women. I use the term 'early Christian' rather broadly, since I shall be concerned not primarily with the New Testament period but with the centuries during which Christianity became the majority religion in the empire, and especially the period from Constantine (AD 306–37) to the sixth century.

The actual role of women in the first Christian communities, especially as seen in the New Testament ('earliest', or 'primitive' Christianity, in the specialist parlance), has been discussed at enormous length.[1] The focus lies especially on what can be deduced from

---

[1] See e. g. Fiorenza 1983; Ruether 1979; Witherington III 1984; 1988—the best recent discussion of the evidence.

the Gospels about Jesus's attitude to women, the passages in the Acts of the Apostles and, for example, the Epistle to the Romans, Chapter 16, which show women as playing an apparently influential role in the first Christian communities, and the various statements made by Paul about the proper place of women and about male/female relationships, especially the injunctions on female behaviour in church in I Corinthians 11, the prescriptions about sexual relationships in I Corinthians 7, and the famous statement of Galatians 3. 28 ('there is neither male nor female; for ye are all one in Christ Jesus'). Whereas the genuine Pauline epistles are extremely early in the development of Christian thinking, even earlier than the Gospels,[2] the so-called Pastoral Epistles (I and II Timothy, Titus) represent a second stage, when Paul's still somewhat ambiguous position has crystallized into a much more developed set of negative attitudes. A large volume of scholarly literature has attempted to square the circle, and to recapture a lost Eden of early Christianity in which women were both active and prominent. No need to emphasize that the purpose behind such enquiries is not completely innocent, even when it is not actually presented in the forthright language of feminist theology; the search cannot be separated from a real and pressing practical issue in the church today, and indeed is sometimes explicitly expressed within the terms of those discussions. Christian feminist writers in particular are placed in a dilemma by the undoubted fact that so much of the later Christian tradition is so negative towards women, or even downright misogynistic, and have been at pains to justify their own agenda by appealing to an earliest phase that was much more positive. The American feminist theologian Elizabeth Schussler Fiorenza, in particular, does so by adopting an explicit methodology of 'remembering' this lost stage of female acceptance which lies buried under centuries of male rejection. It is obvious that the project of studying the origins of a text-based religion to which many scholars are still committed, and in which the place of women is a highly sensitive issue today, is liable to import all kinds of preconceptions. Moreover, it implies the constant reexamination of the same, often ambiguous, texts. Indeed, it seems very doubtful

---

[2] Thus it becomes a critical question to ask just what was Paul's own contribution to this set of ideas, as to Christian interpretation generally.

whether further reexamination at this stage can produce any new results. But we can and should separate the search for the 'real' position of women in the early church from that of the way in which women are represented in early Christian discourse, which is where this chapter takes its starting point (see also Cameron 1990). Leaving aside altogether the question of the role of women in the earliest church, I shall argue here that the concept of woman, in all its aspects, not only constituted a peculiarly problematic area within early Christian discourse but also provided certain convenient polarities round which other ideas could be expressed. This in its turn may help us to understand better the actual role of women in the first centuries of Christianity.

As we have seen, they had become problematic for Christian writers at a very early stage—certainly by the second century AD, when Tertullian was already writing in luridly misogynistic terms.[3] Both Tertullian at the end of the second century and Cyprian of Carthage in the third composed treatises in which women's dress, makeup, and jewellery stood for concealment and deception, with the clear implication that women as such were liable to lead men into temptation.[4] Thus begins an overtly misogynistic strain in ancient and medieval Christian writing that lent itself readily to rhetorical play on real, as distinct from superficial, beauty, and which presented woman in the role of temptress originally associated with Eve (Ruether 1974; Bloch 1987; Pagels 1988). Indeed, the latter theme is also to be found in second-century Christian texts, which already present the Incarnation of Christ as a reversal of the fall of Adam and Eve; for this Eve is given the chief responsibility and, after her, women in general (E. Clark 1983). In this scenario, however, just as Christ was to be the second Adam, so Mary the mother of Jesus took on the role of the second Eve, that is, as Christ redeemed Adam, so Mary's purity was held to have cancelled out the sin of Eve.[5]

Thus even while presenting women in negative terms as the daughters of Eve, the early church also seemed to develop a more positive view, which it expressed in the concept of the Virgin Mary.

[3] See E. Clark 1983 for a very useful collection of texts.
[4] For these and later examples, see Bloch 1987.
[5] Pagels 1988 brings out very well the political implications of this nexus of ideas.

Whether this was actually the case, we shall see later, after we have considered another apparent contradiction in early Christian representation of woman, namely its use of explicit bridal and even sexual imagery juxtaposed with the strong condemnation of female sexuality and promotion of the virginal ideal.

The area of textuality, often neglected in this regard, is of fundamental importance in understanding the development both of early Christian thought and practice. I wish to begin by considering the contrasting modes in which women are presented in early Christian writing. We may start with the condemnation of sexuality which formed such an important part of the strong ascetic ideal in the early church from at least the late first century onwards.[6]

It was not simply female sexuality that was to be abjured; nevertheless, temptation inevitably presented itself in the guise of a female. The classic text is the *Life of Antony* (an ascetic who died in AD 356), perhaps composed by the great fourth-century Father, Athanasius, but in any case one of the most influential of all Christian literary works. This text not only described the life of the man usually considered as the founder of monastic asceticism, but also laid down the parameters of an ascetic ideal for lay Christians of both sexes. Among those deeply influenced by it were Jerome, who brought it to ascetic circles in Rome in an early Latin translation, and Augustine, on whom it had a profound effect, featuring in the account of his conversion which he gives in the *Confessions;* it is interesting that the latter simply assumed that conversion entailed chastity henceforth. However, the influence exerted by the *Life of Antony* also went much wider, and its ideals percolated further than ecclesiastical circles as such.[7] Its vivid descriptions of Antony's struggles against the Devil can be read as representing the soul's desire for God, following on from the teachings of Origen in the third century. But Origen himself had advocated virginity as fundamental to the ascetic life, and Antony's temptations are seen in sharply physical

---

[6] Brown 1988 is the fullest and most vivid discussion. See also Brown 1987 and for the broader background Veyne 1978; 1987; Dodds 1983: 34; Rousselle 1983; Lane Fox 1986, referring to Christian ascetics as 'over-achievers'.

[7] See Harpham 1987: for a good introduction to the work, see Young 1983: 81–3. The *Life of Antony* is the only non-Scriptural work recommended in a prescription for Christian reading laid down by St John Chrysostom.

terms (for Origen, see Crouzel 1989). It is striking that Antony's earliest experience of temptation at once presents him with the image of a seductress: 'The wretched Devil even dared to masquerade as a woman by night, merely in order to deceive Antony.' Ousted on this occasion, the Devil reappears to him in the form of a black boy, who is described as 'the lover of fornication'. It is explained that this first victory of Antony over the Devil represents the New Testament teaching of the primacy of spirit over flesh: thus through his Son, God is said to have 'condemned sin in the flesh'.[8] The conquest of lust for women thus comes early in the stages of Antony's ascetic progress, seen as belonging to the lowest level of the ascetic ascent. In his address to his followers he dismisses it out of hand as merely a preliminary:

as to lusting after women or other sordid pleasure, we shall not entertain such at all, but turn our backs upon it as something transitory—ever fighting on and looking forward to the Day of Judgement. For the fear of greater things involved and the anxiety over torments invariably dissipate the fascination of pleasure and steady the wavering spirit.   (*Ant.* 19)

It is taken for granted that virginity is a mark of Christian virtue, and virgins are ranked together with martyrs as proofs of the faith: 'no one doubts when he sees the martyrs despising death for Christ's sake, or sees the virgins of the Church who for Christ's sake keep their bodies pure and undefiled'.[9]

To judge, however, from the collections of stories about the desert fathers who followed in Antony's footsteps in the late fourth and fifth centuries, it must be said that many seem to have been less successful than he was himself in rising above their susceptibility to the temptations of the female form. Take, for instance, the following passage about a certain John of Lycopolis:

There was a monk, who lived in a cave in the nearest desert and had given proof of the strongest ascetic discipline . . . then the Tempter asked for him,

---

[8] *Life of Antony* (*Ant.*) 5–7; Romans 8. 3f. (cited at *Ant.* 7); cf. *Romans 8. 6*: 'to be carnally minded is death. but to be spiritually minded is life and peace' and see Brown 1988: 213ff.

[9] *Ant.* 79; Antony's sister was given over to nuns by her brother and remained a virgin (3. 54).

as he did with Job, and in the evening presented him the image of a beautiful woman lost in the desert (Ward and Russell 1980: 56–7).

They talk, and the ascetic is won over:

He was frantic by now, like an excited stallion eager to mount a mare. But suddenly she gave a loud cry and vanished from his clutches, slipping away like a shadow. And the air resounded with a great peal of laughter.

The moral is clear: 'Therefore, my children, it is not in our interest to have our dwellings near inhabited places, nor to associate with women'.

The forbidden sexuality, we see, is inextricably identified with the idea of women, who are seen as the bearers of temptation for unwary monks and hermits, and who must therefore be kept away from the places where the latter have made their home. It is a highly coloured view of the relations between the sexes, and one in which women—unless they have adopted the ascetic life themselves, and sometimes even then—occupy the roles of temptress and seductress. Woman was seen, therefore, in terms of sexual allure, both as the object of male desire and as the subject, luring men astray. To insist on virginity was to control the dangers to which men felt themselves exposed. Of the responses of women themselves, we have little direct evidence, since nearly all the literature, including the fourth-century treatises on virginity and the works which praise women ascetics, is written by men,[10] but it is not surprising to find Christian women internalizing this strong message and taking it over into their own lives. Thus in the later fourth century, when the ascetic ideal had taken firm root, we find many examples of Christian women enacting its precepts in their own lives. Significantly, many of those best-known to us (that is, most written-about) are the relatives or associates of the male writers who have recorded their lives. Macrina (d. AD 379), the sister of St Gregory of Nyssa and St Basil, and known to us through the *Life* composed by Gregory himself, is one of the most striking and best-known of these.[11]

---

[10] For an attempt to recapture early Christian women writers see Wilson-Kastner et. al. 1981 and E. Clark 1986: 124–71.

[11] For the *Life*, see Maraval 1983, and Momigliano 1985.

It is very clear that, just as the theme of asceticism itself had allowed the author of the *Life of Antony* to develop certain textual ploys, that of female asceticism gives Gregory still more opportunities for underlining the polarities of gender. Unlike her many brothers, Macrina was of course not sent away from the family estates to be educated; her training, which she received from her mother, was in the Scriptures and the Psalms, her occupation sharing in the domestic work of the house (evidently, however, a very rich one). Thus Gregory can play on the idea that it was she who converted her intellectual and educated brother Basil (by dramatic irony one of the central figures in the development of an eastern monastic rule) to the 'true philosophy' of asceticism. Macrina, as a woman, stands for simplicity, the home rather than the world, the private rather than the public sphere, and the lack of (male) education. The *Life* is heavily indebted to Plato, especially to the *Phaedo*, in its description of Macrina's death, and like Diotima in the *Symposium*, it is Macrina who has the true philosophy of love, which is of course the love of God.[12] Gregory draws on a deep and familiar nexus of Platonic themes and imagery to give us a presentation of his sister which is idealized in every sense; nevertheless, whereas the discourse on love in the *Symposium* takes in the possibility of human and physical love as an allegory of spiritual union, the *Life of Macrina*, assuming from the beginning the rejection of human sexuality as a prerequisite of the spiritual life, finds an added dimension to the by-now familiar theme in that its central character, the model of spiritual knowledge and union with God, is not merely an ascetic but also, and piquantly, a woman.

Since women were inevitably associated with the idea of sex, Macrina had to be virginal in order to represent the spiritual ideal. The thinking was not confined to Christianity; the late third-century Neoplatonist Porphyry, for example, addressed a lengthy treatise commending celibacy to his wife Marcella—we do not know how she reacted on receiving it.[13] Macrina is also presented in the context

[12] See Maraval 1983: intro., 92ff., esp. 98; cf. *Symposium* 204D; for Diotima, see Halperin 1990.
[13] See Wicker 1987; other Neoplatonists also advocated ascetic practices. see e.g. Iamblichus *On the Pythagorean Life* (G. Clark 1989).

of an earlier and longstanding tradition of Christian virginity: Gregory explicitly recalls Thecla, the virgin heroine of the third-century apocryphal *Acts of Paul and Thecla*, set in apostolic times but reflecting a second and third-century enthusiasm for virginity. By now, the unhistorical Thecla had metamorphosed into a saint with an important local cult at Seleucia, but the context of the text in which her story was told was that of a real world of early Christian communities in which virgins, like widows, occupied a special and privileged place.[14] Thus the figure of Macrina as described for us by her brother Gregory draws at one and the same time on a real background of Christian practice, on the common ground of Christian and Neoplatonic thought, and on the textual field of gender and sexuality sharply drawn by previous Christian writers.

The latter in its turn exploited a discourse of love and desire for which the fundamental text was the Scriptural Song of Songs on which Origen had already written a commentary in the third century. In apparently total contrast to the renunciation implied in the texts so far described we here encounter an erotic imagery which is very explicit: 'Let him kiss me with the kisses of his mouth: for thy love is better than wine . . . his left hand is under my head and his right hand doth embrace me' (Song of Songs 1. 2; 2. 6).

The Song of Songs was to become one of the most commented on and most influential texts in the early Christian period.[15] It is a poem about love in a very physical sense, and perhaps at first sight a surprising model for ascetic writers to have chosen. In Origen's exegesis, the soul is the lover (the subject) and God the object of desire;[16] thus the roles are reversed, and the (female) soul is given the burden of desire. In later adaptations the Christian virgin is the subject and Christ both the Beloved and the Lover. Woman is

[14] Thecla, see Brown 1988: 156–9; for apocryphal Acts and virgins in early Christian communities, Davies 1980.

[15] See E. Clark 1986e; Consolino 1984; Cox 1986. Gregory of Nyssa and Jerome were among those who wrote commentaries on the Song. For bridal imagery in the Bible, Frye 1982.

[16] Nevertheless, the erotic language is retained, extending to the use of the *topos* 'wounded by love' (cf. Isaiah 49. 2; Song 2. 5), so reminiscent of the classical Eros with his bow (see Crouzel 1989: 123). Crouzel (1989: 118) rightly warns against attempts to explain such language away.

defined as the desirous subject, and the relation between subject and God as a relation of desire between female and male; the (female) soul desires union with God.

The Greek word *eros*, translated both as 'desire' and as 'love', allows for a reciprocal relation: God's love draws the soul towards union. But the detailed application of the imagery of the Song could produce surprising results, with the virgin envisaged as a nubile young girl, and her relation with Christ, the bridegroom, presented in openly erotic terms. Jerome quotes the very verse cited above in his notorious letter commending virginity; Christ is imagined as approaching the young daughter of Jerome's friend Paula through a crack in her wall (*Epistles* 22. 19). In Jerome's application, the desirous subject manifests itself, as in the original Song, as a young female. But now, paradoxically, the girl must be virginal, while the object of desire is not a human being, but Christ the bridegroom, who nevertheless takes on the attributes and behaviour of a human lover. Although Jerome's own motives may sometimes seem somewhat suspect,[17] he writes within a well-established mode within the field of Christian textuality, according to which the desirous subject is female, while the object is the male God of Christianity or the male person in which He became incarnate (Brown 1985: 274). But not only is the erotic imagery of the Bible utilized, exploited and allegorized in patristic writings; it is stood on its head and made to justify an ethic in which any real sexuality, let alone any actual eroticism, is denied and in which an erotic poem becomes a hymn to virginal spirituality.

The very theme of the Incarnation of Christ, implying physical birth from a woman, ensured that the issue of male–female relations would be enshrined in Christian texts. It was to a young woman that the angel announced the Incarnation, and to a young woman presented as the type of docility and submissiveness. At a very early stage the virtue of Mary, the mother of Jesus, was contrasted with Eve's role as temptress of Adam; as Christ came to save men, represented by the fallen Adam, so Mary quickly became the antithesis of Eve. Already in the second century the nexus is clear, but the logic had been implicit as soon as Paul had linked Christ with Adam; once expressed overtly, the

---

[17] Cf. Kelly 1975, who attributes much to Jerome's 'obsession with sex' and 'his troubled awareness of his sensual nature'.

balancing of Christ and Mary with Adam and Eve ran throughout early Christian and patristic writing.[18] It would be hard to exaggerate the implications for the Christian presentation of the female, but several obvious consequences spring to mind at once. In the first place, it is implied that women are normally to be associated with sin, and specifically with sexual temptation; thus abstinence becomes the logical way of neutralizing this situation. Among others, Elaine Pagels has well described the crystallizing of interpretation of the story of the fall in Genesis around the issue of sexuality, and the baroque excesses to which some Christian thinkers were led (Pagels 1988). Thus the 'clothes of skins' which God gave to the fallen Adam and Eve could be seen as representing sexuality, or even marriage, while the related topics of whether or not they had enjoyed sexual relations in the Garden of Eden, and whether gender would be a part of the resurrection life in Paradise assumed at various times a burning importance. It was also assumed that Christ and Mary must both be virgins par excellence, with the corollary that the virginal life therefore also became the highest to which mere humans could aspire. It is striking that this ideal is thus defined from the beginning in negative terms.

We have so far identified both the negative view of woman in early Christianity, and the way in which erotic discourse could be put to use in reinforcing the ideal of abstinence. But there was yet another Christian presentation of woman, which came eventually to be enshrined in the figure of the Virgin Mary but which also appears in other connections; it is itself the reverse of the negative mode and, since it derives from it and is secondary to it, is correspondingly less common. This is what we may call the image of the saving female, woman as the saviour of man. Found in conjunction with a deep male suspicion of women as temptresses and whores, this too can take different forms, as is clearly apparent in the case of early Christianity. Though it is by no means confined to the discourse about the Virgin Mary, a highly ambivalent figure,[19] it is certainly

---

[18] See Pagels 1988: xxif., 62f.; E. Clark 1986d. For Christ/Adam, see Romans 5. 14. The second-century writer lrenaeus develops the Eve–Mary theme, see the passages cited in E. Clark 1983: ch. 1, esp. 38ff.

[19] Warner 1976, and see Graef 1985; R. Brown et al. 1978—with wider coverage than its title suggests.

immediately recognizable in that connection, especially in the later part of our period. Thus if the Devil was wont to appear in the form of a seductress, the Virgin was wont by that stage to appear as the virtuous woman who saved men from themselves. A young protégé of St Dositheus of Gaza in the sixth century, terrified by a picture of the torments of hell, was visited by a lady, who explained to him what he must do to avoid them: 'you must take up fasting, eat no meat and pray continually' (Dorotheus of Gaza, *Discourses and Sayings*, trans. Wheeler 1977: 37). Similar properties of help and consolation were attributed in the sixth century and later to the Virgin's pictures; in visions she was not usually so recognizable, and tended to appear as a mysterious but always beautiful lady (Cameron 1991: ch. 6). A slightly different approach is found in a story from a seventh-century work, John Moschus' *Spiritual Meadow*, cited with approval by the supporters of icons during the Iconoclastic controversy, according to which a hermit on the Mount of Olives was tormented by a demon of lust who demanded that he stop bowing down to the icon of 'our Lady the Holy Theotokos Mary'; with the help of his abbot, the hermit was able to defy the demon and retain his loyalty to the picture. These stories are comparatively late in date, for the compassionate and maternal aspect of Mary with which we are familiar from so many later representations seems to have developed only gradually alongside the greater emphasis in the early literature on her virginity and her role as 'vessel of the Incarnation'. It is not an exaggeration to say that Thecla, the young virgin who never did become a mother, provided more of a female gender-model for Christianity in the early stages than did Mary. Significantly, the conception of Mary as the saving woman coincides both with the proliferation of icons and other images of Virgin and child which can be found in Byzantine art from the sixth century onwards and with the western collections of 'Mary miracles' (see further, Cameron 1991: ch. 6).

Nonetheless, it was not the only manifestation of an idealized male view of womanhood. We find another version in the immediately popular stories of female saints who had once been prostitutes. Mary Magdalene was the prototype for this group, which included Pelagia and Thais and in particular Mary of Egypt; their popularity is demonstrated by the large number of versions of their stories (Ward 1987; Brock and Harvey 1987). They are typically repentant prostitutes who have become holy women and thus neutralized the dangers inherent in being female by complete renunciation of their sexual side. In doing so, they free the image of woman for safe adoption by male ascetics and by society at large which is why such stories can and typically do coexist with a prevailing discourse which is profoundly negative. Since suspicion of women cannot after all be absolute, or there would be no procreation, it also tends to generate a supporting discourse which legitimates a more favourable view. Here too we may find the Virgin Mary intervening—thus we are told that St Mary of Egypt struggled with temptation for seventeen years, before she was helped by the Mother of God to change her ways and became so holy that she could walk across the waters of the River Jordan. Again, in these stories, the presumed reality of gender is concealed; the woman denies her sex and becomes like a man, sometimes literally so. Thus we often encounter female saints like the prostitute Pelagia who disguised themselves as men—Pelagia did so in order to become a desert hermit. But again, the very existence of such stories and indeed such practices only makes sense in the context of a prevailingly negative context. Like the type of the saving mother, they are secondary to a predominantly misogynistic view. Moreover, unlike the stories about the Virgin in which she appears as consoling and maternal, and thus at least presents a positive female image, these repentant prostitutes, having exploited their sexuality in their former lives, henceforth typically attain holiness by denying it as completely as possible, thus attempting to attain the status of ascetic men. That the image of the 'honorary man' is also encountered frequently in the literature about the prominent Christian woman of the fourth and fifth-century aristocracy (Giannarelli 1980: Consolino 1986) in fact suggests that the image of the saving female, at least as interpreted in a positive sense, is after all less common than we might have thought. Alternatively, it might be confined to the special case of the Virgin Mary, and even then is not obvious in the earlier stages of Christian writing about her. In general, we should perhaps conclude that even while individual Christian women, especially if they belonged to aristocratic circles, could find for themselves an active and honoured role, they must expect as the highest praise possible the statement that they had overcome their sex, or even that they were 'like a man'. The very textual advantages, which, as we have seen, a writer like Gregory of Nyssa could derive from having chosen a female subject, were themselves premised on the very fact that the general supposition about woman was so negative.

The central figure of the Virgin Mary displays features both typical and atypical of this situation. A male God with a virgin mother, attached to a creation story which laid blame for the sin of the whole human race on the first created woman, pointed in certain obvious directions. Women were at once the destroyers and the saviours of men; the latter role however was only to be realized through denial of their sexual side, which alone rendered them safe. There was nothing new about virgin mothers as such in the ancient world, where they appear in several other contexts.[20] But the linkage of the creation story of Adam and Eve, with its emphasis on the role of Eve, to the idea of redemption through the Incarnation meant that the Christian story imported a newly-compelling problematic to the familiar in-gredients. This problematic, while it had already shown itself soon enough in certain quarters, became truly acute with the spreading vogue for asceticism which by the later fourth century was affecting the highest levels of church and society.[21] It was precisely at this time that the Virgin Mary began to attract serious attention in Christian writing and doctrinal discussion, and when in many cases the very same writers addressed themselves to new analyses of the Adam and Eve story in Genesis.[22]

Thus the now intense problems of gender and sexuality in Chris-tian belief and practice were objectified in the figure of Mary, who also began to absorb the softer and safer aspects of womanhood that the desert fathers so roundly disallowed in real women.[23] However, if one can be permitted to differentiate chronologically between the texts of (a) the late fourth and early fifth centuries and (b) the

[20] For the Greek background and for discussion, see Sissa 1987: 97ff. For the problems of the Gospel birth narratives and the Greek word *parthenos*, see R. Brown et al. 1978: 84 f., 111f.; Sissa 1987: 100f.

[21] Christian asceticism: Rousselle 1983; Brown 1988; see also Harpham 1987.

[22] E. Clark 1986d; Pagels 1988; Cameron 1989. Origen had also written a *Com-mentary on Genesis* (see Crouzel 1989: 218).

[23] Carroll 1986 and others see the origins of the importance of the Virgin in the psychological need for the inclusion of a female element in the concept of Christian divinity. The two explanations are not mutually exclusive, but the earlier texts do not in fact lay stress on the maternal aspect.

miracle stories and Marian legends of the sixth and later, the objectification of the Virgin owed most in its first stages to the fact that she
above all was held to have achieved the sublime state of sinlessness
defined as non-sexuality. In contrast, we begin to see the domesti-
cated Virgin in the familiar figure in the hagiography of the fifth,
sixth and seventh centuries, who is also the prototype of the medieval
mater dolorosa and of the blue-robed statues of Our Lady familiar in
the Catholic tradition.[24] For the men who wrote the stories, it was
highly congenial to sanitize the dangerous female element into a
saving maternal figure, not only motherly but also safely virginal.
By the sixth century the Virgin may have taken on these aspects even
in the eyes of Christian women themselves, some of whom seem to
have made her the special object of private devotion (Herrin 1983),
but she had not often been evoked in this way in connection with
Paula, Melania, Olympias, or the other rich ladies of the late fourth
and early fifth centuries.[25]

The overall presentation of woman in early Christian texts is
therefore a negative one, which is also a textual strategy. We can
also see the importance of this textuality in the formation of Christian attitudes and practice in several other areas, some of which have
already been explored. Thus the well-known early Christian rhetoric
of misogyny can plausibly also be related to a rhetoric of power
(Pagels 1988; cf. Mann 1986). As yet, however, there are fewer
analyses of this type of the many treatises on virginity produced
especially in the course of the fourth century, though this would
be a profitable line to follow.[26] More serious attention could also be
given to the treatises on the subject of female dress, make-up, and
adornment, which expound the familiar idea of woman as alluring
and deceitful; the traditional theme provided much scope for rhetorical play on the subject of what constituted real, as opposed to

---

[24] See Kristeva 1982 with 1986: 164–5 (Mary as 'the prototype of love relationships'—based, however, on the later developments in Marian tradition).

[25] For whom see Giannarelli 1980; Consolino 1986; E. Clark 1984; Brown 1988:
280 ff.

[26] See Rousselle 1983: 171ff. Among those who wrote on the subject were Gregory
of Nyssa, Jerome, and Ambrose; it was an easy step from praise of virginity to
denigration of marriage (for which see also Jerome, *Ep.* 22. 22, citing Tertullian,
Cyprian, Damasus, and Ambrose).

superficial, adornment; in the late fourth century Jerome and others, in conscious reversal, seriously expected their ascetic female circle to dress in sackcloth and regarded washing as a sign of undue attachment to sexual allure. Show of all kinds, except religious show, was to be eschewed; similarly the comforts of life—the model was to be Mary, not Martha. We should not underestimate the sheer pull of the rhetorical possibilities offered to a highly-skilled writer by the themes of asceticism and virginity, or, in turn, the powerful influence which this rhetoric exerted on actual behaviour.

Study of the rhetorical strategies of early Christian writing about the Virgin would also repay the effort. Like many of his predecessors, Jerome also links Eve and Mary in relation to discussion of the practice of virginity; as he puts it, 'death comes through Eve, life through Mary' (*Epistle* 22. 21). But while there is a plentiful amount of literature on the figure and cult of the Virgin Mary, much of it has been produced by Catholic scholars with a technical interest in the subject. Useful studies do exist of the various social uses which the cult might serve at different times, and of its diachronic development, but again they tend not to unite psychological and social explanations with consideration of doctrinal and ideological factors; still less do they consider the very striking rhetorical strategies employed in these texts (see especially Warner 1976). In general, again, the subject of the Virgin Mary is not given nearly enough prominence in the majority of the many discussions either of Christian asceticism or of women in early Christianity. On the other hand, we are now witnessing a considerable focusing of interest on the mechanics of charity and renunciation as practised by the wealthy Christian women of the late fourth century, which is producing useful results in terms of the relation of theory and practice; however, though valuable, this discussion again does not usually address the issue as a whole (e.g. Brown 1982; Giardina 1988).

There is some danger in the fragmentation of the approaches which we have surveyed that we may lose sight of some of the basic issues which need to be highlighted in any consideration of the place of the discourse of female desire within early Christianity. I want therefore to return now to some fundamental features in Christian thought which help to explain why such a discourse became central and why gender itself seemed so problematic.

Whatever its origin, and leaving aside the contentious area of Christian origins and the relation of Jewish and Hellenistic elements in Christian thinking, the developed doctrine of the Incarnation rests on the notion of the tension between splitting and union, in Platonic language the problem of the one and the many (Kristeva 1982: 237; 250–1). How God could be divided into two natures, how the divine could relate to the human, and what was to be their relation, henceforth are questions at its heart. We have therefore a set of philosophical problems which are essentially Platonic in nature (Mortley 1981; 1988). But the union/division was in the case of the doctrine of the Incarnation achieved through the primeval means of birth and motherhood—Mary therefore represented the means of separation; yet as Christian theology strove to emphasize the indivisibility of God in Christ, in time Mary herself came to stand for the image of maternal union. The title 'Mother of God' given to her at the Council of Ephesus (AD 431) set the seal on two paradoxes, namely that God could be both divine and human, and that Mary, as his mother, was to be thought of as both fully virgin and fully mother. At the heart of Christianity on this reading are the notions not only of the one and the many but also of the essential splitting that takes place in the process of birth, and which is irrevocably associated with female sexuality. Furthermore, Mary as mother represents reproductive desire, the desire to bear the child of the father; as we have seen. However, the eroticism of motherhood is muted into the paradoxical image of the Virgin as the Mother. The central problems of Christian doctrine focused in this way on the details of human parturition. Thus while it may seem odd or even distasteful to us, it is perfectly logical within the system that the same leading churchmen who debated the story of the fall in Genesis should also have argued over whether or not Mary's hymen remained intact during and after the birth of Jesus. In the same period a whole repertoire of images of marginality—door, ladder, dwelling, vessel, ark, sealed garden—was evolving in order to express the central paradox which she represented, and was fully in place by the time of the Council of Ephesus.

There was also a more philosophical dimension to the discussion expressed in a complex of ideas including those of union with God as the soul's aspiration and desire, love as a joining, putting back

together what has been split, sexuality as an indicator of man's fallen
condition, with asexuality as the heavenly or paradisal state and
androgyny as nearer to that state than male or female sexuality.
Like Christ and the church, so, according to the Letter to the Ephesians, husband and wife become 'one flesh', 'a great mystery' (Ephesians 5. 30–3). But more commonly as time went on, this ideal of
marriage as union gave way to the view that the only way to cancel
out the disadvantages of male and female natures was through the
virginal state itself, the 'life of the angels'. The notion of the virgin
birth of Christ reinforced the notion of gender-difference as indicative of man's fall from grace; from the view that sexuality was part of
man's fallen nature, it was only a small step to the conclusion that
virginity was a necessary condition of success in the soul's desire for
union with God. I would argue indeed that the Platonic language in
which Christian theology was couched, together with its metaphys-
ical arguments, was at least as important as any social factor in
formulating early Christian attitudes to virginity and to women (so
also Mortley 1981: 77).

The concept of union in terms of love and desire is basic to this
Platonizing Christian discourse, and indeed the fact that the dialogue
where Plato's theory of love is most fully expressed is the *Symposium*
was, as we have seen, not lost on Christian authors. At the turn of the
third and fourth centuries, Bishop Methodius of Olympus produced
his own version—a bizarre literary symposium on the theme of
virginity at which the speakers are all female virgins.[27] Two generations later, Gregory of Nyssa describes the dying Macrina's immi-
nent union with the divine in terms of erotic and bridal imagery: she
made plain to those present the 'pure and divine desire (*eros*) for her
invisible husband which she had nurtured hidden in the secret places
of her soul, and revealed her heart's desire to be free of the chains of the
body and hasten to be with the loved one' (Maraval 1983: 22.31ff.,
p. 215); the 'race' which she was running was 'truly towards her
lover'. The description of the union of the soul with God is couched
in the language of the Song of Songs, as Gregory himself expounded
it in his commentary: but it is also the Platonic language of desire and

[27] Musurillo 1963; see Rousselle 1983: 171; Brown 1988: 183–8 (cf. 184: 'a bare-
faced pastiche of Plato's great work'—a strange judgement).

union, based on the idea of the approach towards divine beauty
(above, n. 12). We can begin to see how it is that early Christian
discourse attaches so much importance to the concept of desire, *eros*,
for it is desire which effects unification between human and divine,
as between male and female, and which unites the world of man with
that of the angels, and it is desire again which impels God to create
the world, as it is desire which leads human souls to aspire to reach
the higher beings on the hierarchy. We can also see why the Song of
Songs, in particular with Origen's commentary, assumed such
importance in fourth-century ideas of Christian love and marriage,
for while the model of the bride in the Song of Songs, as representative of the soul in its aspiration towards God, placed the love relation
at the heart of Christian understanding, the neutralization of the
erotic imagery of the Song into an understanding of the virginal
state ensured that a positive Christian theory of marriage would be
extremely difficult to formulate. Nearly all the elements in later
Christian thinking on the subject are already present in Origen,
especially the central idea that religious experience is to be read in
terms of a mystic marriage of soul and God (Crouzel 1989: 141f.;
118ff.; 219f.). He was not afraid to adopt the language of the Song in
all its physical implications, and to use it of mystical experience in a
manner which leads directly to Pseudo-Dionysius the Areopagite and
Maximus Confessor, two founders of orthodox mysticism.[28] Thus
the erotic language of the Song of Songs passed into a profound
religious understanding; at the same time the complex of ideas of
which it was a part, and the language in which they were expressed,
had immediate consequences for early Christian attitudes towards
the real relations between the sexes.

What we have then in early Christianity is a highly complex set of
ideas, language, and assumptions which together tended to focus
suspicious attention on women as sexual beings. It is not just that
early Christianity was misogynistic, or that women did or did not
play a leadership role in the early church. Rather, we should be
looking at the plasticity of the discourse itself as it developed over a
long period, in different places and in different hands. All in all, it

---

[28] See Lossky 1957: 192 and generally. Gregory of Nyssa is also a key author in this
tradition.

does not seem unfair to say that women did occupy a special place in the Christian discourse of desire, very little if any of which of course came from women themselves. The story of Eve, taken over by Christians, encapsulated male suspicions of women, and was far from completely neutralized by the attempts to rehabilitate Eve through Mary. Women continued to be seen both as being particularly desirous and as the objects of men's desire, and the denial of their sexuality as offering the best hopes of rendering them harmless in both guises.

Christianity is a religion heavily dependent on textuality, and I have tried here to emphasize the fundamental role played by Christian discourse in forming social attitudes, in contrast with the more usual scholarly strategy of marginalizing theological writing and claiming that it had little impact outside a closed circle. Such a view both fails to do justice to the importance of the fact that all forms of Christianity presented a coherent and powerful world-view, understood on intellectual, emotional, and practical levels, and forgets that this world-view was passed on orally, above all by preaching, as well as in written form. We have seen that in the case of the Virgin Mary, cult and piety followed on from Christological issues; in the same way perceptions of woman too were shaped by theoretical considerations.

We have seen that gender did become problematic in early Christianity, and for several reasons. The male/female division is a paradigm of the problem of separation/difference implicit in the idea of God being born as man, and the assimilation of a Platonic philosophical vocabulary in which to describe it; the story of Adam and Eve, taken over by Christians from the Old Testament, strongly reinforced the idea of gender separation and all that goes with it, while at an early stage the language of *eros*, and the analogy of sexual love, was applied to spiritual experience. In turn, the increasingly emphasized ideal of asceticism, in which virginity was always a paramount ingredient, provided both a theoretical and a practical objectification of this difference. As a part of the textual basis of early Christianity, asceticism required its own discourse too, which, given the social conditions of the time, was inevitably a discourse made by men. It was, in a paradoxical sense, a discourse of non-desire, neutralizing and deflecting real sexual desire into safer outlets, and serving as a useful diversionary tactic against the actual subversive and revolutionary potential of Christian teaching. The actual discourse of *eros*/desire was reserved for God.

By these means, it became safe to describe religious experience, even the religious experience of young virgin girls, in explicitly erotic language. The relation between this erotic language, the advocacy of renunciation and the psychological influences in individual cases very much needs to be further investigated. Among other things, *eros* used in this way always implies an asymmetrical relation. The (female) soul ascends to knowledge of God. Women were placed low down on the ladder and had few spokesmen ready to promote them. Only with the greatest difficulty did Augustine manage to reach the conclusion that marriage was not actually intrinsically sinful. Not for nothing did the ladder become a symbol of the climb to divine knowledge. For a statement of *eros* in its highest and most intellectual form, but with profound implications for human relations, we may end with a quotation from the sixth-century mystical writer known as Pseudo-Dionysius the Areopagite:

> By *eros*, by which we mean the love which belongs to God or to the angels or the intelligences, or to souls or natures, we understand a power of unification and connection, which impels higher beings to exercise their providence in relation to those below them, those of equal rank to maintain mutual relations and those who are at the bottom of the ladder to turn towards those who have more strength and who are placed above them.
>
> (Ps. Dionysius the Areopagite, *Divine Names* 713A–B)

AFTERWORD (2009)

This paper, published in 1994, raised two main questions: first, why and in what ways were issues surrounding the position of women so prominent in Christian consciousness in this period, and second, how and why was the language of eroticism now applied to Christianity? I had already raised the second of these in a paper called 'Virginity as metaphor' (Cameron 1989), and 'Early Christianity and the discourse of female desire' was also followed by a related paper 'Sacred and profane love: thoughts on Byzantine gender' (Cameron

1997). There has been a torrent of other publications on both my two questions, perhaps most obviously illustrated in many contributions to the *Journal of Early Christian Studies*. Peter Brown's major book (Brown 1988) explored the powerful strand of asceticism in early Christianity and how it played out in gender relations, and the three published volumes of Michel Foucault's *History of Sexuality* (Foucault 1979–86), in particular the second, exerted a powerful influence on the study of early Christian discourse.

The 1990s also saw the appearance of a large collected volume simply entitled *Asceticism* (Wimbush and Valantasis 1995), as well as a modest but ground-breaking book by Gillian Clark (1993). My two questions can perhaps be characterized as dealing respectively with social history and with textuality, of which these two publications deal more with the first. The second question has also been taken up with energy and theoretical sophistication by writers such as Virginia Burrus, for instance in Burrus 2004—*The Sex Lives of Saints: An Erotics of Ancient Hagiography* (see also Coon 1997 and, most recently, Miller 2009). The issues raised in my paper of 1994 have attracted the attention not only of scholars interested in gender in late antiquity, but also of the many who have been influenced by the debates over textuality and literary theory, especially in relation to eroticism and sexuality. Christianity's focus on individual consciousness and the relation of that to the constructed stories of hagiography is another fascinating issue. The question for the present volume is rather different, however, namely how any of this might help us to understand the religious transformations which occurred in the Roman empire in late antiquity, in which they are of course far from being the only issues.

The reasons behind the move of Christianity to centre-stage in late antiquity are many and varied; they include good communication, patronage, visibility, personal advantage and power relationships, as well as personal and psychological issues. The gradual adoption of Christian values and roles by members of the elite is also an important part of the narrative. However, it is perhaps appropriate here to stress a parallel development, namely the extraordinary energy and effort expended by Christians themselves on the project of providing, and also of promoting, a complete and coherent intellectual system which could absorb, replace or as needed supplement the literary and intellectual framework of Roman paganism (see in particular the remarkable Inglebert 2001). That is of course not to say that they fully succeeded in this enterprise, and indeed the effort continued long after the period covered in the present book. But the sheer energy that Christian writers devoted in late antiquity, in a wide variety of literary forms, to systematization, persuasion, argument, and interpretation, is one of the more remarkable features of the religious transformations of Late Antiquity. It is no accident that Christianity's rivals, Judaism and Islam, were themselves not merely religions of the book, like Christianity, but also religions built on interpretation, argument, and dialectic.

BIBLIOGRAPHY

Ariès P. and Duby G. (eds.) (1987). *A History of Private Life From Pagan Rome to Byzantium.* Cambridge, Mass.: Belknap Press of Harvard University Press. [Eng. trans. of *Histoire de la vie privée*, i (1986) Paris: Seuil].

Bloch, R. H. (1987). 'Medieval Misogyny: Woman as Riot', *Representations*, 20: 1–24.

Brock S. P. and Harvey S. A. (1987). *Holy Women of the Syrian Orient.* Berkeley and Los Angeles: University of California Press. [2nd edn. updated, 1998].

Brown, P. R. L. (1982). 'Dalla "Plebs Romana" alla "Plebs dei": aspetti della cristianizzazione di Roma', in P. R. L. Brown, L. Cracco Ruggini, and M. Mazza (eds.), *Governanti e intellettuali, populo di Roma e populo di Dio (I–VI secolo).* Turin: Giappichelli, 123–45.

——(1987). 'Late Antiquity', in Ariès and Duby 1987: 235–311.

——(1988). *The Body and Society: Men, Women and Sexual Renunciation,* Lectures on the History of Religion, new series no. 13. New York: Columbia University Press. [Second edn. 2008, with new introduction.]

Brown R., Donfried K. P., Fitzmeyer J. A., and Reumann, J. (1978). *Mary in the New Testament.* London: Chapman.

Burrus, V. (2004). *The Sex Lives of Saints. An Erotics of Ancient Hagiography.* Philadelphia: University of Pennsylvania Press.

Cameron, A. M. (1989). 'Virginity as Metaphor', in A. M. Cameron (ed.), *History as Text.* London: Duckworth, 184–205.

——(1990). 'Women in Early Christian Interpretation', in R. J. Coggins and R. L. Houlden (eds.), *Dictionary of Biblical Interpretation*. London: SCM Press, 729–31.

——(1991). *Christianity and the Rhetoric of Empire*. Berkeley and Los Angeles: University of California Press.

——(1997) 'Sacred and Profane Love: Thoughts on Byzantine Gender', in L. James (ed.), *Women, Men and Eunuchs: Gender in Byzantium*. London: Routledge, 1–23.

Carroll, M. P. (1986). *The Cult of the Virgin Mary: Psychological Origins*. Princeton, N.J.: Princeton University Press.

Clark, E. A. (1983). *Women in the Early Church*. Wilmington, Del.: Glazier.

——(1986a). *Ascetic Piety and Women's Faith*. Lewiston, N.Y.: Mellen Press.

——(1986b). 'Faltonia Betitia Proba and her Virgilian Poem: The Christian Matron as Artist', in Clark 1986a: 124–52.

——(1986c). 'Jesus as Hero in the Vergilian *Cento* of Faltonia Betitia Proba', in Clark 1986a: 153–71.

——(1986d). 'Heresy, Asceticism, Adam and Eve: Interpretations of Genesis 1–3 in the Later Latin Fathers', in Clark 1986a: 353–85.

——(1986e). 'The Uses of the Song of Songs: Origen and the Later Latin Fathers', in Clark 1986a: 386–427.

Clark, G. (1989). *Iamblichus: On the Pythagorean Life*. Liverpool: Liverpool University Press.

——(1993). *Women in Late Antiquity: Pagan and Christian Lifestyles*. Oxford: Clarendon Press.

Consolino, F. E. (1984). '*Veni huc a Libano*: la sponsa del Cantico degli Cantici come modello per le vergine negli scritti esortatori di Ambrogio', *Athenaeum*, 62: 399–415.

——(1986). 'Modelli di comportamento e modi di santificazione per l'aristocrazia femminile d'Occidente', in A. Giardina (ed.), *Società e impero tardoantico I. Istituzioni, ceti, economie*. Rome: Laterza, 273–306, 684–99.

Coon, L. L. (1997). *Sacred Fictions: Holy Women and Hagiography in Late Antiquity*. Philadelphia, PA: University of Pennsylvania Press.

Cox, P. (1986). 'Pleasure of Text, Text of Pleasure: Origen's Commentary on the Song of Songs', *Journal of the American Academy of Religion*, 54: 241–51.

Crouzel, H. (1989). (Eng. trans.) *Origen*. Edinburgh: T. & T. Clark.

Davies, S. L. (1980). *The Revolt of the Widows: The Social World of the Apocryphal Acts*. Carbondale, London: Southern Illinois University Press; Feffer and Simons.

Dodds, E. R. (1965). *Pagan and Christian in an Age of Anxiety*. Cambridge: Cambridge University Press.

Fiorenza, E. S. (1983). *In Memory of Her: A Feminist Reconstruction of Christian Origins*. New York: Crossroad. [Second edn.: London: SCM Press (1995).]

Foucault, M. (1979–86). *The History of Sexuality.* 1. *An Introduction*; 2. *The Use of Pleasure*; 3. *The Care of the Self*. Eng. trans.: New York: Pantheon and Harmondsworth: Viking.

Frye, N. (1982). *The Great Code. The Bible as Literature*. London: Routledge and Kegan Paul.

Giannarelli, E. (1980). *La tipologia femminile nella biografia e nell'autobiografia cristiana del IV secolo*. Rome: Istituto storico italiano per il Medio Evo.

Giardina, A. (1988). 'Carità eversiva: le donazioni di Melania la giovane e gli equilibri della società tardoromano', *Studi Storici*, 29: 127–42.

Graef, H. (1985). *Mary: A History of Doctrine and Devotion*. London: Sheed and Ward.

Halperin, D. M. (1990). 'Why is Diotima a Woman? Platonic *Eros* and the Figuration of Gender', in D. M. Halperin, J. J. Winkler, and F. I. Zeitlin (eds.), *Before Sexuality: The Construction of Erotic Experience in the Ancient Greek World*. Princeton, NJ: Princeton University Press, 257–308.

Harpham, G. G. (1987). *The Ascetic Imperative in Culture and Criticism*. Chicago, IL: Chicago University Press.

Herrin, J. (1983). 'In Search of Byzantine Women: Three Avenues of Approach', in A. M. Cameron and A. Kuhrt (eds.), *Images of Women in Antiquity*. London: Croom Helm, 167–83.

Inglebert, H. (2001). *Interpretatio christiana: les mutations des savoirs (cosmographie, géographie, ethnographie, histoire) dans l'Antiquite tardive (30–630 après J.C.)*. Paris: Institut d'études augustiniennes.

Kelly, J. N. D. (1975). *Jerome: His Life, Writings and Controversies*. London: Duckworth.

Kristeva, J. (1975/82). 'Maternité selon Giovanni Bellini', in *Polylogue*, Paris: Éditions du Seuil, 409–35; Eng. Trans. as 'Motherhood according to Bellini', in *Desire in Language*. Oxford: Blackwell (1982), 237–70.

——(1986). 'Stabat Mater', in T. Moi (ed.), *The Kristeva Reader*. Oxford: Oxford University Press, 161–86. [First published as 'Hérétique de l'amour', in *Tel Quel*, 74 (1977)].

Lane Fox, R. (1986). *Pagans and Christians*. Harmondsworth: Viking.

Lossky, V. (1957). *The Mystical Theology of the Eastern Church*. Cambridge: J. Clarke.

Mann, M. (1986). *The Sources of Social Power: I. A History of Power from the Beginnings to* AD *1760*. Cambridge: Cambridge University Press.

Maraval, P. (ed.) (1971/1983). *La Vie de Ste. Macrine*, Sources chrétiennes, no. 178. Paris: Éditions du Cerf.

Miller, P. C. (2009). *The Corporeal Imagination: Signifying the Holy in Late Ancient Christianity*. Philadelphia, PA: University of Pennsylvania Press.

Momigliano, A. D. (1985). 'The Life of St. Macrina by Gregory of Nyssa', in J. Ober and J. Eadie (eds.), *The Craft of the Ancient Historian*. Lanham, MD: The University Press of America, 443–58, reprinted in A. D. Momigliano, *Ottavo Contributo alla storia degli studi classici e del mondo antico*. Rome: Edizioni di storia e litteratura (1987), 333–47.

Mortley, R. (ed.) (1981). *Womanhood: The Feminine in Ancient Hellenism, Gnosticism, Christianity and Islam*. Rozelle, N.S.W.: Delacroix Press.

——(1988). *Désir et différence dans la tradition platonicienne*, Histoire des doctrines de l'Antiquité classique 12. Paris: Vrin.

Musurillo, H. (ed.) (1963). *Méthode d'Olympe: Le banquet*, Sources chrétiennes 95. Paris: Éditions du Cerf.

Pagels, E. H. (1988). *Adam, Eve and the Serpent*. London: Weidenfeld and Nicolson.

Rousselle, A. (1983). *Porneia: de la maîtrise du corps à la privation sensorielle, IIe–IVe siècles de l'ère chrétienne*. Paris: Presses Universitaires de France. Eng. trans. as *Porneia: On Desire and the Body in Antiquity*. Oxford; New York: Blackwell (1988).

Ruether, R. R. (ed.) (1974). *Religion and Sexism*. New York: Simon and Schuster.

——(1979). 'Mothers of the Church: Ascetic Women in the Late Patristic Age', in R. R. Ruether and E. McLaughlin (eds.), *Women of Spirit: Female Leadership in the Jewish and Christian Traditions*. New York: Simon and Schuster, 71–98.

Sissa, G. (1987). *Le corps virginale: la virginité féminine en Grèce ancienne*. Paris: Vrin. Eng. trans. (1990) *Greek Virginity*. Cambridge, Mass. and London: Harvard University Press.

Veyne, P. (1978). 'L'amour et la famille dans le haut-empire', *Annales: Économies, Societés, Civilisations*, 33: 35–63.

——(1987). 'The Roman Empire', in Ariès and Duby 1987: 5–234.

Ward, B. (ed.) and Russell, N. (trans.) (1980). *The Lives of the Desert Fathers*. London: Mowbray: Cistercian Publications.

——(ed.) (1987). *Harlots of the Desert: A Study of Repentance in Early Monastic Sources*. London: Mowbray; Kalamazoo, MI.: Cistercian Publications.

Warner, M. (1976). *Alone of All her Sex: The Myth and Cult of the Virgin Mary*. London: Weidenfeld and Nicolson.

Wheeler, E. P. (trans.) (1977). *Dorotheus of Gaza. Discourses and Sayings*. Kalamazoo, Mich.: Cistercian Publications.

Wicker, K. O'B. (1987). *Porphyry the Philosopher: To Marcella*. Atlanta, Ga.: Scholars Press.

Wilson-Kastner, P. et al. (1981). *A Lost Tradition: Women Writers of the Early Church*. Washington, DC: University Press of America.

Wimbush, V. L. and Valantasis, R. (eds.) (1995). *Asceticism*. New York: Oxford University Press.

Witherington III, B. (1984). *Women in the Ministry of Jesus*. Cambridge: Cambridge University Press.

——(1988). *Women in the Earliest Churches*. Cambridge: Cambridge University Press.

Young, F. M. (1983). *From Nicaea to Chalcedon: A Guide to the Literature and its Background*. London: SCM Press.

17

Enjoying the Saints in Late Antiquity

Peter Brown

The discovery at Mainz by François Dolbeau of a new collection of sermons of Augustine has enabled us to study, in far greater detail, the attitude of Augustine to the reform of the cult of the martyrs between 391 and 404. This study aims to understand Augustine's insistence on the need to imitate the martyrs against the background of his views on grace and the relation of such views to the growing differentiation of the Christian community. It also attempts to do justice to the views of those he criticized: others regarded the triumph of the martyrs over pain and death as a unique manifestation of the power of God, in which believers participated, not through imitation but through celebrations reminiscent of the joy of pagan festivals. In this debate, Augustine by no means had the last word. The article attempts to show the continuing tension between notions of the saints as imitable and inimitable figures in the early medieval period, and more briefly, by implication, in all later centuries.[1]

Let us begin with Augustine, preaching in Carthage in 412:

Brethren, see how it is that when a feast of the martyrs or some holy place is mentioned, to which crowds might flow to hold high festival. See how they stir each other up, and say, 'Let us go, let us go.' And each one asks the other, 'Where to?' They say, 'To that place, to that holy place.' They speak to each

---

[1] This article was delivered at the International Medieval Congress at the University of Leeds, 12–15 July 1999.

other, and as if each one of them were set alight, they form together one single blaze.

(Augustine, *Commentaries on the Psalms* 121. 2, ed. Dekkers
and Fraipont 1956: iii. 1802)

Augustine addressed a congregation that needed little encouragement to enjoy such occasions. The Christians of Carthage and elsewhere came from societies which had, for millennia, identified religious festivals with moments of frank remission. In the words of Strabo: 'although it has been said that human beings then act most like the gods when they are doing good to others, yet one may better say that they are closer still to the gods when they are feeling good—when they rejoice and hold high festival' (Strabo, *Geography* 10. 3. 9).

For Plutarch, the high cheer of festivals proved conclusively that the Epicureans were wrong. The gods were not, as the Epicureans claimed, mere persecutory projections of human fears, chill superegos characterized by vengeance and wrath. The relaxed mood of a religious feast proved the exact opposite. On such occasions, human beings stood in the real presence of serene and eminently fun-loving beings (Plutarch, *A Pleasant Life is Impossible* 1101E–1102D). Greek etymologists derived the verb *methuein*, 'to be drunk', from *meta to thuein*, 'to be in on the sacrifices', even from *methienai*, 'to participate'—to share, for a blessed moment, in the heady, joyous essence of the gods (Athenaeus, *Deipnosophistae* 2. 11(40A); Philo, *Noah's Work as a Planter* 163; see esp. Dihle 1992: 323–35).

Given such long-established expectations, it is not a matter for surprise that, in every region and in every period of late antiquity, Christians, too, should just want to have fun. They also were *philheortoi*, impenitent 'lovers of high festival'. In southern Gaul, at saints' festivals in the countryside outside Arles, crowds would stream in from the surrounding villages. They sang songs, they danced, they drank heavily, with many toasts for the saints. The young men fought each other, and their elders settled law suits.[2] It would have been a scene not unlike the great patterns that were still to be seen in early-nineteenth-century Ireland, named, significantly,

---

[2] Caesarius of Arles, *Sermons* 13. 3–4, 47. 5 and 55. 2, ed. Morin 1953: i. 66–7, 214 and 242.

from the *patrún*, the *patronus*, the patron-saint of the region. Such a one was the Pattern of Cloghane, in the Dingle peninsula: 'a day of games, athletics, vaulting over horses, dancing, singing and court-ship, of faction fighting and feasting'. It was a day renowned, also, for its fine meat pies (MacNeill 1962: ii. 104).

At the other end of the Christian world, at the great pilgrimage site of Qala'at Sem'an, the peasants danced around the column of Saint Symeon Stylites. When the first outriders of the Muslim armies fell upon the pilgrims, in 637, Christians of stricter views thought that it had served them right: they had angered God by their drunkenness at the festival (Evagrius, *Church History* 1. 14, *Patrologia Graeca* 86: 2461A; Michael the Syrian, *Chronicle* 11. 6, trans. Chabot 1901: ii. 422).

As this last, sharp remark shows, the enjoyment of the cult of the saints remained a problematic issue in Christian circles, as it had not been, to so great an extent, among pagans. Preachers at such festivals, even at the most euphoric of them, were careful to point out how little Christian occasions resembled what they considered to be the coarser junketings of Jews and pagans. Preaching at Christmas, Gregory Nazianzen enumer-ated in quick succession twenty-two different ways in which the feast was not to be enjoyed (Gregory Nazianzen, *Oration* 38. 5, *Patrologia Graeca* 36: 316A–317B; trans. Browne 1974: vii. 346. See esp. Harl 1981: 129). Twenty-two negative clauses in one paragraph is a lot of negatives—even for a Cappadocian Father. Yet, when it came to the issue of control of the festivals of the saints in late antiquity (in effect, in this case, control of the birthday feasts—the *natalia*, the *natalicia*—of the martyrs) the most prominent figure is, without a doubt, Augustine of Hippo.

We have long known of the determination which Augustine showed, from the moment of his ordination to the priesthood at Hippo, in 391, to reform the manner in which the cult of the martyrs was celebrated in Hippo and Carthage. As a priest, he abolished the songs and solemn drinking associated with the *Laetitia*, the day of solemn good cheer that accompanied the memory of Leontius, a former bishop of Hippo.[3] At the same time, he had gone out of his

---

[3] Augustine, *Letter* 29, to Alypius of Thagaste: see Brown 1981: 26 and 34–5; Saxer 1980: 133–47. It is perhaps important that Leontius was not a martyr: he was celebrated as builder of the basilica. Thus, the Laetitia may have originated as a more 'social' event than was the cult of a martyr. For that reason, the Laetitia may

way to obtain the collaboration of his senior colleague, Aurelius of Carthage and, by implication, of the other Catholic bishops of Africa, in undertaking what was nothing less than a thorough-going reform of Catholic piety, especially as it related to the cult of the martyrs (Augustine, *Letter* 22, to Aurelius of Carthage). The Mainz collection of sermons of Augustine, discovered and now edited by François Dolbeau, has added precious evidence to the dossier of a reform of Christian worship that may have been unique for its times in its determination and trenchancy.[4]

It is certainly the most fully documented example of such a reform in Christian late antiquity. The new sermons have provided us with an unexpected glimpse of Augustine in action, when faced with the long-established religious habits of his fellow-Christians. It is a disturbing glimpse. Here was a Christian preacher who was quite prepared to bring to bear, within his own, Catholic, congregation, a searching critique of 'superstition' and of *imperitia*, of culpable ignorance in matters of religious practice, such as had usually been deployed, by Christians, only against the cultic practices of pagans outside the church (Brown 1998: 367–75, esp. 371–4). In a sermon preached on 23 January 404, Augustine rejoiced that, through the firmness of Aurelius and his colleagues, the exuberant practices (the singing, the drinking and the easy mingling of the sexes in night-long vigils) associated with the shrine of Saint Cyprian—the greatest cult-site in Christian Africa—had been brought to an end: 'Where in those days the din of dirty songs was heard, nowadays it is the singing of hymns that lifts the roof . . . in a word, where God used to be offended, God is now being propitiated' (Augustine, *Sermon Mayence 5/Dolbeau 2*. 5. 95 = Dolbeau 1996: 330, trans. Hill 1997: 334).

In other regions of the late antique Christian world, language such as this would only have been used to celebrate the victory of

---

either have been more rowdy than those at the feast of a martyr, or, alternatively, Augustine may have found it easier to abolish.

[4] Now edited by Dolbeau 1996—using the French name, Mayence, for Mainz—and translated by Hill 1997. The most relevant of these are Mayence 5/Dolbeau 2: *On Obedience*, first edited in Dolbeau 1992a: 50–79; and Mayence 62/Dolbeau 26: *Against the Pagans*, first edited in Dolbeau 1992b: 69–141, now edited in Dolbeau 1996: 315–44 and 345–417, and trans. Hill 1997: 331–42 and 180–237 respectively.

Christian over non-Christian, pagan cult.[5] Faced by what he considered to be disorderly and irreligious behaviour, associated with the
cult of the martyrs, Augustine repeated, over and over again throughout his life, variations of a single, basic formulation: festivals occur,
he said,

ut per eas congregatio membrorum Christi admoneatur imitari martyres
Christi. Haec omnino festivitatis utilitas. Alia non est. (Augustine, *Sermon*
325. 1, *Patrologia Latina* 39: 1447)

(so that through those festivals the congregation made up of members of
Christ should be prompted to imitate the martyrs of Christ. That is the one
and only raison d'être of a festival. There is no other).

For a religious historian, the problem with Augustine is that he is
almost invariably entirely right. It is difficult to gainsay a statement
that is the condensed essence of a religious system which has, to a
large extent, formed the religious common sense of western Europe.
Seen in its eschatological context—that is, as Augustine tended to see
it, from the lofty but ultimate standpoint of the Heavenly Jerusalem,
the City of God—it was obvious that those who wished to join the
martyrs in heaven must, in their own way, follow Christ as the
martyrs had done. In the words of the Visigothic liturgy of Toledo,
those frail worshippers who had tended, in the dangers of the present
life, to look to the saints as guardians and as patrons, as *comites* and
patroni—as sources of help in day-to-day matters rather than as
models of behaviour—must also strive to live in such a way as to
be welcomed into heaven by the saints as their *socii*. They had to
become true companions of the saints, worthy of the company of
Christ, because transformed by Christ's grace in the same manner as
His grace had once, to a high degree, transformed the martyrs of old
(*Liber Sacramentorum* 23. 208, ed. Férotin 1912: 96).

But heaven is a long way off, and western Christendom is a complicated phenomenon, made up of many currents of belief and practice,
spread over an extensive geographical area and subject to constant
change over the millennium of Late Antiquity and the Middle Ages.

---

[5] See the inscription of the church that claimed to have replaced a pagan temple at
Azra'a in Syria: 'Where God was angered once, now God is made content', in *Corpus
Inscriptionum Graecarum* (Berlin, 1877), iv. no. 8627; see Brown 1997: 98.

The clear intuitions of one religious genius can not be expected to embrace such diversity, still less should Augustine's standard of correct worship be allowed, by scholars of late antique and medieval religion, to act as the tacitly-agreed yardstick by which to judge the intrinsic religious worth of the many, various ways in which late antique and medieval persons conducted the cult of the saints.

What strikes the historian of medieval religion is the fact that the notion of the imitation of the saints, though it may seem eminently sensible from a religious point of view, fits awkwardly into the overall development and elaboration of the cult of saints in Europe. The ideal of the imitation of the saints was usually invoked so as to place a check upon powerful opposing notions. Often, it was invoked to spoil the fun—to criticize what were presented, by preachers and moralists, as the more 'earthy', less religious forms of Catholic worship.

In the case of Caesarius of Arles, in the early sixth century, the notion of the imitation of the martyrs was invariably invoked by him so as to attack current practices. He presented such imitation as the only permissible alternative to the rambunctious scenes that we have already described, in connection with saints' festivals in Arles and in the surrounding countryside.[6] With Caesarius (and also with many phrases of the Roman liturgy) one gets the impression that the idea of imitating the saints was interposed, like a screen, to hold the believer back from more exuberantly physical forms of worship. In much the same manner, Gregory the Great had insisted that religious pictures should be *read, ut scriptura*. In so doing, he attempted to substitute a more detached, intellectual activity—the act of reading—for the more direct, physical manifestations of adoration—the bowing, the kissing, the candles and the heavy whiff of incense—usually associated with sacred paintings (Brown 1999: 15–34, at 23–5). In both cases—in the insistence that the martyrs should be 'imitated' and that religious paintings should be 'read'— we are dealing with a formula of control that privileged the intellectual over the physical, and that insisted that contemplation of the meaning of objects of Christian worship was superior to all other forms of access to them—whether this was unmediated participation in the joy of festivals or loving 'adoration' of holy images.

---

[6] See above, n. 2 and *Sermon* 233. 1–2, p. 882.

We must, therefore, make an effort of the imagination to recover something of the full religious weight of the expectations of those who, in fourth-century North Africa and, indeed, in all subsequent centuries of the western Middle Ages, enjoyed the saints without necessarily feeling obliged to imitate them. I use the word 'religious' advisedly. The effect of Augustine's rhetoric has been to drain away from our image of such feasts the heavy charge of sacrality that lay at their centre. He singled out for denunciation the elements of moral disorder and of inappropriate excitement associated with the cult of the martyrs. The impression that he leaves is that the *hommes moyens sensuels* of Carthage came to the feasts to have fun, when they should have come to have religion. As a former *jeune homme sensuel*, Augustine knew of what he spoke. I never dreamed, until the publication of the Dolbeau sermon *On Obedience*, that I would hear Augustine, the Catholic bishop in 404, speak with such candour about his own behaviour in the 370s: 'When I went to vigils as a student in this city, I spent the night rubbing up beside women, along with other boys anxious to make an impression on them and, who knows, should the opportunity present itself, to 'make it' with them.'[7]

But such engaging candour on Augustine's part should not cause us to forget that such 'happenings' belonged to the highly-specific excitement of a specific occasion: disorderly though they were, they were only the outermost shock waves, on the fringes of the martyr's festival, that registered the detonation, in its midst, of a heavy charge of religious feeling, associated with a particular notion of the sacred. Let us attempt to measure the mass of this charge, set up by a structure of distinct imaginative associations, connected with the cult of the martyrs throughout the fourth-century Christian Mediterranean.

It is best to begin with a remark of the wry pagan, Ammianus Marcellinus. Everyone, so he implied, knew what Christian martyrs had been like: though forced to abandon their beliefs, they had found their way to a 'glorious death' brought about by *cruciabiles poenae*—

---

[7] Augustine, Mayence 5/Dolbeau 2, *On Obedience* 5. 79 = Dolbeau 1996: 330; Hill 1997: 333. On the strength of a discreet mention in *Confessions* 3. 3. 5, I had proposed (as befitted a young Oxford don of the early 1960s) a considerably more chaste interpretation: see Brown 1967: 41.

by 'excruciating torments'.[8] It is the image of the *cruciabiles poenae*, of the excruciating torments which had accompanied the deaths of the martyrs, that surged forwards, in the late fourth century if not earlier, to take centre stage. We move, within a century, from the curt, judicial records of the martyrs of the time of the Great Persecution—where torture is used only to discover information, in the 'aseptic' manner of a late Roman *cognitio* procedure—to a world awash with blood.[9] To Shenute of Atripe, in the first part of the fifth century, it was easy to distinguish between authentic and inauthentic accounts of the martyrs. Any account that did not recount how the martyr had died under great torments, that did not report that the martyr's eyes had been torn out, that the martyr's body had been chopped limb from limb, that did not describe how scorching fires had been applied to the martyr's sides, and that did not conclude with an account of how the martyr had been weighted down with stones and thrown, in vain of course, into the river Nile—such an account could not be authentic: it was a *martyros ñnoudj*, an account of a martyr based on lies (Horn 1986: 8 and, in general, Baumeister 1972). It was the same for Victricius of Rouen when he preached in around 396 (that is, at the time when, in distant Africa, Augustine and his colleagues had embarked on their reforms): 'Let there be no day, dearest brothers, on which we do not meditate on these stories. This one did not pale before the tortures...this one greedily swallowed the flames...another was cut to pieces, yet remained whole' (Victricius of Rouen, *In Praise of the Saints* 12, *Patrologia Latina* 20: 456CD, trans. Hillgarth 1986: 27–8).

---

[8] Ammianus Marcellinus, *Res gestae* 21. 11. 10. Ammianus wrote as he did so as to ensure that the lynching of George, the high-handed Christian bishop of Alexandria, would not be considered as a 'true' martyrdom: see Barnes 1998: 236. His criteria, therefore, were not dissimilar from those of Shenute!

[9] As is shown in the newly discovered *Acta Gallonii*: Chiesa 1996: 241–68, at 252. On judicial torture in the later Roman Empire, see now Harries 1999: 122–9. A similar, curt original account of an Egyptian martyrdom has been discovered among the papyri of Duke University: Van Minnen 1995: 13–38. It is significant that, in a tantalizingly incomplete letter, newly discovered by Johannes Divjak, Augustine expressed his strong preference for such *Acta*, over and against contemporary attempts to re-write the tales of the martyrs: Divjak 1987: 414–16; trans. Eno 1989: 193–5.

Those who came to the feasts of the martyrs came to participate in the unearthly 'glory' of a moment of total triumph over pain and death. Men and women alike, the bodies of the martyrs stood out as the centre of attention. For the martyrs had been rendered immune by God to the horrors inflicted on their flesh. In the words of an inscription of the martyrs at Haïdra (Ammaedera), they were the ones 'cui divinitus inspirare hoc in animo dignatus est' 'to whom God has deigned to place in their soul the breath of divine spirit' (Duval 1982: nos. 51A and 52 at pp. 108 and 110–12).

The emotion which the sight of the violated yet unmoved bodies of the martyrs evoked was not one of sympathy and admiration for human courage. It was, rather, a sense of awe such as had always fallen heavily on the hearts of ancient persons, when confronted with a fellow-human being in whose strangely altered body they sensed the presence of a mighty god. This is what made Saint Eulalia so stunning to the readers of the *Peristephanon* of Prudentius (written in around 400). In applying to the words of Eulalia before her persecutors the classical phrase *infremuit . . . spiritus*, 'her spirit raged', Prudentius chose to use the language of the ancient oracles, to describe the raw 'frenzy' of a young girl's spirit, that had 'breathed in' the power of God (Prudentius, *Peristephanon* 3. 31–4, ed. Thomson 1961: ii. 144).

Prudentius, I suspect, shared with many of his contemporaries what has been somewhat unfairly labelled (in comparison to the Neo-Platonic notions of Augustine) as a 'material' view of the soul. It is better to talk of a 'localized' view of the soul. For Prudentius, the soul lay in the depths of the body, beyond the reach of human probing. With the martyrs, this inner soul finally 'leapt free', unscathed, to regain its home beyond the stars.[10] The notion of a 'localized' soul gave rock-like, ontological solidity to the belief that the martyr, possessed by God, had remained throughout inviolate: 'There is another, within the body, whom no man is able to outrage . . . free, undisturbed, unharmed, exempt from grievous pain' (Prudentius,

---

[10] Prudentius, *Peristephanon* 1. 30, p. 100. See esp. Fontaine 1982: 55–67. The notion of a 'material' soul was more widespread than we realize: see Fortin 1995; Di Marco 1995. The effect of this notion on late antique Christian piety has not been fully explored.

Peristephanon 5. 157, p. 178). The body of Eulalia was 'painted scarlet with new blood' (Prudentius, *Peristephanon* 3. 143, p. 152). But that blood had touched her hidden, inner self as little as a wash of red paint affected the cool, smooth surface of a wall down which it dripped.

The miracle of impassivity, associated with the torments of the martyrs, tilted over into a yet greater miracle. So great was the disjuncture between the observed, outside state of the martyr, brought into contact with sources of excruciating pain, and the inviolate state of his or her inner being, that the associations of human pain, as it were, passed through the looking glass: pain was transformed into its very opposite. The searing flames outside became like cooling water to the soul; or they came to seem as cold as ice compared to the firestorm of the spirit of God that raged within the martyr.[11] In a dream-like moment of God-possessed dissociation, all meanings became reversed. The martyrs lay upon the burning coals of their bonfire as if they were reclining 'amid red roses' (John Chrysostom, *On the Holy Martyrs* 1, *Patrologia Graeca* 49: 708).

We can catch a hint of the crackle of awe generated by so total a disjuncture between observed torment and the miracle worked by God's presence in the martyr if we look at Byzantine illuminations of just such scenes. Leslie Brubaker has remarked, most acutely, of ninth-century renderings of the deaths of the martyrs, that these were models of classical restraint: 'the dying saints...seem to us detached; they do not elicit our sympathy'. Yet Byzantines expected that to contemplate just such illuminations would provoke an outburst of 'warm tears' (Brubaker 1989: 23–93, at 24–5; see now Brubaker 1999: 260). For in the miniatures, one was given a glimpse of the bodies of the martyrs as they appeared, at the time of torment, to the souls of the martyrs. The believer would supply the rest. We are dealing, here, with an exquisitely late-antique structuring of the emotions, by which a scene in which one element is uncannily absent acts as a trigger, to unleash the full horror and wonder of a moment charged with the presence of God. For this was how martyrs were thought to feel their own martyrdom. His mind and soul filled with God, the martyr Dativus (from Abitina, near Carthage, in 304) 'viewed

---

[11] e.g. *Liber Sacramentorum* 47. 880, ed. Férotin 1912: 393: an image constantly employed on the martyrdom of Saint Laurence.

the ruin of his body all the while like a spectator, rather than feeling its pain' (*Passion of the Martyrs of Abitina* 10, ed. Maier, 1987: i. 72).

What matters, in such an imaginative structuring of the cult of the martyrs, is that the martyr (as, later, the ascetic or the saintly bishop) stands isolated. He or she is sheathed in the majesty of the full presence of God. The martyr's festival was a *spectaculum* in the most profound and ancient sense: it was a showing of God. The sufferings of the martyrs were offered to believers—in a manner that I am tempted to speak of with a term more usually applied to late medieval Eucharistic devotion—as a *heilbringende Schau*, a sight which in and of itself unleashed salvation. It was a *spectaculum*, also, in that the believers were drawn by the deeper imaginative logic of the occasion to participate in the glory of the martyrs rather than to imitate them. They gathered so as to share, for a time of high celebration, in the original, death-defying moment of 'glory' associated with God's triumph in the saint. In that way, the cult of the saints took up, and rendered that much more physical, more local, and more frequent the supreme moment of Christ's triumph over death, celebrated every year at the feast of Easter. Easter, also, was an occasion for a frank explosion of physical joy and, among some believers, for heavy use of the bottle.[12] As with Easter, there was a strong, non-verbal element in such participation. One was expected to join, body and soul, in a great event that shook, for a moment, the boundaries of the possible. The high cheer and 'oceanic' feelings induced by wine; the chanted songs (songs whose wild pitch, rather than their words, may have shocked stricter, ancient ears as 'obscene'); the potential for the breaking of the boundaries between the sexes; and, above all, the gravity-defying leaps of the dancers: these were physical expressions of a moment of vast release, that marked the passing of a great soul, through torments, to beyond the stars. Equally non-verbal and equally dramatic were the healings which the saint was believed (in all later centuries) to bestow on the faithful, throughout the year but most especially at the high moment of the festival of the saint. For this was the moment when the iron constraints of pain and death, that held the lives of the

---

[12] Gregory the Great, *Dialogues* 4. 33. 1–2 (ed. de Vogüé 1980: 108) gives an example of drunkenness after the Easter Vigil and of its chilling consequences.

faithful in their grip, had suddenly sprung open, for the martyr, at the touch of God (Brown 1981: 80–5).

It was to the isolation of the martyrs from other members of the faithful, implied in this powerful model—and hence to the essentially participatory relationship established between the martyrs and their devotees—that Augustine addressed the full force of his own, most deeply meditated religious convictions. He aimed to leave the imprint of a very different notion of God's grace—a notion equally dramatic but more evenly distributed between martyrs and faithful—on the burgeoning cult of the saints. Put very briefly, while never denying for a moment the majesty of God's presence in the martyrs, he went out of his way to insist that the martyrs did not enjoy an outright monopoly of the overwhelming grace of God. The working of God's grace in every heart was, in itself, a miracle. It was surrounded by the same sense of amazement as was the blood-soaked glory of a Lawrence, a Cyprian, or a Eulalia.

Much recent scholarship, now ably interpreted by Carole Straw, has stressed the extent to which, from his very first years as a bishop, Augustine's thought on grace grew out of the deep taproot of his daily involvement in the African cult of the martyrs (Straw 1999: 538–42. See also Hombert 1996, with Brown 1999b). The martyrs were spectacularly visible creatures of God's grace. They owed their 'glory' to God alone. Nobody doubted that for a moment. They were the 'predestinate' members of the elect *par excellence*, made plainly visible on earth by the nature of their lives and by the glory of their passing.[13] Everyone agreed with that. What Augustine went on to say, as often as he could, was that exactly the same grace might stir—discreetly at first but eventually, perhaps, triumphantly—in the hearts of every one of his hearers: 'God who gave grace to them can give it to us . . . By that grace they became his friends; we can, at least, by the same grace become his servants . . . and, why not, then also his friends: through his grace, that is, not through our own will' (Augustine, *Sermon* 335H, *Revue bénédictine*, 68 (1958), 103 = *Patrologia Latina Supplementum* 2: 831).

---

[13] Augustine, *Sermon* 312. 6, 1422, on Saint Cyprian; compare the mid-fourth-century Donatist *Passio Marculi* 2, ed. Maier 1987: 278: 'Ille . . . olim praeelectus et praedestinatus a domino'.

At one stroke, Augustine had taken possession of the reservoir of raw charisma, associated with the persons of the martyrs, and had led it, along innumerable, hidden paths, into the lives of every Catholic Christian. He did it, largely, by placing the martyrs in the larger context of the Church. All Catholics were subject to the command to 'follow' Christ. All were bound to Christ—even if with widely varying degrees of prominence—as 'members' of his body, the church (Augustine, *Sermon* 280. 6, 1283).

At Upenna (Henchir Chigarnia in modern Tunis), a list of otherwise unknown and local martyrs was given new majesty, at some time in the fifth century, by being copied on to a mosaic, in such a way that they now appeared ranged on either side of a great, jewelled cross (Duval 1982: no. 29, fig. 42 at p. 65).

In the same way, in Augustine's vision of the church, the faithful were encouraged to crowd in behind the martyrs, because equally dwarfed by that great Cross, ranged behind the image of Christ to which all believers, in their different ways, strained to conform themselves:

The martyrs followed Christ right up to the shedding of their blood, up to a likeness of His own Passion. They followed him, but they did not do so alone. It is not as if, once they passed, that bridge would be lifted; nor, once they had drunk of the fountain [of God's grace] that fountain had dried up (Augustine, *Sermon* 304. 2. 2, 1396).

Augustine's notion of the 'imitation of the martyrs', therefore, was founded on the need to throw a bridge across the crevasse that appeared to separate the martyrs from the faithful. It was based, in part, on his extraordinary ability to reduce the spiritual struggle to a universal common denominator. On that theme, Augustine could be trusted to wax eloquent: 'We have always drawn attention to this, brethren. We have never ceased to say it. We have never been silent: life eternal is what we should love; this present life, what we should scorn' (Augustine, *Sermon* 302. 9, 1389). Before grace had worked upon them, the hearts of the martyrs had been divided by just such a conflict between two loves as was the heart of the simplest Christian. It was not the distant, blood-stained bodies of the martyrs that spoke most directly to the faithful: the martyrs, rather, spoke heart to heart to every believer of a struggle that they also had experienced—the struggle between the love of God and the deep, fierce love of the soul for its own body and for the present life (e.g. Augustine, *Sermon* 284. 4, 1279 and *Sermon Frangipane* 6. 2, ed. Morin 1930: i. 221).

Thus, when it came to the issue as to how exactly each individual saint might be imitated, Augustine remained gloriously unspecific. Apart from the occasional praise of women martyrs, so as to shame the men and to prove that any woman might expect to enjoy the full measure of God's grace (Augustine, *Sermon Denis* 13. 2, ed. Morin 1930: 56); apart, also, from a pointed reference to martyrs who had been married women and mothers of children, so as to rebuke nuns who were tempted to despise married persons (Augustine, *On Virginity* 44. 45), Augustine never offered the behaviour of any specific saint for imitation by any specific group. He felt that he did not need to do so. All the faithful should admire and imitate all the saints, for they all had faced the same, basic struggle as they faced themselves. The struggle of the love of God to overcome love of the world was the only confrontation that mattered. All must face it, as the martyrs had faced it, irrespective of class, race, or gender; and no one could hope to triumph in that struggle unless they came as utter paupers, stripped of social and cultural particularity, to the rich banquet of God's grace (Augustine, *Sermon Mayence 24/Dolbeau 9* 5. 123, ed. Dolbeau 1996: 33, trans. Hill 1997: 51).

We should remember that Augustine, for all his brilliance and considerable idiosyncrasy, was a man of his generation and the inheritor of a dense Christian tradition. His insistence on Christ as the primary model and the only help of the martyrs both followed the teachings of Cyprian and also echoed faithfully the *Epigrammata* of his near-contemporary, Pope Damasus: 'possit quid gloria Christi' 'believe then what Christ's glory can achieve'.[14] What is significant, however, is the difference between the physical setting in which such piety was shown. The piety of Damasus was elaborated in little masterpieces of calligraphic style, discreetly displayed in quiet burial chambers for the benefit of literate visitors of meditative disposition (Guyon 1995: 157–77). Augustine wished to impose such views, also, on large, tumultuous assemblies.

---

[14] Damasus, *Epigrams* 8. 9; cf. Vergil, *Aeneid* 11. 386: 'possit qui virida virtus'. See esp. Fontaine, 1986: 134. On Cyprian, see esp. Deléani 1979: 75–95, 106–110.

One can sense, in Augustine's insistence on the personal workings of grace that made the examples of the martyrs directly relevant to ordinary persons, the ground-swell of an African Christian community that had become ever more complex in its social and intellectual structures. Differing groups of the laity pressed forwards for special attention. Among the well-to-do, especially, one may suspect that there were many who did not want to feel as distant from the martyrs as everybody else, because equally deprived of the supreme charisma of their unearthly death. They did not wish to lose their identities by sinking back into the crowd, in great, participatory rituals. They wanted their own, more personal share in the 'portion of the saints'.

To take one small but revealing example of these pressures. In the higher empire, the educated gentry began to accord to their own beloved forms of funerary remembrance modelled on the cult of the gods and of the heroes of old. Private 'heroization' became widespread (Marrou 1938: 231–57; Wrede 1981).

It is possible to talk, for the late fourth century, of a similar drift towards a 'martyrization' of the deceased. Take the example of the young Christian lady Proiecta. Proiecta may have been buried, in Rome, in a chamber as impressive as that of any martyr. Damasus had no hesitation about writing of her as if she were already in heaven, with the martyrs, and even hinted that, from heaven, she now brought comfort to her entire family (Guyon 1995: 177–9). At Thabarka, in North Africa, the deacon Crescentinus was portrayed, in the mosaic above his tomb, trotting jauntily across the countryside. But the inscription speaks of him in such florid terms, as 'guest of the angels, companion of the martyrs', that it is only recently that Professor Yvette Duval has struck him from the register of saints, placing the young deacon, firmly, in an appendix devoted to 'faux martyrs' (Duval 1982: 208–9, fig. 281 at p. 431). Crescentinus had been 'martyrized' by his loved ones, much as his pagan predecessors had 'heroized' their dead. Furthermore, the increasing practice of *depositio ad sanctos*, burial beside the saints, points in the direction of a sincere wish on the part of the deceased (and not only on the part of those who preserved their memory) to draw closer to the martyrs by imitation. Burial beside the saints was not only an occasion for the rich and for the clergy to show their special status in the community:

for some pious persons, it marked the end of a life characterized by continuous effort to imitate their chosen saints (Duval 1988: 54–62).

Altogether, religious history would be immeasurably poorer if it were not for the unflagging pretentiousness of members of the sub-elites. Augustine's world was marked by the constant presence of relatively well-to-do persons, inhabitants of the fluid urban worlds of Carthage and of Hippo—women quite as much as men, married persons quite as much as celibates, and members of the laity quite as much as those associated with the clergy. The discreet upward pressure of so many little groups of men and women ensured that Augustine's system of grace maintained a strong 'democratic' flavour. For Augustine's insistence on the accessibility of the grace that rendered possible the spiritual struggle and, so, the imitation of the martyrs, was a challenge addressed to all categories of persons within the Catholic church. There were always some persons, at least (often from a surprisingly wide range of social and cultural backgrounds: by no means invariably educated or of clerical background), who took Augustine at his word.

It is necessary to linger upon Augustine so as to conjure up the distinctive profile of his attitude to the cult of the martyrs. It is, indeed, so distinctive that it should come as no surprise to learn that, in the centuries immediately following his death, Augustine had considerably less influence on the religious behaviour of Latin Christians than many modern estimates of his work would lead us to suppose. He was a striking figure, but one figure only, in a large and well-populated landscape. Without being in any way less intelligent or spiritually more obtuse than the bishop of Hippo, many Christians, in many regions, thought very differently on how they might relate to the saints.

If we turn, for instance, to the Visigothic liturgies of the late sixth and seventh centuries, we find ourselves among the nameless authors of great prayers. These men were acquainted with the works of Augustine and Caesarius. They were masters of the art of sacred rhetoric. They came from a world not so very different from the *studiolo* of Augustine (Diaz y Diaz 1980: 61–76 and Hillgarth 1980: 23–5). But what they offered, in the prayers preserved in the Mozarabic Sacramentary of Toledo, was nothing less than a weighty evocation of the sheer 'magic' of the feasts. Imitation of the martyrs, such as Augustine proposed, had its place in these liturgies, as was also the case, and to a greater degree, in the Roman–Frankish liturgies of the eighth and ninth centuries. But the notion of imitation was a recessive colour. It was overshadowed by the vibrant phrases that gravitated incessantly around themes that came straight from the poems of Prudentius and from the glory days of the fourth-century cult of the 'unconquerable', inimitable martyrs.

Reading the Mozarabic Sacramentary, we are left in no doubt that we are dealing with a book of potent rituals. These rituals derived their power from an incantatory deployment of charged metaphors, associated with the miraculous circumstances of the sufferings of the great martyrs. In these prayers, the believers did not strain to join their hearts to the martyrs, as if to prototypes for their own hope of victory. Rather, they offered their souls (and, often, the souls of their dead kin) as passive objects, on which God would work the great transformation of pain into delight, of constraint into freedom, as he had done in the miraculous bodies of the martyrs:

Eternal God, by whose grace the virgin Eulalia stood protected and blushed not to confess amidst the flames, for, through your promise, you caused her to be scorched by the fire of your love. So may you protect us, through her prayers, amidst the treacherous wall of flame that is this world . . .

And so may God [the bishop would proclaim], who once covered her naked body with a drift of pure white snow, make you all snow white and pure from every sin and misdemeanour (*Liber Sacramentorum* 11. 95 and 100, ed. Férotin 1912: 47, 49).

In such prayers, one is struck by a contrast. On the one hand, the prayers evoked insistently, in language worthy of Prudentius, the unparalleled sufferings of the bodies of the martyrs. These sufferings marked out the saints as unique and utterly otherworldly beings. On the other hand, the prayers called upon the saints to answer all and every prayer for safety and for success in this life (e.g. *Liber Sacramentorum* 28. 247, ed. Férotin: 1912: 113—to Saint Vincent of Saragossa). Confronted by so stark a juxtaposition between otherworldly heroes and the impenitently earthly desires of their devotees, one cannot help but be reminded of the rituals by which modern Buddhist monks in Sri Lanka bless the peasantry. The chants of blessing, the *parittâ*, consist of recitations, in Pali, of the melodramatic scenes that accompanied each stage of the renunciation of the Buddha. Yet these chants are performed so as to bestow 'long life, good health and a fair complexion'. 'The intriguing paradox', writes Professor Tambiah, 'is that the conquests of the Buddha which relate to the withdrawal from life are in the process of transference transmuted into an affirmation of life' (Tambiah 1968: 181).

Anyone who wishes to understand how and why the saints came to be enjoyed in late antiquity and in the early Middle Ages must grapple, at some time or other, with that paradox. When I wrote my book on the *Cult of Saints*, now almost twenty years ago, I had not done that. I had entered with gusto into one aspect of the cult of the saints in late antique Italy and Gaul. My book attempted to do justice to the impressive religious, cultural, and artistic energy deployed around the notion of the saints as *patroni*, as protectors and intercessors, on a frankly late Roman, aristocratic model of the exercise of spiritual power (Brown 1981: esp. 54–68). I explained how the saints worked, as *patroni*, in terms that were easily available to contemporaries, and that were, for that reason, easy for them to verbalize. On looking back, I realize that I did not delve as deeply as I might have done into the other side of the problem, for which late Roman contemporaries did not have a ready language. I did not address the deeper, more implicit imaginative structures that explained not only how the saints worked (a subject on which late Roman Christians could be trusted to wax eloquent) but why the saints worked and, above all, on what objects.

Why was it that those whose lives and deaths were associated with such prolonged suffering that they had been, as it were, drastically 'cauterized' from all contact with the 'world', re-entered the same 'world', after death, not only as lordly figures, but as figures deeply implicated in all that was most earthy and most irreducibly profane in the life of the world? One can understand how a Roman patron might be interested in the welfare of his clients. But overwhelming and meticulous concern for semi-feral pigs, for horse herds, for the wombs of women, and for the thick, rich mud of the Nile are not interests one automatically associates with late Roman aristocrats.[15] A different model has to be invoked to explain that aspect of the relation between the saint and the world.

---

[15] See Brown 1995: 76–8, where I attempt to address this problem in relation to eastern hagiography.

For the evidence appears to show that it was precisely by keeping the saints inimitable—and, above all, inimitable in their physical sufferings—that the Christians of late antiquity and the early Middle Ages kept the saints sacred. For, in keeping the saints sacred, they felt able to bring them back into worldly affairs, as invulnerable presences, capable of reaching into the deepest, most potentially polluted and polluting levels of daily life. To build a frail bridge of imitation between oneself and such persons was the exact opposite of what one wanted from them. It did far more than destroy the fun of the festivals. It brought the saints down to the level of their imitators, and, in so doing, it undermined the fundamental antithesis between the sacred and the profane. For if sacred figures such as the saints were no longer seen as utterly, inimitably different from the profane, then the very life-force of the profane world, which depended on intermittent contact with the sacred, would wither away.[16]

In her study of certain, extreme forms of late medieval hagiography, Brigitte Cazelles has suggested that the working of such imaginative structures—above all, the need to establish a clear antithesis between the sacred and the profane—accounted for the continued demand for lives of inimitable, heroic saints. Her insights can be fruitfully applied to the late antique and early medieval periods. But a historian of the cult of the saints in the early Middle Ages cannot be content with a clear cut either/or. Imitation of the saints was often combined with a sharp sense of their uniquely sacred qualities. Much can be learned from figures who combined such a strong sense of sacrality with fervent belief that heroic sainthood could and should be replicated in their own times.

Gregory of Tours was one such person. He insisted that the faithful should imitate the martyrs. *Tu, o homo mortalis, . . . non agonizas,* 'you, mortal being, do not struggle': human beings, in fact, must always struggle against the allurements of the world (Gregory of Tours, *Book on the Glory of the Martyrs* 105, ed. Krusch 1885: 111; trans. Van Dam 1988: 132). And they could struggle successfully. All that the Christian needed to do was to make the sign of the Cross

---

[16] On this issue, Cazelles 1982: esp. 64 and 78. I am indebted to Professor Caroline Bynum for having urged this book upon my attention.

with serious intent—*viriliter et non tepide* (the two words, manfully and vigorously, speak volumes on Gregory's view of life)—and to trust in Christ: 'For, as I have often said, the Lord himself struggles and triumphs in the martyrs' (Gregory of Tours, *Book on the Glory of the Martyrs* 106, ed. Krusch 1885: 111; trans. Van Dam 1988: 133).

Christ would 'struggle and triumph' once again in those who were faithful to him. Gregory felt that he lived in a world that dearly needed saints, to challenge the complacency of modern times. When he stated, in the *Preface* of his *History*, that he wrote 'propter eos, qui adpropinquantem finem mundi disperant', we misunderstand late Latin if we translate the phrase, as we so often do, as if it meant that Gregory wrote for those 'who are losing hope [or: who are driven to despair] as they see the end of the world coming nearer and nearer'.[17] In fact, *disperare* means, rather, 'to give up all hope', 'to expect no longer'.[18] What worried Gregory was that, apart from himself and his few pious friends—persons who took the approach of the end of the world with deadly seriousness—nobody seemed to give any thought to that distant event. Their conduct showed this only too clearly. Gregory, then, did not look out at a society shrinking beneath the chill shadow of the approach of the Apocalypse. What he saw, rather, was a Merovingian Gaul more like the world that recent scholarship has presented to us. He surveyed, with religious disquiet, a basically secure and sophisticated post-Roman society, still confidently profane in many of its reflexes, the majority of whose members were stolidly indifferent to the approach of the Last Judgement. A large part of his literary work was devoted to making the saints 'stand out'. They were the only truly active and vibrant figures in a

[17] Gregory of Tours, *Decem Libri Historiarum* 1, praef., ed. Krusch 1951: 2; trans. Thorpe 1974: 67. See Breukelaar 1994: esp. 300 and n. 23, with 52–5 and 169–74; Heinzelmann 1994: 69–101, both accepting the conventional translation.

[18] For Gregory's use of *disperare* to mean 'not expect, lose hope of', cf. *Decem Libri historiarum* 4. 12, ed. Krusch 1951: 142 with n. 2, citing Sidonius Apollinaris, *Letter* 2. 1: 'nec accipiebat instrumenta desperans'; trans. Dalton 1915: i. 35: 'nor does he trouble to furnish himself with deeds, knowing it hopeless to prove a title'. See also, *Sortes Sangallenses* 33, R.8: 'Habebis spem fidei, sed de disperato', in Dold 1948: 24 with note on p. 110: 'from someone you do not expect'. By contrast to the insouciance castigated by Gregory, expectation of the coming end of the world was the attitude expected of religiously minded persons: e.g. the formula for a legacy to a pious foundation: Marculf, *Formulae* 2. 3, ed. Uddholm 1962: 178.

world where nothing else moved, becalmed as it was in the windless, moral doldrums of the *saeculum*.

Not only was sanctity needed; it was possible. But this was an ancient sanctity, modelled on the martyrs and on the great ascetics. For nobody had yet told the bishop of Tours about the *Adelsheiligen* (the holy through nobility). He did not know that such creatures existed. He did not believe that aristocratic lineage, nor even that a well-established family tradition of episcopal rule, conveyed sanctity. Indeed, like any pensive observer of the Roman governing class, from Seneca to Ammianus Marcellinus, Gregory had a low view of the moral fibre of the majority of his peers. Violence, sensuality and a weakness for the bottle seemed to characterize only too many of his well-born contemporaries. Descent *de stemmate Romanorum*, from the ancestry of the Romans, was no guarantee in itself that a bishop would show the high degree of physical courage, the integrity, and the self-control that were necessary for a bishop's tasks.

What conveyed these qualities was grace, and a somewhat old-fashioned grace at that. For Gregory had inherited from Augustine, perhaps through Augustine's Gallic admirers, that streak in the Augustinian system that emphasized that the *saeculum* still needed heroes—persons endowed with the gift of perseverance: 'strong figures who could tame the unjust powers of the world' (Muhlberger 1990: 131). This was not the fluid, bubbling grace that had encouraged so many humble groups—women as well as men, married as well as celibate, lay persons as well as clergy—to strive towards the martyrs, as in the churches of Augustine's Africa. It was the grace required by a human icebreaker, before whose solid prow the ice-floes of the *saeculum* broke and gave way.

But, for Gregory, such grace was still active in Gaul. It was a matter of pride to him that it had come to members of his own family. Nicetius, bishop of Lyons from 552 to 573, was the uncle of his mother. Here, plainly, was a man predestinate. He had been blessed from the womb. Nicetius was one of those who had received 'the first and basic act of pity shown by a merciful God, who heaps the wealth of grace upon the undeserving and who sanctifies the one who is not yet born' (Gregory of Tours, *Book on the Life of the Fathers* 8 pref., ed. Krusch, p. 241; trans. James 1985: 65). And how did Gregory know this? Nicetius had picked up little Gregory, then aged eight, and had sat him on his knee, but not before adjusting his robe: 'holding his fingers on the edge of his garment he covered himself with it so well that my body was never touched by his blessed limbs' (Gregory of Tours, *Book on the Life of the Fathers* 8.2, ed. Krusch, p. 242, trans. James 1985: 67). Would that all clergymen had such *cautela*—so deeply internalized a sense of clerical decorum! The gesture showed the 'wealth of grace' that God had 'heaped' upon the bishop's soul.

With Gregory we can glimpse how a religious person of the late sixth century strove to make his own the awesome qualities of the saints of old. Their sacrality and fierce deaths did not hold them at a distance from him. Gregory grew up talking about saints with his mother at the fireside (Gregory of Tours, *Book on the Glory of the Confessors* 3, ed. Krusch, p. 300, trans. Van Dam 1988: 20). His first lessons in reading and writing from the Scriptures enabled him to copy out a remedy with which to heal his father's gout (Gregory of Tours, *Book on the Glory of the Confessors* 39, ed. Krusch, p. 322, trans. Van Dam 1988: 51). He lived among persons whom he admired especially for the reverent awe with which they would pass on stories of the saints (Gregory of Tours, *Book on the Life of the Fathers* 17 pref., ed. Krusch, trans. James 1985: 114). He wrote profusely so as to do the same himself. He was an active member of what we might call a 'hagiological subculture'. Faced by a man such as Gregory and his many tales of the saints, we must remember what the cognitive psychologists tell us. The very act of thought contains a strong narrative element. 'Asleep and awake it is just the same: we are telling ourselves stories all the time' (Hudson 1980: 85, from Carrithers 1983: 86). There is no reason not to suppose that the stories told so often by Gregory did not become part of his own story to himself about himself. The raw dramas of the lives of the saints entered the thought flow of an entire group of men and women, such as Gregory himself, who had created for themselves a 'hagiological subculture'. Ethnographers can see this happening, over the years in a living society, as the Buddhist monks in modern Sri Lanka absorb dramatic tales of the trials of the Buddha. Even as lay persons, they had taken these archaic narratives, set in a distant time, often characterized by redundant, barely explicable violence against the self, into their own thought flow and, hence, into their own inner narrative about themselves. Of the great monk Paññânda, Michael Carrithers can write:

'having so much hagiography about him to begin with, he easily became the stuff of hagiography itself' (Carrithers 1983: 88).

One such person, perhaps, was the lady Blatta, who was buried in Rome in the church of Saint Anastasia in 688.

et quia marturibus Christi studiosa cohaesit,
Christigeri meruit marturis esse comes.

And because with zeal she clung to the martyrs of Christ, she has deserved to be the companion [perhaps through *ad sanctos* burial] of the Christ-bearing martyr herself.   (Diehl 1925–67: no. 201B, lines 23–4)

Historians should not underestimate persons like the lady Blatta, although they barely appear in the sources for the religious history of the early Middle Ages. But they were there. Sixty years old, Blatta had been loyal to priests and generous to the poor. She had instilled *pudicitia* in all her children. She was the sort of grandmother, a true *nonna*, who would have fostered many a little Gregory of Tours. Ethnographers of living Buddhist societies still find themselves challenged to understand 'the actual replication of a living tradition' (Carrithers 1983: 74). Medievalists, I think, face a similar challenge. Persons such as Gregory and the lady Blatta are so welcome to us, as they give a hint of how a section of the religious world of the early Middle Ages set about the 'replication of a living tradition' by establishing a constant, warm relation with the saints.

With a date such as 688, we have reached the end of late antiquity. But recent studies of the hagiography of the medieval west indicate that the story continues. The medieval cult of the saints owed its contours to the continued grinding together of two massive tectonic plates—the urge to imitate and the urge to admire. The monumental study of André Vauchez, *La sainteté en Occident*, published in 1981, dealt with the change in attitudes to sanctity in the later Middle Ages, that led to the emergence, in the thirteenth and fourteenth centuries, of 'les saints imitables'—of imitable saints, cut to a more human measure, presented as models of Christian behaviour appropriate to a more complex and urbanized society.[19] Within a year, however, the brilliant analysis of vernacular saints' lives in northern France, *Le*

[19] Vauchez 1981; see also his most illuminating second thoughts on the subject: Vauchez 1991: 161–72. See also Geary 1996: 1–22.

corps de sainteté by Brigitte Cazelles, drew attention to a strong
current of devotion that flowed in the opposite direction. She
pointed out the extent to which an 'archaic' image of sanctity
continued to feed the imagination of believers on utterly *in*imitable
figures, conjured up from the distant, late antique past. Saint Catherine,
Saint Margaret, Saint Christina and Jehan Bouche d'Or—Saint John
Chrysostom as the wild hermit—are troubling revenants. They are
avatars from a very ancient Christian east (Cazelles 1982: 19), they fit
awkwardly into our image of a tidy, *bourgeois* Gothic Europe, where
each group can be supposed to have enjoyed its own, made-to-measure
saint, and where the cunning of the medievalist can be fruitfully
deployed in matching the aspirations, the social codes and the needs
for empowerment of each group in medieval society to an appropriate
'role model' saint. This juxtaposition, within the same high medieval
society, of two very different images of sanctity, calls for a few, necessarily brief, concluding observations. The first is that the tenacity of 'late
antique' forms of the image of the saints, revealed in studies such as
those of Brigitte Cazelles, should cause us, perhaps, to redefine the
boundaries of Western Europe. Throughout this period, Catholic Western Europe was flanked by Christian societies that had not lost touch
with the late antique imaginative structures that had favoured, on the
whole, the emergence of inimitable saints. No Augustine had come to
spoil the fun of the festivals, and to cause the shadow of his austere
insistence on the imitation of the saints to fall between the faithful and
more ancient forms of the enjoyment of the saints, through heady
participation in their triumph. Such post-Augustinian developments
did not occur in Greece, in the Balkans, in Ethiopia, and in medieval
and early modern Russia. And yet western and eastern Christendom
never became entirely separate worlds. Both were the heirs of late
antiquity. In the year 1400, in a continuum that stretched from Novgorod to London, the Christian imagination continued to be fed by
legends whose dramatic structures, whose insistent physicality, and
whose notions of the sacred still carried with them the distinctive
flavour of fifth-century Syria and of Coptic Egypt.[20]

---

[20] e.g. Heffernan 1988: 280–91, on the English vernacular legends of Saint Christina; Lenhoff 1989: 60–1, on the cult of Saint Christina in Novgorod, later replaced by
the equally dramatic Passion of Boris and Gleb.

We should not isolate the hagiography of western Europe, by privileging only its more distinctive and original features. There is no denying that the sudden development of the notion of imitable saints in the later medieval west was a notable phenomenon. In recent years, the notion that late medieval saints were expected to function as 'role models' has stimulated a series of historiographical endeavours. Historians of literature and society have attempted to do justice to the full complexity of the relationships between saints, their patrons and their audiences in the differing regions of western Europe. But, seen from the viewing point of a wider Christian world, the notion of imitable sanctity is a theme as vivid and as colourful, but as superficial, as a growth of lichen across an ancient rock. If we listen to what Byzantinists and students of medieval and early modern Russia (and even students of medieval and modern Ethiopia) can tell us about how the saints were perceived in those Christian regions, western medievalists may find an answer, through the valid comparison of cognate imaginative structures, to many of the mysteries which still perplex them.

Last but not least, the greatest mystery of all remains: how do saints produce saints? That is, how, for many religious persons, does the inimitable come to be absorbed in such a way as to provide a glimpse of wider, heroic horizons beyond the cramped confines of their normal life? On this issue, it is a relief to learn that the saints tend to give as many different answers to that question as do professors. For they also were products of very different spiritual landscapes, formed by the differing pressures of the tectonic plates to which we have referred. To take a few examples. In the months before the death of Saint Thérèse of Lisieux, in 1897, the companion of her bedside, Sister Agnès de Jésus (in fact, Thérèse's elder sister) spoke to her of certain saints who had lived extraordinary lives, such as Saint Symeon Stylites. Thérèse was unimpressed. She wished, rather, for saints who had fear of nothing in this world, such as Saint Cecilia, who had not feared even to be married.[21] The late antique historian

---

[21] Thérèse de Lisieux 1971: 233 (= 1977: 69)—30th June no. 1; see also, 1971: 390 (= 1977: 161)—21st August, no. 3, about the Virgin Mary: 'On la montre inabordable, il faudrait la montrer imitable'.

(who tends to have a soft spot for Syrian holy-men of melodramatic disposition) is chastened by such words.

Thérèse of Lisieux was an exquisite example of a very modern Catholic piety. For when we draw nearer to the culture of the later Middle Ages, we meet persons for whom the ancient, inimitable saints had lost nothing of their appeal. In his autobiography, Ignatius of Loyola describes how, when still at Manresa, in 1522, he had tested his mind. Always the fine psychologist, he observed that:

> When he was thinking about things of the world, he took delight in them, but afterwards, when he was tired and put them aside he found that he was dry and discontented. But when he thought of going to Jerusalem barefoot and eating nothing but herbs and undergoing all the rigours that he saw the saints had endured [and by these saints, Ignatius meant the formidable Desert Fathers of early Byzantium, transferred to the west in all their archaic ferocity in books such as the *Golden Legend* of Jacobus de Voragine] not only was he consoled when he had these thoughts, but even after putting them aside, he remained content and happy.
>
> (*The Autobiography of St. Ignatius Loyola*, trans. Olin and O'Callaghan 1974: 240)

Heroic saints, their unearthly image transmitted from the days of Prudentius, were still available, also, to give courage and a sense of drama to the lives of lesser figures. In 1576, a young girl from Seville, recruited as a nun by Saint Teresa of Avila, confessed to Teresa that while she was being brutally battered by her parents for refusing to marry, 'she had felt almost nothing, for she thought of what Saint Agnes had suffered, a thought which the Lord brought into her memory' (Teresa of Avila, ed. Madre de Dios and Steggink: 1967, cap. 26. 8, p. 591; trans. Kavanaugh and Rodriguez: 1985, 237–8). Somehow, Ignatius and the unknown nun from Seville had, like Gregory of Tours a thousand years before them, absorbed the inimitable. By the manner in which they had remembered the saints, they had contributed to 'the actual replication of a living tradition'.

It is the purpose of this article to suggest to medievalists that the continuous tension, evident in medieval hagiography, between imitation of the saints and other forms of imaginative appropriation of their power, goes back directly to the late antique period. It is a tension that can be traced back to the fact that, for men such as Augustine and the poet Prudentius, differing images of the martyrs and differing attitudes to their festivals implied divergent views, also, on the relation between grace and human nature, on the possible relations between members of the Christian community and its shared heroes, and, ultimately, on the nature of the boundary between the sacred and the profane. These were weighty topics. A debate upon them, begun around the year 400, was by no means concluded by the year 1500. It is this unresolved, late antique debate that goes some way to explain the remarkable diversity in function and in imaginative content that characterized the medieval cult of saints.

BIBLIOGRAPHY

Barnes, T. D. (1998). *Ammianus Marcellinus and the Representation of Historical Reality*. Ithaca, NY; London: Cornell University Press.

Baumeister, T. (1972). *Martyr Invictus: der Martyrer als Sinnbild der Erlösung in der Legende und im Kult der frühen koptischen Kirche*. Münster: Regensberg.

Breukelaar, A. H. B. (1994). *Historiography and Episcopal Authority in Sixth-Century Gaul. The Histories of Gregory of Tours Interpreted in Historical Context*, Forschungen zur Kirchen- und Dogmengeschichte 57. Göttingen: Vanderhoeck & Ruprecht.

Brown, P. (1967/2000). *Augustine of Hippo*. London: Faber and Faber. Reprinted 2000 (London: Faber and Faber), with Epilogue, 441–520.

—— (1981). *The Cult of the Saints. Its Rise and Function in Latin Christianity*. Chicago: University of Chicago Press; London: SCM Press.

—— (1995). *Authority and the Sacred. Aspects of the Christianization of the Roman World*. Cambridge: Cambridge University Press.

—— (1997). *The Rise of Western Christendom*. Oxford: Blackwell.

—— (1998). 'Qui adorant columnas in ecclesia. Saint Augustine and a practice of the imperiti', in G. Madec (ed.), *Augustin Prédicateur (395–411)*. Paris: Institut d'Études Augustiniennes, 367–75, esp. 371–74.

—— (1999a). 'Images as a Substitute for Writing', in E. Chrysos and I. Wood (eds.), *East and West: Modes of Communication*. Leiden: Brill.

Brown, P. (1999b). 'The New Augustine', *New York Review of Books*, 46: 11 (24 June).

Browne, C. G. (1974). *Gregory of Nazianzen*, in Library of the Nicene and Post-Nicene Fathers. Grand Rapids, MI: Eerdmans; Edinburgh: T. & T. Clark.

Brubaker, L. (1989). 'Byzantine Art in the Ninth Century: Theory, Practice and Culture', *Byzantine and Modern Greek Studies*, 13: 23–94.

——(1999). *Vision and Meaning in Ninth-Century Byzantium. Image as Exegesis in the Homilies of Gregory of Nazianzus*. Cambridge: Cambridge University Press.

Carrithers, M. (1983). *The Forest Monks of Sri Lanka. An Anthropological and Historical Study*. Delhi; London: Oxford University Press.

Cazelles, B. (1982). *Le corps de sainteté d'après Jean Bouche d'Or, Jehan Paulus et quelques vies des xiie et xiiie siècles*. Geneva: Droz.

Chabot, J. B. (1901). *Le Chronique de Michel le Syrien*. Paris: Ernest Leroux.

Chiesa, P. (1996). 'Un testo agiografico africano ad Aquileia. Gli Acta di Gallonio e dei martiri di Timida Regia', *Analecta Bollandiana*, 114: 241–68.

Dalton, O. M. (1915). *The Letters of Sidonius*. Oxford: Clarendon Press.

Deléani, S. (1979). *Christum Sequi. Étude d'un thème dans l'oeuvre de saint Cyprien*. Paris: Études Augustiniennes.

de Vogüé, A. (ed.) (1980). *Grégoire le Grand: Les Dialogues*, iii, Sources chrétiennes 265. Paris: Les Éditions du Cerf.

Diaz y Diaz, M. C. (1980). 'Literary Aspects of the Visigothic Liturgy', in E. James (ed.), *Visigothic Spain: New Approaches*. Oxford: Clarendon Press; New York: Oxford University Press.

Diehl, E. (ed.) (1925–67). *Inscriptiones Latinae Christianae Veteres*. Berlin: Weidmann.

Divjak, J. (1987). *Oeuvres de Saint Augustin 46B: Lettres 1–29*. Paris: Études Augustiniennes.

Di Marco, M. (1995). *La polemica sull'anima tra 'Fausto di Riez' e Claudiano Mamerto*, Studia Ephemeridis Augustinianum 51. Rome: Institutum Patristicum Augustinianum.

Dolbeau, F. (1992a). 'Nouveaux sermons de saint Augustin pour la conversion des païens et des donatistes (III)', *Revue des études augustiniennes*, 38: 50–79, re-edited in Dolbeau 1996.

——(1992b). 'Nouveaux sermons de saint Augustin pour la conversion des païens et des donatistes (IV)', *Recherches augustiniennes*, 26: 69–141, re-edited in Dolbeau 1996.

——(1996). *Vingt-Six Sermons au Peuple d'Afrique*. Paris: Institut d'études augustiniennes.

Dold, A. (1948). *Die Orakelsprüche im St. Galler Palimpsestcodex* 908, Österreichische Akademie der Wissenschaften: Sitzungsberichte 225: 4.

Duval, Y. (1982). *Loca sanctorum Africae. Le culte des martyrs en Afrique du ive au viie siècle,* Collection de l'École française de Rome 58. Rome: École française de Rome.

——(1988). *Auprès des saints corps et âme. L'inhumation 'ad sanctos' dans la chrétienté d'Orient et d'Occident du iiie au viie siècle.* Paris: Études Augustiniennes.

Eno, R. B. (1989). *Saint Augustine. Letters* VI (I*–29*), Fathers of the Church 81. Washington, DC: Catholic University of America Press.

Férotin, M. (1912). *Le Liber Mozarabicorum Sacramentorum.* Paris: Firmin-Didot.

Fontaine, J. (1982). 'Images virgiliennes de l'ascension céleste dans la poésie latine chrétienne', *Gedenkschrift für Alfred Stuiber,* Jahrbuch für Antike und Christentum Supp. 9. Münster: Aschendorff, 55–67.

——(1986). 'Damase poète théodosien: l'imaginaire poétique des epigrammata', in *Saecularia Damasiana.* Vatican City: Pontificio istituto di archeologia cristiana, 115–45.

Fortin, E. L. (1959). *Christianisme et culture philosophique au ve siècle. La querelle de l'âme humain en Occident.* Paris: Études Augustiniennes.

Geary, P. (1996). 'Saints, Scholars and Society. The Elusive Goal', in S. Sticca (ed.), *Saints: Studies in Hagiography,* Medieval and Renaissance Texts and Studies 141. Binghamton, NY: Medieval and Renaissance Texts and Studies.

Guyon, J. (1995). 'Damase et l'illustration des martyrs. Les accents de la dévotion et l'enjeu d'une pastorale', in M. Lamberigts and P. Van Deun (eds.), *Martyrium in a Multidisciplinary Perspective. Memorial Louis Reekmans.* Louvain: Louvain University Press.

Harl, M. (1981). 'La dénonciation des festivités profanes dans le discours épiscopal et monastique, en Orient chrétien, à la fin du IVe siècle', *La fête, pratique et discours,* Annales de l'Université de Besançon 262. Paris: Presses universitaires de Franche-Comté, 123–47.

Harries, J. (1999). *Law and Empire in Late Antiquity.* Cambridge: Cambridge University Press.

Heffernan, T. J. (1988). *Sacred Biography. Saints and their Biographers in the Middle Ages.* Oxford: Oxford University Press.

Heinzelmann, M. (1994). *Gregor von Tours (538–594). 'Zehn Bücher der Geschichte'. Historiographie und Gesellschaftskonzept im 6. Jht.* Darmstadt: Wissenschaftliche Buchgesellschaft.

Hillgarth, J. N. (1980). 'Popular Religion in Visigothic Spain', in E. James (ed.), *Visigothic Spain: New Approaches.* Oxford: Clarendon Press.

Hill, E. (1997). *Newly Discovered Sermons: Translations and Notes,* The Complete Works of Saint Augustine: A Translation for the Twenty-First Century. Sermons III/1. Hyde Park, NY: New City Press.

Hombert, P.-M. (1996). *Gloria Gratiae. Se glorifier en Dieu: principe et fin de la théologie augustinienne de la grâce.* Paris: Institut d'études augustiniennes.

Horn, J. (1986). *Studien zu den Märtyrern des nordlichen Oberägyptens. 1 Märtyrerverehrung und Märtyrerlegende im Werk des Schenute,* Göttinger Orientforschungen, Series 4: Aegypten, 15. Wiesbaden: Harrassowitz.

Hudson, L. (1980). in *Times Literary Supplement,* 25 January 1980, p. 85, cited by Carrithers 1983: 86.

James, E. (1985). *Gregory of Tours. Life of the Fathers.* Liverpool: Liverpool University Press.

Krusch, B. (ed.) (1885). *Monumenta Germaniae Historica,* Scriptores rerum Merovingicarum 1: 2. Hanover: Bibliopolii Hahniani.

——(ed.) (1951). *Gregorii Episcopi Turonensis Historiarum libri X,* 2nd edn., Monumenta Germaniae Historica, Scriptores rerum Merovingicarum 1:1 fasc. 3. Hanover: Bibliopolii Hahniani.

Lenhoff, G (1989). *The Martyred Princes Boris and Gleb: A Socio-Cultural Study of the Cult and the Texts,* UCLA Slavic Studies 19. Columbus, OH: Slavica Publishers.

MacNeill, M. (1962). *The Festival of Lughnasa.* Oxford: Oxford University Press.

Madre de Dios, E. de la and Steggink, O. (eds.) (1967). *Teresa de Avila: Obras completas.* Second edn., Madrid: Biblioteca de autores cristianos. Translated by K. Kavanaugh and O. Rodriguez, *The Collected Works of Teresa of Avila,* iii. Washington, DC: ICS Publications (1985).

Maier, J.-L. (1987). *Le Dossier du Donatisme.* Berlin: Akademie-Verlag.

Marrou, H. I. (1938). *MOYCIKOC ANHP. Étude sur les scènes de la vie intellectuelle figurants sur les monuments funéraires romains.* Grenoble: Didier & Richard. [Repr. Roma: 'L'Erma' di Bretschneider (1964).]

Morin, G. (1930). *Miscellanea Agostiniana: Studi e Testi.* Rome: Tipografia poliglotta vaticana.

——(ed.) (1953). Caesarius of Arles, *Sermons,* Corpus Christianorum Series Latina 103. Turnhout: Brepols.

Muhlberger, S. (1990). *The Fifth Century Chroniclers,* ARCA Monographs 27. Leeds: Francis Cairns.

Olin, J. C. and O'Callaghan, J. F. (translators) (1974). *The Autobiography of St. Ignatius Loyola.* New York: Harper.

Saxer, V. (1980). *Morts, martyrs, reliques en Afrique chrétienne aux premiers siècles,* Théologie Historique 55. Paris: Éditions Beauchesne.

Straw, C. (1999). 'Martyrdom', in A. D. Fitzgerald (ed.), *Augustine through the Ages. An Encyclopedia.* Grand Rapids, MI: Eerdmans.

Tambiah, S. J. (1968). 'The Magical Power of Words', *Man*, 3: 175–208.

Thérèse de Lisieux (1971). *Derniers entretiens avec ses sœurs.* Paris: Desclée de Brouwer; Éditions du Cerf. [Eng. trans. by J. Clark, as *Her Last Conversations.* Washington, DC: ICS Publications (1977)].

Thomson, H. J. (ed.) (1961). Prudentius *Peristephanon.* Cambridge, MA: Harvard University Press.

Thorpe, L. (trans.) (1974). *Gregory of Tours. The History of the Franks.* Harmondsworth: Penguin.

Uddholm, A. (ed.) (1962). Marculfi *Formularum Libri duo.* Uppsala: Eranos.

Van Dam, R. (1988). *Gregory of Tours: Glory of the Martyr,* Translated Texts for Historians, Latin Series 4. Liverpool: Liverpool University Press.

Van Minnen, P. (1995). 'The Earliest Account of a Martyrdom in Coptic', *Analecta Bollandiana*, 113, 13–38.

Vauchez, A. (1981). *La sainteté en Occident aux derniers siècles du Moyen Age,* Bibliothèque de l'École française de Rome 241. Rome: École française de Rome.

——(1991). 'Saints admirables et saints imitables: les fonctions de l'hagiographie ont-elles change aux derniers siècles du Moyen Age?', in *Les fonctions des saints dans le monde occidental (iiie–xiiie siècle)*, Collection de l'École française de Rome 149. Rome: École française de Rome, 161–72.

Wrede, H. (1981). Consecratio in formam deorum. *Vergöttlichte Privatpersonen in der römischen Kaiserzeit.* Mainz: Zabern.

Details of Original Publication

Permission to reprint the following items is gratefully acknowledged.

1. Jörg Rüpke, 'Römische Religion und "Reichsreligion": Begriffsgeschichtliche und methodische Bemerkungen', in H. Cancik and J Rüpke (eds.), *Römische Reichsreligion und Provinzialreligion* (Tübingen: Mohr Siebeck, 1997), 3–24.

2. Richard Gordon, 'The Roman Imperial Cult and the Question of Power', in L. Golden (ed.), *Raising the Eyebrow: John Onians and World Art Studies: An Album Amicorum in his Honour*, BAR International Series 996 (Oxford: Archaeopress, 2001), 107–22.

3. James B. Rives, 'Magic in Roman Law: The Reconstruction of a Crime', *Classical Antiquity*, 22.2 (2003), 313–39.

4. William Van Andringa, 'Nouvelles combinaisons, nouveaux statuts: les dieux indigènes dans les panthéons des cités de Gaule romaine', in D. Paunier (ed.), *La romanisation et la question de l'héritage celtique* (Glux-en-Glenne: Bibracte, Centre archéologique européen, 2006), 219–32.

5. Nicole Belayche, '*Hypsistos*. Une voie de l'exaltation des dieux dans le polythéisme gréco-romain', in *Archiv für Religionsgeschichte*, 7 (2005), 34–55.

6. Andeas Bendlin, 'Vom Nutzen und Nachteil der Mantik. Orakel im Medium von Handlung und Literatur in der Zeit der Zweiten Sophistik', in D. Elm von der Osten, J. Rüpke, and K. Waldner (eds.), *Texte als Medium und Reflexion von Religion im römischen Reich*, Potsdamer altertumswissenschaftliche Beiträge 14 (Stuttgart: Steiner, 2006), 159–207.

7. Simon Price, 'Homogénéité et diversité dans les religions à Rome', *Archiv für Religionsgeschichte*, 5 (2003), 180–97.

8. Giulia Sfameni Gasparro, 'Misteri e culti orientali: un problema storico-religioso', in C. Bonnet, J. Rüpke, and P. Scarpi (eds.), *Religions orientales—culti misterici—neue Perspektiven—nouvelles perspectives—prospettive nuove* (Stuttgart: Steiner, 2006), 181–210.

9. Richard Gordon, 'Ritual and Hierarchy in the Mysteries of Mithras', *ARYS. Antigüedad: religiones y sociedades*, 4 (2001), 245–73.

10. John Scheid, 'Communauté et communauté. Réflexions sur quelques ambiguïtés d'après l'exemple des thiases de l'Egypte romaine', in Nicole Belayche and Simon C. Mimouni (eds.), *Les communautés religieuses dans le monde gréco-romain: essais de définition*. Bibliothèque de l'École des hautes études. Section des sciences religieuses, 117 (Turnhout: Brepols, 2003), 61–74.

11. Philip A. Harland, 'Acculturation and Identity in the Diaspora: A Jewish Family and 'Pagan' Guilds at Hierapolis', *Journal of Jewish Studies*, 57 (2006), 222–44.

12. Martin Goodman, 'Josephus and Variety in First Century Judaism', *The Israel Academy of Sciences and Humanities. Proceedings*, 7, No. 6. Jerusalem, 2000, 201–13, repr, in M. Goodman, *Judaism in the Roman World: Collected Essays* (Leiden: Brill, 2007), 33–46.

13. Judith Lieu, 'The Forging of Christian Identity and the *Letter to Diognetus*', *Mediterranean Archaeology*, 11 (1998), 71–82 (as revised in her *Neither Jew nor Greek?* (Edinburgh: T. & T. Clark, 2002), 171–89).

14. Guy G. Stroumsa, 'Purification and its Discontents: Mani's Rejection of Baptism', in J. Assmann and G. Stroumsa (eds.), *Transformations of the Inner Self in Ancient Religions* (Leiden: Brill, 1999), 405–20.

15. John North, 'Pagans, Polytheists and the Pendulum', in W. V. Harris (ed.), *The Spread of Christianity in the First Four Centuries: Studies in Explanation* (Leiden: Brill, 2005), 125–43.

16. Averil Cameron, 'Early Christianity and the Discourse of Female Desire', in L. J. Archer, S. Fischler, and M. Wyke (eds.), *Women in Ancient Societies* (Basingstoke: Macmillan, 1994), 152–68.

17. Peter Brown, 'Enjoying the Saints in Late Antiquity', *Early Medieval Europe*, 9 (2000), 1–24.

Suggestions for Further Reading

As this book is aimed at an Anglophone readership, we limit our suggestions to works published in English. Good general introductions are offered by:

Beard, M., North, J., and Price S. (1998). *Religions of Rome*. Cambridge: Cambridge University Press, i, chs. 4–8, are on religious life in the imperial period, including Jews and Christians.

Clark, G. (2004). *Christianity and Roman Society*. Cambridge: Cambridge University Press, a thematic study, short and to the point.

Feeney, D. C. (1998). *Literature and Religion at Rome*. Cambridge: Cambridge University Press, on the Augustan period, raises important methodological questions.

North, J. A. (2000). *Roman Religion*, Greece and Rome New Survey 30. Oxford: Oxford University Press, ranging more widely than its title might suggest.

Rives, J. B. (2006). *Religion in the Roman Empire*. Oxford: Blackwell, a thematic study.

Rüpke, J. (ed.) (2007). *A Companion to Roman Religion*. Malden, MA and Oxford: Blackwell, for background information on a wide range of topics.

Scheid, J. (2003). *An Introduction to Roman Religion*. Edinburgh: Edinburgh University Press, on the cults of Rome.

Schiffman, L. H. (1991). *From Text to Tradition: A History of Second Temple and Rabbinic Judaism*. Hoboken, NJ: Ktav, a good starting point.

We also give some more detailed suggestions, using the four headings employed in this book.

I: Changes in Religious Life: Roman and Civic Cults

Ando, C. (2008). *The Matter of the Gods: Religion and the Roman Empire*. Berkeley, CA: University of California Press, makes some good points.

Athanassiadi, P. and Frede, M. (eds.) (1999). *Pagan Monotheism in Late Antiquity*. Oxford: Clarendon, 1–20, a good exposition of the case rejected by Belayche (above, Ch. 5) and North (above, Ch. 15).

Beard, M. and North, J. A. (eds.) (1990). *Pagan Priests*. London: Duckworth, includes important chapters by R. L. Gordon on imperial-period priesthoods.

Liebeschuetz, J. H. W. G. (1979). *Continuity and Change in Roman Religion*. Oxford: Clarendon, is an accessible account of the literary sources, tracing religious changes in the imperial period up to Constantine.

Hekster, O., Schmidt-Hofner, S. and Witschel, Chr. (eds.) (2009). *Ritual Dynamics and Religious Change in the Roman Empire*. Leiden: Brill, a wide-ranging volume of conference papers, many in English.

Price, S. R. F. (1984). *Rituals and Power: The Roman Imperial Cult in Asia Minor*. Cambridge: Cambridge University Press, and Beard/North/Price, *Religions of Rome*, i, 206–10, 348–63, are useful complements to Gordon (above, Ch. 2).

Rives, J. B. (1995). *Religion and Authority in Roman Carthage*. Oxford: Clarendon, a case-study of Roman traditions in the *colonia* of Carthage, including interactions with Christianity.

On oracles and divination (discussed in Bendlin, above, Ch. 6), see:

Fontenrose, J. E. (1988). *Didyma: Apollo's Oracle, Cult and Companions*, Berkeley, CA and London: University of California Press.

Lane Fox, R. (1986). *Pagans and Christians in the Mediterranean World from the Second Century* AD *to the Conversion of Constantine*. Harmondsworth: Viking, 168–261.

Potter, D. S. (1994). *Prophets and Emperors: Human and Divine Authority from Augustus to Theodosius*. Cambridge, MA and London: Harvard University Press.

On magic (regulations against which are discussed by Rives, above, Ch. 3):

Gager, J. G. (1992). *Cursing Tablets and Binding Spells*. New York and Oxford: Oxford University Press.

Gordon, R. L. (1999). 'Imagining Greek and Roman Magic', in B. Ankarloo and S. Clark (eds.), *Witchcraft and Magic in Europe: Ancient Greece and Rome*. Philadelphia, PA and London: University of Pennsylvania Press, 159–276.

—— and Simón, F. M. (eds.) (2010). *Magical Practice in the Latin West*. Leiden: Brill, an important collection of conference papers.

Ogden, D. (2009). *Magic, Witchcraft, and Ghosts in the Greek and Roman Worlds: A Sourcebook*, 2nd edn. Oxford: Oxford University Press, an excellent collection of material.

II: Elective Cults

On Asclepius:

Petsalis-Diomidis, A. (2010). *Truly beyond Wonders: Aelius Aristides and the Cult of Asklepios.* Oxford: Oxford University Press, cleverly marries archaeological and textual evidence, especially on the cult at Pergamum.

On Isis (discussed by Sfameni Gasparro, above, Ch. 8):

Turcan, R. (1996). *The Cults of the Roman Empire.* Oxford: Blackwell, misleadingly titled, in fact outlines evidence on 'Oriental cults', including Isis.

Readers will need to consider carefully the nature of Apuleius' evidence. The following offer three different positions:

Harrison, S. J. (2000). *Apuleius, A Latin Sophist.* Oxford: Oxford University Press, ch. 6.

Nock, A. D. (1933). *Conversion: The Old and the New in Religion from Alexander the Great to Augustine of Hippo.* Oxford: Clarendon, 1–16, 138–55.

Winkler, J. J. (1985). *Auctor & Actor: A Narratological Reading of Apuleius' Golden Ass.* Berkeley, CA: University of California Press, 215–21.

On the cult of Mithras (discussed by Gordon, above, Ch. 9):

Beck, R. L. (2006). *The Religion of the Mithras Cult in the Roman Empire.* Oxford: Oxford University Press, discusses the conceptual world of Mithraism.

Clauss, M. (2000). *The Roman Cult of Mithras.* Edinburgh: Edinburgh University Press, the most straightforward starting-point, but readers need to be aware that the author seriously downplays visual evidence.

Gordon, R. L. (1996). *Image and Value in the Graeco–Roman World.* Aldershot: Variorum, a collection of his important articles on Mithraism.

III: Co-existence of Religions, Old and New

Edwards, M., Goodman, M., and Price, S. (eds.) (1999). *Apologetics in the Roman Empire.* Oxford: Clarendon, includes chapters on pagan, Jewish, and Christian apologetics.

Elsner, J. (2007). 'Viewing and Resistance: Art and Religion at Dura Europos', in his *Roman Eyes: Visuality and Subjectivity in Art and Text.* Princeton, NJ: Princeton University Press, 253–87 (revised version of his

(2001) 'Cultural Resistance and the Visual Image: The Case of Dura
Europos', *Classical Philology*, 96: 269–304), examines the possible interactions between cults of pagans, Jews, and Christians in one town at the
boundary of the Empire, Dura Europos.

Lane Fox, R. (1986). *Pagans and Christians* (above, I), presents the evidence
for the vitality of Greek cults of the imperial period, and outlines parallel
Christian developments.

Lieu, J. M. (2004). *Christian Identity in the Jewish and Graeco–Roman World.*
Oxford: Oxford University Press, chs. 2, 3, and 8.

Price, S. (1999). *Religions of the Ancient Greeks.* Cambridge: Cambridge
University Press, 143–71, on reactions to Greek religion by Romans,
Jews, and Christians.

Versnel, H. S. (ed.) (1981). *Faith, Hope and Worship: Aspects of Religious
Mentality in the Ancient World.* Leiden: Brill, a fine collection of essays,
which include much on Greek religion of the imperial period.

On Judaism (discussed by Harland, above, Ch. 11 and Goodman, above, Ch. 12):

Fonrobert, C. E. and Jaffee M. S. (eds.) (2007). *The Cambridge Companion to
the Talmud and Rabbinic Literature.* Cambridge: Cambridge University
Press.

Golb, N. (1995). *Who Wrote the Dead Sea Scrolls?: The Search for the Secret of
Qumran.* London: Michael O'Mara, is a rational account, though for a
different view, see next entry.

Lieu, J. M. (1996). *Image and Reality: The Jews in the World of the Christians
in the Second Century.* Edinburgh: T. & T. Clark.

Lieu, J., North, J., and Rajak, T. (eds.) (1992). *The Jews among Pagans and
Christians.* London: Routledge.

Maccoby, H. (1988). *Early Rabbinic Writings.* Cambridge: Cambridge
University Press, is a good introduction to texts of the second and third
centuries.

Sanders, E. P. (1992). *Judaism: Practice and Belief, 63 BCE–66 CE.* London:
SCM and Philadelphia, PA: Trinity Press International, chs. 5–8, emphasizes the centrality of temple cult.

Schwarz, S. (2010). *Were the Jews a Mediterranean Society?: Reciprocity and
Solidarity in Ancient Judaism.* Princeton, NJ: Princeton University Press,
ch. 5: 'Roman Values, Palestinian Rabbis'.

de Vaux, R. (1973). *Archaeology and the Dead Sea Scrolls.* London: British
Academy, outlines the archaeological evidence.

Vermes, G. and Goodman, M. (1989). *The Essenes According to the Classical
Sources.* Sheffield: Oxford Centre for Postgraduate Hebrew Studies,

presents the evidence that the Essenes were the authors of the Dead Sea Scrolls (on which see also, below, Vermes 2004).

On early Christianity (discussed by Lieu, above, Ch. 13 and Cameron, above, Ch. 16):

Balch, D. L. and Osiek, C. (2003). *Early Christian Families in Context: An Interdisciplinary Dialogue.* Grand Rapids, MI and Cambridge: Eerdmans.

Goodman, M. (1994). *Mission and Conversion: Proselytizing in the Religious History of the Roman Empire.* Oxford: Clarendon, ch. 5.

Harris, W. V. (ed.) (2005). *The Spread of Christianity in the First Four Centuries: Essays in Explanation,* Leiden: Brill, chs. by Rives and Sandwell.

Hopkins, K. (1998). 'Christian Number and Its Implications', *Journal of Early Christian Studies,* 6.2: 185–226 (also available online), the best exploration of possible numbers.

—— (1999). *A World Full of Gods: Pagans, Jews and Christians in the Roman Empire.* London: Weidenfield and Nicholson, ch. 3, an experimental essay.

Lieu, J. M. (2004). *Christian Identity in the Jewish and Graeco–Roman World.* Oxford: Oxford University Press, ch.1.

Williams, R. (ed.) (1989). *The Making of Orthodoxy* Cambridge: Cambridge University Press, ch. 1, on developing ideas of Christian 'orthodoxy'.

On Manichaeism (discussed by Stroumsa, above, Ch. 14):

Lieu, S. N. C. (1992). *Manichaeism in the Later Roman Empire and Medieval China,* 2nd edn. Tübingen: Mohr Siebeck.

On 'women's religions' in various traditions (discussed by Cameron, above, Ch. 16):

Beard, M. (1980). 'The Sexual Status of Vestal Virgins', *Journal of Roman Studies,* 70 (1980), 12–27, with her second thoughts in (1995), 'Re-reading (Vestal) Virginity', in R. Hawley and B. Levick (eds.), *Women in Antiquity: New Assessments.* London and New York: Routledge, 166–77.

Flemming, R. (2007). 'Festus and the Role of Women in Roman Religion', in F. Glinister and C. Woods (eds.), *Verrius, Festus, and Paul: Lexicography, Scholarship and Society,* Bulletin of the Institute of Classical Studies, Supp. 93, London: Institute of Classical Studies, 87–108 (to be included in J. North and S. Price (eds.), *Oxford Readings in Roman Republican Religion: Rome and Italy).*

Fonrobert, C. E. (2007). 'The Human Body in Rabbinic Legal Discourse', in Fonrobert and Jaffee (eds.) 2007 (above, under Judaism): 270–94.

Kraemer, R. S. (2004). *Women's Religions in the Greco–Roman World: A Sourcebook.* Oxford: Oxford University Press, a wide-ranging work.

Nixon, L. F. (1995). 'The Cults of Demeter and Kore', in R. Hawley and
    B. Levick (eds.), *Women in Antiquity: New Assessments*. London and New
    York: Routledge, 75–96.
Price, S. (1999). *Religions of the Ancient Greeks*. Cambridge: Cambridge
    University Press, 67–73, 89–100, on women in Greek religion.
Scheid, J. (1992). 'The Religious Roles of Roman Women', in P. Schmitt
    Pantel (ed.), *A History of Women: From Ancient Goddesses to Christian
    Saints*. Cambridge, MA and London: Belknap, 377–408, is wide-ranging,
    but the central argument has been rejected by Flemming.

IV: Late Antiquity

Beard, M., North, J., and Price, S. *Religions of Rome*, i, ch. 8.
Bowersock, G. W. (1990). *Hellenism in Late Antiquity*. Cambridge: Cam-
    bridge University Press, includes much on late paganism.
——(2006). *Mosaics as History: The Near East from Late Antiquity to Islam*.
    Cambridge, MA and London: Harvard University Press, an imaginative
    study of the mix of cultural traditions in the Levant.
Brown, P. (2003). *The Rise of Western Christendom: Triumph and Diversity,
    AD 200–1000*, 2nd edn. Oxford: Blackwell, chs. 1–5.
Drake, H. A. (2000). *Constantine and the Bishops: The Politics of Intolerance*.
    Baltimore, ND and London: Johns Hopkins University Press.
Doig, A. (2008). *Liturgy and Architecture from the Early Church to the Middle
    Ages*. Aldershot and Burlington, VT: Variorum, chs. 1–2, on the relation
    between church building and liturgy.
Millar, F. (1992). 'The Jews of the Graeco–Roman Diaspora between Paganism
    and Christianity, 312–438', in Lieu et al. 1992 (above section III, under
    Judaism): 97–123.
Rajak, T. (2001). 'Jews, Pagans and Christians in Late Antique Sardis: Models
    of Interaction', in her *The Jewish Dialogue with Greece and Rome: Studies
    in Social and Cultural Interaction*. Leiden: Brill, 447–62.
Stroumsa, G. G. (2009). *The End of Sacrifice: Religious Transformations in
    Late Antiquity*. Chicago, IL and London: Chicago University Press.

Those wanting access to the full range of modern scholarship on the
religious history of the Roman Empire should consult the extraordinary,
multi-authored bulletins published in the *Archiv für Religionsgeschichte*
every five years.

For those wanting access to some of the primary evidence, there are two possible routes. The first is via a sourcebook.

Beard, M., North, J., and Price, S. (1998). *Religions of Rome*. Cambridge: Cambridge University Press, ii, includes both texts and material evidence, on pagans, Jews, and Christians, with annotation and further bibliography.

MacMullen, R. and Lane, E. N. (eds.) (1992). *Paganism and Christianity, 100–425 CE: A Sourcebook*. Minneapolis: Fortress, includes a good range of Greek inscriptions.

Valantasis, R. (ed.) (2000). *Religions of Late Antiquity in Practice*. Princeton, NJ and Oxford: Princeton University Press, a sourcebook.

The second route is via individual ancient texts. In teaching this topic, we have found the following to be useful:

Acts of the Apostles (New English Bible; ed. J. A. Fitzmyer (New York: Doubleday, 1998); or C. K. Barrett, *A Critical and Exegetical Commentary on the Acts of the Apostles*, 2 vols, (Edinburgh: T&T Clark, 1994–8)), a gripping narrative of the early spread of Christianity, a narrative which needs to be read with caution.

Aelius Aristides, *Oration* 48 (= *Sacred Tales* 2) (trans. with notes by C. A. Behr, *The Complete Works* (Leiden: Brill, 1981–6), ii. 318–39; also in C. A. Behr, Aelius *Aristides and the Sacred Tales* (Leiden: Brill, 1968), 253–77), part of Aristides account of his 'salvation' by Asclepius (see Petsalis-Diomidis 2010, above, Section II).

Apuleius, *Metamorphoses* 11 (Hanson, Loeb); commentary and translation by J. G. Griffiths, *The Isis-Book* (Leiden: Brill, 1975), the vivid account of the hero's 'salvation' by Isis (see above Section II).

Augustine, *City of God*, 4–10 (Penguin, 1984), polemically contrasting Roman religion and Christianity.

Josephus, *Against Apion* 2 (Loeb), a presentation to a gentile audience of what Josephus saw as the main features of Judaism.

Lucian, *Alexander* (Loeb), on the allegedly bogus founder of a healing oracle (cf. Bendlin, above, Ch. 6, but see also Petsalis-Diomidis 2010, above Section II); *Peregrinus* (Loeb), on a wandering sage, who allegedly dabbled in Christianity.

Minucius Felix, *Octavius* (Loeb, with Tertullian); translation with excellent introduction and notes by G. W. Clarke (Ancient Christian Writers series, 1974), a fictional debate between a pagan and a Christian, resulting in the pagan's conversion.

Musurillo, H. A. (1972). *Acts of the Christian Martyrs.* Oxford: Clarendon, a collection of the allegedly authentic accounts of Christian martyrdoms.
Ovid, *Fasti* 4 (Loeb; ed. E. Fantham, Cambridge: Cambridge University Press, 1998), which offers a poetical response to the civic cults of Augustan Rome (see above, Feeney 1998, in the introductory section).
Plutarch, *Decline of Oracles* (Loeb).
Vermes, G. (2004). *The Complete Dead Sea Scrolls in English,* revised edn. London: Penguin, of which the best starting points are: Community Rule (1QS) and the Damascus Document (CD), with the War Scroll for enthusiasts (above Section III on authorship and context).

Index